INFLORESCENCE TYPES

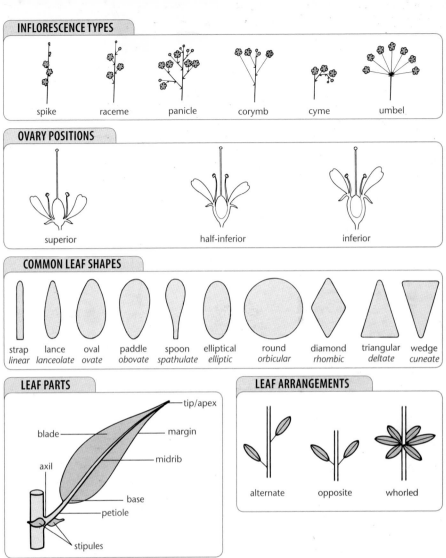

spike   raceme   panicle   corymb   cyme   umbel

OVARY POSITIONS

superior   half-inferior   inferior

COMMON LEAF SHAPES

strap	lance	oval	paddle	spoon	elliptical	round	diamond	triangular	wedge
linear	*lanceolate*	*ovate*	*obovate*	*spathulate*	*elliptic*	*orbicular*	*rhombic*	*deltate*	*cuneate*

LEAF PARTS

tip/apex
blade
margin
midrib
axil
base
petiole
stipules

LEAF ARRANGEMENTS

alternate   opposite   whorled

LEAF TYPES

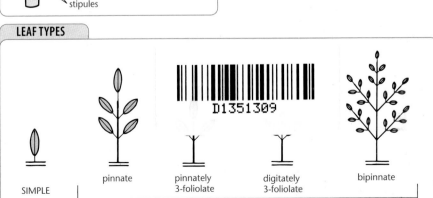

D1351309

SIMPLE   pinnate   pinnately 3-foliolate   digitately 3-foliolate   bipinnate

COMPOUND

FIE

W

RS

OF S

ND

Joh

21/5/10.

10/6/10

O/L CHESHIRE
UNITY
2367590
DB 23 MAR 2012

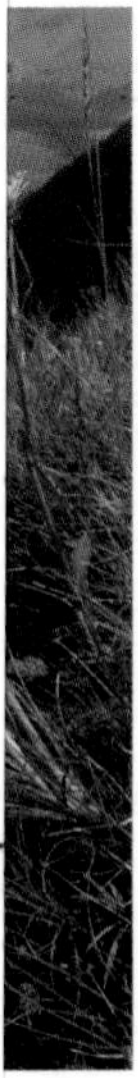

DEDICATION
For my fellow adventurers, E, R, M, T, G and H.

Published by Struik Nature
(an imprint of Random House Struik (Pty) Ltd)
Reg. No. 1966/003153/07
80 McKenzie Street, Cape Town 8001
PO Box 1144, Cape Town 8000, South Africa
www.randomstruik.co.za

Log on to our photographic website **www.imagesofafrica.co.za**
for an African experience.

First published in 2009

1 3 5 7 9 10 8 6 4 2

Publisher: Pippa Parker
Managing editor: Helen de Villiers
Project manager: Leni Martin
Editor: Marthina Mössmer
Proofreader: Cynthia Kemp
Designer: Martin Endemann
Illustrator: John Manning

Reproduction by Hirt & Carter Cape (Pty) Ltd
Printed and bound by Times Offset (M) Sdn Bhd

ISBN 978 1 77007 758 4

Photographs:
FRONT COVER: *Berkheya purpurea*
PREVIOUS PAGE: *Gazania lichtensteinii* and *Felicia* sp. (left),
Erica viscaria (middle), *Kniphofia thodei* and *Berkheya rhapontica* (right)
THIS PAGE: *Impatiens sylvicola* (top), *Drosanthemum speciosum*
(middle), *Sparaxis grandiflora* (bottom)
FOLLOWING PAGE: *Argyroderma pearsonii* in the Knersvlakte

The author and publisher are grateful to the Parker family of
Elandsberg Nature Reserve for their generous sponsorship.

ABOUT THIS BOOK

Almost 20 000 different wild flowers are indigenous in South Africa, constituting as much as 10 per cent of all flowering plant species known throughout the world, and the number continues to grow each year as new species are discovered and described. A great many of them produce attractive flowers. Notable exceptions are grasses, sedges, reeds and rushes, together comprising some 1 800 species in South Africa, and most trees, which number an additional 1 000 or so species. The flowers of these groups are mostly small or insignificant, and the species require specialist knowledge for their identification. Excluding them still leaves about 17 000 species of flowering herbs and shrubs.

Trying to identify this staggering variety is a daunting undertaking. No single book can hope to cover more than a fraction of all the species, but *Field Guide to Wild Flowers of South Africa* approaches the problem by providing the tools and knowledge that will enable the user to identify wild flowers with greater confidence and skill. More than 1 100 species from across the region are illustrated, with descriptive text that has been carefully formulated to emphasise those characters that are most important in distinguishing each species. At a higher level, each genus and family are carefully diagnosed, enabling the user to correctly classify to those levels even plants that have not been included.

ACKNOWLEDGEMENTS

This guide was commissioned by Pippa Parker of Struik Nature and produced by her expert team: designer Martin Endemann, project manager Leni Martin and freelance editor Tina Mössmer. The great bulk of the photographs were taken on the many wild-flower safaris that I participated in over the past decade with Minoru Tomiyama and the Shinwa Wildflower Touring Company. Without these opportunities this book would not have been possible. I owe another special debt of gratitude to Elizabeth Parker of Elandsberg Nature Reserve, who supported several additional field trips and contributed materially to the publication of this book. Her commitment to the conservation of some of South Africa's most endangered wild flowers is an inspiration. Additional sponsorship was provided by the Mia Karsten bequest to the Compton Herbarium and by the Botanical Society of South Africa.

The map of major vegetation types was developed specially for this book by Les Powrie of the South African National Biodiversity Institute, and the species distribution maps that are such an important part of the guide were very kindly generated by Hester Steyn from specimen data held in the PRECIS database of SANBI. Thanks also to everyone who helped me in the field, especially John and Sandie Burrows, Cameron McMaster, Rose Smuts, Mervyn Berowsky, Tex and Gretel, and Hippo, and to my colleagues at the Compton Herbarium for their assistance.

national
biodiversity
institute
S A N B I

ELANDSBERG
NATURE RESERVE

CONTENTS

INTRODUCTION	**8**
SOUTH AFRICAN WILD FLOWERS	8
FLORAL REGIONS	10
VEGETATION TYPES	11
THE NAMES OF PLANTS	18
HOW TO USE THIS BOOK	**20**
IDENTIFYING PLANTS	20
WHERE TO BEGIN	20
FINDING THE RIGHT GROUP	23
PICTORIAL GUIDE TO WILD-FLOWER FAMILIES	24
DESCRIPTIONS OF WILD-FLOWER FAMILIES	30
THE QUICK FAMILY FINDER	**40**
HOW TO USE THE FAMILY FINDER	40
SPECIES DESCRIPTIONS	**46**
GROUP ONE	**46**
GROUP TWO	**50**
GROUP THREE	**52**
GROUP FOUR	**66**
GROUP FIVE	**104**
GROUP SIX	**166**
GROUP SEVEN	**234**
GROUP EIGHT	**270**
GROUP NINE	**304**
GROUP TEN	**416**
GLOSSARY OF TERMS	**470**
FURTHER READING	**472**
INDEX	**473**
ILLUSTRATED GLOSSARY	**IFC and IBC**

SOUTH AFRICAN WILD FLOWERS

Who would have thought the stern and sombre veld
Could nourish things so delicately fair?

FE WALROND (1875–1948)

South Africa is famous for the diversity and beauty of its native wild flowers. Its botanical riches, which have been known and utilised by indigenous people since the dawn of humankind, attracted the attention of European naturalists and scientists almost from the moment that voyagers from the northern hemisphere set foot on the subcontinent. The first major collections of southern African plants reached the scientific fraternity of Europe in the late seventeenth and early eighteenth centuries. Their arrival caused a sensation. Botanists unpacking the specimens were confronted with plants from another world – the very first proteas, ericas, restios and brunias known to science, as well as numbers of strange succulents and beautiful bulbs. Many of them attracted the eager attentions of horticulturists and remain highly sought after today.

The earliest collections originated from the southwestern Cape, where passing ships made landfall to refresh their stores. It was only a hundred years later, at the beginning of the nineteenth century, that collectors began to penetrate beyond the Cape settlement into the hinterland. Soon afterwards, plants from the interior of the subcontinent – from the subtropical East Coast to the high Drakensberg – began to make their appearance in hothouses and gardens in England and Europe.

Today South African plants of a great many kinds adorn gardens throughout the world. Cape Honeysuckle, Plumbago and crane flowers are widely grown shrubs in subtropical and Mediterranean gardens; agapanthus, aloes, clivias, dietes and red-hot pokers are staples of landscape gardeners in warmer climates around the world; vases of freesias, gerberas, gladioli and arum lilies grace homes across the globe; and miniature succulents from the drier parts of the region are avidly sought by specialist collectors in many countries. South African wild flowers have made their way into the hearts and gardens of people everywhere.

South Africa has a remarkably rich flora. The region represents less than one per cent of the world's land surface but may account for as many as 10 per cent of the known species of flowering plants. A high proportion of these plant species is endemic, found naturally only here.

Patterns of diversity

Africa's plants are distributed very unevenly across the continent, with high concentrations of species in some regions contrasting with a relative paucity in others. At a regional level, the flora of southern Africa is the most diverse on the continent. With nearly 20 000 species of seed plants, it is far richer than the floras of either East Africa, which has fewer than 12 000 species, or West Africa, with about 7 000 species, despite the apparent advantages afforded these regions by their more tropical climates. More broadly, the flora of the whole of tropical Africa, which covers an area of 20 million km^2, is estimated at 30 000–40 000 species. Southern Africa, with a surface area of 2.5 million km^2 and lying entirely outside the tropics, accounts for between a third and a half of the wild flowers of sub-Saharan Africa in just 10 per cent of the land area.

At a local level, however, there is no doubt that the richest concentrations of indigenous plants on the continent are to be found mostly in tropical Africa. Plant geographers have identified seven centres of plant diversity in sub-Saharan Africa. Six of these regions of exceptionally high species richness are located in tropical Africa. The single exception is the Cape Floral Region in the extreme southwest of the continent, home to the unique vegetation known as Cape fynbos.

Levels of biological diversity are generally highest at the equator and decrease towards the poles. In Africa this attenuation in species richness is less marked in the southern hemisphere than in the north. Plant diversity at the tropic of Capricorn (23–24°S) is about half that at the equator and drops to a third of equatorial levels by 30°S. In a startling reversal of the global trend, by 34°S the botanical diversity rises to a level comparable to that found at about 20°S. This anomaly in patterns of plant diversity is due to the extraordinary variety of plants found in the Cape Floral Region.

The proportion of endemic species in South Africa – 80 per cent of the total flowering plant species – is exceptionally high and more like the levels that characterise isolated oceanic islands than those of a continental region. Southern Africa's flora as a whole has a distinct character, a consequence of the unusual predominance of certain plant families. A large part of this is due to groups that are typical of the Cape Floral Region, notably the Ice Plant, Iris and Erica families, as well as parts of the Pea, Hyacinth and Milkweed families. These plant groups are concentrated in the southwest and make a disproportionately large contribution to the flora because of the exceptional numbers of fynbos and succulent karoo species. They are not characteristic of most of the country, which has more tropical affinities.

The richness of southern Africa's plant life is closely linked to the diversity of landscape and climate that characterises the region. At the largest scale this is evident in the recognition by plant ecologists of nine major vegetation types, or biomes, in the subcontinent, each with its own complement of plant species. Adjacent areas of tropical Africa typically harbour just two or three biomes.

Plant diversity in southern Africa is richest in the south and east, where the higher and more regular rainfall encourages relatively lush growth. West of this, the rainfall becomes sparser and more erratic and plant diversity decreases. The subtropical forest and thicket vegetation along the East Coast gives way inland to more seasonal savanna and grassland, interspersed with relict patches of temperate forest.

Much of the drier interior of the country is covered with semi-arid karroid shrubland, but even this drought-adapted vegetation cannot survive in the hyper-arid conditions that prevail along the West Coast. Here sparse desert vegetation ekes out an existence,

Grasslands dominate the high interior plateau, where winter cold and frequent fires encourage a diverse bulb flora, including *Moraea moggii*.

THE 10 LARGEST PLANT FAMILIES IN SOUTH AFRICA		
Family	Number of species	Endemic (%)
DAISY	2 300	87
ICE PLANT	1 700	94
PEA	1 700	75
IRIS	1 050	97
ERICA	800	99
GRASS	750	44
SUTERA	700	87
MILKWEED	700	87
ORCHID	470	81
HYACINTH	410	70

FLORAL REGIONS

The nearly 20 000 species of wild flower found in southern Africa do not form a single botanical unit but are distributed among four main floral regions. The best known of these, the Cape Floral Region, is the only one confined to the subcontinent. In its traditional sense, it occupies the coastal plain and adjacent Cape Fold Mountains in the extreme southwest of Africa, from near Vanrhynsdorp southwards to the Cape Peninsula and eastwards along the southern Cape to Port Elizabeth.

Treated for many years as a distinct floral kingdom with the same status as the rest of the flora of sub-Saharan Africa, the Cape Floral Region is home to the world's richest and most distinctive temperate flora, dominated by fine-leaved fynbos heathland and associated Mediterranean shrublands. It has recently been realised that these plant communities have close links to the succulent shrublands of the West Coast and neighbouring interior. This has led to the recognition of an enlarged Greater Cape Floral Region that encompasses both fynbos and succulent karoo vegetation, thus extending the original floral region northwards into southern Namibia. Being unusually rich in species, the Greater Cape Floral Region makes the single largest contribution to South Africa's floral wealth and gives it much of its distinctive character.

Much of South Africa's drier interior inland of the Cape Fold Mountains and across the central plateau, along with coastal Namibia and southern Angola, forms the Karoo-Namib Floral Region. Relatively poor in species, this arid or semidesert region is dominated by small shrubs and grasses. It contrasts sharply with the well-watered coastal regions of the east that constitute the subtropical forest zone of the Swahilian–Pondoland Floral Region, which extends from Port Elizabeth northwards to Kenya. This floral region includes many endemic species, mainly trees.

The remaining portion of the country, comprising the grasslands and savannas of the north and northeast, is the southern extent of the vast Sudano–Zambesian Floral Region. This, the largest floral region on the continent, includes all the rest of sub-Saharan Africa with the exception of the tropical forests of West Africa. Not unnaturally for such a large region, it has a rich and diverse flora.

sustained by coastal fog. South of the Namib Desert the climate becomes progressively more Mediterranean and a specialised type of semi-arid shrubland dominated by a diversity of succulents makes its appearance. The extreme southwest of the country, where rainfall is higher and soils are acidic and poor in nutrients, is the bastion of the rich fynbos heathlands.

The success of each of these life forms, as well as their prevalence in the vegetation, reflects the influence of climate, fire and soil fertility. Most of the major vegetation types in southern Africa are distributed primarily according to climate, in particular the average annual rainfall, the season in which it falls and the severity of summer drought. A combination of these factors generally determines the type of vegetation that will thrive in a particular region.

Two striking exceptions to the paramount influence of climate are the hard-leaved fynbos shrublands, which develop on nutrient-poor soils over a relatively wide range of climatic conditions, and grassland, which dominates in upland areas where a combination of winter cold and frequent fires prevents woody plants from establishing themselves. Fire is also important in maintaining savanna and in the recycling of nutrients in fynbos, while grazing and browsing have a significant impact in both grassland and savanna.

VEGETATION TYPES

The dominant growth strategy – or life form – developed among the plants that make up each community defines the major vegetation types, or biomes. Typical life forms of plants include trees, shrubs, long-lived grasses and other soft perennials, annual herbs, and geophytes (plants with underground storage organs). Biomes, therefore, are defined by the structure of the vegetation and not by the identity of the component species. Thus all forests are dominated by trees, just as all grasslands are dominated by grasses, although different types of forests or grasslands vary greatly in the individual species of trees or grasses found in each. The boundaries between biomes may be very sharp, like that between fynbos and succulent karoo at the foot of the mountains in the southwestern Cape, or between forest patches and surrounding grasslands. More usually, however, they occur as gradual transitions extending over several kilometres. In rare cases the boundaries between biomes are vague, such as that between grassland and savanna in KwaZulu-Natal, reflecting a relatively elastic interface that stretches and shrinks in response to changes in climate over time.

Fynbos

Although fynbos takes its name from the dominant plant communities in the region, it actually comprises three quite different, naturally fragmented vegetation types: fynbos heathland, renosterveld shrubland and strandveld shrubland. For its size, it is the richest temperate vegetation type in the world: in just 6.6 per cent of the southern African land surface, it harbours a staggering one-third to one-half of all the

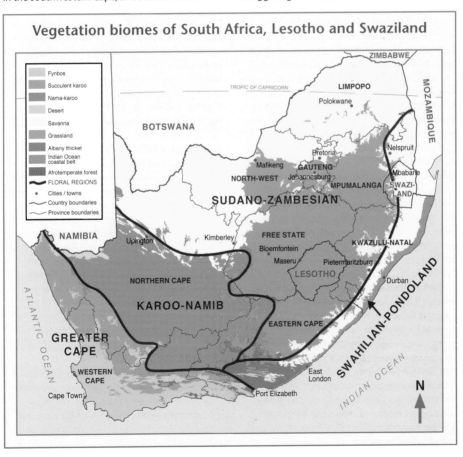

Vegetation biomes of South Africa, Lesotho and Swaziland

11

Fynbos has proportionally the richest species diversity in South Africa.

plant species recorded from the region. The distribution of fynbos coincides largely with the extensive outcrops of sandstone soils of the Cape System. Its development, unlike that of other vegetation types, is determined by a combination of soils and climate, in the form of nutrient-poor soils with moderate to high winter rainfall, and moderate to high summer aridity. Much of fynbos vegetation occupies areas that are climatically suitable for afrotemperate forest, and it is mainly the aridity and the frequency of fires in the region that prevent forest from taking over.

An open or dense shrubland dominated by leathery- and often small-leaved shrubs and perennials, fynbos has a high representation (almost one-fifth of the species) of plants with bulbs and corms. Although seldom more than 3 m high, it is more or less distinctly three-layered, combining a canopy of medium or tall shrubs, primarily members of the Protea, Erica and Daisy families, with a middle layer of restios, shrublets and occasionally grasses, and an understorey of herbaceous perennials and bulbs. This basic structure varies with the age of the vegetation, which is determined by the interval between successive fires. Periodic fires are critical for rejuvenating the vegetation and most fynbos plants are adapted to burning, typically every 10–25 years. It has even been proposed that the finely branched architecture of many shrubs has evolved to encourage periodic burning.

Fynbos is easily the most bewildering of the vegetation types. The sheer number of species, between 7 000 and 8 000, coupled with the small ranges over which many of them occur, makes fynbos a frustrating floral paradise for anyone trying to identify its plants. It is rich in small-leaved shrublets in the Citrus, Daisy, Erica and Pea families; leathery-leaved pelargoniums and proteas; succulent-leaved shrublets in the Crassula and Ice Plant families; and diverse annuals in the Mustard and Sutera families. Its crowning glory, however, is its wealth of beautiful bulbs. Colourful species in the Amaryllis, Hyacinth, Iris and Stargrass families are supplemented by equally attractive tuberous or bulbous members of the Geranium and Oxalis families – together contributing almost one-fifth of all fynbos species.

Fine tracts of montane fynbos cover the mountains of the southwestern Cape, most obviously in the Table Mountain National Park but also in several other reserves. Coastal fynbos communities are conserved in the West Coast National Park and De Hoop Nature Reserve.

Succulent karoo

The richest semidesert in the world, succulent karoo includes more species of succulent plants than any other vegetation type on the planet. It occupies low-lying country, mainly in a band below the western rim of the central escarpment in Namaqualand and southern Namibia, and in

Namaqualand in the succulent karoo is known for its seasonal displays of annuals, especially daisies.

flowers that appear along road verges, on rocky outcrops and among the small shrubs studding the landscape. The full range includes numerous species in the Bellflower, Sunflax and Sutera families, a host of colourful bulbs in the Iris, Hyacinth, Colchicum and Lady's Hand families, uncountable numbers of succulents in the Ice Plant, Crassula and Geranium families, and a rich mixture of flowering shrubs and perennials.

Seasonal displays of annuals and other wild flowers can be seen in the Namaqualand National Park and the Goegap Reserve.

Nama-karoo

the rain shadow of the Cape Fold Mountains. Succulent karoo covers 6.5 per cent of southern Africa, in regions with a winter rainfall below 200 mm – too low to support the development of fynbos – and extreme summer aridity. Fog is common near the coast and several specialised plant communities rely on it for survival.

Succulent karoo is characterised by a sparse growth of low, succulent shrubs and supports a unique assemblage of dwarf succulents, mainly members of the Ice Plant, Crassula and Euphorbia families. Several annuals are common, but perennial grasses are relatively rare.

Namaqualand's succulent karoo is renowned for its spring displays of annual wild flowers, most especially the fields of orange, yellow and mauve daisies. These displays are only the most conspicuous exhibition of the true diversity of

Poor in species but showing many intriguing evolutionary relationships with its six neighbouring biomes, Nama-karoo occurs across the drier western half of southern Africa's central plateau and through the low-lying basin of the Great Karoo in the rain shadow of the Cape Fold Mountains. The biome covers just under 20 per cent of South Africa, developing where the summer rainfall is between 100 and 520 mm per year. The generally low rainfall is unreliable and droughts are frequent and sometimes prolonged.

Nama-karoo is an open, grassy, dwarf shrubland in which deciduous shrubs predominate and fire is a rare event. Historically, large nomadic or migratory herds of springbok and other herbivores traversed the region, continually moving between the patches of fresh vegetation that flourished after local showers of rain. Today, less mobile herds of sheep, goats and cattle all too often strip the veld of palatable grasses and herbage.

Flowering plants respond quickly to sporadic rainfall events in the dwarf shrubland of the Nama-karoo.

13

Wild flowers are few and their appearance unpredictable, but when rain does fall the shrubs quickly become covered with flowers, among them the yellow Karoo Rhigozum (*Rhigozum obovatum*) and pink Karoo Rose (*Hermannia grandiflora*). The ephemeral moisture also stimulates the germination of some striking desert annuals, including the pagoda-like Rogeria (*Rogeria longiflora*), and several colourful daisies, most conspicuously the yellow *Gazania lichtensteinii* and white to orange *Arctotis leiocarpa*.

Desert

The Namib, southern Africa's only true desert, occupies a broad belt along the west coast of Namibia and extends into southern Africa along the lower reaches of the Orange River to cover just 0.5 per cent of the subcontinent. It is the driest of the summer-rainfall biomes, enduring extreme aridity and receiving a mere 13–70 mm of rain per year. Coastal fogs, which penetrate deep inshore, are frequent, and most of the desert's plants are adapted to make use of this critically important source of moisture, some absorbing it directly through their leaves. Plant diversity in the desert is the lowest of all the biomes.

A sparse cover of shrubs dominates the scant desert vegetation, but annual herbs, especially grasses, are the most diverse in the number of

their species. An ephemeral component of the vegetation, they avoid drought by existing for most of the time in the form of dormant seeds. These opportunistic plants respond to infrequent and irregular falls of rain by germinating quickly and flowering soon afterwards.

Although poor in wild flowers, desert vegetation includes some iconic species such as Halfmens (*Pachypodium namaquensis*), which is best seen in southern Africa in the Richtersveld National Park.

Savanna

The largest biome in Africa, savanna typifies the continent's vegetation in the popular consciousness. It covers almost one-third of southern Africa, dominating the landscape in the north and northeast and extending in a more fragmented form down the east coast in frost-free areas below the escarpment. A strongly seasonal climate, with dry winters and an average summer rainfall of 235–1 000 mm, delimits the biome.

Savanna is characterised by a grassy ground layer overtopped by a distinct but discontinuous upper layer of woody plants that typically includes thorny trees, especially acacias. The shrub or tree layer varies significantly in height (1–20 m) and by its stature defines different savanna subtypes that are known variously as shrubveld, bushveld or woodland. Grazing and

Plant cover in the desert biome is sparse, but includes drought-adapted species such as *Didelta carnosa*.

Savanna is characterised by a combination of grass cover and woody plants such as *Greyia sutherlandii*, as well as a rich diversity of aloes.

browsing are important natural determinants of savanna, as are frequent fires, and almost all savanna plant species are adapted to burning.

This vegetation type is especially rich in flowering shrubs, including the orange Pride of De Kaap *(Bauhinia galpinii)*, a host of yellow-flowered hibiscus species with purple eyes, numerous perennial daisies, such as the Barberton Daisy *(Gerbera jamesonii)*, and several bulbs, notably *Ornithogalum saundersii* and the yellowish form of the Flame Lily *(Gloriosa superba)*. In winter, the bright orange spikes of many aloe species punctuate the dry veld, and the leafless stems of the Impala Lily *(Adenium multiflorum)* sprout white and cerise trumpets.

Large tracts of unspoiled savanna vegetation are found in the many game reserves along the northern and eastern borders of South Africa.

Grassland

Poorly represented on the continent beyond southern Africa, grassland blankets almost 28 per cent of South Africa's surface. It includes a great number of species that are particular to the region and covers much of the high central plateau and inland areas in the eastern part of the subcontinent. Grasslands develop in moister, seasonal parts of the summer-rainfall region, where the annual rainfall is between 400 and 2 000 mm and the winters are dry and cold. A combination of frequent fires, cold winter temperatures and high levels of grazing maintains the dominance of grasses and other herbaceous perennials by inhibiting the growth

of woody species that would otherwise convert large areas into woodland or forest.

A single-layered sward with a rich assortment of associated perennial herbs characterises grassland. Shrubs and trees are restricted to localised habitats such as rock outcrops and sheltered ravines, where they can avoid fire and frost. Grassland flowering plants are adapted to survive and actually thrive with regular, even annual, winter burning. Many protect their renewal buds from fire and cold damage by insulating them underground in bulbs, corms or other woody rootstocks. These subterranean organs also store nutrients, enabling the plants

Gladiolus dalenii is a widespread grassland species.

to sprout rapidly in spring before the grass cover can re-establish itself. Grasslands are pre-eminent among the summer-rainfall vegetation types in the diversity of their bulbs.

Grassland ranks with fynbos and succulent karoo as one of the best vegetation types in which to see wild flowers. In spring after a winter burn, large numbers of geophytes in the Amaryllis, Iris, Hyacinth and Stargrass families come into flower, as do associated grassland plants that resprout from underground rootstocks, such as members of the Mint, Daisy, Acanthus, Daphne and Pea families. Later, in summer, larger bulbs like agapanthus, gladioli and orchids, become evident, as well as the curiously shaped flowers of several attractive milkweeds.

Large tracts of pristine grassland can be found along the KwaZulu-Natal Drakensberg in the Ukhahlamba National Park, and also along parts of the Mpumalanga escarpment.

Albany thicket

Albany thicket borders on no fewer than seven different biomes and combines plant forms

Albany thicket is a thorny, semi-succulent vegetation transitional between forest, shrubland and grassland.

from savanna and Nama-karoo with subtropical forest. Thicket occupies a little over two per cent of South Africa's land surface in the southeast of the country, in a highly dissected landscape formed by numerous river valleys. It occupies the interface between winter- and summer-rainfall climates in a semi-arid region that receives an annual rainfall of 200–900 mm throughout the year, but with peaks in spring and autumn.

Generally a dense, woody, semi-succulent and thorny vegetation, Albany thicket averages 2–3 m in height and in a pristine state is almost impenetrable. Its diverse vegetation includes a wide range of growth forms, including leaf and stem succulents, deciduous and semi-deciduous shrubs, dwarf shrubs, geophytes, annuals and grasses. The understorey typically includes various dwarf succulent shrubs, especially members of the Crassula and Ice Plant families, many of which are rare and highly localised. A distinct group of spiny or thorny shrubs with arching branches occurs in certain types of thicket, their unusual architecture forming an impassable barricade to larger animals.

The wide range of growth forms found in Albany thicket reflects its transitional nature between forest, evergreen and deciduous shrublands, and grassland. Among the more spectacular shrubs are the Bitter Aloe (*Aloe ferox*), with flowering candelabras carried above a mop of ferociously prickly leaves, the exotic spikes of Bird-of-paradise or Crane Flower (*Strelitzia reginae*), several succulent *Cotyledon* species with paddle-like leaves and nodding, tubular flowers, and two garden stalwarts, Plumbago (*Plumbago auriculata*) with ice-blue flowers and the brazen orange Cape Honeysuckle (*Tecoma capensis*).

The largest areas of Albany thicket are found in the valleys of the lower reaches of the Sundays, Fish and Kei rivers. Smaller patches of this intriguing vegetation type occur in the southern Cape from Riversdale eastwards, in the Little Karoo around Oudtshoorn, in the Baviaanskloof wilderness and around the Zuurberg.

Indian Ocean coastal belt

Representing the southernmost occurrence of the wet forests of the East African tropics, the Indian Ocean coastal belt occupies a little over one per cent of the surface area of the subcontinent. It forms a strip that ranges in width from 10 to

Scadoxus multiflorus flowers brighten the forest gloom in the Indian Ocean coastal belt.

35 km and extends along the east coast of South Africa as far south as the mouth of the Kei River. The climate is subtropical, with high humidity and an annual rainfall of 820–1 200 mm, most of which falls in summer. The absence of a definite dry period distinguishes the climate of the Indian Ocean coastal belt from that of savanna.

Trees, lianas and epiphytes in the wooded portions give the vegetation an unmistakably tropical appearance. It contains several distinct types of forest, mostly subtropical but also mangroves, swamp forest and riverine forest. These form a mosaic with more open vegetation types, like grasslands, wetlands and estuaries, and are fringed along the coastal margins by true seashore vegetation.

The forest and coastal thicket include flowering shrubs such as Wild Banana (*Strelitzia nicolai*) and blue-purple *Barleria obtusa*, along with striking bulbs, such as Flame Lily (*Gloriosa superba*) and Blood Lily (*Scadoxus multiflorus*). The associated grasslands are rich in members of the Daisy, Coffee, Iris, Orchid, Pea and Milkweed families.

Small enclaves of coastal belt vegetation survive all along the East Coast between numerous resort developments.

Afrotemperate forest

Afrotemperate forests form part of the global warm-temperate forest biome. In southern Africa they are patchy in distribution, covering barely 0.3 per cent of the land surface. They are found only in frost-free areas which have an average annual rainfall of more than 525 mm in the winter-rainfall region and more than 725 mm in summer-rainfall areas. Scattered along the southern coast of the country and inland along the edge of the eastern escarpment, they are sensitive to fire and persist only in places where burns are rare or absent, in moist coastal areas or on protected slopes.

Forests are characterised by their continuous canopy of mostly evergreen trees, below which shelters a multi-layered understorey of smaller trees and shrubs. The dense shade beneath the canopy prevents a distinct layer of herbs from developing at ground level. Some 650 different woody species and a similar number of herbaceous ones have been recorded in the forests of southern Africa.

Dominated as they are by trees, forests are relatively poor in flowering perennials and herbs. Most wild flowers are concentrated at the margins and in open spaces, where sunlight can reach the floor. They include numerous varieties of spur-sage (*Plectranthus*) in shades of blue and purple, the tangerine and pink flowers of begonias, native species of wild impatiens with pink, butterfly-like flowers, the orange showers of Falling Stars (*Crocosmia aurea*) and various kinds of Forest Iris (*Dietes*) and clivias. Among the few plants that favour the shaded forest floor itself

In afrotemperate forest, wild flowers are concentrated in clearings and at margins, where sunlight penetrates the canopy.

are numerous *Streptocarpus* species, with their velvety, ruffled leaves and sky-blue blooms.

The most accessible patches of afrotemperate forest are to be found in the vicinity of Knysna in the Western Cape, in the river valleys of the KwaZulu-Natal Drakensberg and around Sabie in Mpumalanga.

THE NAMES OF PLANTS

Names are a form of shorthand for objects around us. They are also the heading under which all recorded information about a particular object is stored. For names to function optimally in these roles it is necessary that they are both accessible and universal. At a local level, each culture or community develops its own system of nomenclature, leading to a multitude of common or vernacular names. This contrasts with the need for a single name that is consistently applied by all, and which is the origin of the botanical name.

These sometimes conflicting demands can create a tension between the two systems of names that is unnecessary. Vernacular and botanical names are each appropriate to their place and use. Far from being mutually exclusive, they complement one another and help make botany comprehensive to more of us.

Botanical names

The botanical name of a species comprises two words. The first, traditionally derived from Greek, is the name of the genus to which the species belongs and functions much like a surname. It always begins with a capital letter. The second, traditionally derived from Latin, is particular to that species and functions like a given name. It is written entirely in lower-case letters. The scientific name of a plant constitutes a powerful key that not only identifies the species, but also gives some indication of its relationships to others.

Botanical Latin is essentially a written language, but the scientific names of plants are often spoken. This can give rise to some anxiety about pronouncing them correctly. The best words on the subject remain those of Professor William Stearn, a botanist, Classics scholar and the author of *Botanical Latin*: 'How [botanical names] are pronounced really matters little provided they sound pleasant and are understood by all concerned.' Nevertheless, he qualified this advice by instructing us that this is most likely to be attained by pronouncing the names in accordance with the rules of classical Latin pronunciation – an injunction that does not help those of us who have not studied the subject.

In English-speaking countries, most botanists and gardeners favour a system of pronunciation derived from English rather than that used by classical scholars. Here are some guidelines.

- Words containing more than one vowel or diphthong (i.e. two successive vowels that are pronounced as one, such as *ei* or *au*) are divided into syllables: *al-bus*, *al-bi-dus*, *au-re-a* and *lei-o-po-da*.
- Every vowel is pronounced: *va-ri-a-bi-le* and not *variable*, and *thyrs-o-i-des*, not *thyrs-oi-des*.
- Vowels may be short, as in *sick*, or long, as in *site*. Diphthongs are treated as long vowels: *ei* as in *rein*. However, when two vowels come together without forming a diphthong, the first vowel is short: the *ne* in *car-ne-us* is pronounced as in *pet*.
- In words of two or more syllables, the stress generally falls on the second-last syllable: *mi-ni-**a**-ta* or *mi-tri-**for**-mis*. However, if this syllable is short, the stress falls on the third-last syllable: *la-ti-**fo**-li-us*. Words in which the last two vowels are separated by two consonants follow the normal rule: *cru-**en**-tus*.
- Consonants are generally pronounced as they are in English.

Vernacular names

Whenever possible, this book provides common or vernacular names, especially for genera. Most come from Christo Smith's incomparable *Common Names of South African Plants*, and others from the many popular guides produced over the past century. In many cases a selection has been made from among several alternatives, discarding those names that are seldom used or are not especially applicable. Where the names have been suggested by some obvious visible attribute of the plants, their derivation has not been given; in cases where their origin is more obscure, this is explained. Many of the common names are originally Dutch or Afrikaans, reflecting the language spoken by early settlers in the country. Others derive from indigenous Khoisan terms and represent just a fraction of the original indigenous plant taxonomy.

Common names were used by early inhabitants of the country primarily to identify plants by their useful attributes, which were often medicinal or edible. For this reason they were sometimes applied indiscriminately to several different species with similar properties. In addition, various names may have been applied to the same plant by different people and in different regions. Given the diversity of wild-flower species in South Africa, and with new ones still being discovered each year, it is not possible to assign a unique common name to each species.

Although rarely specific, the vernacular names are invariably colourful, usually informative and often as familiar to the local inhabitants as the scientific names are to botanists. They represent a rich cultural heritage that deserves to prosper.

A solitary orange Jakkalsbietou (*Dimorphotheca pinnata*) among pale yellow Pietsnot (*Grielum humifusum*) in Namaqualand.

IDENTIFYING PLANTS

South Africa's wealth of wild flowers makes the identification of all but the most distinctive species a daunting challenge. To make the task easier, this guide provides information at several levels, ranging from species through genus to family. The primary aim is to provide the general user with the skills and knowledge to identify the wild flowers that are featured in any flower guide, not only this one.

Field Guide to Wild Flowers of South Africa assists users in naming the more common plant families, genera and species by identifying the features that characterise each of the categories. Familiarity with plant families and genera, and the kinds of features that are important in identifying them, is an essential first step in beginning the more complex task of identifying individual species. Once you have mastered this basic knowledge, you will be able to approach the species accounts in this and other guides with greater ease and confidence.

More than 1 100 indigenous species are featured in this book. Although this number represents just a fraction of the nearly 20 000 plant species that occur in South Africa, it includes the more common and conspicuous ones – those that are prevalent in well-visited areas, and especially those with showy blooms that attract attention. Essentially, this excludes any plants with flowers or flowerheads less than 10 mm across. The choice of species was driven by experience gained over two decades of fieldwork across many thousands of kilometres. Parts of the country that are most accessible and regularly visited by wild-flower enthusiasts have been given precedence over those that are inaccessible or poor in wild flowers.

Many plant families have had to be excluded. Among them are all the trees, for which many specialist guides exist and field identification is in any case based primarily on vegetative features, mainly foliage. Also not covered are the grasses and related families, including the Cape reeds, or restios, and the sedges. Although very important ecologically and economically, these families require specialist knowledge and microscopic study for their identification. Even among the genera that are included, the coverage of the species is necessarily uneven. Comprehensive identification of even a representative sample of species in very large genera, such as *Erica* (860 spp.), *Senecio* (±300 South African spp.), *Aspalathus* (±280 spp.) and *Helichrysum* (250 South African spp.) is beyond the scope of a guide such as this.

WHERE TO BEGIN

The arrangement of plant families, genera and species in this guide is an artificial one devised to aid identification at each level. To identify a family, turn first to 'Finding the Right Group' (p. 23), where flowering plants have been divided into three convenient categories: unusual families (comprising ancient dicotyledons plus three anomalous monocotyledon families: Aponogeton, Arum and Crane Flower); typical monocotyledons; and true dicotyledons. Within these categories, the plants have been sorted further into 10 groups. Each of these represents an assemblage of plant families which have selected characteristics in common.

When you have identified the group to which your specimen probably belongs, consult the 'Pictorial Guide to Wild-flower Families' (p. 24), where a short summary of the families within each of the groups is given, along with a photograph of a species from each family. At this point you can select what appears to be the appropriate family and then turn to 'Descriptions of Wild-flower Families' (p.30) to check all the characteristic features. Now turn to the relevant family in the main body of the book (for an example, see opposite).

Alternatively, you can identify the family to which your specimen belongs by making use of 'The Quick Family Finder' (p. 40).

Within the larger families, the genera are grouped into subfamilies or informal groups as an additional aid to identification. Follow the leads to the appropriate subfamily or informal group of genera in each family. Read the descriptions of each genus in the section, paying particular attention to italicised text, which describes the critical characteristics that define each genus. The number of South African species in each genus is an indication of how many species of that particular genus are likely to be featured in this guide.

Within the larger genera, the species are also sometimes arranged in clusters by some obvious

HOW TO USE THIS BOOK

GROUP FIVE

IRIDACEAE Iris family

▸ SUBFAMILY NIVENIOIDEAE SHRUBS WITH WOODY STEMS, LEATHERY LEAVES WITHOUT MIDRIB
▸▸ FLOWERS IN CLUSTERS, TRUMPET- OR SALVER-SHAPED, WITH A TUBE

Witsenia **WITSENIA, BOKMAKIERIESTERT**
(Named for Nicholas Witsen, 18th-century Dutch patron of botany) Evergreen shrub. Leaves in tight fans at the branch tips, sword-shaped and fibrous, *without a midrib. Flowers in pairs,* enclosed by leathery bracts, *tubular,* greenish-black with velvety yellow tepals; style 3-notched. Southwestern Cape: 1 sp. The vernacular name *bokmakieriestert* derives from the resemblance of the yellow and black inflorescence to the tail of the shrike-like Bokmakierie.

① *Witsenia maura* Waaiertjie   J F M A M J J A S O N D
Slender woody shrub to 2 m, with fans of tough, narrowly sword-shaped leaves, and clusters of tubular, blackish-green flowers with bright yellow, velvety tepals, 60–70 mm long. Marshes and seeps in the southwestern Cape.

Nivenia **BUSH IRIS** *(Named for David James Niven, 1774–1826, Scottish gardener and plant collector)*
Evergreen shrubs. Leaves *in tight fans at the branch tips,* sword-shaped and fibrous, *without a midrib. Flowers solitary or in pairs,* enclosed by firm, dry or papery bracts, arranged in *flat-topped panicles or clusters, salver-shaped with a long tube, bright blue to mauve;* style with 3 short branches. Southwestern Cape: 10 spp.

② *Nivenia stokoei*   J F M A M J J A S O N D
(=*Nivenia woodii*) Evergreen shrub 40–60 cm, with fans of sword-shaped leaves, and clusters of large, pale to deep blue or mauve flowers with a tube 27–37 mm long. Rocky sandstone ridges in fynbos in the southwestern Cape.

▸ SUBFAMILY ARISTEOIDEAE RHIZOMATOUS HERBS WITH LEATHERY LEAVES WITHOUT A MIDRIB; FLOWERS IN CLUSTERS, STAR-SHAPED WITHOUT A TUBE, BLUE, SHORT-LIVED

Aristea **ARISTEA, BLOUSUURKANOL**
(Greek, arista, *an awn, referring to the fringed spathes and bracts)* Rhizomatous perennials. Leaves in a basal fan, *tough and fibrous, without a midrib.* Flowers in clusters enclosed by brownish or green bracts, or spathes, *blue to mauve,* lasting less than a day and shrivelling in the early afternoon, *star-shaped with almost separate tepals;* style flexed to the side, either minutely notched or 3-lobed at the tip. Africa and Madagascar: ±55 spp.; South Africa: 45 spp.

▸ STYLE MINUTELY NOTCHED
▸▸ FLOWERS IRIS-LIKE WITH SPEAR-SHAPED INNER TEPALS

③ *Aristea bakeri* Klatt   J F M A M J J A S O N D
Robust perennial to 1 m, with cylindrical, usually well-branched stems and narrow, fibrous leaves, and blue flowers, 20–25 mm in diameter, with a simple style; the spathes dry and rusty brown with transparent margins, usually minutely hairy towards the base; the fruits oblong and 3-winged, woody. Stony lower sandstone slopes from the southwestern to the Eastern Cape. *Aristea spiralis* from the southern Cape has sessile flower clusters.

1. Family group for identification
2. Family botanical name
3. First-tier lead to genus identification
4. Second-tier lead to genus identification
5. Genus botanical name
6. Genus vernacular name: English
7. Genus vernacular name: Afrikaans
8. Explanation of genus name
9. Family common name
10. Species number: photograph

11. Species photograph
12. Species distribution map
13. First-tier lead to species identification
14. Second-tier lead to species identification
15. Species number
16. Species botanical name
17. Old name (following reclassification)
18. Species vernacular name
19. Similar species
20. Flowering months

21

characteristic. The species descriptions focus on the features of the plant that are diagnostic. Read the description carefully and check the accompanying distribution map, the flowering season and the numbered photograph on the opposite page before deciding on the identity of your plant. In some cases, similar species are mentioned at the end of the description. An illustrated glossary (inside front and back covers) and a text glossary (p.470) are supplied to help interpret botanical terms.

The circumscription of families and genera used in this guide reflects the most modern understanding of plant relationships, based on recent advances in DNA-based studies. Species from 72 families are included, 18 from the group of plants known as monocotyledons and the remaining 54 representing the dicotyledons. The waterlilies are one of several ancient groups of flowering plants that are now known to predate the origin of the monocotyledons and the modern dicotyledons, both of which diverged from a common early dicotyledon ancestor. Modern, or true, dicotyledons are thus more immediately related to monocotyledons than they are to ancient dicotyledons.

In some cases these new interpretations of relationships can lead to changes in the names of families, genera and species. Such changes can be confusing but they are evidence of the ongoing advances in our understanding of the natural world. These changes are due either to a change in the circumscription of a species or group, or to the discovery of a previously overlooked name. Where a species' name has changed recently, it is listed under its new name, with the old name given in brackets, e.g. *Ipomoea oblongata* (=*Turbina oblongata*). Where dimensions are given in the descriptions, the usual range is indicated, from the smallest to the largest (unusually small or large sizes are inserted in parentheses before or after the normal range). Likely flowering months are indicated by a calendar bar above each species description. Where there is space, extra images have sometimes been included (as in 2A, 2B), showing other colour forms.

The Cape Floral Region, with 9 000 plant species in 150 families, has one of the richest floras in the world.

FINDING THE RIGHT GROUP

For this guide, plants have been assembled in 10 groups of families with selected characteristics in common. To find the group to which your unidentified plant belongs, select the appropriate category on the left. Proceed along the branches of the diagram, making selections based on the generalised descriptions at each stage. You should then arrive at one of the 10 plant family groups on the right. Once the group is selected, you can identify the family in the 'Pictorial Guide to Wild-flower Families' (p.24), confirm details in 'Descriptions of Wild-flower Families' (p.30) and find the right genus and then species in the species descriptions starting on p.46.

UNUSUAL FAMILIES

Aquatic or robust terrestrial perennials, tufted or palm-like, with large, petiolate leaves and distinctive flowers.

GROUP ONE

TYPICAL MONOCOTYLEDONS

Herbs, rarely tree-like. Leaves with parallel venation, often strap-shaped. Flowers with parts in multiples of 3, often with undifferentiated sepals and petals (= tepals).

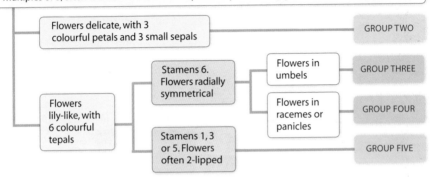

Flowers delicate, with 3 colourful petals and 3 small sepals — GROUP TWO

Flowers lily-like, with 6 colourful tepals

Stamens 6. Flowers radially symmetrical

Flowers in umbels — GROUP THREE

Flowers in racemes or panicles — GROUP FOUR

Stamens 1, 3 or 5. Flowers often 2-lipped — GROUP FIVE

TRUE DICOTYLEDONS

Herbs, shrubs or trees. Leaves with netted or herring-bone venation, often toothed or lobed. Flowers with parts in multiples of 4 or 5, usually with separate sepals and petals.

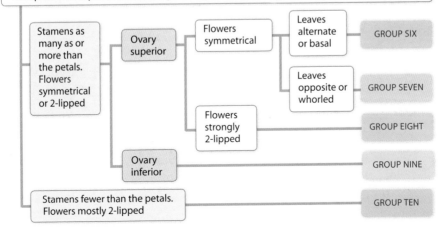

Stamens as many as or more than the petals. Flowers symmetrical or 2-lipped

Ovary superior

Flowers symmetrical

Leaves alternate or basal — GROUP SIX

Leaves opposite or whorled — GROUP SEVEN

Flowers strongly 2-lipped — GROUP EIGHT

Ovary inferior — GROUP NINE

Stamens fewer than the petals. Flowers mostly 2-lipped — GROUP TEN

PICTORIAL GUIDE TO WILD-FLOWER FAMILIES

Aquatic or robust terrestrial perennials, tufted or tree-like, with large, petiolate leaves and distinctive flowers.

WATERLILY FAMILY
Aquatic herbs with floating, umbrella-like leaves and solitary, large blue flowers.

APONOGETON FAMILY
Aquatic herbs with floating, oblong leaves and crowded, small white flowers.

ARUM FAMILY
Arum-like plants with soft, spongy, petiolate leaves.

CRANE FLOWER FAMILY
Banana-like plants with large, leathery, petiolate leaves.

Flowers delicate, with 3 colourful petals and 3 small sepals.

COMMELINA FAMILY
Flowers with 3 delicate petals, withering within a day.

Flowers in umbels, lily-like, with 6 stamens.

ONION FAMILY
Plants smelling of onion or garlic.

AGAPANTHUS FAMILY
Flowers blue, with deflexed stamens.

AMARYLLIS FAMILY
Ovary inferior.

Flowers in racemes or panicles, lily-like, with 6 stamens.

ANTHERICUM FAMILY
Flowers on jointed pedicels, several per bract.

ALOE FAMILY
Succulent perennials with yellow sap.

HYACINTH FAMILY
Bulbous perennials; flowers on leafless scapes.

LANARIA FAMILY
Tough evergreen perennial; flowers in dense woolly clusters; hairs branched.

BLACK-STICK LILY FAMILY
Fibrous shrublets; ovary glandular or bristly.

STARGRASS FAMILY
Leaves 3-ranked; flowers mostly yellow; ovary inferior.

COLCHICUM FAMILY
Cormous perennials; flowers usually opposite the bracts.

CYANELLA FAMILY
Stamens clustered, with apical pores; ovary half-inferior.

Flowers lily-like or orchid-like, often 2-lipped, with 1 or 3 stamens.

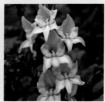

BLOODROOT FAMILY
Rootstock bright orange; leaves oriented edgewise, often hairy; stamens 3, opposite the inner tepals.

IRIS FAMILY
Leaves usually oriented edgewise; stamens 3, opposite the outer tepals; ovary inferior.

ORCHID FAMILY
Flowers 2-lipped, often spurred; stamen 1, joined to the style.

Flowers symmetrical; stamens as many as the petals or more; ovary superior; leaves alternate.

PROTEA FAMILY
Flowers in heads or spikes; sepals 4, slender; petals absent; anthers sessile on the sepals.

RANUNCULUS FAMILY
Leaves divided; stamens many; ovary of many separate carpels.

POPPY FAMILY
Sap milky or coloured; petals 4, crumpled in bud.

SUNDEW FAMILY
Insectivorous, covered with reddish gland-tipped hairs; styles 3–5.

MUSTARD FAMILY
Often with a sulphurous, cabbage-like smell; petals 4; stamens 6.

TWINLEAF FAMILY
Stems jointed; leaves divided into 2 oblique leaflets, fleshy; stipules hard and sharp; stamens 8–10.

OXALIS FAMILY
Rootstock a scaly bulb; leaves 3- (rarely up to 10-) lobed; petals furled in bud; stamens 10 in 2 dissimilar whorls; styles 5.

GERANIUM FAMILY
Leaves often lobed; flowers in umbel-like clusters; stamens 10 or 15; fruits beak-like.

CITRUS FAMILY
Leaves gland-dotted and aromatic; ovary deeply lobed, often horned.

TURNERA FAMILY
Petals furled in bud; styles 3; fruits slender and ± beaded.

HIBISCUS FAMILY
Leaves or stems rough with star-shaped hairs; petals furled in bud; stamens often joined into a tube.

CONVOLVULUS FAMILY
Twining climbers; leaves lobed; petals furled in bud like an umbrella.

PLUMBAGO FAMILY
Stems and leaves often scurfy; calyx persistent and papery; petals furled in bud; styles 5 or deeply 5-lobed.

POTATO FAMILY
Flowers often opposite the leaves; stamens sometimes opening by apical pores; fruit fleshy.

FORGET-ME-NOT FAMILY
Leaves often bristly; inflorescence 1-sided and coiled; ovary 4-lobed.

EUPHORBIA FAMILY
Succulents with milky sap; flowers unisexual, minute; fruit splitting into 3 1-seeded segments.

Flowers symmetrical; stamens as many as the petals or more; ovary superior; leaves opposite.

CRASSULA FAMILY
Succulents with opposite leaves; ovary of 5 separate carpels.

ERICA FAMILY
Heath-like shrubs; leaves whorled; flowers tubular, 4-lobed; anthers 8, with pores and tails.

PENAEA FAMILY
Leaves 4-ranked, overlapping; flowers tubular, leathery; sepals 4; petals absent.

DAPHNE FAMILY
Heath-like shrubs with string-like bark; sepals 4 (5), joined into a tube; petals inconspicuous; style lateral.

CARNATION FAMILY
Leaves opposite, narrow; sepals joined into a tube; petals notched or fringed.

ST JOHN'S WORT FAMILY
Petals furled in bud, short-lived; stamens numerous; styles 3–5.

GENTIAN FAMILY
Leaves opposite; flowers tubular, petals furled in bud; fruits splitting along the joints.

MILKWEED FAMILY
Often succulent, with clear or milky sap; leaves opposite; flowers leathery; anthers fused to style.

BUDDLEJA FAMILY
Leaves opposite; petals and stamens 4.

Flowers 2-lipped; stamens as many as the petals or more; ovary superior.

FUMITORY FAMILY
Twiners with lobed leaves; sepals 2, deciduous; petals 4, separate.

VIOLET FAMILY
Flowers violet-like, spurred or pouched; anthers joined around ovary, with glands.

BALSAM FAMILY
Leaf teeth with slender appendages; lower sepal spurred; anthers joined into a deciduous cap.

MELIANTHUS FAMILY
Leaves regularly divided, with axillary stipules; calyx pouched; petals 4, dissimilar.

POLYGALA FAMILY
Flowers sweetpea-shaped with a fringed crest on the keel; sepals separate, dissimilar; stamens 5–8.

PEA FAMILY
Flowers often sweetpea-shaped; stamens ±10; fruit a pod.

Flowers mostly symmetrical; stamens as many as the petals or more; ovary inferior.

ICE PLANT FAMILY
Succulents; leaves opposite, ± cylindrical; stamens and petals numerous.

MONTINIA FAMILY
Flowers unisexual; petals 4.

BEGONIA FAMILY
Flowers unisexual; styles 3; ovary 3-winged.

CUCUMBER FAMILY
Flowers unisexual; plants tendrilled, climbing.

27

DESERT PRIMROSE FAMILY
Hairy, mucilaginous annuals; flowers axillary, solitary; styles 5–10.

COFFEE FAMILY
Leaves opposite with interpetiolar stipules; flowers tubular.

TIBOUCHINA FAMILY
Leaves opposite, parallel-veined from the base; stamens flexed, with an appendage; anthers with pores.

BELLFLOWER FAMILY
Flowers tubular, sometimes split; anthers shedding pollen onto style, either withered at maturity or joined into a ring.

FAN FLOWER FAMILY
Flowers tubular, split to form a fan; stigma enclosed within a fringed cup.

CARROT FAMILY
Plants with an aromatic parsley-like smell; leaves often divided; flowers in umbels.

BRUNIA FAMILY
Heath-like shrubs; leaves with minute black tip; flowers tubular.

DAISY FAMILY
Inflorescence a head surrounded by scale-like bracts; florets tubular; anthers joined into a collar.

Flowers mostly 2-lipped; stamens fewer than the petals.

SCABIOUS FAMILY
Leaves opposite, lobed or divided; flowers in heads; ovary inferior.

VERBENA FAMILY
Leaves opposite on 4-angled stems; flowers weakly 2-lipped.

MINT FAMILY
Leaves opposite on 4-angled stems, often glandular; fruit 4-lobed.

BLADDERWORT FAMILY
Delicate, apparently leafless insectivores; flowers spurred; stamens 2.

ACANTHUS FAMILY
Shrubs with simple, opposite leaves; seeds borne on hardened, hook-like funicles.

SESAME FAMILY
Plants covered in mucilage glands; fruit woody, horned.

BIGNONIA FAMILY
Leaves compound; seeds flattened and winged.

AFRICAN VIOLET FAMILY
Stemless plants with quilted, velvety leaves.

BROOMRAPE FAMILY
Parasitic plants, turning black when damaged; leaves scale-like, fleshy, yellowish.

SUTERA FAMILY
Leaves often with gland-tipped hairs; flowers often thin-textured; stamens 2 or 4.

Drip Disa (*Disa longicornu*) is a member of the Orchid family.

DESCRIPTIONS OF WILD-FLOWER FAMILIES

ANCIENT DICOTYLEDONS

WATERLILY FAMILY *Nymphaeaceae* – p.46
Rhizomatous aquatic perennials with floating leaves. Leaves basal, spirally arranged, petiolate, round or heart-shaped. Inflorescence of solitary, large, emergent flowers on a long peduncle. Flowers blue, white, yellow or pink, showy, regular, scented; sepals 4; petals 5–many, in several series; stamens many, spirally arranged, outermost with broad, petal-like filaments; ovary sunk in the receptacle, stigmas radiating from a central boss. Fruit a large berry. Worldwide in tropics and subtropics: ±60 spp. Widely cultivated.

MONOCOTYLEDONS

AGAPANTHUS FAMILY *Agapanthaceae* – p.52
Rhizomatous perennials with slimy sap. Leaves basal, in 2 ranks, strap-like and channelled with a thickened midrib. Inflorescence an umbel borne on a leafless scape, enclosed in bud by 2 large membranous or papery bracts. Flowers blue, spreading on slender pedicels, funnel-shaped with 6 tepals joined at the base in a short tube; stamens 6, arising at the top of the tube, of 2 lengths, flexed slightly downwards and arched up at the ends; ovary superior, the style slender and flexed downwards but turned up at the tip. Fruit 3-angled, dry at maturity, flexed sharply downward on the pedicels. Restricted to temperate southern Africa: 10 spp.

ALOE FAMILY *Asphodelaceae* – p.66
Rhizomatous perennials, often with swollen or tuberous roots, or single-stemmed to branched shrubs or trees, rarely annuals, the roots usually with yellow sap. Leaves usually succulent, in a spiral or in 2 ranks, channelled, flat or cylindrical, the margins often spiny. Inflorescence a simple or branched raceme or spike, sometimes crowded into a head. Flowers white, yellow, orange or red, star-like or tubular, with 6 tepals that are separate or joined into a tube; stamens 6, arising at the base of the ovary; ovary superior, style slender. Fruit mostly leathery or dry, rarely a fleshy berry. Old World, most diverse in southern Africa: ±750 spp.

AMARYLLIS FAMILY *Amaryllidaceae* – p.54
Bulbous or rhizomatous perennials with slimy sap. Leaves basal, spirally arranged or more usually in 2 ranks, often strap-like, or slender to broad and usually without a midrib, sometimes spreading on the ground, rarely hairy. Inflorescence an umbel borne on a leafless scape, sometimes 1-flowered or rarely subterranean, enclosed in bud by 2 or more large papery or leafy bracts. Flowers variously coloured, often red, pink or yellow, star- or funnel-shaped to tubular, with 6 tepals that are separate or joined at the base into a short to long tube; stamens 6 (rarely more), arising at the top of the tube, all similar or of 2 lengths, spreading or arching downward; ovary inferior, the style slender and straight or arching downward. Fruit dry or fleshy at maturity. Worldwide, mainly tropical and subtropical, and most diverse in southern Africa: ±850 spp. Includes many horticultural species, such as daffodil, narcissus, snowdrop and hippeastrum.

ANTHERICUM FAMILY *Anthericaceae* – p.66
Rhizomatous or tuberous perennials, sometimes with stiff or swollen roots, usually with leafy stems. Leaves in 2 ranks or in a basal rosette, narrow and channelled, fleshy or firm-textured, often fibrous at the base. Inflorescence a branched or simple raceme, with 1–few flowers at each node. Flowers on jointed pedicels, white, star-like, with 6 separate tepals; stamens 6, the filaments sometimes rough; ovary superior, the style slender. Fruit dry and usually 3-winged. Widespread, mainly tropical: ±250 spp.

APONOGETON FAMILY *Aponogetonaceae* – p.46
Rhizomatous or tuberous, aquatic perennials. Leaves basal, submerged or floating on long petioles, slender to oblong, mostly with a midrib. Inflorescence a small, simple or forked spike, often fleshy. Flowers usually whitish, sometimes unisexual, with 1 or 2 (rarely up to 6) separate tepals; stamens 6 (rarely more); ovary superior, of 3–6 separate carpels, the styles short and curved. Fruit membranous. Old World tropics, mainly in seasonal freshwater pools: 43 spp. The fruiting spikes of *Aponogeton distachyos* are used as a pot herb.

ARUM FAMILY *Araceae* – p.46
Rhizomatous or tuberous perennial herbs or climbers, or minute floating aquatics. Leaves petiolate, the blades simple or variously divided, with watery sap. Inflorescence usually a fleshy column, surrounded by a large coloured or mottled bract. Flowers tiny, often unisexual, with 0–8 minute greenish tepals that are usually separate; stamens 1–7 (sometimes absent), separate or joined; ovary superior, style short. Fruit usually fleshy or leathery. Widespread and largely tropical or subtropical: ±3 300 spp. Most species contain bundles of needle-like crystals of oxalic acid that make them

unpalatable or toxic; *Zantedeschia aethiopica* is important as a cut-flower.

BLACK-STICK LILY FAMILY *Velloziaceae* – p.94

Tufted or shrubby perennials with stems protected by fibrous leaf bases. Leaves tufted at the branch tips, fibrous. Inflorescence of 1–few flowers among the leaves. Flowers mauve or white, star-like, with 6 tepals that are separate or joined into a short tube; stamens 6 on short filaments; ovary inferior, style cylindrical. Fruit 3-lobed and dry. Africa, Madagascar and South America: ±80 spp.

BLOODROOT FAMILY *Haemodoraceae* – p.104

Rhizomatous or cormous perennials with bright orange sap. Leaves basal, oriented edgewise to the stem in 2 ranks forming a fan, flat or pleated, mostly hairy. Inflorescence a cylindrical or flat-topped panicle, often hairy or glandular. Flowers mauve or yellowish, irregular or star-like, with 6 tepals that are separate (Cape species) or joined into a tube; stamens 3, opposite the inner whorl of tepals, all similar or of 2 lengths; ovary superior or inferior, style slender and ± strongly flexed to 1 side. Fruit 3-lobed and dry. Southern Africa, Australia and tropical America: ±100 spp.

COLCHICUM FAMILY *Colchicaceae* – p.98

Cormous or tuberous perennials, sometimes twining. Leaves basal or in a loose spiral up the stem and then sometimes drawn into tendrils, usually thin-textured and mostly lance-shaped. Inflorescence a raceme or spike, or crowded into a head, sometimes 1-flowered. Flowers variously coloured, star-like or cup-shaped, with 6 tepals that are separate or joined at the base and often narrowed below, and bearing a nectar gland; stamens 6; ovary superior, styles 3 or united below but forked above. Fruit dry or leathery. Old World, especially southwestern Cape: ±170 spp. Most species contain the toxic alkaloid colchicine; several are cultivated as ornamentals.

COMMELINA FAMILY *Commelinaceae* – p.50

Rhizomatous perennials or annuals. Leaves basal or scattered up the stem, usually with a closed sheath fringed at the mouth. Inflorescence a terminal and axillary cluster of flowers, sometimes enclosed in boat-shaped spathes. Flowers mauve, blue or yellow, star-shaped or very irregular, with 3 sepals and 3 fragile petals that wither within a few hours; stamens 6, all fertile or some modified into staminodes, with smooth or bearded filaments; ovary superior, style slender, undivided. Fruit either dry or fleshy. Widespread in the tropics and subtropics: ±650 spp.

CRANE FLOWER FAMILY *Strelitziaceae* – p.48

Large perennials or banana-like trees. Leaves in 2 ranks, tough and leathery, petiolate, the blades elliptical, often becoming torn. Inflorescence axillary, pedunculate, crowded within a leathery, boat-like spathe. Flowers white or orange, and blue or mauve, very irregular, with 3 petal-like sepals and 3 petals, the lower 2 joined to form an arrow-shaped blade containing the stamens and style in a central channel; stamens 5; ovary inferior, style 3-branched. Seeds with a woolly tuft. Tropical: ±7 spp. Widely cultivated.

CYANELLA FAMILY *Tecophilaeaceae* – p.102

Cormous or tuberous perennials, rarely climbing. Leaves basal or scattered along the stem, usually spirally arranged, lance-shaped, sometimes with tendrils. Inflorescence a raceme or panicle, or 1-flowered, mostly borne on leafy stems. Flowers white, mauve or yellow, star- or cup-shaped, with 6 tepals that are separate or joined at the base; stamens 6, usually clustered together on short filaments, the anthers with apical pores; ovary half-inferior, style slender, central or flexed to 1 side. Fruit dry and spherical. Tropical and temperate Africa, Chile and California: 25 spp.

HYACINTH FAMILY *Hyacinthaceae* – p.82

Bulbous perennials with slimy sap. Leaves basal, mostly channelled but without a midrib, fleshy, sometimes hairy. Inflorescence a simple raceme or spike borne on a leafless stem, sometimes the stem reduced and the flowers crowded between the leaves. Flowers variously coloured, star-like or funnel-shaped to tubular, with 6 tepals that are separate or united into a short or long tube; stamens 6, arising below the ovary or in the tube when present; ovary superior, style short or slender. Fruit 3-lobed and dry. Mainly subtropical and temperate Africa and Eurasia, most diverse in southern Africa: ±900 spp. Many species are important in horticulture.

IRIS FAMILY *Iridaceae* – p.106

Rhizomatous, cormous or bulbous perennials, rarely shrubs. Leaves mostly sword-shaped and oriented edgewise to the stem in 2 ranks forming a fan, sometimes facing the stem and channelled, sometimes hairy. Inflorence either a spike or the flowers enclosed in leafy bracts, usually on leafy stems, sometimes borne at ground level. Flowers variously coloured, often irregular, star-shaped, iris-like or funnel-shaped to tubular, with 6 tepals that are separate or joined into a short to long tube; stamens 3, opposite the outer whorl of tepals, arising at the mouth of the tube when present, sometimes joined at the base into a column; ovary inferior, style slender and usually divided above, sometimes the branches petal-like. Widespread but most diverse in southern Africa: ±1 800 spp. Many species are grown in gardens, and *Freesia*, *Gladiolus* and *Iris* are widely grown for the cut-flower trade.

LANARIA FAMILY *Lanariaceae* – p.94
Rhizomatous, evergreen perennial. Leaves basal, tough and fibrous, strap-shaped and channelled, hairy below. Inflorescence a dense, flat-topped panicle, densely white-hairy. Flowers small, mauve, densely white-hairy on the outside, funnel-shaped with 6 tepals joined into a tube; stamens 6, arising at the mouth of the tube; ovary inferior, style slender. Fruit papery, with 1 large, pea-like seed. Restricted to South Africa, mainly in grassy fynbos: 1 sp.

ONION FAMILY *Alliaceae* – p.52
Rhizomatous or bulbous perennials with slimy sap, producing an onion or garlic smell when crushed. Leaves basal, usually strap-like. Inflorescence an umbel borne on a leafless scape, enclosed in bud by 2 large membranous or papery bracts. Flowers usually white, blue or pink, spreading on slender pedicels, star- or funnel-shaped, with 6 tepals separate or joined at the base into a short tube; stamens 6, arising at the top of the tube; ovary superior. Fruit 3-angled, dry at maturity. Worldwide, mainly northern hemisphere: ±720 spp. The genus *Allium* is very important economically as the source of onions, garlic, leeks and shallots.

ORCHID FAMILY *Orchidaceae* – p.146
Tuberous or rhizomatous perennials, or epiphytes with fleshy roots. Leaves often in 2 ranks, in terrestrial species mostly spreading on the ground. Inflorescence a spike, raceme or panicle. Flowers variously coloured, long-lasting, mostly 2-lipped, with 6 ± separate tepals, the lowermost often enlarged into a lip and spurred; stamen 1, united with the style to form a thick column, the pollen grains aggregated into pollinia; ovary inferior, often twisted. Fruit leathery or papery, containing numerous minute seeds. Worldwide, especially in the tropics: ±20 000 spp. The family second in size only to the daisies. Many species are cultivated for their ornamental flowers; the genus *Vanilla* is the source of vanilla.

STARGRASS FAMILY *Hypoxidaceae* – p.94
Rhizomatous or cormous perennials. Leaves basal, in 3 ranks, strap-shaped and channelled or pleated, often hairy, with fibrous bases. Inflorescence of 1–several flowers on branched leafless stalks in loose clusters arising from a common point, or the flower stalk reduced and flowers borne at ground level. Flowers white or yellow, occasionally pink to red, often green on the underside, star-shaped, with 6 tepals that are separate or joined into a tube; stamens 6, rarely 3, with short filaments; ovary inferior, sometimes drawn into a long, solid beak, style short, undivided. Fruit dry and opening from a lidded top or a fleshy berry. Widespread in the tropics and subtropics, most diverse in southern Africa: ±130 spp. Species of *Hypoxis* are used medicinally.

TRUE DICOTYLEDONS

ACANTHUS FAMILY *Acanthaceae* – p.430
Herbs, shrubs or trees. Leaves opposite, rarely toothed. Inflorescence an axillary cluster. Flowers variously coloured, funnel- or trumpet-shaped and 2-lipped; sepals mostly 4 or 5, joined into a tube; petals 5, joined into a tube; stamens usually 4, rarely 2, the anther lobes often dissimilar and spurred or crested; ovary superior, style slender, simple or 2-lobed. Fruit dry and often opening explosively, the seeds borne on hardened, hook-like funicles. Worldwide in the tropics and subtropics: ±4 350 spp. Many species are cultivated as ornamentals.

AFRICAN VIOLET FAMILY *Gesneriaceae* – p.442
Annual or perennial herbs, usually stemless. Leaves 1 or more, and then usually opposite, mostly velvety and quilted. Inflorescence 1- or more-flowered. Flowers variously coloured, often blue or mauve, funnel- or trumpet-shaped and 2-lipped; sepals 5, joined into a short tube; petals 5, joined into a long tube; stamens 2, the anther lobes cohering face to face; ovary superior, style slender. Fruit dry, opening spirally. Worldwide in the tropics: ±2 900 spp. Many species are popular indoor or shade plants.

BALSAM FAMILY *Balsaminaceae* – p.272
Soft, brittle, succulent herbs or shrublets. Leaves opposite, alternate or whorled, usually toothed, the teeth usually with a slender, glandular appendage. Inflorescence axillary, 1–few-flowered. Flowers brightly coloured, strongly 2-lipped; sepals 3, the lower one spurred; petals 5, joined at the base, the side ones often lobed; stamens 5, the anthers joined into a deciduous cap over the ovary; ovary superior, style absent. Fruit fleshy, opening explosively. Worldwide in the tropics and subtropics: ±850 spp.; South Africa: 4 spp.

BEGONIA FAMILY *Begoniaceae* – p.320
Unisexual herbs or shrublets, mostly fleshy. Leaves alternate, petiolate, usually asymmetrical with radiating veins, toothed or lobed. Inflorescence an

axillary cluster. Flowers white, pink, red or orange, regular or irregular; sepals and petals not differentiated, showy and petal-like, 2 or 4 in male flowers, usually 5 or 6 in female flowers; stamens many; ovary inferior, 3-winged, styles mostly 3. Fruit 3-winged. Tropical: ±900 spp. Popular as ornamentals.

BELLFLOWER FAMILY *Campanulaceae* – p.326
Mostly shrubs and perennials, sometimes annuals, often with milky sap. Leaves usually alternate, often toothed. Inflorescence usually a raceme, sometimes 1-flowered. Flowers mostly blue, cup-shaped or 2-lipped; sepals mostly 5; petals 4 or 5, united into a short or long tube that is sometimes split down the top or sides; stamens as many as the petals, either withered at maturity (cup-shaped flowers) or clustered into a tube (2-lipped flowers), shedding pollen directly onto the style; ovary mostly inferior, style slender, 2–10-lobed. Fruit dry, opening by apical valves. Worldwide, especially temperate: ±1 700 spp.

BIGNONIA FAMILY *Bignoniaceae* – p.440
Trees or shrubs, often scrambling or climbing. Leaves opposite, usually compound and divided into leaflets. Inflorescence a terminal or lateral cluster. Flowers variously coloured, funnel- or trumpet-shaped and 2-lipped; sepals mostly 5, joined into a short tube; petals 5, joined into a long tube, often hairy within at the base of the stamens; stamens usually 4, of 2 lengths; ovary superior, style slender, 2-lobed. Fruit usually dry, with flat, winged seeds. Worldwide in the tropics: ±750 spp. Many species are popular garden plants.

BLADDERWORT FAMILY *Utriculariaceae* – p.430
Delicate, insectivorous perennials or annuals growing in wet places. Leaves inconspicuous, basal or scattered on creeping stems, some developed into insect traps. Inflorescence a raceme. Flowers white, mauve or yellow, 2-lipped; sepals 2 or 5; petals 5, joined into a 2-lipped corolla, the lower lip larger and spurred at the base; stamens 2, arising from the base of the tube on short, curved filaments; ovary superior, style slender, 2-lobed. Fruit dry, often opening by a lid. Worldwide in wet places: ±245 spp.

BROOMRAPE FAMILY *Orobanchaceae* – p.442
Parasitic or hemiparasitic perennials or annuals, often fleshy and hairy, frequently turning black when drying. Leaves opposite, alternate or whorled, sometimes reduced and scale-like, often yellowish and lacking chlorophyll. Inflorescence a raceme or spike, rarely a solitary flower in an upper axil.

Flowers variously coloured, often conspicuous, irregular or 2-lipped; sepals 4 or 5, joined into a cup; petals 4 or 5 (rarely 3), joined into a 2-lipped corolla, in bud the upper lip entirely or partially enclosed by the lower; stamens 2 or 4, of 2 lengths, arising within the corolla tube; ovary superior, style slender. Fruit usually dry. Worldwide: ±600 spp. Complete or partial root parasites on various shrubs and grasses; some, like witchweed (*Striga*) and broomrape (*Orobanche*), are pests of crops.

BRUNIA FAMILY *Bruniaceae* – p.340
Shrubs, mostly heath-like. Leaves spirally arranged, small, ± needle-like, always with a minute, dry, black tip. Inflorescence often a small, dense, rounded head, sometimes a spike or panicle. Flowers mostly small, often cream-coloured or white, star- or cup-shaped; sepals 5, separate or joined at the base; petals 5, mostly separate but sometimes joined below; stamens 5; ovary ± inferior, styles 1 or 2, short. Fruit dry. South Africa, mostly southwestern Cape in fynbos: ±64 spp.

BUDDLEJA FAMILY *Buddlejaceae* – p.268
Shrubs or trees. Leaves opposite, alternate or whorled, with stipules present or represented by a ridge between the bases of opposite leaves. Inflorescence a panicle or raceme. Flowers cup- or funnel-shaped; sepals 4, joined at the base; petals 4, joined into a short or longer tube, sometimes bearded in the throat; stamens 4; ovary superior, hairy, style 1. Widespread in the tropics: ±120 spp.

CARNATION FAMILY *Caryophyllaceae* – p.252
Annuals, perennials or small shrublets. Leaves mostly opposite, often narrow. Inflorescence varied, ± branched, the branching evenly forked. Flowers mostly pink or white, star- or salver-shaped; sepals 4 or 5, mostly joined into a tube; petals 4 or 5, separate, sometimes narrowed below, often lobed or fringed; stamens 4, 5 or 10, arising below the ovary; ovary superior, styles 2–5, slender. Fruit dry and splitting from the apex. Worldwide, mainly north temperate: ±2 200 spp. *Dianthus* is the florists' carnation.

CARROT FAMILY *Apiaceae* – p.338
Tuberous perennials or annuals, occasionally shrubs or small trees, often aromatic (parsley or celery). Leaves alternate, the petioles sheathing at the base, mostly lobed or divided, often into fine segments. Inflorescence a simple or compound umbel. Flowers small, usually white to yellow, star-shaped, mostly on wiry pedicels; sepals 5; petals 5, separate, often keeled, short-lived; stamens 5; ovary inferior, styles 2, usually short. Fruit dividing into 2 segments,

containing oil ducts. Worldwide, mainly temperate: ±3 500 spp. Includes many culinary herbs and food plants such as the carrot, parsnip, fennel, parsley and celery; some, such as hemlock, are deadly.

CITRUS FAMILY *Rutaceae* – p.210
Trees, shrubs or shrublets, often aromatic, rarely unisexual, frequently heath-like. Leaves opposite or alternate, often small and leathery or needle-like, sometimes divided, dotted with translucent oil glands and aromatic. Inflorescence a terminal or axillary cluster or raceme, sometimes 1-flowered. Flowers mostly white to pink, star-shaped; sepals 5 (rarely 4), separate or joined at the base; petals 5 (rarely 4), separate, often narrowed below, very rarely absent; stamens 5 (rarely 10), arising at the base of the ovary or on the disc, sometimes alternating with petal-like staminodes; ovary superior, surrounded by a fleshy, nectar-secreting disc, deeply lobed or divided into separate carpels, style slender. Fruit dry and splitting into segments, or fleshy. Worldwide, mostly tropical but many in the southwestern Cape: ±1 650 spp. Includes lemons, oranges and grapefruit; *Agathosma* species (buchu) are important flavourants and medicines.

COFFEE FAMILY *Rubiaceae* – p.324
Trees, shrubs or herbs. Leaves opposite or whorled, simple, with interpetiolar stipules on each side of the stem between the 2 leaves of each pair. Inflorescence mostly a terminal or axillary cluster. Flowers often white, symmetrical, funnel- or salver-shaped; sepals mostly 4 or 5, joined into a tube; petals mostly 4 or 5, joined into a tube; stamens as many as the petals; ovary inferior, style slender, 2-lobed, often heterostylous. Fruit dry or fleshy, sometimes crowned with the persistent sepals. Worldwide, especially tropical: ±10 200 spp. Valuable as the source of quinine (*Cinchona*) and coffee (*Coffea*); also widely cultivated as ornamentals.

CONVOLVULUS FAMILY *Convolvulaceae* – p.222
Herbs or shrubs, often twining, rarely parasitic. Leaves alternate, often palmately lobed. Inflorescence mostly few-flowered and axillary. Flowers variously coloured, often showy, funnel-shaped, short-lived; sepals mostly 5, joined below into a cup; petals 5, joined into a narrow to wide tube that in bud is rolled like an umbrella, thin-textured; stamens 5, arising from the base of the corolla tube; ovary superior, styles 1 or 2, slender. Fruit dry. Worldwide, especially tropical: ±1 700 spp.

CRASSULA FAMILY *Crassulaceae* – p.234
Mostly succulent shrubs, perennials or annuals. Leaves opposite or alternate, sometimes in rosettes, flat to cylindrical, succulent. Inflorescence usually branched, often flat-topped. Flowers variously coloured, mostly white or pink, star- or cup-shaped to tubular; sepals 3–5, separate or joined; petals 3–5, separate or joined into a tube; stamens as many as or twice as many as the petals, arising at the base or on the petals; ovary superior, of 3–5 separate carpels, tapering into the styles. Fruit dry, with 5 separate segments. Worldwide, with centres of diversity in southern Africa and Central America: ±1 500 spp. Widely cultivated as ornamentals.

CUCUMBER FAMILY *Cucurbitaceae* – p.322
Herbs or shrubs, climbing by means of tendrils, usually roughly hairy. Leaves alternate, usually palmately lobed. Flowers usually unisexual, symmetrical, mostly solitary, white or yellow; sepals 5, separate; petals 5, separate or joined at the base; male flowers usually with 3 stamens; female flowers with an inferior ovary; style simple or divided. Fruit a fleshy or corky berry. Worldwide, mainly tropical and subtropical: ±735 spp. Grown for the edible fruits, including melons, cucumbers, pumpkins and squash.

DAISY FAMILY *Asteraceae* – p.344
Small trees, shrubs, perennials or annuals, often aromatic. Leaves alternate or opposite, sometimes lobed or divided, hairless or hairy. Inflorescence a head surrounded by scale-like bracts. Flowers (florets) small, often yellow or purple, funnel-shaped or the outer row forming petal-like rays; sepals absent or represented by minute scales or bristles, petals 4 or 5, joined into a narrow tube; stamens 4 or 5, the anthers usually united into a tube around the style; ovary inferior, style slender, usually forked at the tip. Fruit a dry nutlet, often crowned with scales or bristles, rarely fleshy. Worldwide: ±25 000 spp. (the largest plant family). Widely grown for medicinal purposes and food, and as ornamentals.

DAPHNE FAMILY *Thymelaeaceae* – p.246
Small trees or shrubs, often heath-like, with tough bark that strips into strings. Leaves alternate or opposite, often narrow or needle-like and pressed against the stems, often covered with silvery hairs. Inflorescence a spike or head, rarely 1-flowered. Flowers usually white to yellow, or pinkish, tubular; sepals 4 or 5, joined into a slender or funnel-shaped tube, often coloured; petals absent or represented by small scales inserted at the mouth of the tube, as many as or twice as many as the sepals; stamens 4, 8 or 10, arising in the tube and often hidden within it; ovary superior, style arising laterally, slender. Fruit enclosed within the calyx.

Worldwide, especially Africa and Australia: ±600 spp. Many members of the family are poisonous.

DESERT PRIMROSE FAMILY *Neuradaceae* – p.322
Prostrate, hairy annuals with a taproot and slimy or mucilaginous sap. Leaves alternate, toothed or deeply lobed, leathery and hairy. Inflorescence 1-flowered, axillary. Flowers yellow, cup-shaped; sepals 5, joined into a cup; petals 5, separate; stamens 10, arising on the calyx cup; ovary ± inferior, styles 5–10, short. Fruit woody and disc-like, often spiny on top. Dry regions of Africa and western Asia to India: 9 spp.

ERICA FAMILY *Ericaceae* – p.240
Heath-like shrubs, shrublets or small trees. Leaves mostly whorled, usually ± needle-like, hard, the margins tightly rolled under. Inflorescence a raceme or whorl, or a small cluster on a short shoot. Flowers brightly coloured, often shades of pink, sometimes sticky, cup-shaped to tubular, leathery; sepals 4, joined below, sometimes coloured and larger than the petals; petals 4, joined into a short or long tube; stamens mostly 8, arising below the ovary, anthers often opening by basal pores and often tailed; ovary superior, style mostly slender. Fruit usually small and dry. Worldwide: ±4 500 spp. In southern Africa represented mainly by the large genus *Erica*.

EUPHORBIA FAMILY *Euphorbiaceae* – p.232
Trees, shrubs or herbs, often succulent, with milky latex. Leaves usually alternate, undivided, sometimes rudimentary. Inflorescence varied, often surrounded by fleshy, petal-like bracts. Flowers often unisexual, tiny, greenish; sepals and petals small, sometimes absent; stamens 1–many; ovary superior. Fruit usually dry and 3-chambered, with 1 seed per chamber, splitting between the lobes. Worldwide, mainly tropical and often in dry areas: ±7 000 spp. Many species are toxic.

FAN FLOWER FAMILY *Goodeniaceae* – p.338
Shrublets. Leaves alternate or basal. Inflorescence an axillary cluster. Flowers white, pink or blue, 2-lipped; sepals 5; petals 5, joined in a tube that is split to the base and hairy within; stamens 5, anthers crested; ovary inferior, style thick, stigma enclosed within a fringed cup. Fruit hard, not splitting open. Southern hemisphere, mainly Australasia: ±430 spp.

FORGET-ME-NOT FAMILY *Boraginaceae* – p.228
Trees, shrubs, perennials and annuals, often harshly hairy or bristly. Leaves mostly alternate, simple. Inflorescence usually a branched, 1-sided raceme coiling at the tips. Flowers often shades of blue, cup-shaped; sepals 5, joined below into a cup; petals 5, joined into a short tube, sometimes with scales or folds in the throat; stamens 5, arising in the floral tube; ovary superior, often deeply 4-lobed, style slender, sometimes forked above. Fruit fragmenting into several small, often spiny nutlets, rarely fleshy. Worldwide, especially the Mediterranean: ±2 500 spp.

FUMITORY FAMILY *Fumariaceae* – p.270
Glaucous, brittle annuals or perennials, often sprawling or climbing, with watery sap. Leaves finely divided and often ending in a tendril. Inflorescence a raceme. Flowers mostly pink or yellow, 2-lipped; sepals 2, scale-like, short-lived; petals 4, in 2 dissimilar pairs, the outer 2 sometimes pouched or spurred at the base; stamens 2–6, separate or joined in 2 bundles; ovary superior, style slender, 2-lobed. Fruit dry, sometimes bladder-like. Mostly north temperate: ±530 spp. Closely related to and sometimes included in the Poppy family.

GENTIAN FAMILY *Gentianaceae* – p.254
Shrubs, perennials or annuals. Leaves mostly opposite or in a basal rosette, simple. Inflorescence mostly few-flowered. Flowers mostly pink or yellow, often showy, cup- or salver-shaped; sepals 4 or 5, joined into a cup; petals mostly 4 or 5, joined into a tube, in bud furled like an umbrella; stamens as many as the petals, arising in the tube; ovary superior, style short and thick. Fruit dry, rarely fleshy. Worldwide, mainly temperate and subtropical: ±1 200 spp. Important commercially as the source of bitters.

GERANIUM FAMILY *Geraniaceae* – p.200
Shrubs, perennials or annuals, often hairy and aromatic, sometimes succulent. Leaves alternate or opposite, usually lobed or divided. Inflorescence an axillary umbel, sometimes few-flowered. Flowers variously coloured, often pink to purple with darker veins, star-shaped or 2-lipped; sepals 5, separate or joined below; petals 5 (or fewer), separate, often notched at the tips; stamens 10 or 15, sometimes not all fertile, filaments sometimes joined at the base; ovary superior, style dividing into 3–5 branches. Fruit with a long beak, fragmenting into segments that curl up from the base. Widespread in temperate and subtropical regions: ±800 spp. Includes many horticultural subjects in the genera *Geranium* and *Pelargonium*.

HIBISCUS FAMILY *Malvaceae* (=*Sterculiaceae, Tiliaceae*) – p.214
Trees, shrubs and perennials, with mealy, star-shaped hairs. Leaves alternate, often palmately lobed or divided and with toothed margins, often with

conspicuous stipules. Inflorescence an axillary cluster or 1-flowered. Flowers variously coloured, often yellow or pink, cup-shaped or furled, with or without a whorl of sepal-like bracts beneath the calyx; sepals 3–5, joined below into a cup; petals 5, separate but often joined to the base of the staminal column, in bud furled like an umbrella; stamens 5–many, the filaments often joined into a tubular column; ovary superior, style often branched. Fruit dry, often fragmenting into segments. Worldwide, especially tropical: ±3 500 spp. The family now includes the Cola family (Sterculiaceae) and the Linden family (Tiliaceae). Many genera are cultivated, notably *Althaea* (hollyhock), *Abutilon* and *Hibiscus*; the tropical *Gossypium* is the source of cotton.

ICE PLANT FAMILY *Aizoaceae* (=*Mesembryanthemaceae*) – p.304
Succulent shrubs, perennials or annuals. Leaves mostly opposite, sometimes in rosettes, usually cylindrical or 3-angled in cross section. Inflorescence a small or large cluster, or 1-flowered. Flowers variously coloured, often brilliant red, purple or pink, symmetrical; sepals 4–6; petals absent or more often numerous and narrow; stamens 4–many, often numerous, sometimes with staminodes; ovary inferior, style often short or absent. Fruit a woody capsule, often opening when damp by pointed flaps, then star-like. Worldwide but mostly southwestern Cape: ±2 000 spp. A characteristic element of succulent karoo shrublands.

MELIANTHUS FAMILY *Melianthaceae* – p.272
Trees, shrubs or subshrubs, often foetid. Leaves alternate, divided into many, evenly toothed leaflets, axis ± winged, with conspicuous axillary stipules. Inflorescence a raceme. Flowers greenish, brown or red, 2-lipped, twisting through 180° at flowering; sepals 5, of 2 types, joined into a cup, pouched below; petals 4 or 5, separate, narrowed below, of 2 types; stamens 4, separate or joined, arising below the ovary within a fleshy, nectar-secreting disc, short and often bent forward; ovary superior, style slender, hairy at the base. Fruit leathery, lantern-like, 4-lobed or -winged. Sub-Saharan Africa: ±20 spp.

MILKWEED FAMILY *Apocynaceae* (=*Asclepiadaceae*) – p.258
Trees, shrubs, perennials or annuals, sometimes vines, often succulents, with milky or clear sap. Leaves opposite with successive pairs at right angles to one another, sometimes in whorls or occasionally reduced or absent. Inflorescence

mostly a few-flowered terminal or axillary cluster, often flat-topped. Flowers variously coloured, sometimes showy, cup-shaped to tubular, leathery; sepals 5, separate or joined below into a cup, petals 5, joined below into a narrow to wide tube, often with scales or hairs in the throat; stamens 5, sometimes united with the stigmas into a fleshy body; ovary superior, sometimes with 2 separate carpels, style 1 or 2, joined at the tips. Fruit dry or fleshy, sometimes with paired, often horn-like segments, the seeds often plumed. Worldwide, mostly tropical: ±4 800 spp. Many contain poisonous alkaloids; the stapeliads, or carrion-flowers, are popular among succulent collectors.

MINT FAMILY *Lamiaceae* – p.418
Small trees, shrubs and perennials, sometimes annuals, mostly glandular and aromatic with essential oils; the stems often square in cross section. Leaves opposite or whorled, mostly toothed. Inflorescence usually raceme- or spike-like, with flowers in loose or tight whorls. Flowers variously coloured, often white or pink to blue, irregular, mostly 2-lipped; sepals 5, joined into a cup-like calyx, sometimes variously lipped; petals 5, joined into a 2-lipped corolla, the lower lip often largest, sometimes boat-shaped; stamens 2 or 4, arising in the tube; ovary superior, deeply 4-lobed above, style slender, often 2-lobed at the tip. Fruit of 4 1-seeded nutlets. Worldwide, especially subtropical and Mediterranean: ±7 000 spp. Contains many culinary herbs, including basil, rosemary, sage and mint, as well as several garden plants.

MONTINIA FAMILY *Montiniaceae* – p.320
Unisexual shrubs or small trees. Leaves alternate, simple, glaucous and leathery. Inflorescence 1–few-flowered in terminal clusters. Flowers white, regular, star-shaped; sepals 4, joined into a cup with very short lobes; petals 4, separate, leathery, stamens 4 in male flowers, arising at the base of a fleshy, nectar-secreting disc or basin, short; ovary inferior, absent in male flowers, style short, 2-branched. Fruit leathery, flask-shaped. Eastern and southern Africa and Madagascar: ±4 spp.

MUSTARD FAMILY *Brassicaceae* (=*Capparaceae*) – p.190
Perennials, annuals, shrubs or small trees, often tasting and smelling of mustard or sulphur. Leaves mostly alternate, often lobed or divided. Inflorescence usually a slender raceme, sometimes ± flat-topped. Flowers often yellow, white or blue, cross-shaped; sepals 4 in 2 pairs, the inner often sac-like or spurred, petals 4 (rarely absent), separate, usually narrow at the base; stamens usually 6 with

the outer 2 shorter (rarely numerous); ovary superior, sometimes stalked, style usually short. Fruit dry and papery, short or long, the outer wall splitting into 2 halves, leaving the seeds attached to a central partition. Worldwide, mostly northern hemisphere: ±3 000 spp. Includes many ornamentals as well as food plants such as cabbage, broccoli and mustard.

OXALIS FAMILY *Oxalidaceae* – p.198
Bulbous perennials, rarely annuals, often stemless, brittle and sour-tasting. Leaves alternate or basal, usually digitately divided into 3–several leaflets that often fold closed at night. Inflorescence an umbel or 1-flowered. Flowers variously coloured, often pink or yellow, with a yellow centre, funnel-shaped; sepals 5, separate; petals 5, narrowed below and joined at the base, in bud furled like an umbrella; stamens 10 in 2 dissimilar whorls, joined at the base; ovary superior, styles 5, slender. Fruit fleshy, splitting explosively. Nearly cosmopolitan, mainly South America and southern Africa, especially southwestern Cape: ±900 spp. The characteristic sour taste comes from oxalic acid crystals in the cells.

PEA FAMILY *Fabaceae* – p.276
Trees, shrubs, perennials or annuals. Leaves mostly alternate, usually compound, sometimes needle-like, often with conspicuous stipules. Inflorescence usually a raceme, sometimes tightly clustered. Flowers mostly yellow, or pink to purple, regular or irregular, often sweetpea-shaped; sepals mostly 5, often joined into a cup; petals mostly 5, separate at the base, uppermost largest, forming a flag, the lower 2 joined along the edge into a keel hiding the stamens and style, the 2 laterals forming wings; stamens mostly twice as many as the petals, frequently joined into a split tube; ovary superior, style slender, usually hooked at the tip. Fruit a pod with seeds arranged in a single row. Worldwide: ±18 000 spp. Characterised by the presence of nitrogen-fixing bacteria in specialised root nodules; includes many important food plants, such as beans, peas and lentils.

PENAEA FAMILY *Penaeaceae* – p.244
Shrubs or shrublets, mostly hairless. Leaves opposite and in 4 ranks, simple and leathery, usually overlapping. Inflorescence a spike or small head-like cluster, sometimes 1-flowered. Flowers mostly yellow or pink, sometimes bicoloured, tubular or bell-shaped, leathery; sepals 4, brightly coloured and petal-like, joined into a fleshy tube; petals absent; stamens 4, with short fleshy filaments and anthers, arising in the throat of the tube; ovary superior, style slender, sometimes ridged or winged. Fruit dry. Southwestern Cape in fynbos: 23 spp.

PLUMBAGO FAMILY *Plumbaginaceae* – p.226
Shrubs or perennials. Leaves alternate or in a basal rosette, stiff and leathery, sometimes reduced to scales, usually with scattered, scurfy chalk glands. Inflorescence a raceme or flat-topped panicle. Flowers mostly pink to blue, sometimes bicoloured, funnel- or salver-shaped; sepals 5, joined into a 5–15-ribbed tube, often papery and coloured, or glandular; petals 5, joined below into a short or long tube, in bud furled like an umbrella; stamens 5, arising at the base of the tube or below the ovary; ovary superior, styles 1 or 5, slender. Fruit dry, enclosed by the persistent calyx. Worldwide, especially the Mediterranean and Near East, mainly maritime and arid areas in saline conditions: ±650 spp. Excess calcium salts are excreted through the specialised chalk glands; plumbago (*Plumbago auriculata*) is widely grown as an ornamental in South Africa.

POLYGALA FAMILY *Polygalaceae* – p.274
Small trees, shrubs or perennials, often ericoid. Leaves mostly alternate, sometimes tufted, simple and often needle-like. Inflorescence usually 1-flowered, often in racemes. Flowers mostly pink to purple, 2-lipped and sweetpea-shaped; sepals 5, separate, the lateral ones sometimes wing-like; petals 3 or 5, joined at the base to the stamens, the lowermost forming a keel with a fringe or crest near the tip; stamens 5–8, the filaments usually joined into a split tube, curved at the ends; ovary superior, style slender, often flattened and lobed at the tip. Fruit dry, rarely fleshy. Nearly worldwide: ±950 spp. Some species of *Polygala* are popular garden plants.

POPPY FAMILY *Papaveraceae* – p.188
Annuals or perennials, hairless, hairy or prickly, with milky or coloured sap. Leaves alternate, mostly basal, often lobed or divided and often bristly or prickly. Inflorescence often 1-flowered. Flowers brightly coloured, regular; sepals mostly 2, separate or joined, short-lived; petals mostly 4, separate, crumpled in bud; stamens many, separate; ovary superior, style absent or short. Fruit dry, opening by valves or pores at the top. Mostly north temperate: ±240 spp. Several species are cultivated; the Opium Poppy (*Papaver somniferum*) is the source of opium.

POTATO FAMILY *Solanaceae* – p.226
Trees, shrubs, perennials or annuals, erect or climbing, sometimes prickly. Leaves alternate or in tufts, often ± lobed. Inflorescence mostly a small

lateral cluster arising opposite or alongside the leaves, or 1-flowered. Flowers variously coloured but often shades of blue, star-shaped to funnel-shaped; sepals usually 4 or 5, joined below into a cup; petals 4 or 5, joined at the base or into a short or long tube; stamens 4 or 5, arising in the corolla tube, often clustered and opening by apical pores; ovary superior, 2-chambered, the cross-wall diagonally orientated relative to the stem, style slender or stout. Fruit often a fleshy berry. Worldwide, mainly tropical and subtropical: ±2 600 spp. Includes many important food plants, such as the tomato (*Lycopersicon esculentum*), potato (*Solanum tuberosum*), aubergine (*S. melongena*) and peppers (*Capsicum* spp.); ornamentals like petunia; and tobacco (*Nicotiana tabacum*). Many species contain poisonous alkaloids.

PROTEA FAMILY *Proteaceae* – p.166
Trees, shrubs or shrublets, erect or creeping, sometimes with the sexes on separate plants. Leaves mostly alternate, or in whorls, sometimes divided into needle-like segments, flat or thread-like, leathery, often turned sideways. Inflorescence a raceme, panicle or head and then often surrounded by coloured bracts. Flowers usually whitish, regular or irregular, slender, often hairy; sepals 4, separate or joined below into a tube, narrow or thread-like; petals absent; stamens 4, the anthers often stalkless and arising near the tips of the sepals; ovary superior, style stiff, often swollen or needle-like at the tip. Fruit cone-like or a woody nutlet. Southern continents, mainly Australia and southern Africa: ±1 350 spp. Several species and hybrids of protea (*Protea*) and pincushion (*Leucospermum*) are grown as ornamentals or cut-flowers.

RANUNCULUS FAMILY *Ranunculaceae* – p.186
Annuals or perennials, sometimes shrubs or climbers, rarely aquatic. Leaves usually alternate or crowded basally, often divided, usually sheathing at the base. Inflorescence a panicle, often flat-topped, or 1-flowered. Flowers variously coloured, often star-shaped; sepals 3–many, separate, often deciduous, sometimes petal-like; petals 0–many, separate; stamens many, separate, arising below the ovary; ovary usually of many separate carpels, styles slender or absent. Fruit comprising many nutlets, rarely fleshy. Worldwide, mainly temperate: ±1 750 spp. Many genera, including *Anemone*, *Delphinium* and *Ranunculus*, are cultivated in gardens and as cut-flowers.

SCABIOUS FAMILY *Dipsacaceae* – p.416
Shrublets, perennials or annuals. Leaves usually opposite, often lobed and divided. Inflorescence a small head surrounded by scale-like bracts. Flowers small, white or lilac, funnel-shaped and ± 2-lipped; sepals 5–20 and bristle-like or joined into a collar; petals 5, usually hairy, joined into a wide tube; stamens 4 (rarely 5), arising in the corolla tube; ovary inferior, style slender. Fruit an achene topped with bristles or a crown. Africa and Eurasia, mainly Mediterranean: 350–400 spp.

SESAME FAMILY *Pedaliaceae* – p.438
Annual or perennial herbs, shrubs or small trees, usually covered in short, glandular hairs and foetid-smelling. Leaves ± opposite, or upper leaves alternate, often lobed. Inflorescence usually axillary, sometimes a raceme. Flowers often pink or mauve, funnel-shaped, irregular and weakly 2-lipped, usually with 2 small spherical extrafloral nectaries at the base of the pedicels; sepals 5, joined into a short tube; petals 5, joined into a tube, sometimes sac-like or spurred at the base; stamens 4, of 2 lengths; ovary superior, surrounded by a nectar-secreting disc; style 1, slender, 2-lobed. Fruit woody, often spiny or horned, with sculptured and winged seeds. Tropical: ±85 spp. Sesame (*Sesamum orientale*), originally from India, is cultivated for its seeds.

ST JOHN'S WORT FAMILY *Hypericaceae* – p.252
Trees, shrubs or herbs. Leaves opposite, simple, dotted or streaked with glands. Inflorescence with 1 or more flowers, terminal. Flowers mostly yellow, often tinged with red, star-shaped; sepals 5, often dotted with glands and with stalked glands on the margins; petals 5, separate, short-lived, gland-dotted, in bud furled like an umbrella; stamens numerous, joined in clusters at the base; ovary superior, styles 3–5, sometimes joined at the base. Fruit dry, splitting between the lobes. Widespread: ±1 000 spp.

SUNDEW FAMILY *Droseraceae* – p.190
Insectivorous perennials or annuals. Leaves basal and/or scattered along the stem, with sticky reddish glands and tentacles. Inflorescence 1–few-flowered, often coiled in bud. Flowers usually pink or white, star-shaped; sepals 5; petals 5, separate; stamens 5; ovary superior, styles 3–5, sometimes deeply divided. Worldwide, especially in moist, acidic soils: ±100 spp.

SUTERA FAMILY *Scrophulariaceae* – p.450
Trees, shrubs, perennials or annuals. Leaves usually opposite, sometimes tufted, often toothed, frequently glandular and foetid. Inflorescence a raceme, spike, head or panicle. Flowers variously coloured, often blue, mauve or white, usually irregular, often 2-lipped; sepals 4 or 5, joined into

a short tube, sometimes with dissimilar lobes; petals 4 or 5, joined into a short or long tube; stamens usually 4, of 2 lengths, sometimes with the anther lobes joined; ovary superior, style slender. Fruit dry or fleshy. Worldwide, mainly Africa: ±2 000 spp. Includes ornamentals such as *Nemesia*. The family has recently undergone a radical reclassification and many northern hemisphere genera with 2-lipped flowers previously considered to belong here, such as Foxglove (*Digitalis*), Snapdragon (*Antirrhinum*) and Beardtongue (*Penstemon*), are now classified in a separate family with the plantains (*Plantago*).

TIBOUCHINA FAMILY *Melastomataceae* – p.324
Herbs, shrubs or trees. Leaves opposite or whorled, with 3–9 parallel veins from the base. Inflorescence a spike or panicle, sometimes a head-like cluster. Flowers pink to purple, regular; sepals 4 or 5; petals 4 or 5, separate; stamens as many as or, more usually, twice as many as the petals, sometimes of 2 lengths, usually with a joint or appendage; ovary inferior, style slender, unlobed. Fruit dry or fleshy. Worldwide, tropics and subtropics: ±3 000 spp.

TURNERA FAMILY *Turneraceae* – p.212
Trees, shrubs or herbs, often bristly. Leaves alternate, often variously cut or toothed. Inflorescence a raceme or 1-flowered. Flowers yellow or orange, regular; sepals 5, joined below; petals 5, separate, in bud furled like an umbrella; stamens 5, separate; ovary superior, styles 3, slender, often heterostylous. Fruit slender or egg-shaped, dry. Tropical: ±190 spp.

TWINLEAF FAMILY *Zygophyllaceae* – p.194
Shrubs, perennials or annuals, often with jointed branches. Leaves usually opposite, often somewhat fleshy, frequently divided into 2 oblique leaflets, stipules often hard and sharp. Inflorescence with 1 or 2 flowers, axillary. Flowers mostly yellow, star-shaped; sepals 5, separate or joined at the base; petals 4 or 5, separate; stamens as many as or twice as many as the petals, often with scales or appendages at the base; ovary superior, often surrounded by a fleshy, lobed disc at the base, styles 1–5, slender. Fruit dry and 5-lobed, rarely fleshy. Widespread in the tropics and subtropics, mostly deserts and arid regions: ±250 spp.

VERBENA FAMILY *Verbenaceae* – p.416
Trees, shrubs and perennials, sometimes glandular and aromatic with essential oils; the stems often square in cross section. Leaves opposite or whorled, sometimes toothed. Inflorescence clustered, raceme- or spike-like. Flowers variously coloured, often white or pink, irregular, weakly 2-lipped; sepals 4 or 5, joined into a cup-like calyx; petals 4 or 5, joined into a tubular corolla; stamens 4, arising in the tube; ovary superior, style slender. Fruit fleshy or leathery, with 4 1-seeded nutlets. Worldwide, especially tropical and subtropical: ±1 000 spp. Contains several ornamentals.

VIOLET FAMILY *Violaceae* – p.270
Perennials, annuals, shrubs or trees. Leaves alternate, simple, often toothed. Inflorescence 1-flowered, axillary. Flowers often blue or yellow, 2-lipped; sepals 5, usually separate; petals 5, separate, the lower ones often spurred or pouched; stamens 5, arising below the ovary, anthers joined into a ring around the ovary, with glands or nectaries on the back; ovary superior, style often swollen above. Fruit often splitting open explosively. Widespread in the tropics: ±830 spp. The mainly temperate genus *Viola* is widely cultivated.

Members of the Oxalis family are characteristically sour-tasting.

HOW TO USE THE FAMILY FINDER

The family finder makes use of characteristics that are relatively rare or diagnostic for certain South African wild-flower families and are thus valuable for identification. To find the family of an unfamiliar plant, first determine whether the plant in question is a monocotyledon or a dicotyledon by reading the descriptions under the relevant headings below and on page 42. Select the appropriate chart, then look at the key below it and choose an obvious character shown by your plant. The numbers in the key correspond to the numbers across the top of the chart. Match the number of your chosen character to a number at the top of the chart and read down the column to discover

MONOCOTYLEDONS

Herbs, rarely tree-like. Leaves with parallel venation, often strap-shaped.
Flowers with parts in multiples of 3, often with undifferentiated sepals and petals.

FAMILY	1	2	3	4	5	6	7	8	9	10	11	12	13	14
Agapanthus														
Aloe		●	◐		◐					◐		◐	●	
Amaryllis						◐								
Anthericum														
Aponogeton	●								●					
Arum									●	◐				
Black-stick Lily							●							
Bloodroot							◐	●			◐		●	
Colchicum					◐	◐								
Commelina					◐		●		◐					
Crane Flower			●						●					
Cyanella														
Hyacinth		◐				◐	◐		◐	◐				
Iris			◐			◐		◐						
Lanaria							●							
Onion														●
Orchid				◐					◐	◐				
Stargrass	◐					◐	◐				◐			
	1	2	3	4	5	6	7	8	9	10	11	12	13	14

KEY TO NUMBERING

Growth form
1 Aquatic
2 Succulent
3 Tree or shrub
4 Epiphyte
5 Climber or scrambler
6 Stemless

Leaves
7 Stem and/or leaves hairy
8 Oriented edgewise to the stem, fan-like
9 Petiolate
10 Spotted or blotched
11 Pleated

12 Toothed
13 Sap yellow or orange
14 Garlic or onion smell

Inflorescence
15 Peduncle without scattered leaves or bracts

the families to which your plant could belong. Note them down; with luck, your list may comprise just one or two families. Check the relevant family descriptions (p.30) to make a final decision.

If your list contains several families, select another character from the key and repeat the process, referring back to your shortlist of families that show the first character. In your shortlist, underline each family name that also shows the second character. You should now have a much reduced list of underlined possibilities. Each time you repeat this exercise with a new character, you will reduce the list of options. Finally, check the relevant family descriptions to confirm your identification.

● indicates that all species in a family have the feature   ◐ indicates that only some species have the feature

15	16	17	18	19	20	21	22	23	24	25	26	27	28	29	FAMILY
●			●												Agapanthus
					◐					◐					Aloe
●		●	◐									●			Amaryllis
	●		●												Anthericum
		●											●	●	Aponogeton
●		●								●			●		Arum
●				●				●				●		●	Black-stick Lily
					◐	◐	●	●				●			Bloodroot
												●			Colchicum
					●	◐			◐						Commelina
						●						●		●	Crane Flower
	●			◐								●			Cyanella
●	◐			◐						◐			◐		Hyacinth
	◐			◐	◐	◐		●		◐	●			●	Iris
							●					●			Lanaria
●			●												Onion
	●					●						●	●		Orchid
				◐			◐	◐				●	●		Stargrass
15	16	17	18	19	20	21	22	23	24	25	26	27	28	29	

16 Pedicels jointed or with a bracteole midway
17 Spike
18 Umbel
19 Solitary-flowered

Flowers
20 Lasting a single day
21 Petals dissimilar
22 Petals hairy
23 Stamens 3
24 Stamen filaments hairy or bearded

25 Pollen shed through pores
26 Ovary inferior
27 Styles 3
28 Style short and stout
29 Style branched

DICOTYLEDONS

Herbs, shrubs or trees. Leaves with netted or herring-bone venation, often toothed or lobed. Flowers with parts in multiples of 4 or 5, usually with separate sepals and petals.

FAMILY	1	2	3	4	5	6	7	8	9	10	11	12	13	14	15
Acanthus				◑			◑				●				
African Violet															
Balsam											●				
Begonia															
Bellflower		◑		◑					●						
Bignonia				◑			◑				●	◑			
Bladderwort						●			◑						
Broomrape				◑	●						●	◑			
Brunia															
Buddleja											●				
Carnation											●				
Carrot													◑		●
Citrus													◑	●	●
Coffee											●				
Convolvulus				●									◑		
Crassula		◑	◑								◑				
Cucumber				●				●					◑		
Daisy		◑	◑	◑			◑			◑	◑		◑		◑
Daphne											●				
Desert Primrose	●												●		
Erica											●				
Euphorbia			●				◑		●	◑					
Fan Flower															
Forget-me-not							◑								
Fumitory		◑		●				●				●	◑		
Gentian		◑									●				
	1	2	3	4	5	6	7	8	9	10	11	12	13	14	15

KEY TO NUMBERING

Habit
1 Submerged aquatic
2 Annual
3 Succulent
4 Climbers or twiner
5 Root parasite
6 Carnivorous, often covered in reddish glandular hairs
7 Spiny or thorny
8 Tendrils present
9 Sap milky

Leaves
10 Reduced and plants apparently leafless
11 Opposite or whorled
12 Compound
13 Deeply and finely divided
14 Gland-dotted
15 Aromatic when crushed

16	17	18	19	20	21	22	23	24	25	26	27	28	29	30	FAMILY
◐		●					●		●	◐			◐		Acanthus
		●					●		●	●					African Violet
		●								●					Balsam
	●				◐						●	●			Begonia
◐		◐					●			◐	●		◐	◐	Bellflower
		●					●		●				●		Bignonia
		●					●		●				●		Bladderwort
		●			◐		●		●						Broomrape
●							●				●	◐			Brunia
					●		●								Buddleja
												●			Carnation
◐	◐										●	●			Carrot
															Citrus
					◐		●				●		●		Coffee
							●	●				◐			Convolvulus
					◐		◐					●			Crassula
	●						●			◐	●			◐	Cucumber
●	◐	◐			◐		●			●	●		◐		Daisy
◐			●		◐		●								Daphne
											●	●			Desert Primrose
					●		●								Erica
	◐			◐											Euphorbia
		●					●				●				Fan Flower
							●			●			◐		Forget-me-not
		●			●					◐					Fumitory
					◐		●	●							Gentian
16	17	18	19	20	21	22	23	24	25	26	27	28	29	30	

Inflorescence
16 Head of sessile flowers, often surrounded by coloured bracts

Flowers
17 Unisexual
18 Irregular or 2-lipped
19 Pea-like
20 Petals absent
21 Petals 4
22 Petals indeterminate in number
23 Petals joined into a short or long tube
24 Petals furled in bud like an umbrella
25 Stamens fewer than petals
26 Stamens partially/ fully joined
27 Ovary inferior
28 Styles more than 1
29 Stigma 2-branched
30 Stigma ≥ 3-branched

DICOTYLEDONS continued

FAMILY	1	2	3	4	5	6	7	8	9	10	11	12	13	14	15
Geranium			◐				◐				◐		◐		◐
Hibiscus							◐								
Ice Plant	◐		●								◐				
Melianthus												●			●
Milkweed			◐	◐			◐		◐	◐	●				
Mint											●			●	●
Montinia															
Mustard		◐								◐			◐		◐
Oxalis												●		●	
Pea				◐			◐					◐		◐	
Penaea											●				
Plumbago															
Polygala															
Poppy		◐					◐		◐						
Potato				◐			◐								
Protea													◐		
Ranunculus				◐								◐	◐		
Scabious											◐				
Sesame		◐									●				●
St John's Wort											●				
Sundew						●									
Sutera		◐					◐				◐		◐		◐
Tibouchina											●				
Turnera							◐								
Twinleaf				◐							●	●			
Verbena											●				◐
Violet															
Waterlily	●														
	1	2	3	4	5	6	7	8	9	10	11	12	13	14	15

KEY TO NUMBERING

Habit
1 Submerged aquatic
2 Annual
3 Succulent
4 Climbers or twiner
5 Root parasite
6 Carnivorous, often covered in reddish glandular hairs
7 Spiny or thorny
8 Tendrils present
9 Sap milky

Leaves
10 Reduced and plants apparently leafless
11 Opposite or whorled
12 Compound
13 Deeply and finely divided
14 Gland-dotted
15 Aromatic when crushed

● indicates that all species in a family have the feature　◑ indicates that only some species have the feature

16	17	18	19	20	21	22	23	24	25	26	27	28	29	30	FAMILY
◑		◑						◑		◑		●			Geranium
							●	●		◑		◑		●	Hibiscus
				◑		●					●	●		●	Ice Plant
		●			●					◑					Melianthus
							●	◑		◑		◑			Milkweed
		●					●		●				●		Mint
	●				●							●		●	Montinia
		◑			●					◑					Mustard
								●				●			Oxalis
		◑	◑							◑					Pea
					●		●								Penaea
							●	●				◑			Plumbago
		●	●							◑			◑		Polygala
					●										Poppy
							●			◑					Potato
●		◑		●	●										Protea
												●			Ranunculus
●		◑					●		●			●			Scabious
		●					●		●				●		Sesame
								◑				●			St John's Wort
												●			Sundew
		●					●		●	◑			◑		Sutera
											●				Tibouchina
								●				●			Turnera
				◑									◑		Twinleaf
		◑					●		●						Verbena
		●					●			●					Violet
						●						●			Waterlily
16	17	18	19	20	21	22	23	24	25	26	27	28	29	30	

Inflorescence
16 Head of sessile flowers, often surrounded by coloured bracts

Flowers
17 Unisexual
18 Irregular or 2-lipped
19 Pea-like
20 Petals absent
21 Petals 4
22 Petals indeterminate in number
23 Petals joined into a short or long tube
24 Petals furled in bud like an umbrella
25 Stamens fewer than petals
26 Stamens partially/ fully joined
27 Ovary inferior
28 Styles more than 1
29 Stigma 2-branched
30 Stigma ≥ 3-branched

45

NYMPHAEACEAE
Waterlily family

Nymphaea **WATERLILY** *(Greek nymphe, goddess of springs)*

Aquatic perennials with floating, round or heart-shaped leaves on long petioles. *Flowers solitary, large and showy, with numerous petals and numerous, spirally inserted stamens.* Worldwide tropical and subtropical: ±60 spp.; South Africa: 2 spp. Tubers eaten by animals and humans; used medicinally and grown as an ornamental.

1 *Nymphaea nouchali* **Blue Waterlily**   J F M A M J J A S O N D
Robust, submerged aquatic with floating, heart-shaped leaves, toothed on the margins, and solitary, fragrant, lilac to blue flowers, 100–120 mm in diameter, closing in the afternoon. Rivers, lakes and pools through southern and eastern South and tropical Africa and India.

APONOGETONACEAE
Aponogeton family

Aponogeton **PONDBLOSSOM, WATERBLOMMETJIE**

(Derived from Potamogeton, another aquatic plant genus) Rhizomatous or tuberous *aquatic perennials.* Leaves basal, submerged or floating on long petioles. Inflorescence a small, simple or forked spike. *Flowers with 1 or 2 tepals,* fleshy; stamens (4–)6 or more; *ovary of 3–6 separate carpels.* Old World tropics, mainly in seasonal freshwater pools: 43 spp.; South Africa: 7 spp. *Aponogeton distachyos* is cultivated in the Western Cape for its edible fruiting spikes, traditionally used in mutton stew.

2 *Aponogeton distachyos*   J F M A M J J A S O N D
Water Hawthorn, Waterblommetjie Submerged aquatic herb with oblong, floating leaves and fragrant white flowers in forked spikes; tepals 1 and stamens >6 per flower. Pools and ditches in the southwestern Cape. *Aponogeton angustifolius* is smaller, with 2 tepals and 6 stamens per flower.

ARACEAE
Arum family

Stylochaeton **BUSHVELD ARUM**

(Greek stylos, stylus; chiton, covering, referring to the enveloping floral spathe) Rhizomatous perennials. Leaves basal, petiolate with an arrow- or heart-shaped blade. Inflorescence *on a short peduncle at ground level,* surrounded by a narrow *spathe with the margins joined into a tube at the base.* Tropical and subtropical Africa: ±15 spp.; South Africa: 1 sp. The roots and leaves were used medicinally.

3 *Stylochaeton natalensis*   J F M A M J J A S O N D
Deciduous perennial to 45 cm, with conspicuously veined, heart- or arrow-shaped leaves that are mottled on the petiole, and a narrowly funnel-shaped, greenish or dull yellowish floral spathe at ground level. Rocky grassland and open woodland through eastern South and tropical Africa.

Zantedeschia ARUM LILY, CALLA *(Named for Italian botanist, Francesco Zantedeschi, 1773–1846)*

Rhizomatous or tuberous perennials. Leaves basal, with a *spongy petiole and a spear- or arrow-shaped blade*. Inflorescence *on a long peduncle*, surrounded by a conspicuous, *flaring spathe with the margins overlapping at the base*. Southern Africa, mostly the eastern grasslands: 8 spp., all South Africa. *Zantedeschia aethiopica* is a popular garden plant that has become naturalised in California and elsewhere; the tubers are relished by porcupines, and the boiled leaves were used medicinally.

❶ *Zantedeschia rehmannii*

J F M A M J J A S O N D

Dwarf Arum Lily, Pienkvarkoor Deciduous perennial, 20–60 cm, with spear-shaped leaves, and a narrowly funnel-shaped, white to pink floral spathe. Rocky grassland and bush margins in northeastern South Africa.

❷ *Zantedeschia aethiopica*

J F M A M J J A S O N D

White Arum Lily, Varklelie Evergreen or deciduous perennial, 60–100 cm, often massed, with plain green, arrow-shaped leaves, and a large, pure white floral spathe; the fruiting stems remaining erect. Seasonally wet vleis and stream sides through southwestern and eastern South Africa.

❸ *Zantedeschia albomaculata*

J F M A M J J A S O N D

Spotted-leaved Arum Lily Deciduous perennial, 60–80 cm, with plain green or white-spotted, arrow-shaped leaves, and a large, cream-coloured floral spathe, usually with a deep purple eye; the fruiting stems bent over. Marshy flats and grassy mountainsides through eastern South Africa.

❹ *Zantedeschia pentlandii*

J F M A M J J A S O N D

Yellow Arum Lily, Geelvarkoor Deciduous perennial, 40–60 cm, with plain green, arrow-shaped leaves, and a large, bright yellow floral spathe with a dark purple eye. Rocky grassland and open woodland among dolerite boulders near Lydenburg. *Zantedeschia jucunda* has speckled, sharply pointed leaves.

STRELITZIACEAE   Crane Flower family

Strelitzia CRANE FLOWER, BIRD-OF-PARADISE FLOWER
(Named for Queen Charlotte, wife of George III, from the House of Mecklenburg-Strelitz) Robust, stemless perennials or banana-like trees. *Leaves large and leathery, petiolate*, blade elliptical, rarely reduced. *Flowers clustered within large, boat-shaped spathes*, very irregular; sepals 3, large and petal-like, orange or white; petals 3, mauve or blue, lower 2 joined in an arrow-shaped structure. Southern and subtropical Africa: 5 spp., all South Africa.

❺ *Strelitzia reginae*

J F M A M J J A S O N D

Crane Flower, Geel Piesang Evergreen, stemless perennial to 1.5 m, with large, elliptical leaves on long petioles, and orange and blue flowers in a leathery, boat-shaped spathe 12–20 cm long. Coastal bush and thicket in the Eastern Cape and KwaZulu-Natal. *Strelitzia juncea* from Humansdorp has poker-like leaves without blades.

❻ *Strelitzia nicolai* Wild Banana

J F M A M J J A S O N D

Tree to 9 m, clump-forming, with large, petiolate leaves, often tattered by the wind, and multiple inflorescences of white and mauve flowers enclosed in leathery, boat-shaped spathes, 20–30 cm long; the base of the arrow-shaped petal-keel pointed. Coastal bush in the Eastern Cape and KwaZulu-Natal. *Strelitzia alba* from the southern Cape has the base of the petal-keel rounded; *S. caudata* from Swaziland and northern South Africa has a small tooth projecting from the middle of the keel on the lower sepal.

COMMELINACEAE   Commelina family

Aneilema   ANEILEMA   *(Greek an, without; eilema, involucre, i.e. lacking the spathes found in Commelina)*

Perennial or annual herbs. Leaves petiolate or sessile. Flowers *without enclosing spathes*, white, yellow, pink or blue, open only in the morning, *irregular*, with 2 large paddle-shaped upper petals plus 1 smaller lower petal; 3 fertile stamens alternating with 3 staminodes. Africa: ±60 spp.; South Africa: 11 spp. Eaten as a vegetable.

1 *Aneilema aequinoctiale*

J F M A M J **J A** S O N D

Climbing Aneilema Trailing perennial, with 2-ranked leaves, the sheaths 'sticky' from hooked hairs, and panicles of bright yellow flowers with purple style, 15 mm in diameter; the lower stamen filaments bearded. Moist forest margins through eastern South and tropical Africa.

Commelina   COMMELINA
(Named for the Commelin brothers, Dutch botanists who were active at the end of the 17th century) Perennial herbs. *Leaves with a sheathing base.* Flowers in *clusters enclosed in large, boat-shaped spathes*, blue or yellow, open only in the morning, *irregular*, with 2 large, paddle-shaped upper petals plus 1 small scale-like lower petal; *lower 3 stamens fertile, upper 3 sterile*, the *filaments smooth*. Old World tropics: ±170 spp.; South Africa: 16 spp. Used medicinally and as a vegetable.

2 *Commelina africana*

J F M A M J J A S O N D

Yellow Commelina Spreading perennial, hairless or hairy, with narrow or broader, flat or folded leaves, and yellow flowers, 10–15 mm in diameter; the spathes simply folded. Stony grassland through southern and eastern South and tropical Africa.

3 *Commelina erecta*

J F M A M J J A S O N D

Blue Commelina Erect or spreading perennial, hairless or minutely hairy, with lance-shaped leaves, and bright blue flowers, 10–15 mm in diameter; the spathes stalked, with the lower margins joined, and some fruit segments 2-seeded. Coastal and inland scrub in eastern South Africa.

4 *Commelina eckloniana*

J F M A **M J J** A S O N D

Ecklon's Commelina Spreading perennial, almost hairless, with narrow leaves, and pale blue flowers, 10–15 mm in diameter; the spathes stalked, with the lower margins joined, and the fruit segments 1-seeded. Rocky slopes in scrub, through eastern South and tropical Africa. *Commelina benghalensis* is an annual with sessile spathes.

Cyanotis   DOLL'S POWDERPUFF   *(Greek kyanos, blue; otis, ear, alluding to the petals)*

Hairy perennials, often with separate leafing and flowering shoots. *Leaves sessile.* Flowers mauve to blue, open only in the morning, *symmetrical* with 3 small sepals and 3 large petals joined into a short tube; *stamens all fertile*, white or mauve, the *filaments thickly bearded*. Old World tropics: ±50 spp.; South Africa: 7 spp. The roots were used medicinally.

5 *Cyanotis speciosa*

J F M A M J J A S O N D

Erect, hairy perennial to 50 cm, with separate leafing shoots, and flowering stems with clusters of mauve to blue flowers among folded spathes, 10 mm in diameter, lasting one morning, with bearded stamen filaments. Grassland through eastern South and tropical Africa. *Cyanotis lapidosa* is a creeping plant of rock ledges.

ALLIACEAE   Onion family

Tulbaghia WILD GARLIC (Named for Ryk Tulbagh, Dutch governor at the Cape from 1751 to 1771)

Rhizomatous perennials. Flowers in umbels on a leafless scape, *funnel-shaped with a fleshy collar or crown at the mouth*; the stamens enclosed within the tube. Africa: ±20 spp.; South Africa: 18 spp. Used as a culinary ingredient and medicinally; mauve-flowered *Tulbaghia violacea* is a common garden plant.

1 *Tulbaghia capensis* **Cape Garlic**   J F M **A M J J A S O N** D

Perennial, 15–35 cm, strongly aromatic, with strap-like leaves, 4–12 mm wide, and brownish to purplish flowers with an orange, 6-toothed crown in the mouth, 10 mm in diameter, honey-scented at night. Stony flats and slopes in the south-western Cape. *Tulbaghia alliacea* has a collar-like crown.

2 *Tulbaghia cernua*   J F M A M J **J** A **S O N** D

Perennial to 50 cm, strongly aromatic, with strap-like leaves, 8–15 mm wide, and greenish flowers with an orange, short-lobed crown in the mouth, 10 mm in diameter, scented at night. Rocky grassland through eastern South Africa. *Tulbaghia acutiloba* has narrower leaves, 3–4 mm wide.

AGAPANTHACEAE   Agapanthus family

Agapanthus AGAPANTHUS, BLOULELIE

(Greek agape, *love;* anthos, *flower, presumably an allusion to their beauty*)   Rhizomatous perennials. Leaves strap-shaped, keeled. *Inflorescence an umbel* on a leafless scape. *Flowers blue*, funnel-shaped or cylindrical, the tepals joined below into a short tube; stamens 6, of 2 types, flexed slightly downwards and arched up at the tips. Southern Africa: 7 spp. The evergreen *Agapanthus praecox* from the southern coastal regions is the widely grown agapanthus of horticulture. Decoctions of the underground parts are used as a mild purgative.

3 *Agapanthus africanus*   J **F** M **A M J J A S** O N **D**

Cape Agapanthus Evergreen perennial, 25–70 cm, with strap-shaped leaves and deep blue, widely funnel-shaped flowers, 25–40 mm long, with a tube less than half as long. Rocky slopes on the coastal mountains of the southwestern Cape, flowering mainly after fire.

4 *Agapanthus praecox*   J **F** M A M J **J** A **S** O N **D**

Common Agapanthus Evergreen perennial, 40–100 cm, with strap-shaped leaves and white to blue, funnel-shaped flowers, 30–70 mm long, with a tube up to half as long. Rocky outcrops and stream banks in coastal thicket and scrub through southeastern South Africa.

5 *Agapanthus campanulatus*   J F M **A M J J A S** O N **D**

Bell Agapanthus Deciduous perennial, 40–100 cm, with strap-shaped leaves and blue, widely funnel-shaped flowers, 20–35 mm long, with a tube less than one-third as long. Rocky slopes in montane grassland through eastern South Africa.

53

1 *Agapanthus inapertus*

Drooping Agapanthus Deciduous perennial, 40–180 cm, with strap-shaped leaves and nodding, blue, tubular to narrowly funnel-shaped flowers, 30–50 mm long, with a tube half to two-thirds as long. Damp slopes or stream sides in montane grassland in northeastern South Africa.

AMARYLLIDACEAE Amaryllis family

▶ FLOWERS LONGER THAN THE PEDICELS; STAMEN FILAMENTS SEPARATE

Cyrtanthus   FIRE LILY, VUURLELIE

(Greek kyrtos, curved; anthos, flower, alluding to the characteristic shape) Deciduous bulbous perennials. Leaves *slender and strap-shaped*, sometimes twisted, *often with a midrib*. Flowers borne on a *hollow scape*, funnel-shaped to tubular and *often curved*, sometimes 2-lipped, variously coloured, spreading or nodding on very short pedicels, stamens arising in the tube in *2 series at different heights*, separate. Fruit ellipsoid with *flattened, black seeds*. Southern Africa, mainly the eastern seaboard: ±50 spp., all South Africa.

2 *Cyrtanthus sanguineus*   J F M **A** M J J **A** S O N D

Inanda Lily, Kei Lily Deciduous perennial to 30 cm, in clumps, with lance-shaped leaves ±20 mm wide, and stems of 1 or 2 broadly funnel-shaped, red flowers with a paler throat streaked with dark red, ±100 mm long; the stamens not protruding beyond the throat. On rock faces near water through eastern South and tropical Africa.

3 *Cyrtanthus elatus*   J F **M A** M J J A S **O N** D

George Lily, Knysna Lily Deciduous perennial to 45 cm, with bright green, strap-like leaves, 10–25 mm wide, and stems of 2–9 broadly funnel-shaped scarlet or rarely pink flowers, 70–100 mm long; the stamens protruding well beyond the throat. Forest margins and moist mountain slopes in the southern Cape, flowering well after fire.

4 *Cyrtanthus angustifolius*   J F M A M J J A S **O N** D

Deciduous perennial to 45 cm, with narrow, strap-like leaves, 7–15 mm wide, and stems of 4–10 nodding, narrowly trumpet-shaped, scarlet flowers, 30–70 mm long; the stamens protruding beyond the throat. Mountain slopes and flats in seasonal streams and vleis in the southwestern and southern Cape, flowering after fire.

5 *Cyrtanthus ventricosus* Vuurlelie   J F M **A M** J J A S O **N** D

Deciduous perennial, 10–20 cm, with strap-like leaves appearing after flowering, and stems of 2–12 nodding, trumpet-shaped, vermilion to bright red flowers, 40–50 mm long; the stamens arising at the base of the tube and protruding beyond the throat. Cool, south-facing mountain slopes in the southwestern Cape, flowering within 2 weeks after summer fires.

6 *Cyrtanthus tuckii*   J F M A M J J **A S O** N D

Green-tipped Fire Lily Deciduous perennial to 45 cm, with strap-like leaves ±9 mm wide appearing after flowering, and stems of 5–15 nodding, tubular, reddish or green-tipped flowers, ±60 mm long, with erect tepals; the stamens protruding slightly beyond the throat. Montane grasslands through eastern South Africa, flowering after fire.

① *Cyrtanthus flanaganii*
J F M A M J J **A S O N** D

Yellow Dobo Lily Deciduous perennial to 20 cm, with strap-like leaves ±20 mm wide, and stems of 4–7 narrowly trumpet-shaped, yellow flowers, 55–75 mm long; the stamens not protruding beyond the throat. Wet cliffs and seeps along the high Drakensberg.

② *Cyrtanthus breviflorus*
J F M A M J J A S **O N D**

Yellow Fire Lily Very variable, deciduous perennial, 7–30 cm, with slender or strap-like leaves, 1–14 mm wide, present or absent at flowering, and stems of 1–10 (rarely 20) funnel-shaped, yellow flowers, 25–35 mm long with tepals; the stamens protruding shortly beyond the throat. Marshes and moist grassland through eastern South and tropical Africa.

Clivia CLIVIA, BUSH LILY *(Named for Lady Charlotte Clive, d. 1866)*

Evergreen *rhizomatous* perennials. Leaves *strap-like, leathery, often with minutely toothed margins*. Flowers borne on a *flattened, 2-edged scape*, funnel-shaped to tubular, orange or with green tips, spreading or nodding on shorter pedicels. Fruit spherical and fleshy. Southern Africa, mainly the eastern seaboard: 5 spp., all South Africa. Popular garden plants, also used medicinally.

③ *Clivia caulescens*
J F M A M J J A S **O N** D

Transvaal Clivia Evergreen perennial forming sprawling, leafy stems rooting along their length, with strap-like leaves, and stalks of ±20 nodding, tubular, orange flowers with green tips, ±30 mm long. Rocky forest floor in northern Drakensberg. *Clivia gardenia* from KwaZulu-Natal and *C. nobilis* from the Eastern Cape both lack the well-developed leafy stem.

④ *Clivia miniata* Clivia
J F M A M J J **A S O** N D

Evergreen perennial to 80 cm, forming clumps, with strap-like leaves, and stalks of ±30 funnel-shaped, orange flowers with flaring tepals, ±70 mm in diameter. Forest and bush clumps in partial shade, mainly coastal, through eastern South Africa.

Scadoxus BLOOD LILY *(Greek skiadion, parasol; doxa, glory, referring to the umbels)*

Deciduous or evergreen, rhizomatous or partially bulbous perennials. Leaves *petiolate with a thin-textured, oval to lance-shaped blade with a prominent midrib*. Flowers in a *compact head surrounded by several large, green or brown bracts*, narrowly funnel- or salver-shaped, erect or spreading on very short pedicels, orange to red, stamens erect or spreading, separate. Fruit a red berry. Southern and tropical Africa: 9 spp.; South Africa: 3 spp. The rootstock is poisonous but has been used medicinally.

⑤ *Scadoxus membranaceus*
J F M **A** M J J A S O N **D**

Dwarf Blood Lily Evergreen perennial to 50 cm, with the leaves arising directly from the bulb, and a brush-like head ±5 cm in diameter, of erect, orange flowers surrounded by large greenish bracts. Coastal and dune forest along the eastern seaboard of South Africa.

① *Scadoxus puniceus* Blood Lily J F M A M J J A S O N D

Robust, deciduous perennial to 1 m, with the leaf cluster forming a false stem, often not fully developed at flowering, and a brush-like head, ±15 cm in diameter, of erect, orange flowers surrounded by large brownish bracts. Savanna and forest margins from the southern Cape to tropical Africa.

② *Scadoxus multiflorus* J F M A M J J A S O N D

Fireball Lily, Blood Flower Robust, deciduous perennial to 1 m, with the leaf cluster forming a false stem, and a rounded head, 15–25 cm in diameter, of spreading, pinkish-red flowers. Coastal and swamp forest and savanna through eastern South and tropical Africa.

Haemanthus PAINTBRUSH LILY, KWASLELIE

(Greek haima, blood; anthos, flower, for the colour of most species) Deciduous or evergreen bulbous perennials. Leaves *mostly 2*, erect or prostrate, *tongue-shaped and leathery*, sometimes hairy, often *barred or spotted* with purple beneath. Flowers in a *brush-like head* surrounded by several *large, red or pink fleshy bracts*, funnel-shaped with very short pedicels, white, pink or red, rarely white, stamens ± erect, separate. Fruit a soft, translucent berry. Southern Africa: 22 spp. The bulbs were used medicinally.

③ *Haemanthus humilis* J F M A M J J A S O N D

Rabbit's Ears Perennial to 30 cm, with ± erect, mostly velvety leaves, present or developing at flowering, and white or pink flowers surrounded by membranous, pink bracts on a ± hairy peduncle. Rocky outcrops in grassland, through eastern and central South Africa.

④ *Haemanthus albiflos* J F M A M J J A S O N D

White Paintbrush Lily Evergreen perennial to 40 cm, often forming clumps, with ± erect leaves often spotted with white, present at flowering, and white flowers surrounded by leathery, white and green bracts on a smooth or hairy, green peduncle. Forest and thicket, mostly coastal, southern and eastern South Africa.

⑤ *Haemanthus coccineus* Misryblom J F M A M J J A S O N D

Perennial, 6–20 cm, often forming large clumps, with spreading or ± erect leaves usually speckled with red beneath, dry at flowering, and scarlet flowers surrounded by leathery, red bracts on a spotted peduncle. Widespread in coastal scrub and on rocky slopes, often in large clumps, in western and southern South Africa.

⑥ *Haemanthus sanguineus* J F M A M J J A S O N D

April Fool, Veldskoenblaar Perennial, 5–30 cm, with prostrate, leathery leaves often outlined with red, dry at flowering, and red or pink flowers surrounded by leathery, red bracts on a plain red peduncle. Lower slopes in the southwestern, southern and Eastern Cape.

Ammocharis MALGAS LILY, MALGASLELIE

(Greek ammos, sand; charis, delight, alluding to the habitat) Deciduous bulbous perennials. Leaves *in a prostrate fan*, sickle-shaped, with a *blunt, often withered tip*. Flowers funnel-shaped, white to red, on stout pedicels about as long as the flowers, stamens spreading, *separate to the base*. Africa, mainly semi-arid areas: 6 spp.; South Africa: 2 spp.

1 *Ammocharis coranica*

J F M A M J J A S O N D

Ground Lily Perennial, 25–30 cm, with a spreading fan of blunt, sickle-shaped leaves, green or developing at flowering, and star-like, pink, sweetly-scented flowers, 50–70 mm long; the stamens ± as long as the tepals, and the fruits not developing into a tumbleweed. Hot, dry flats from the southern and Eastern Cape to northern South Africa.

2 *Ammocharis longifolia*

J F M A M J J A S O N D

(=*Cybistetes longifolia*) **Malgas Lily** Perennial, 25–35 cm, with a spreading fan of blunt, sickle-shaped leaves, green or dry at flowering, and widely funnel-shaped, cream-coloured to pink, lily-scented flowers, 50–70 mm long; the stamens ± half as long as the tepals, and the fruits maturing into a large tumbleweed. Sandy and loamy flats in Namaqualand and the southwestern Cape.

Crinum RIVER LILY *(Latin crinon, crinum, lily)*

Deciduous or evergreen bulbous perennials. Leaves strap-shaped, with a *blunt, often withered tip*. Flowers fragrant at night, trumpet- or salver-shaped with a *long, straight or curved tube*, white to pink, on *short pedicels*, stamens *separate to the base*. Worldwide in the tropics and subtropics: ±65 spp.; South Africa: 20 spp.

3 *Crinum moorei*

J F M A M J J A S O N D

Moore's River Lily, Natal River Lily Perennial to 1.6 m, with soft-textured leaves with a distinct midrib, 60–120 mm wide, forming a false stem, and pale pink, funnel-shaped flowers, with a tube 80–100 mm long; the stamens arching downwards, with black anthers. Marshy areas in shaded situations, mainly coastal, through eastern South Africa.

4 *Crinum macowanii* **River Lily**

J F M A M J J A S O N D

Perennial to 1 m, with channelled leaves, 20–160 mm wide, and white to pale pink, funnel-shaped flowers, with a tube 30–110 mm long; the stamens arching downwards, with black anthers, and the fruits strongly beaked. Rocky grassland near rivers through eastern South and subtropical Africa.

5 *Crinum bulbispermum*

J F M A M J J A S O N D

Orange River Lily Perennial to 1 m, with channelled leaves to 110 mm wide, and narrowly funnel-shaped white to pink flowers striped with red, with a tube 50–110 mm long; the stamens arching downwards, with greyish or light brown anthers. Seasonal wetlands and along streams through central South Africa.

6 *Crinum variabile*

J F M A M J J A S O N D

Namaqua River Lily Perennial to 60 cm, with channelled leaves, 20–50 mm wide, and funnel-shaped flowers, white striped with pink, with a tube 20–40 mm long; the stamens arching downwards, with cream-coloured anthers. Seasonal streambeds along the western escarpment.

61

① *Crinum campanulatum* J F M A M J J **A S O** N D

Albany Vlei Lily Perennial to 80 cm, with narrow, channelled leaves, 10–25 mm wide, and cup-shaped flowers, white flushed with pink in the centre, with a tube ±50 mm long; the stamens symmetrically arranged, with yellow anthers. Seasonal marshes and pans in the Eastern Cape.

▸ FLOWERS USUALLY SHORTER THAN THE PEDICELS; STAMEN FILAMENTS ± JOINED TOGETHER AT THE BASE

Amaryllis BELLADONNA, MAARTBLOM

(Named for the mythological Greek shepherdess, Amaryllus) Robust, deciduous, bulbous perennial. Leaves *strap-shaped with a distinct midrib*, soft-textured. *Flowers large, funnel-shaped, pink*, borne on *short, stout pedicels*; stamens of 2 lengths, flexed downwards and arched up at the tips, *joined at the base*. Fruit spherical, papery, with fleshy, *pink seeds*. Western and southwestern South Africa: 2 spp.

② *Amaryllis belladonna* J **F M A M** J J J A S O N D

Robust perennial to 90 cm, with strap-shaped leaves that are dry or absent at flowering, and a cluster of large, funnel-shaped, pink flowers, 80–100 mm long, narcissus-scented. Loamy soils in lowlands of the southwestern and southern Cape, often in seasonal vleis.

Brunsvigia CANDELABRA LILY, KANDELAAR *(Named for the House of Brunswick)*

Deciduous bulbous perennials. Leaves erect or prostrate, *broadly tongue-shaped, leathery*, often with reddish *cartilaginous margins*. Flowers funnel-shaped, *mostly irregular*, pink or red, on stout pedicels as long as or much longer than the flowers, stamens all similar or of 2 lengths, *flexed downwards* or rarely erect, *joined at the base*. Fruit *developing into a tumbleweed*. Widespread through southern Africa, in mainly semi-arid areas: ±20 spp.

③ *Brunsvigia grandiflora* J F M **A M J J A S** O N D

Giant Candelabra Lily Perennial to 80 cm, with 10–15 erect, wavy leaves that are present at flowering, and pink, irregularly funnel-shaped flowers, 50–70 mm long; the fruits bluntly 3-angled. Grassland through eastern South Africa.

④ *Brunsvigia radulosa* J **F M A M J J A S O N D**

Common Candelabra Lily Perennial to 80 cm, with 4–6 prostrate leaves that are green or emerging at flowering, and pink or wine-red, irregularly funnel-shaped flowers, 50–60 mm long; the fruits 3-angled. Grassland through eastern and central South Africa.

⑤ *Brunsvigia bosmaniae* J F **M A** M J J **A S O** N D

Fragrant Candelabra Lily Perennial to 50 cm, with 5 or 6 prostrate leaves, dry at flowering, and pink, narcissus-scented, irregularly funnel-shaped flowers, 20–40 mm long; the fruits 3-winged and heavily ribbed. Stony flats in western South Africa.

⑥ *Brunsvigia orientalis* J **F M** A M J J **A S** O N D

Koningskandelaar Perennial, 40–50 cm, with 5 or 6 prostrate leaves that are dry at flowering, and red, very irregular flowers with the tepals rolled back, 40–65 mm long; the fruits 3-winged and heavily ribbed. Sandy flats, mainly coastal, in southwestern South Africa. *Brunsvigia josephinae* is larger, with erect, wavy leaves.

① *Brunsvigia marginata*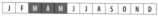

False Nerine Perennial to 20 cm, with 4 prostrate leaves that are dry at flowering, and a tight head of bright scarlet, funnel-shaped flowers, 25–40 mm long; the fruits 3-winged. Rocky sandstone slopes in the mountains of the southwestern Cape.

Nerine NERINE, NERINA

(Nerine was a mythological sea nymph, an allusion to the mistaken belief that Nerine sarniensis *washed ashore on Guernsey from a foundered ship)* Deciduous or evergreen bulbous perennials. Leaves *thread-like to strap-shaped, succulent.* Flowers *mostly irregular,* pink or rarely white or red, with *narrow, ± wavy or crinkly tepals,* on pedicels a little longer than the flowers, stamens of 2 lengths, flexed downwards or rarely erect, *joined at the base.* Fruit spherical, membranous, with fleshy, green or brown seeds. Southern Africa: ±23 spp.

▶ FLOWER STALK HAIRLESS

② *Nerine sarniensis*

Guernsey Lily, Red Nerine Perennial, 25–45 cm, with smooth peduncle and strap-shaped leaves, 8–20 mm wide, dry at flowering, and symmetrical, red (rarely pink or white) flowers with erect stamens, 40 mm long. Mountain slopes in the southwestern Cape.

③ *Nerine humilis*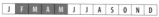

Common Cape Nerine Bulbous perennial, 15–35 cm, with smooth peduncle and strap-shaped leaves, 4–10 mm wide, dry or just emerging at flowering, and irregular, pale to dark pink flowers, 25–30 mm long. Rocky slopes in the southwestern and southern Cape.

④ *Nerine bowdenii* Giant Nerine

Robust perennial to 70 cm, with smooth peduncle and strap-shaped leaves, 15–30 mm wide, and irregular, pink flowers, 50–70 mm long. Wet cliff faces in the high Drakensberg. *Nerine krigei* from northern South Africa has erect, twisted leaves 10–15 mm wide.

▶ FLOWER STALK HAIRY

⑤ *Nerine angustifolia*

Ribbon-leaved Nerine Perennial to 1 m, with hairy peduncle and pedicels and ribbon-shaped leaves, 3–5 mm wide, and irregular, pink flowers, 30–40 mm long. Marshy grassland through eastern South Africa.

⑥ *Nerine appendiculata*

Grass-leaved Nerine Perennial to 80 cm, with hairy peduncle and pedicels and channelled, grass-like leaves, 3–5 mm wide, and irregular, pink flowers, 25–30 mm long. Marshy grassland in eastern South Africa.

ANTHERICACEAE Anthericum family

Chlorophytum GRASS LILY, GRASLELIE (*Greek* chloros, *yellowish-green;* phytum, *plant*)

Rhizomatous, tufted perennials, either with stiff, tapering roots or long, slender roots with tuberous swellings. Leaves narrow and channelled, *often fibrous at the base*. Flowers in leafy racemes or panicles, usually *with more than 1 at each node, on jointed pedicels*, star-shaped with separate tepals, *each lasting a day*. Fruit usually *3-winged*. Widespread in Africa, Eurasia and the Americas, mainly tropical: ±165 spp.; South Africa: 36 spp.

❶ _Chlorophytum triflorum_

| J | F | M | A | M | J | J | A | S | O | N | D |

Variable perennial to 80 cm, with hard, tapering roots, leaves that are often minutely fringed on the margins, and unbranched stems with white flowers, 20 mm in diameter. Sandy slopes and flats in the southwestern Cape.

❷ _Chlorophytum undulatum_

| J | F | M | A | M | J | J | A | S | O | N | D |

Perennial to 50 cm, with slender roots and numerous small tubers, leaves that are often minutely fringed on the margins, and unbranched stems with white flowers, 20 mm in diameter. Widespread on stony flats and slopes in Namaqualand and the southwestern Cape.

❸ _Chlorophytum cooperi_

| J | F | M | A | M | J | J | A | S | O | N | D |

Perennial to 50 cm, with wiry roots, some with small tubers at the ends, narrow leaves that are often minutely fringed on the margins, and heads of white flowers, 20 mm in diameter, on flattened, 2-winged stems; the fruits ribbed. Stony grassland through eastern South Africa.

❹ _Chlorophytum comosum_

| J | F | M | A | M | J | J | A | S | O | N | D |

Hen-and-chickens Perennial to 80 cm, with slender roots swollen near the tip, a loose rosette of narrow leaves, and a slender, unbranched stem of white flowers, 20 mm in diameter, bending over and developing plantlets from the tip. Forest floor and margins in moist places, through southern and eastern South Africa. The variegated form is widely cultivated.

❺ _Chlorophytum bowkeri_

| J | F | M | A | M | J | J | A | S | O | N | D |

Robust perennial to 1 m, clumped, with wiry roots, broadly lance-shaped leaves, and an unbranched stem of closely packed, white flowers, 20 mm in diameter. Damp, rocky grassland and forest margins through eastern South and subtropical Africa. *Chlorophytum krookianum* is even larger, up to 2 m, with branching flowering stems.

ASPHODELACEAE Aloe family

▸ FLOWERS STAR-SHAPED, MOSTLY WHITE OR YELLOW

Bulbine BULBINE, KOPIEVA
(*Greek* bolbos, *bulb;* inus, *resembling, referring to the swollen stem base*) Tufted perennials, rarely annuals or shrublets, with wiry or swollen roots. Leaves succulent or fleshy. Flowers *yellow to orange, star-like, each lasting a day*, the stamen filaments densely *hairy or bearded*. Africa and Australia, mainly southern Africa: ±50 spp.; South Africa: 46 spp. The leaf sap of several species was widely used as an antiseptic and emollient.

❶ *Bulbine capitata*

J F M A M J J **A S O N** D

Narrow-leaved Bulbine Tufted perennial to 30 cm, with narrow, bright green, quill-like leaves with broad membranous bases that decay into membranous strips with age, and head-like racemes of bright yellow flowers, 10 mm in diameter. Open grassland in northeastern South Africa, conspicuous after fire. *Bulbine abyssinica* is similar, but the leaves are pink at the base and do not decay into membranous strips, and the raceme is conical or cylindrical.

❷ *Bulbine narcissifolia*

J F **M A** M J J A S **O N** D

Strap-leaved Bulbine Tufted perennial to 30 cm, with a fan of grey, twisted, strap-like leaves decaying into fine fibres at the base, and a conical raceme of pale, canary-yellow flowers, 10 mm in diameter. Open grassland, common on overgrazed rangeland, in central South Africa.

❸ *Bulbine annua* Annual Bulbine

J F M A M J J A **S O N D**

Tufted annual, 15–40 cm, with wiry roots and many quill-like leaves, and dense racemes of yellow flowers, 10 mm in diameter; the fruits spherical and spreading on long pedicels. Sandy soils along the coast in the southwestern Cape.

❹ *Bulbine praemorsa* Kopieva

J F M A M **J J A** S O N D

Slender or stout perennial, 40–60 cm, with a small tuber and fleshy, channelled leaves decaying into fine fibres at the base, and a loose raceme of yellow or orange flowers, 10 mm in diameter; the fruits elliptical and held upright on bent pedicels. Common and widespread, mostly on rocky sandstone slopes in western South Africa.

Trachyandra TRACHYANDRA, VELDKOOL

(Greek *trachy*, rough; *andros*, male, referring to the bristly stamen filaments) Tufted, rhizomatous or tuberous perennials or shrublets, with wiry or swollen roots. Leaves succulent or fleshy, often surrounded at the base by tubular, membranous or papery sheaths. Flowers star-like, *white or pinkish, each lasting 1 afternoon*, the stamen *filaments rough or bristly*. Africa, mainly winter-rainfall southern Africa: ±50 spp.; South Africa: 49 spp. The young flower spikes of some species are edible.

❺ *Trachyandra saltii*

J F M **A M J J A S O N** D

Tufted perennial to 50 cm, with narrow, grass-like leaves not wrapped with papery sheaths at the base, and spreading, unbranched stems of pure white flowers, 15 mm in diameter. Grassland through eastern and central South and tropical Africa. *Trachyandra asperata* has ± hairy or bristly fruit.

❻ *Trachyandra falcata*

J F M A M J **J A S O** N D

Stout perennial to 1 m, with sickle-shaped, mostly hairless, leaves collectively wrapped with brown, papery sheaths at the base, and an unbranched or sparsely branched stem of crowded, pure white or pinkish flowers, 15 mm in diameter, with a large encircling bract at the branch. Sandy or clay flats and lower slopes in Namaqualand and the Western Cape.

❶ *Trachyandra muricata*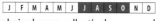

Perennial to 90 cm, with sickle-shaped, roughly hairy leaves collectively wrapped with brown, papery sheaths at the base, and a widely branched stem, bristly at the base, with nodding, white flowers with yellow marks at the centre, 10 mm in diameter, with the tepals curled back. Stony clay or granite slopes in open scrub in Namaqualand and the southwestern Cape.

❷ *Trachyandra revoluta* J F M A M J J A S O N D

Perennial to 90 cm, with quill-like, roughly hairy leaves individually wrapped with brown, papery sheaths at the base, and a widely branching panicle stem, roughly hairy at the base, with nodding, white flowers with yellow marks at the centre, 10 mm in diameter, with the tepals curled back. Sandy flats and lower slopes from Namaqualand to the southern Cape.

❸ *Trachyandra divaricata* J F M A M J J A S O N D

Stout, clumped perennial to 90 cm, with bright green, hairless, quill-like leaves individually wrapped with brown, papery sheaths at the base, and a widely branched stem of nodding white flowers with yellow marks at the centre, 10 mm in diameter, with the tepals curled back. Coastal dunes and sand flats from southern Namibia to the Eastern Cape.

Bulbinella BULBINELLA, KATSTERT *(Diminutive of Bulbine)*

Tufted, rhizomatous perennials, with wiry or swollen roots. Leaves soft or firm-textured but *not succulent*, narrow and quill-like or grass-like and channelled, decaying into *prominent, often netted fibres at the base*. Flowers star-like, white or pinkish, yellow or orange. Fruit with *1 or 2 shield-shaped seeds* per chamber. Mainly winter-rainfall southern Africa with a few species in New Zealand: 22 spp.; South Africa: 17 spp.

❹ *Bulbinella latifolia* J F M A M J J A S O N D

Robust perennial to 1 m, with bright green, broadly strap-shaped leaves to 65 mm wide, and a cylindrical raceme of deep yellow or orange flowers, 7 mm in diameter. Seasonally damp slopes and flats along the western escarpment.

❺ *Bulbinella nutans* J F M A M J J A S O N D

Perennial to 1 m, with bright green, narrow, channelled leaves to 15 mm wide, and a conical raceme of yellow or cream-coloured flowers, 7 mm in diameter. Stony or peaty soils or seasonal marshes in the southwestern Cape.

❻ *Bulbinella caudafelis* J F M A M J J A S O N D

Perennial to 80 cm, with greyish, grass-like, channelled leaves, sometimes finely toothed on the margins, and a narrowly conical raceme of white flowers with a pink tinge, 7 mm in diameter. Widespread on damp sandstone, granite or clay slopes in southwestern South Africa.

Kniphofia RED-HOT POKER, VUURPYL

(Named for German professor of botany, Johan Kniphof, 1704–1763) Tufted, rhizomatous perennials. Leaves soft or fibrous, narrow and *V-shaped* in cross section, often with minutely toothed margins. Flowers *tubular,* white, yellow or red, the *buds often differently coloured; the stamens often protrude at flowering but are later withdrawn.* Africa and southern Arabia: ±70 spp.; South Africa: 48 spp. Several species and hybrids are popular garden plants.

▶ STAMENS PROTRUDING CONSPICUOUSLY AND PERSISTENTLY

❶ *Kniphofia caulescens*

J F M A M J J A S O N D

Grey-leaved Poker Robust, short-stemmed, clumped perennial to 1 m, with greyish leaves, 25–50 mm wide, and a dense, bicoloured, conical raceme of nodding, tubular flowers, reddish in bud and opening creamy-yellow, 22–24 mm long, with persistently protruding stamens; the bracts narrow and pointed. Peaty seeps on rock sheets at high altitude in the Drakensberg.

❷ *Kniphofia ensifolia*

J F M A M J J A S O N D

Highveld Marsh Poker Robust, clump-forming perennial to 2 m, with greyish leaves, 15–45 mm wide, and a dense, bicoloured, cylindrical raceme of nodding, tubular flowers, tinged red in bud and opening greenish-cream, 15–21 mm long, with persistently protruding stamens; the bracts narrow and pointed. Marshes and stream banks in central South Africa.

❸ *Kniphofia tysonii* Tyson's Poker

J F M A M J J A S O N D

Robust, clump-forming perennial to 2 m, with dull green leaves, 12–40 mm wide, and a dense, bicoloured raceme of nodding, tubular flowers, red in bud and opening orange or yellow, 20–28 mm long, with conspicuously protruding stamens; the bracts broad and blunt. Rank grassland at lower altitudes in eastern South Africa.

▶ STAMENS PROTRUDING AT FIRST BUT LATER WITHDRAWN

❹ *Kniphofia linearifolia*

J F M A M J J A S O N D

Common Marsh Poker Robust, clump-forming perennial to 1.5 m, with dull green leaves, 12–28 mm wide, and a dense, bicoloured raceme of nodding, tubular flowers, reddish in bud and opening greenish to orange, 25–35 mm long, with shortly protruding stamens later withdrawn; the bracts broad and blunt. Marshes and stream banks through eastern South Africa.

❺ *Kniphofia uvaria* Cape Poker

J F M A M J J A S O N D

Perennial to 1.2 m, often in small clumps, with leaves 6–18 mm wide, and a dense, bicoloured raceme of nodding, tubular flowers, reddish in bud and opening yellow or orange, 30–40 mm long, with shortly protruding stamens; the bracts broad and blunt. Seeps, marshes and stream banks from Namaqualand to the Eastern Cape.

❻ *Kniphofia ritualis* Lesotho Poker

J F M A M J J A S O N D

Perennial to 80 cm, solitary or in small groups, with green, finely toothed leaves, 12–24 mm wide, and a dense, bicoloured raceme of nodding, tubular flowers, red in bud and opening yellow, 25–30 mm long, with scarcely protruding stamens later withdrawn; the bracts narrow and pointed. Grassy slopes at high altitude in the Drakensberg and Maluti Mountains. *Kniphofia hirsuta* from Lesotho has leaves with hairy keels.

❶ *Kniphofia sarmentosa*

`J` `F` `M` `A` `M` `J` `J` `A` `S` `O` `N` `D`

Roggeveld Poker Clump-forming perennial to 1 m, with greyish leaves, 8–30 mm wide, and a loose, bicoloured raceme of nodding, tubular flowers, reddish in bud and opening creamy pink, 20–35 mm long, with shortly protruding stamens later withdrawn; the bracts narrow and pointed. Stream sides in the mountains of the southwestern Cape interior.

❷ *Kniphofia fluviatilis* River Poker

`J` `F` `M` `A` `M` `J` `J` `A` `S` `O` `N` `D`

Clumped perennial to 60 cm, with dull, greyish leaves, 8–25 mm wide, and a dense, rounded, bicoloured raceme of nodding, tubular flowers, red in bud and opening orange to yellow, 42–50 mm long, with shortly protruding stamens later withdrawn; the bracts sharp. Widespread in grassy vleis at higher altitudes in eastern South Africa. *Kniphofia porphyrantha* has softer, green leaves and flowers 30–42 mm long.

❸ *Kniphofia triangularis*

`J` `F` `M` `A` `M` `J` `J` `A` `S` `O` `N` `D`

Mandarin Poker Dainty perennial to 60 cm, with grass-like leaves, 2–8 mm wide, and a dense raceme of tubular, yellowish-orange to reddish flowers, 24–35 mm long, with shortly protruding stamens later withdrawn; the bracts narrow and pointed. Peaty mountainsides through eastern South Africa.

❹ *Kniphofia thodei* Thode's Poker

`J` `F` `M` `A` `M` `J` `J` `A` `S` `O` `N` `D`

Dainty perennial to 50 cm, with grass-like leaves, 2–5 mm wide, and a dense, bicoloured raceme of tubular flowers, red in bud and opening white, 20–35 mm long, with the stamens not protruding; the bracts narrow and pointed. Peaty mountainsides at high altitude in the Drakensberg.

❺ *Kniphofia laxiflora* Slender Poker

`J` `F` `M` `A` `M` `J` `J` `A` `S` `O` `N` `D`

Slender perennial to 1 m, with narrow, grass-like leaves, 6–12 mm wide, and a loose raceme of nodding, tubular, greenish or yellow to red flowers, 24–35 mm long, constricted near the base, with scarcely protruding stamens; the bracts broad and blunt. Rocky grassland throughout KwaZulu-Natal.

❻ *Kniphofia buchananii*

`J` `F` `M` `A` `M` `J` `J` `A` `S` `O` `N` `D`

Small White Poker Slender perennial to 80 cm, with grass-like leaves, 3–4 mm wide, and a narrow raceme of spreading, shortly tubular, whitish flowers, 4–6 mm long, with shortly protruding stamens. Grassy slopes at lower altitude in KwaZulu-Natal.

Aloe ALOE, AALWYN *(Greek aloe, the dried sap of aloes)*

Tufted shrubs or trees. Leaves *succulent, curved in cross section,* usually with *sharp, horny teeth on the margins.* Flowers *tubular,* white, yellow or orange. Africa and Arabia: ±500 spp.; South Africa: ±130 spp. The sap of the North African *Aloe vera* is an important cosmetic and medicine and *A. ferox* fulfils the same role in southern Africa; many species are cultivated.

75

▶ TREES WITH BRANCHED STEMS

❶ *Aloe dichotoma* Kokerboom

| J | F | M | A | M | J | J | A | S | O | N | D |

Stout, densely branched shrub or tree to 9 m, with tufts of finely toothed leaves at the branch tips, and short panicles of spreading, tubular, yellow flowers, 30–40 mm long, with conspicuously projecting orange stamens. Dry and rocky slopes in Namibia and northwestern South Africa. *Aloe pillansii* from the Richtersveld has drooping panicles.

❷ *Aloe plicatilis* Cape Kokerboom

| J | F | M | A | M | J | J | A | S | O | N | D |

Stout, dichotomously branched shrub or small tree to 5 m, with tight fans of oblong, thornless leaves at the branch tips, and short, rather loose racemes of nodding orange flowers, 35–45 mm long, with shortly projecting stamens. Sheltered valleys in the mountains of the southwestern Cape.

▶ ERECT, SINGLE-STEMMED PLANTS

❸ *Aloe ferox* Bitteraalwyn

| J | F | M | A | M | J | J | A | S | O | N | D |

Single-stemmed shrub to 3 m, with large, broadly lance-shaped leaves, toothed on the margins and often beneath, and branched racemes of slightly upcurved, orange to red flowers, 23–35 mm long, with conspicuously protruding stamens. Dry, rocky slopes in scrub and savanna through southeastern South Africa.

❹ *Aloe marlothii* Mountain Aloe

| J | F | M | A | M | J | J | A | S | O | N | D |

Single-stemmed shrub to 4 m, with large, broadly lance-shaped leaves, toothed on the margins and often beneath, and slanted or horizontal, branched racemes of spreading, tubular, yellow to red flowers, 23–35 mm long, with conspicuously protruding stamens. Dry, rocky slopes in savanna through northeastern South and tropical Africa.

❺ *Aloe castanea* Cat's-tail Aloe

| J | F | M | A | M | J | J | A | S | O | N | D |

Single-stemmed shrub to 2 m, branching above, with narrowly lance-shaped leaves, finely toothed on the margins, and long, slender, sinuous spikes of ± sessile chestnut flowers, 15–18 mm long, with conspicuously protruding orange stamens and brown nectar. Dry bushveld north of Lydenburg.

❻ *Aloe alooides* Graskop Aloe

| J | F | M | A | M | J | J | A | S | O | N | D |

Single-stemmed shrub to 2 m, with long, narrow, drooping leaves, toothed on the margins, and long, slender, bottlebrush-like spikes of sessile, bell-shaped, yellow flowers to 10 mm long. Open dolomite ridges around Graskop.

❼ *Aloe lineata* Striped Aloe

| J | F | M | A | M | J | J | A | S | O | N | D |

Single-stemmed shrub to 2 m, with a dense crown of longitudinally striped leaves with finely toothed margins, and conical racemes of nodding, tubular, pink to red flowers, 25–30 mm long. Thicket in the southern and southeastern Cape.

▶ MULTI-STEMMED SHRUBS AND RAMBLERS

❶ *Aloe arborescens* Kransaalwyn

| J | F | M | A | M | J | J | A | S | O | N | D |

Many-branched shrub to 3 m, with narrow, sharply toothed leaves, and mostly unbranched, conical racemes of nodding, tubular, reddish flowers, 30–40 mm long, with shortly protruding stamens. Widespread through southern and eastern South Africa in bush and forest.

❷ *Aloe ciliaris*

| J | F | M | A | M | J | J | A | S | O | N | D |

Many-branched rambler to 6 m, with scattered leaves fringed with white, bristle-like thorns, and short, dense racemes of nodding, tubular, red flowers tipped with yellow, 25–40 mm long, with shortly protruding stamens. Thicket and coastal scrub in the Eastern Cape.

❸ *Aloe tenuior*

| J | F | M | A | M | J | J | A | S | O | N | D |

Untidy, sprawling shrublet to 3 m, with terminal tufts of greyish-green leaves, finely toothed on the margins, and racemes of spreading, shortly tubular, yellow to red flowers, 10–20 mm long, with shortly protruding stamens. Open savanna in southeastern South Africa.

▶ CREEPING SHRUBLETS

❹ *Aloe perfoliata*

| J | F | M | A | M | J | J | A | S | O | N | D |

(=*Aloe mitriformis*) **Mitre Aloe** Sprawling, often branched shrublet with stems 1–2 m long, leaves closely overlapping, oval, plain or sparsely speckled, sharply toothed, and branched, head-like racemes of nodding, tubular, scarlet flowers, 25–45 mm long, with scarcely protruding stamens. Rocky slopes and cliffs in southwestern South Africa.

▶ GRASS ALOES WITH SOFT LEAVES

❺ *Aloe cooperi* Cooper's Grass Aloe

| J | F | M | A | M | J | J | A | S | O | N | D |

Tufted perennial to 1 m, often in small groups, with bright green, narrow, finely toothed leaves, spotted at the base, and a conical raceme of nodding, tubular, pinkish flowers, 25–30 mm long, with enclosed or scarcely protruding stamens. Rocky and marshy grassland through eastern South Africa.

❻ *Aloe ecklonis*

| J | F | M | A | M | J | J | A | S | O | N | D |

(=*Aloe boylei*) **Broad-leaved Grass Aloe** Tufted perennial to 1 m, often in small groups, with strap-like, bright green, finely toothed leaves, and a head-like raceme of nodding, shortly tubular, yellow to red flowers, 14–24 mm long, with shortly protruding stamens. Open grassland through eastern South Africa.

❼ *Aloe kniphofioides*

| J | F | M | A | M | J | J | A | S | O | N | D |

Poker Grass Aloe Tufted perennial to 60 cm, with narrow, grass-like, finely toothed leaves swollen at the base into a bulb, and a sparse raceme of nodding, tubular, red flowers, 30–50 mm long, with enclosed or scarcely protruding stamens. Montane grassland in northeastern South Africa.

❽ *Aloe nubigena*

| J | F | M | A | M | J | J | A | S | O | N | D |

Graskop Cloud Aloe Clump-forming, short-stemmed plants to 20 cm, with drooping, bright green, finely toothed leaves, and slanting, head-like racemes of nodding, tubular, orange flowers tipped green, 17–27 mm long, with scarcely protruding anthers. Wet cliffs around Graskop.

▶ STEMLESS PLANTS WITH TUBULAR FLOWERS

❶ *Aloe petricola*

J F M A M J J A S O N D

Nelspruit Rock Aloe Stemless succulent to 1 m, with a rounded rosette of greyish leaves, toothed on the margin and both surfaces, and a dense, bicoloured, poker-like raceme of slightly upcurved, tubular flowers, dull red in bud and opening yellow to ivory, 20–30 mm long, with conspicuously protruding purple stamens. Granite outcrops around Nelspruit.

❷ *Aloe melanacantha*

J F M A M J J A S O N D

Black-thorned Aloe Stemless succulent to 1 m, with a rounded rosette of leaves bearing long black thorns on the margins and lower keel, and a bicoloured, conical raceme of densely packed, nodding, tubular flowers, red in bud and opening yellowish, 35–45 mm long, with shortly protruding stamens. Arid rocky hillsides in Namaqualand.

❸ *Aloe krapohliana* Banded Aloe

J F M A M J J A S O N D

Stemless succulent to 50 cm, with narrow, minutely white-toothed leaves banded with greyish-brown, and a dense, oblong raceme of nodding, reddish flowers tipped green, 25–35 mm long, with enclosed or scarcely protruding stamens. Arid rocky flats in western South Africa.

❹ *Aloe microstigma*

J F M A M J J A S O N D

(=*Aloe framesii, A. khamiesensis*) **Cape Speckled Aloe** Stemless or short-stemmed succulent, with densely spotted, brown-toothed leaves and conical, mostly bicoloured racemes of tubular flowers, reddish in bud and opening orange or yellow, 20–30 mm long, with shortly protruding stamens. Dry karroid slopes from Namaqualand to the Eastern Cape.

▶ STEMLESS PLANTS WITH FLASK-SHAPED FLOWERS SWOLLEN AT THE BASE

❺ *Aloe striata*

J F M A M J J A S O N D

Coral Aloe, Blouaalwyn Stemless succulent to 1 m, with broad, pale bluish, longitudinally striped leaves without marginal teeth, and well-branched panicles of flask-shaped, coral-red flowers, 20–30 mm long, with shortly protruding stamens. Stony hillsides and open shrubland in southern and northwestern South Africa.

❻ *Aloe variegata*

J F M A M J J A S O N D

Partridge Aloe, Kanniedood Stemless, clumped succulent to 50 cm, with thick, triangular, white-spotted leaves, and loose racemes of nodding, ± flask-shaped, pinkish-red flowers, 22–45 mm long, with shortly protruding stamens. Arid open scrubland through the western interior of South Africa.

❼ *Aloe maculata*

J F M A M J J A S O N D

Soap Aloe, Bontaalwyn Stemless succulent to 80 cm, with heavily spotted, brown-toothed leaves, and sparsely branched, flat-topped racemes of nodding, flask-shaped, yellow to red flowers, 20–45 mm long, with scarcely protruding stamens. Grassland and open savanna in southern and eastern South and subtropical Africa.

① *Aloe mudenensis*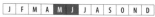
Muden Spotted Aloe Short-stemmed succulent to 1 m, the leaf sap purple, with bluish, toothed leaves spotted above and streaked beneath, and sparsely branched, egg-shaped racemes of nodding, flask-shaped, orange to red flowers, 20–35 mm long, with scarcely protruding stamens. Rocky savanna in central KwaZulu-Natal.

② *Aloe fosteri* **Foster's Spotted Aloe**
Stemless succulent to 1.5 m, the leaf sap purple, with dark green, toothed leaves streaked and banded only above, and well-branched, elongated racemes of nodding, flask-shaped, yellow, orange or red flowers, 20–38 mm long, with shortly protruding stamens. Locally common on stony soils in savanna and woodland in northeastern South Africa.

③ *Aloe affinis* (=*Aloe immaculata*)
Stemless succulent to 30 cm, with ± unspotted leaves with hard, brownish margins, and branched, conical racemes of nodding, flask-shaped, orange to red flowers, 25–45 mm long, with scarcely protruding stamens. Hot bushveld in northeastern South Africa.

④ *Aloe greatheadii*
(=*Aloe longibracteata, A. verdoorniae*) **Common Spotted Aloe** Stemless succulent to 1.5 m, with spotted, toothed leaves (the sap drying yellow), and branched, densely conical racemes of nodding, flask-shaped, pink to cream-coloured flowers, 22–35 mm long, with scarcely protruding stamens. Rocky outcrops in highveld grassland in northern South and tropical Africa. *Aloe parvibracteata* has more open racemes and the sap usually dries purple.

HYACINTHACEAE Hyacinth family

Drimia POISON SQUILL, BRANDUI
(Greek drimys, acrid, as many species are poisonous or irritant) Bulbous perennials. *Leaves often dry at flowering.* Flowers in heads or racemes, with at least the *lower bracts spurred at the base, each flower lasting only up to 1 day.* Africa and Eurasia: ±100 spp.; South Africa: 60 spp. The bulbs are highly poisonous or irritant and were used medicinally; the fleshy, sap-filled leaves of larger species were used as a substitute for soap.

⑤ *Drimia capensis* **Maerman**
Stout perennial to 2 m, with a large tuft of oblong to elliptical leaves, dry at flowering, and a narrow spike of white or cream-coloured flowers in dense whorls, 10 mm in diameter, with the petals curled back. Clay and lime soils in the southwestern and southern Cape.

⑥ *Drimia altissima*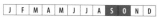
Tall White Squill, Jeukbol Stout perennial to 1 m, with a large tuft of lance-shaped leaves, dry at flowering, and a cylindrical raceme of white or greenish flowers, 10 mm in diameter, on long, wiry pedicels. Hot bushveld and open thicket through western, eastern and northern South and tropical Africa.

83

❶ _Drimia macrocentra_

Large Snake-head, Slangkop Stout perennial to 1 m, with a solitary, hollow, cylindrical leaf not present in flowering plants, and a dense raceme of white or greenish flowers, 10 mm in diameter, the lowermost bracts with a flat spur 30–40 mm long. Damp or marshy montane grassland near streams in the Drakensberg.

Albuca SLIME LILY, SLYMLELIE, TAMARAK

(Latin albicans, becoming white, referring to the flowers of Albuca canadensis) Bulbous perennials. Leaves 1–several. Flowers in slender or flat-topped racemes, *often nodding*, with *thick-textured petals, white to yellowish with a green longitudinal band, the inner petals usually erect and differing from the outer in having a thickened, hooded or flap-like tip.* Fruit usually *with diverging crests on each side.* Africa: ±60 spp.; South Africa: ±50 spp. One or two of the species, especially *Albuca nelsonii*, are grown horticulturally. The vernacular name *tamarak(ka)* is derived from the Khoisan name.

❷ _Albuca abyssinica_

Bushveld Slime Lily, Bosveld Slymlelie Perennial to 1 m, with strap-shaped leaves that are hairy on the underside towards the base, and a narrow raceme of green flowers with darker keels, ±20 mm long, on short, spreading pedicels; inner tepals weakly cupped at the tip. Rocky slopes on forest margins and shaded cliffs in northeastern South and tropical Africa.

❸ _Albuca setosa_ Fibrous Slime Lily

Perennial to 50 cm, the bulb with a conspicuous fibrous collar at the tip, with narrow, channelled leaves, and a flat-topped raceme of white flowers with green keels, scented of spicy vanilla, 15–20 mm long, on long, erect pedicels; inner tepals erect and distinctly fleshy at the tips. Widespread through South and tropical Africa in open habitats.

❹ _Albuca nelsonii_ Nelson's Slime Lily

Robust perennial to 1 m high, growing in clumps, with strap-shaped leaves, and stout, fat-topped racemes of white flowers with green keels, 25–35 mm long, on long, erect, pedicels; inner tepals erect and distinctly fleshy at the tip. Grassland, especially near the coast, through eastern South Africa.

❺ _Albuca flaccida_ Slime Lily, Slymlelie

Perennial, 40–100 cm, with fleshy, channelled leaves clasping the base of the stem, and a raceme of fragrant, nodding, yellowish flowers with broad green keels, 15–25 mm long; inner tepals erect, with a hinged flap at the tip, and outer stamens sterile. Mostly coastal in deep sandy soils in the southwestern Cape.

❻ _Albuca canadensis_

(=*Albuca maxima*) **Wittamarak** Perennial, 40–150 cm, the outer bulb tunics slightly fibrous at the top, with fleshy, channelled leaves clasping the base of the stem, and long racemes of weakly nodding, white flowers with broad green keels, 15–25 mm long; the inner tepals are erect, with a hinged flap at the tip, and the outer stamens are sterile. Rocky flats in Namaqualand and southwestern South Africa.

Ornithogalum CHINCHERINCHEE, TJIENK *(Origin unclear)*

Bulbous perennials. Leaves usually lance-shaped. Flowers in slender or flat-topped racemes, star-, cup- or bell-shaped, *pale greenish, white, yellow or orange, sometimes with a dark eye*. Fruit egg- or spindle-shaped *with flattened or angled seeds*. Widespread through Africa and Eurasia into India: ±160 spp.; South Africa: ±80 spp. Several species are extremely poisonous and may cause stock losses; some of the larger-flowered species are important in horticulture. The vernacular name *tjienkerientjee* is an onomatopoeic rendering of the squeaking sound produced when the stems are drawn across one another.

❶ *Ornithogalum xanthochlorum* | J | F | M | A | M | J | J | **A** | **S** | O | N | D |

Giant Chincherinchee, Slangkop Robust perennial to 60 cm, with glossy, strap-shaped leaves, and a cylindrical raceme of waxy, green and white, scented flowers, 25 mm in diameter. Dry sandy or gravelly flats and lower slopes in Namaqualand.

❷ *Ornithogalum regale* | J | **F** | M | A | M | J | J | A | S | O | N | D |

(=*Galtonia regalis*) **Royal Berg Lily** Robust perennial to 80 cm, with strap- or lance-shaped leaves, and a conical raceme of nodding, bell-shaped, greenish flowers, 25–40 mm long; stamens 9–10 mm long. Wet cliffs at high altitude in the Drakensberg.

❸ *Ornithogalum candicans* | J | F | M | **A** | M | J | J | A | S | O | N | D |

(=*Galtonia candicans*) **White Berg Lily** Robust perennial to 1.5 m, with strap- or lance-shaped leaves, and a conical raceme of nodding, bell-shaped, white or cream-coloured flowers, 30–45 mm long; stamens 18–19 mm long. Rough grassland along streams and forest margins in eastern South Africa.

❹ *Ornithogalum saundersiae* | **J** | F | **M** | A | M | J | J | A | S | O | N | **D** |

Black-eyed Berg Lily, Giant White Ornithogalum Robust perennial, 1–1.5 m, with lance-shaped leaves and a rounded or flat-topped raceme of white flowers with a blackish ovary, 15 mm in diameter, on long pedicels. Localised on rocky banks and outcrops in thicket in northeastern South Africa.

❺ *Ornithogalum pruinosum* | J | F | M | A | M | J | J | A | **S** | **O** | N | D |

Grey-leaved Chincherinchee Perennial, 10–50 cm, the outer bulb tunics hard and dark, with oblong, greyish leaves, often with wavy margins, and a conical or rounded raceme of glossy white flowers, 15–25 mm in diameter. Stony slopes in Namaqualand.

❻ *Ornithogalum dubium* Geeltjienk | J | F | M | A | M | J | **J** | **A** | **S** | **O** | **N** | **D** |

Perennial, 10–50 cm, the outer bulb tunics dark black, with spreading, oblong leaves with finely fringed margins, sometimes dry at flowering, and a rounded raceme of glossy white, yellow or orange flowers, often with a green or brown centre, 15–25 mm in diameter; inner stamen filaments sometimes winged at the base, and the style sometimes very short. Stony clay flats and slopes from the southwestern to the Eastern Cape.

❼ *Ornithogalum thyrsoides* | J | F | M | A | M | J | J | A | S | **O** | **N** | D |

Chincherinchee Perennial, 20–80 cm, the outer bulb tunics soft and whitish, with ± erect, lance-shaped leaves, and a conical or rounded raceme of glossy white flowers, often with a blackish centre, 15–25 mm in diameter; inner stamen filaments with broad membranous wings at the base. Sandy flats and lower slopes in the southwestern Cape.

Schizocarphus WHITE SQUILL

(Greek schizein, to split; karpos, fruit, referring to the deeply 3-lobed fruits) Bulbous perennial, the *bulb with coarse, fibrous outer tunics.* Leaves tough, with thickened margins. Flowers in a conical or cylindrical raceme on *long, wiry pedicels, white with a blackish ovary,* star-shaped. Southern and south tropical Africa: 1 sp. Used medicinally.

❶ *Schizocarphus nervosus*

J F M A M J J A S O N D

White Squill Perennial to 40 cm, the bulb covered with fibrous sheaths, with strap- or lance-shaped, stiff and often twisted leaves with thickened margins, and a raceme of white to cream-coloured flowers on wiry pedicels, with a green or blackish ovary, 5–8 mm in diameter. Stony or open grassland through eastern South and tropical Africa.

Merwilla BLUE SQUILL

(Named for South African amateur botanist, Frederick van der Merwe, 1894–1968) Bulbous perennial, the *bulb with brown, cartilaginous outer tunics.* Leaves hairless or hairy. Flowers in a conical or cylindrical raceme, *blue or mauve,* star-shaped. Southern and south tropical Africa: 3 spp.; South Africa: 2 spp. Poisonous but used medicinally, and also to make soap.

❷ *Merwilla plumbea*

J F M A M J J A S O N D

(=*Scilla natalensis*) **Large Blue Squill** Slender to stout perennial, 20–100 cm, with lance-shaped, smooth or velvety leaves, and a cylindrical raceme of blue to mauve flowers with white filaments, 10 mm in diameter. Rocky grassland through eastern South Africa. *Merwilla dracomontana* is a dwarf species with hairy stems.

Ledebouria SPOTTED SQUILL

(Named for Carl Friedrich von Ledebour, 1785–1851, professor of botany at Dorpat (Tartu), Estonia) Bulbous perennials. Leaves spotted or streaked with purple or dark green, hairless or hairy. Flowers in sprawling racemes without bracts, often >1 per bulb, pink or greyish, star-shaped, often with magenta stamen filaments. Africa and India: ±50 spp.; South Africa: ±40 spp. Used medicinally.

❸ *Ledebouria socialis*

J F M A M J J A S O N D

Social Ledebouria Small, clump-forming perennial to 7 cm, with exposed bulbs, silvery leaves spotted with purple, and racemes of grey or pinkish flowers, 4 mm in diameter, with magenta stamens. Rock sheets and shallow soil beneath trees in river valleys in the Eastern Cape.

❹ *Ledebouria cooperi*

J F M A M J J A S O N D

Cooper's Ledebouria Perennial to 25 cm, with bright green leaves longitudinally streaked with purple beneath, and racemes of pink flowers, 5 mm in diameter, with magenta filaments. Wet and marshy grassland through southern and eastern South Africa.

❺ *Ledebouria revoluta*

J F M A M J J A S O N D

Common Ledebouria Perennial to 15 cm, with dull green leaves spotted or blotched with purple or dark green, and racemes of greyish flowers, ±5 mm in diameter, with magenta filaments. Stony grassland and open woodland through southern and eastern South Africa.

① *Ledebouria zebrina*   J F M A M J J A S O N D

Giant Ledebouria Perennial to 30 cm, with the leaves streaked or barred with purple, and sprawling racemes of greenish flowers, 5 mm in diameter, with green stamens. Moist savanna through eastern South Africa.

Eucomis   PINEAPPLE LILY, WILDEPYNAPPEL

(Greek eukomes, beautifully haired, referring to the crown of bracts) Bulbous perennials. Leaves hairless, sometimes barred or spotted with purple beneath. Flowers in dense racemes on plain or mottled stalks, *topped with a crown of long, leafy bracts*, star-shaped, white or greenish, sometimes speckled with purple. *Seeds spherical.* Sub-Saharan Africa: 10 spp., all South Africa. Several species and hybrids are cultivated.

② *Eucomis autumnalis*   J F M A M J J A S O N D

Common Pineapple Lily Perennial, 6–30 cm, with a plain green stem, plain green, wavy or crinkled leaves, and a dense raceme of white to greenish flowers, 15–20 mm in diameter, on spreading pedicels 3–9 mm long. Open grassland, among rocks or in swamps through eastern South and tropical Africa.

③ *Eucomis humilis*   J F M A M J J A S O N D

Dwarf Pineapple Lily Perennial, 12–35 cm, with a purple-blotched stem, tightly crinkled and toothed leaves speckled with purple beneath, and a loose raceme of white to greenish and purple flowers, 20–30 mm in diameter, on spreading or drooping pedicels 5–11 mm long. Montane and subalpine grassland in the Drakensberg.

④ *Eucomis pallidiflora*   J F M A M J J A S O N D

Giant Pineapple Lily Perennial, 45–120 cm, with a plain green stem, plain green, wavy leaves, and a loose or dense raceme of greenish flowers, 20–30 mm in diameter, on ± erect pedicels 15–50 mm long. Montane marshes and coastal grassland through eastern South Africa. *Eucomis comosa* has purple-spotted stems and flowers.

⑤ *Eucomis bicolor*   J F M A M J J A S O N D

Bicoloured Pineapple Lily Perennial 20–60 cm, with a purple-blotched stem, wavy or crinkled leaves spotted with purple beneath, and a short, dense raceme of creamy white and purple flowers, ±20 mm in diameter, on drooping pedicels 13–50 mm long. Montane grassland along streams and damp cliffs in the Drakensberg.

Lachenalia   LACHENALIA, VIOOLTJIE

(Named for Werner de Lachenal, 1736–1800, professor of botany at Basle) Bulbous perennials. Leaves *often barred or spotted, surrounded at the base below ground level by a transparent, membranous collar.* Flowers in spikes or racemes, *with the lower bracts often reduced, often with sterile upper flowers,* spreading or nodding, funnel-shaped to tubular, with the *tepals joined below,* variously coloured, the outer petals *often with a swollen, darkly coloured tip. Seeds spherical.* Southern Africa, mainly the winter-rainfall parts: ±110 spp., all South Africa. Several of the larger species are cultivated. The vernacular name *viooltjie* derives from the squeaking sound produced when the stems are drawn across one another.

❶ *Lachenalia pustulata*

J F M A M J J **A S O** N D

Perennial, 15–35 cm, with 1 or 2 lance-shaped, mostly densely warty leaves, and a raceme of shortly cylindrical flowers, 7–9 mm long, shades of cream-coloured, blue or pink, with green or brownish markings; the anthers shortly or well exposed beyond the flowers. On sandy flats in the southwestern Cape, often in large colonies.

❷ *Lachenalia mutabilis* Bontviooltjie

J F M A M J **J A** S O N D

Perennial, 10–45 cm, with 1 erect, lance-shaped leaf with crinkly margins, and a spike of sessile, shortly cylindrical to urn-shaped flowers, 8–10 mm long, pale blue and white with yellow tips, or yellowish-green, with brown markings, always with several lilac to bright purplish sterile upper flowers; the anthers concealed within the flowers. Sandy and stony slopes in Namaqualand and the southwestern Cape.

❸ *Lachenalia aloides*

J F M **A M J J A S O** N D

Cape Cowslip, Vierkleurtjie Perennial, 5–31 cm, with 1 or 2 lance-shaped, plain or spotted leaves, and a raceme of nodding, cylindrical flowers, 20–35 mm long, in combinations of orange, red, yellow or greenish-blue, with greenish markings, the inner tepals much longer than the outer, and the anthers concealed within the flowers. Rocky outcrops in the southwestern Cape.

❹ *Lachenalia bulbifera* Rooinaeltjie

J F M **A M J J A S** O N D

Perennial, 8–30 cm, with 1 or 2 lance-shaped, plain or spotted leaves, and a raceme of nodding, cylindrical flowers, 20–35 mm long, orange to red, with darker red or brown markings and green tips; the inner tepals only slightly longer than the outer, and the anthers concealed within the flowers. Sandy slopes and flats, mainly coastal, in the southwestern Cape.

❺ *Lachenalia rubida* Sandviooltjie

J F **M A M J J** A S O N D

Perennial, 6–25 cm, with 1 or 2 lance-shaped, plain or spotted leaves, and a raceme of nodding, cylindrical, pink to red flowers, 20–32 mm long, plain or densely spotted with pink or red; the inner tepals much longer than the outer, and the anthers concealed within the flowers. Sandy flats and slopes, mainly coastal, in the southwestern Cape.

Veltheimia VELTHEIMIA

(Named for Count Frederick von Veltheim, 1741–1801, German patron of botany) Robust bulbous perennials. Leaves *often wavy or crinkly*. Flowers in a dense raceme, *nodding, tubular, with the tepals joined for most of their length*, pinkish; *the stamens arise obliquely near the middle of the tube*. Fruit *large and 3-winged*. Southern Africa: 2 spp. *Veltheimia bracteata* is a popular garden plant.

❻ *Veltheimia capensis* Sandlelie

J F **M A M J J** A S O N D

Robust bulbous perennial, 20–50 cm, with dull greyish, wavy or crinkly leaves, and a dense raceme of nodding, tubular, pinkish flowers, 20–35 mm long. Sandy flats and rocky slopes in Namaqualand and southwestern South Africa. *Veltheimia bracteata*, from coastal parts of the southern and Eastern Cape, has glossy green leaves and flowers in spring.

93

LANARIACEAE
Lanaria family

Lanaria KAPOK LILY, PERDEKAPOK
(Greek lana, wool; aria, connected with, referring to the woolly flowering stems) Rhizomatous, evergreen perennial. Leaves *strap-shaped and channelled with coarse hairs at the base*, the margins finely toothed. Flowers small, in a dense, *white-haired, flat-topped panicle*, mauve, funnel-shaped, densely white-felted on the outside. Southwestern South Africa: 1 sp.

1 *Lanaria lanata*   J F M A M J J A S O N D

Evergreen perennial, 30–80 cm, with fibrous, grass-like leaves finely toothed along the margins, and a dense, woolly panicle of mauve flowers, 10 mm in diameter. Stony slopes from the southwestern to the Eastern Cape.

VELLOZIACEAE
Black-stick Lily family

Xerophyta BLACK-STICK LILY *(Greek xeros, dry; phytos, plant, alluding to their tough habit)*
Fibrous shrublets. Leaves narrow and grass-like, tough and dying back to the base. Flowers solitary, mauve, with a *coarsely hairy or spiny ovary*. Widespread: 30–40 spp.; South Africa: 7 spp. Stems used as pot scourers and to make rope; also used in traditional medicine.

2 *Xerophyta retinervis*   J F M A M J J A S O N D

Black-stick Lily, Bobbejaanstert Shrublet to 1.8 m, with tufts of grass-like leaves at the ends of erect, black stems, and pale to deep mauve flowers, 80 mm in diameter; ovary and flower stalks covered with coarse, brownish hairs. Rocky outcrops in dry areas through northeastern South Africa, flowering especially after fire.

3 *Xerophyta viscosa*   J F M A M J J A S O N D

Small Black-stick Lily Tufted dwarf shrublet to 60 cm, with tough, grass-like leaves that are coarsely fringed on the margins, and mauve flowers, 80 mm in diameter; ovary and flower stalks covered with sticky black glands. Rocky outcrops in eastern and northern South and subtropical Africa.

HYPOXIDACEAE
Stargrass family

Hypoxis STARGRASS *(A classical Greek plant name)*
Cormous perennials. Leaves *3-ranked*, narrow or lance-shaped, *sparsely or densely hairy*. Flowers on a slender or stout peduncle, *yellow or white*, star-shaped, often closing around midday. Worldwide through the tropics: ±90 spp.; South Africa: ±40 spp. Widely used medicinally, both traditionally and in modern medicine; the fibrous leaves make a tough rope.

4 *Hypoxis rigidula*   J F M A M J J A S O N D

Stiff-leaved Stargrass, Silver-leaved Stargrass Erect perennial to 90 cm with stiffly erect, narrow, fibrous leaves, 3–15 mm wide, covered with white hairs, sometimes densely so, and clusters of yellow flowers, ±30 mm in diameter, on erect stems. Stony grassland through eastern South and subtropical Africa.

95

❶ *Hypoxis hemerocallidea*

J F M A M J J A S O N D

Common Stargrass, African Potato Perennial to 40 cm, with 3 ranks of sickle-shaped, sharply channelled leaves, 10–50 mm wide, the margins and lower surface densely covered with white hairs, and sloped or sprawling stems of yellow flowers, ±40 mm in diameter. Widespread in grassland and open woodland through eastern South and tropical Africa.

❷ *Hypoxis colchicifolia*

J F M A M J J A S O N D

Broad-leaved Stargrass Robust perennial to 60 cm, with broad, lance-shaped leaves, 30–110 mm wide, almost hairless or hairy on the margins, and yellow flowers, 30–40 mm in diameter. Thick grassland and open woodland in eastern South Africa.

Rhodohypoxis RED STAR, ROOISTERRETJIE
(Greek rhodo, rose red; the genus Hypoxis) Cormous perennials. Leaves narrow and channelled, *usually hairy*. Flowers 1 or 2 on a slender peduncle, *red, pink or white*, with the *tepals erect at the base to form a throat enclosing the stamens*. High-altitude grassland and rock flushes in the Drakensberg. South Africa: 6 spp.

❸ *Rhodohypoxis baurii*

J F M A M J J A S O N D

Dwarf mat-forming perennial, 5–10 cm high, with narrow, grass-like leaves covered with conspicuous hairs, and white, pink or red flowers, 20–30 mm in diameter, on hairy stalks. Rock sheets and damp ledges in short grassland along the eastern escarpment. *Rhodohypoxis milloides* from seeps and stream sides has hairless leaves.

Empodium AUTUMN STAR, PLOEGTYDBLOMMETJIE
(Greek em, within; pod, foot, referring to the underground ovary) Cormous, often stemless perennials. *Leaves usually pleated* and hairless, often developing after flowering. *Flowers solitary, often at ground level*, yellow, star-shaped with a well-developed *solid tube, or beak, above the ovary. Fruit fleshy, spindle-shaped, 1-chambered*. Southern Africa, mainly winter-rainfall parts: ±9 spp. The vernacular name *ploegtydblommetjie* is a colourful reminder of the importance to early farmers of natural signs of the changing seasons.

❹ *Empodium plicatum*

J F M A M J J A S O N D

Dwarf, stemless perennial, 10–30 cm, with narrow, pleated leaves surrounded at the base by pale sheaths, sometimes absent or just emerging at flowering, and bright yellow flowers at ground level, 30–40 mm in diameter; the ovary hidden among the leaf sheaths. Damp flats and lower slopes in the southwestern Cape.

Spiloxene CAPE STAR, STERRETJIE
(Greek spilos, spot; xenos, host, alluding to the markings on the tepals in some species) Cormous perennials. Leaves broad to thread-like, usually channelled, *hairless*. Flowers 1–6 in a cluster on a slender peduncle with 1 or 2 bracts, white, yellow or orange, star-shaped with separate tepals. Fruit a dry, 3-chambered capsule *opening from a lidded top*. Winter-rainfall southern Africa: ±25 spp.

1 *Spiloxene aquatica* Watersterretjie J F M A M **J J A S O N** D
Aquatic perennial, 10–30 cm, with firm, quill-like leaves, and clusters of 2–7 white flowers with green reverse, 15 mm in diameter; with 2 leaf-like bracts. Seasonal pools and marshes in the southwestern Cape.

2 *Spiloxene capensis* Peacock Flower J F M A M J **J A S O N** D
Perennial, 10–30 cm, with narrow, grass-like leaves V-shaped in section, and solitary, yellow or white to pink flowers, striped on the reverse and usually with an iridescent green or dull black centre, 30–50 mm in diameter; with 1 leaf-like bract. Seasonally wet flats in the southwestern Cape. *Spiloxene canaliculata* from near Darling has orange flowers and unusual J-shaped seeds.

3 *Spiloxene serrata* J F M A **M J J A S O** N D
Perennial, 6–20 cm, with narrow, grass-like leaves minutely toothed along the margins, and solitary yellow, orange or white flowers with green reverse, 20–30 mm in diameter; with 2 thread-like bracts. Seasonally damp flats and lower slopes in the southwestern Cape.

COLCHICACEAE   Colchicum family

Gloriosa FLAME LILY *(Latin gloriosus, glorious)*

Cormous perennials, climbing or erect. Leaves alternate or the lower whorled, lance-shaped *with 3 main veins, often narrowed into a tendril at the tip*. Flowers often nodding on long pedicels, *inserted next to or between the upper leaves, yellow or orange to red*, the tepals separate. Africa and Asia: 14 spp.; South Africa: 3 spp. Plants are poisonous but have been used medicinally and are cultivated commercially for chemicals and as ornamentals; the colourful seeds are used as beads.

4 *Gloriosa modesta* J F M A M J J A S O **N D**
(=*Littonia modesta*) **Littonia, Geelklokkie** Erect or scrambling perennial to 2 m, with the lower leaves in whorls of 3 or 4, sometimes drawn into a tendril, and nodding, cup-shaped, orange flowers, 20–30 mm in diameter. Damp and rank grassland on the edge of forests and bush clumps through eastern South Africa.

5 *Gloriosa superba* Flame Lily J **F M** A M J J A S O **N D**
Sprawling or climbing perennial to 2 m, with the leaves drawn into a tendril, and nodding flowers shaped like a Turk's-cap lily, yellowish or red and yellow, 50–60 mm in diameter, with curved-back petals crinkled along the margins. Coastal dunes and inland thicket and bush through eastern South and tropical Africa to India.

Sandersonia CHRISTMAS BELLS, CHINESE LANTERN LILY
(Named for John Sanderson, d. 1881, who discovered the species) Cormous perennial, usually climbing. Leaves lance-shaped *with 3 main veins, often narrowed into a tendril at the tip*. Flowers nodding on long pedicels, *inserted next to or between the upper leaves, yellow or orange, lantern-shaped*. South Africa: 1 sp. Plants have been used medicinally and are cultivated commercially as a cut-flower.

6 *Sandersonia aurantiaca* J F M A M J J A S O **N D**
Christmas Bells, Geelklokkie Climbing or sprawling perennial to 1.5 m, with the leaves sometimes drawn into a tendril, and nodding, orange, lantern-like flowers, ±25 mm long. Damp grassland, often on the margins of bush, through eastern South Africa.

Colchicum   MEN-IN-A-BOAT, PATRYSBLOM   (Of Colchis, on the Black Sea)

Cormous perennials, mostly with an *underground* or very short stem. Leaves 2–few, lance-shaped to oval, often *spreading on the ground*. Flowers 1–few, clustered in a *head and concealed among enlarged and often coloured bracts*, pale greenish or white to pink, the tepals usually separate and narrowed towards the base and *often cupped above*, the stamens *with a swollen, nectar-secreting base*. Africa and the Mediterranean, mostly winter-rainfall southern Africa: ±90 spp.; South Africa: ±30 spp. The vernacular name *patrysblom* may refer to the belief that the corms were scratched out by francolins but they have also been recorded as being toxic to crows. Another possibility is that the attractively marked bracts of some species suggested the speckling on the breasts of the birds. Recent study has included the genus *Androcymbium* within *Colchicum*.

❶ *Colchicum melanthioides*

J F M A M J J A S **O N** D

(=*Androcymbium melanthioides*) **Pyjama Flower**   Short-stemmed perennial, 10–20 cm, with narrow, channelled leaves, and large, creamy-white or lilac bracts conspicuously striped with green veins; the stamen filaments 8–10 mm long. Stony montane and alpine grassland through central and northern South and tropical Africa. *Colchicum orienticapense* has shorter stamen filaments, 4–5 mm long.

❷ *Colchicum coloratum*

J F M A M **J J A** S O N D

(=*Androcymbium latifolium*) **Patrysblom**   Stemless perennial with lance-shaped leaves, and large, white or red bracts; the stamens longer than the tepals. Clay flats in the southwestern Cape.

Baeometra   BEETLE LILY, KEWERLELIE

(Greek baios, small; metron, measure, referring to its size)   Cormous perennial with a *stiffly erect stem with several narrow leaves*. Flowers in a spike with the *lower flowers in the axils of narrow bracts, yellow to orange* with reddish reverse. Fruit very *long and cylindrical*. Winter-rainfall Western Cape: 1 sp. Reported to be poisonous to cattle.

❸ *Baeometra uniflora*

J F M A M J **J A** S O N D

Erect perennial to 25 cm, with several narrow leaves, and a spike of yellow to orange flowers with a black centre, 20–25 mm in diameter. Damp slopes and flats in the southwestern Cape.

Wurmbea   SPIKE LILY, WITKOPPIE   (Named for F. von Wurmb, a Dutch merchant in Java)

Cormous perennials. *Leaves 3*, lance-shaped and channelled. Flowers in spikes *without bracts*, green or white to pink, sometimes dark reddish-purple, the *tepals often with paired or solitary dark markings at the base of the stamens*. Africa and Australia, mainly Western Cape: 40 spp.; South Africa: 21 spp. Recent study has included the genus *Onixotis* in *Wurmbea*.

❹ *Wurmbea elatior*

J F M A M J J A S O N D

Pepper-and-salt Flower   Slender perennial to 40 cm, with 3 narrow, channelled leaves, and a spike of white flowers with glossy purple marks on the tepals, 15 mm in diameter, musk-scented. Seeps and stream banks in montane grassland through the Drakensberg.

❺ *Wurmbea stricta*

J F M A M J J **A S** O N D

(=*Onixotis stricta*) **Meadow Flower, Rysblommetjie**   Slender perennial, 20–50 cm, with 3 quill-like leaves, triangular in section, the upper 2 leaves just below the flower spike, and spikes of pale pink flowers darkly marked in the centre, 15 mm in diameter. Marshes and seasonal pools in Namaqualand and the southwestern Cape.

TECOPHILAEACEAE
Cyanella family

Cyanella LADY'S HAND, RAAPTOL
(Latin cyaneus, greenish-blue; ella, diminutive) *Cormous* perennials. Leaves mostly in a basal tuft, lance-shaped to thread-like. Flowers in simple or branched racemes, on *slender pedicels with a small bracteole near the middle*, white, yellow, pink or blue, the *stamens in 2 groups with the upper anthers smaller, and the style directed to one side*. Southern Africa, mainly winter-rainfall: 7 spp., all South Africa. The roasted corms are edible and the vernacular name *raaptol* derives from their resemblance either to a turnip *(raap)* or a top *(tol)*.

❶ *Cyanella alba*

J F M A M J J A S O N D

Perennial, 12–25 cm, with thread-like leaves, and fragrant, yellow or white flowers, 20 mm in diameter, on long pedicels arising directly among the leaves, with 5 upper and 1 larger lower stamen. Stony flats in the southwestern Cape interior.

❷ *Cyanella hyacinthoides*

J F M A M J J A S O N D

Perennial, 25–40 cm, with narrowly lance-shaped leaves that are sometimes velvety, and branched racemes of mauve flowers, 10 mm in diameter, on spreading pedicels, with 5 upper and 1 larger lower stamen. Stony slopes and flats in western South Africa. *Cyanella lutea* has bright yellow flowers.

❸ *Cyanella orchidiformis*

J F M A M J J A S O N D

Perennial, 30–40 cm, with soft, often wavy, lance-shaped leaves, and mostly unbranched racemes of fragrant mauve flowers with a darker centre, 15 mm in diameter, on ± erect pedicels, with 3 upper and 3 larger lower stamens. Rocky flats and lower slopes, often in damper places, in Namaqualand.

103

HAEMODORACEAE — Bloodroot family

Dilatris BLOODROOT, BLOEDWORTEL

(Greek di, two; latris, servants, alluding to the two smaller anthers as 'servants' of the larger one) Rhizomatous perennials.

Leaves in a dense fan, oriented edgewise to the stem, flat and fibrous. Flowers in a *dense, rounded or flat-topped panicle on a grey-haired or reddish-glandular stem*, mauve or yellowish, star-shaped, with 1 stamen *shorter than the others and with a larger anther*. Winter-rainfall Western Cape: 4 spp.

❶ *Dilatris ixioides*

| J | F | M | A | M | J | J | A | S | O | N | D |

Perennial, 20–40 cm, with grey-haired stems and narrow, grass-like leaves, and a flat-topped or rounded panicle of mauve flowers, 10 mm in diameter; the 2 long stamens twice as long as the tepals. Rocky mountainsides in southwestern South Africa. *Dilatris corymbosa* has the long stamens about as long as the tepals; *D. pillansii* has all 3 stamens shorter than the tepals.

❷ *Dilatris viscosa*

| J | F | M | A | M | J | J | A | S | O | N | D |

Perennial, 45–60 cm, with stems covered with glandular hairs, sword-shaped leaves, and a rounded or flat-topped panicle of dull orange or yellow flowers, 15 mm in diameter; the long stamens slightly longer than the tepals. Montane marshes and seeps in the southwestern Cape.

Wachendorfia BUTTERFLY LILY, ROOIKANOL

(Named for E.J. Wachendorff, 18th-century professor of botany and chemistry at Utrecht) Rhizomatous perennials.

Leaves in a loose fan, oriented edgewise to the stem, pleated. Flowers in a cylindrical or open panicle on a ± hairy stem, yellow to brownish with dark markings at the base of the upper 3 tepals, *slightly irregular, lasting a day or less*, stamens all similar. Winter-rainfall South Africa: 4 spp.

❸ *Wachendorfia paniculata*

| J | F | M | A | M | J | J | A | S | O | N | D |

Perennial, mostly 20–70 cm, with mostly hairy leaves, and an open panicle of pale apricot to yellow flowers, 25–30 mm in diameter. Damp slopes and flats in southwestern South Africa, flowering best after fire. *Wachendorfia multiflora* has a short, dense panicle of yellow to brownish flowers with narrow tepals.

❹ *Wachendorfia thyrsiflora*

| J | F | M | A | M | J | J | A | S | O | N | D |

Robust perennial, 1–2 m, with broad, hairless leaves, and a dense, cylindrical panicle of golden-yellow flowers, 25–30 mm in diameter. Permanent marshes and stream banks in the southwestern and southern Cape.

IRIDACEAE Iris family

▶ **SUBFAMILY NIVENIOIDEAE** SHRUBS WITH WOODY STEMS AND LEATHERY LEAVES WITHOUT A MIDRIB; FLOWERS IN CLUSTERS, TRUMPET- OR SALVER-SHAPED, WITH A TUBE

Witsenia WITSENIA, BOKMAKIERIESTERT
(Named for Nicholas Witsen, 18th-century Dutch patron of botany) *Evergreen shrub.* Leaves *in tight fans at the branch tips*, sword-shaped and *fibrous, without a midrib*. Flowers *in pairs*, enclosed by leathery bracts, *tubular*, greenish-black with velvety yellow tepals; style 3-notched. Southwestern Cape: 1 sp. The vernacular name *bokmakieriestert* derives from the resemblance of the yellow and black inflorescence to the tail of the shrike-like Bokmakierie.

① *Witsenia maura* **Waaiertjie** | J | F | **M** | **A** | **M** | **J** | **J** | **A** | S | O | N | D |

Slender woody shrub to 2 m, with fans of tough, narrowly sword-shaped leaves, and clusters of tubular, blackish-green flowers with bright yellow, velvety tepals, 60–70 mm long. Marshes and seeps in the southwestern Cape.

Nivenia BUSH IRIS   *(Named for David James Niven, 1774–1826, Scottish gardener and plant collector)*
Evergreen shrubs. Leaves *in tight fans at the branch tips*, sword-shaped and *fibrous, without a midrib*. Flowers *solitary or in pairs*, enclosed by firm, dry or papery bracts, arranged in *flat-topped panicles or clusters, salver-shaped with a long tube*, bright blue to mauve; style with 3 short branches. Southwestern Cape: 10 spp.

② *Nivenia stokoei* | J | **F** | **M** | A | M | J | J | A | S | O | N | D |

Evergreen shrub 40–60 cm, with fans of sword-shaped leaves, and clusters of large, pale to deep blue or mauve flowers with a tube 27–37 mm long. Rocky sandstone ridges in fynbos in the southwestern Cape.

▶ **SUBFAMILY ARISTEOIDEAE** RHIZOMATOUS HERBS WITH LEATHERY LEAVES WITHOUT A MIDRIB; FLOWERS IN CLUSTERS, STAR-SHAPED WITHOUT A TUBE, BLUE, SHORT-LIVED

Aristea ARISTEA, BLOUSUURKANOL
(Greek, arista, an awn, referring to the fringed spathes and bracts) *Rhizomatous perennials*. Leaves in a basal fan, *tough and fibrous, without a midrib*. Flowers in clusters enclosed by brownish or green bracts, or spathes, *blue to mauve, lasting less than a day and shrivelling in the early afternoon, star-shaped with almost separate tepals; style flexed to the side*, either minutely notched or 3-lobed at the tip. Africa and Madagascar: ±55 spp.; South Africa: 45 spp.

▶ **STYLE MINUTELY NOTCHED**

③ *Aristea bakeri* | J | F | M | A | M | J | J | A | **S** | **O** | **N** | **D** |

Robust perennial to 1 m, with cylindrical, usually well-branched stems and narrow, fibrous leaves, and blue flowers, 20–25 mm in diameter, with a simple style; the spathes dry and rusty brown with transparent margins, usually minutely hairy towards the base; the fruits oblong and 3-winged, woody. Stony sandstone slopes from the southwestern to the Eastern Cape, flowering mainly after fire.

④ *Aristea capitata* | J | F | M | A | M | J | J | A | **S** | **O** | **N** | **D** |

(=*Aristea major*) **Blue Sceptre** Robust, often clump-forming perennial to 1.5 m, with cylindrical stems shortly branched above, and strap-like leaves, and overlapping clusters of blue flowers, 15–20 mm in diameter, with a simple style; the spathes membranous and translucent with dark keels; the fruits short and 3-winged. Mountain slopes in moist places in the southwestern and southern Cape.

▶ **STYLE DISTINCTLY 3-LOBED**

① *Aristea africana* Maagbossie   J F M A M J J A S **O N D**

Small, usually branched perennial, mostly 10–15 cm, with flattened stems and narrow leaves, and small heads of blue flowers, 15–20 mm in diameter, with fringed stigma lobes; the bracts translucent, with dark keels and finely fringed ends; the fruits short and 3-winged. Sandy flats and mountain slopes in the southwestern Cape.

② *Aristea dichotoma*   J **F** M A M J J A S O **N** D

Highly branched, cushion-forming perennial, 15–30 cm, with cylindrical stems and narrow, greyish leaves, and blue flowers, 15–20 mm in diameter, with fringed stigma lobes; the bracts narrow and translucent with dark keels; the fruits short, 3-winged and translucent with dark ribs. Sandy flats and lower slopes in Namaqualand and the southwestern Cape.

③ *Aristea abyssinica* Blue-eyed Grass   J F M A M J J A S O **N** D

Slender perennial, 10–15 cm, with an unbranched, leafless, flattened stem and narrow basal leaves, and a cluster of blue flowers, 10–15 mm in diameter, with fringed stigma lobes; the bracts dry and torn; the fruits egg-shaped. Grassland through eastern South and tropical Africa.

④ *Aristea torulosa*   J **F** M A M J J A **S O N D**

(=*Aristea woodii*) **Common Grass Aristea, Wood's Aristea** Perennial to 80 cm, with an unbranched stem and narrow leaves, and scattered clusters of blue flowers, 10–15 mm in diameter, with fringed stigma lobes; the bracts translucent with dark keels and deeply torn; the fruits short and oblong. Grassland through eastern South and subtropical Africa.

⑤ *Aristea compressa*   J **F** M A M J J A **S O N** D

Perennial, 60–100 cm, with a loosely branched, flattened stem and narrow leaves, and small clusters of pale to deep blue flowers, 10–15 mm in diameter, with fringed stigma lobes; the bracts translucent, with dark keels; the fruits short and oblong. Damp and rocky grassland in eastern South Africa. The more widespread *Aristea angolensis* has cylindrical stems.

▶ **SUBFAMILY IRIDOIDEAE** PERENNIAL HERBS WITH CYLINDRICAL, FLAT OR CHANNELLED LEAVES, WITHOUT A MIDRIB; FLOWERS IN CLUSTERS, INDIVIDUALLY STALKED, MOSTLY IRIS-LIKE

Bobartia **RUSH IRIS, BLOMBIESIE** *(Named for German gardener, Jacob Bobart, 1641–1719)*

Rhizomatous perennials. Leaves in a basal tuft, tough and fibrous, *mostly long and cylindrical.* Flowers on a long, leafless stem in a *terminal head enclosed by a leaf-like or dry spathe,* yellow, *lasting less than a day,* star-like, *on hairy pedicels; style divided into 3 long, thread-like branches.* Southwestern and Eastern Cape: 14 spp.

⑥ *Bobartia indica*   J F M A M J J A S **O N D**

Tufted perennial to 1 m or more, with trailing, cylindrical leaves longer than the stems, and yellow, star-shaped flowers in a dense head enclosed by a green spathe with a long, needle-like tip. Sandy flats and rocky slopes in the extreme southwestern Cape, flowering mainly after fire.

① *Bobartia orientalis* J F M A M J J **A S O** N D

Tufted perennial, 40–130 cm, with stiff, quill-like leaves, and yellow, star-shaped flowers, 20–30 mm in diameter, in a dense head enclosed by a green spathe. Mainly dry, stony, sandstone slopes, often in large colonies, in the southern and Eastern Cape.

Dietes DIETES, FOREST IRIS
(Greek dis, twice; etes, associated, referring to its resemblance to both Iris *and* Moraea*)* Rhizomatous perennials.
Leaves in a basal fan, tough and fibrous, sword-shaped without a midrib. Flowers in clusters enclosed by leathery, leaf-like spathes, yellow, or white and blue, *iris-like*; stamens separate or joined below; style branches *flattened and petal-like*, concealing the anthers. Africa and Australasia: 6 spp.; South Africa: 5 spp. Widely cultivated.

② *Dietes iridoides* Small Forest Iris J F M A M J J **A S O N D**

Tufted perennial to 60 cm, with fans of sword-shaped leaves, and clusters of white, iris-like flowers, 60 mm in diameter, with violet style branches, withering at midday; the fruits often beaked or pointed. Forest margins and understorey, through southern and eastern South and tropical Africa.

③ *Dietes grandiflora* J F M A M J J A **S O N D**

Large White Forest Iris Tufted perennial to 1 m, with fans of long, sword-shaped leaves, and clusters of white flowers, ±80–100 mm in diameter, with violet style branches and brow markings on the outer tepals, lasting 2–3 days; the fruits blunt. Margins of evergreen thicket, Eastern Cape to KwaZulu-Natal.

Ferraria SPIDER LILY, SPINNEKOPBLOM
(Named for Giovanni Batista Ferrari, 1584–1653, Italian botanical writer) Perennials with naked, disc-like
corms. Leaves leathery and sword-shaped, usually with a raised midrib. Flowers in clusters enclosed by large, leathery, leaf-like spathes, *cup-shaped, dull-coloured and speckled with separate tepals crinkly or ruffled on the margins*; stamen filaments joined in a cylindrical column; *style branches deeply fringed* and concealing the anthers. Africa: 13 spp.; South Africa: 12 spp.

④ *Ferraria crispa* Inkpotjie, Krulletjie J F M A M J J **A S** O N D

Robust, often densely branched perennial, 40–100 cm, with narrow leaves, and clusters of shallowly cup-shaped, cream-coloured to yellowish flowers sparsely to densely speckled with brown (rarely plain brown), scented of cocoa, 30–40 mm in diameter; the anther lobes parallel. Mainly coastal in deep sands or granite outcrops in the southwestern Cape.

Moraea MORAEA, TULP   *(Named by Carl Linnaeus in 1753 for his wife, Sara Elisabeth née Morea)*

Perennials, sometimes stemless, with corms covered in fibrous, herringbone-patterned tunics. Leaves usually grass-like and *channelled without a midrib*. Flowers in clusters enclosed by leathery, leaf-like spathes, variously coloured and marked, *iris-like, cup-shaped or star-like*, with the tepals mostly separate; stamen filaments separate or more usually *joined in a cylindrical column*; style branches often *flattened and petal-like or thread-like*. Africa and Middle East: 195 spp.; South Africa: ±180 spp. The corms of certain species, such as *Moraea fugax*, formed an important part of the diet of local hunter-gatherers in the past but several others, notably the *tulps* (previously placed in *Homeria*), are poisonous to livestock.

▶ FLOWERS CUP-SHAPED WITH ALL THE TEPALS SIMILAR

① *Moraea fugacissima*

(=*Galaxia fugacissima*) **Clockflower** Stemless perennial, 3–6 cm, with narrow or needle-like leaves, and cup-shaped, bright yellow flowers, 15–20 mm in diameter, with the tepals all similar, and fringed stigmas; the flowers lasting from about 10h30 to 16h00. Wet sand and clay flats from Namaqualand to the southern Cape. *Moraea galaxia* has broad leaves with fringed margins.

② *Moraea lewisiae*

(=*Hexaglottis lewisiae*) **Volstruisuintjie** Slender perennial, 20–90 cm, with 1–3 long, narrow, trailing leaves, and star-shaped, yellow flowers, 20–30 mm in diameter, with the tepals all similar, and the style divided into 6 thread-like arms spreading between the anthers; the flowers lasting from about 15h30 to 19h00; the fruits narrowly ellipsoid and projecting from the floral bracts. Various soils and habitats, mostly in dry sites, from Namaqualand to the southern Cape.

③ *Moraea miniata*

(=*Homeria miniata*) **Tulp** Perennial, 15–60 cm, with 2 or 3 narrow, trailing leaves, and star-shaped, salmon-orange or sometimes yellow or white flowers minutely speckled in the centre, 20–30 mm in diameter, with all tepals similar and spreading, and the anthers prominently displayed. Mainly clay slopes in Namaqualand and southwestern South Africa.

④ *Moraea ochroleuca*

(=*Homeria ochroleuca*) **Aas-uintjie** Perennial, 35–75 cm, with 1, rarely 2, trailing leaves, and widely cup-shaped, yellow or orange, scented flowers, 40–50 mm in diameter, with all tepals similar. Rocky slopes in the southwestern Cape, flowering only after fire.

▶ FLOWERS IRIS-LIKE WITH LANCE- OR SPEAR-SHAPED INNER TEPALS

⑤ *Moraea ciliata*

Stemless perennial, 5–10(–20) cm, with 3–5 hairy, usually grey leaves, sometimes with crinkly margins, and blue or yellow, rarely white, strongly vanilla-scented, iris-like flowers, 40–50 mm in diameter, with narrow, ± erect inner tepals and lance-shaped style crests; the flowers lasting from midday to late afternoon. Sandy and clay slopes in Namaqualand, the Western Cape and the Eastern Cape.

⑥ *Moraea serpentina*

Serpentine Moraea Perennial with 1–5 narrow, coiled or twisted leaves, and white to yellow and bluish, iris-like flowers, 30–40 mm in diameter, with erect, paddle-shaped inner tepals; the flowers lasting most of the day. Stony flats and lower slopes in Namaqualand.

⑦ *Moraea neglecta*

Erect perennial with a rod-like stem, 20–50 cm, sticky at the nodes, with a solitary, quill-like leaf, and large, yellow, iris-like flowers with the nectar guide streaked with dots, 50–60 mm in diameter, and narrow inner tepals; the stamen filaments joined only at the base, and the style crests shorter than the style branches; the flowers lasting from early afternoon to sunset. Usually deep sandy soils in the southwestern Cape. *Moraea angusta* has paler, brownish flowers with clear yellow nectar guides; *M. anomala* has the stamens joined in a column at the base.

113

① *Moraea fugax*

J F M A M J J A S O N D

Soetuintjie, Hottentotsuintjie   Perennial with short, crowded branches, 12–80 cm, with 1 or 2 narrow, trailing leaves on the stem well above ground, just below the branches, and blue, white or yellow, iris-like, vanilla-scented flowers, 50–60 mm in diameter, with lance-shaped inner tepals; the flowers lasting from early afternoon to sunset; the fruits characteristically pointed. Deep sands and rocky soils in Namaqualand and the southwestern Cape.

② *Moraea ramosissima* Vlei-uintjie

J F M A M J J A S O N D

Robust, well-branched perennial, 50–120 cm, with several to many leaves in a fan, and highly branched stems of bright yellow iris-like flowers with red anthers, 20–30 mm in diameter, and tepals that are all similar; the flowers lasting from midday to late afternoon. Along streams and in seeps in the southwestern and southern Cape, flowering only after fire.

③ *Moraea spathulata*

J F M A M J J A S O N D

Large Yellow Moraea   Robust perennial to 1 m high, solitary or growing in small clumps, with a solitary, leathery, flat or channelled leaf, often bent and trailing above, and large, bright yellow, iris-like flowers with dark yellow nectar guides, 50–70 mm in diameter, and erect, spatula-shaped inner tepals. Grassland, often among rocks, through eastern South and tropical Africa. *Moraea moggii* has a distinctly grey leaf; *M. alticola* has a netted sheath around the stem base.

④ *Moraea huttonii*

J F M A M J J A S O N D

Golden Vlei Moraea   Robust, clumped perennial to 1 m high, with a solitary, leathery, flat or channelled leaf, often bent and trailing above, and large, bright yellow, iris-like flowers with dark yellow nectar guides and a brown blotch on the style branches, 50–70 mm in diameter, and erect, spatula-shaped inner tepals. Stream sides and river beds through eastern South Africa.

⑤ *Moraea polystachya* Karoo Iris

J F M A M J J A S O N D

Branched perennial to 80 cm, with several narrow, trailing leaves, and mauve to blue, iris-like flowers with yellow nectar guides, 40–50 mm in diameter, and paddle-shaped inner tepals. Stony slopes and flats through much of interior South Africa. *Moraea bipartita* from the Little Karoo has smaller flowers, 30–40 mm in diameter.

⑥ *Moraea elliotii* Blue Tulp

J F M A M J J A S O N D

Slender perennial, 20–50 cm, with a single, narrow, channelled basal leaf, and blue to mauve, iris-like flowers with yellow nectar guides and yellow pollen, 30–40 mm in diameter, with tongue-shaped inner tepals. Stony and moist grassland through eastern South Africa.

⑦ *Moraea inclinata*

J F M A M J J A S O N D

Common Blue Moraea   Slender perennial, 30–90 cm, with a single, narrow, channelled leaf inserted well up the stem, which is sharply bent above, and mauve to violet, iris-like flowers with yellow and purple nectar guides and bright red pollen, 30–40 mm in diameter, with spreading, tongue-shaped inner tepals. Montane grassland in eastern South Africa.

▶ FLOWERS IRIS-LIKE WITH PEG-LIKE OR 3-LOBED INNER TEPALS

① *Moraea tripetala* Blou-uintjie

J F M A M J J A S O N D

Slender perennial, 20–45 cm, with a single, narrow leaf that is occasionally hairy below, and blue to violet or rarely white flowers, with the outer tepals bent backwards and minute, cusp-like inner tepals; the stamens separate almost to the base and tightly pressed against the stalk-like bases of the outer tepals. Common and widespread in rocky sandstone and clay soils in the southwestern Cape.

② *Moraea brevistyla* Partridge Moraea

J F M A M J J A S O N D

Slender perennial, 20–50 cm, with a single, narrow leaf, and white, iris-like flowers, ±20 mm in diameter, with the outer tepals bent sharply backwards and with small inner tepals, each similarly 3-fingered; the flowers lasting several days. Moist grassland and seeps in the Drakensberg. *Moraea trifida* from the Drakensberg and *M. unguiculata* from the southwestern Cape have short side lobes on the inner tepals.

③ *Moraea villosa*

J F M A M J J A S O N D

Peacock Moraea Perennial with softly hairy stems, 30–40 cm, with a solitary, hairy leaf, and large, mauve or pale orange iris-like flowers with conspicuous iridescent nectar guides, 50–70 mm in diameter, with broad, spreading outer tepals and small, 3-lobed inner tepals. Stony slopes and flats in the southwestern Cape.

▶ SUBFAMILY CROCOIDEAE PERENNIAL HERBS; LEAVES WITH A MIDRIB, OFTEN RIBBED; FLOWERS IN SPIKES OR SOLITARY, INDIVIDUALLY STALKLESS, OFTEN 2-LIPPED

▶▶ EACH STYLE BRANCH DEEPLY FORKED, THE STYLE THUS WITH 6 BRANCHES

Watsonia **WATSONIA, SUURKANOL**
(Named for Sir William Watson, 1715–1787, London physician and naturalist) Robust cormous perennials. Leaves tough and fibrous, sword-shaped with a prominent midrib and margins. Flowers in a 2-sided, spirally twisted spike, with *dry, firm-textured or leathery bracts*, usually 2-lipped, and the tepals joined into a short to long tube; the style dividing into *3 branches that are in turn forked for half their length*. Southern Africa: 52 spp. The vernacular name alludes to the rather sour taste of the corms.

▶ FLOWERS FUNNEL-SHAPED OR CYLINDRICAL

④ *Watsonia laccata*

J F M A M J J A S O N D

Dwarf perennial, 30–40 cm, with short, sword-shaped leaves, and pink to orange, funnel-shaped flowers with a flared tube, ±20 mm long, the stamens lying on the lower tepal, with filaments to 18 mm long; the fruits narrow and tapering. Stony lower slopes in the southern Cape.

⑤ *Watsonia aletroides*

J F M A M J J A S O N D

Dwarf perennial to 45 cm, with short, sword-shaped leaves, and nodding, red to pinkish, cylindrical flowers with very small tepals, with a tube 35–45 mm long and filaments 30–35 mm long; the fruits narrow and tapering. Hybridises with *Watsonia laccata*. Stony lower slopes in the southern Cape.

① *Watsonia borbonica*

J F M A M J J A S O N D

Robust, branched perennial, 50–200 cm, often with purple stems, and with bright apple-green, sword-shaped leaves, and magenta-pink, funnel-shaped flowers with a flared tube, 20–40 mm long, the stamens lying either under the upper or on the lower tepal, with filaments 13–20 mm long; the fruits blunt. Rocky slopes in the southwestern Cape, flowering well after fire.

② *Watsonia strubeniae*

J F M A M J J A S O N D

Sabie Watsonia Perennial to 1 m, with sword-shaped leaves, and pink, funnel-shaped flowers with a flared tube, ±15 mm long, and filaments 6–7 mm long. Moist grassland around Sabie in Mpumalanga.

③ *Watsonia lepida*

J F M A M J J A S O N D

Drakensberg Watsonia Erect perennial to 65 cm, solitary, with sword-shaped leaves, and pink, funnel-shaped flowers with a flared tube, 28–35 mm long, and closely overlapping, dry, brown bracts, and filaments 12–16 mm long. Montane grasslands in the Drakensberg and Maluti Mountains.

④ *Watsonia densiflora*

J F M A M J J A S O N D

Large Pink Watsonia Robust, clump-forming perennial with inclined stems to 1.5 m, with sword-shaped leaves, and pink, funnel-shaped flowers with a flared tube, 20–30 mm long, and closely overlapping, dry, brown, pale-veined bracts, and filaments 10–12 mm long. Mainly coastal and midland grassland in KwaZulu-Natal and the Eastern Cape.

⑤ *Watsonia watsonioides*

J F M A M J J A S O N D

Yellow Watsonia Perennial to 1 m, with sword-shaped leaves, and drooping, pale yellow, funnel-shaped flowers with a flared tube, 16–18 mm long, and filaments 10–12 mm long. Stony grassland in northeastern South Africa.

▶ FLOWERS TRUMPET-SHAPED

⑥ *Watsonia fourcadei*

J F M A M J J A S O N D

Perennial to 2 m, with sword-shaped leaves, and orange to red, rarely pink or purple flowers with a cylindrical tube, 40–50 mm long, and filaments 38–45 mm long; the inner bracts deeply forked, and the fruits tapering. Rocky sandstone slopes in the southwestern and southern Cape.

⑦ *Watsonia knysnana*

J F M A M J J A S O N D

Robust perennial to 1.6 m, with sword-shaped leaves, and pink to purple flowers with a cylindrical tube, 30–45 mm long, and filaments 16–28 mm long; the fruits blunt. Sandstone slopes in the southern and Eastern Cape. Hybridises with *Watsonia pillansii* in the southern Cape.

❶ *Watsonia pillansii*

J F M A M J J A S O **N D**

Robust perennial to 1.6 m, forming colonies, with sword-shaped leaves, and orange flowers with a cylindrical tube, 36–50 mm long, and filaments 30–40 mm long; the fruits blunt. Rocky slopes in grassland in southern and eastern South Africa. Hybridises with *Watsonia knysnana* in the southern Cape.

❷ *Watsonia tabularis*

J F **M A** M J J A S O **N D**

Table Mountain Watsonia Perennial to 1.5 m, with sword-shaped leaves and conspicuously inflated stem leaves, and salmon-pink flowers with a cylindrical tube, 40–50 mm long, and filaments 35–40 mm long; the fruits blunt. Rocky sandstone slopes on the Cape Peninsula.

❸ *Watsonia meriana* **Waspypie**

J F M A M J J **A S** O **N** D

Robust perennial, 60–200 cm, sometimes bearing cormlets on the stems, with sword-shaped leaves, and dull orange, pink or mauve flowers with a cylindrical tube, 42–50 mm long, and filaments 35–45 mm long; the inner bracts are as long or longer than the outer; the fruits blunt. Sandy soils, often in vleis and stream banks, in the southwestern Cape, sometimes forming dense colonies.

❹ *Watsonia schlechteri*

J **F** M A M J J A S O **N D**

Perennial, 40–100 cm, with sword-shaped leaves with very thick margins, and scarlet flowers with a cylindrical tube, 40–50 mm long, and filaments 35–45 mm long; the fruits short and blunt. Rocky sandstone slopes in fynbos in the southwestern and southern Cape, flowering mainly after fire.

Freesia **FREESIA, FLISSIE** *(Named for German physician, F. Freese, d. 1876)*

Cormous perennials. Leaves in a close fan, sword-shaped and finely veined with a raised midrib and often with *blunt or rounded tips*, soft-textured. *Flowers in a 1-ranked, horizontal and scalloped spike*, with green or dry bracts, 2-lipped with the tepals united into a long, funnel-shaped or cylindrical tube; the stamens arching together and the *style divided into 3 deeply forked branches*. Eastern parts of southern and tropical Africa: 17 spp.

❺ *Freesia laxa*

J **F M A M** J J A S O **N D**

Woodland Painted Petals Slender perennial to 30 cm, with sword-shaped leaves, and salver-shaped, red, pink or pale blue flowers, 20 mm in diameter, with dark marks on the lower tepals and very short stamens. Woodland and thicket through eastern South and tropical Africa. *Freesia grandiflora* has larger flowers with long, protruding stamens.

❻ *Freesia caryophyllacea*

J F M **A M** J J A S O N D

Dwarf perennial, 5–10 cm, with blunt leaves, often spreading on the ground, and fragrant, funnel-shaped white flowers with yellow markings on the lower tepals. Stony lower flats in the southwestern Cape.

❼ *Freesia alba*

J F M A M J **J A S** O N D

Erect perennial, 12–40 cm, with sharply pointed leaves that develop cormlets in the axils along the stem, and fragrant, funnel-shaped, white or pale yellow flowers flushed dull purple and with yellow markings on the lower tepals. Coastal sands in the southern Cape.

Dierama HAIRBELL, DIERAMA (*Greek* dierama, *funnel, referring to the flowers*)

Cormous perennials with slender, wiry stems, often forming small or large clumps. Leaves narrowly sword-shaped, fibrous and without a midrib. Flowers nodding in an arching, branched, wand-like spike, with large, translucent, membranous bracts, often ± speckled with brown, often with a dark eye, radially symmetrical, the tepals joined into a short funnel-shaped tube; the stamens erect in the centre of the flower; the style dividing into 3 short branches. South and subtropical Africa: 44 spp.; South Africa: 40 spp.

❶ *Dierama floriferum*

| J | F | M | A | M | J | J | A | S | O | N | D |

Small, clump-forming perennial to 75 cm, with leaves 3–5 mm wide, and mauve or pinkish-purple flowers, 16–21 mm long, and brown-flecked bracts, often with white tips. Montane grasslands in eastern South Africa.

❷ *Dierama argyreum*

| J | F | M | A | M | J | J | A | S | O | N | D |

Perennial to 1 m, 1–few stems, with strap-like leaves, 3–7 mm wide, and creamy white or pale yellow flowers, sometimes pink-tinged, 18–30 mm long, and pure white bracts. Stony grassland in southern KwaZulu-Natal. *Dierama pallidum* from central KwaZulu-Natal has smaller flowers, 15–18 mm long.

❸ *Dierama latifolium*

| J | F | M | A | M | J | J | A | S | O | N | D |

Robust, clump-forming perennial to 2.5 m, with strap-like leaves, 5–15 mm wide, and pink to claret flowers, 24–33 mm long, and ± pure white bracts. Open grassland in eastern South Africa.

Ixia IXIA, KALOSSIE (*Named from a classical plant of ancient Greece*)

Cormous perennials with slender, *wiry stems*. Leaves sword-shaped, often rather short. Flowers in a spike, spirally arranged, with *short, pale or translucent, membranous bracts, often 3-toothed at the tips*, colourful and *often with a dark eye, radially symmetrical*, the tepals joined into a short or long tube; the stamens erect in the centre of the flower; the *style dividing into 3 short branches below the top of the anthers*. Winter-rainfall South Africa: ±50 spp. Flowers mostly close at night or in inclement weather. The vernacular name derives from the Afrikaans *kalotjie*, originally a skull-cap but applied to the headdress worn by Malay slaves in early Cape Town, which the flowers were thought to resemble.

▸ FLORAL TUBE CYLINDRICAL OR FUNNEL-SHAPED

❹ *Ixia paniculata* Pypkalossie

| J | F | M | A | M | J | J | A | S | O | N | D |

Perennial, 40–100 cm, with sword-shaped leaves, and salver-shaped, cream- to buff-coloured flowers with a cylindrical tube, 35–70 mm long, partially enclosing the purple anthers. Seeps and stream banks in the southwestern Cape.

❺ *Ixia rapunculoides* Bloukalossie

| J | F | M | A | M | J | J | A | S | O | N | D |

Perennial, 15–70 cm, usually branched, with sword-shaped leaves, and blue, mauve or pink flowers with a funnel-shaped tube, 6–15 mm long, partially enclosing the anthers. Stony flats along the western escarpment.

▶ **FLORAL TUBE THREAD-LIKE**

❶ *Ixia dubia*

J F M A M J J A S **O** **N** **D**

Perennial, 25–60 cm, with narrow, sword-shaped leaves, and orange to yellow flowers with a small dark centre, flushed reddish on the reverse, with a thread-like tube, 5–15 mm long, and partly or entirely black stamen filaments; the bracts translucent pink. Moist flats and lower slopes in the southwestern Cape.

❷ *Ixia maculata*

J F M A M J J A **S** **O** N D

Perennial, 20–50 cm, with sword-shaped leaves, and yellow to orange flowers with a large dark centre, often with a yellowish star-like marking in the middle, with a thread-like tube, 5–20 mm long, and stamen filaments that are partially or wholly joined together; the bracts papery and rusty-brown. Stony flats and lower slopes along the West Coast.

❸ *Ixia polystachya* Koringblommetjie

J F M A M J J A S **O** **N** **D**

Wiry perennial, 40–80 cm, often branched, with narrow leaves, and white or pink to mauve flowers, sometimes with a small dark centre, with a thread-like tube, 5–15 mm long. Stony flats and slopes in the southwestern Cape.

Sparaxis **SPARAXIS, FLUWEELTJIE** (*Greek sparasso, torn, referring to the fringed bracts*)

Cormous perennials. Leaves sword-shaped in a closely set fan and *finely veined*, with a prominent midrib. Flowers few to many in a 1-sided or spiral spike, with *dry, papery or crinkly bracts, irregularly fringed and streaked with brown*, 2-lipped or bowl-shaped, the tepals joined into a short to long tube; the style dividing into 3 short branches. Winter-rainfall South Africa: 15 spp. Hybrids between a few of the colourfully marked, symmetrically-flowered species are popularly cultivated as spring bulbs.

❹ *Sparaxis bulbifera*

J F M A M J J A **S** **O** N D

Branching perennial, 15–45 cm, developing axillary cormlets after blooming with sword-shaped leaves, and nearly symmetrical, cup-shaped, white to cream-coloured flowers, often purplish on the reverse, 30–40 mm in diameter. Seasonally wet sandy flats, often in roadside ditches, in the southwestern Cape. *Sparaxis grandiflora*, with white, yellow or purple flowers, is never branched and has no axillary cormlets on the stem.

❺ *Sparaxis tricolor* Harlequin-flower

J F M A M J J A **S** **O** N D

Cormous perennial, 10–30 cm, with sword-shaped leaves, and symmetrical, reddish-orange flowers with a large yellow and black cup and yellow anthers, 35–40 mm in diameter. Seasonally moist stony flats around Nieuwoudtville, often along streams. *Sparaxis pillansii* has pinkish-red flowers with brown or black anthers.

❻ *Sparaxis elegans*

J F M A M J J **A** S O N D

Streptanthera, Pale Harlequin-flower Cormous perennial, 10–20 cm, with sword-shaped leaves, and symmetrical, salmon-pink or white flowers with a purple cup edged in black and yellow and coiled, purple anthers, 40–50 mm in diameter. Stony clay flats around Nieuwoudtville.

❼ *Sparaxis villosa*

J F M A M J J **A** S O N D

Perennial, 12–35 cm, with sword-shaped, often blunt, leaves, and small 2-lipped, yellow flowers with purple upper tepals and a tube ±16 mm long. Clay and granite slopes along the West Coast. *Sparaxis variegata* has larger flowers.

125

Tritonia TRITONIA, AGRETJIE

(Latin triton, *weathercock, alluding to the variable positions of the stamens)* Cormous perennials. Leaves usually sword-shaped in a closely set fan, with a prominent midrib. Flowers 1–many in a 1-sided or spiral spike, with *dry, firm-textured or papery, often 3-toothed bracts*, 2-lipped or bowl-shaped, the tepals joined into a short to long tube; the style dividing into 3 short branches. Eastern and southern Africa: 28 spp. The vernacular name derives from the French *aigrette*, an allusion to the plume-like appearance of the flower spikes of some species.

❶ *Tritonia deusta* Kalkoentjie

| J | F | M | A | M | J | J | A | S | O | N | D |

Perennial, 25–50 cm, with sword-shaped leaves, and large, bowl-shaped, orange flowers with reddish-black blotches, 30–40 mm in diameter. Stony flats in the southwestern Cape. *Tritonia crocata* (orange flowers) and *T. squalida* (pink flowers) have translucent, window-like patches on the tepals.

❷ *Tritonia disticha* Red Tritonia

| J | F | M | A | M | J | J | A | S | O | N | D |

Perennial, 20–80 cm, with sword-shaped leaves with a prominent vein near the margin, and 2-lipped, orange to red flowers with yellow blotches on the lower tepals, the tube 10–15 mm long. Grassland through eastern South Africa.

❸ *Tritonia gladioloides*

| J | F | M | A | M | J | J | A | S | O | N | D |

(=*Tritonia lineata*) **Pencilled Tritonia** Like *Tritonia disticha* but with pale yellow to pale apricot, darkly veined flowers appearing in spring.

❹ *Tritonia drakensbergensis*

| J | F | M | A | M | J | J | A | S | O | N | D |

Drakensberg Tritonia Perennial to 30 cm, with sword-shaped leaves with a prominent vein near the margin, and 2-lipped, pinkish-red flowers with a triangular yellow crest on each lower tepal, the tube 8–10 mm long. Montane grasslands and cliffs in the southern Drakensberg.

❺ *Tritonia securigera* Orange Tritonia

| J | F | M | A | M | J | J | A | S | O | N | D |

Perennial, 15–40 cm, with sword-shaped, sometimes crisped leaves, and 2-lipped, reddish to orange flowers with a large, yellow, tooth-like crest on each lower tepal, the tube 10–20 mm long. Clay slopes in the southern and Eastern Cape. *Tritonia laxifolia* flowers in late summer and autumn; *T. nelsonii* from the northern provinces has narrower leaves to 5 mm wide.

❻ *Tritonia pallida* Katjietee

| J | F | M | A | M | J | J | A | S | O | N | D |

Perennial, 20–40 cm, with sword-shaped leaves, and long-tubed, cream-coloured or pink to pale lilac flowers with a small, yellowish-green tooth on each lower tepal, the tube 30–70 mm long; the bracts fairly short. Sandstone and clay slopes, often in large communities, in the Little Karoo. *Tritonia flabellifolia* from the southwestern Cape has long, tapering bracts.

Romulea **ROMULEA, FROETANG** *(After Romulus, co-founder of Rome, where some species grow)*

Cormous perennials, *often stemless, the corm mostly asymmetrical, with woody coats. Leaves quill-like, with narrow longitudinal grooves.* Flowers *solitary at the tip of each branch*, with green bracts, often with transparent margins, *usually white or yellow in the centre, radially symmetrical and cup-shaped*, the tepals joined into a short tube; the stamens erect in the centre of the flower; the style *dividing into several short branches below the top of the anthers.* Southern Africa to southern Europe and Middle East: ±95 spp.; South Africa: 80 spp. Accurate species identification requires careful examination of the corm. The young fruits are juicy and were eaten by children, and the vernacular name *froetang* is a Malay corruption of the Portuguese *fruta*.

1 *Romulea tabularis*

J F M A M J J A S O N D

Perennial to 10 cm, branching above ground, with an oblique corm and 1 or 2 quill-like leaves from the base of the stem, and pale blue flowers with a wide yellow cup, often blotched on the reverse and sometimes fragrant, 15–20 mm in diameter. Damp or marshy coastal flats in Namaqualand and the southwestern Cape.

2 *Romulea hirsuta*

J F M A M J J A S O N D

Perennial to 10 cm, usually branching above ground, with a bell-shaped corm and 2 quill-like leaves from the base of the stem, and pink to rose or coppery-orange flowers with dark marks at the edge of a yellow cup, 15–30 mm in diameter. Damp flats and lower slopes in the southwestern Cape.

3 *Romulea cruciata*

J F M A M J J A S O N D

Stemless perennial, 5–12 cm, with a pointed corm and several quill-like leaves, and magenta to lilac flowers with dark blotches at the edges of a yellow cup, 15–20 mm in diameter. Stony slopes and flats in the southwestern Cape.

4 *Romulea rosea* **Knikkertjie**

J F M A M J J A S O N D

Stemless perennial, 10–40 cm, with a rounded corm and several quill-like leaves, and pink to purple flowers with a yellow cup and purple feathering on the reverse, 15–20 mm in diameter. Sandy and stony slopes and flats in the southwestern and southern Cape.

5 *Romulea sabulosa*

J F M A M J J A S O N D

Stemless perennial, 10–40 cm, with a rounded corm and several quill-like leaves, and red flowers with black markings in a greenish cup, 20–40 mm in diameter. Stony flats around Nieuwoudtville. *Romulea monadelpha* has thick black filaments.

Geissorhiza SATINFLOWER, SYBLOM

(Greek geisson, tile; rhiza, root, alluding to the overlapping corm tunics) Cormous perennials with *woody corm coats*. Leaves mostly narrow, with a raised midrib, sometimes ribbed or quill-like. Flowers few to many in a spike, spirally arranged, with *green, soft-textured bracts*, blue, usually *salver-shaped*, the tepals joined in a short to long tube; the stamens either erect or flexed downward, sometimes one shorter than the remaining two; the style divided into 3 short branches. Winter-rainfall parts of South Africa: 85 spp.

▶ **LEAVES FLAT OR WITH SLIGHTLY THICKENED MARGINS**

1 *Geissorhiza aspera*

| J | F | M | A | M | J | J | A | S | O | N | D |

Sysie, Blue Sequins Perennial with a finely velvety stem, 10–35 cm, with sword-shaped leaves, and blue to violet flowers, 10–15 mm in diameter, with a very short tube, 1–2 mm long, and 1 stamen slightly shorter than the others; the bracts dry and brown in the upper half. Mostly sandy soils in the southwestern Cape.

2 *Geissorhiza monanthos* **Bloukelkie**

| J | F | M | A | M | J | J | A | S | O | N | D |

Perennial with velvety stems, 6–20 cm, with narrow, flat leaves, and glossy dark blue flowers paler in the centre with a dark ring, 15–20 mm in diameter, with a short tube, 2 mm long; stamens downward-arching. Sandy slopes and granite outcrops along the West Coast. *Geissorhiza splendidissima* from Nieuwoudtville has ribbed, quill-like leaves.

3 *Geissorhiza ovata*

| J | F | M | A | M | J | J | A | S | O | N | D |

Perennial, 6–15 cm, with oval, leathery leaves spread on the ground, and white flowers, flushed pink or reddish on the outside, 15–20 mm in diameter, with a well-developed tube, mostly 10–20 mm long. Sandstone slopes and flats in the southwestern Cape, flowering mainly after fire.

▶ **LEAVES QUILL-LIKE AND RIBBED OR WITH THICKENED OR WINGED MARGINS**

4 *Geissorhiza radians* **Wynkelkie**

| J | F | M | A | M | J | J | A | S | O | N | D |

Perennial, 8–16 cm, with narrow, ridged leaves, the uppermost leaf with a swollen, ribbed sheath, and ± cupped, deep blue flowers with a red centre outlined with a white ring, 15–20 mm in diameter, with a tube 6–8 mm long; stamens downward-arching and bent up at the ends. Damp sandy soils along the West Coast.

5 *Geissorhiza exscapa*

| J | F | M | A | M | J | J | A | S | O | N | D |

Perennial, 18–30 cm, with narrow or quill-like, sticky leaves, H-shaped in cross section, and large, creamy-white flowers with darker veins, flushed reddish on the outside, 40–50 mm in diameter, with a very long tube, 40–80 mm long, and protruding stamens; the bracts about half as long as the tube. Deep sandy soils along the Western Cape coast.

Hesperantha HESPERANTHA, AANDBLOM

(Greek hesperos, evening; anthos, flower, referring to the many night-flowering species) Cormous perennials with *woody corm coats*. Leaves mostly narrow or sword-shaped. Flowers few to many in a spike, spirally arranged, with green, soft-textured bracts, mostly pink or white, radially symmetrical, usually *salver-shaped*, the tepals joined in a short to long tube; the stamens either erect or flexed downward; the *style dividing at the top of the tube into 3 long, spreading, thread-like branches*. Sub-Saharan Africa: ±80 spp. Corms of some species were eaten.

① *Hesperantha bachmannii* **Ballerina** J F M A M J J A S O N D
Slender perennial, 15–30 cm, with narrow leaves, and nodding white flowers with a curved tube, 10 mm long, and tepals bent sharply backwards, 15 mm in diameter, opening in the afternoon and sweetly scented. Stony slopes in Namaqualand and the southwestern Cape and in the Eastern Cape.

② *Hesperantha falcata* **Bontrokkie** J F M A M J J A S O N D
Perennial, 6–30 cm, with bell-shaped corm and sword- or sickle-shaped leaves, and white or yellow flowers flushed red to brown on the reverse, 15–20 mm in diameter, with a straight tube, 4–9 mm long, opening in the afternoon and early evening. Stony flats and lower slopes in the southwestern and southern Cape. *Hesperantha cucullata* from Nieuwoudtville to Sutherland has an oblique, pointed corm.

③ *Hesperantha baurii* J F M A M J J A S O N D
Baur's Hesperantha Perennial, 15–50 cm, with 4 narrow leaves, the lower 2 basal, and bright pink flowers, 20–30 mm in diameter, with a straight tube 7–10 mm long, opening during the day. Moist, mainly montane grassland in eastern South Africa.

④ *Hesperantha scopulosa* J F M A M J J A S O N D
Drakensberg Cliff Hesperantha Drooping perennial, 10–25 cm, with 3 or 4 drooping leaves, and bright pink flowers, 20–30 mm in diameter, with a straight, narrow tube, 25–40 mm long, opening during the day. Wet cliffs in the high Drakensberg.

⑤ *Hesperantha coccinea* J F M A M J J A S O N D
(=*Schizostylis coccinea*) **Scarlet River Lily** Clump-forming perennial to 60 cm, with sickle-shaped leaves, and scarlet or pink flowers, 30–40 mm in diameter, with a straight tube, 30–40 mm long. Montane river banks through eastern South and subtropical Africa.

▶▶ STYLE 3-BRANCHED; FLOWERS MOSTLY 2-LIPPED; CORMS ROUNDED, THE TUNICS MOSTLY FIBROUS; BRACTS GREEN, SOMETIMES WITH MEMBRANOUS MARGINS

Babiana **BABIANA, BOBBEJAANTJIE**
(From the Dutch name for baboons, which are partial to the corms) Cormous perennials, often with *hairy stems and leaves*. Leaves sword- or wedge-shaped, *pleated and usually hairy*. Flowers in a 2-ranked or spiral spike, with *green, usually hairy bracts with dry tips*, usually 2-lipped, rarely bowl-shaped, the tepals united into a short or long tube; the style dividing into 3 short branches. Southern Africa: 86 spp. The corms are favoured by baboons and porcupines, hence the vernacular name *bobbejaantjie*.

▶ INNER BRACTS SPLIT TO THE BASE, AND THUS APPARENTLY PAIRED; OVARY HAIRY OR HAIRLESS

⑥ *Babiana stricta* J F M A M J J A S O N D
Slender, erect perennial, 10–20 cm, with narrow, stiff, shortly hairy leaves, and almost salver-shaped, mauve to violet or white to pale yellow flowers, often with darker markings and dark blue or black, arrow-shaped anthers, with a tube 8–18 mm long; the ovary hairy, and the inner bracts paired. Moist stony flats in the southwestern Cape.

133

① *Babiana angustifolia*

| J | F | M | A | M | J | J | A | S | O | N | D |

Perennial, 10–20 cm, with stiff, shortly hairy leaves, and cup-shaped, weakly 2-lipped, dark blue to violet flowers with red or black markings and dark anthers, with a tube 11–17 mm long; the ovary hairy, and the inner bracts paired. Damp flats and lower slopes in the southwestern Cape.

② *Babiana ambigua*

| J | F | M | A | M | J | J | A | S | O | N | D |

Dwarf perennial, 5–8 cm, with narrow, softly hairy leaves often longer than the stem, and fragrant, 2-lipped, blue to mauve flowers with white to cream-coloured markings, with a short tube, 10–19 mm long; the ovary hairless, and the inner bracts paired. Sandy or gravelly flats and lower slopes in the southwestern Cape.

③ *Babiana scabrifolia*

| J | F | M | A | M | J | J | A | S | O | N | D |

Short perennial, 5–9 cm, with soft-textured, lance-shaped, shortly hairy leaves longer than the stem and twisted or coiled when young, and sweet-scented, 2-lipped, blue to lilac flowers with yellow and purple markings, with a tube 12–18 mm long; the ovary thinly hairy, and the inner bracts paired. Sandy soils in dry fynbos in the Olifants River valley.

④ *Babiana mucronata*

| J | F | M | A | M | J | J | A | S | O | N | D |

Perennial, 5–15 cm, with lance-shaped, shortly hairy leaves, and acrid-scented, 2-lipped, pale blue flowers with yellow markings, with a tube mostly 12–20 mm long; the ovary densely hairy, and the inner bracts paired. Rocky slopes, mainly in the Olifants River valley.

▶ **INNER BRACTS FORKED BUT EVIDENTLY SINGLE; OVARY ALWAYS HAIRLESS**

⑤ *Babiana nana*

| J | F | M | A | M | J | J | A | S | O | N | D |

Dwarf perennial, 3–10 cm, with soft-textured, softly hairy, often short and broad leaves, and large, fragrant, 2-lipped, blue or violet flowers with white markings, with a tube 12–17 mm long. Sandy coastal flats and dunes in the southwestern Cape.

⑥ *Babiana bainesii*

| J | F | M | A | M | J | J | A | S | O | N | D |

Stemless perennial to 25 cm, with pleated, narrow, smooth or hairy leaves, and fragrant, long-tubed, purple flowers with white and red markings, with a slender tube, 40–70 mm long. Dry grassland and savanna through central and northeastern South and tropical Africa.

⑦ *Babiana curviscapa*

| J | F | M | A | M | J | J | A | S | O | N | D |

Dwarf perennial with short, horizontal stems to 10 cm, stiffly pleated, velvety leaves, and long-tubed, purple or magenta flowers with white markings, with a slender tube, 35–45 mm long, sharply bent near the top. Sandy and gravelly flats in open scrub in Namaqualand. *Babiana attenuata* has larger flowers with a proportionately shorter tube; *B. dregei* has hard, needle-like leaves.

⑧ *Babiana hirsuta*

| J | F | M | A | M | J | J | A | S | O | N | D |

(=*Babiana thunbergii*) **Rooibobbejaantjie, Strandlelie** Robust perennial, 40–70 cm, with short, horizontal branches, stiff, minutely hairy leaves, and strongly 2-lipped, red flowers with a curved tube, 30–40 mm long. Sandy coastal flats and dunes in Namaqualand and on the West Coast.

① *Babiana ringens* Rotstert

J F M A M J J **A S** O N D

Perennial, 15–40 cm, with the main stem sterile and forming a perch, bearing flowers on a short side branch at ground level, with narrow, very stiff, hairless or minutely hairy leaves, and strongly 2-lipped, red flowers, with a curved tube, 30–45 mm long. Sandy flats, often coastal, in the southwestern Cape.

Crocosmia CROCOSMIA, MONTBRETIA

(Greek krokos, crocus; osme, scent, alluding to the saffron-like smell of the infused flowers) Robust cormous perennials. Leaves in a basal fan, sword-shaped with a raised midrib, or lance-shaped and pleated. Flowers in a 2-ranked spike, with *small, leathery, green bracts with dry tips, orange*, usually 2-lipped, the tepals joined into a long, funnel-shaped or gradually flared tube; the style dividing into 3 short branches. Seeds *spherical, ± smooth*, black or reddish-brown. Sub-Saharan Africa: 8 spp.

② *Crocosmia aurea* Falling Stars

J **F M A** M J J A S O N D

Perennial, 40–70 cm, with sword-shaped leaves, 10–30 mm wide, and nodding, salver-shaped flowers, 25–50 mm in diameter, with a curved tube, 10–20 mm long. Forest margins and floors through eastern South and tropical Africa. *Crocosmia pottsii* has small, funnel-shaped flowers.

③ *Crocosmia paniculata*

J **F** M A M J J A S O N **D**

Zig-zag Crocosmia, Aunt Eliza Robust, clump-forming perennial, 1–1.5 m, with lance-shaped, pleated leaves, and a branched, zigzag stem of orange, trumpet-shaped flowers with a cylindrical tube, 30–40 mm long. Marshy grassland, stream margins and rocky outcrops in eastern South and tropical Africa. *Crocosmia mathewsii* from Graskop has small, funnel-shaped flowers; *C. pearsei* from the high Drakensberg is smaller and solitary with unbranched stems.

Chasmanthe COBRA LILY, PIEMPIEMPIE

(Greek chasme, gaping; anthos, flower, alluding to the 2-lipped flowers) Robust cormous perennials. Leaves in a basal fan, sword-shaped with a raised midrib, *soft-textured*. Flowers in a 1- or 2-ranked spike, with *small, leathery green bracts with dry tips, orange*, very *dissimilarly 2-lipped*, the tepals joined into a *long tube that is very narrow and usually twisted below and cylindrical above*; the stamens arched together beneath the *spoon-shaped dorsal tepal*; the style dividing into 3 short branches. Seeds *spherical, ± smooth*, orange or reddish-brown. Southern South Africa: 3 spp. The vernacular name is possibly an onomatopoeic rendition of the squeaking sound produced by rubbing the stems together.

④ *Chasmanthe aethiopica*

J F M **A M J J** A S O N D

Perennial, 40–65 cm, with soft-textured leaves, and orange flowers in a 1-ranked spike, the tube flaring abruptly and almost pouched above the twisted lower portion; the fruits large and reddish-purple within, containing pea-sized, thinly fleshy, orange seeds. Mainly coastal in bush and forest margins in the southwestern and Eastern Cape, spreading by runners and often forming large colonies.

⑤ *Chasmanthe floribunda*

J F M A M J **J A S** O N D

Robust perennial, 45–100 cm, with soft-textured leaves, and orange (rarely watery-yellow) flowers in a 2-ranked, often branched spike, the tube flaring gradually above the almost straight lower portion; the fruits small and brown, containing small, hard, reddish-brown seeds. Rocky slopes in scrub in the southwestern Cape.

Tritoniopsis TRITONIOPSIS, RIETPYPIE *(Resembling the genus* Tritonia*)*

Evergreen or deciduous, cormous perennials. Leaves green or dry at flowering, sword-shaped with *2 or more, equally strong, main veins*. Flowers in a spirally twisted spike, with *dry, firm-textured or leathery bracts with the inner longer than the outer*, 2-lipped, the tepals joined into a short to long tube; the stamens usually arched together under the upper tepal, *curving back when old*; the style dividing into 3 short branches. Winter-rainfall South Africa: 24 spp.

1 *Tritoniopsis antholyza* **Karkaarblom** | J | F | M | A | M | J | J | A | S | O | N | D |

Robust perennial to 90 cm, with 3–6-veined, sword-shaped leaves, and trumpet-shaped yellowish-pink to red flowers with a tube 25–30 mm long. Rocky slopes in the southwestern and southern Cape.

2 *Tritoniopsis burchellii* | J | F | M | A | M | J | J | A | S | O | N | D |

Rooibergpypie Stiffly erect perennial, 50–90 cm, with 3-veined, lance-shaped basal leaves, narrowed below into a petiole, and long, awn-like stem leaves, with trumpet-shaped scarlet flowers with a tube 30–40 mm long. Rocky sandstone slopes in the southwestern Cape. *Tritoniopsis triticea* has smaller flowers with a tube 25–30 mm long.

Gladiolus GLADIOLUS, PYPIE *(From the Latin for a small sword, alluding to the leaves)*

Cormous perennials. Leaves sword- or strap-shaped, or quill-like and longitudinally grooved, sometimes hairy. Flowers few to many in a 1- (rarely 2-) ranked spike, with *green, soft-textured bracts, mostly 2-lipped*, the tepals joined into a short to long tube; the style dividing into 3 *short branches widened at the tips; the seeds flattened, with a broad, membranous wing*. Africa and Madagascar into Eurasia: ±260 spp.; South Africa: 170 spp. Some hybrids are widely grown as cut-flowers.

▸ **LEAVES REDUCED, BRACT-LIKE AND CLASPING THE STEM**

3 *Gladiolus brevifolius* **Herfspypie** | J | F | M | A | M | J | J | A | S | O | N | D |

Slender perennial, 15–50 cm, with reduced, bract-like leaves sheathing the stem, the true foliage leaves narrowly sword-shaped and hairy, dry at flowering, and mostly unscented, pink to grey flowers with yellow and red markings, with a tube 11–13 mm long. Stony slopes and flats in the southwestern Cape. *Gladiolus monticola* from the Cape Peninsula has a longer cylindrical floral tube, 22–30 mm long.

4 *Gladiolus carmineus* **Cliff Gladiolus** | J | F | M | A | M | J | J | A | S | O | N | D |

Perennial to 35 cm, with reduced leaves sheathing the stem, rarely with a short, sword-shaped blade, and funnel-shaped, deep pink flowers with white streaks, with a tube 30–35 mm long. Coastal cliffs and rocks around Hermanus.

▸ **LEAVES X- OR H-SHAPED IN CROSS SECTION, OR RIBBED, OR QUILL-LIKE WITH RAISED MARGINS**

5 *Gladiolus inflatus* | J | F | M | A | M | J | J | A | S | O | N | D |

Tulbagh Bell, Blouklokkie Slender perennial, 25–60 cm, the lowermost leaf quill-like with 4 longitudinal grooves, and nodding, unscented, bell- or funnel-shaped, mauve or pink flowers with red markings, with a curved tube, 12–25 mm long. Rocky sandstone slopes in the southwestern Cape. *Gladiolus patersoniae* from the Little Karoo has a shorter floral tube.

139

❶ *Gladiolus gracilis* Bloupypie

J F M A M **J J** A S O N D

Slender perennial, 30–60 cm, with stiff, narrow leaves, 1.5–2.5 mm wide, H-shaped in cross section, and fragrant, blue to grey, pink or yellow flowers with dark streaks, on a flexed stem, with a tube 12–18 mm long. Stony flats and lower slopes in the southwestern Cape. *Gladiolus caeruleus* from Saldanha Bay has wider leaves and spotted flowers.

❷ *Gladiolus liliaceus*

J F M A M J J **A S O N** D

Large Brown Afrikaner, Ribbokblom Perennial, 35–70 cm, with the lowermost leaf long and narrow, 2–5 mm wide, with thickened margins and midrib, and long-tubed, funnel-shaped, brown to russet or beige flowers, turning mauve in the evening and becoming strongly fragrant of cloves, with a tube 40–55 mm long, enclosed within long, tapering bracts. Stony flats and lower slopes in the southwestern and southern Cape.

❸ *Gladiolus tristis*

J F M A M J J **A S O** N D

Marsh Afrikaner, Trompetters Stiffly erect perennial, 40–150 cm, the lowermost leaf long and slender and X-shaped in cross section, 2–4 mm in diameter, with large, trumpet-shaped, cream-coloured flowers, often with brown shading, with a tube 40–65 mm long, and a spicy fragrance at night. Seasonally moist or marshy places in the southwestern and southern Cape.

❹ *Gladiolus watsonius* Rooi Afrikaner

J F M A M J J **A S** O N D

Stiffly erect perennial, 30–50 cm, with the lowermost leaf narrow and H-shaped in cross section, 3–6 mm wide, and red to orange, trumpet-shaped flowers with a cylindrical tube, 45–55 mm long, narrowed in the lower part. Stony flats and lower slopes in the southwestern Cape. *Gladiolus teretifolius* from the southern Cape is a more delicate plant with narrower leaves, 1–2 mm wide.

❺ *Gladiolus alatus* Kalkoentjie

J F M A M J J **A S** O N D

Compact perennial, 8–25 cm, with longitudinally ribbed, sickle-shaped leaves, 2–9 mm wide, and a ridged or winged stem of strongly 2-lipped, orange flowers with the upper tepal held upright and the lower 3 tepals greenish-yellow towards the base, with a short tube, 10–14 mm long. Sandy flats and slopes in the southwestern Cape. One of 3 similar fynbos species, distinguished in part by whether the leaves are flat or ribbed and the dorsal tepal erect or arching.

❻ *Gladiolus equitans*

J F M A M J J **A S** O N D

Namaqua Kalkoentjie Compact perennial, 15–30 cm, with leathery, sickle-shaped leaves, 20–40 mm wide, with thickened, reddish margins, and a ridged or winged stem of strongly 2-lipped, orange flowers with the upper tepal arching and the lower 3 tepals greenish-yellow towards the base, with a short tube, 10–15 mm long. Stony hills in Namaqualand.

❼ *Gladiolus watermeyeri*

J F M A M J **J A S** O N D

Soetkalkoentjie Perennial, 10–30 cm, with narrow, ribbed leaves, 3–11 mm wide, and highly fragrant, strongly 2-lipped, pearly-grey flowers with chocolate brown feathering and yellowish-green lower tepals, with the upper tepal arched, and a tube 14–16 mm long. Sandstone rock sheets around Nieuwoudtville. *Gladiolus virescens* from the southwestern and southern Cape has narrower leaves, 1–3 mm wide, and an erect upper tepal.

▶ LEAVES STRAP- OR SWORD-SHAPED

1 *Gladiolus cunonius* **Lepelblom** J F M A M J J A **S O** N D
Perennial, 20–45 cm, with a fan of soft-textured, narrowly sword-shaped leaves, 5–12 mm wide, and strongly asymmetrical, bright red, tubular flowers with a long, spoon-shaped upper tepal and minute, greenish lower tepals, with a cylindrical tube, 12–15 mm long, narrowed below. Coastal sands in the southwestern and southern Cape.

2 *Gladiolus saccatus* **Suikerkannetjie** J F M A M J **J A** S O N D
Stiffly branched perennial, 20–100 cm, with a fan of greyish, narrowly sword-shaped leaves, 3–15 mm wide, and strongly asymmetrical, bright red, tubular flowers with a long, spoon-shaped upper tepal and minute, greenish lower tepals, with a cylindrical tube, 12–20 mm long, with a sac near the top. Seasonally moist, stony slopes and flats through western South Africa and Namibia.

3 *Gladiolus debilis* **Little Painted Lady** J F M A M J J A **S O** N D
Slender perennial, 35–50 cm, with narrow leaves thickened on the margins and midrib, 1–2 mm wide, and long-tubed white flowers with red markings, with a cylindrical tube, 15–22 mm long, and short, ribbed bracts. Rocky sandstone slopes in the southwestern Cape.

4 *Gladiolus venustus* **Perskalkoentjie** J F M A M J J **A** S **O** N D
Perennial, 20–60 cm, with grass-like leaves, 2–5 mm wide, and fragrant, 2-lipped, pink to purple flowers with greenish tips, the lower tepals strongly pinched at the base and sharply flexed downwards, with a tube 12–17 mm long. Sandstone and clay slopes in the southwestern Cape. *Gladiolus scullyi* from Namaqualand has gently arched lower tepals.

5 *Gladiolus caryophyllaceus* J F M A M J J **A** S O N D
Sandpypie Robust perennial, 18–75 cm, with hairy, sword-shaped leaves with thickened, often reddish margins, 10–25 mm wide, and large, fragrant, funnel-shaped, pink to mauve flowers streaked and speckled with red, with a tube 30–40 mm long. Sandy flats and slopes in the southwestern Cape.

6 *Gladiolus carinatus* **Blou Afrikaner** J F M A M J J **A** S O N D
Perennial, 30–60 cm, the base of the stem mottled purple and white, with narrow leaves, 3–9 mm wide, and fragrant, 2-lipped, blue or yellow (occasionally pink) flowers marked with yellow and blue, with a short tube, 6–10 mm long. Deep sands and lower slopes in southwestern South Africa.

7 *Gladiolus carneus* J F M A M J J A S **O** N D
White Afrikaner, Painted Lady Perennial, 25–60 cm, with narrowly sword-shaped leaves, 6–20 mm wide, and funnel-shaped, pink or white flowers, often with dark pink markings, with a tube 20–40 mm long. Rocky slopes, often in damp sites in the southwestern Cape.

1 *Gladiolus undulatus* Vleipypie

J F M A M J J A S O **N D**

Robust perennial, 30–150 cm, with sword-shaped leaves, 5–12 mm wide, and long-tubed, greenish-white to cream-coloured flowers with long, tapering, often crinkly tepals, with a slender tube, 50–75 mm long. Marshes and stream sides in the southwestern Cape. *Gladiolus angustus* from the West Coast has relatively blunt tepals with the lower 3 tepals much smaller than the upper ones.

2 *Gladiolus floribundus*

J F M A M J J A **S O N** D

Stout perennial, 15–45 cm, with a fan of leathery, sword-shaped leaves, 12–20 mm wide, and long-tubed white to pink flowers with a dark central streak on each tepal, the lower ones much smaller, with a slender tube, 40–70 mm long. Dry stony flats and slopes in the southern and Eastern Cape.

3 *Gladiolus cardinalis* New Year Lily

J F M A M J J A S O **N D**

Perennial, 60–120 cm, with a fan of narrowly sword-shaped leaves, 11–20 mm wide, and an inclined or drooping stem of large, red, funnel-shaped flowers with white splashes, with a tube 30–40 mm long. Waterfalls and wet cliffs in the southwestern Cape.

4 *Gladiolus saundersii*

J **F M** A M J J A S O N D

Lesotho Cornflag Robust perennial, 30–60 cm, with a fan of stiff, sword-shaped leaves, 15–25 mm wide, and large, nodding, flared, scarlet flowers mottled with white, with a curved tube, 33–37 mm long. Alpine hillsides and fields in the Drakensberg and Maluti Mountains.

5 *Gladiolus dalenii*

J F **M A M** J J **A S O N** D

Parrot Gladiolus, Natal Lily Robust perennial to 1.5 m, with a fan of sword-shaped leaves, 10–50 mm wide, and hooded orange, red or greenish, speckled flowers, with a tube 30–50 mm long, and large bracts 40–70 mm long. Grassland and woodland through eastern South and tropical Africa. *Gladiolus aurantiacus* has short leaves scattered up the stem.

6 *Gladiolus ecklonii*

J **F** M **A M** J J A S O **N D**

Common Speckled Gladiolus Perennial, 15–50 cm, with a fan of sword-shaped leaves, 15–50 mm wide, and an inclined stem of hooded flowers, densely speckled with pink or brown, with a tube 15–20 mm long, and large, keeled bracts 40–50 mm long. Grasslands through eastern South Africa.

7 *Gladiolus crassifolius*

J **F M** A M J J A S O N D

Small Wild Gladiolus Perennial 30–100 cm, with a fan of long, slender leaves, 5–12 mm wide, and an inclined spike of many, funnel-shaped, pinkish to mauve flowers with dark markings, with a tube 9–15 mm long. Stony grassland through eastern South and tropical Africa. *Gladiolus densiflorus* has leaves with fine, closely placed veins.

145

1 *Gladiolus mortonius*

| J | F | M | A | M | J | J | A | S | O | N | D |

Small Salmon Gladiolus Perennial, 40–70 cm, with a fan of sword-shaped leaves, 15–25 mm wide, and a flexed spike of pink to salmon, funnel-shaped flowers streaked with red, with a tube 30–45 mm long. Stony grassland in the Eastern Cape.

2 *Gladiolus oppositiflorus*

| J | F | M | A | M | J | J | A | S | O | N | D |

Large Salmon Gladiolus Robust perennial, 50–150 cm, with a fan of sword-shaped, smooth or velvety leaves, 12–20 mm wide, and a 2-ranked spike of pink to salmon, funnel-shaped flowers streaked with red, with a slender tube, 30–55 mm long, and tubular inner bracts. Seasonally moist, stony, grassy slopes in southeastern South Africa.

3 *Gladiolus papilio* **Butterfly Gladiolus**

| J | F | M | A | M | J | J | A | S | O | N | D |

Slender perennial, 40–100 cm, with a fan of thin-textured, sword-shaped leaves, 10–15 mm wide, and an inclined spike of nodding, bell-shaped, greenish or mauve flowers with large, dark blotches on the lower tepals, with a tube 20 mm long. Damp grassland, marshes and seeps through eastern South Africa.

ORCHIDACEAE   Orchid family

▶ **SUBFAMILY EPIDENDROIDEAE** EPIPHYTIC OR TERRESTRIAL PLANTS; POLLEN AGGREGATED INTO 2 HARD WAXY BODIES BENEATH A DECIDUOUS ANTHER CAP AT THE TIP OF A CYLINDRICAL COLUMN

▶▶ EPIPHYTIC PLANTS; LEAVES TOUGH AND LEATHERY WITH NOTCHED TIPS

Polystachya   **SNOUT ORCHID**   *(Greek polys, many; stachys, spike)*

Rhizomatous, *epiphytic perennials with the base of the stems swollen to form pseudobulbs.* Leaves 1–6, leathery, often notched. Flowers in a terminal spike, white, yellow, orange or pink, *with the lip uppermost*; the lip is 3-lobed and hinged at the base, without a spur. Pan-tropical, mostly Africa: ±200 spp.; South Africa: 11 spp. Used traditionally as a protective and love charm.

4 *Polystachya pubescens*

| J | F | M | A | M | J | J | A | S | O | N | D |

Epiphyte or lithophyte to 20 cm, with clusters of egg-shaped pseudobulbs, 20–60 mm long, with 1–3 oblong leaves, and loose spikes of open, deep yellow flowers with reddish stripes, 15–20 mm in diameter. Forests or forest margins, often coastal, from the Eastern Cape to Zimbabwe.

Mystacidium   **TREE ORCHID**   *(Greek mystax, moustache, for the fringed lip of the side lobes)*

Epiphytic perennials. Leaves 2-ranked, channelled and notched. Flowers in spreading or drooping, lateral spikes produced from below the leaves, white, with sharply pointed lip bearing a slender spur tapering from a wide mouth. Africa, mainly southern Africa: 9 spp.; South Africa: 7 spp.

5 *Mystacidium venosum*

| J | F | M | A | M | J | J | A | S | O | N | D |

Epiphyte with a fan of oblong, channelled leaves, 15–45 mm long, notched at the tip, and hanging spikes of white flowers, 20–30 mm in diameter; the spur slender, 20–45 mm long. Coastal forest and savanna in eastern South Africa. *Mystacidium capense* flowers in spring and summer and has larger leaves and a spur 35–60 mm long.

147

Eulophia HARLEQUIN ORCHID *(Greek eu, truly; lophos, crested, referring to the lip crests)*

Rhizomatous perennials with underground corms or aerial pseudobulbs. Leaves absent or present at flowering, on a separate shoot. Flowers in spikes *borne to the base of the leafing shoots*, variously coloured and marked, with the *lip bearing crests or warts* and usually a short spur at the base. Pan-tropical and subtropical: ±250 spp.; South Africa: 42 spp. Some species used traditionally as love charms.

▸ LIP CRESTS OF LOW FLESHY RIDGES TAPERING GRADUALLY TO THE LIP APEX

① *Eulophia streptopetala*

| J | F | M | A | M | J | J | A | S | O | N | D |

Robust perennial to 2 m, with partly exposed pseudobulbs and pleated, lance-shaped leaves, and a loose spike of flowers, 25–35 mm in diameter, the sepals green mottled with brown, and the petals and lip yellow; the lip crests forming low, fleshy ridges, and the spur 1.5–2.0 mm long. Bush and savanna through eastern South and tropical Africa.

② *Eulophia speciosa*

| J | F | M | A | M | J | J | A | S | O | N | D |

Robust perennial to 80 cm, with subterranean or partly exposed corms/pseudobulbs and channelled, leathery or succulent leaves, and a loose spike of yellow flowers, 20–30 mm in diameter; the lip crests forming broad fleshy ridges, and the spur conical, 1–3 mm long. Mostly coastal bushveld through southern and eastern South and tropical Africa.

▸ LIP CRESTS OF WARTS OR RIDGES ENDING ABRUPTLY ON THE OUTER THIRD OF THE LIP

③ *Eulophia angolensis* Vlei Orchid

| J | F | M | A | M | J | J | A | S | O | N | D |

Robust perennial to 1 m, with stiffly pleated leaves, and a spike of yellow and brownish flowers, 20–30 mm long; the lip crests forming narrow ridges, and the spur very small or absent. Marshy grassland and savanna through eastern South and tropical Africa.

④ *Eulophia parvilabris*

| J | F | M | A | M | J | J | A | S | O | N | D |

Robust perennial to 80 cm, with channelled leaves and a dense spike of creamy-yellow flowers with a dark red eye, 40–50 mm in diameter; the lip uppermost, with crests forming ridges on the lower third, and the spur cylindrical, 5–6 mm long. Moist and marshy grassland in eastern South Africa.

⑤ *Eulophia welwitschii*

| J | F | M | A | M | J | J | A | S | O | N | D |

Robust perennial to 80 cm, with pleated leaves partly to fully developed at flowering, and a dense head of bright yellow, funnel-shaped flowers with dark red side lobes on the lip, 20–40 mm long; the lip crests forming slender warts in the middle of the lip, and the spur slender, 4–7 mm long. Dry or moist grassland through eastern South and tropical Africa.

⑥ *Eulophia ensata*

| J | F | M | A | M | J | J | A | S | O | N | D |

Robust perennial to 80 cm, with pleated leaves partly to fully developed at flowering, and a dense head of yellow, funnel-shaped flowers, 15–25 mm long; the lip crests forming slender warts to the end of the lip; the spur slender, 3–7 mm long. Open grassland and savanna in eastern South Africa.

❶ *Eulophia clavicornis* J F M A M J J **A S O N** D

Slender perennial to 70 cm, with narrow, channelled leaves that are often not fully developed at flowering, and a loose spike of white, purplish or yellow and brown flowers, 8–18 mm long; the lip crests forming narrow, toothed ridges, and the spur slender, 2–9 mm long. Grassland through eastern South Africa.

❷ *Eulophia ovalis* J F **M A M J J** J A S **O N** D

Perennial to 65 cm, with narrow, channelled leaves, and a loose spike of purple and white flowers, 14–36 mm long; the lip crests forming ridges and slender warts, and the spur 1–5.5 mm long. Open grassland through eastern South and tropical Africa.

❸ *Eulophia zeyheriana* J F M A M J J J A S O N D

Slender perennial to 70 cm, with narrow, channelled leaves, and a loose spike of purplish and blue flowers, 7–10 mm long; the lip crests forming fleshy ridges, and the spur cylindrical, 2–3 mm long. Montane grassland, mainly in KwaZulu-Natal.

▶ **SUBFAMILY ORCHIDOIDEAE** TERRESTRIAL PLANTS; POLLEN AGGREGATED INTO 2 CRUMBLY, GRANULAR BODIES WITHIN PERSISTENT ANTHER SACS
▶▶ **LIP SPURRED**

Bonatea **WOOD ORCHID** (Named for Giuseppe Bonata, 1753–1836, professor of botany at Padua)

Tuberous perennials. Leaves often crowded toward the base of the stem, sometimes withered at flowering. Flowers green and white, with the upper 3 tepals cohering to form a hood; the *petals are deeply forked* and the *lip is deeply 3-lobed with a slender spur at the base; the stigmas are 2 slender stalks joined to the lip*, with a hood-like rostellum lobe above. Africa and Arabia: 14 spp.; South Africa: 10 spp.

❹ *Bonatea speciosa* J F **M A M** J J **J A S O N** D

Green Wood Orchid, Oktoberlelie Robust herb to 1 m, with oblong leaves and green and white, spider-like flowers, highly fragrant at night; the lip spur 20–57 mm long. Coastal scrub and forest margins along the southern and eastern seaboard of South Africa.

Habenaria **GHOST ORCHID** (Latin habena, strap; aria, possessing, referring to the slender lip spur)

Perennials. Leaves scattered along the stem or basal. Flowers green or yellowish or partially white; the petals are unlobed or *deeply forked and the lip is usually deeply 3-lobed with a slender spur at the base; the stigmas are 2 slender stalks* not joined to the lip, with a flat rostellum lobe above. Worldwide, mainly tropical and subtropical: ±800 spp.; South Africa: 35 spp.

▶ **PETALS UNLOBED**

❺ *Habenaria epipactidea* J F **M A M J J A S O N** D

Stout herb to 50 cm, with a densely leafy stem and a spike of spreading, pale green and white flowers, fragrant at night; the petals broad and unlobed, and the lip with a pair of small whiskers at the base and a club-shaped spur, 20–60 mm long. Grassland and moist savanna through eastern and subtropical South Africa.

151

① *Habenaria falcicornis*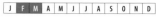

Stout herb, 20–80 cm, with a leafy stem and a cylindrical spike of spider-like, green and white flowers, fragrant at night; the petals divided, with the narrow upper lobe minutely hairy and the lower lobe ovate or lance-shaped; the lip spur slender, 23–43 mm long, and the stigma arms 2–4 mm long. Grassland through eastern South and tropical Africa.

② *Habenaria clavata*

Stout herb, 20–80 cm, with a leafy stem and an open spike of large, spider-like, green and white flowers, fragrant at night; the petals divided, with the long lower lobe curved and horn-like; the lip spur club-shaped, 30–50 mm long, and the stigma arms 8–12 mm long. Grassland through eastern South and tropical Africa. *Habenaria cornuta* has short stigma arms, 3–8 mm long.

③ *Habenaria lithophila*

Slender herb, 10–30 cm, with a pair of round leaves pressed to the ground and a dense spike of small green flowers, fragrant at night; the petals divided into 2 equally long, narrow lobes; the lip spur club-shaped, 8–11 mm long. Moist grassland in eastern South Africa. *Habenaria dregeana* has a tapering spur that widens at the mouth.

Bartholina **SPIDER ORCHID** (Named for Danish botanist, Thomas Bartholin, 1616–1680)

Small, tuberous perennials with a hairy stem. Leaf *solitary, hairy, pressed against the ground*. Flower *large, solitary, white to mauve*, with a *deeply fringed lip bearing a slender spur at the base*. Winter-rainfall southern Africa: 2 spp., both South Africa.

④ *Bartholina burmanniana* J F M A M J J A S O N D

Slender herb to 20 cm, with a hairy stem and a solitary, rounded, hairy leaf pressed to the ground, with a solitary white and pale mauve flower with the lip deeply divided into narrow, pointed segments. Clay slopes and flats in southwestern and southern South Africa, flowering mostly after fire.

Satyrium **SATYR ORCHID, TREWWA**
(From the mythological satyr, half-man, half-goat, alluding to the pair of horn-like spurs on the lip) Tuberous perennials.

Leaves scattered along the stem and sheathing it or crowded toward the base, the lowermost sometimes pressed to the ground. Flowers in a dense, sometimes head-like raceme, *often with leafy, downflexed bracts*, mostly white to greenish or pink; the *ovary not twisted*, the *lip uppermost and hooded, with 2 long or short spurs, the remaining tepals smaller and ± similar, the column long and slender*. Africa and Madagascar, extending into Asia, mainly southern Africa: ±88 spp.; South Africa: 40 spp.

▸ FLOWERS GREENISH; LIP ENTRANCE VERY SMALL

⑤ *Satyrium parviflorum* Devil Orchid J F M A M J J A S O N D

Slender to stout herb to 1 m, with basal leaves in a separate tuft or absent, and a long spike of green or brownish flowers, 5 mm in diameter, scented at night; the lip globular with a narrow entrance and slender spurs, 5–15 mm long, about as long as the ovary. Rank grassland and forest margins throughout eastern South Africa.

① *Satyrium odorum* Ruik-trewwa `J F M A M J J A S O N D`

Stout herb to 55 cm, with 2–6 oval, fleshy leaves and a moderately dense spike of yellowish-green flowers, sometimes with a purple tinge, 10 mm in diameter, with a strong scent at night; the lip sac-like with a narrow entrance and slender spurs, 13–18 mm long, longer than the ovary. Rocky slopes in scrub in the southwestern and southern Cape.

▶ FLOWERS COLOURFUL; LIP SPURS SHORTER THAN THE OVARY

② *Satyrium coriifolium* Rooitrewwa `J F M A M J J A S O N D`

Stout perennial to 80 cm, with 2–4 elliptical leaves clustered at the base of the stem, purple-spotted towards the bottom, and a dense spike of bright yellow to orange flowers; the lip taller than wide, with a crest, and slender spurs, 9–12 mm long, shorter than the ovary. Moist clay and sand in the southwestern and southern Cape.

③ *Satyrium erectum* Pienk-trewwa `J F M A M J J A S O N D`

Herb to 60 cm, with 2 fleshy, oval or elliptical leaves pressed to the ground, and a dense spike of fragrant, pale to deep pink flowers with darker tinges and spots; the spurs slender and 5–11 mm long, shorter than the ovary. Dry sandstone and clay flats in the southwestern and southern Cape.

④ *Satyrium cristatum* `J F M A M J J A S O N D`

Slender herb, 20–50 cm, with 2 or 3 leaves spreading near the ground, and a spike of white flowers streaked and blotched with red or brown; the lip shallow and taller than wide, with spurs 3–12 mm long, half the length of the ovary. Moist and marshy grassland through eastern South Africa.

▶ FLOWERS COLOURFUL; LIP SPURS LONGER THAN THE OVARY

⑤ *Satyrium carneum* Rooikappie `J F M A M J J A S O N D`

Stout perennial to 80 cm, with 2–4 fleshy leaves, the lowest 2 somewhat spreading, and a dense spike of pale pink to rose or sometimes white flowers; the lip somewhat keeled, with slender spurs, 14–20 mm long, longer than the ovary. Sandy, coastal flats and slopes in the southwestern and southern Cape.

⑥ *Satyrium hallackii* `J F M A M J J A S O N D`

Stout herb, 30–60 cm, with 4–6 basal leaves grading into the stem leaves, and with a dense spike of pink flowers, fragrant at night; the lip with a crest and slender spurs, 7–31 mm long, longer than the ovary. Marshy grassland through eastern South Africa.

⑦ *Satyrium neglectum* `J F M A M J J A S O N D`

Pink Candle Orchid Herb 20–80 cm, with 2 leaves in a separate shoot next to the stem, and a dense spike of fragrant, pink to deep rose flowers; the lip with a hairless flap and slender spurs, 6–19 mm long, longer than the ovary. Grassland through eastern South Africa.

⑧ *Satyrium longicauda* `J F M A M J J A S O N D`

Blushing Bride Orchid Herb 20–80 cm, with 1 or 2 leaves in a separate shoot next to the stem, and a dense spike of fragrant, white to pink flowers; the lip with a minutely hairy flap and slender spurs, 15–46 mm long, longer than the ovary. Grassland through eastern South Africa.

▶▶ LIP NOT SPURRED, PARTIALLY JOINED TO THE ANTHER COLUMN; PETALS JOINED TO THE MIDDLE SEPAL TO FORM A HOOD

Pterygodium　BONNET ORCHID, MOEDERKAPPIE

(Greek pterygodes, wing-like, from the spreading lip lobes of some species)　Tuberous perennials. Leaves few, elliptical to lance-shaped. Flowers mostly in a loose spike, yellow to cream-coloured or greenish, with the upper 3 tepals cohering to form a *shallow hood, and the lip bearing a tall, conical or funnel-shaped appendage*. East and southern Africa, mainly winter-rainfall: 18 spp.; South Africa: 17 spp.

❶ *Pterygodium magnum*
J F M A M J J A S O N **D**
Robust herb to 1.5 m, with many lance-shaped leaves grading into the floral bracts, which are flexed downwards, and a dense, cylindrical spike of buff flowers densely speckled with red; the petals and lip fringed. Marshy grassland and river banks along the eastern escarpment.

❷ *Pterygodium alatum*
J F M A M J J **A** S O N D
Herb to 20 cm, with narrowly elliptical leaves clustered towards the base, and a loose spike of pale greenish-yellow flowers, 15 mm in diameter, fragrant; the lip with 2 broad, spreading side lobes on either side of a small pointed midlobe, and a spoon-shaped appendage. Sandy flats and slopes in the southwestern and southern Cape.

❸ *Pterygodium catholicum*
J F M A M J J A **S O N** D
Cowled Friar　Herb to 35 cm, with oblong leaves, and a loose spike of yellowish-green flowers, often flushed with red, 15 mm in diameter; the lip appendage minutely toothed at the tip. Clay flats in renosterveld in the southwestern and southern Cape, flowering mostly after fire.

Corycium　MONKSHOOD ORCHID

(Greek koros, helmet; ium, resembling, for the shape of the flowers)　Tuberous perennials. Leaves *numerous, narrow, overlapping up the stem*. Flowers many in a dense spike, yellow to greenish, or maroon to brown, with the *3 upper tepals cohering to form a deep hood, the lateral sepals ± joined together, and the lip bearing a shield-shaped appendage that spreads over the anther*. East tropical and southern Africa, mainly Western Cape: 14 spp., all occurring in South Africa.

❹ *Corycium carnosum*
J **F** M **A** M J J A S **O N D**
Herb to 55 cm, turning black when dry, with a dense spike of dull pink, deeply hooded flowers, ±7 mm in diameter; the lateral sepals not joined. Seeps in fynbos in the southwestern and southern Cape.

❺ *Corycium orobanchoides*
J F M A M J J A **S O** N D
Slender herb to 42 cm, the lower leaves barred with red towards the base, with a dense spike of deeply cup-shaped, yellowish-green flowers with purple or black tips to the petals, ±5 mm in diameter, fragrant; the lateral sepals joined. Sandy flats in the southwestern Cape. *Corycium crispum* has bright yellow flowers and crinkly leaves.

❻ *Corycium nigrescens*
J F **M** A M J J A S O N **D**
Black-faced Orchid　Slender herb to 55 cm, turning black when dry, with a dense spike of globular, black or dark maroon flowers, ±5 mm in diameter; the lateral sepals joined, and the lip appendages curled and tapering. Montane grassland through eastern South Africa. *Corycium dracomontanum* has blunt lip appendages.

157

Disperis WITCH ORCHID, MOEDERKAPPIE

(Greek dis, double; pera, pouch, referring to the spurs on the sepals) Small, tuberous perennials, sometimes with hairy stems. Leaves few, lance- to heart-shaped. Flowers 1–few in a loose spike, yellow to greenish or pink to purple, with the upper 3 tepals cohering to form a deep hood, *the lateral tepals each with a conical or club-shaped spur, and the lip flexed back into the hood and bearing a slender, often hairy, tail-like appendage.* Sub-Saharan Africa and Old World tropics: ±84 spp.; South Africa: 26 spp.

① *Disperis stenoplectron*

J F M A M J J A S O N D

Herb 14–20 cm, with 3 or 4 lance-shaped leaves and a dense, 1-sided spike of pink or purple flowers, 15–20 mm in diameter, with a sac-like hood, 9 mm deep. Moist montane grassland along the eastern escarpment.

② *Disperis capensis*

J F M A M J J A S O N D

Slender herb to 50 cm, with a softly hairy stem and 2 lance-shaped leaves, and a solitary green and magenta or cream-coloured flower, 20–30 mm in diameter, with conspicuously tailed sepals and a 2-pouched hood, 2–5 mm deep. Fynbos seeps and moist flats in the southwestern and southern Cape.

③ *Disperis wealei*

J F M A M J J A S O N D

Slender herb, 15–30 cm, with 2–5 lance-shaped leaves scattered up the stem, and a loose spike of white, bonnet-shaped flowers, 20–30 mm in diameter, with a bell-shaped hood, 4–5 mm deep. Marshes and grassy stream banks throughout eastern South Africa.

④ *Disperis fanniniae*

J F M A M J J A S O N D

Granny Bonnet, Moederkappie Slender herb, 15–30 cm, with 3 lance-shaped leaves scattered up the stem, and a loose spike of white, bonnet-shaped flowers, 20–30 mm in diameter, with a sac-like hood, 10–16 mm deep. Leaf litter and on rocks on the forest floor in eastern South Africa.

▶▶ LIP SEPARATE FROM THE ANTHER COLUMN AND NOT SPURRED; PETALS NOT JOINED TO THE MIDDLE SEPAL BUT SOMETIMES ENCLOSED WITHIN IT

Brownleea BROWNLEEA

(Named for the Rev. John Brownlee, 1791–1871, who collected plants from around King William's Town) Tuberous perennials. Leaves scattered up the stem. Flowers in a cylindrical or rounded spike, white to mauve, with the *upper, or median, tepal hooded and with a spur,* the petals usually smaller and enclosed within the dorsal tepal, the *lip minute and erect in front of the flower.* Southern and tropical Africa: 7 spp.; South Africa: 5 spp.

⑤ *Brownleea macroceras*

J F M A M J J A S O N D

Slender perennial, 10–50 cm, with 1–3 leaves and a loose spike of pale mauve flowers with a slender curved spur, 20–40 mm long. Rock ledges and outcrops in high-altitude montane grassland in the Drakensberg.

Disa DISA *(Probably honouring Dis, an early Greek mother-goddess)*

Tuberous perennials. Leaves scattered up the stem or basal, sometimes on a separate shoot, green or dry at flowering. Flowers in a loose or dense, cylindrical or flat-topped spike, variously coloured, with the *upper, or median, tepal hooded and with a spur, the petals usually smaller and enclosed within the dorsal tepal,* the lip small or large, sometimes fringed. Africa and the Arabian Peninsula, mainly southern Africa: ±162 spp.; South Africa: ±130 spp.

▶ **FLORAL SPUR 0–10 MM LONG**

❶ Disa chrysostachya

J F M A M J J A S O **N D**

Robust perennial to 1 m, with closely leafy stems and a dense, cylindrical spike of tightly packed, orange flowers, ±8 mm in diameter; the spur swollen and longer than the sepal, 5–11 mm long. Damp or marshy grassland through eastern South and tropical Africa. *Disa polygonoides* has red flowers with a spur 1.5–4 mm long; *D. woodii* has yellow flowers with a spur 1–2.5 mm long.

❷ Disa versicolor

J **F** M A M J J A S O N D

Apple-blossom Orchid   Robust perennial, 20–70 cm, with a leafy stem and separate leafy shoot, and a dense spike of closely packed, fragrant, pink and brown flowers, ±10 mm; the spur sharply bent, 5–7 mm long. Grassland through eastern South and subtropical Africa.

❸ Disa atricapilla

J F M A M J J A S O **N D**

Perennial to 30 cm, with narrow leaves in a basal tuft, and a flat-topped cluster of bicoloured flowers, 20–30 mm in diameter, the lateral sepals sharply keeled and red or black, and white, and the petals and lip maroon; the spur very small or absent. Seeps and moist sandstone slopes in the southwestern Cape, flowering mostly after fire.

❹ Disa bivalvata

J **F M A M J J A** S O N D

Perennial to 30 cm, with narrow leaves in a basal tuft, and a flat-topped cluster of bicoloured flowers, 20–30 mm in diameter, the sepals white, and the petals and lip maroon; the spur very small or absent. Moist sandstone slopes and seeps in the southwestern and southern Cape, flowering mostly after fire.

❺ Disa racemosa Vlei Disa

J F M A M J J A S O **N D**

Slender perennial to 1 m, with narrow leaves in a basal tuft, and a loose spike of pale pink flowers with darker veins, 30–40 mm in diameter; the upper sepal dish-shaped, with a very small or absent spur. Sandstone seeps and marshes from the southwestern to Eastern Cape, flowering mainly after fire.

❻ Disa tenuifolia

J F M A M J J A S O **N D**

Slender perennial to 30 cm, with narrow, grass-like leaves in a basal tuft and broader stem leaves, and an open spike of yellow flowers, 15–20 mm in diameter; the spur very small or absent. Mountain seeps in the southwestern Cape, flowering mostly after fire.

❶ *Disa flexuosa*

J F M A M J J A **S O** N D

(=*Schizodium flexuosum*) **Fried Egg Orchid** Slender perennial to 30 cm, with the leaves clustered at the base of the wiry, flexed stem, and a few white flowers with bright yellow petals, and the lip spotted with black, 15–20 mm in diameter; the spur 2–4 mm long. Seasonally moist, sandy flats in the southwestern Cape.

❷ *Disa graminifolia*

J F **M** A M J J A S O N D

(=*Herschelia graminifolia*) **Blue Disa** Slender perennial to 60 cm, with a basal tuft of grass-like leaves that are dry at flowering, and a loose spike of blue to violet flowers with a flat lip and lime-green petals; the spur club-shaped, 2–4 mm long. Sandstone mountains among rocks in the southwestern and southern Cape. *Disa purpurascens* has a lip with curled margins, and a tapering spur.

▸ **FLORAL SPUR 10–20 MM LONG**

❸ *Disa ferruginea* **Cluster Disa**

J **F** M A M J J A S O N D

Slender perennial to 45 cm, with a basal cluster of narrow leaves that are dry at flowering, and a crowded, head-like spike of bright red to orange flowers with dry bracts, 10–15 mm in diameter; the dorsal tepal narrowing gradually into a slender spur, 7–20 mm long. Sandstone mountain slopes in the southwestern and southern Cape.

❹ *Disa uniflora* **Red Disa**

J **F M** A M J J A S O N D

Perennial to 60 cm, with narrowly lance-shaped leaves clustered towards the base, and 1–few large, carmine-red to orange flowers, 60–120 mm in diameter, with the upper sepal streaked with red; the spur wedge-shaped, 10–15 mm long. Wet cliffs, stream sides and seeps in the mountains of the southwestern Cape..

❺ *Disa cornuta* **Golden Orchid**

J F **M A M** J J A **S O N** D

Robust perennial to 60 cm, with a closely leaved stem, and a dense spike of purple and silvery-green flowers with a black lip, 15–20 mm in diameter; the spur 10–20 mm long. Sandstone slopes and grassland from the southwestern Cape to tropical Africa.

❻ *Disa nervosa*

J **F** M A M J J A S O N D

Robust perennial, 40–80 cm, with a leafy stem and a dense spike of spreading, pink flowers, 30–45 mm in diameter, with a thread-like lip; the spur slender, 12–20 mm long. Dry, stony, montane grassland in eastern South Africa.

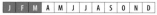

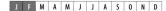

▶ FLORAL SPUR >20 MM LONG

❶ *Disa harveiana* Lilac Disa

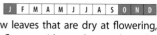

Perennial to 30 cm, with a basal tuft of narrow leaves that are dry at flowering, and a loose spike of cream-coloured or mauve flowers with purple or red streaks, 20–30 mm in diameter; the dorsal tepal not completely enclosing the petals and drawn into a slender spur, 20–90 mm long. Sandstone mountain slopes in the southwestern Cape. *Disa draconis* from the West Coast has a paddle-shaped dorsal tepal that completely encloses the petals.

❷ *Disa cooperi*

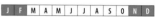

Robust perennial, 40–70 cm, with a leafy stem and a separate leafy shoot, and a dense spike of down-facing, white or cream-coloured flowers with a green, spade-shaped lip, 15 mm in diameter, fragrant at night; the spur slender, 35–45 mm long. Montane grassland along the Drakensberg. *Disa scullyi* has a narrow, elliptical lip.

❸ *Disa crassicornis*

Robust perennial to 1 m, with a leafy stem and a spike of large, pale pink, mottled flowers, ±50 mm in diameter, sweetly scented; the spur tapered and arched or sharply bent, 30–40 mm long. Damp, montane grassland and bush clumps in eastern South Africa. *Disa thodei* is smaller, with tepals up to 20 mm long.

❹ *Disa longicornu* Drip Disa

Perennial with an arching stem to 20 cm, with a basal tuft of narrowly elliptical leaves and a solitary, pale greyish-blue flower, 40–50 mm in diameter; the spur horn-like, 20–35 mm long. Wet cliffs on Table Mountain and in the Jonkershoek Mountains.

PROTEACEAE

Protea family

Protea PROTEA, SUGARBUSH

(Thought to derive from the god Proteus, who assumed multifarious forms) Shrubs or small trees. Leaves mostly elliptical, rarely needle-like. *Flowers clustered into heads surrounded by enlarged, colourful bracts;* the individual flowers or florets are 2-lipped, with 3 of the petals joined into a sheath and the fourth separate, sometimes tipped with a beard of hairs. Southern and tropical Africa, mainly southwestern Cape: 115 spp.; South Africa: 83 spp. Many species and hybrids are popular in gardens and as cut-flowers. The vernacular name *suikerbos* (sugarbush) was applied originally to *Protea repens* on account of the copious sugary nectar that was collected and boiled down to make syrup (*bossiestroop*).

▶ **STYLE 12–35 MM LONG**

❶ *Protea acaulos* Ground Protea

J F M A M J J A S O N D

Mat-forming shrublet, with erect, hairless, narrowly lance-shaped to oval leaves, 60–250 mm long, and cup-shaped flowerheads, 30–60 mm in diameter; the floral bracts hairless and green with red tips; the style 25–35 mm long. Sandy flats and lower slopes in the southwestern Cape.

❷ *Protea amplexicaulis*

J F M A M J J A S O N D

Sprawling shrublet to 40 cm, with greyish, hairless, heart-shaped leaves, 30–80 mm long, clasping the stems, and cup-shaped flowerheads, 60–80 mm in diameter, near the base of the branches; the floral bracts smooth and ivory above and chocolate-velvety beneath; the style 25–30 mm long. Sandstone slopes in the southwestern Cape.

❸ *Protea nana* Mountain Rose

J F M A M J J A S O N D

Shrub to 1.3 m, with hairless, bright green, needle-like leaves, 20–30 mm long, and nodding, cup-shaped flowerheads, 30–45 mm in diameter; the floral bracts red to green and fringed; the style 20–25 mm long. Moist sandstone slopes in the southwestern Cape.

❹ *Protea scolymocephala* Skollie

J F M A M J J A S O N D

Erect shrub to 1.5 m, with hairless, narrowly spoon-shaped leaves, 35–90 mm long, and bowl-shaped flowerheads, 35–45 mm in diameter; the floral bracts hairless and creamy green; the style 12–25 mm long. Sandy flats and lower slopes in the southwestern Cape.

▶ **STYLE 40–100 MM LONG AND MUCH LONGER OR MORE CONSPICUOUS THAN THE FLORAL BRACTS**

❺ *Protea aurea*

J F M A M J J A S O N D

Shrub or tree to 5 m, with hairless, oblong to oval leaves, 40–90 mm long, with a lobed base, and shuttlecock-like flowerheads, 90–120 mm long; the floral bracts silky and pink to creamy green; the style 85–105 mm long. South-facing mountain slopes in the southern Cape.

❶ *Protea nitida* Waboom

J F M A **M J J** A S O N D

Tree 5–10 m, with olive-green to silvery-grey, hairless, elliptical leaves, 80–180 mm long, and cup-shaped flowerheads, 80–160 mm in diameter; the floral bracts short, sometimes silky, and silver-grey; the style 60–80 mm long, not kinked at the tip. Sandstone slopes in the southwestern and southern Cape.

❷ *Protea glabra* Chestnut Sugarbush

J F M A M J J **J A S** O N D

Multi-stemmed shrub or tree to 5 m, with greyish, hairless, elliptical leaves, 40–75 mm long, and bowl-shaped flowerheads, 70–120 mm in diameter; the floral bracts short, hairless or velvety, and dull brown; the style 40–50 mm long, not kinked at the tip. Dry sandstone slopes and plateaus on the interior mountains of the West Coast.

❸ *Protea punctata*

J F **M A M** J J A S O N D

Shrub to 4 m, with greyish, oval leaves, 35–80 mm long, hairless when mature, and bowl-shaped flowerheads, 20–25 mm in diameter; the floral bracts silky, and pink or white with fringing hairs that spread outwards; the style ±50 mm long. Rocky slopes in the interior mountains of the southwestern and southern Cape.

▸ **STYLE 40–70(–90) MM LONG BUT SHORTER AND LESS CONSPICUOUS THAN THE FLORAL BRACTS**

▸▸ **INNER FLORAL BRACTS WITHOUT A DISTINCT BEARD**

❹ *Protea gaguedi* African Sugarbush

J F M A M J J A S O N **D**

Gnarled shrub to 3 m, hairy on the young stems, with oblong to sickle-shaped leaves, 80–200 mm long, greyish and hairless when mature, and bowl-shaped flowerheads, 50–110 mm in diameter; the floral bracts cream-coloured with silvery hairs; the style 40–65 mm long. Mainly drier grassy slopes, rocky outcrops and *Protea* woodland through eastern South and tropical Africa. *Protea welwitschii* has rusty hairs on the bracts.

❺ *Protea caffra*

J F M A M J J A S **O N D**

Common Grassland Sugarbush Multi-stemmed shrub or small tree to 8 m, with hairless, pale green to silvery leaves, 70–250 mm long, and cup-shaped flowerheads, 45–80 mm in diameter; the floral bracts hairless or hairy when young and cream-coloured to carmine; the style 40–60 mm long. Coastal and inland grassy slopes and *Protea* savanna through eastern South and tropical Africa.

❻ *Protea simplex*

J F M A M J J A S O **N D**

Dwarf Grassland Sugarbush Multi-stemmed shrublet to 1 m, the stems slender, 2–5 mm in diameter, pinkish when young and dying after a few years, with hairless, oblong leaves, 60–120 mm long, and cup-shaped flowerheads, 35–60 mm in diameter; the floral bracts hairless and green or cream-coloured to carmine; the style 20–40 mm long, not kinked at the tip. Stony grasslands in eastern South Africa, flowering after fire.

❶ *Protea dracomontana*

`J F M A M J J A S O N D`

Drakensberg Sugarbush Shrub to 1.5 m, the stems reddish and 5–10 mm in diameter, with hairless, greyish, oblong leaves, 80–140 mm long, and cup-shaped flowerheads, 40–60 mm in diameter; the floral bracts hairless with fringed margins and cream-coloured to carmine; the style 45–60 mm long. Subalpine grassland on basalt rock in the Drakensberg and Zimbabwe.

❷ *Protea subvestita* **Waterlily Sugarbush**

`J F M A M J J A S O N D`

Small tree to 5 m, with elliptical leaves, 50–110 mm long, and woolly when young, curved upwards, and cylindrical flowerheads, 55–70 mm long; the floral bracts hairless or silky but with shaggy margins and cream-coloured to pink, the inner ones bent out at the tips; the style 55–60 mm long. Montane grassland on sandstone rock through southern and eastern South Africa.

❸ *Protea roupelliae* **Silver Sugarbush**

`J F M A M J J A S O N D`

Rounded tree, 3–8 m, with hairless or shaggy, narrow to oval leaves, 60–170 mm long, curved upwards, and cup-shaped flowerheads, 80–120 mm long; the floral bracts silky and pink to brownish, the inner ones spoon-shaped; the style 50–65 mm long. Grassy slopes and *Protea* woodland in eastern South Africa.

❹ *Protea compacta* **Bot River Protea**

`J F M A M J J A S O N D`

Lanky shrub to 3.5 m, with oblong to oval leaves, 50–130 mm long, curved upwards and lobed at the base, hairless when mature, and narrowly cup-shaped flowerheads, 90–120 mm long; the floral bracts downy and pink or white, the inner ones spoon-shaped; the style 60–70 mm long. Coastal slopes and flats in the extreme southwestern Cape.

❺ *Protea eximia*

`J F M A M J J A S O N D`

Broad-leaved Sugarbush Shrub to 5 m, with hairless, oval to oblong leaves, 60–100 mm long, spreading and lobed at the base, and narrowly cup-shaped flowerheads, 100–140 mm long; the floral bracts downy and pink, the inner ones spoon-shaped, and the florets tipped with purple or black velvety hairs; the style 60–75 mm long. Sandstone slopes in the mountains of the southern Cape.

❻ *Protea cynaroides* **King Protea**

`J F M A M J J A S O N D`

Multi-stemmed, resprouting shrub to 3 m, with hairless, long-petioled leaves with an elliptical to rounded blade 120–300 mm long, and large, cup-shaped flowerheads, 120–300 mm in diameter; the floral bracts pale or deep pink and often silky outside; the style 80–95 mm long. Moist sandstone slopes in the southwestern and southern Cape.

❼ *Protea repens* **Sugarbush, Suikerbos**

`J F M A M J J A S O N D`

Shrub or tree to 4.5 m, with hairless, narrow to spoon-shaped leaves, 50–150 mm long, and narrowly cup-shaped flowerheads, 100–160 mm long; the floral bracts cream-coloured to red, or bicoloured, and covered with a sticky gum; the style 70–90 mm long. Sandstone and clay flats and slopes from the southwestern to Eastern Cape.

171

1 *Protea obtusifolia*

J F M A M **J J J A** S O N D

Large shrub to 4 m, with elliptical to lance-shaped leaves, 100–150 mm long, curved upwards and tapering at the base, hairless when mature, and narrowly cup-shaped flowerheads, 90–120 mm long; the floral bracts downy, cream-coloured to red, the inner ones spoon-shaped; the style ±65 mm long. Limestone flats and hills on the Agulhas Plain in the southern Cape.

2 *Protea susannae* Stinkblaarsuikerbos

J F M **A M J J** A S O N D

Shrub to 3 m, with elliptical leaves, 80–160 mm long, curved upwards and tapering at the base with a sulphurous odour, and narrowly cup-shaped flowerheads, 80–100 mm long; the floral bracts pinkish-brown and covered with a sticky, brown varnish; the style 60–70 mm long. Coastal limestone and sand on the Agulhas Plain in the southern Cape.

3 *Protea longifolia*

J F M A M **J J** A S O N D

Sprawling shrub to 1.5 m, with hairless, narrow to spoon-shaped leaves, 90–20 mm long, curved upwards and tapering at the base, and narrowly cup-shaped flowerheads, 80–160×40–90 mm, with the florets forming a black woolly cone longer than the bracts; the floral bracts hairless and greenish to pink, the innermost thread-like and densely fringed; the style 40–65 mm long. Stony flats and lower slopes in the southwestern Cape.

▶▶ INNER FLORAL BRACTS WITH A DISTINCT BEARD

4 *Protea burchellii* Burchell's Sugarbush

J F M A M **J J J A** S O N D

Shrub to 2 m, with narrow to spoon-shaped leaves, 70–170 mm long, and narrowly cup-shaped flowerheads, 90–100 mm long; the floral bracts shiny and cream-coloured to carmine, the inner ones fringed or bearded; the style 55–65 mm long. Mainly clay slopes and loamy flats in the southwestern Cape.

5 *Protea laurifolia*

J F M A **M J J** A S O N D

Grey-leaved Sugarbush Small tree to 8 m, with elliptical, greyish leaves, 80–140 mm long, hairless when mature, with a horny margin and midrib, and cylindrical flowerheads, 100–130 mm long; the floral bracts silky and cream-coloured to pink, the outer ones with brown horny margins and the inner ones with a dense blackish beard; the style 65–70 mm long. Sandstone slopes in the southwestern Cape.

6 *Protea neriifolia*

J F M A M J J A S O N **D**

Narrow-leaved Sugarbush Shrub to 3 m, with oblong, green leaves, 100–180 mm long, hairless when mature, and cylindrical flowerheads, 100–130 mm long; the floral bracts silky and cream-coloured to pink, the outer ones with brown, horny margins and the inner ones with a dense white or black beard, with fine silvery hairs below the beard; the style 55–70 mm long. Sandstone and clay slopes in the southwestern and southern Cape.

① *Protea lepidocarpodendron*   J F M **A M J J A** S O N D

Black-bearded Protea   Similar to *Protea neriifolia* but with black hairs below the beard on the inner floral bracts. Mainly sandstone slopes in the extreme southwestern Cape.

② *Protea coronata* **Green Sugarbush**   J F M **A M J** J A S O N D

Erect shrub or small tree to 5 m, with elliptical, green leaves, 70–120 mm long, hairless or silky, and cylindrical flowerheads ±100 mm long; the floral bracts bright green with the tips curved inwards and fringed with a white beard; the style ±60 mm long. Clay slopes in the extreme southwestern and southern Cape.

③ *Protea lorifolia*   J F M **A M J** J A S O N D

Strap-leaved Sugarbush   Rounded shrub or small tree to 3(–5) m, with narrowly elliptical, bluish-grey leaves, 120–250 mm long, with thickened, reddish or yellow margins and midrib, hairless when mature, and egg-shaped flowerheads, 70–130 mm long, partially concealed among the leaves; the floral bracts silky and dull pink or cream-coloured with a white or brown beard; the style 55–65 mm long. Dry sandstone slopes in the Western and southern Cape.

Leucadendron   CONE BUSH, TOLBOS

(Greek leukos, white; dendron, tree, alluding to the silvery leaves of some species)   Shrubs or trees, *with the sexes on separate plants.* Leaves mostly elliptical but sometimes needle-like. *Flowers in dense spikes at the branch tips; the male florets in small rounded or conical heads and the female florets in cones formed by overlapping woody bracts, often scented.* Fruiting cones either remain intact until burned or the individual scales open when mature to expose the fruits. South Africa, mainly southwestern Cape: 83 spp. The vernacular name *tolbos* alludes to the tendency of the woody fruiting cones of many species to spin like a top when dropped or kicked.

▸ **FLORAL LEAVES SIMILAR TO THE FOLIAGE LEAVES**

④ *Leucadendron argenteum*   J F M A M J J A **S O** N D

Silver Tree, Witteboom   Tree to 10 m, with silvery, silky, lance-shaped leaves to 150 mm long, with the floral leaves similar; male flowerheads ±50 mm and female heads ±40 mm in diameter. Granite and clay slopes on the Cape Peninsula, Paarl Mountain and the Helderberg.

⑤ *Leucadendron salicifolium*   J F M A M J **J A** S O N D

Single-stemmed shrub to 3 m, with hairless, narrowly sickle-shaped leaves to 60 mm long and twisted below, with the floral leaves few, similar and creamy yellow but the involucral bracts conspicuously spreading and yellow; the flowerheads 9–10 mm in diameter and slightly fruit-scented. Streams and seeps on flats and slopes in the southwestern Cape.

▶ FLORAL LEAVES BRIGHTLY COLOURED AND MORE CONSPICUOUS THAN THE FOLIAGE LEAVES

▶▶ CONE SCALES CURVING BACK AND OPENING WITHIN A SEASON TO SHED THE FRUITS

❶ *Leucadendron daphnoides*

| J | F | M | A | M | J | J | A | S | O | N | D |

Single-stemmed shrub to 1.5 m, with hairless, elliptical to lance-shaped leaves to 60 mm long, with the floral leaves broader and yellow, turning ivory-white and then red; male flowerheads ±42 mm and female heads ±23 mm in diameter, with a citrus scent. Granite slopes in the extreme southwestern Cape, especially on Dutoitskloof Pass.

❷ *Leucadendron sessile*

| J | F | M | A | M | J | J | A | S | O | N | D |

Single-stemmed shrub to 1.5 m, with hairless, narrowly elliptical leaves to 64 mm long (male) or to 80 mm long (female), with the floral leaves similar and yellow or red; male flowerheads ±35 mm in diameter, with erect, brown bracts, and female heads 14–18 mm in diameter, lemon-scented. Granitic slopes and flats in the southwestern Cape, especially visible on Sir Lowry's Pass.

▶▶ CONE SCALES REMAINING TIGHTLY CLOSED AND RETAINING THE FRUITS FOR SEVERAL SEASONS UNTIL BURNED

❸ *Leucadendron spissifolium*

| J | F | M | A | M | J | J | A | S | O | N | D |

Multi-stemmed shrub to 1.3 m, with hairless, narrowly paddle-shaped leaves, 25–63 mm long (male) or 27–80 mm long (female) and twisted at the base, with the floral leaves larger and ivory or pale green; male flowerheads ±18 mm and female heads 13–15 mm in diameter, lemon-scented. Sandstone slopes in the southwestern and southern Cape, and in the Eastern Cape and KwaZulu-Natal.

❹ *Leucadendron salignum*

| J | F | M | A | M | J | J | A | S | O | N | D |

Sprawling or erect, multi-stemmed shrub to 1(–2) m, with hairless, narrowly paddle-shaped leaves, 20–47 mm long (male) or 48–58 mm long (female) and twisted below, with the male floral leaves slightly longer and yellow or sometimes red and the female leaves larger and ivory or red; male flowerheads 10–14 mm and female heads 9–12 mm in diameter, sweet or yeast-scented. Sandy and clay slopes and flats throughout the southwestern and southern Cape.

❺ *Leucadendron meridianum*

| J | F | M | A | M | J | J | A | S | O | N | D |

Densely branched, single-stemmed shrub to 2 m, with silky or hairless, narrowly paddle-shaped leaves, ±40 mm long, with the floral leaves longer and yellow; the flowerheads ±12 mm in diameter, slightly scented. Limestone flats on the Agulhas Plain in the southern Cape.

❻ *Leucadendron xanthoconus*

| J | F | M | A | M | J | J | A | S | O | N | D |

Single-stemmed shrub to 2 m, with narrowly oblong or sickle-shaped leaves to 65 mm long, twisted at the base and silky when young but hairless when mature, with the floral leaves larger and yellow; the flowerheads 10–11 mm in diameter. Sandstone slopes in the extreme southwestern Cape.

1 *Leucadendron laureolum* J F M A M **J J** A S O N D

Single-stemmed shrub to 2 m, with oblong leaves to 75 mm long (male) or 95 mm long (female), hairless when mature, with the floral leaves larger, yellow and concealing the young heads; male flowerheads ±20 mm and female heads ±14 mm in diameter, slightly fruit-scented; the cones with a spiral of 8 shallow grooves. Sandstone slopes in the extreme southwestern Cape.

Mimetes PAGODA BUSH, STOMPIE *(Greek mimete, mimic; the allusion is unclear)*

Shrubs or trees. Leaves usually silky, elliptical to oblong *with 1 or more horny teeth at the tips. Flowers in headlets arranged in dense spikes at the branch tips, either surrounded individually by coloured floral bracts or in the axils of enlarged, often coloured inflorescence leaves.* Southwestern Cape in fynbos: 13 spp. The vernacular name *stompie*, also applied to *Brunia*, refers to the stumps that invariably remain after the woody shrubs have burned down in periodic veld fires.

2 *Mimetes hirtus* Marsh Pagoda J F M A M J **J A** S O N D

Single-stemmed shrub to 2 m, with ± hairless, oval to lance-shaped foliage leaves, 25–45 mm long, and similar inflorescence leaves; the flower spikes comprising headlets of 9–14 white flowers surrounded by bright yellow floral bracts, 15–40 mm long, with red tips; the style red and 50–55 mm long. Peaty marshes in the extreme southwestern Cape.

3 *Mimetes cucullatus* J F M A M J J A S O N D

Common Pagoda, Rooistompie Multi-stemmed shrub to 1.4 m, resprouting from a woody base, with hairless, oblong to elliptical leaves, 25–55 mm long, and red, spoon-shaped inflorescence leaves; the flower spikes comprising headlets of 4–7 white flowers surrounded by small bracts; the style red and 45–50 mm long. Sandstone slopes and flats in the southwestern and southern Cape.

4 *Mimetes fimbriifolius* Tree Pagoda J F M A M J **J A S O N D**

Tree to 4 m, with oblong to elliptical leaves, 40–70 mm long, densely fringed with hairs, and with dull reddish-yellow, spoon-shaped inflorescence leaves; the flower spikes comprising headlets of 4–7 white flowers surrounded by small bracts; the style yellow with a red tip and 55–60 mm long. Rocky slopes on the Cape Peninsula.

5 *Mimetes argenteus* Silver Pagoda J F **M A M J** J A S O N D

Single-stemmed shrub to 3.5 m, with spreading, silvery, silky, elliptical leaves, 40–65 mm long, and with carmine to pale mauve, spoon-shaped inflorescence leaves; the flower spikes comprising headlets of 6–9 pink flowers surrounded by small bracts; the style yellow, 40–45 mm long, with a kink at the tip. Moist, south-facing mountainsides in the extreme southwestern Cape.

Serruria SPIDERHEAD, SPINNEKOPBOS

(Named for early 18th-century Dutch botanist James Serrurier) Shrubs or shrublets, erect or creeping. *Leaves needle-like or divided into narrow or needle-like segments. Flowers clustered in 1 or more small heads at branch tips, usually pink or silvery.* Southwestern Cape: ±50 spp. The vernacular names derive from the finely divided, silky leaves that give the impression of being covered with spiders' webs.

▶ FLOWERHEADS CLUSTERED

① *Serruria decipiens*

J F M A M J **J A S O** N D

Sandveld Spiderhead Rounded shrublet to 1 m, with almost hairless, finely divided leaves, 30–45 mm long, and a very short, thick peduncle bearing clusters of 5–10 flowerheads of 6–10 creamy white, fragrant flowers, without floral bracts; the style 8–9 mm long. Sandy flats and slopes, mainly along the West Coast.

② *Serruria fasciflora*

J F M A **M J J A S O N D**

Common Pin Spiderhead Sprawling to erect shrublet to 1 m, with sparsely hairy, finely divided leaves, 30–70 mm long, and a short, hairy peduncle bearing clusters of many flowerheads of 5–7 silvery-pink, sweetly-scented flowers, with lance-shaped floral bracts; the style 5–7 mm long. Sandy flats and lower slopes in the southwestern Cape.

▶ FLOWERHEADS SOLITARY

③ *Serruria fucifolia* **Northern Spiderhead**

J F M A M J J **A S O** N D

Rounded shrub to 1.5 m, with grey-haired, finely divided leaves, 35–60 mm long, and a hairy peduncle, 20–60 mm long, bearing a solitary flowerhead of 20–30 silvery-grey to purple, sweetly-scented flowers, with lance-shaped floral bracts; the style ±9 mm long. Sandy flats and lower slopes along the West Coast.

④ *Serruria acrocarpa*

J F M A M J **J A S O N D**

Common Rootstock Spiderhead Rounded, resprouting shrublet to 50 cm, with almost hairless, finely divided leaves, 20–50 mm long, and a hairy peduncle, 10–32 mm long, bearing a solitary flowerhead of 10–25 silvery-pink to greenish, sweetly-scented flowers, with oval floral bracts; the style ±7 mm long. Sandy flats and slopes in the southwestern Cape.

⑤ *Serruria villosa* **Golden Spiderhead**

J F M **A M J J** A S O N D

Compact, rounded shrublet to 80 cm, with silky, finely divided leaves, 20–40 mm long, and a solitary, sessile flowerhead of 18–22 yellow, fragrant flowers nestled among the leaves, with lance-shaped floral bracts; the style ±10 mm long. Sandstone slopes and flats on the southern Cape Peninsula.

Diastella **SILKYPUFF** *(Greek diastellein, to separate, referring to the very short floral tube)*

Shrublets, erect or creeping. *Leaves overlapping, oval to needle-like. Flowers clustered in a small head at the branch tips, usually pink.* Southwestern Cape: ±7 spp.

⑥ *Diastella divaricata*

J F M A M J **J A S O** N D

Common Silkypuff Sprawling, single-stemmed shrublet, 0.5×3 m, with elliptical leaves, 2–18×2–7 mm, bearing pink flowerheads, 10–15 mm in diameter. Sandstone flats and slopes in the extreme southwestern Cape. *Diastella proteoides* has narrow leaves, 5–15×1–2 mm, which are hairy when young.

181

Leucospermum PINCUSHION, SPELDEKUSSING

(Greek leukos, white; spermum, seed, referring to the pale, waxy aril that covers the seeds) Shrubs or trees, erect or creeping. *Leaves oval to narrow, with 1 or more horny teeth at the tips. Flowers clustered at the branch tips in a medium-sized to large head containing >15 florets, often yellow to red;* South Africa to Zimbabwe, mainly southwestern Cape: 48 spp. Several species and their hybrids are popular garden subjects and cut-flowers. The vernacular name *luisiesbos* refers to the resemblance of the nutlets of several species to lice.

▶ **STYLE 10–35 MM LONG**

1 *Leucospermum oleifolium*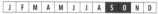

Overberg Pincushion   Rounded shrub to 1 m, with hairless or hairy, oval to lanceolate leaves, 40–60 mm long, with 1–5 apical teeth, and flat-topped flowerheads, 25–40 mm in diameter, yellow-green, fading to red; the style straight, 25–30 mm long. Sandstone slopes in the southwestern Cape.

2 *Leucospermum calligerum*

Arid Pincushion   Shrub to 2 m, with grey-haired, lance-shaped to elliptical leaves, 12–36 mm long, with 1(–3) apical teeth, and spherical flowerheads, 20–35 mm in diameter, cream-coloured, fading to dull red; the style slightly curved inwards, 21–25 mm long. Dry sandy slopes in the southwestern Cape.

3 *Leucospermum bolusii*

Gordon's Bay Pincushion   Rounded shrub to 1.5 m, with ± hairless, oval to elliptical leaves, 25–45 mm long, with 1 apical tooth, and rounded flowerheads ±20 mm in diameter, cream-coloured, fading to pale pink; the style straight, 15–20 mm long. Rocky sandstone slopes above Gordon's Bay in the southwestern Cape.

4 *Leucospermum rodolentum*

Sandveld Pincushion   Erect or spreading shrub to 3 m, with grey, velvety, elliptical to wedge-shaped leaves, 40–65 mm long, with 3–6 apical teeth, and spherical flowerheads, 30–35 mm in diameter, bright yellow; the style usually straight, 15–25 mm long. Sandy flats and lower slopes in Namaqualand and the southwestern Cape.

5 *Leucospermum tomentosum*

Saldanha Pincushion   Sprawling, multi-stemmed shrub to 1 m, with grey, velvety, narrowly channelled leaves, 45–60 mm long, with 1–3 apical teeth, and spherical flowerheads, 30–35 mm in diameter, yellow; the style straight, 17–20 mm long. Coastal sands on the West Coast.

6 *Leucospermum muirii*

Albertinia Pincushion   Rounded shrub to 2 m, with almost hairless, narrowly wedge-shaped leaves, 40–60 mm long, with 3–7 apical teeth, and spherical flowerheads, 20–30 mm in diameter, yellow, fading to orange; the style straight, 13–22 mm long. Coastal limey sands around Still Bay in the southern Cape. *Leucospermum truncatum* from west of Still Bay has leaves with only 3 apical teeth and larger flowerheads, 30–40 mm in diameter.

183

❶ *Leucospermum prostratum*
Yellow Trailing Pincushion Mat-forming shrublet to 4 m in diameter, with ± hairless, narrow leaves, 20–40 mm long, all pointing upwards, with 1 apical tooth, and spherical flowerheads, 20–25 mm in diameter, rose-scented, yellow, fading to orange; the style 12–15 mm long. Mainly coastal sands in the southwestern Cape.

❷ *Leucospermum hypophyllocarpodendron*
Snake-stemmed Pincushion Trailing or creeping shrublet with hairless or grey-felted, narrow and channelled to lance-shaped leaves, 40–130 mm long, all pointing upwards, with 2–4 apical teeth, and flattened-spherical flowerheads, 30–40 mm in diameter, bright yellow; the style straight or slightly curved inwards, 20–26 mm long. Sandy coastal flats in the southwestern Cape.

▶ **STYLE 30–60 MM LONG**

❸ *Leucospermum cuneiforme*
Warty-stemmed Pincushion Multi-stemmed shrub to 2 m, resprouting from a woody rootstock with the stems warty below, with hairless, wedge-shaped leaves, 45–110 mm long, with 3–10 apical teeth, and oval flowerheads, 50–90 mm in diameter, yellow, fading to red; the style slightly curved, 38–55 mm long. Sandstone slopes and flats in the southern and Eastern Cape.

❹ *Leucospermum conocarpodendron*
Kreupelhout Rounded shrub or tree to 5 m, with thickly hairy branches and almost hairless or felted, elliptical to wedge-shaped leaves, 60–115 mm long, with 3–10 apical teeth, and spherical to oval flowerheads, 70–90 mm in diameter, bright yellow; the style slightly curved, 45–55 mm long. Dry rocky slopes in the extreme southwestern Cape.

❺ *Leucospermum tottum*
Ribbon Pincushion Rounded shrub with spreading branches to 1.3 m, with hairless, oblong to lance-shaped leaves, 25–60 mm long, with 1–3 apical teeth, and flattened-spherical flowerheads, 90–150 mm in diameter, pinkish; the style curved inwards at first but later spreading and ±50 mm long. Rocky slopes in the mountains along the West Coast.

❻ *Leucospermum lineare*
Needle-leaved Pincushion Erect to sprawling shrub to 2 m, with hairless, narrow and often channelled leaves, 40–100 mm long, with 1–3 apical teeth, and flattened-spherical flowerheads, 60–90 mm in diameter, yellow to red; the style curved inwards, 50–60 mm long. Clay slopes in the extreme southwestern Cape.

❼ *Leucospermum cordifolium*
Pincushion Rounded shrub with drooping branches to 1.5 m, with almost hairless, oval leaves, 20–80 mm long, lobed at the base, with 1–6 apical teeth, and flattened-spherical flowerheads, 100–120 mm in diameter, orange to scarlet, and at right angles to the stem; the style spreading to curved inwards, 45–60 mm long. Rocky sandstone slopes in the extreme southwestern Cape. *Leucospermum patersonii* from coastal limestones around Stanford in the southwestern Cape is a tree to 4 m, with erect flowerheads and silky floral tubes.

① *Leucospermum vestitum*

J F M A M J J A S O N D

Silky-haired Pincushion Rounded shrub to 2.5 m, with hairless, oval to elliptical leaves, 50–70 mm long, with 2–4 apical teeth, and rounded flowerheads, 70–90 mm in diameter, orange to scarlet with silky floral tubes; the style curved inwards, 50–60 mm long. Rocky sandstone slopes on the interior mountains of the West Coast.

▸ **STYLE 70–90 MM LONG**

② *Leucospermum reflexum* J F M A M J J A S O N D

Rocket Pincushion Single-stemmed shrub to 3 m, with grey-felted, elliptical leaves, 20–55 mm long, with 2 or 3 apical teeth, and spherical flowerheads, 80–100 mm in diameter, scarlet; the style sharply bent down, 70–75 mm long. Near streams in the Cedarberg.

③ *Leucospermum catherinae* J F M A M J J A S O N D

Catherine-wheel Pincushion Shrub to 3 m, with hairless, elliptical leaves, 90–135 mm long, with 3 or 4 apical teeth, and disc-shaped flowerheads, ±150 mm in diameter, orange to coppery bronze; the style flexed and twisted clockwise near the tip, 70–80 mm long. Sandstone slopes along streams in the interior mountains of the West Coast.

RANUNCULACEAE   Ranunculus family

Ranunculus BUTTERCUP
(Diminutive of Greek rana, frog, alluding to the damp habitat) Annual or perennial herbs. *Leaves often basal* and usually divided or lobed and toothed. Flowers yellow or white, often glossy, with *3–5 green sepals and as many petals.* Cosmopolitan: ±250 spp.; South Africa: 7 spp. The acrid juice was used medicinally.

④ *Ranunculus multifidus* J F M A M J J A S O N D

Common Buttercup Perennial herb, 20–50 cm, with silky leaves divided into toothed leaflets, and bright, glossy yellow flowers, 10–15 mm in diameter. Damp ground near streams or marshes throughout Africa.

⑤ *Ranunculus baurii* J F M A M J J A S O N D

Nasturtium-leaved Buttercup Perennial herb, 60–120 cm, with a basal tuft of circular, finely toothed, umbrella-like leaves on slender petioles, and bright, glossy yellow flowers, 10–25 mm in diameter. Along waterfalls and stream sides at high altitude through the Drakensberg.

Anemone ANEMONE, ANEMOON *(From the classical Greek name for the genus)*

Perennials. *Leaves basal* and usually much divided or lobed, with 1 or more *whorls of bract-like leaves forming a collar below each flower.* Flowers often large and showy, the *sepals 4–20 and petal-like,* deciduous, no true petals. Cosmopolitan, mainly temperate: ±120 spp.; South Africa: 15 spp. The fresh leaves and roots of some species are an irritant, causing blistering, and were used medicinally.

1 *Anemone transvaalensis*

(=*Knowltonia transvaalensis*) **Transvaal Blister-leaf, Transvaal Anemone** Slender perennial herb, 40–100 cm, with a basal tuft of deeply lobed, coarsely toothed leaves, and clusters of white flowers, 15–20 mm in diameter, on branching stems. Damp grassy slopes and river banks in northeastern South Africa.

2 *Anemone fanniniae* **Giant Anemone**

Perennial herb to 1.2 m high, with a basal tuft of leathery, 5–7-lobed, finely toothed leaves on long petioles, the blades velvety above and silky beneath, and 1–3 creamy-white flowers, 80–100 mm in diameter, on simple or sparsely branched stems. Moist depressions along drainage lines and stream sides in the Drakensberg.

3 *Anemone tenuifolia* **Cape Anemone**

Tufted perennial to 40 cm, with leathery leaves divided 2 or 3 times into triangular, 3-toothed segments, with the margins rolled under, and solitary, large, pinkish-white flowers, silky beneath, 50–70 mm in diameter. Moist sandstone slopes in the southwestern Cape.

Clematis **CLEMATIS, TRAVELLER'S JOY** *(From the classical Greek name for the genus)*

Woody climbers or scramblers. Leaves opposite, scattered up the stem, divided or lobed, with the axis twining. Flowers with *4 petal-like sepals,* true petals short or absent. *Fruits with slender, feathery styles.* Cosmopolitan, mainly temperate: ±230 spp.; South Africa: 4 spp. The dried leaves were used medicinally.

4 *Clematis brachiata* **Lemoenbloeisels**

Climber or scrambler to several metres, with opposite leaves divided into oval, coarsely toothed leaflets, sparsely hairy beneath, and clusters of hairy, fragrant white flowers, 20 mm in diameter. Scrub and forest margins through South and tropical Africa.

PAPAVERACEAE ·   Poppy family

Papaver **POPPY** *(From the classical Latin name for the genus)*

Annual or perennial herbs. Leaves mainly basal, sometimes spiny. Flowers solitary, *nodding in bud,* pink, *orange* or red. *Seeds shed through a ring of pores beneath the stigma.* Mostly northern hemisphere: ±80 spp.; South Africa: 1 sp.

5 *Papaver aculeatum*

Orange Poppy, Doringpapawer Tufted annual to 1 m, with deeply lobed and toothed leaves, covered in stiff yellow prickles, and solitary orange flowers on slender stalks, 50 mm in diameter. Scree and disturbed ground through central and eastern South Africa.

DROSERACEAE

Sundew family

Drosera   SUNDEW, DOUBLOM   *(Greek droseros, dewy, alluding to the leaf glands)*

Glandular, insectivorous perennials or annuals. Leaves basal or scattered along the stem, *covered in sticky glands and tentacles.* Flowering stem short or slender, coiled at the tip when young; flowers usually pink, mauve or white, closing at night. Worldwide, mainly southern hemisphere: ±80 spp.; South Africa: 20 spp.

1 *Drosera pauciflora*

J F M A M J J **A S O** N D

Tufted perennial to 20 cm, with a basal rosette of paddle-shaped leaves, and pink or mauve flowers with a dark centre, 30–40 mm in diameter. Damp loamy or sandy flats in the southwestern Cape.

2 *Drosera cistiflora*

J F M A M J J **A S** O N D

Poppy-flowered Sundew, Snotrosie Slender perennial to 40 cm, with or without basal leaves but always with slender leaves scattered up the stem, and white, creamy yellow, pink, mauve, purple or red flowers with a dark centre, 30–40 mm in diameter. Damp sandy flats and seeps in southwestern South Africa.

BRASSICACEAE

Mustard family

Cadaba   CADABA   *(From khadab, the Arabic name for one of the species)*

Shrubs, sometimes leafless or spiny. *Leaves simple,* alternate or tufted on short shoots. Flowers solitary or in clusters; sepals 4, coloured and petal-like; petals mostly absent; *stamens 5–8, joined to the stalk of the ovary to form a long, combined cylindrical structure with the ovary at the tip.* Africa to Australasia: ±30 spp.; South Africa: 4 spp.

3 *Cadaba aphylla*

J F **M A** M J J **A S O** N D

Bobbejaanarm, Swartstormbos   Leafless, often tangled shrub with purplish branches to 2 m, often thorny at the tips, and clusters of greenish to red flowers on side shoots, ±10 mm long, with stamens and style protruding 30–40 mm. Dry bushveld and semidesert through central South and subtropical Africa.

Cleome   CLEOME   *(From a classical Greek plant name)*

Annual or perennial herbs. Leaves usually digitately divided. Flowers in racemes, *highly irregular;* sepals 4; petals 4, *often very dissimilar with 2 large and paddle-shaped;* stamens 4–many, all fertile or *some sterile and whisker-like.* Fruit cylindrical and opening to shed the seeds. Worldwide in the tropics: ±150 spp.; South Africa: 21 spp.

4 *Cleome angustifolia*

J F **M A** M J J A S O **N D**

Yellow Mouse-whiskers, Peultjiesbos   Erect annual herb with wand-like stems to 1.5 m, covered in conical, whitish protuberances, with leaves digitately divided into 3–13 thread-like leaflets, and a slender raceme of yellow flowers with purple marks at the base of the 2 largest petals, closing at midday, 20 mm in diameter. Savanna and open scrub through the northern parts of South Africa and tropical Africa.

5 *Cleome hirta*

J F M A M J **J A S O N D**

Erect annual herb with glandular, wand-like stems to 1.5 m, leaves digitately divided into 5–9 narrow leaflets, and a leafy raceme of mauve flowers with yellow blotches on the 2 largest petals, 20 mm in diameter. Savanna and open scrub through the northern parts of South Africa and tropical Africa.

Heliophila SUNFLAX, SPORRIE

(Greek helios, sun; philein, loving; the flowers open in sunny weather) Shrubs, perennials or annuals. Leaves narrow or broad, often lobed or divided. Flowers *mostly mauve or blue*, sometimes pink or white, closing at night and in cool weather. *Fruit often slender and beaded, tipped by the swollen style*. Southern Africa, mainly southwestern Cape: 85 spp. The genus has recently been expanded to include several smaller genera that were distinguished by their differently shaped fruits, including the wild stock, *Brachycarpaea*.

▶ PERENNIALS OR SHRUBLETS

1 *Heliophila rigidiuscula*

| J | F | M | A | M | J | J | A | S | O | N | D |

Grassland Cross-flower Perennial with erect annual stems to 90 cm from a woody base, with scattered, narrow leaves, and racemes of drooping, pale mauve to purple flowers with a pale eye and hairless sepals, 10–20 mm in diameter; the fruits narrow and unbeaded, 30–70 mm long. Grassland through eastern South Africa. *Heliophila formosa* forms large clumps, with broader, basal leaves and trailing flowering stems.

2 *Heliophila cornuta*

| J | F | M | A | M | J | J | A | S | O | N | D |

Willowy or straggling shrublet to 1.5 m, with narrow or thread-like, leathery leaves, and white, mauve or blue flowers, with the petals flexed back and with hairless or minutely hairy sepals, 10–15 mm in diameter; the fruits lightly beaded, 30–100 mm long. Rocky slopes in arid fynbos from southern Namibia to the Eastern Cape.

3 *Heliophila elata*

| J | F | M | A | M | J | J | A | S | O | N | D |

Willowy shrublet to 1 m, with thread-like, sometimes lobed, leaves, and blue to mauve flowers with ± hairless sepals, ±10 mm in diameter; the fruits lightly beaded, 20–80 mm long. Sandy flats and slopes in arid fynbos in the southwestern Cape.

4 *Heliophila carnosa*

| J | F | M | A | M | J | J | A | S | O | N | D |

Tussock-forming shrublets with annual stems to 60 cm from a woody base, with thread-like leaves, and large, white, pink or violet flowers, 15–20 mm in diameter; the fruits oblong, 25–80 mm long. Dry hillsides from Namibia to the southern seaboard and to Gauteng.

5 *Heliophila juncea*

| J | F | M | A | M | J | J | A | S | O | N | D |

(=*Brachycarpaea juncea*) **Wild Stock, Blouriet** Wand-like shrublet to 1 m, with narrow to oblong leaves, and racemes of white, pink or purple flowers with narrowly paddle-shaped petals 8–20 mm long; the fruits disc-shaped and warty. Rocky sandstone slopes from the southwestern to Eastern Cape, flowering best after fire; very variable in growth form and flower size.

193

① *Heliophila africana*

J F M A M J J **A S O N** D

Roughly hairy annual herb to 40 cm, often somewhat sprawling, with lance-shaped, often lobed or toothed leaves, and blue or mauve flowers with hairless or hairy sepals, 10 mm in diameter; the fruits narrow and unbeaded, 13–100 mm long. Sandy flats in the southwestern Cape.

② *Heliophila arenaria*

J F M A M J **J A S** O N D

Almost hairless or hairy annual herb with stiffly erect stems to 50 cm, with thread-like, sometimes lobed leaves, and blue flowers with hairy sepals, 10–15 mm in diameter; the fruits beaded, 15–55 mm long. Sandstone slopes in the northern Western Cape.

③ *Heliophila coronopifolia*

J F M A M J J **A S O** N D

Annual herb with stiffly erect stems to 60 cm, roughly hairy towards the base, with thread-like or variously lobed leaves, and blue flowers with a white or greenish centre and hairless, purplish sepals, 10–20 mm in diameter; the fruits beaded, 30–90 mm long. Widespread on sandy flats and slopes, often forming massed displays, in Namaqualand and the southwestern Cape.

④ *Heliophila variabilis*

J F M A M J **J A S** O N D

Wit Sporrie Minutely hairy annual herb to 30 cm, with finely lobed leaves, and white flowers turning pinkish with age, 10–15 mm in diameter; the fruits lightly beaded, 20–40 mm long. Sandy or gravelly flats in Namaqualand.

ZYGOPHYLLACEAE Twinleaf family

Sisyndite DESERT BROOM *(Origin obscure)*

Greyish, broom-like shrubs. Leaves mostly opposite, pinnately compound with deciduous leaflets. Flowers solitary in the branch forks, yellow, *with a silky ovary. Fruit silky.* Drier western parts of southern Africa: 1 sp.

⑤ *Sisyndite spartea*

J F **M A M J J** A S O N D

Greyish, broom-like shrub to 2 m, with small, deciduous leaflets on branch-like leaves, and mostly solitary, pale yellow flowers, 30–50 mm in diameter, with a silky ovary and fruits. Gravelly flats, washes and dry river beds in the dry northwest of South Africa.

Tribulus DEVIL'S-THORN *(Greek tri, three; bolos, point, alluding to the spiny fruits)*

Spreading annual or perennial herbs. Leaves opposite, 1 usually markedly smaller than the other, divided into 5–10 pairs of slightly unequally sized leaflets. Flowers solitary in the axils of the smaller leaves, yellow. *Fruit splitting into 5 winged or spiny segments.* Worldwide in arid areas: ±25 spp.; South Africa: 4 spp.

⑥ *Tribulus terrestris*

J F M A M J J A S O N D

Common Devil's-thorn Prostrate annual with radiating stems up to 1.5 m, compound leaves, and clear yellow flowers with petals 3–12 mm long; fruit segments each with 4 long spines plus small spinules. Sandy flats and roadsides through southern Africa. *Tribulus zeyheri* has large flowers and fruits with numerous, ± similar spines or warts.

❶ *Tribulus cristatus* J F **M A M** J J A S O N D

Winged Devil's-thorn Prostrate annual with radiating stems to 1 m, compound leaves, and pale yellow flowers with petals to 25 mm long; fruit segments each with 4 broad, crested wings. Sandy flats and roadsides through western South Africa.

Roepera TWINLEAF, SPEKBOS *(Named for German botanist, J. Roeper, 1801–1885)*

Shrubs with jointed stems. *Leaves opposite, fleshy, divided into 2 leaflets.* Flowers 1 or 2 together, mostly yellow or white, with reddish marks at the base of the petals, the stamen *filaments with appendages at the base. Fruit with 4 or 5 ridges or wings.* Mainly drier parts of southern Africa, especially the southwestern Cape: ±50 spp. The southern African species were previously included in the North African genus *Zygophyllum*. The vernacular name *spekbos* alludes to the value of the plants as fodder; the leaves and seeds are poisonous.

❷ *Roepera morgsana* J F **M A M J J A S O** N D

(=*Zygophyllum morgsana*) **Slymbos** Shrub or shrublet to 1.5 m, with petiolate leaves divided into 2 asymmetrical, oval leaflets, and watery yellow flowers with only 4 petals, 20 mm in diameter; fruits large, conspicuously 4-winged. Sandy and stony slopes and flats, mostly coastal, from southern Namibia to the Eastern Cape.

❸ *Roepera foetida* J F M A M J **J A S O** N D

(=*Zygophyllum foetidum*) **Scrambling Twinleaf, Skilpadbos** Sprawling or climbing shrub to 2 m or more, foetid when crushed, with petiolate leaves divided into 2 asymmetrical, broad leaflets, and yellow flowers with 5 petals, 20 mm in diameter; fruits 5-lobed, with prominent bony ribs when dry. Bush patches and stream banks through the Northern, southwestern and Eastern Cape.

❹ *Roepera cordifolia* J F M **A M J J A S O** N D

(=*Zygophyllum cordifolium*) **Penny-leaved Twinleaf, Sjielingbos, Geldjiesbos** Shrublet to 70 cm, with sessile, almost circular leaves, and pairs of yellow flowers with 5 petals, 20 mm in diameter; fruits narrowly 5-winged when dry. Sandy or gravelly flats, often coastal, in Namibia and the far western Cape.

❺ *Roepera flexuosa* J F M A M **J J A S** O N D

(=*Zygophyllum flexuosum*) **Maerbos** Sprawling shrublet to 70 cm, with sessile leaves divided into 2 oval leaflets, and yellow flowers with 5 petals, 20 mm in diameter; fruits spherical when fresh and 5-angled when dry. Coastal sands in the southwestern Cape.

197

OXALIDACEAE
Oxalis family

Oxalis **SORREL, SURING** (*Greek oxys, acid, alluding to the oxalic acid content*)

Mostly stemless herbs, with sour sap. Leaves in a basal tuft or alternate, *divided into 3 (or more) leaflets that are often 2-lobed or notched at the tips, drooping and closing at night.* Flowers solitary or in umbels, funnel-shaped and furled at night, mostly pink, yellow or white; the *stamens in 2 series at different heights with the stigmas at a third level.* Cosmopolitan, mainly South America and the southwestern Cape: ±500 spp.; South Africa: ±200 spp. Plants have been used in cooking and as a treatment for intestinal worms.

▶ **FLOWERS IN UMBELS**

❶ *Oxalis semiloba* **Common Pink Sorrel**   J F M A M J J A S O N D
Stemless perennial, with the leaves in a basal tuft, divided into 3 wedge-shaped, notched, usually hairless leaflets, and clusters of 3–12 pink flowers with a greenish tube, 15–20 mm in diameter. Grassland through eastern South and tropical Africa.

❷ *Oxalis pes-caprae* **Geelsuring**   J F M A M J J A S O N D
Stemless perennial, with the leaves mostly in a basal tuft, divided into 3 wedge-shaped, notched leaflets, usually hairless above and hairy beneath, and clusters of 3–20 canary-yellow flowers, 15–20 mm in diameter. Widespread and common in the Northern, southwestern and Eastern Cape, often along verges and in fields.

▶ **FLOWERS SOLITARY; LEAFLETS WEDGE-SHAPED TO ROUNDED**

❸ *Oxalis luteola* **Sandsuring**   J F M A M J J A S O N D
Stemless perennial with the leaves divided into 3 broadly wedge-shaped, hairless or hairy leaflets, conspicuously veined and often purple beneath, and bright yellow flowers on a jointed stalk, 15–20 mm in diameter. Sandy flats and lower slopes in the southwestern Cape.

❹ *Oxalis melanosticta*   J F M A M J J A S O N D
Stemless perennial with the leaves divided into wedge-shaped, notched leaflets with fringed margins, black-dotted when dry, and yellow to red flowers with a yellow tube, 20–25 mm in diameter. Dry mountain slopes in the southwestern Cape interior.

❺ *Oxalis obtusa* **Geeloogsuring**   J F M A M J J A S O N D
Stemless perennial with the leaves divided into 3 broadly wedge- or heart-shaped leaflets, hairless or hairy, and pink, brick-red, yellow or white flowers, with darker veins and a yellow tube on a jointed stalk covered in down-facing hairs, 15–20 mm in diameter. Mostly damp clay slopes in the Northern, southwestern and Eastern Cape.

❻ *Oxalis obliquifolia*   J F M A M J J A S O N D
Fleshy-leaved Pink Sorrel Stemless perennial with the leaves divided into fleshy, broadly wedge-shaped, rounded leaflets, hairless or slightly hairy, and solitary pink flowers with a yellow tube, 15–25 mm in diameter. Grassland through eastern South and tropical Africa.

❼ *Oxalis purpurea* **Grand Duchess Sorrel**   J F M A M J J A S O N D
Stemless perennial with the leaves divided into 3 broadly heart-shaped leaflets, finely fringed on the margins and purple beneath, and large, purple, pink, yellow or white flowers with a yellow tube, 25–40 mm in diameter. Widespread and common on damp flats and slopes from Namaqualand to the Eastern Cape.

► FLOWERS SOLITARY; LEAFLETS THREAD-LIKE TO NARROWLY ELLIPTICAL

❶ *Oxalis flava* Bobbejaanuintjie

J F M A **M J** J A S O N D

Stemless perennial with the leaves often not fully expanded at flowering, divided into 2–12 narrow to elliptical, folded leaflets, hairless and leathery with large brown stipules, and solitary, yellow, white or pale lilac flowers, 20–30 mm in diameter. Flats and lower slopes, often on sand, in the southwestern Cape.

❷ *Oxalis polyphylla*

J F **M A M J** J A S O N D

Thread-leaved Sorrel Perennial with a slender stem to 20 cm, with the leaves divided into 3(–7) thread-like, folded leaflets, sometimes thinly hairy beneath, and rose, lilac or white flowers with a yellow tube and often slightly darker margins, 15–20 mm in diameter. Flats and rocky outcrops from the southwestern to the Eastern Cape.

❸ *Oxalis pardalis* Spotted Sorrel

J F M A **M J J** A S O N D

Perennial with a slender stem to 30 cm, with the leaves often not fully expanded at flowering, divided into 3 narrowly elliptical leaflets, hairless or hairy and black-streaked, and orange, reddish-purple, pink, yellow or white flowers with a yellow tube, 15–20 mm in diameter. Flats, often in large numbers, through the southwestern Cape.

❹ *Oxalis hirta*

J F M **A M J** J A S O N D

Perennial with a leafy stem 5–30 cm, often branching, with ± sessile, grey-green leaves divided into 3 narrowly elliptical, folded leaflets, hairy beneath, and mauve, magenta or white flowers with a yellow, sometimes elongated tube, 15–25 mm in diameter. Flats and lower slopes in the southwestern Cape.

GERANIACEAE　　Geranium family

***Geranium*　GERANIUM, CRANE'S-BILL** *(Greek geranos, crane, referring to the beak-like fruit)*

Annual or perennial herbs, often with jointed stems. Leaves palmately lobed or divided and toothed. Flowers *radially symmetrical*, white or pink to purple, *with notched petals; stamens 10*. Fruit segments with a mostly hairless awn. Worldwide: 300 spp.; South Africa: 31 spp. Used as a tea and medicinally.

► LEAVES DIVIDED TO THE BASE

❺ *Geranium incanum* Wild Geranium

J F M A M J J **A S O** N D

Loose, trailing perennial to 50 cm, with leaves divided to the base into 3–7 deeply and narrowly lobed segments, densely white-haired beneath, and pink to mauve flowers with petals 10–15 mm long. Sandy and stony soils along the southern and Eastern Cape coast.

❻ *Geranium robustum*

J F M A M J J A S O **N D**

Shrublet to 1 m, with leaves divided to the base into 3–5 irregularly toothed lobes, densely silver-haired beneath, and purple flowers with petals mostly 15–20 mm long. Streamsides and moist mountain slopes in eastern South Africa.

▶ LEAVES NOT DIVIDED TO THE BASE

❶ *Geranium pulchrum* Showy Geranium `J F M A M J J A S O N D`
Shrublet to 1.2 m, with leaves deeply divided into 5–7 toothed lobes, densely silver-haired, especially beneath, and mauve to purple flowers with petals 17–22 mm long; hairs on petioles facing downwards. Mountain streams and drainage lines in the Drakensberg.

❷ *Geranium flanaganii* `J F M A M J J A S O N D`
Flanagan's Geranium Sprawling perennial to 1 m, with leaves deeply divided into 5 toothed lobes, softly hairy on both surfaces, and pale to deep pink flowers with petals 10–16 mm long; hairs on petioles facing downwards. Mainly on forest margins through southeastern South Africa.

❸ *Geranium brycei* Bryce's Geranium `J F M A M J J A S O N D`
Shrublet to 1 m, with leaves deeply divided into 5–7 toothed lobes, white-felted beneath, and purple or bluish flowers with petals 14–20 mm long. Damp rocky cliffs and ravines at high altitude in the Drakensberg.

❹ *Geranium schlechteri* `J F M A M J J A S O N D`
Schlechter's Geranium Loose, trailing perennial to 1 m, covered in gland-tipped hairs, with leaves divided about two-thirds to the base into 5 toothed lobes, sparsely hairy beneath, and pale or deep pink flowers with petals 9–12 mm long. Moist grasslands, often among rocks, through eastern South Africa.

❺ *Geranium wakkerstroomianum* `J F M A M J J A S O N D`
White Geranium Loose, trailing perennial to 1 m, with leaves divided about two-thirds to the base into 5 toothed lobes, sparsely to densely hairy beneath, and white flowers, veined with red, with deeply notched petals 7–15 mm long. Forest margins, marshes and rocky outcrops through eastern South Africa.

Monsonia MONSONIA, BOESMANSKERS
(Named for amateur botanist, Lady Anne Monson, 1714–1776) Annual or perennial herbs, or spiny, succulent shrublets with waxy bark. *Leaves often dissimilar*, some either smaller or on longer petioles that become spiny, palmately toothed or lobed. *Flowers radially symmetrical*, white, yellow or pink, usually with the *petals irregularly toothed at the tips; stamens 15*. Fruit segments with a crested or fringed awn. Africa and Asia: ±40 spp.; South Africa: 20 spp.

▶ HERBACEOUS PERENNIALS

❻ *Monsonia speciosa* Sambreeltjie `J F M A M J J A S O N D`
Sprawling perennial with annual stems to 10 cm, with toothed to finely divided, ± hairless leaves, and large, white to pink flowers, 25–65 mm in diameter, deep pink on the reverse. Stony slopes and flats in the southwestern Cape.

❼ *Monsonia attenuata* `J F M A M J J A S O N D`
Common Grassland Monsonia Tufted perennial with annual stems to 50 cm, with crowded, narrow, channelled, finely toothed, white-haired leaves, 3–10 mm wide, and greyish-white flowers strongly net-veined with grey beneath, 30–40 mm in diameter. Grassland and rocky hillsides in eastern South Africa.

1 *Monsonia glauca* **Bushveld Monsonia** `J F M A M J J A S O N D`
Tufted perennial to 50 cm, with upper leaves opposite, narrowly oval, channelled, finely toothed, ± hairy, with small white pockets at the base of the teeth, 3–20 mm wide, and white or creamy flowers, 30–40 mm in diameter. Hot savanna and bushveld across South Africa.

▶ SUCCULENT SHRUBLETS

2 *Monsonia camdeboense* `J F M A M J J A S O N D`
(=*Sarcocaulon camdeboense*) **Bushman's Candle, Kersbos** Spiny succulent shrublet to 50 cm, with rounded and notched, hairless leaves, and pale creamy-yellow flowers to 35 mm in diameter. Rocky hillsides in the dry southern interior of South Africa. *Monsonia salmoniflora* from the western interior has very slender branches and pink flowers; *M. spinosa* from Namaqualand has bright yellow flowers.

3 *Monsonia patersonii* `J F M A M J J A S O N D`
(=*Sarcocaulon patersonii*) **Hellthorn** Spiny succulent shrublet to 50 cm, with greyish, rounded and notched, hairless leaves, and pink to purple flowers to 35 mm in diameter. Dry, stony and sandy coastal flats in northwestern South Africa.

4 *Monsonia multifida* `J F M A M J J A S O N D`
(=*Sarcocaulon multifidum*) **Cistus-flowered Bushman's Candle** Dwarf, succulent shrublet to 10 cm, with greyish, finely divided, hairy leaves, and white or pale to deep pink flowers with darker markings in the throat, to 35 mm in diameter. Dry, stony flats at the mouth of the Orange River.

5 *Monsonia crassicaule* `J F M A M J J A S O N D`
(=*Sarcocaulon crassicaule*) **Bushman's Candle** Spiny succulent shrublet to 50 cm, branches >10 mm in diameter, with oval, irregularly lobed and toothed, usually hairy leaves, and pale to bright yellow flowers to 55 mm in diameter. Dry, rocky or stony slopes in western South Africa. *Monsonia ciliata* from inland Namaqualand has thinner branches and petals fringed with long hairs.

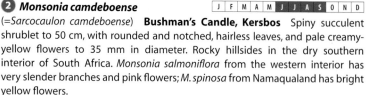

Pelargonium **PELARGONIUM, MALVA** (*Greek pelargos, a stork, referring to the beak-like fruit*)
Perennial herbs or shrubs, rarely annuals. Leaves usually lobed or divided, often hairy or glandular and aromatic. Flowers *zygomorphic or 2-lipped*, in *umbels*, variously coloured, *the upper sepal forming a hollow spur joined to the top of the pedicel*; stamens 10, *usually only 2–7 fertile*. Fruit segments with a crested or fringed awn. Widespread, mainly southwestern Cape: ±270 spp.; South Africa: 220 spp. Hybrids of various South African species are widely grown as the florists' geranium; the scented oils from certain species are important in the fragrance industry, and some species were used medicinally.

▶ TUBEROUS PERENNIALS WITH LEAVES IN A BASAL TUFT

6 *Pelargonium triste* **Kaneeltjie** `J F M A M J J A S O N D`
Tuberous perennial with a basal cluster of softly hairy leaves, finely divided 2 or 3 times, to 300 mm in diameter, and long peduncles of up to 20 pale yellow flowers, variously marked with maroon or black, 15–18 mm in diameter, clove-scented at night; the floral tube 25–35 mm long. Sandy flats and lower slopes, often coastal, in Namaqualand and the southwestern Cape. *Pelargonium lobatum* has broadly lobed leaves.

1 *Pelargonium schlechteri*

J F M A M J J A S **O N D**

Two-tiered Pelargonium Tuberous perennial with a basal tuft of coarsely lobed and toothed, hairy leaves, and a long, stout peduncle of mostly 2-tiered heads of up to 60 bicoloured yellowish flowers strongly marked with maroon, 15–20 mm in diameter; the floral tube ±30 mm long. Moist grasslands in eastern South Africa.

2 *Pelargonium luridum*

J F M A M J J A S **O N D**

Starburst Pelargonium Tuberous perennial with a basal tuft of variously lobed, softly hairy leaves with broad or ribbon-like lobes, and a long, stout peduncle of up to 60 pink or pale yellowish to whitish flowers, 20–25 mm in diameter; the floral tube ±30 mm long. Moist grasslands through eastern South and tropical Africa.

3 *Pelargonium incrassatum*

J F M A M J J **A S** O N D

Namaqua Stork's-bill, Namaqualand Beauty Tuberous perennial with a basal tuft of irregularly lobed, silky leaves with a silvery sheen, and 1 or more peduncles of 20–40 bright magenta-pink flowers, with the upper 2 petals largest, ±20 mm in diameter; the floral tube 30–40 mm long. Rock outcrops and gravelly slopes in Namaqualand.

▸ **SOFT-STEMMED PERENNIALS**

4 *Pelargonium alchemilloides*

J F M A M J J A S **O N D**

Pink Trailing Pelargonium Sprawling perennial to 20 cm, with round, hairy, usually lobed leaves, 70 mm in diameter, with broadly oval stipules and often with reddish zonal marking, and long-stalked clusters of 3–6(–15) white, yellow or pink flowers, 15–20 mm in diameter; the floral tube 12–35 mm long and much longer than the pedicel. Grassland and rocky places through much of southern and eastern South and tropical Africa.

5 *Pelargonium ovale*

J F M A M J **J A S O N D**

Tufted, rhizomatous shrublet to 30 cm, with densely hairy, elliptical, toothed leaves ±40×10–30 mm, and clusters of up to 7 white to pink flowers on well-developed, branching stems, 25–40 mm in diameter, with the upper 2 petals much larger and overlapping; the floral tube 2–13 mm long. Open places on mountains from the southwestern to Eastern Cape.

6 *Pelargonium elegans*

J **F M A M J J A S O N D**

Tufted perennial to 45 cm, with hairless or hairy, somewhat leathery, elliptical leaves, ±30×25 mm, and clusters of up to 7 pink flowers, ±50 mm in diameter; the floral tube 10–15 mm long and shorter than the pedicel. Coastal fynbos in the southern and Eastern Cape.

7 *Pelargonium myrrhifolium*

J **F M A M J J A S O N D**

Sprawling, soft-stemmed shrublet to 50 cm, with leaves divided 2 times into thread- to ribbon-shaped segments, ±50×30 mm, and clusters of up to 5 white, pink or purple flowers, 20–25 mm in diameter, with the upper 4 petals markedly wider; the floral tube 4–10 mm long. Open places on stony sand from the southwestern to Eastern Cape.

① *Pelargonium suburbanum* J F M A M J J A S O N D

Sprawling shrublet to 50 cm, with leaves divided 1 or 2 times, 30–70 mm in diameter, and clusters of up to 6 cream-coloured to purple flowers, 30–40 mm in diameter, with the upper 2 petals much wider; the floral tube 8–50 mm long. Coastal dunes from the southwestern to Eastern Cape.

② *Pelargonium tongaense* J F M A M J J A S O N D

Perennial to 40 cm, with leathery, sparsely hairy, sharply lobed leaves, 40–60 mm in diameter, and lone-stalked clusters of scarlet flowers, 20–30 mm in diameter; the floral tube 30–40 mm long. Coastal woodland in northeastern KwaZulu-Natal.

▶ **SUCCULENT-STEMMED SHRUBLETS**

③ *Pelargonium inquinans* J F M A M J J A S O N D

Scarlet Pelargonium Softly woody shrub to 2 m, with velvety young branches, rounded, shallowly lobed, velvety leaves, mostly 40–80 mm in diameter, and stalked clusters of 5–30 white, pink or scarlet flowers, 20 mm in diameter; the floral tube 30–40 mm long. Margins of coastal bush and in thicket in the Eastern Cape.

④ *Pelargonium zonale* J F M A M J J A S O N D

Zonal Pelargonium Softly woody shrub to 2 m, with rounded, shallowly lobed leaves, usually with reddish zonal marking, mostly 40–80 mm in diameter, and stalked clusters of up to 70 pink flowers, ±30 mm in diameter; the floral tube 25–45 mm long. Stony slopes, riversides and forest margins in the southwestern and Eastern Cape.

⑤ *Pelargonium fulgidum* **Rooimalva** J F M A M J J A S O N D

Succulent-stemmed shrublet to 40 cm, with lobed, densely silver, silky leaves to 100×70 mm, and clusters of 4–9 scarlet flowers, 15–20 mm in diameter; the floral tube 20–40 mm long. Rocky slopes, often coastal granite, in the Northern and Western Cape.

⑥ *Pelargonium peltatum* J F M A M J J A S O N D

Ivy-leaved Geranium Scrambling, semisucculent shrublet to 4 m, with leathery, rounded, often 5–7-lobed leaves with reddish zonal marking, and clusters of 2–9 pale pink to purple flowers, 40–50 mm in diameter; the floral tube 30–50 mm long. Coastal or succulent scrub from the southwestern to Eastern Cape.

▶ WOODY-STEMMED SHRUBS, USUALLY WITH AROMATIC LEAVES

❶ *Pelargonium crispum* J F **M** A **M** J J **A S O** ʘ D

Shrublet to 70 cm, with 2-ranked, small, rough, fan-shaped leaves with crinkly margins, up to 10 mm in diameter, often lemon-scented, and short-stalked clusters of 1–3 pink flowers, ±25 mm in diameter; the floral tube 5–8 mm long. Rocky lower slopes in the southwestern Cape.

❷ *Pelargonium scabrum* Hoenderbos J F M A M J J **A S O N** D

Roughly hairy, aromatic shrub to 1.2 m, with deeply lobed, roughly hairy, lemon-scented leaves, ±50 mm in diameter, and clusters of up to 6 white to pink flowers, ±20 mm in diameter; the floral tube 3–12 mm long. Rocky sandstone slopes from the southwestern to Eastern Cape.

❸ *Pelargonium betulinum* Kanferblaar J F M A M J J **A S O N** D

Shrub to 1.5 m, with oval to elliptical, somewhat leathery leaves, ±20 mm long, and clusters of up to 6 white to pink flowers, ±50 mm in diameter; the floral tube 3–8 mm long. Coastal dunes in the southwestern and southern Cape.

❹ *Pelargonium cucullatum* J **F** M A M J J **A S O N D**

Wildemalva Roughly hairy shrub to 2 m, with ± round, toothed leaves, ±70 mm in diameter, and clusters of up to 13 pinkish-purple flowers, ±40 mm in diameter, with widely overlapping petals; the floral tube 5–12 mm long. Sandstone and granite slopes along the coast in the southwestern Cape.

❺ *Pelargonium capitatum* Kusmalva J F M A M J J A **S O** N D

Sprawling, softly velvety shrublet to 50 cm, with aromatic, rounded, lobed and crinkly leaves, ±50 mm in diameter, and clusters of up to 20 pink to purple flowers, 15–25 mm in diameter; the floral tube 3–8 mm long. Coastal dunes and flats from the southwestern Cape to KwaZulu-Natal.

RUTACEAE   Citrus family

Adenandra CHINA FLOWER, PORSELEINBLOM
(Greek aden, gland; andra, man, referring to the anther glands) Ericoid shrublets. Leaves elliptical or needle-like. Flowers 1–few at the branch tips, glistening white (rarely pink) above and pink to red beneath; the *stamens each tipped with a stalked gland*, alternating with hairy, thread-like staminodes; ovary surrounded by a cup-shaped nectar-disc; the style shorter than the petals. Southwestern Cape: 18 spp.

❻ *Adenandra uniflora* J F M A M J J **A S O** N D

Aromatic shrublet to 50 cm, with oblong to lanceolate leaves, 4–14 mm long, with the margins rolled under, and solitary (rarely more) white to pink flowers, reddish on the reverse, 6–16 mm long. Sandstone slopes in the southwestern Cape. Very similar to *Adenandra villosa* and thought to hybridise with it on the Cape Peninsula.

Agathosma BUCHU, BOEGOE *(Greek agathis, good; osme, scent, referring to the aromatic leaves)*

Ericoid shrubs or shrublets. Leaves needle-like to orbicular. Flowers 1–few in the axils or in clusters at the branch tips, white, pink or mauve; stamens usually with a terminal gland, *alternating with variously shaped staminodes, these often petal-like*; ovary surrounded by a deeply cup-shaped nectar-disc; *the style longer than the petals*. Southern Africa: ±150 spp. Among the most important traditional medicines in the Cape pharmacopoeia. The vernacular name derives from the original Khoi name for several species of shrubby members of the family, the dried leaves of which were used medicinally or ceremonially.

❶ *Agathosma bisulca* Steenbokboegoe   J F M A M **J J A** S O N D
Rounded shrub to over 1 m, with needle-like to lance-shaped leaves, mostly 10–12 mm long and often 2-grooved beneath, and clusters of white flowers, 5–6 mm long, with thread- or paddle-shaped staminodes; the fruits 2- or 3-segmented. Lower slopes and flats in deep sand in the southwestern Cape.

❷ *Agathosma thymifolia*   J F M A M J J **A S O** N D
Shrub to over 1 m, with broadly rounded leaves, 3.5–4 mm long, and clusters of pink or mauve flowers, 4 mm long, with paddle-shaped staminodes; the fruits 3- or 4-segmented. Coastal sand and dunes on limestone near Langebaan in the Western Cape.

❸ *Agathosma capensis*   **J F M A M J J A S O N D**
Coppicing shrub to 90 cm, with needle-like to oval leaves, 1.5–7 mm long, and clusters of white, pink or purple flowers, 3–5 mm long, with peg-like or lance-shaped staminodes; the fruits 3-segmented. Slopes and flats in southwestern South Africa.

TURNERACEAE   Turnera family

Tricliceras LION'S EYE *(Greek tri, three; kleis, bolt; ceras, horn, referring to the three styles)*

Annual or perennial herbs, often bristly and glandular-haired. Leaves variously toothed or lobed. Flowers in racemes, *orange. Fruits slender and cylindrical, ± beaded*. Africa: ±11 spp.; South Africa: 7 spp.

❹ *Tricliceras lacerata*   J F M A M J J **A S O** N D
Perennial to 30 cm, covered with coarse, greenish bristles, with narrow, deeply lobed and toothed leaves, and few-flowered racemes of orange flowers, 40 mm in diameter; the minutely bristly fruits flexed downwards. Subtropical woodland in northeastern South Africa. *Tricliceras longipedunculata* has spreading, reddish hairs, only slightly toothed leaves, and ± hairless fruits.

MALVACEAE
Hibiscus family

▶ **SUBFAMILY BYTTNERIOIDEAE** STAMENS 5, SEPARATE

Hermannia DOLL'S ROSE, POPROSIE
(Named for German botanist and traveller, Paul Hermann, 1640–1695) Shrublets or perennials. Leaves unlobed, toothed or variously divided, usually with *leaf-like stipules*. Flowers axillary, *often in raceme- or panicle-like inflorescences*, yellow to red or pink, the sepals forming a *spherical to bell-shaped calyx* and the *petals spirally twisted*; stamens 5, opposite the petals, the *filaments winged or lobed* and the *anthers tapering to a pointed or hairy tip*. Africa, Australasia and America: ±180 spp.; South Africa: 162 spp.

❶ *Hermannia saccifera*

J F M A M J J **A S O** N D

Hairless, sticky, sprawling shrublet to 40 cm, with regularly toothed, elliptical to oblong leaves, and axillary pairs of yellow, bell-shaped flowers, 10 mm in diameter, with the bracts joined into a small cup below the calyx; the stamen filaments cross-shaped and bearded. Stony clay slopes from the southwestern to the Eastern Cape.

❷ *Hermannia grandiflora*

J F M A M J J **A S O N D**

Karoo Rose, Klokkiebos Slender-stemmed shrublet to 60 cm, with oblong, toothed leaves, and pairs of nodding, pink to reddish flowers on long slender pedicels, 15–20 mm in diameter; the fruits small and rounded. Dry, stony slopes in south-central South Africa.

❸ *Hermannia stricta* Desert Rose

J F M A M **J J A S** O N D

Rounded, slender-stemmed shrublet to 60 cm, with oblong, toothed leaves, and solitary, nodding, flared, pink to reddish flowers, 15–20 mm in diameter; the fruits with 5 pairs of long, spreading horns. Dry, rocky slopes and flats along the lower reaches of the Orange River.

❹ *Hermannia cristata*

J F M A M J J A S **O N D**

Crested Hermannia Low-growing herb to 30 cm, resprouting from a woody rootstock, with elliptical, toothed leaves, and elongated racemes of nodding, bell-shaped, reddish-orange flowers, 8–10 mm in diameter; the fruit large and 5-angled, with fringed crests along the angles. Stony grassland through eastern South Africa.

❺ *Hermannia geniculata*

J F M A M J J A S O N **D**

White Hermannia Low-growing, trailing herb to 30 cm, resprouting from a woody rootstock, with oval to elliptical, finely toothed leaves, paler and densely felted beneath, with fringed stipules, and racemes of nodding, bell-shaped, white to creamy yellow flowers, 10–20 mm long. Grassland through eastern South Africa.

❻ *Hermannia scabra*

J F M A M J **J A S** O N D

Sprawling, roughly hairy shrublet to 60 cm, with shortly petiolate, wedge-shaped leaves, coarsely toothed above with the terminal tooth curved back, and yellow, bell-shaped flowers, 8 mm in diameter, in small clusters along slender, raceme-like terminal branches. Sandy slopes and flats in the southwestern Cape.

1 *Hermannia alnifolia*

J F M A M J **J A S O** N D

Rounded, grey-mealy shrub to 1 m, the young branchlets hairy, with wedge-shaped to oval leaves, toothed above and pale-mealy beneath, and elongated clusters of numerous, small, yellow, bell-shaped flowers, 5 mm in diameter. Stony slopes in the southwestern Cape.

2 *Hermannia althaeifolia*

J F M A M J J **A S O** N D

Softly hairy and mealy, grey-green shrublet to 50 cm, with petiolate, oval to elliptical, toothed and crinkly leaves with broad, leafy stipules, and terminal and axillary clusters of yellow, bell-shaped flowers, 8 mm in diameter, with a swollen calyx, reddish, fading to cream-coloured. Stony slopes in southwestern South Africa.

3 *Hermannia trifurca* Purple Hermannia

J F M A M J J **A S O** N D

Roughly hairy shrublet to 1.5 m, with oblong leaves, 3-toothed above, and horizontal 1-sided racemes of bell-shaped, mauve flowers with dark venation, 8 mm in diameter. Stony and sandy soils in the Northern and Western Cape.

4 *Hermannia hyssopifolia*

J F M A M J J A **S O** N D

Pokkiesblom Pale-mealy, twiggy shrub to 2 m, with wedge-shaped leaves toothed above, and dense terminal clusters of cream-coloured to pale yellow flowers, 10 mm in diameter, with a pin-hole throat and a swollen, urn-shaped, papery calyx. Stony slopes from the southwestern to Eastern Cape.

▶ **SUBFAMILY MALVOIDEAE** STAMENS NUMEROUS, PARTIALLY JOINED INTO A TUBE

Pavonia **PAVONIA** *(Named for Don José Pavón, d. 1844, Spanish botanist and explorer)*

Shrubs or perennials, often velvety. Leaves usually heart-shaped and lobed, petiolate. Flowers mostly solitary in the axils, *yellow or orange, lasting a day, with a collar (epicalyx) of 5–16 bracts; stamens many, joined into a staminal column that is blunt at the top; style branches twice as many as the carpels, 10. Fruit splitting into 1-seeded segments.* Cosmopolitan in the tropics: 150+ spp.; South Africa: 11 spp.

5 *Pavonia burchellii* Dainty Pavonia

J F **M A** M J J A S O N D

Shrubby, foetid perennial to 1 m, with softly hairy, shallowly palmately 3–5-lobed leaves, with toothed or scalloped margins, on long petioles, and solitary yellow or orange flowers, 30 mm in diameter, on long, axillary pedicels, with an epicalyx of 5 oval bracts. Forest margins and bush through eastern South and tropical Africa.

Anisodontea **AFRICAN MALLOW, BERGROOS**

(Greek aniso, unequal; odontus, toothed, referring to the leaves) Shrubs or perennials, often roughly hairy. Leaves unlobed or 3–7-lobed. Flowers 1–several in the axils, *white, pink or magenta, lasting a day, with a collar (epicalyx) of 3–10 bracts; stamens many, joined into a staminal column that is split at the top into numerous filaments; style branches as many as the carpels, 5–26. Fruit splitting into 1–3-seeded segments.* South Africa and Lesotho, mainly in the drier parts: 21 spp.

6 *Anisodontea scabrosa* Sandroos

J F M A M J J A **S O** N D

Thinly to densely glandular-hairy shrub to 2 m, with somewhat 3-lobed or elliptical, toothed leaves, and 1–few pink flowers in the axils, 30–35 mm in diameter, with an epicalyx of 3 bracts; the fruit segments 1-seeded. Coastal sands and granite outcrops from the southwestern Cape to KwaZulu-Natal.

217

❶ *Anisodontea elegans*   J F M A M J J **A S O** N D
Twiggy, white-haired shrublet to 1.5 m, with 3–5-lobed, deeply cut leaves, and 1–few white to pink flowers in the axils, 40 mm in diameter, with an epicalyx of 3 bracts; the fruit segments 1- or 2-seeded. Stony slopes in the southwestern Cape interior.

❷ *Anisodontea julii* Mountain Mallow   J **F** M A M J J A S O N D
Slender shrub to 2 m, with 3–5-lobed, coarsely toothed leaves, velvety when young, and slender stalks of 2 or 3 pink flowers in the axils, 40–50 mm in diameter, with an epicalyx of 4–10 bracts; the fruit segments are 2-seeded. Scrub, often among boulders, and roadsides in the KwaZulu-Natal Drakensberg, Free State and Lesotho.

Hibiscus HIBISCUS, WILDESTOKROOS
(Classical Latin name for the related genus, Althaea*)*   Shrubs, subshrubs, or annual or perennial herbs. Leaves unlobed or lobed. Flowers usually solitary in the axils, *often large*, usually *yellow or pink with a dark eye*, lasting a day, *with a collar (epicalyx) of 5–20 bracts*; stamens many, *joined into a staminal column*; style branches as many as the carpels, 4 or 5, the stigmas usually disc-like. Fruits not splitting into segments. Worldwide in the tropics and subtropics: ±300 spp.; South Africa: ±50 spp. Used in traditional medicine. The bark of some species was used as twine; *Hibiscus cannabinus* is grown as a fibre plant in India.

▶ SEEDS WITH SILKY FLOSS

❸ *Hibiscus pedunculatus*   J **F M A M** J J A S **O** N **D**
Pink Forest Hibiscus Slender shrublet to 2 m, with 3-lobed, roughly hairy leaves, and pink flowers, 60–70 mm in diameter, on long, slender pedicels in the axils, with an epicalyx of 7 or 8 bracts; the seeds with a cotton-like floss. Thicket and forest margins, mainly low-lying, through eastern South Africa and Mozambique.

❹ *Hibiscus coddii* Red Hibiscus   J F M A M J J A S **O N** D
Perennial with annual stems to 1.5 m, with oval, toothed, roughly hairy leaves, and open, red flowers, 20–30 mm in diameter, in the axils in raceme-like branches, with an epicalyx of 6–9 bracts and a stamen tube 7–10 mm long; the seeds with a silky white floss. Rocky woodland in northern South and tropical Africa. *Hibiscus barbosae* has deeply 3-lobed leaves and flowers 30–35 mm in diameter, with a stamen tube 5–6 mm long.

❺ *Hibiscus pusillus*   J **F M A M** J J A S O N D
Dark-eyed Dwarf Hibiscus Sprawling perennial with annual stems to 30 cm, with oval to deeply 3–5-lobed, ± hairless or roughly hairy leaves with prominent veins, and cream-coloured, yellow or pink flowers, usually with a dark eye, 50–60 mm in diameter, on short or long pedicels in the axils, with an epicalyx of 8–11 bracts; the seeds with a silky floss. Stony grassland and savanna through South and tropical Africa.

① *Hibiscus aethiopicus* Dwarf Hibiscus   J F M A M J J A S O N D

Sprawling perennial with annual stems to 30 cm, with oval to elliptical, ± hairless or roughly hairy leaves, and cream-coloured, yellow or pink flowers without a dark eye, 40–50 mm in diameter, with an epicalyx of 10–12 narrow, fringed bracts; the seeds velvety. Grassland and open scrub through South and tropical Africa.

② *Hibiscus saxatilis*   J F M A M J J A S O N D

Tawny-haired Dwarf Hibiscus   Sprawling perennial with tawny-haired, annual stems to 30 cm, with oval to elliptical, tawny-haired leaves, and rather closed, white or yellow flowers with a dark eye, 30–50 mm in diameter, on long, tawny-haired pedicels, with an epicalyx of 8–10 leaf-like bracts longer than the calyx. Open woodland in eastern South Africa.

③ *Hibiscus dongolensis*   J F M A M J J A S O N D

Dongola Hibiscus   Shrub or woody perennial with erect, ± hairless stems to 2 m, with oval, mostly unlobed, ± hairless leaves, and drooping, rather closed, pale yellow flowers with a dark eye, borne in the axils, with an epicalyx of 5 bracts; the seeds mealy. Open woodland and coastal savanna, in northeastern South and tropical Africa.

④ *Hibiscus vitifolius*   J F M A M J J A S O N D

Vine-leaved Hibiscus   Straggling shrub or woody perennial to 1.5 m, with oval or 3–5-lobed leaves, ± hairless or roughly hairy, and pale yellow flowers with a dark eye, 50–90 mm in diameter, on short pedicels, with an epicalyx of 10 bracts; the fruit deeply 4- or 5-lobed or -winged, and the seeds hairless. Woodland near watercourses, through eastern South and tropical Africa.

⑤ *Hibiscus calyphyllus*   J F M A M J J A S O N D

Large Yellow Wild Hibiscus   Shrub or softly woody herb to 2 m, the older branches ± hairless, with heart-shaped or 3–5-lobed, roughly hairy leaves, and yellow flowers with a dark eye, 100–120 mm in diameter, on very short pedicels in the axils, with an epicalyx of 5 bracts; the seeds velvety. Forest and bush margins and thicket through eastern South and tropical Africa.

⑥ *Hibiscus engleri* Stinging Hibiscus   J F M A M J J A S O N D

Perennial or shrub with erect stems to 1.5 m covered in velvety or bristly, irritating hairs, with 3–5-lobed or -angled, velvety leaves, and pale yellow flowers with a large, dark red eye, on long pedicels in the upper axils, 50–60 mm in diameter, with an epicalyx of 7–10 relatively short, narrow bracts below the calyx; the seeds mealy. Dry bush and savanna through northern South and subtropical Africa.

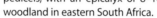

⑦ *Hibiscus trionum*   J F M A M J J A S O N D

Bladder Hibiscus, Terblansbossie   Annual herb to 1.5 m, with 3–5-lobed leaves, ± hairless except on the margins, and cream-coloured to pale yellow flowers with a dark eye, 30–40 mm in diameter, with an epicalyx of 12 thread-like bracts below the swollen, bladder-like calyx. Widespread and often weedy through South Africa and in Asia and Australia.

① *Hibiscus cannabinus* J F **M A M** J J A S O N D

Hemp-leaved Hibiscus, Wilde Stokroos Annual herb with tall, rod-like stems to 2 m, sparsely covered in small prickles, with deeply 3–7-lobed, minutely prickly leaves, and ± sessile, whitish or pale greyish-yellow flowers with a large, purple eye, up to 100 mm in diameter, with an epicalyx of 7 or 8 prickly, thread-like bracts below the calyx; the seeds mealy. Roadsides and disturbed ground through northern South and tropical Africa and in India.

CONVOLVULACEAE   Convolvulus family

Convolvulus BINDWEED, KLIMOP *(Latin convolvere, to twine)*

Sprawling or *twining perennials*. Leaves often *heart- or arrow-shaped*, sometimes lobed. Flowers 1–few in the leaf axils, funnel- to cup-shaped, white to pink or magenta; *style with 2 slender stigma lobes*. The flowers each last a single day. Worldwide, mainly temperate and subtropical: ±250 spp.; South Africa: 9 spp.

② *Convolvulus capensis* Cape Bindweed J F M A M J J **A S O** N D

Thinly hairy climber or creeper to 2 m, with arrow-shaped to deeply lobed, often toothed leaves, and white to pink flowers, 15–35 mm in diameter; the sepals blunt and usually silky. Widespread on dry, stony slopes through the southwestern to Eastern Cape.

Xenostegia THREAD-LEAVED BINDWEED

(Greek xenos, strange; stege, shelter, evidently due to the unusual characters of the genus) Climbing or creeping *perennials*. Leaves *slender or narrowly arrow-shaped with basal lobes*. Flowers 1–few in the leaf axils, funnel- to bell-shaped, *white or pale yellow, often with a purple eye; style with 2 spherical stigma lobes*. Tropical: 2 spp.; South Africa: 1 sp. Used medicinally, possibly toxic.

③ *Xenostegia tridentata* J F **M A M** J J A S O N D

(=*Merremia tridentata*) Hairless, creeping or ± twining perennial to 1 m, with ± sessile, very narrow leaves with toothed ears at the base, and pale to bright yellow flowers, often with a purple throat, 15–20 mm in diameter. Grassland and open woodland through northern and central South and tropical Africa.

Merremia BLACK-EYED BINDWEED *(Named for Professor B. Merrem, 1784–1824)*

Climbing or creeping perennials. Leaves heart-shaped or variously lobed. Flowers 1–few in the leaf axils, funnel- to bell-shaped, *white or pale yellow, often with a purple eye; anthers twisted; style with 2 spherical stigma lobes*. Tropical: ±80 spp.; South Africa: 9 spp. Used medicinally, possibly toxic.

④ *Merremia kentrocaulos* J F **M A** M J J A **S O** N D

Hairless, creeping or twining perennial to 15 m, with deeply lobed and jaggedly toothed leaves, and white to buff flowers with a purple throat, 60–80 mm in diameter. Rocky places in savanna and bushveld from northern South Africa to the Sahara and in India.

Ipomoea MORNING GLORY

(Greek ips, bindweed; omoios, resembling, referring to the similarity to Convolvulus*)* Shrublets or *climbing or creeping perennials.* Leaves *oblong or heart-shaped,* sometimes deeply lobed. Flowers 1–few in the leaf axils, funnel- to salver-shaped, *mostly pink to purple; style with 2 or 3 spherical stigma lobes.* Worldwide in the tropics and subtropics: 500 spp.; South Africa: ±40 spp. Used medicinally and cultivated ornamentally; the tubers are edible.

1 *Ipomoea obscura*

`J F M A M J J A S O N D`

Yellow Morning Glory Creeping or climbing perennial with hairless or hairy stems to 3 m, with heart-shaped leaves, and 1–few, pale yellow or white flowers in the axils, 15–25 mm in diameter; all the sepals similar, oval. Widespread in grassland, bushveld and savanna, often along roadsides or cultivated ground, through eastern South and tropical Africa.

2 *Ipomoea pes-caprae*

`J F M A M J J A S O N D`

Dune Morning Glory Robust, hairless, creeping perennial with hollow stems to 30 m, with 2-lobed, leathery leaves, and 1–few, pink to magenta flowers with a darker centre, 30–55 mm in diameter; the sepals all similar or of 2 types and broadly oval. On sandy beaches, often forming large mats, from the Eastern Cape throughout the tropics.

3 *Ipomoea pellita*

`J F M A M J J A S O N D`

Golden-haired Morning Glory Creeping perennial with robust, bristly stems to 2 m, with oblong to oval leaves, densely golden-haired on the margins, and clusters of magenta flowers at the branch tips, 40–70 mm in diameter; the bracts and sepals very narrow and bristly. Grassland through eastern South Africa.

4 *Ipomoea oblongata*

`J F M A M J J A S O N D`

(=*Turbina oblongata*) **Turbina** Creeping perennial with robust, hairless or bristly stems to 2 m, with narrowly oblong to oval leaves, fringed on the margins, and 1 or more magenta flowers in the axils, 40–70 mm in diameter; the sepals all ± similar, oval or lance-shaped. Very common and widespread in grasslands and savanna through eastern South and subtropical Africa.

5 *Ipomoea holubii*

`J F M A M J J A S O N D`

(=*Turbina holubii*) **Bush Turbina** Multi-stemmed shrub with woody stems to 2.5 m, sprawling over small trees, with rounded to heart-shaped, greyish, silky leaves, and clusters of mauve to pinkish flowers, 40–50 mm in diameter; the sepals greyish and oblong to paddle-shaped. Very conspicuous in savanna and woodland in northern South and tropical Africa.

6 *Ipomoea crassipes*

`J F M A M J J A S O N D`

Leafy-flowered Morning Glory Creeping perennial with hairless or hairy stems to 1 m, with oblong to heart-shaped leaves, and solitary mauve to purple flowers (rarely white with a purple throat) in the axils, 36–60 mm in diameter, with leafy bracts; the sepals dissimilar, the outer pair large and leaf-like. Grassland and savanna through eastern South and tropical Africa.

PLUMBAGINACEAE　　　Plumbago family

Limonium　SEA-PINK, PAPIERBLOM　*(From the Greek name for the plants, leimonion)*

Perennial herbs or shrubs, with *rough, scurfy stems*. Leaves often in rosettes or tufted, spoon- or paddle-shaped. Flowers in flat-topped or rounded panicles made up *of 1-sided spikes*; calyx funnel-shaped or tubular, and ribbed, often *expanded at the top and umbrella-like, persisting and papery in fruit*; petals separate or shortly joined at the base; *styles 5, separate*. Old World maritime and arid regions, mainly Mediterranean: ±350 spp.; South Africa: ±20 spp.

1 *Limonium capense*　J F M A M J J A S O **N D**

Rounded, densely leafy shrublet to 60 cm, with scurfy, minutely pitted, paddle-shaped leaves, 18–25×3–4 mm, and spikes of pink flowers, 17 mm in diameter. Limestone flats around Saldanha Bay on the West Coast.

2 *Limonium perigrinum*　J F M A M J J **A S O N** D

Strandroos, Papierblom Shrub to 1 m, with rough, sometimes pitted, paddle-shaped leaves, 40–80×10–20 mm, at the branch tips, and flat-topped clusters of pink and magenta flowers, 15–17 mm in diameter. Coastal dunes in the Western Cape.

Plumbago　PLUMBAGO, LEADWORT
(Latin plumbum, lead; the plants were a supposed cure for lead poisoning)　Shrubs. Leaves alternate, often *eared at the base*. Flowers in spikes or racemes, *salver-shaped*; calyx tubular, glandular-haired; petals joined in a long tube; *style 5-lobed*. Worldwide: ±24 spp.; South Africa: 5 spp. Used medicinally. *Plumbago auriculata* is widely cultivated.

3 *Plumbago auriculata* Blousyselbos　J F M A M **J J A S O N D**

Shrub or scrambler to 2 m, with oblong or paddle-shaped leaves bearing lobes or ears at the base, and spikes of pale blue, salver-shaped flowers with a slender tube, 20–30 mm long. Thicket and scrub through eastern South Africa. *Plumbago zeylanica* from interior northern South and tropical Africa has petiolate leaves without basal ears, and smaller, white flowers with a tube 25 mm long.

SOLANACEAE　　　Potato family

Solanum　NIGHTSHADE, BITTERAPPEL　*(Latin name for the nightshade)*

Herbs or shrubs, sometimes climbing, thornless or prickly. *Leaves sometimes lobed*. Flowers in *branched clusters*, 5-lobed, white or mauve to purple, *usually saucer-shaped*, sometimes with a cup-shaped tube; the calyx is 5–10-lobed; the *stamens are inserted at the mouth of the tube* and the *pollen is shed through apical pores or slits*. Cosmopolitan, mainly tropical, with many weedy species: ±1 400 spp.; South Africa: 25 native spp. plus many naturalised weeds. Certain species are toxic.

4 *Solanum africanum* Dronkbessie　J F M A M J J **A S O** N D

Scrambling or creeping, semi-succulent shrub to 3 m, the stems squared when young, with lance-shaped to oval leaves to 6 cm long, the lower ones often lobed, and terminal clusters of ±30 white, mauve or purple flowers, 10 mm in diameter; the berries purplish-black. Coastal bush from the Cape Peninsula to KwaZulu-Natal.

❶ *Solanum guineense*

Erect or sprawling shrub to 1.5 m, with softly leathery, oval to elliptical leaves to 7 cm long, and axillary clusters of 1–few mauve to light blue flowers to 18 mm in diameter; the berries yellow, orange or red. Coastal dunes, slopes and river banks from the southwestern to Eastern Cape.

BORAGINACEAE Forget-me-not family

Codon CODON, SUIKERKELK *(Greek kodon, a bell, referring to the flowers)*

Perennial herbs or shrubs, *covered in white or yellowish prickles*. Leaves oval to lance-shaped, prickly. Flowers bell-shaped, *yellow or white, striped on the outside*; calyx 10–12-lobed; *corolla 10–12-lobed; stamens 10–12, attached to the base of the corolla.* Fruit many-seeded, *splitting into 2 halves.* Namibia and southern Africa: 2 spp.; South Africa: 1 sp.

❷ *Codon royenii*

Roughly hairy shrublet to 1.5 m high, covered in straight, white prickles, with elliptical prickly leaves, and large, bell-shaped, cream-coloured to yellow flowers with purple stripes, 25 mm long. Dry and stony slopes in Namibia and northwestern South Africa.

Lobostemon LOBOSTEMON, AGTDAEGENEESBOS

(Greek lobos, lobe; stemon, thread, referring to the stamens being opposite the petal lobes) *Shrubs or shrublets,* usually roughly hairy. *Leaves alternate, scattered on the stems*, often roughly hairy. Flowers *bell- or funnel-shaped, usually blue to pink, rarely red*; stamens either included within the tube or projecting beyond it, with *hairy scales or ridges at their base. Fruit of 4 almost smooth to wrinkled nutlets.* Winter-rainfall South Africa: 30 spp. Decoctions of the plant were used as an antiseptic.

▸ **FLOWERS MOSTLY UP TO 15 MM LONG; STAMINAL SCALES WITH WELL-DEVELOPED LATERAL LOBES**

❸ *Lobostemon glaucophyllus*

Shrublet, 30–80 cm, with hairless branches and narrowly lance-shaped leaves that are hairy only along the midrib and margins, and blue to pink flowers, 7–15 mm long, hairless outside; the staminal scales rounded, with hairy lateral lobes. Sandy flats and slopes in the southwestern Cape.

❹ *Lobostemon dorotheae*

Shrublet, 30–80 cm, with hairless branches, and narrowly lance-shaped leaves that are hairy only along the midrib and margins, and blue to pink flowers, 7–15 mm long, hairless outside, with dissimilar sepals and the stamens protruding and curved at the tips; the staminal scales triangular, with hairy lateral lobes. Rocky sandstone slopes in the southwestern Cape.

❺ *Lobostemon trichotomus*

Shrublet, 30–100 cm, with hairy, somewhat leathery, narrowly lance-shaped leaves, and white or blue flowers, 7–25 mm long, hairless or hairy outside, with dissimilar, velvety sepals; the staminal scales slightly triangular, with lateral lobes. Sandy slopes and flats in the southwestern Cape.

① *Lobostemon echioides* J F M A M J J **A S O** N D

Shrublet, 20–80 cm, with oblong to elliptical, softly silvery-haired leaves, and small, salver-shaped, blue flowers, 7–15 mm long, hairy outside with prominently projecting stamens; the staminal scales triangular, with hairy lateral lobes. Stony slopes and flats in western and southern South Africa.

▶ **FLOWERS MOSTLY >15 MM LONG; STAMINAL SCALES REDUCED TO RIDGES WITHOUT LATERAL LOBES**

② *Lobostemon fruticosus* J F M **A M J J A S O N D**

Douwurmbos, Luisbos Shrublet, 50–80 cm, with hairy, elliptical or oval leaves, and blue to pink flowers, 15–25 mm long, hairy outside; the staminal scales ridge-like, without lateral lobes. Sandy flats on the West Coast and in the southwestern Cape.

③ *Lobostemon montanus* J F M A M J **J A S** O N D

Shrub, 0.8–1.2 m, with silvery-haired, oval to lance-shaped leaves, and blue or turquoise flowers, 15–25 mm long, hairy outside; the staminal scales ridge-like, without lateral lobes. Coastal sandstone in the extreme southwestern Cape.

④ *Lobostemon argenteus* **J F** M A M J **J A S O** N D

Shrublet, 30–60 cm, with hairy, narrowly lance-shaped leaves rolled under along the margins, and blue flowers, 15–25 mm long, in a false spike with 1 flower per bract, hairy outside on the midveins and margins; the staminal scales ridge-like. Shale slopes from the southwestern to Eastern Cape.

***Myosotis* FORGET-ME-NOT** *(Greek myos, mouse; otis, ear, alluding to the shape of the leaves)*

Annual or perennial herbs. Leaves alternate, basal ones petiolate. Flowers blue or white, with a cylindrical tube *usually blocked at the mouth by 5 hairy scales opposite the petals; petals in bud furled like an umbrella; anthers with a sharp point*, concealed within the tube or protruding. *Fruit of 4 smooth, glossy nutlets.* Worldwide temperate: ±100 spp.; South Africa: 7 spp. Used medicinally.

⑤ *Myosotis afropalustris* J F M **A** M J J A S **O** N D

Roughly hairy perennial to 60 cm, with narrow leaves, and branched racemes of pale blue flowers, 5 mm in diameter, with the mouth almost blocked by small yellow scales. Damp soil in scrub and among rocks in the Drakensberg.

Anchusa CAPE FORGET-ME-NOT, OSSETONG

(Greek anchousa, a cosmetic paint obtained from Anchusa tinctoria) Annual or perennial herbs. Leaves mostly basal, narrow, rough. Flowers blue or white, with a cylindrical tube *blocked at the mouth by 5 hairy scales opposite the petals; anthers blunt, concealed within the tube. Fruit of 4 wrinkled nutlets,* rounded on the back with a *rim or wing around the margin.* Africa and Eurasia: ±35 spp.; South Africa: 1 sp.

❶ *Anchusa capensis*

| J | F | M | A | M | J | J | A | S | O | N | D |

Softly or roughly hairy annual to 1 m, with narrowly lance-shaped leaves in a basal tuft, and blue flowers, 5–8 mm in diameter, in coiled racemes that lengthen in fruit. Sandy flats, often in disturbed places and along roadsides, throughout the drier parts of southern Africa.

EUPHORBIACEAE   Euphorbia family

Euphorbia EUPHORBIA, MELKBOS

(Named for Euphorbias, 1st-century physician to King Juba of Mauritania) Trees, shrubs or herbs, often succulent and sometimes spiny, *usually with milky latex.* Leaves often reduced or soon lost. Flowers *unisexual,* minute, arranged in *a small, cup-like, 'false flower' (cyathium) surrounded by 5 fleshy, petal-like glands.* Worldwide, predominantly succulent in drier areas: ±2 000 spp.; South Africa: ±300 spp. The milky sap of several species is highly irritant and toxic, but plants have been used medicinally, and also as birdlime.

❷ *Euphorbia mauritanica*

| J | F | M | A | M | J | J | A | S | O | N | D |

Beesmelkbos, Geelmelkbos Erect shrub to 2 m, with smooth, bright green stems 3–6 mm in diameter, and clusters of false flowers comprising a central male 'flower' surrounded by 5–7 bisexual 'flowers', 7–15 mm in diameter, each surrounded by bright yellow, fleshy glands. Sandy coastal flats from Namibia to Eastern Cape and stony slopes in the drier interior.

❸ *Euphorbia caput-medusae*

| J | F | M | A | M | J | J | A | S | O | N | D |

Medusa's Head, Vingerpol Sprawling shrublet with a rosette of warty, ± club-shaped branches, 10–30 mm in diameter, and large, false flowers, 10–18 mm in diameter, each surrounded by deeply fringed, pale yellow or cream-coloured and green glands. Sandy flats and stony slopes in the southwestern Cape.

CRASSULACEAE   Crassula family

▶ LEAVES OPPOSITE AND ± JOINED AT THE BASE; STAMENS USUALLY 5, AS MANY AS THE PETALS

Crassula **CRASSULA, STONECROP** *(Latin crassus, thick, for the succulent leaves)*

Shrubs, perennials or annuals, mostly succulent, sometimes tuberous. Leaves opposite, often crowded in rosettes, *each leaf pair ± joined at the base around the stem.* Flowers 1–many in simple or branched clusters, variously coloured, mostly white or pink, *usually with 5 petals that are separate or joined at the base into a cup- or urn-shaped tube; stamens usually 5.* Worldwide, mainly drier areas: 300+ spp.; South Africa: ±150 spp. Popular among succulent collectors.

▶ FLOWERS TO 15 MM LONG

① *Crassula columnaris* | J | F | M | A | M | J | J | A | S | O | N | D |

Khakibutton, Sentkannetjie Dwarf succulent perennial or biennial to 10 cm, with pairs of scale-like leaves closely overlapping in 4 rows to form a column, and a round head of tubular, white to yellow flowers, sometimes tinged reddish, 7–13 mm long, highly fragrant at night. Rock pavements and quartz patches in western South Africa.

② *Crassula rupestris* | J | F | M | A | M | J | J | A | S | O | N | D |

Concertina Plant, Sosaties Shrublet to 50 cm, with pairs of fleshy, oval to lance-shaped, greyish or pinkish leaves with red or yellow, horny margins, and short-stalked, rounded clusters of whitish star-shaped flowers tinged pink, 4–6 mm long. Dry stony slopes from Namibia to the Eastern Cape.

③ *Crassula setulosa* | J | F | M | A | M | J | J | A | S | O | N | D |

Dwarf, cushion-forming perennial to 20 cm, with closely packed rosettes of smooth or hairy, elliptical leaves, and clusters of white, cup-shaped flowers often tinged red, 3–4 mm long. Seasonally wet rock faces in the Drakensberg and eastern interior of South Africa.

④ *Crassula vaginata* | J | F | M | A | M | J | J | A | S | O | N | D |

White Stonecrop, Yellow Crassula Erect perennial to 50 cm, with narrow, lance-shaped leaves grading down in size up the stem, smooth or hairy and fringed along the margins with white, club-shaped hairs, and a flat-topped cluster of yellow or white, fragrant, cup-shaped flowers, 4–6 mm long. Moist grassland through eastern South Africa. *Crassula acinaciformis* from northeastern South Africa is larger, with smooth leaf margins, and flowers in winter.

⑤ *Crassula perfoliata* **Red Treasure** | J | F | M | A | M | J | J | A | S | O | N | D |

Perennial to 1.5 m, with fans of closely overlapping, oblong or triangular leaves, flattened from the sides, and flat-topped clusters of white or pink to red, cup-shaped flowers, 5–8 mm long. Dry stony slopes in scrub in eastern South Africa.

▶ **FLOWERS 20–40 MM LONG**

❶ *Crassula coccinea* | J | F | M | A | M | J | J | A | S | O | N | D |

Red Crassula, Keiserkroon Shrublet to 60 cm, with oval to elliptical leaves, and flat-topped heads of bright red, tubular flowers, 30–45 mm long. Sandstone outcrops in the southwestern Cape.

❷ *Crassula fascicularis* Ruiksissie | J | F | M | A | M | J | J | A | S | O | N | D |

Shrublet to 40 cm, with ± erect, narrow to lance-shaped leaves, usually with curved-back hairs on the margins, and flat-topped clusters of tubular, cream-coloured to yellow-green flowers, 20–32 mm long, fragrant at night. Sandstone slopes in the southwestern Cape.

❸ *Crassula obtusa* Klipblom | J | F | M | A | M | J | J | A | S | O | N | D |

Sprawling shrublet to 15 cm, the branches often rooting at the nodes, with oblong to paddle-shaped leaves with hairy margins, and clusters of 1–5 tubular, white flowers tinged pinkish, 30–40 mm long, fragrant at night. Sandstone ledges from the southwestern to Eastern Cape.

▶ **LEAVES SPIRALLY ARRANGED OR OPPOSITE BUT NOT JOINED AT THE BASE; STAMENS 10, TWICE AS MANY AS THE PETALS**

Tylecodon TYLECODON, BANDJIESBOS

(Anagram of Cotyledon, in which the species were first placed) Shrublets, sometimes tree-like with a thick fleshy trunk, the branches covered with knobbly leaf scars. *Leaves spirally arranged, deciduous or dry at flowering.* Flowers on simple or branched peduncles, variously coloured, often nodding, with *5 petals joined in an urn-shaped or cylindrical tube usually longer than the lobes; stamens 10.* Southern Africa: 41 spp. The vernacular name derives from the fanciful resemblance of the tufted leaves to ribbons, or *bandjies*, tied to the end of a stick.

❹ *Tylecodon grandiflorus* | J | F | M | A | M | J | J | A | S | O | N | D |

Rooisuikerblom Succulent, often sprawling, shrublet to 50 cm, with bright green, narrow leaves rolled upwards on the margins, withered at flowering, and arching, ± 1-sided clusters of curved, tubular, reddish flowers, 40–50 mm long. Rocky outcrops along the West Coast.

❺ *Tylecodon paniculatus* Botterboom | J | F | M | A | M | J | J | A | S | O | N | D |

Succulent shrublet with stout, peeling stems to 1.5 m, with bright green, paddle-shaped leaves, absent at flowering, and branched stems of nodding, urn-shaped, yellowish to red flowers, 15–20 mm long. Rocky slopes from Namibia to the southwestern Cape. Hybridises with *Tylecodon wallichii*.

❻ *Tylecodon wallichii* Kandelaarbos | J | F | M | A | M | J | J | A | S | O | N | D |

Succulent shrublet with warty stems to 1 m, with spindle-shaped leaves, absent at flowering, and branched stems of nodding, urn-shaped, greenish-yellow flowers, 15–20 mm long. Dry stony flats and slopes through Namaqualand and the interior of the Western Cape. Hybridises with *Tylecodon paniculatus*.

Cotyledon COTYLEDON, VARKOOR

(From the similarity of the fleshy leaves to the first leaves, or cotyledons, of many plants) Shrubs, mostly succulent.
Leaves opposite, succulent, persistent. Flowers usually nodding on a stout peduncle, red to yellowish, with *5 petals joined in an urn-shaped or cylindrical tube longer than the lobes; stamens 10.* Africa and Arabia: 9 spp., all South Africa. Although toxic, the juice is used medicinally.

❶ *Cotyledon barbeyi*

| J | F | M | A | M | J | J | A | S | O | N | D |

Succulent shrublet to 2 m, with hairless or glandular-haired, paddle-shaped to spindle-shaped leaves, and clusters of nodding, dull reddish, tubular flowers, 20–30 mm long, on stout stems; the tube bulging at the base. Widespread through northeastern South and tropical Africa in scrub.

❷ *Cotyledon velutina*

| J | F | M | A | M | J | J | A | S | O | N | D |

Succulent shrublet to 1 m, with hairless or velvety, paddle-shaped leaves, and clusters of nodding, orange to copper-coloured, tubular flowers, 14–20 mm long; the tube bulging at the base. Thicket and scrub in the Eastern Cape.

❸ *Cotyledon orbiculata* Kouteriebos

| J | F | M | A | M | J | J | A | S | O | N | D |

Succulent shrublet to 1 m, with hairless or velvety, broadly paddle-shaped to spindle-shaped leaves, and clusters of nodding, dull reddish, tubular flowers, 15–40 mm long, on stout stems; the tube cylindrical. Widespread through South and tropical Africa on sandy or stony soils in scrub.

❹ *Cotyledon woodii*

| J | F | M | A | M | J | J | A | S | O | N | D |

Slender, highly branched shrublet to 1 m, with elliptical leaves at the branch tips, and mostly solitary, nodding, reddish, tubular flowers, 15–20 mm; the tube ± cylindrical. Sheltered kloofs and bush margins among rocks in the southern and Eastern Cape.

Kalanchoe KALANCHOE *(The Chinese name for one of the species)*

Shrubs, somewhat woody. Leaves opposite. Flowers erect or spreading, red to yellowish, with *4 petals joined in an urn-shaped or cylindrical tube longer than the lobes; stamens 8.* Old World tropics: ±200 spp.; South Africa: 13 spp.

❺ *Kalanchoe thyrsiflora* White Lady

| J | F | M | A | M | J | J | A | S | O | N | D |

Erect, single-stemmed perennial to 1.5 m, with elliptical leaves covered in a white bloom, tinged red on the margins, and a dense, cylindrical cluster of tubular flowers, 15–20 mm long, with bright yellow petals, fragrant. Rocky grassland and savanna in eastern South Africa.

❻ *Kalanchoe luciae* Northern White Lady

| J | F | M | A | M | J | J | A | S | O | N | D |

Erect, single-stemmed perennial to 1.5 m, with elliptical leaves tinged red on the margins, and a narrow, cylindrical cluster of tubular flowers, 10–15 mm long, with white or pale greenish petals. Rocky grassland and savanna in northeastern South Africa.

239

1 *Kalanchoe rotundifolia* **Kalanchoe** | J | F | M | A | M | J | J | A | S | O | N | D |
Slender, erect perennial to 1 m, with scattered, elliptical leaves, often ± toothed, and an open, flat-topped cluster of orange to red, urn-shaped flowers, 8–15 mm long; the sepals 1–2 mm long. Widespread through Africa in light shade in scrub and savanna. *Kalanchoe crenata* has consistently toothed or scalloped leaves and longer sepals, 3–5 mm long.

ERICACEAE   Erica family

Erica   HEATH, HEIDE   *(From the classical Greek name for heath)*

Shrublets or rarely small trees. *Leaves mostly in whorls of 3 or 4*, small and leathery, often *needle-like, with the margins rolled under*. Flowers in axillary clusters or racemes, variously coloured, cup-shaped to tubular, usually with 4 sepals and a *firm-textured, long-lived, 4-lobed corolla*; stamens usually 8, *pollen shed through small slits or pores in the anthers*. Africa, Madagascar and Europe, mainly southwestern Cape: ±860 spp.; South Africa: ±780 spp. Several species are cultivated.

▶ **ANTHERS PROTRUDING CONSPICUOUSLY**

2 *Erica coccinea* | J | F | M | A | M | J | J | A | S | O | N | D |
Erect, stiff shrub to 1.2 m, with tufts of hairless or shortly fringed, needle-like leaves, 3–8 mm long, and tubular, yellow, orange or red flowers, 6–17 mm long, with conspicuously protruding anthers; bracts sepal-like, pressed against the calyx. Common on rocky flats and mountains in the southwestern and southern Cape.

3 *Erica plukenetii* **Hangertjie** | J | F | M | A | M | J | J | A | S | O | N | D |
Erect shrub to 2 m, with whorls of 3 hairless or shortly fringed, needle-like leaves, 12–20 mm long, and swollen-tubular, white, pink, red, green or yellow flowers, (7–)13–18 mm long, with conspicuously protruding anthers; bracts small, inserted well below the calyx. Widespread in the southwestern Cape.

▶ **ANTHERS HIDDEN OR JUST PROTRUDING; FLOWERS NOT STICKY**

4 *Erica cerinthoides* | J | F | M | A | M | J | J | A | S | O | N | D |
Fire Heath, Rooihaartjie Compact, multi-stemmed shrublet to 30 cm, rarely sparse and to 1.2 m, with whorls of 4–6 hairy, needle-like leaves, 6–16 mm long, and tight clusters of velvety, swollen-tubular, orange-red or creamy-pink flowers, 22–35 mm long. Sandy flats and slopes from the southwestern Cape to northern South Africa, flowering especially after fire.

5 *Erica mammosa* | J | F | M | A | M | J | J | A | S | O | N | D |
Ninepin Heath, Rooiklossieheide Erect shrub to 1.5 m, with whorls of 4 hairless, needle-like leaves, 6–10 mm long, and swollen-tubular, hairless flowers with a narrow mouth and dimples at the base, cream-coloured, pale green, pink, orange or red, 15–25 mm long. Sandy flats and lower mountain slopes in the southwestern Cape.

❶ *Erica vestita* J F M A M J J A S O N D

Trembling Heath, Trilheide Compact, erect shrublet to 1 m, with whorls of 6 slender, delicate, needle-like leaves, 12–35 mm long, and tubular, ± hairy, red, white or pink flowers, 17–25 mm long. Mountain slopes in the southwestern Cape.

❷ *Erica curviflora* J F M A M J J A S O N D

Water Heath, Waterbos Erect, willowy shrub to 1.6 m, with whorls of 4 hairless or hairy, needle-like leaves, 3–7 mm long, and tubular, hairy or hairless, orange, red or yellow flowers, 20–30 mm long. Widespread in damp or wet areas on flats to high altitude, from the southwestern to Eastern Cape.

❸ *Erica perspicua* J F M A M J J A S O N D

Prince-of-Wales Heath, Veerheide Erect shrub to 2 m, with whorls of 4 hairless or hairy, needle-like leaves, 3–7 mm long, and tubular, hairy, white or pink flowers with white tips, 10–20 mm long. Marshy slopes and flats between Betty's Bay and Hermanus.

❹ *Erica pinea* J F M A M J J A S O N D

Erect shrublet to 1.5 m, with whorls of 4 hairless, needle-like leaves, 5–10 mm long, and tubular, hairless, white or yellow flowers with white tips (rarely purplish-pink), with the anthers just protruding from the mouth, 20–24 mm long. Rocky slopes and plateaus in the extreme southwestern Cape.

❺ *Erica patersonii* J F M A M J J A S O N D

(=*Erica patersonia*) **Mealie Heath, Mielieheide** Erect, sparsely branched shrublet to 1 m, with whorls of 4 hairless, needle-like leaves, and dense, cylindrical spikes of tubular, yellow, hairless flowers, 14–18 mm long. Marshy coastal flats in the extreme southwestern Cape.

❻ *Erica sessiliflora* Green Heath J F M A M J J A S O N D

Erect shrub to 2 m, with whorls of 6 hairless or hairy, needle-like leaves, 4–14 mm long, and dense spikes of tubular, hairless, light green flowers, 16–30 mm long, and distinctive, fleshy fruiting inflorescences on the older branches. Moist flats and seeps on lower slopes from the southwestern to Eastern Cape.

▸ ANTHERS HIDDEN; FLOWERS STICKY

❼ *Erica massonii* J F M A M J J A S O N D

Erect shrublet to 1 m, with whorls of 4–6 needle-like leaves with hairy margins, and whorls of tubular, very sticky, red flowers with a green tip, ±25 mm long. Rocky mountain slopes in the southwestern Cape.

❽ *Erica regia* J F M A M J J A S O N D

(=*Erica mariae*) **Elim Heath** Straggling or erect shrublet to 2 m, with whorls of 6 hairless or minutely hairy, needle-like leaves, 6–12 mm long, and tubular, sticky, orange, red or white flowers with reddish tips, 14–24 mm long. Sandy or gravelly coastal flats and limestone hills in the southwestern Cape.

1 *Erica densifolia*

Erect shrub to 1.5 m, with densely packed, needle-like leaves, 3–5 mm long, and tubular, curved, hairy and sticky, red flowers with greenish-yellow lobes, 24–30 mm long. Lower and middle slopes on the mountains of the southern Cape.

2 *Erica discolor* (=*Erica speciosa*)

Dense, multi-stemmed shrublet to 1 m, with whorls of 3 needle-like leaves, 3–10 mm long, and clusters of tubular, hairless and sticky, pink to dark red flowers with pale tips, 18–24 mm long. Flats and lower mountain slopes from the southwestern to Eastern Cape.

3 *Erica versicolor*

Erect or sprawling shrub to over 2 m, with whorls of 4 needle-like leaves, and tubular, hairless and sticky, pink or red flowers with paler or greenish tips, 22–28 mm long. Sandstone slopes in the mountains from the southwestern to Eastern Cape.

4 *Erica abietina*

(=*Erica grandiflora, E. phylicifolia, E. purpurea*) **Red Heath, Rooiheide** Erect shrublet to 1.5 m, with whorls of 4 hairless or hairy, needle-like leaves, 10–40 mm long, and compact spikes of hairless or hairy, slightly sticky, tubular, yellow, orange, red or magenta flowers, (10–)20–35 mm long, sometimes with protruding anthers. Dry lower to middle slopes in the southwestern Cape.

5 *Erica viscaria*

(=*Erica longifolia*) **Sticky Heath** Erect shrublet to 1 m, with whorls of 6 usually hairless, needle-like leaves, 8–12 mm long, and tubular, hairy and sticky, white, yellow, orange, red, purple or greenish (sometimes bicoloured) flowers, 12–22 mm long. Sandy or stony slopes in the extreme southwestern Cape.

PENAEACEAE
Penaea family

Saltera **SALTERA, VLIEËBOSSIE** (*Named for amateur botanist, T.M. Salter, 1883–1969*)

Sparsely branched shrublets with 4-ridged branches. Leaves leathery and overlapping in 4 ranks, oval. Flowers *glossy pink*, the floral tube cylindrical and *20–30 mm long*; the *bracts broader than the leaves and gummy, with minutely fringed margins*. Southwestern Cape in fynbos: 1 sp. The bright pink flowers are pollinated by Orange-breasted Sunbirds.

6 *Saltera sarcocolla*

Sparsely branched shrub with slender stems to 1.5 m, coppicing from a woody base, with leathery, closely overlapping, oval to almost diamond-shaped leaves, and large, glossy pink flowers, 20–30 mm long, in the axils of sticky bracts with fringed margins. Rocky sandstone slopes in the extreme southwestern Cape.

245

THYMELAEACEAE Daphne family

Gnidia   SAFFRON BUSH, SAFFRAAN   *(Derivation uncertain)*

Shrublets or shrubs, often ericoid. Flowers usually in heads surrounded by involucral leaves, sometimes solitary or in short spikes, usually white to yellow; sepals 4 or 5, joined in a long, cylindrical or funnel-shaped tube with *membranous or fleshy petal-scales in the mouth; stamens 8 or 10, in 2 whorls* at different heights within the tube. Mainly Africa, also India: ±130 spp.; South Africa: ±100 spp. The yellow flowers of *Gnidia deserticola* were used as a source of saffron-coloured dye for leather; several species are poisonous but were used medicinally.

▸ FLOWERS 5-LOBED

① *Gnidia anthylloides* Brandbossie   J F M A M J J A S O N D

Shrublet with slender, softly hairy branches to 60 cm, with overlapping, silky, lance-shaped leaves, and heads of 10–20 glossy yellow, 5-lobed flowers, with a silky tube and minute or absent petal-scales in the mouth. Grassland and open scrub in eastern South Africa.

② *Gnidia caffra* Gifbossie   J F M A M J J A S O N D

Multi-stemmed shrublet to 1 m, resprouting from a woody base, with lance-shaped leaves, hairless or silky beneath, and heads of 3–10 glossy yellow, 5-lobed flowers, with a silky tube and 4 small petal-scales in the mouth. Grassland and rock outcrops through eastern South Africa.

③ *Gnidia capitata*   J F M A M J J A S O N D

Gifbossie, Kerriebossie   Multi-stemmed perennial to 70 cm, resprouting from a woody base, with bluish-grey, narrowly lance-shaped leaves, hairless or silky beneath, and distinctly stalked heads of 10–15 glossy mustard-yellow, 5-lobed flowers surrounded by a collar of wider leaves, with a silky tube and 4 small petal-scales in the mouth. Rocky grassland through eastern South Africa.

④ *Gnidia kraussiana*   J F M A M J J A S O N D

Lesser Yellow-head   Multi-stemmed perennial to 70 cm, resprouting from a woody base, with lance-shaped leaves, hairless or silky beneath, and distinctly stalked heads of 15–30 glossy yellow, 5-lobed, scented flowers surrounded by a collar of wider leaves, with a silky tube and 4 large, membranous petal-scales in the mouth. Grassland and coastal scrub through eastern South and tropical Africa.

⑤ *Gnidia deserticola* Saffraan   J F M A M J J A S O N D

Twiggy shrub to 30 cm, with minutely hairy, oblong to oval leaves, and clusters of 5–7 ochre-yellow flowers, with a silky tube developing long, spreading hairs at the base in fruit, and 5 membranous petal-scales in the mouth. Dry stony flats and lower slopes in the interior southwestern and Eastern Cape.

▸ FLOWERS 4-LOBED, WITHOUT PETAL-SCALES IN THE MOUTH

⑥ *Gnidia compacta*   J F M A M J J A S O N D

Alpine Saffron Bush   Gnarled dwarf shrublet forming mats to 30 cm across, with silky, elliptical leaves, and clusters of 4–6 bright yellow flowers, with a silky tube and no petal-scales in the mouth. Rock sheets and basalt ground at high altitude in the Drakensberg.

▸ FLOWERS 4-LOBED, WITH 4 PETAL-SCALES IN THE MOUTH

① *Gnidia juniperifolia*　　　J F M A M J J A S O N D

Erect or spreading shrublet to 50 cm, with scattered, alternate, hairless, narrow to awl-shaped leaves, and pairs of yellow flowers, with a hairless, funnel-shaped tube and 4 membranous petal-scales in the mouth. Mountain slopes in the southwestern Cape. *Gnidia simplex* has clusters of 2–4 flowers.

② *Gnidia pinifolia*　　　J F M A M J J A S O N D

Shrub to 1 m, with crowded, alternate, hairless, needle-like to narrowly oblong, ± sharply pointed leaves, and clusters of ±10 white flowers, scented at night, with a silky tube and 4 fleshy, densely silky petal-scales in the mouth. Sandy flats and lower slopes from the southwestern to Eastern Cape..

③ *Gnidia tomentosa*　　　J F M A M J J A S O N D

Shrub to 1 m, with alternate, oval to lance-shaped leaves, silky when young but hairless later and warty beneath, and clusters of ±6 white flowers, scented at night, with a silky tube and 4 fleshy, hairy, yellow petal-scales in the mouth. Marshy sandstone slopes in the southwestern Cape.

④ *Gnidia oppositifolia* Basbos　　　J F M A M J J A S O N D

Erect, willowy shrub to 3 m, with opposite, hairless, lance-shaped leaves, the uppermost broader and edged with purple, and 4–6 pale yellow flowers, with a velvety tube and 4 fleshy petal-scales in the mouth that turn brown when dry. Sandstone slopes from the southwestern to Eastern Cape.

⑤ *Gnidia geminiflora*　　　J F M A M J J A S O N D

Erect shrub to 60 cm, with opposite, narrowly lance-shaped leaves, hairless or silky above, and pairs of creamy-yellow flowers at the branch tips, scented at night, with a silky tube and 4 fleshy, 2-lobed petal-scales in the mouth. Sandy flats in the Western Cape.

▸ FLOWERS 4-LOBED, WITH >4 PETAL-SCALES IN THE MOUTH

⑥ *Gnidia penicillata*　　　J F M A M J J A S O N D

Shrublet to 40 cm, with narrow leaves, at first with densely fringed margins, and 2–6 bright blue or pink flowers at the branch tips, with a silky tube and 16 minute, hairy petal-scales in the mouth. Marshy flats and lower slopes in the extreme southwestern Cape.

⑦ *Gnidia squarrosa*　　　J F M A M J J A S O N D

Slender, willowy shrub to 2 m, with alternate, narrowly lance-shaped, hairless leaves, and clusters of pale creamy-green flowers tinged with pink, scented at night, with a hairy tube and 8 finger-like petal-scales in the mouth. Coastal limestone and sandy slopes from the southwestern to Eastern Cape.

Struthiola FEATHERHEAD, VEERTJIE, JUFFERTJIE-ROER-BY-DIE-NAG

(Greek strouthos, ostrich, possibly alluding to the feathery or plume-like flower spikes) Shrublets or shrubs, often ericoid. *Flowers solitary in the upper axils, forming long spikes*, usually white or cream-coloured; sepals 4, joined in a long, cylindrical tube with *fleshy petal-scales and tufts of stiff hairs in the mouth*; *stamens 4, in 1 whorl* within the tube. South Africa, mostly southwestern Cape: ±40 spp. The flowers are fragrant at night, and the vernacular name *veertjie* refers either to the plumose flower spikes or, more probably, to the usage of the flexible stems as dusters (*vee*, wipe or sweep).

▸ **PETAL-SCALES 4**

1 *Struthiola striata* Roemanaggie J F M A M J J A S O N D

Shrub to 1 m, hairy on the young branches, with overlapping, lance-shaped leaves, strongly ridged beneath and fringed along the margins at first, and cream-coloured, yellow or pinkish flowers, scented at night, with a hairless tube and 4 petal-scales in the mouth. Flats and lower slopes in the southwestern and southern Cape and in the Eastern Cape.

▸ **PETAL-SCALES 8**

2 *Struthiola ciliata* Stroopbossie J F M A M J J A S O N D

Shrub to 1.5 m, with hairy or woolly branches and pointed, narrowly lance-shaped to oval leaves, usually erect and overlapping, faintly ribbed beneath and fringed on the margins, and cream-coloured, pink or reddish flowers, scented at night, with a sparsely hairy or silky tube and 8 petal-scales in the mouth. Sandy flats and lower slopes in western South Africa.

3 *Struthiola leptantha* J F M A M J J A S O N D

Shrub to 2 m, with densely to sparsely hairy branches and rather blunt, narrowly elliptical leaves, often ± spreading, hairy beneath when young but later hairless, and cream-coloured or reddish flowers, scented at night, with a silky tube and 8 petal-scales in the mouth. Stony flats and mountain slopes in western South Africa.

4 *Struthiola myrsinites* J F M A M J J A S O N D

Erect shrub to 2 m, with hairless and narrowly elliptical leaves, lightly keeled beneath, and white or pale pink flowers, scented at night, with a long, hairless tube and 8 petal-scales in the mouth. Sandstone slopes from the southwestern to the Eastern Cape.

5 *Struthiola dodecandra* Soetgonna J F M A M J J A S O N D

Erect shrub to 80 cm, with wand-like branches, and hairless, lance-shaped leaves, smooth or faintly ribbed beneath, and white or pink flowers with a hairless tube and 8 petal-scales in the mouth. Stony flats and lower slopes in the southwestern and in the southern Cape.

▸ **PETAL-SCALES 12**

6 *Struthiola tomentosa* J F M A M J J A S O N D

Slender shrublet to 60 cm, with woolly branches and overlapping, elliptical to oval leaves, woolly beneath, and yellow to pale orange flowers, vanilla-scented at night, with a woolly tube and 12 narrow petal-scales in the mouth. Mainly lower rocky sandstone slopes in the southwestern and southern Cape. *Struthiola argentea* has leaves with densely fringed margins.

251

CARYOPHYLLACEAE
Carnation family

Dianthus   PINK, ANGELIER
(Greek dios, divine; anthos, flower, probably referring to the heavenly scent) Annuals or softly woody shrublets. Leaves opposite, *narrow and grass-like, hairless, each pair joined at the base into a short sheath.* Flowers 1–few, white, pink or red; sepals *joined into a long calyx tube with several bracts at the base;* petals usually *fringed or toothed.* Old World: ±300 spp.; South Africa: 15 spp. Used in traditional medicine and magic.

❶ *Dianthus basuticus*   J F M **A M J J A** S O N D

Drakensberg Carnation Densely tufted, cushion-forming perennial to 15 cm, with narrow leaves, and pink flowers with finely toothed petals, the blade 10–12 mm long; the calyx 15–20 mm long. Rocky grassland at high altitudes through eastern South Africa. *Dianthus mooiensis* from northeastern South Africa has a narrower, fringed blade, ± twice as long as wide.

❷ *Dianthus zeyheri* Wild Carnation   J F M **A M** J J **A** S O N D

Erect perennial to 80 cm, with narrow leaves, and white to pale pink flowers with fringed petals, the blade 15–25 mm long; the calyx 30–45 mm long. Stony grassland through eastern South Africa.

HYPERICACEAE
St John's Wort family

Hypericum   ST JOHN'S WORT   *(Original Greek and Latin name for the genus)*

Trees, shrubs or herbs. Leaves opposite, dotted or streaked with translucent glands. Flowers 1 or more, *yellow or orange,* the *petals gland-dotted and in bud rolled like an umbrella, short-lived; stamens* numerous, often joined in clusters; *styles 3–5, separate or partially joined.* Worldwide: ±400 spp.; South Africa: 10 spp. Used medicinally.

❸ *Hypericum aethiopicum*   J F M A M J J A S **O N D**

Small St John's Wort Perennial herb to 50 cm, with rounded stems from a woody rootstock, elliptical leaves, and loosely branched clusters of yellow flowers, reddish in bud, 10 mm in diameter, with separate styles. Stony grassland in the southern and eastern South and tropical Africa. *Hypericum lalandii* has stems that are square in cross section.

❹ *Hypericum revolutum*   J F M A M J J **A S O N D**

Curry Bush, Forest Primrose Shrub to 2 m, with elliptical leaves rolled under along the margins, 8–25 mm long, giving off a curry-like smell when crushed, and solitary, deep yellow flowers, 30–40 mm in diameter, with the styles joined together below. Stream banks and forest margins in eastern South and tropical Africa. *Hypericum roeperanum* from Graskop has leaves 40–85 mm long and clusters of flowers.

GENTIANACEAE Gentian family

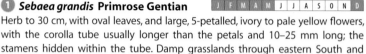

Sebaea **SEBAEA** *(Named for Dutch naturalist, Albert Seba, 1665–1736)*

Annual, biennial or perennial herbs. Leaves basal or scattered along the stem, well-developed or reduced, narrow to round. Flowers *few to many in flat-topped cymes, yellow or white; sepals usually keeled or winged; anthers often tipped with a yellow or black, fleshy gland*. Old World tropics and subtropics, mainly Africa, in damp situations: ±60 spp.; South Africa: ±50 spp. Used medicinally.

▸ STAMENS HIDDEN WITHIN THE FLOWER TUBE

❶ *Sebaea grandis* Primrose Gentian

Herb to 30 cm, with oval leaves, and large, 5-petalled, ivory to pale yellow flowers, with the corolla tube usually longer than the petals and 10–25 mm long; the stamens hidden within the tube. Damp grasslands through eastern South and tropical Africa.

❷ *Sebaea exacoides*

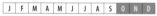

Annual herb to 30 cm, with oval leaves, and 5-petalled, yellow or ivory flowers with orange streaks in the throat, the corolla tube ± as long as the lobes and 6–19 mm long; the stamens hidden within the tube. Moist sandy flats and slopes in southwestern South Africa.

▸ ANTHERS PROTRUDING, TIPPED WITH A LARGE DARK GLAND

❸ *Sebaea spathulata*

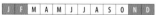

Tufted perennial to 60 cm, with a rosette of oblong or spoon-shaped leaves, and head-like or elongated clusters of narrowly 5-petalled, white flowers, with the corolla tube longer than the petals and 8–11 mm long; the anthers tipped with dark glands. Moist grassy slopes at high altitude in the Drakensberg.

❹ *Sebaea marlothii*

Small, mat-forming perennial, with broad leaves, and almost sessile, 5-petalled, yellow flowers, with the corolla tube ± as long as the petals and 5–10 mm long; the anthers tipped with blackish glands. Alpine meadows in the Drakensberg.

▸ ANTHERS PROTRUDING, TIPPED WITH A SMALL OR YELLOW GLAND

❺ *Sebaea aurea*

Annual herb to 30 cm, with oval leaves, and 4-petalled, yellow or white flowers, with the corolla tube shorter than the petals and 2–6 mm long. Moist sandy flats and slopes from the southwestern to Eastern Cape. *Sebaea albens* has sepals rounded on the back.

❻ *Sebaea sedoides*

Herb with annual stems from a woody root, oval to round leaves, and 5-petalled, yellow flowers, with the corolla tube ± as long as the petals and 3–8 mm long. Grasslands through eastern South and tropical Africa. *Sebaea natalensis* has conspicuously winged sepals.

Chironia CENTAURY, BITTERWORTEL

(After the mythological Chiron, the centaur who studied medicine, astronomy and the arts) Annual or perennial herbs. Leaves scattered along the stem and in a basal rosette but the basal ones sometimes dry at flowering, sometimes reduced. Flowers *few to many in a flat-topped cluster, pink to magenta, rarely white; sepals keeled; anthers sometimes twisted*. Africa and Madagascar, in moist or saline situations: ±30 spp.; South Africa: 16 spp. Used medicinally.

① *Chironia baccifera*

J F **M A M J J A S O N D**

Christmas Berry, Aambeibossie Tangled shrublet to 1 m, with narrow, spreading leaves, and small, pink flowers with a bottle-shaped tube, 3–5 mm long, and a knob-like stigma; the fruits bright red berries. Sandy flats and slopes, often coastal, from Namaqualand to KwaZulu-Natal.

② *Chironia linoides*

J **F M A M J J A S O N D**

Shrublet to 90 cm, with narrow, erect or spreading leaves, and pink flowers with a cylindrical tube, 3–5 mm long, and a knob-like stigma. Sandy or marshy flats and slopes in Namaqualand and the southwestern Cape.

③ *Chironia jasminoides*

J **F M A M J J A S O N D**

Shrublet to 90 cm, with erect, narrow to oval leaves, and pink flowers with a cylindrical tube, 9–14 mm long, and a knob-like stigma. Marshy slopes in the southwestern and southern Cape. *Chironia tetragona* has the sepals joined more than halfway and a thickened collar in the throat of the flower.

④ *Chironia purpurascens*

J F **M A M J J A S O N D**

Purple Chironia Willowy perennial to 80 cm, with scattered, narrow leaves, and magenta-pink flowers with a cylindrical tube, 3–5 mm long, very slender, tapering sepals, a narrowly 2-lobed stigma, and twisted anthers. Damp and marshy grassland through eastern South and tropical Africa. *Chironia palustris* has paler pink flowers with shorter sepals.

Orphium SEA ROSE *(After the mythological Orpheus, without an obvious reason)*

Shrublet with finely velvety stem. Leaves crowded, *leathery and finely velvety*. Flowers *solitary in the upper axils or in clusters, glossy pink*; sepals *rounded on the back*; anthers twisted. Western Cape in coastal areas: 1 sp.

⑤ *Orphium frutescens*

J F **M A M J J A S O N D**

Velvety shrublet to 80 cm, with paddle-shaped, velvety leaves, rolled under at the margins, and 1 or 2 glossy pink flowers in the upper leaf axils, 20–30 mm in diameter; the anthers twisted and open at the tips. Coastal sands and pans in southwestern South Africa.

APOCYNACEAE   Milkweed family

▶ **THICK-STEMMED SHRUBLETS WITH CLEAR, WATERY SAP**

Adenium   ADENIUM   *(From the Arab name for the genus)*

Shrubs or shrublets with swollen, succulent stems, with clear sap. Leaves *alternate, often in tufts, without spine-like stipules.* Flowers clustered at the branch tips, funnel- or bell-shaped, white or pink to purple; *the stamens separate but joined in a cone to the stigma, with long, tail-like tips.* Africa and Arabia: 5 spp.; South Africa: ±4 spp. Plants are toxic and a source of fish and arrow poisons.

① *Adenium multiflorum*

| J | F | M | A | M | J | J | A | S | O | N | D |

Impala Lily, Sabie Star   Sparsely branched shrublet to 3 m, with a swollen stem, leafless at flowering, the leaves paddle-shaped and hairless, and clusters of funnel-shaped flowers, 40–55 mm long, velvety inside, white with dark pink, crinkly margins. Dry woodland among rocks or on sandy flats through northeastern South and tropical Africa. *Adenium swazicum* has pink to purple flowers that are hairless inside.

Pachypodium   PACHYPODIUM   *(Greek pachys, thick; podos, foot, referring to the swollen stem)*

Shrubs or small trees with swollen, succulent stems, with clear sap. Leaves *alternate, often in tufts, with paired stipules transformed into spines.* Flowers clustered at the branch tips, funnel- or bell-shaped, yellow, white or pink to purple; *the stamens separate but joined in a cone to the stigma, with short tips.* Africa and Madagascar: ±20 spp.; South Africa: 5 spp.

② *Pachypodium saundersii*

| J | F | M | A | M | J | J | A | S | O | N | D |

Kudu Lily   Sparsely branched shrublet to 1.5 m, with a swollen stem, the leaves paddle-shaped, hairless or with hairy margins, and clusters of salver-shaped flowers, 25–35 mm long, white flushed with reddish-purple outside. Dry woodland in crevices on rock outcrops through northeastern South and subtropical Africa.

③ *Pachypodium namaquanum*

| J | F | M | A | M | J | J | A | S | O | N | D |

Elephant Trunk, Halfmens   Mostly single-stemmed trees to 3 m, with a tapering, swollen stem covered in spine-tipped warts, topped with a cluster of elliptical, densely velvety leaves with wavy margins, and bell-shaped flowers clustered among the leaves, yellowish-green but reddish inside, 40–55 mm long. Arid, rocky slopes in southern Namibia and the Richtersveld.

▶ **SOFTLY WOODY, LEAFY PERENNIALS WITH WHITE, MILKY SAP**

Raphionacme   RAPHIONACME

(Greek raphis, needle; acme, highest point; the allusion is unclear)   *Sprawling or climbing* perennials *with milky sap.* Leaves opposite, narrow to oval and shortly stalked. Flowers in clusters next to the leaf axils and at the branch tips, *with a short tube,* variously coloured; *the stamens separate but joined to scale-like corona lobes in the mouth of the tube.* Fruit paired or solitary by abortion, narrow. Sub-Saharan Africa and Arabia: 36 spp.; South Africa: ±20 spp. The tubers were used medicinally.

④ *Raphionacme hirsuta*

| J | F | M | A | M | J | J | A | S | O | N | D |

False Gentian   Branched perennial to 30 cm from a tuberous rootstock, with elliptical to oval, hairless or hairy leaves, and clusters of pink to purple flowers, 10–15 mm in diameter, with toothed corona lobes; fruits solitary or paired, erect or spreading, spindle-shaped, 4–11 cm long. Grassland and savanna through eastern South Africa, often flowering after fire.

① *Raphionacme palustris*

Long-horned False Gentian Like *Raphionacme hirsuta* but the corona lobes with long, tail-like tips and the fruits normally solitary, erect and horn-like, 18–27 cm long. Moist and marshy grassland in eastern South Africa.

Pachycarpus **PACHYCARPUS**
(Greek pachys, thick; karpos, fruit, alluding to the large, leathery fruits) *Erect, often robust* perennials *with milky sap.* Leaves opposite, mostly elliptical and shortly stalked. Flowers in *upright or nodding clusters next to the leaf axils* and at the branch tips, star- or cup-shaped with spreading or curving petals; the *corona lobes spread horizontally at the base and are flattened with crests.* Fruit usually solitary by abortion, smooth and crested. Africa: ±30 spp.; South Africa: ±25 spp.

② *Pachycarpus campanulatus*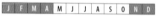

Fairy-bell Pachycarpus Slender-stemmed perennial to 60 cm, with narrow, almost thread-like leaves, with the margins rolled under, hairless or finely haired, and clusters of nodding, spherical, pale green flowers, 20–40 mm in diameter, the petals joined more than halfway; fruit slender. Montane grassland through eastern South Africa, mainly after fire.

③ *Pachycarpus grandiflorus*

Grand Pachycarpus Robust perennial to 60 cm, with elliptical to oval leaves, shortly or softly haired, and tight clusters of nodding, spherical, purple- or brown-spotted flowers, 20–40 mm in diameter, the petals joined less than halfway. Rocky grassland through eastern South Africa.

④ *Pachycarpus schinzianus*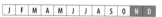

Lilac Pachycarpus Erect perennial to 50 cm, with narrowly lance-shaped leaves, usually with wavy margins, ± hairy, and erect clusters of cup-shaped, pale lilac-tinged flowers with black marks on the corona lobes, 20–40 mm in diameter, the petals joined at the base. Stony grassland in northeastern South Africa.

⑤ *Pachycarpus concolor*

Astral Pachycarpus Erect perennial to 70 cm, with elliptical, rough-haired leaves, and mostly pairs of spreading, shallowly cup-shaped, greenish, yellowish or brown flowers, 20–40 mm in diameter, the petals separate to the base. Open grassland through eastern South Africa.

⑥ *Pachycarpus scaber*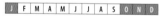

Large White Pachycarpus Erect perennial to 70 cm, with elliptical, ± hairy leaves, and erect clusters of honey-scented, star-shaped, white to cream-coloured flowers, 20–30 mm in diameter, the petals separate to the base and the corona lobes with long, hooked tips forming a cage-like structure. Stony grassland through eastern South Africa.

Xysmalobium MILKWORT *(Greek xusma, fragments; lobos, lobe, referring to the corona lobes)*

Erect, often robust perennials *with milky sap.* Leaves opposite, mostly elliptical. Flowers in *upright or nodding clusters next to the leaf axils or at the branch tips,* star- or cup-shaped with spreading or curving petals; the *corona lobes fleshy without crests or hollows.* Fruits usually solitary by abortion, and smooth or with fleshy projections. Africa: ±40 spp.; South Africa: ±20 spp. Widely used medicinally.

1 *Xysmalobium undulatum* Uzura   J F M A M J J A S O N D

Robust perennial to 1.5 m, with hairy, often wavy leaves, and clusters of cup-shaped, greenish flowers with the petals curled back at the tips and covered with stout white hairs, 10–15 mm in diameter; the fruits large, balloon-like and covered with stout, soft bristles. Grassland and roadsides throughout eastern South and tropical Africa.

Asclepias MILKWEED, WILDE KAPOK *(From the mythical Greek physician, Asklepios)*

Sprawling perennials or annuals *with milky sap.* Leaves opposite, often narrow, ± *coarsely haired.* Flowers in *upright, flat-topped clusters next to the leaf axils and at the branch tips,* star-shaped with spreading petals; the *corona lobes hollowed and boat-shaped.* Fruits usually solitary by abortion, and smooth or with fleshy projections. Africa and America: ±150 spp.; South Africa: ±50 spp. The dried leaves were used medicinally.

2 *Asclepias cucullata*   J F M A M J J A S O N D

Hooded Meadow-star Perennial with slender, sprawling stems to 30 cm from a woody rootstock, narrow, rough-haired leaves, rolled under along the margins, and loose clusters of greyish flowers with a purple and white corona, ±10 mm in diameter. Stony grassland through eastern South Africa, flowering mainly after fire.

Gomphocarpus WILD COTTON, KATOENBOS *(Greek gomphos, club; karpos, fruit)*

Erect perennials or shrublets *with milky sap.* Leaves opposite, narrow or broad. Flowers in *nodding, flat-topped clusters next to the axils and at the branch tips,* star-shaped with spreading petals; the *corona lobes hollowed and boat-shaped.* Fruits usually *inflated and balloon-like,* with fleshy projections. Africa and Asia: ±30 spp.; South Africa: 7 spp.

3 *Gomphocarpus cancellatus*   J F M A M J J A S O N D

Gansiebos Robust shrub to 1.5 m, with rough-haired, leathery, oblong to elliptical leaves, rounded at the base, and nodding clusters of cream-coloured flowers, ±8 mm in diameter; the fruits swollen, with tapering tips. Stony slopes from southern Namibia to Eastern Cape.

4 *Gomphocarpus fruticosus*   J F M A M J J A S O N D

Vleiklapper Slender shrub, 1–3 m, branching mainly from the base, with narrow leaves tapering gradually towards the base, and nodding clusters of cream-coloured flowers, ±8 mm in diameter; the fruits swollen, with tapering tips. Disturbed areas through southern Africa and elsewhere. *Gomphocarpus physocarpus* has willowy, unbranched stems and rounded, balloon-like fruits.

Ceropegia CEROPEGIA

(Greek keros, wax; pege, fountain, alluding to the texture and form of the flowers) Climbers or sprawling perennials with clear sap. Leaves opposite, narrow or broad. Flowers in small clusters outside the leaf axils, tubular to urn-shaped, greenish and often speckled, the *tips of the petals usually closing over the tube like a cage.* Africa to Australasia, mainly arid areas: 160+ spp.; South Africa: ±50 spp.

① *Ceropegia ampliata*

| J | F | M | A | M | J | J | A | S | O | N | D |

Elephantine Ceropegia, Boesmanpyp Succulent, apparently leafless vine, with clusters of 2–4 pale greenish, finely striped, fragrant, flask-shaped flowers, 50–70 mm long. Hot, dry savanna through eastern South and tropical Africa.

Microloma WAX CREEPER, MELKTOU

(Greek micro, small; loma, fringe, referring to the tufts of hairs in the corolla) Climbers or twiggy shrublets with clear sap. Leaves opposite, *narrow,* erect to hanging. Flowers in small clusters outside the leaf axils, tubular to urn-shaped and ribbed, greenish-yellow, *orange, red or pink,* the *petals usually closing the mouth of the tube.* Fruit hanging. Southern Africa, mainly arid areas: 10 spp.

② *Microloma calycinum*

| J | F | M | A | M | J | J | A | S | O | N | D |

Bokhorinkies Twiggy shrublet with drooping, narrowly oblong leaves tapering below, 6–18 mm long, and clusters of tapering, finely haired, pink to red flowers, 5–8 mm long, with pointed petals. Drier, stony and sandy slopes and flats in Namaqualand.

③ *Microloma sagittatum*

| J | F | M | A | M | J | J | A | S | O | N | D |

Bokhorinkies Slender climber or twiggy shrublet with narrowly arrow-shaped leaves lobed below, 7–35 mm long, and clusters of tapering, finely haired, pink to red flowers, 5–11 mm long, with pointed petals. Drier, stony and sandy slopes and flats through Western and Eastern Cape.

④ *Microloma tenuifolium*

| J | F | M | A | M | J | J | A | S | O | N | D |

Kannetjies Slender climber with drooping, narrow or thread-like leaves, 20–70 mm long, densely hairy beneath, and clusters of shiny, hairless, urn-shaped, orange to red flowers, 6–8 mm long, with rounded petals. Moister mountain slopes and stony hills in the southwestern and Eastern Cape.

⑤ *Microloma namaquense*

| J | F | M | A | M | J | J | A | S | O | N | D |

Namakwakannetjies Slender climber with mainly ascending, narrow or thread-like leaves, 10–35 mm long, thinly hairy on both surfaces, and clusters of smooth, bright red flowers, 6–8 mm long, with rounded petals. Rocky slopes west of Springbok in Namaqualand.

Stapelia CARRION-FLOWER, AASBLOM

(Named for Dutch physician, B.J. van Stapel, d. 1636) Clumped or mat-forming, leafless succulents with *velvety stems bearing 4–6 rows of tubercles and clear sap.* Flowers star- to funnel-shaped, usually with *wrinkled and often hairy petals*, yellowish to brownish and foetid. Africa, mainly drier parts of southern Africa: 43 spp.; South Africa: 24 spp. The stench of the flowers attracts carrion flies, which act as pollinators.

❶ *Stapelia hirsuta* Haasoor   J F **M A M J J A S O** N D

Leafless, usually finely hairy succulent with 4-angled stems, 10–20 mm in diameter, forming dense clumps, with reddish to purple flowers, 50–110 mm in diameter, hairless or softly hairy around the centre and along the petal margins, smelling of rotting fish. Stony, often sandstone slopes, in western and southern South Africa.

❷ *Stapelia grandiflora*   J F **M A M J J A S O** N D

Large Stapelia Leafless, finely hairy succulent with 4-angled stems, 20–40 mm in diameter, forming dense clumps, with reddish to purple flowers, 80–220 mm in diameter, softly hairy along the petal margins, smelling of rotting fish. Stony, often sandstone slopes, in southern and south–central South Africa.

❸ *Stapelia gigantea*   **J F M** A M J J A **S O N D**

Giant Stapelia Leafless, often finely hairy succulent with 4-angled stems, 15–35 mm in diameter, forming dense clumps, with pale yellowish-brown to reddish flowers with the tips of the petals drawn into long, tapering points, 125–400 mm in diameter, softly hairy on the inner surface and along the petal margins, smelling of rotting fish. Stony slopes and loamy flats through northeastern South and tropical Africa.

Orbea TOAD PLANT, AASBLOM

(Latin orbis, circle or disc, referring to the thickened ring on the flower) Clumped or mat-forming, leafless succulents with *hairless stems bearing 4 rows of tubercles and clear sap.* Flowers usually >30 mm in diameter, with smooth or wrinkled petals, often with a *thickened ring* in the centre, yellowish to brownish and foetid. Southern Africa, mainly drier parts: 20 spp., all South Africa. The stench of the flowers attracts carrion flies, which act as pollinators.

❹ *Orbea variegata*   **J F M A M J J A S** O **N D**

Mat-forming, leafless succulent with clear sap, the stems 15–25 mm in diameter, with conical tubercles loosely arranged in 4 rows, and large, speckled flowers, 70–110 mm in diameter, with a raised, shallowly bowl-shaped centre surrounded by a ± flat, disc-like rim. Mainly coastal on granite or shale outcrops in the southwestern and southern Cape. *Orbea verrucosa* from the Eastern Cape has a low, warty rim around the centre.

267

➊ *Orbea namaquensis*

J F M A M J J A S **O N** D

Clump-forming, leafless succulent with clear sap, the stems 20–40 mm in diameter, with conical tubercles loosely arranged in 4 rows, and large, speckled flowers, 70–100 mm in diameter, with a raised, deeply bowl-shaped centre surrounded by a doughnut-like rim with the edge curved under. Gravelly flats in Namaqualand.

Hoodia **HOODIA, GHAAP** *(Named for Mr Hood, an early 19th-century collector of succulents)*

Spiny, leafless succulents with *11–17-angled stems bearing spiny tubercles and clear sap*. Flowers saucer- to bowl-shaped, yellowish to brownish and foetid. Africa, mainly drier parts of southern Africa: 13 spp.; South Africa: 9 spp.

➋ *Hoodia gordonii*

J F M A **M** J J **A** S O N D

Muishondghaap, Wolweghaap Spiny, cactus-like, leafless succulent to 1 m, with 11–17-angled stems forming dense clumps, and dish-like, flesh-coloured, somewhat foul-smelling flowers, 40–100 mm in diameter. Dry, stony slopes and flats in Namibia and western South Africa.

BUDDLEJACEAE Buddleja family

Gomphostigma **RIVER STARS, OTTERBOSSIE**
(Greek gomphos, club, referring to the shape of the stigma) Willowy shrublet covered in greyish scales. Leaves narrow. Flowers in racemes, pure white. Africa: 2 spp. Used medicinally.

➌ *Gomphostigma virgatum*

J F **M** A M J J A S O N **D**

Willowy shrublet with smooth or silvery grey-haired, wand-like stems to 2 m, with narrow, opposite leaves and racemes of white flowers with 4 petals, ±12 mm in diameter. Rocky mountain streambeds, often in flowing water, in eastern, central and northwestern South and tropical Africa.

FUMARIACEAE **Fumitory family**

Cysticapnos **AFRICAN FUMITORY**
(Greek kystis, bladder; kapnos, smoke, applied to the allied genus Fumaria*)* *Brittle, climbing or scrambling herbs with watery sap. Leaves divided 2 times* with the *apical leaflet often developed into a tendril. Fruits dry and papery, many-seeded.* Southern Africa: 4 spp.

❶ *Cysticapnos pruinosa*   J F **M** A M J J A S O N **D**

Mountain Fumitory, Wild Fumaria Scrambling perennial herb to 1 m, with finely divided, carrot-like leaves, the uppermost developing tendrils, and long racemes of pink flowers, 7–8 mm long; the fruits diamond-shaped and bent. Mountainsides and boulder beds at high altitude in the Drakensberg. *Cysticapnos cracca* from the southwestern Cape has smaller flowers and straight, lance-shaped fruits.

❷ *Cysticapnos vesicaria* Klappertjies   J F M A M J J **A S O** N D

Straggling annual herb to 1 m, with leaves divided 2 times, the uppermost developing tendrils, and short racemes of pink flowers, 6–7 mm; the fruits swollen and balloon-like. Sandy flats and slopes in western South Africa.

VIOLACEAE **Violet family**

Hybanthus **LADY'S SLIPPER**   *(Greek hybos, hump; anthos, flower, referring to the spur or pouch)*

Erect or trailing herbs or shrublets. Leaves entire or toothed. Flowers usually solitary in the axils *on jointed pedicels,* 2-lipped with the *lower petal much larger than the others, with or without a spur at the base.* Mainly South and Central America: ±100 spp.; South Africa: 4 spp.

❸ *Hybanthus enneaspermus*   J F **M** A M J J A **S O N D**

Pink Lady's Slipper Erect or trailing perennial to 20 cm, with narrow or elliptical, hairless or thinly hairy leaves, and solitary, pink or lilac flowers in the axils, 10–20 mm in diameter, with a very large lower lip pouched at the base. Moist grassland in eastern South Africa. *Hybanthus capensis* has no spur or pouch.

Viola **VIOLET**   *(From the classical Latin name for the genus)*

Erect or trailing herbs or shrublets. Leaves entire or toothed. Flowers usually solitary in the axils, 2-lipped with the *lower petal smaller than the others and spurred or pouched at the base.* Worldwide, mainly northern hemisphere: ±300 spp.; South Africa: 2 spp. The Pansy, *Viola odorata,* and Heartsease, *V. tricolor,* are popular garden plants.

❹ *Viola decumbens* Wild Violet   J F M A M J **J A S O N D**

Slender shrublet to 25 cm, with narrow or thread-like leaves, and solitary, nodding, faintly scented mauve to purple, violet-like flowers in the axils, 10–15 mm in diameter. Damp sandstone slopes in the extreme southwestern Cape.

BALSAMINACEAE Balsam family

Impatiens IMPATIENS *(Latin impatiens, impatient, referring to the explosive bursting of the fruits)*

Brittle-stemmed, semi-succulent annuals or perennials. Leaves mostly toothed, the teeth usually tipped with a slender appendage. Flowers usually solitary in the upper axils, 2-lipped with the *lower sepal spurred and the lower 2 petals 2-lobed.* Worldwide in the tropics and subtropics: ±850 spp.; South Africa: 4 spp. Several species are popular garden plants.

❶ *Impatiens hochstetteri*　　J F M A M J J A S O N D

Wild Balsam　Soft annual or perennial herb to 50 cm, with oval, thinly hairy leaves, scalloped on the margins, and pale pink or mauve flowers with yellow blotches in the centre, 20 mm in diameter, with deeply 2-lobed lower petals and a thread-like spur, (10–)16–24 mm long. Forested patches in damp places, especially along streams, through eastern South and tropical Africa.

❷ *Impatiens sylvicola*　　J F M A M J J A S O N D

Transvaal Balsam　Soft annual or perennial herb to 50 cm, with oval, thinly hairy leaves, scalloped on the margins, and pink to purple flowers with dark red blotches in the centre, 20 mm in diameter, with shallowly notched lower petals and a thread-like spur, 11–18 mm long. Forest margins in damp places in northeastern South and tropical Africa.

MELIANTHACEAE Melianthus family

Melianthus TURKEY BUSH, KRUIDJIE-ROER-MY-NIE
(Greek meli, honey; anthos, flower, referring to the copious nectar) Shrubs, *often foetid.* Leaves with *leafy stipules,* *pinnately divided into unequal-sided, toothed leaflets, with a winged axis.* Flowers in racemes with 1–4 flowers at each node, reddish to greenish, with a *5-lobed calyx, the lobes dissimilar,* sometimes with a pouch at the base, and *with 5 dissimilar petals.* Southern Africa: 6 spp. The flowers are visited by birds for nectar; the plants are toxic but were used as an antiseptic.

❸ *Melianthus comosus*　　J F M A M J J A S O N D

Common Turkey Bush　Shrub to 2 m, with leathery leaves divided into flat, toothed leaflets, thinly hairy above and white-felted beneath, and drooping racemes in the leaf axils with a single flower at each node, the petals red in bud and brown in flower and longer than the sepals; the ovary and fruits velvety. Stony slopes and stream banks from Namibia to the Eastern Cape.

❹ *Melianthus pectinatus*　　J F M A M J J A S O N D

Namaqua Turkey Bush　Shrub to 2 m, with leathery leaves divided into narrow, often toothed leaflets, the margins rolled under, hairless above and felted beneath, and flowers in whorls of 2–4 in erect racemes among the leaves, the petals red in bud, turning brown at maturity and appearing to be withered, 20–25 mm long; the ovary and fruits hairless. Rocky outcrops in Namaqualand. *Melianthus elongatus* from the West Coast has velvety fruits.

❺ *Melianthus major*　　J F M A M J J A S O N D

Honeyflower, Heuningblom　Foetid shrub to 2 m, with large leaves divided into toothed leaflets with a distinct greyish bloom, and robust, pedunculate racemes with 2–4 flowers at each node, the petals reddish and shorter than the maroon to greenish sepals; the ovary and fruits hairless. Mostly along streams in the southwestern and Eastern Cape.

273

POLYGALACEAE
Polygala family

Polygala BUTTERFLY BUSH, ERTJIEBOS

(Greek poly, many; gala, milk; some species were supposed to stimulate milk production) Shrubs or perennials. Leaves small or large. Flowers pink to purple; *the inner 2 sepals are enlarged and petal-like, spreading like wings*; the lower petal is keeled with an apical crest and the *lateral 2 petals are usually reduced and sometimes 2-lobed. Fruit dry and flattened.* Worldwide in temperate and warm countries: ±600 spp.; South Africa: ±88 spp. Some species are cultivated.

① *Polygala fruticosa*

| J | F | M | A | M | J | J | A | S | O | N | D |

Shrub to 2 m, with opposite, ± heart-shaped leaves, and short racemes of pale greenish or purple flowers, 10–15 mm long, with deeply 2-lobed lateral petals. Stony slopes from the southwestern Cape to KwaZulu-Natal.

② *Polygala myrtifolia* Septemberbos

| J | F | M | A | M | J | J | A | S | O | N | D |

Sprawling or erect shrub to 2 m, often velvety on the young stems, with narrow or elliptical leaves, the margins sometimes rolled under, and short racemes of purple flowers, 15–20 mm long, with 2-lobed lateral petals. Rocky slopes from the southwestern to Eastern Cape.

③ *Polygala virgata*

| J | F | M | A | M | J | J | A | S | O | N | D |

Willowy, single-stemmed shrub branching above, sometimes to 2 m, only leafy at the top, mostly with elliptical leaves, and slender racemes of purple flowers, 10–15 mm long, with unlobed lateral petals. Margins of forest and bush clumps through eastern South and tropical Africa.

Muraltia PURPLE GORSE, KROESBOSSIE

(Named for 16th-century Swiss botanist, J. von Muralt) Mainly *ericoid* shrublets or shrubs. Leaves small and often sharply pointed or spine-tipped, often in tufts. Flowers purple, pink or white, with all 5 sepals similar in size or the inner 2 sepals larger and petal-like; the lower petal is keeled with an apical crest and the lateral 2 petals are narrow. *Fruit dry, usually with 4 horns or warts, or rounded and fleshy.* Africa, mainly southwestern Cape: ±120 spp., all South Africa. The fleshy-fruited species were used medicinally, and the fruits are edible. The vernacular name *kroesbossie* derives from the tufted, curly arrangement of the leaves of many of the species, suggestive of the hair of the Khoisan people.

④ *Muraltia spinosa*

| J | F | M | A | M | J | J | A | S | O | N | D |

(=*Nylandtia spinosa*) **Nylandtia, Skilpadbessie** Stiffly-branched, thorny shrub to 1 m, with small, oblong leaves, and purplish or pink and white flowers with the inner 2 sepals large and petal-like, 8 mm long; the fruits red or orange and fleshy. Sandy flats and rocky slopes in the southwestern and Eastern Cape. *Muraltia scoparia* is a large, willowy shrub to 3 m.

⑤ *Muraltia heisteria*

| J | F | M | A | M | J | J | A | S | O | N | D |

Erect shrub with wand-like stems to 1.5 m, closely covered in tufts of hard, spine-tipped leaves, and with small, purple and white flowers, 5–8 mm long; the fruits with long, slender horns. Rocky, mainly sandstone slopes in fynbos in the southwestern Cape.

FABACEAE
Pea family

▶ **SUBFAMILY CAESALPINIOIDEAE** FLOWERS IRREGULAR BUT NOT SWEETPEA-LIKE

Chamaecrista DWARF CASSIA
(Greek chamai, on the ground; Latin crista, crest, alluding to the plants' herbaceous nature) Mostly perennial or annual herbs. Leaves *pinnately compound, leaflets many, often with wart-like nectaries on the axes.* Flowers in racemes in the leaf axils, irregular, *yellow;* stamens all similar or slightly dissimilar, *opening by a pore or short slit.* Pods papery or leathery. Widespread through the tropics: ±250 spp.; South Africa: 9 spp.

1 *Chamaecrista comosa*

J F **M A M J** J **A S** O **N** D

Trailing Dwarf Cassia Sprawling perennial herb with stems to 50 cm from a woody rootstock, pinnate leaves of 11–35 pairs of narrow leaflets, with the leaf axis grooved above, and loose clusters of yellow flowers with a reddish calyx, ±20 mm in diameter. Stony and rocky grassland, often roadsides, through eastern South and tropical Africa. *Chamaecrista mimosoides* (annual) and *C. plumosa* (perennial) have crested leaf axes.

Bauhinia BAUHINIA   *(Commemorating the 16th-century Bauhin brothers in the paired leaflets)*
Trees or shrubs. Leaves *simple, usually 2-lobed.* Flowers solitary or in racemes in the leaf axils, irregular, yellow, white, magenta or red; *calyx spathe-like, splitting along 1 side;* stamens 10, all fertile or some sterile. Pods woody or papery. Widespread through the tropics: ±150 spp.; South Africa: 6 spp.

2 *Bauhinia galpinii*

J F **M** A **M** J J A S O **N** D

Pride-of-De Kaap, Vlam-van-die-vlakte Sprawling shrub to 5 m, with broad, deeply notched leaves, and axillary clusters of dull reddish flowers with stalked petals, 40 mm in diameter, on brown, velvety pedicels. Scrambling among bushveld and scrub through eastern South and subtropical Africa.

▶ **SUBFAMILY PAPILIONOIDEAE** FLOWERS SWEETPEA-LIKE
▶▶ LEAVES PINNATELY COMPOUND, NOT GLAND-DOTTED; FLOWERS PINK OR RED

Lessertia BALLOON PEA, BLAASERTJIE
(Named for French businessman and amateur botanist, Jules Lessert, 1773–1847) Herbs or shrubs. Leaves *pinnately compound, leaflets many;* stipules present. Flowers in racemes in the leaf axils, *pink to purple or red;* calyx with slightly dissimilar lobes; stamens joined, with the upper one separate, all similar. *Pods membranous, flat or ± swollen, opening at the tip;* seeds rough. Southern and eastern tropical Africa: ±55 spp.; South Africa: ±50 spp. The leaves of *Lessertia frutescens* are widely used as a tonic under the name *Sutherlandia.*

3 *Lessertia perennans*

J **F M A M J J A S** O **N** D

Erect shrublet to 1 m, with pinnate leaves of 8–10 pairs of oblong leaflets, and loose racemes of pink flowers, ±6 mm in diameter, on peduncles longer than the leaves; pods elliptical, flat and papery. Grassy stream banks and boulder beds through eastern South Africa.

❶ *Lessertia frutescens*   J F M A M J **J A S O N D**

(=*Sutherlandia frutescens*) **Sutherlandia, Kankerbos** Erect or sprawling shrublet to 1 m, with pinnate leaves of 6–10 pairs of oblong to heart-shaped leaflets, hairless or thinly hairy above, and racemes of red flowers, 25–35 mm long, with very small wing petals hidden within the calyx; pods large, swollen and papery. Stony and sandy places, often along roadsides, throughout southern and central South Africa. *Lessertia canescens* from coastal sands in the southwestern Cape has leaflets with dense silvery hairs on both surfaces.

Indigofera **INDIGO**   (Greek *indikos, indigo;* Latin, *feros, bearing;* Indigofera tinctoria *is the source of the dye*)

Herbs or shrubs, mostly covered with forked hairs. Leaves pinnately (1–)3(–9)-foliolate, sometimes reduced to scales; stipules present. Flowers in axillary or terminal racemes, *pink, petals often deciduous, the keel petals each with a pouch or spur on the side and a fringed upper margin;* calyx with ± similar lobes; stamens joined with the upper one separate, the *anthers distinctly pointed.* Pods narrow or broad. Worldwide in the tropics and subtropics: ±730 spp.; South Africa: 200+ spp.

▶ **TRAILING OR SPRAWLING PERENNIALS WITH 3 LEAFLETS PER LEAF**

❷ *Indigofera heterophylla*   J **F** M A **M** J J A S O N D

Sprawling shrublet to 1 m, with pinnately or digitately 3-foliolate leaves of lance-shaped to oval, thinly hairy leaflets, and stalked racemes of orange-pink to reddish-purple flowers, ±10 mm in diameter; calyx thinly hairy with awl-like lobes up to 3 times as long as the tube. Stony flats and slopes from Namaqualand to the Eastern Cape.

❸ *Indigofera procumbens* Lewertjie   J F M A M **J J A S O** N D

Spreading or trailing perennial to 10 cm, with the stems often running underground, with digitately 3-foliolate leaves of oval or rhomboidal leaflets, hairless or thinly hairy above, and stalked racemes of orange, copper, rose, or purple flowers, ±10 mm in diameter. Sandy coastal flats in the southwestern Cape.

▶ **PERENNIALS OR SHRUBLETS WITH 5–17 LEAFLETS PER LEAF**

❹ *Indigofera brachystachya*   J F M A M J J A S **O** N D

Dense, mass-flowering shrub to 1.5 m, with ± stalkless, pinnate leaves of 3–5 pairs of narrowly wedge-shaped leaflets, densely grey-haired beneath, with the margins strongly rolled under, and dense, short-stalked racemes shorter than the leaves, of ± sessile, mauve to pink flowers, ±8 mm in diameter. Coastal fynbos and limestone in the southwestern Cape.

❺ *Indigofera hedyantha*   J **F** M A M J J A S **O N** D

Black-bud Indigo Shrublet to 90 cm, with pinnate leaves of 3–5 pairs of narrowly elliptical, thinly hairy leaflets, and slender-stalked racemes, longer than the leaves, of reddish-pink flowers, ±10 mm in diameter. Rocky grassland and boulder beds through eastern South and tropical Africa.

❻ *Indigofera hilaris*   J F M A M J **J A S O N D**

Red Bush Indigo Perennial with erect, annual stems to 60 cm from a woody rootstock, with pinnate leaves of 1–4 pairs of narrowly elliptical, silky leaflets, and short-stalked racemes, scarcely longer than the leaves, of reddish-pink flowers, ±6 mm in diameter. Grassland through eastern South and tropical Africa, flowering especially after fire.

① *Indigofera oxytropis* Keeled Indigo | J | F | M | A | M | J | J | A | S | **O** | **N** | **D** |

Perennial with creeping stems from a woody rootstock, with pinnate leaves of 5–8 pairs of elliptical leaflets, silky beneath, and stalked racemes, longer than the leaves, of reddish-pink flowers, ±6 mm in diameter. Grassland in northeastern South Africa.

Pseudarthria VELVET BEAN
(Greek pseudes, false; arthria, joint, referring to the imperfectly segmented fruits) Herbs or shrubs. Leaves *pinnately 3-foliolate*; stipules present. *Flowers in panicles, pink*; calyx 2-lipped; stamens joined, with the upper one separate, all similar. *Pods oblong, woody, jointed but not breaking into segments.* Africa and Asia: ±6 spp.; South Africa: 1 sp.

② *Pseudarthria hookeriana* | J | F | M | A | M | J | J | A | S | **O** | **N** | **D** |

Bug-catcher Bush Erect shrub to 3 m, with 3-foliolate leaves of leathery leaflets, rough above, pale and velvety beneath, and panicles of bright pink flowers, ±8 mm in diameter, with a velvety brown or mauve calyx; pods narrowly oblong, jointed and glandular-haired. Damp hillsides and forest margins through eastern South and tropical Africa.

Desmodium DESMODIUM *(Greek desmos, bundle, referring to the joined stamens)*
Herbs or shrubs. Leaves *pinnately (rarely digitately) 3-foliolate*; stipules present. *Flowers in panicles, pink, purple or orange*; calyx 2-lipped; stamens joined, with the upper one separate, all similar. *Pods oblong, woody, jointed and breaking into segments.* Worldwide in the tropics: ±300 spp.; South Africa: 10 spp.

③ *Desmodium repandum* | J | F | M | A | M | J | J | A | S | O | N | **D** |

Orange Desmodium Scrambling shrublet to 1.5 m, with 3-foliolate leaves of oval or diamond-shaped, dark green leaflets with a shining blotch on the upper surface, and sparse panicles of orange flowers, ±14 mm in diameter; pods narrowly oblong, glandular-haired, woody and breaking into segments. Bush and forest margins through eastern South and tropical Africa.

Tephrosia TEPHROSIA *(Greek tephros, ashen, referring to the grey-haired leaves of many species)*
Herbs or shrubs. Leaves *pinnately or digitately 3–5-foliolate, with fine, closely parallel veins reaching the margins*; stipules present. *Flowers in racemes in the leaf axils, magenta or rarely orange*; calyx 2-lipped; stamens joined, with or without the upper one separate, all similar. *Pods oblong, woody.* Widespread in the tropics: 400+ spp.; South Africa: ±50 spp. The roots of *Tephrosia macropoda* were used as a fish poison.

④ *Tephrosia grandiflora* | J | F | M | A | M | J | J | **A** | **S** | O | N | D |

Large-flowered Tephrosia Shrublet to 1.5 m, with large, oval stipules, pinnate leaves of 5–7 pairs of elliptic to oblong, many-veined leaflets, and long-stalked, rounded racemes of pink or magenta flowers, 15–20 mm in diameter. Scrub and forest margins through eastern South Africa.

⑤ *Tephrosia macropoda* | J | F | M | A | M | J | J | A | S | **O** | **N** | **D** |

Fish Bean, Visboontjie Creeping, mat-forming perennial, with large, oval stipules, long-petioled, pinnate leaves of 2–3 pairs of elliptic to oblong, many-veined leaflets, and long-stalked, rounded racemes of pink or magenta flowers, 15–20 mm in diameter. Open and rocky grassland through eastern South Africa.

▸▸ CLIMBERS OR CREEPERS WITH PINNATELY 3-FOLIOLATE LEAVES, USUALLY WITH ASYMMETRICAL LATERAL LEAFLETS; FLOWERS PINK OR MAUVE, LARGE AND SWEETPEA-LIKE

Dipogon CAPE SWEETPEA, BOSKLIMOP

(Greek di, two; pogon, beard, referring to the bearded style) *Perennial climber.* Leaves pinnately 3-foliolate with diamond-shaped leaflets, *the lateral leaflets asymmetrical*; stipules present. Flowers in short racemes on long peduncles, magenta; calyx with *very short, blunt lobes, all similar*; stamens joined in a tube with the upper one separate; *style S-shaped, thickly bearded on the upper side near the tip.* Pods oblong. Western and Eastern Cape: 1 sp.

❶ *Dipogon lignosus* J F M A M J J A S O N D

Woody climber, with pinnately 3-foliolate leaves with diamond-shaped leaflets, greyish beneath, and long-stalked racemes of magenta or pink flowers, 15–20 mm in diameter. Scrub or forest margins from the southwestern to Eastern Cape.

Vigna COWPEA *(Commemorating the classical Greek commentator of this name)*

Annual or perennial climbers or creepers. Leaves pinnately 3-foliolate with diamond-shaped leaflets, *the lateral leaflets asymmetrical*; stipules present. Flowers in short racemes on long peduncles, shades of pink to purple; calyx 2-lipped; *keel twisted*; stamens joined in a tube with the upper one joined or separate; *style coiled, thickly bearded on the upper side near the tip, with the stigma lateral.* Pods narrow or cylindrical. Worldwide in the tropics: ±160 spp.; South Africa: ±18 spp. The seeds and tubers are edible.

❷ *Vigna vexillata* Wild Sweetpea J F M A M J J A S O N D

Trailing creeper, with 3-foliolate leaves of narrow to oval leaflets, not lobed at the base, and long-stalked, greenish flowers flushed purple, ±25 mm in diameter, with a twisted keel. Grassland and open woodland through eastern South and tropical Africa.

❸ *Vigna unguiculata* Wild Cowpea J F M A M J J A S O N D

Trailing creeper, with 3-foliolate leaves of narrow to oval leaflets, bulging or lobed at the base, and long-stalked, greenish flowers flushed purple, ±25 mm in diameter, with a twisted keel. Grassland and woodland through eastern South and tropical Africa.

Canavalia CANAVALIA *(From the Malabar name for the genus)*

Perennial creepers or lianas. Leaves pinnately 3-foliolate with elliptical leaflets; stipules small, deciduous. Flowers in racemes in the leaf axils, magenta; calyx 2-lipped; keel sometimes twisted; stamens joined in a tube. *Pods large*, woody, oblong. Widespread in the tropics: ±50 spp.; South Africa: 6 spp.

❹ *Canavalia rosea* Beach-bean J F M A M J J A S O N D

Robust climber or creeper with stems to 10 m, with 3-foliolate leaves of broadly oval leaflets, and racemes of scented, magenta flowers with a yellow eye, ±25 mm in diameter; pods 11–20 cm long. Coastal dunes and estuaries throughout the tropics.

Otholobium OTHOLOBIUM, SKAAPBOSTEE

(Greek otho, to burst; lobos, lobe, alluding to the pods appearing to push out of the calyx) Shrubs or perennials.

Leaves 3-foliolate, *dotted with black or translucent glands*; stipules streaked with glands and hairy, sometimes joined to the base of the petiole. Flowers ± sessile, in 2s or 3s in the axil of a single bract and aggregated in spikes, white, pale blue or yellow; calyx 2-lipped; stamens joined in a tube with the upper one separate, all similar. Pods *1-seeded, glandular-haired* and swollen. South Africa: ±60 spp. Some species have been used medicinally.

❶ *Otholobium bracteolatum*

J F M A M J J A S O N D

Sprawling shrub to 2 m, with digitately 3-foliolate of glandular, wedge-shaped leaflets with fringed, glandular stipules, and dense spikes of blue, white and violet flowers, ±6 mm in diameter. Coastal slopes and flats from the southwestern to Eastern Cape.

Psoralea BLUE PEA, BLOUKEURTJIE

(Greek psoraleos, warty, referring to the glands on the plants) Shrubs or small trees. Leaves 3-foliolate or pinnate, sometimes reduced, *dotted with black or red glands*; stipules clasping the stem and joined to the base of the petiole. Flowers in groups of 1–5, each in the axil of a lobed cupule that is itself enclosed within 2 bracts, usually blue or lilac with a dark-tipped keel; calyx ± 2-lipped; stamens joined in a tube, mostly with the upper one separate. *Pods 1-seeded and glandular, included within the calyx at maturity.* Southern Africa: ±50 spp.

❷ *Psoralea aculeata*

J F M A M J J A S O N D

Tree-like shrub to 2 m, with 3-foliolate leaves of leathery, wedge-shaped leaflets to 8 mm long, with downcurved tips, and clusters of mauve and white flowers on pedicels to 13 mm long; calyx hairless. Rocky slopes in fynbos in the extreme southwestern Cape.

❸ *Psoralea pinnata*

J F M A M J J A S O N D

Willowy tree to 4 m, with 7–9-foliolate leaves of thread-like leaflets to 50 mm long, with small stipules, and clusters of blue flowers on pedicels up to 25 mm long; calyx hairless or hairy. Mountain fynbos, forest margins and riverbeds, in the extreme southwestern Cape. *Psoralea affinis* from the southwestern and southern Cape has a distinctly black-haired calyx.

❹ *Psoralea aphylla* Fonteinbos

J F M A M J J A S O N D

Erect, broom-like shrub to 4 m, with drooping branches, with very small, scale-like leaves, 5–17 mm long, present only on the young branches, and clusters of blue and white flowers; calyx hairless. Mountain and lowland fynbos, often along stream banks, in the southwestern Cape.

▶▶ LEAVES DIGITATELY OR PINNATELY 3-FOLIOLATE, SOMETIMES TUFTED, NEVER GLAND-DOTTED

Trifolium CLOVER *(Latin tri, three; folium, leaf)*

Annual or perennial herbs. Leaves digitately 3–9-foliolate, *leaflets often minutely toothed; stipules frequently joined to the base of the petiole.* Flowers in pedunculate spikes or heads variously coloured, *drying and remaining on the fruit; stamens joined in a tube with the upper separate, widened at the tips,* all similar. Pods short, hidden within the dried flower. Worldwide: ±250 spp.; South Africa: 3 spp.

▶ FLOWERS 5-LOBED

❶ *Trifolium burchellianum*   J F M **A M J J A** S O N D

Burchell's Clover Creeping perennial herb to 60 cm, ± hairless, with 3-foliolate leaves of broadly wedge- or heart-shaped, finely toothed leaflets, and heads of purple flowers. Grassland and forest margins through southern and eastern South and tropical Africa.

❷ *Trifolium africanum* African Clover   J F **M A M J J A S O N** D

Creeping perennial herb to 60 cm, ± hairy, with 3-foliolate leaves of narrowly wedge-shaped, finely toothed leaflets, and heads of reddish flowers. Moist and marshy grassland through eastern South Africa.

Rhynchosia RHYNCHOSIA *(Greek rhynchos, beak, referring to the style)*

Twining or creeping perennials. Leaves *pinnately 3-foliolate*, rarely reduced to a single leaflet; stipules present. *Flowers in pedunculate racemes in the leaf axils,* yellow to orange; calyx lobed, with all lobes similar; stamens joined in a tube split down the top, *with the upper one separate and curved or swollen at the base,* all similar. *Pods short and flattened, hairy, 2-seeded; seed funicle attached in the middle of the hilum.* Widespread in the tropics: ±200 spp.; South Africa: ±70 spp. Used medicinally.

❸ *Rhynchosia villosa* Giant Rhynchosia   J F M A M J J A **S O N D**

Robust, trailing herb, with 3-foliolate leaves of broadly oval leaflets, and long-stalked racemes of yellow flowers with red veins, ±15 mm in diameter, in the axils of small, papery brown bracts. Grassland in eastern South Africa.

❹ *Rhynchosia cooperi*   J **F M** A M J J A S **O N** D

Cooper's Rhynchosia Trailing herb, with 3-foliolate leaves of broadly oval leaflets, and long-stalked racemes of yellow flowers, ±15 mm in diameter. Grassland in eastern South Africa.

❺ *Rhynchosia monophylla*   J F M A M J **J A S O N** D

Trailing herb, with mainly 1-foliolate leaves of a solitary, rounded leaflet, and mostly solitary, yellow and orange flowers in the axils, ±15 mm in diameter. Rocky grassland in northeastern South and tropical Africa.

Eriosema ERIOSEMA

(Greek erion, woolly; sema, a token, referring to the shaggy calyx and fruit in many species) Perennial herbs or shrublets, *most erect*. Leaves *pinnately 3-foliolate*, rarely reduced to a single leaflet; stipules present. *Flowers in pedunculate racemes in the leaf axils*, yellow to orange; calyx lobed, with all lobes similar; stamens joined in a tube split down the top, *with the upper one separate and curved or swollen at the base*, all similar. *Pods short and flattened, hairy, 2-seeded; seed funicle attached at one end of the long hilum*. Widespread in the tropics: ±130 spp.; South Africa: ±36 spp. Used medicinally.

❶ *Eriosema distinctum*

J F M **A M** J J **A S O N D**

Scarlet Eriosema Clumped perennial with sprawling annual stems from a woody rootstock, with 3-foliolate leaves of elliptical to oval leaflets, and racemes of orange to red flowers, ±14 mm in diameter. Grasslands through eastern South Africa, flowering after fire or in overgrazed pastures.

❷ *Eriosema cordatum*

J F M A M J J A S O N D

Heart-leaved Eriosema Perennial with trailing annual stems from a woody rootstock, with 1–3-foliolate leaves of oval leaflets, and racemes of down-facing, yellow or reddish flowers, ±10 mm in diameter. Grasslands through eastern South Africa. Commonly hybridises with *Eriosema salignum*.

❸ *Eriosema kraussianum*

J F M A M J J A **S O N** D

Pale Yellow Eriosema Perennial with clumps of erect, unbranched stems from a woody rootstock, with 3-foliolate leaves of thinly silky, narrowly elliptical leaflets, green on both surfaces, and with brown, papery stipules, and racemes of down-facing, pale yellow flowers, ±12 mm in diameter; calyx rusty-haired. Stony grassland through eastern South Africa, flowering well after fire.

❹ *Eriosema salignum*

J F M **A M J** J **A S O N D**

Willow-leaved Eriosema, Brown Bonnets Perennial with ± solitary, slender, erect, ± unbranched stems, with 3-foliolate leaves of narrowly elliptical leaflets, green and ± hairless above but densely silver-haired beneath, and with large, brown papery stipules, and racemes of down-facing, yellow to orange flowers, ±12 mm in diameter; calyx silvery silky. Grassland through eastern South Africa.

❺ *Eriosema psoraleoides*

J F M **A M** J J **A S O N D**

Shrubby Eriosema Shrublet with branched stems to 2 m, with 3-foliolate leaves of narrowly elliptical leaflets, green and ± hairless above but densely silver-haired beneath, with small, leafy stipules, and racemes of down-facing, yellow flowers, ±12 mm in diameter; calyx greyish. Grassland and woodland through eastern South and tropical Africa.

Argyrolobium LIQUORICE BEAN

(Greek argyros, silver; lobos, pod, referring to the silver-haired pods of some species) Perennial herbs, *sometimes turning black when dry.* Leaves digitately 3-foliolate; stipules present, sometimes joined. *Flowers in racemes that are terminal or opposite the leaves,* yellow becoming reddish; *calyx 2-lipped with lower 3 sepals ± joined; stamens joined in a tube slit down the top, of 2 types.* Pods narrow. Africa: ±70 spp.; South Africa: ±50 spp.

❶ *Argyrolobium baptisioides*

| J | F | M | A | M | J | J | A | S | O | N | D |

(=*Argyrolobium sandersonii*) **Common Liquorice Bean** Bushy perennial with annual stems to 60 cm from a woody rootstock, with 3-foliolate leaves of hairless, narrowly elliptical leaflets, and elongated racemes of bright yellow, scented flowers, 10 mm in diameter, with narrowly wedge-shaped flag petals. Grassland in southeastern South Africa, flowering especially after fire.

❷ *Argyrolobium robustum*

| J | F | M | A | M | J | J | A | S | O | N | D |

Large Liquorice Bean Bushy perennial with annual stems to 60 cm from a woody rootstock, with 3-foliolate leaves of broadly elliptical, hairless leaflets, and cylindrical racemes of scented, pale yellowish and orange flowers with darker veins, 10 mm in diameter, with rounded flag petals. Grassland in eastern South Africa, flowering especially after fire.

Lebeckia LEBECKIA *(Commemorating H.J. Lebeck, an 18th-century botanist, traveller and plant collector)*

Shrubs or herbs, sometimes spiny. Leaves usually digitately 3-foliolate, rarely reduced to a single leaflet, leaflets thread-like to oval; *stipules absent.* Flowers in pedunculate racemes, yellow; *calyx lobed, with all lobes similar; stamens joined in a tube split down the top,* of 2 types. Pods narrow, many-seeded. Southern Africa: ±45 spp.

▶ LEAVES UNDIVIDED, THREAD-LIKE

❸ *Lebeckia plukenetiana*

| J | F | M | A | M | J | J | A | S | O | N | D |

Sprawling shrublet to 40 cm, with unjointed, thread-like leaves, and racemes of yellow flowers, 10 mm in diameter, with the keel shorter than the standard petal and the calyx lobes shorter than the tube. Sandy flats along the West Coast, flowering especially after fire.

❹ *Lebeckia sepiaria*

| J | F | M | A | M | J | J | A | S | O | N | D |

(=*Lebeckia simsiana*) **Wildeviolette** Spreading shrublet to 50 cm, with jointed, thread-like leaves, and racemes of yellow flowers, 10 mm in diameter, with the keel as long as or longer than the standard petal and the calyx lobes shorter than the tube; pods spongy, up to 40 mm long. Sandy flats in the southwestern Cape.

▶ LEAVES 3-FOLIOLATE

❶ *Lebeckia sericea*

J F M A M J **J A S** O N D

Shrub to 1.5 m, with 3-foliolate leaves of silky, elliptical leaflets, and racemes of bright yellow or cream-coloured flowers with a silky calyx and pods. Dry stony slopes and coastal thicket in Namaqualand and the southwestern Cape.

❷ *Lebeckia cytisoides*

J F M A M J **J A S O N D**

Shrub or small tree to 2 m, with 3-foliolate leaves of silky, elliptical leaflets, and racemes of bright yellow flowers with a hairless calyx and pods. Stony slopes in the southwestern Cape.

Crotalaria RATTLE POD *(Greek krotalon, castanet, alluding to the rattling seeds when the pod is shaken)*

Herbs or shrubs. Leaves usually digitately 3-foliolate; stipules usually present. Flowers solitary or in racemes, *opposite the leaves,* yellow; calyx lobed, with all lobes ± similar; *keel sharply angled and beaked; stamens joined in a tube slit down the top,* of 2 types. *Pods swollen and woody.* Widespread in the tropics and subtropics: 600+ spp.; South Africa: ±60 spp.

❸ *Crotalaria capensis*

J F M A **M J J A S O N D**

Forest Rattle Pod Shrub to 3 m, with 3-foliolate leaves of oval, thinly hairy leaflets, with the stipules similar or sometimes absent, and short, horizontal, terminal racemes of yellow flowers, 15 mm in diameter. Woodland and forest margins in southern and eastern South Africa.

❹ *Crotalaria laburnifolia* Birdflower

J F M A M J J A S O N D

Shrubby perennial to 2 m, with hairless, 3-foliolate leaves of elliptical leaflets, and terminal racemes of large, yellow flowers with a brown eye, 20–30 mm long. Bushveld and roadsides through northeastern South and tropical Africa to Australasia.

❺ *Crotalaria globifera*

J F M A M **J J A S** O N D

Round-pod Rattle Bush, Jaagsiektebossie Clumped perennial with erect, annual stems to 60 cm high from a woody rootstock, with 3-foliolate leaves of narrow leaflets folded along the midline, and racemes of yellow flowers, 10 mm long. Pods spherical. Drier grassland through eastern South Africa, flowering especially after fire.

❻ *Crotalaria excisa*

J F M A M J J **A S O** N D

Perennial with sprawling stems from a woody rootstock, with 3-foliolate leaves of elliptical, thinly hairy leaflets, and 1 or 2 yellow flowers, 10 mm in diameter, on slender stems. Stony flats in Namaqualand and the southwestern Cape.

293

Lotononis **LOTONONIS** *(Combination of 2 other leguminous generic names, Lotus and Ononis)*

Herbs or shrubs. Leaves usually digitately 3-foliolate; *stipules usually solitary at each node*. Flowers axillary or terminal, solitary or in heads, yellow or blue, *without bracteoles; calyx usually with the upper 4 lobes joined and the lower narrower; stamens joined in a tube slit down the top*, of 2 types. Pods narrow or broad; seeds on long funicles. Southern and eastern Africa, Eurasia and Pakistan: ±150 spp.; South Africa: ±144 spp.

▶ FLOWERS YELLOW

❶ *Lotononis prostrata*

| J | F | M | A | M | J | J | **A** | **S** | O | N | D |

Prostrate or creeping shrublet, with 3-foliolate leaves of thinly hairy, wedge-shaped leaflets, with solitary or dissimilar stipules, and solitary, long-stemmed yellow flowers, 10 mm in diameter. Stony slopes in the southwestern Cape.

❷ *Lotononis umbellata*

| J | F | M | A | **M** | **J** | **J** | **A** | **S** | O | N | D |

Prostrate shrublet with thick, woody branches to 10 cm, with 3-foliolate leaves of thinly hairy, wedge-shaped leaflets, with solitary stipules, and slender-stemmed, flat clusters of a few yellow flowers, 10 mm in diameter. Stony slopes in the southwestern and southern Cape.

❸ *Lotononis corymbosa*

| J | F | M | A | M | J | **J** | **A** | **S** | O | **N** | D |

Pincushion Lotononis Sprawling perennial with annual branches to 30 cm high from a woody rootstock, 3-foliolate leaves of elliptical leaflets, hairless above and silky beneath, and ± 1-sided heads of yellow flowers, 10 mm long, nestled in the upper leaves. Grassland in eastern South Africa, flowering especially after fire.

▶ FLOWERS BLUE

❹ *Lotononis galpinii*

| **J** | **F** | M | A | M | J | J | A | S | O | N | **D** |

Rounded, cushion-like or sprawling, mat-forming shrublet to 60 cm, with 3-foliolate leaves of ± hairy, elliptical leaflets, 3–5×3 mm, and purple flowers with a yellow eye; standard and wing petals shorter than the keel, and calyx lobed, with all lobes ± similar. Rocky slopes, streambeds and gravelly patches in the Drakensberg.

❺ *Lotononis sericophylla*

| **J** | **F** | M | A | M | J | J | A | S | O | N | **D** |

Erect, sometimes willowy shrublet to 1.5 m, with 3-foliolate leaves of elliptical leaflets, densely silvery silky on both surfaces, ±10×4 mm, and wisteria-blue flowers with a yellow eye; standard and wing petals shorter than the keel, and calyx lobed; the calyx lobes dissimilar and the upper lobes closely joined in pairs. Grassy ridges and boulder beds in the Drakensberg. *Lotononis divaricata* has sparsely hairy upper leaf surfaces.

❻ *Lotononis lotononoides*

| **J** | **F** | M | A | M | J | J | A | S | O | N | **D** |

Perennial with erect stems to 50 cm, with 3-foliolate leaves of sparsely hairy, oval leaflets, ±20×8 mm, and mauve flowers with a yellow eye; standard and hairless wing petals longer than the hairless keel. Moist, rocky grassland in the Drakensberg.

❼ *Lotononis pulchella*

| **J** | F | M | A | M | J | J | A | S | O | **N** | **D** |

Shrublet to 1 m, with 3-foliolate leaves of silver-haired, oval leaflets, ±13×8 mm, and flat clusters of blue flowers with a yellow eye; standard and hairy wing petals longer than the hairy keel. Grassy ridges and boulder beds in the Drakensberg.

Aspalathus CAPE GORSE *(From the ancient Greek name for a similar, spiny bush)*

Prostrate to erect shrubs, *often spiny. Leaves usually in clusters, sessile,* simple or 3-foliolate, needle-like to almost round, fleshy or leathery and often spine-tipped; *stipules absent.* Flowers usually in heads or racemes, usually yellow, rarely lilac, pink or white; calyx lobed, usually with all lobes ± similar; *stamens joined in a tube slit down the top,* of 2 types. *Pods 1-seeded,* narrow to broad. South Africa, mainly winter-rainfall region: 278 spp. *Aspalathus linearis* is the source of rooibos tea.

▶ LEAVES UNDIVIDED, NEVER TUFTED

❶ *Aspalathus cordata*

J F M A M J J A **S O N D**

Stiff shrub to 1 m, with hard, spine-tipped, oval to heart-shaped leaves, 12–25 mm long and 11–21-veined from the base, and clusters of bright yellow flowers, fading to bright red, with a white-haired calyx and hairy keel. Lower mountain slopes in the southwestern Cape.

❷ *Aspalathus crenata* Stekeltee

J F M A M J J A **S O N D**

Erect or sprawling shrub to 1 m, with leathery, spine-tipped, oval to heart-shaped leaves, 10–40 mm long, with minutely toothed margins and 7–11-veined from the base, and clusters of yellow flowers, fading to red or brown, with a hairless calyx and keel. Mountain fynbos in the southwestern Cape.

▶ LEAFLETS STIFF, SHARP AND NEEDLE-LIKE

❸ *Aspalathus astroites*

J F M A M J J A S **O N** D

Erect shrub to 1.3 m, with whitish-haired branch tips, with 3-foliolate leaves of sharp, tufted, needle-like leaflets, 6–15 mm long, and small heads of bright yellow flowers, fading to orange, with a hairless or thinly hairy calyx with spiny lobes and a beak-like keel. Lowland fynbos in the extreme southwestern Cape.

❹ *Aspalathus chenopoda*

J F M A M J J **A S O N D**

Stiff shrub to 2 m, with densely hairy branches, with 3-foliolate leaves of sharp, needle-like, hairless or whiskered leaflets, 4–15 mm long, and heads of bright yellow flowers that have a densely woolly calyx with needle-like lobes and a hairless keel. Mountain fynbos on lower slopes in the extreme southwestern Cape.

▶ LEAFLETS CYLINDRICAL AND ± FLESHY, NOT SHARP AND NEEDLE-LIKE

❺ *Aspalathus ericifolia*

J F M A M J J A **S O N** D

Erect or sprawling shrublet to 60 cm, with 3-foliolate leaves with ± cylindrical, hairy or hairless leaflets, 1–6 mm long, and scattered, pale or bright yellow flowers, usually with a shortly hairy calyx with slender, thread-like lobes and a hairy keel. Mountain and lowland fynbos in the southwestern Cape.

❻ *Aspalathus capensis*

J F M A M J **J A S O N D**

Stiffly erect shrub to 3 m, with 3-foliolate leaves of fleshy, needle-like leaflets, 5–10 mm long, and heads of 1–3 large, bright yellow flowers, with a fleshy, hairless calyx with oval lobes and a hairless keel. Lowland fynbos on the southern Cape Peninsula.

297

❶ Aspalathus capitata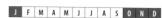

Erect shrub or small tree to 2 m, with 3-foliolate leaves of fleshy, sparsely hairy, needle-like leaflets, 7–15 mm long, and heads of bright yellow flowers, with a fleshy, ± hairless calyx with oval lobes and a pointed, beak-like keel. Lowland and mountain fynbos on the northern Cape Peninsula.

❷ Aspalathus callosa

Erect shrublet, 15–60 cm, with 3-foliolate leaves of fleshy, needle-like leaflets, 4–15 mm long, and heads of yellow flowers, with a hairless calyx with pointed lobes and a hairless keel. Lower slopes in the southwestern Cape.

❸ Aspalathus cephalotes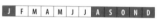

Shrub to 1 m, with 3-foliolate leaves of thread-like or very narrow, sparsely hairy leaflets, 4–10 mm long, and spikes or heads of pale violet or rose, rarely almost white, flowers, with a silky calyx with awl-like lobes and a silky keel. Lower mountain slopes in the southwestern Cape. *Aspalathus nigra* has slate-blue to violet flowers and calyx lobes mostly shorter than 3 mm.

▸ LEAFLETS ± FLAT

❹ Aspalathus quinquefolia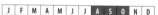

Erect or sprawling shrub to 1.5 m, with 3-foliolate leaves of grey-silky or almost hairless, oblong to elliptical leaflets, 3–10 mm long, and spikes of pale to bright yellow flowers, with a silky calyx and keel. Coastal flats and lower slopes in the southwestern Cape.

Wiborgia **PENNYPOD** *(Named for Danish botanist, Eric Viborg, 1759–1822)*

Shrubs, often spiny. Leaves digitately 3-foliolate; *stipules small or absent*. Flowers in terminal, *often 1-sided racemes*, creamy-yellow to bright yellow; calyx ± 2-lipped; *stamens joined in a tube that is slit down the top*, of 2 types. *Pods woody and indehiscent*, elliptical to spherical *with a peripheral wing along the upper side*. Winter-rainfall South Africa: 10 spp.

❺ Wiborgia fusca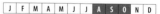

Erect or spreading, somewhat thorny shrub to 1.5 m, with hairless, greyish branches, 3-foliolate leaves of elliptical, pointed leaflets, and racemes of pale greenish-yellow flowers; pods with a wing along the upper side, 12–30×9–15 mm. Mountain and lowland fynbos in Namaqualand and along the West Coast.

❻ Wiborgia mucronata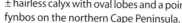

Erect or spreading, thorny shrub to 1.5 m, with hairless branches, 3-foliolate leaves of elliptical leaflets, and terminal racemes of yellow flowers; pods irregularly ridged, with a wing along the upper side, 12–30×9–15 mm. Stony slopes in Namaqualand and the southwestern Cape.

① Wiborgia obcordata

J F M A M J J **A S O** N D

Slender, stiffly branched or willowy shrub to 3 m, with velvety branches when young, 3-foliolate leaves of wedge-shaped leaflets, sparsely hairy beneath, and racemes of bright yellow flowers; pods with a narrow crest along the upper side, 7–12×4–7 mm. Sandy flats and slopes in the southwestern Cape.

Cyclopia BUSH TEA, BOERTEE *(Greek kuklos, circle; pous, foot, referring to the distinctive calyx)*

Erect shrubs. Leaves digitately or palmately *3-foliolate*, leaflets narrow or broad, hairless or hairy, often with the margins rolled under. Flowers solitary in the axils, yellow; calyx pushed in at the base; *stamens separate or joined only at the base* with the *filaments widened at the base.* Pods oblong; seeds with a waxy appendage. South Africa, southwestern and southern Cape: 23 spp. *Cyclopia genistoides* is the original *heuningtee,* or honeybush tea, but today other species, including *C. subternata*, are harvested commercially.

② *Cyclopia genistoides*

J F M A M J J A **S O** N D

Honeybush Tea, Heuningtee Erect, resprouting shrub to 2 m, with 3-foliolate leaves of narrow, needle-like leaflets, with the margins rolled under, and clusters of yellow flowers. Seasonally marshy flats and lower slopes in the southwestern Cape.

▸▸ LEAVES SIMPLE, ± SESSILE; STIPULES SMALL OR ABSENT

Rafnia INK PEA *(Named for Danish botanist, Karl Rafn, 1769–1808)*

Shrubs, *completely hairless and usually bluish or grey, often drying black.* Leaves simple, hairless; *stipules absent.* Flowers solitary or in racemes, yellow; calyx usually with the lowest lobe narrower; *stamens joined in a tube that is slit down the top,* of 2 types. Pods narrow. South Africa, mainly winter-rainfall region: 19 spp. The roots of *Rafnia amplexicaulis* were used as a liquorice substitute, and a decoction of *R. perfoliata* as a diuretic.

③ *Rafnia angulata*

J **F** M A M J J A **S O** N D

Erect or sprawling shrublet with wand-like stems to 2 m, with needle-like to oval leaves, and racemes of 1–6 yellow flowers in the leaf axils, 8–20 mm long, with a sharp, beak-like keel. Stony slopes in the southwestern Cape.

④ *Rafnia perfoliata*

J F M **A** M J J A **S O** N D

Prostrate or trailing shrublet to 30 cm high, forming clumps to 1 m in diameter, with heart-shaped leaves, often clasping the stem and opposite on flowering branches, and solitary, yellow flowers, 9–14 mm long, with a sharp, beak-like keel. Stony slopes in the mountains of the southwestern Cape.

Liparia MOUNTAIN PEA *(Greek liparos, oily or shiny, referring to the leaves)*

Shrubs or shrublets. *Leaves simple,* narrow to round, *3- or more-veined from the base,* often drying black; stipules small. Flowers in terminal heads, yellow to orange, *with large, leaf-like bracts; calyx pushed in at the base,* with long lobes, the upper 4 often partly joined and the *lowermost much larger;* stamens joined in a tube with the upper one separate, of 2 types. Pods oval or oblong, thinly hairy; seeds with a fleshy appendage. Winter-rainfall South Africa: 20 spp. The striking flowers of *Liparia splendens* are pollinated by sunbirds.

① Liparia splendens

| J | F | M | A | M | J | J | A | S | O | N | D |

Mountain Dahlia, Skaamblom Erect or creeping shrublet to 1 m, with elliptical leaves, and nodding heads of 15–17 orange to red flowers among conspicuous, dark reddish-brown bracts. Mountain and lowland fynbos in the southwestern Cape.

Podalyria CAPE SWEETPEA, KEURTJIE
(Named for Podaleirios, son of the Greek god of healing, Asklepios) Silky or silver-haired shrubs. Leaves simple, narrow to almost round. *Flowers 1–4 on axillary peduncles,* pink, purple or white; *calyx shaggy and pushed in at the base,* sometimes split on 1 side; *stamens joined only at the base,* with the filaments widened at the base. Pods shaggy; seeds with a fleshy collar. Mainly winter-rainfall South Africa: 19 spp.

② Podalyria sericea

| J | F | M | A | M | J | J | A | S | O | N | D |

Single-stemmed shrublet to 1 m, with elliptical leaflets, silky on both surfaces, and small, pink and white flowers, ±10 mm in diameter, in the axils of lance-shaped bracts. Sandstone and granite outcrops along the West Coast.

③ Podalyria myrtillifolia

| J | F | M | A | M | J | J | A | S | O | N | D |

Rounded, single-stemmed or sometimes resprouting shrub to 2 m, with oval or paddle-shaped leaves, silky on both surfaces, and pink and white flowers, 10–15 mm in diameter, in the axils of lance-shaped bracts. Stony lower slopes from the southwestern to Eastern Cape.

④ Podalyria calyptrata

| J | F | M | A | M | J | J | A | S | O | N | D |

Small tree to 5 m, with oval leaves, silky on both surfaces, and bright pink and white flowers, ±15 mm in diameter, in the axils of very broad bracts that are joined into a cap or sheath. Sandstone slopes in marshy places in the extreme southwestern Cape.

AIZOACEAE

Ice Plant family

▶ LEAVES ± FLAT AND COVERED WITH GLISTENING BLADDER CELLS

Mesembryanthemum ICE PLANT, BRAKSLAAI
(Greek mesembria, midday; anthemon, flower, as the flowers open only in full sunlight) *Annual or perennial herbs, often sprawling, with angled or winged stems.* Leaves opposite or alternate, *flat and petiolate to club-shaped, covered with rounded or flattened, glistening bladder cells.* Flowers solitary or clustered, pink, yellow or white, 10–60 mm in diameter, open in sunlight. Fruit 5-segmented. Dry parts of southern Africa: 110 spp.

❶ *Mesembryanthemum guerichianum* J F M A M J J A S O N D
Sprawling annual with oval or paddle-shaped leaves forming a small rosette at the base, covered with small bladder cells, and white or pinkish flowers, 25–55 mm in diameter. Sandy flats and roadsides in the drier parts of southern Africa.

❷ *Mesembryanthemum eurystigmatum* J F M A M J J A S O N D
(=*Eurystigma clavatum*) Sprawling, rounded annual with cylindrical leaves covered with small bladder cells, and pale yellow flowers, 40–60 mm in diameter. Dry gravelly flats in the interior southwestern Cape.

Dorotheanthus DOROTHEANTHUS, BOKBAAIVYGIE
(Named for Dorothea Schwantes, mother of German succulent expert, Dr Gustav Schwantes, 1881–1960) *Small annual herbs.* Leaves *mostly alternate in a basal tuft, flat and petiolate, covered in glistening bladder cells.* Flowers solitary on long, leafless pedicels, opening in sunlight, white, yellow, orange, red or pink, with *a dark centre,* to 40 mm in diameter; *petals in 2 series; stamens sometimes brown or reddish.* Fruit 5-segmented. Winter-rainfall South Africa: 7 spp. The vernacular name *bokbaaivygie* alludes to the prevalence of the plants on the sands around Bokbaai on the West Coast.

❸ *Dorotheanthus bellidiformis* J F M A M J J A S O N D
Livingstone Daisy Tufted annual herb with strap-shaped to narrowly paddle-shaped leaves covered in bladder cells, and red, yellow, pink or white flowers, usually with a dark centre, 40–50 mm in diameter. Mostly on sandy flats in the southwestern Cape and Namaqualand.

❹ *Dorotheanthus maughanii* J F M A M J J A S O N D
Karoo Snow Tufted annual herb with broadly paddle-shaped leaves, warty and covered in bladder cells, and white flowers with a red centre and glistening, knob-like stigmas, 40–60 mm in diameter. Dry gravelly clay in karroid scrub in the Northern Cape. *Dorotheanthus booysenii* has plain white flowers without knob-like stigmas.

❺ *Dorotheanthus rourkei* J F M A M J J A S O N D
Tufted annual herb with narrowly paddle-shaped leaves covered in bladder cells, and red to orange flowers with a dark centre and sharply pointed petals, 20–40 mm in diameter. Red sandy flats in Namaqualand.

Cleretum   CLERETUM   *(Derivation uncertain)*

Small annual herbs. Leaves *opposite, flat and petiolate, sometimes lobed, covered in glistening bladder cells.* Flowers solitary and ± *sessile,* yellow or white, to 40 mm in diameter, opening in sunlight; *petals in 1–3 series.* Fruit 5-segmented, *ridged on top.* Winter-rainfall South Africa: 3 spp.

❶ Cleretum papulosum   J F M A M J **J A S O** N D

Tufted annual with paddle-shaped leaves covered in bladder cells, and yellow flowers, 10–40 mm in diameter. Sandy and gravelly flats in western South Africa.

▸ **ANNUALS OR TRAILING PERENNIALS WITH SMOOTH OR HAIRY LEAVES; FLOWERS LARGE, OFTEN YELLOW; STIGMAS AND FRUIT SEGMENTS >6**

Apatesia   APATESIA, VETKOUSIE

(Greek apatesis, *deception, from its similarity to the genus* Hymenogyne*)* Sprawling annual herb. Leaves opposite, flattened with a petiole clasping the stem at the base, covered with waxy flakes. Flowers solitary on long pedicels, yellow, opening in sunlight; petals in 4 or 5 series, with minutely hairy margins. Fruit 8–12-segmented. Southwestern Cape: 3 spp.

❷ *Apatesia pillansii*   J F M A M J J A **S O** N D

Annual herb to 15 cm, with flat, slightly succulent leaves, and yellow flowers, 40–60 mm in diameter; the fruits slightly domed above; the seeds slightly warty. Coastal dunes along the West Coast. *Apatesia helianthoides* from further inland has fruits that are conical above, with smooth seeds.

Carpanthea   CARPANTHEA, VETKOUSIE

(Greek karpos, *fruit;* anthos, *flower, alluding to the edible flowers and fruit)* *Annual herb* with *glistening, hairy stems.* Leaves opposite, *flat, with scattered white hairs and fringed margins.* Flowers 1–3 at the stem tips, *golden-yellow,* opening in sunlight; petals narrow. *Fruit 12–18-segmented.* Southwestern Cape: 1 sp. The vernacular name *vetkousie* is part corruption and part translation of the original Khoi name. The leaves and flowers may be used as a vegetable in stews.

❸ *Carpanthea pomeridiana*   J F M A M J J A **S O N** D

Annual succulent to 20 cm, with softly hairy stems, flat, slightly succulent leaves with hair-like papillae on the margins, and yellow flowers with hair-like papillae on the calyx. Sandy flats in the southwestern Cape.

Conicosia   CONICOSIA, GANSIES   *(Greek* konicos, *conical, referring to the fruit)*

Perennial or biennial herbs with trailing branches, often tuberous. Leaves opposite, in a basal tuft and scattered along the branches, 3-angled in cross section, smooth, elongated, *up to 40 cm long.* *Flowers solitary at the branch tips on long pedicels, yellow or whitish,* to 100 mm in diameter, *opening in the afternoon, often unpleasantly scented;* petals narrow. *Fruit cone-shaped, 10–25-segmented, opening when dry.* Winter-rainfall South Africa: 2 spp.

❹ *Conicosia pugioniformis* Varkslaai   J F M A M J J A **S O N** D

Sprawling perennial to 40 cm, with long trailing branches bearing long, 3-angled leaves, and solitary, yellow flowers opening in the afternoon, 60–100 mm in diameter. Sandy flats, mostly coastal, from Namaqualand to the Eastern Cape.

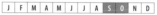

① *Conicosia elongata*

J F M A M J J A S O N D

Tufted, cushion-like perennial to 20 cm, with short branches bearing long, ± cylindrical leaves, and solitary, pale yellow flowers opening in the afternoon, 60–130 mm in diameter. Sandy and gravelly flats, often along the coast, in western South Africa.

Carpobrotus SOUR FIG, SUURVY *(Greek karpos, fruit; brotos, edible)*

Robust, trailing perennials, often forming large mats, with angled or narrowly winged stems. Leaves opposite, smooth and sharply 3-angled in cross section, *with cartilaginous, often reddish, toothed keel and margins, up to 130 mm long.* Flowers solitary at the branch tips, *up to 150 mm in diameter,* white, yellow, pink or magenta; *ovary 2-ridged* and tapering into the pedicel. *Fruit fleshy, 4–20-segmented.* Southern Africa, Chile, California and Australia: 13 spp.; South Africa: 7 spp. The sap was used as an antiseptic and the fruits are made into jam.

▶ BASE OF FLOWER TAPERING GRADUALLY INTO THE PEDICEL

② *Carpobrotus edulis*

J F M A M J J A S O N D

Succulent perennial with trailing stems to 2 m long, with straight or slightly curved leaves, 8–18 mm in diameter, and yellow flowers, fading to pink with age, 50–80 mm in diameter, the base tapering gradually into the pedicel. Coastal and inland slopes in southwestern and southern South Africa. *Carpobrotus mellei* from the southwestern Cape interior has pink or magenta flowers, with the stigmas longer than the stamens.

③ *Carpobrotus dimidiatus*

J F M A M J J A S O N D

Succulent perennial with trailing stems to 2.5 m long, with slender, straight or slightly curved leaves, 5–12 mm in diameter, and magenta, pink or white flowers, 40–60 mm in diameter, the base tapering gradually into the pedicel. Coastal dunes and rocks in eastern South Africa.

▶ BASE OF FLOWER NARROWING ABRUPTLY INTO THE PEDICEL

④ *Carpobrotus deliciosus*

J F M A M J J A S O N D

Succulent perennial with trailing stems to 2.5 m, with ± straight leaves 12–18 mm in diameter, and purple, pink or white flowers, 60–80 mm in diameter, the base narrowing abruptly into the pedicel, the ovary with the centre raised. Sand dunes and rocky grassland in the southern and Eastern Cape.

⑤ *Carpobrotus acinaciformis*

J F M A M J J A S O N D

Succulent perennial with trailing stems to 2 m long, with robust, sabre-shaped leaves, 15–25 mm in diameter, and magenta flowers, 70–100 mm in diameter, the base narrowing abruptly into the pedicel. Coastal sands in the southwestern and southern Cape. *Carpobrotus muirii* has narrow leaves, 5–7 mm in diameter.

⑥ *Carpobrotus quadrifidus*

J F M A M J J A S O N D

Succulent perennial with trailing stems to 2.5 m long, with robust, straight or slightly curved leaves, 18–25 mm in diameter, and magenta flowers, 120–150 mm in diameter, the base narrowing abruptly into the pedicel. Coastal sands along the western seaboard of South Africa.

Jordaaniella JORDAANIELLA, STRANDVYGIE

(Named for Pieter Jordaan, professor of botany at Stellenbosch University, 1953–1979) Prostrate perennials with orange or yellow stem segments. *Leaves spindle-shaped (tapering at both ends)*. Flowers solitary on short side branches, yellow to purple, rarely white, opening at midday. *Fruit 10–25-segmented.* Winter-rainfall South Africa: 6 spp.

❶ *Jordaaniella spongiosa*

| J | F | M | A | M | J | J | A | S | O | N | D |

(=Cephalophyllum spongiosum) **Giant Vygie, Volstruisvygie** Robust, sprawling or trailing perennial to 1 m long, with large, finger-shaped leaves, and large flowers, 70–100 mm in diameter, red or magenta with a yellow centre, on short side branches. Sandy flats in coastal scrub in Namaqualand.

❷ *Jordaaniella cuprea*

| J | F | M | A | M | J | J | A | S | O | N | D |

Creeping succulent forming compact mats, with spindle-shaped leaves, 50–100 mm long, and pale yellow to salmon-coloured flowers with orange to pink edges, 30–100 mm in diameter; fruit on horizontal stalks, 14–20-segmented. Coastal sands in northern Namaqualand.

❸ *Jordaaniella dubia*

| J | F | M | A | M | J | J | A | S | O | N | D |

Prostrate succulent with slender, spindle-shaped leaves, 20–50 mm long, and bright yellow flowers, 30–40 mm in diameter; fruit 10–15-segmented. Coastal sands in the southwestern Cape.

Cephalophyllum CEPHALOPHYLLUM

(Greek kephale, head; phyllon, leaf, alluding to the head-like tufts of leaves) Compact or creeping perennials. Leaves opposite, ± 3-angled in cross section. Flowers *terminal, colourful*, opening at midday. *Fruit 10–21-segmented.* Winter-rainfall southern Africa: 33 spp.

❹ *Cephalophyllum pillansii*

| J | F | M | A | M | J | J | A | S | O | N | D |

Namaqua Creeping Vygie Succulent shrublet to 10 cm, with creeping annual stems, erect, greyish, cylindrical leaves, and pale yellow flowers with a red centre, 60 mm in diameter. Gravelly flats, often along road verges, in Namaqualand.

❺ *Cephalophyllum spissum*

| J | F | M | A | M | J | J | A | S | O | N | D |

Compact, cushion-forming perennial to 10 cm, with finger-shaped, 3-sided leaves, and pink to purple flowers with a paler halo and centre, 30–40 mm in diameter. Quartz patches on the Knersvlakte near Vanrhynsdorp.

❻ *Cephalophyllum caespitosum*

| J | F | M | A | M | J | J | A | S | O | N | D |

Compact, cushion-forming perennial to 10 cm, with finger-shaped, 3-sided leaves, and orange to red flowers with a paler halo and red centre, 30–40 mm in diameter. Quartz patches near Vanrhynsdorp.

Delosperma DELOSPERMA, SKAAPVYGIE

(Greek delos, visible; spermum, seed, alluding to the lack of concealing membranes over the seeds) Shrublets or perennials, *often with sprawling annual branches*, sometimes tuberous. Leaves opposite, sometimes hairy or prickly and with bladder cells, 3-angled to cylindrical, *usually soft, often bright green*. Flowers solitary or in 3s, white to pink or purple, rarely yellow or reddish; petals in 1–4 series. Fruit usually 5-segmented. Mainly South Africa, especially eastern parts: ±158 spp.

① *Delosperma cooperi*

| J | F | M | A | M | J | J | A | S | O | N | D |

Mat-forming perennial with rough, bluish, 3-angled leaves, and magenta flowers, 20 mm in diameter. Rock sheets and outcrops at high altitude in central South Africa and Lesotho.

② *Delosperma wethamae*

| J | F | M | A | M | J | J | A | S | O | N | D |

Mat-forming perennial with rough, green, 3-angled leaves, and white flowers, 20 mm in diameter. Rock sheets and outcrops at high altitude in the Drakensberg.

Drosanthemum DROSANTHEMUM, DOUVYGIE

(Greek drosos, dew; anthos, flower, referring to the glittering leaf papillae) Shrublets or loosely branched shrubs, *often prostrate, with distinctly segmented, often bristly stems*. Leaves opposite, *not joined at the base and easily shed, rounded at the tips* and up to ±50 mm long, *covered with glistening papillae or bladder cells*. Flowers solitary or in clusters, white, orange, red, pink or magenta, opening at midday; petals in 1 or 2 series. Fruit 5-segmented. Mainly winter-rainfall southern Africa: 110 spp.

③ *Drosanthemum hispidum*

| J | F | M | A | M | J | J | A | S | O | N | D |

Erect or spreading shrublet to 60 cm, with bristly, red branches and blunt, cylindrical leaves mostly bending downwards and covered with glittering bladder cells, and magenta flowers, 15 mm in diameter. Pioneer of disturbed areas and roadsides in the drier parts of southern Africa.

④ *Drosanthemum bicolor*

| J | F | M | A | M | J | J | A | S | O | N | D |

Erect shrub to 1 m, with rough stems and blunt, cylindrical leaves with small bladder cells, and golden-yellow flowers with maroon tips, 20 mm in diameter. Stony sandstone slopes in the Little Karoo.

⑤ *Drosanthemum speciosum*

| J | F | M | A | M | J | J | A | S | O | N | D |

Erect shrublet to 60 cm, with rough stems and blunt, cylindrical leaves with glittering bladder cells when young, and red to orange flowers, 20–30 mm in diameter. Shale slopes between Worcester and Barrydale.

Lampranthus LAMPRANTHUS, VYGIE *(Greek lampros, bright; anthos, flower)*

Creeping or erect shrublets with smooth stems. Leaves opposite, *usually cylindrical, mostly smooth*, up to 50 mm long. Flowers solitary or in clusters, white, yellow, orange or pink to magenta, 7–70 mm in diameter, opening in sunlight. Fruit 5-segmented. Mainly winter-rainfall southern Africa: ±150 spp. The vernacular name derives from the Dutch diminutive for fig, applied originally to the edible fruits of *Carpobrotus*.

① *Lampranthus aureus*

| J | F | M | A | M | J | J | A | S | O | N | D |

Erect shrublet to 40 cm, with greyish leaves joined at the base, to 50 mm long, and shiny orange flowers to 60 mm in diameter. Granite outcrops around Saldanha Bay in the Western Cape.

② *Lampranthus bicolor*

| J | F | M | A | M | J | J | A | S | O | N | D |

Stiffly branched, erect shrublet to 30 cm, with rough, green, almost 3-angled leaves, 12–25 mm long, and groups of 1–3 yellow flowers with scarlet or copper undersides. Sandy flats or slopes in the extreme southwestern Cape.

③ *Lampranthus amoenus*

| J | F | M | A | M | J | J | A | S | O | N | D |

Shrublet to 40 cm, with weakly spreading, cylindrical to 3-angled, shortly pointed leaves to 40 mm long, and white to purple flowers, 35–40 mm in diameter. Sandy flats along the West Coast.

④ *Lampranthus watermeyeri*

| J | F | M | A | M | J | J | A | S | O | N | D |

Erect shrublet to 50 cm, with cylindrical leaves joined at the base, 20–40×6 mm, and mostly solitary magenta or white flowers on long pedicels, to 70 mm in diameter. Rocky outcrops in Namaqualand and the southwestern Cape.

Ruschia RUSCHIA, VYGIE *(Named for Namibian farmer and plant collector, Ernst Rusch, 1867–1957)*

Shrubs or shrublets, usually erect but sometimes creeping. Leaves opposite, *sometimes joined in pairs at the base*, 3-angled in cross section, *bluish-green and usually with darker spots*. Flowers usually in clusters, white or pink to purple, opening in sunlight; *stamens arranged in a cone*. Fruit 5- (rarely 6-) segmented. Widespread through the dry parts of southern Africa: ±400 described species but probably fewer.

⑤ *Ruschia tumidula*

| J | F | M | A | M | J | J | A | S | O | N | D |

Erect shrublet to 40 cm, with reddish branches, almost cylindrical, slightly rough leaves, and many-flowered clusters of white to pink flowers, 20 mm in diameter. Sandy coastal flats in the extreme southwestern Cape.

⑥ *Ruschia tecta*

| J | F | M | A | M | J | J | A | S | O | N | D |

Erect shrub to 1 m, with erect, S-shaped leaves joined together below in a long, slightly swollen sheath, and clusters of purplish flowers with a white centre, ±20 mm in diameter; fruit 6-segmented. Sandy flats along the West Coast.

Oscularia OSCULARIA *(Latin osculum, small mouth, alluding to the toothed leaves)*

Dense shrublets with *reddish stems*. Leaves opposite, *3-angled in cross section, short, up to ±20 mm long, mostly with toothed keel and margins, waxy and greyish-green to pale blue*. Flowers up to ±15 mm in diameter, *remaining open, almond-scented*, white to pink; *petals in ±1 series; stamens and staminodes arranged in a cone*. Fruit 5-segmented. Winter-rainfall South Africa: ±25 spp.

① *Oscularia deltoides* Bergvygie   J F M A M J J A S **O N D**

Sprawling or rounded shrublet to 20 cm, with reddish, shining branches, triangular, greyish leaves with toothed keel and margins, and clusters of pale pink flowers, 15 mm in diameter. Sandstone rocks in the southwestern Cape.

▶ **TUFTED OR CUSHION-FORMING PERENNIALS; STYLES AND FRUIT SEGMENTS 10–20**

Cheiridopsis CHEIRIDOPSIS

(Greek cheiris, sheath; opsis, resembling, referring to the papery leaf sheaths) Compact, tufted dwarf shrublets.
Leaves opposite, *only 1 or 2 pairs per branch, joined at the base, with 1 pair withering to form a papery sleeve*, short or long, 3-angled in cross section, often with a few teeth along the keel or near the tip. *Flowers solitary at the branch tips, usually yellow*, rarely purple or red, 10–100 mm in diameter, opening at midday. Fruit 10–20-segmented. Winter-rainfall southern Africa: 23 spp.

② *Cheiridopsis rostrata*   J F M A M J **J A S** O N D

Compact, cushion-forming succulent to 5 cm, with leaves triangular in cross section and covered with translucent spots on the underside, and yellow flowers, fading to red, 30–40 mm in diameter. Granite outcrops on the West Coast.

③ *Cheiridopsis namaquensis*   J F M A M J **J A S** O N D

Cigarettes Compact, cushion-forming succulent to 5 cm, with pincer-like leaves, triangular in cross section and slightly warty on the keel and margins, and yellow flowers, fading to red, 30–45 mm in diameter. Stony slopes and rock crevices on the western escarpment.

④ *Cheiridopsis denticulata*   J F M A M J **J A S** O N D

Compact, cushion-forming succulent to 10 cm, with leaves triangular in cross section and slightly warty on the keel and margins, and cream-coloured to pale yellow flowers, often apricot or purplish towards the edges, 60–70 mm in diameter. Sandy and gravelly flats, often in seasonal washes, in northwestern South Africa.

Monilaria BEADED ICE PLANT, MONILARIA

(Latin monile, necklace, alluding to the jointed or beaded stems) Compact, dwarf shrublets with *short, beaded stems*. Leaves opposite, of 2 types, the first pair short and collar-like, the second pair *soft and cylindrical, covered in glistening warts*, joined at the base. Flowers solitary at the branch tips on long pedicels, white, yellow or magenta, 30–50 mm in diameter, opening at midday. Fruit 10–20-segmented. Winter-rainfall southern Africa: 5 spp.

⑤ *Monilaria moniliformis*   J F M A M J **J** A S O N D

Cushion-forming succulent to 15 cm, with beaded stems, glistening, finger-shaped leaves, and solitary white flowers on long stalks, 35–40 mm in diameter. Quartz patches and stony quartzite in the northern Western Cape.

▶ **DWARF 'STONE PLANTS' WITH 1 OR 2 LEAF PAIRS**

Oophytum PEBBLE PLANT *(Greek oion, egg; phyton, plant)*

Dwarf, stemless, clumped perennials. *Leaves 4 per branch, glistening,* the lower pair forming a collar and the *upper pair united in a cylindrical body with a small, mouth-like opening at the top.* Flowers solitary, emerging from the central opening of the leaf body, white to magenta, opening during the day. Fruit 6-segmented. Winter-rainfall southern Africa: 3 spp.

❶ *Oophytum nanum*

Dwarf succulent perennial, clump-forming, with rounded leaf bodies 10 mm long, and pink flowers with a white centre, 20 mm in diameter. Quartz patches and stony slopes in Namaqualand.

Conophytum CONE PLANT, TOONTJIES *(Greek konos, cone; phyton, plant)*

Dwarf, stemless perennials, solitary or clumped. *Leaves 2 per branch, united in a top-shaped or cylindrical body with a small, mouth-like opening at the top,* often spotted or lined. Flowers solitary, emerging from the central opening of the leaf body, *with an elongated floral tube,* variously coloured, opening during the day or at night. Fruit 3–8-segmented. Winter-rainfall southern Africa: 86 spp. Popular with succulent collectors.

❷ *Conophytum minutum*

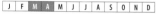

Common Cone Plant Dwarf succulent perennial, clump-forming, with leaf bodies 15–20 mm long, often flattened and spotted, and magenta to pink (rarely white) flowers with a white tube, 10–15 mm in diameter. Quartz patches and stony slopes in Namaqualand.

❸ *Conophytum minusculum*

Dwarf succulent perennial, clump-forming, with leaf bodies 5–15 mm long, often flattened or slightly keeled and spotted and streaked, and magenta (rarely white) flowers with a yellow tube, 10–15 mm in diameter. Sandstone slopes and pavement in the mountains of the West Coast.

❹ *Conophytum subfenestratum*

Fenestrate Cone Plant Dwarf succulent perennial, usually solitary, with leaf bodies 20–25 mm long, flattened and soft with a translucent window at the top, and pink flowers with a white tube, 15–20 mm in diameter. Quartz patches on the Knersvlakte near Vanrhynsdorp.

319

Argyroderma STONE PLANT, BABABOUDJIES (*Greek argyros, silver; derma, skin*)

Dwarf, stemless perennials, solitary or clumped. *Leaves 2 per branch, united below, thumb-shaped or rounded, silvery-grey and smooth.* Flowers solitary, emerging from beween the leaf pair, *with a cup-shaped tube*, variously coloured, opening during the day. Fruit 12–25-segmented. Winter-rainfall southern Africa: 11 spp. Popular with succulent collectors.

① *Argyroderma fissum*
| J | F | M | A | M | J | J | A | S | O | N | D |

Tufted Stone Plant Tufted succulent to 15 cm, usually clumped, with a pair of finger-like leaves, often flattened on the upper side, and solitary magenta flowers with a white centre, 30–40 mm in diameter. White quartz gravel patches on the Knersvlakte near Vanrhynsdorp.

② *Argyroderma delaetii* Stone Plant
| J | F | M | A | M | J | J | A | S | O | N | D |

Dwarf succulent to 5 cm high, solitary or clump-forming, with a pair of ± spherical, silver-skinned leaves, and solitary yellow or white to purple flowers, 30–40 mm in diameter. White quartz gravel patches on the Knersvlakte near Vanrhynsdorp.

MONTINIACEAE   Montinia family

Montinia MONTINIA, PEPERBOS (*Named for Swedish botanist, Laurence Montin*)

Shrubs or shrublets *with the sexes on separate plants.* Leaves elliptical and leathery. Flowers cup-shaped, white, with *4 petals.* Fruit *dry and shuttle-shaped*, the husk splitting into 2 halves. Dry parts of southern Africa: 1 sp. The vernacular name *peperbos* alludes to the acrid taste of the foliage.

③ *Montinia caryophyllacea*
| J | F | M | A | M | J | J | A | S | O | N | D |

Upright, greyish shrub to 1.5 m, with leathery, elliptical leaves, and white flowers, 6–10 mm in diameter, either in loose clusters in male plants, or 1 or 2 in female plants. Drier rocky slopes through southwestern parts of southern Africa.

BEGONIACEAE   Begonia family

Begonia BEGONIA
(*Named for Michel Begon, 1638–1710, French governor of San Domingo and patron of botany*) Fleshy herbs or shrublets with *unisexual flowers on the same plant. Leaves asymmetrical, with radiating veins,* lobed or toothed. Flowers in clusters, *male flowers with 2 or 4 tepals, female flowers with 5 or 6 tepals.* Fruit *3-winged.* Tropical: ±900 spp.; South Africa: 5 or 6 spp.

④ *Begonia sonderiana*
| J | F | M | A | M | J | J | A | S | O | N | D |

Sonder's Begonia Stout, brittle-stemmed perennial to 1 m, with obliquely 5–7-lobed, irregularly toothed leaves, and pink flowers up to 30 mm in diameter. Moist banks and rock falls in forest in northeastern South and subtropical Africa. *Begonia homonyma* from southeastern South Africa is similar.

⑤ *Begonia sutherlandii*
| J | F | M | A | M | J | J | A | S | O | N | D |

Wild Orange Begonia Brittle-stemmed perennial to 50 cm, with very oblique, often lobed, and toothed leaves, and orange flowers up to 30 mm in diameter. Mossy banks and forest floor through eastern South and tropical Africa.

CUCURBITACEAE Cucumber family

Momordica BALSAM APPLE, BURSTING BEAUTY

(Latin mordeo, bite, alluding to the jagged seeds) Climbers with unisexual flowers on the same plant, *foul-smelling when bruised.* Leaves unlobed or 3–5-lobed, often toothed. *Flowers white or cream-coloured*, male flowers in racemes, female flowers solitary. *Fruit ellipsoid, usually covered in fleshy spines or protuberances, splitting open to reveal the seeds; seeds often sculptured.* Africa and Asia: ±40 spp.; South Africa: 9 spp.

① *Momordica foetida*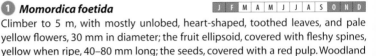
Climber to 5 m, with mostly unlobed, heart-shaped, toothed leaves, and pale yellow flowers, 30 mm in diameter; the fruit ellipsoid, covered with fleshy spines, yellow when ripe, 40–80 mm long; the seeds, covered with a red pulp. Woodland and riverine bush and forest, through eastern South and tropical Africa.

Coccinea WILD CUCUMBER

(Latin coccinus, scarlet, alluding to the characteristic colour of the fruit) Climbers, the sexes on separate plants. Leaves 3–5-lobed, often toothed. *Flowers white or cream-coloured*, male flowers in racemes, female flowers solitary. *Fruit cylindrical or ellipsoid, smooth, red when ripe;* seeds flattened, triangular. Africa and Asia: ±30 spp.; South Africa: 7 spp.

② *Coccinea palmata*
Wild Cucumber Climber up to 8 m, with forked tendrils and hairless, deeply 5-lobed, toothed leaves, and pale yellow, cup-shaped flowers, 30 mm in diameter; the fruit ellipsoid and pointed, red when ripe, 50–80 mm long. Forest and thicket margins through eastern South Africa. *Coccinea adoensis* is similar but has simple tendrils.

NEURADACEAE Desert Primrose family

Grielum DESERT PRIMROSE, DUIKERWORTEL

(Greek greilos, old, alluding to the grey-haired leaves) Creeping, ± white-woolly annuals with a *mucilaginous taproot and stems.* Leaves deeply lobed or divided. Flowers large, solitary in the axils, yellow, cup-shaped, with the petals furled in bud; stamens 10. *Fruit flattened and pentagonal with a peripheral wing and central knobs.* Drier parts of southern Africa: ±6 spp.; South Africa: 4 spp. The vernacular name *duikerwortel* refers to duikers' predilection for the succulent rootstock.

③ *Grielum grandiflorum*
Creeping annual herb, often mat-forming, with white-woolly leaves, divided 1 or 2 times, with pointed lobes, and glistening, pale yellow flowers with a green eye. Coastal from southern Namibia to the West Coast.

④ *Grielum humifusum*
Maritzwater, Pietsnot Creeping annual herb, often mat-forming, with deeply divided, thinly white-woolly leaves, almost hairless above, with rounded lobes, and glistening, pale yellow flowers with a white eye or central ring. Sandy lower slopes from southern Namibia to the southwestern Cape.

RUBIACEAE   Coffee family

Conostomium   WILD PENTAS

(Greek konos, cone; stoma, mouth, from the ring of anthers at the mouth of the tube) Erect subshrubs. Flowers in terminal clusters, white or blue, not heterostylous; *sepals 4, all similar; petals 4; anthers concealed in the mouth of the tube. Seeds numerous in each chamber.* Africa: 9 spp.; South Africa: 2 spp. Traditionally used in magic rituals.

❶ *Conostomium natalense*

J F **M A** M J J A **S** O N **D**

Erect, slightly woody subshrub to 1 m, with narrow, opposite leaves and leafy clusters of white to mauve, salver-shaped flowers with 4 petals, 20 mm long. Forest margins through eastern South Africa.

Pentanisia   PENTANISIA   *(Greek pente, five; anisos, unequal, from the dissimilar sepals)*

Perennials, resprouting from a woody rootstock. Flowers in terminal clusters, blue, *heterostylous; sepals 3–5, dissimilar; petals 5; anthers of some flowers concealed in the tube but protruding in others. Seeds 1 in each chamber.* Africa: 15 spp.; South Africa: 3 spp. Used medicinally.

❷ *Pentanisia prunelloides*

J F **M A** M J J A **S** O N **D**

Broad-leaved Pentanisia Perennial to 60 cm, resprouting from a woody base, with lance-shaped, hairless or hairy, opposite leaves, and heads of mauve to blue, salver-shaped flowers with 5 petals, 20 mm long, heterostylous with long-styled (pin) or short-styled (thrum) forms. Grasslands through eastern South and tropical Africa, flowering well in spring after fire. *Pentanisia angustifolia* has very narrow, hairless leaves and a more slender inflorescence.

MELASTOMATACEAE   Tibouchina family

Antherotoma   ANTHEROTOMA

(Greek antheros, anther; tomos, slice or piece, alluding to the cut-off tips of the anthers) Annual or perennial herbs. Leaves opposite, 3–7-veined. *Flowers in heads surrounded by a whorl of leaves,* magenta to purple; calyx with *4 lobes alternating with bristly teeth; petals 4; stamens all ± similar or of 2 types, the longer filaments spurred or horned, opening by a pore at the tip.* Africa: ±10 spp.; South Africa: 3 spp.

❸ *Antherotoma phaeotricha*

J F M A M J J A **S** O N **D**

(=*Dissotis phaeotricha*) **Dwarf Dissotis** Perennial herb with erect, rod-like stems to 60 cm, covered in spreading, tawny hairs, with pairs of bristly leaves at each node, 3–5-veined from the base and 10–60 mm long, and heads of mauve flowers, ±30 mm in diameter; the filament spurs slender. Marshy grasslands through eastern South and tropical Africa. *Antherotoma debilis* is an annual with short, pale bristles pressed to the stems and forked filament spurs.

Dissotis DISSOTIS *(Greek dissos, twofold, alluding to the 2 types of anthers)*

Herbs or shrubs. Leaves opposite, 3–7-veined. Flowers in heads or panicles, magenta to purple; calyx with 5 *lobes alternating with bristly teeth or thick appendages; petals 5; stamens of 2 types, with the longer filaments spurred or horned, opening by a pore at the tip.* Africa: ±120 spp.; South Africa: 2 spp.

1 *Dissotis canescens* **Marsh Dissotis**   J F M A M J J A S O N D
Erect shrub to 1.5 m, with pairs of leaves at each node, 3–7-veined from the base and 20–80 mm long, and clusters of magenta flowers, 34–45 mm in diameter, the sepals remaining on the fruits. Marshy grassland through eastern South and tropical Africa.

2 *Dissotis princeps*   J F M A M J J A S O N D
Wild Tibouchina Softly woody shrub to 3 m, with 2 or 3 large leaves at each node, 5–7-veined from the base and 30–140 mm long, and clusters of purple flowers, 50–60 mm in diameter, the sepals deciduous. Stream sides in bush and on forest margins in eastern South and tropical Africa.

CAMPANULACEAE   Bellflower family

▶ **SUBFAMILY CAMPANULOIDEAE** FLOWERS SYMMETRICAL, THE ANTHERS MOSTLY WITHERED AT FLOWERING

Wahlenbergia AFRICAN BLUE-BELL, BLOUKLOKKIE
(Named for Dr Georg Wahlenberg, 1780–1851, professor at Uppsala University, Sweden) Annual or perennial herbs or shrublets. Leaves mostly alternate, narrow and stiff to broad and soft. Flowers solitary or in panicles, white to blue, star-shaped to deeply cup-shaped; stamens attached to the base of the petals, withered at flowering; *ovary ± half inferior; stigma with 2-5 lobes alternating with the petals. Fruit opening by 5 flaps at the tip.* Mainly southern temperate: ±180 spp.; South Africa: ±170 spp.

▶ **ANNUAL HERBS**

3 *Wahlenbergia androsacea*   J F M A M J J A S O N D
Lesser Bellflower Tufted annual herb to 40 cm, with roughly hairy, paddle-shaped leaves with wavy or crinkly margins, mostly in a basal tuft, and flat-topped panicles of white to pale blue, cup-shaped flowers, 5–15 mm in diameter, with a hairless ovary. Sandy flats from southern Namibia to tropical Africa.

4 *Wahlenbergia annularis*   J F M A M J J A S O N D
Greater Bellflower Tufted annual herb to 40 cm, with roughly hairy, paddle-shaped leaves with wavy or crinkly margins, mostly in a basal tuft, and flat-topped panicles of white to pale blue, bowl-shaped flowers, 15–20 mm in diameter, with a hairless ovary and the style less than half as long as the corolla. Sandy flats and lower slopes in Namaqualand.

5 *Wahlenbergia capensis*   J F M A M J J A S O N D
Dark-eyed Bellflower Hairy annual herb to 50 cm, with paddle-shaped to elliptical, wavy or toothed leaves, mostly scattered up the stem, and solitary, bowl-shaped flowers, pale blue with a darker centre, on long stems, with a densely hairy ovary and 5 broad stigma lobes. Sandstone slopes and flats in southwestern South Africa.

▶ PERENNIAL HERBS

① *Wahlenbergia undulata*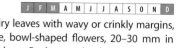
Perennial herb to 60 cm, with elliptical, hairy leaves with wavy or crinkly margins, and loosely branched stems of pale blue, bowl-shaped flowers, 20–30 mm in diameter, with triangular sepals, 3–4 mm long. Rocky grassland in eastern and southern South Africa.

② *Wahlenbergia cuspidata*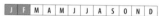
Perennial herb to 60 cm, with elliptical, hairy leaves with wavy or crinkly margins, and loosely branched stems of pale blue, bowl-shaped flowers, 20–30 mm in diameter, with slender, tapering sepals, 9–17 mm long. Damp cliffs or rocky slopes in the Drakensberg.

③ *Wahlenbergia polytrichifolia*
Moss-leaved Bellflower Creeping, mat-forming perennial with crowded, awl-shaped leaves, and blue, bell-shaped flowers, often with dark markings in the throat, ±10 mm in diameter. Gravelly patches on rock sheets in the Drakensberg.

Craterocapsa CARPET BELLFLOWER
(Greek krateros, strong; capsa, box, alluding to the hard fruits) *Creeping, mat-forming perennial herbs.* Leaves stiff. Flowers *sessile, solitary or in clusters at the branch tips*, blue or white, bell-shaped; stamens deciduous at flowering; stigma divided into *3 fleshy lobes*. Fruit opening by a lid at the top. Southern Africa: 4 spp.

④ *Craterocapsa tarsodes*
Mat-forming perennial herb with tufts of lance-shaped leaves at the branch tips, and small clusters of blue or white, bell-shaped flowers, ±20 mm in diameter, opening one at a time and soon overtopped by new shoots. Rock outcrops and stony grassland in the Drakensberg.

Roella ROELLA *(Named for G. Roelle, 18th-century Dutch professor of anatomy)*
Shrublets or creeping perennials. Leaves stiff, *with coarse white bristles on the margins, the uppermost leaves below the flowers (floral bracts) often larger*. Flowers *sessile, solitary or in clusters at the branch tips*, white to blue, rarely pink, *sometimes with dark blotches*, bell-shaped; stamens deciduous at flowering; stigma divided into *2 fleshy lobes*. Fruit opening by a lid at the top. South Africa, mainly southwestern Cape: 20 spp.

⑤ *Roella incurva*
Shrublet to 40 cm, with stiff, awl-like leaves, prickly-toothed and bristly on the margins, the midrib thickened beneath, and 1–3 white or blue, rarely pink or red flowers, 20–30 mm in diameter, mostly with dark spots on the petals; the ovary hairless, and the floral bracts longer than the leaves. Sandy lower slopes in the southwestern Cape.

⑥ *Roella ciliata*
Shrublet to 50 cm, with stiff, awl-like leaves, bristly on the margins, the midrib thickened beneath, and solitary, white or blue flowers, 20–30 mm in diameter, with a dark ring or spots on the petals; the ovary hairless, and the floral bracts larger than the leaves and fringed with white bristles. Stony slopes in the southwestern Cape.

① *Roella triflora*   J **F** M A **M** J J A S O N **D**

Shrublet to 20 cm, with stiff, awl-like leaves, prickly-toothed on the margins and bristly towards the base, and 1–3 pale blue flowers, 15–20 mm in diameter, with a dark eye; the calyx and ovary hairy, the floral bracts larger than the leaves and finely hairy, with stiff, wire-like hairs on the margins. Sandy lower slopes in the Cape Peninsula. *Roella maculata* from the southwestern coast has large dark spots in the gaps between the petals.

Prismatocarpus   PRISMATOCARPUS, STEELVRUG

(Greek prisma, *sawn or cut;* karpos, *fruit, referring to the slender, prism-like fruits*)   Slender-stemmed shrublets or perennial herbs. Leaves often narrow and leathery. Flowers *usually on wiry stems*, white to blue, *funnel- or salver-shaped*; stamens deciduous at flowering; stigma divided into 2 fleshy lobes. *Fruit cylindrical, splitting longitudinally into 5 strips*. South Africa, mainly southwestern Cape: 31 spp.

② *Prismatocarpus fruticosus*   J **F** **M** A M J J A S O N **D**

Shrublet to 50 cm, with needle-like leaves coarsely hairy on the margins at the base, and a leafless, branching inflorescence of deeply cup- or funnel-shaped, white flowers with brown or purple reverse, 10–15 mm in diameter. Sandy flats and lower slopes in the southwestern Cape.

③ *Prismatocarpus diffusus*   J **F** M A M J J A S O N **D**

Shrublet to 45 cm, with needle-like leaves sparsely hairy on the margins at the base, and a leafless, branching inflorescence of salver-shaped, blue or white flowers with a slender, cylindrical tube, ±10 mm long. Rocky slopes in the southwestern Cape, flowering well after fire.

▶ **SUBFAMILY CYPHIOIDEAE** FLOWERS ± 2-LIPPED, THE ANTHERS PRESENT AT FLOWERING AND ± SEPARATE

Cyphia   CYPHIA, BAROE, AARDBOONTJIE

(Greek kyphos, *curved, referring to the shape of the stigma*)   Erect or twining perennial herbs, often with a tuber. Leaves basal or scattered along the stem, lance-shaped or deeply divided, usually toothed. Flowers in racemes or 1–few in the upper leaf axils, white to mauve or purple, 5-lobed or 2-lipped, lobes ± similar, usually *split down the sides*; stamens not attached to the petals, with the anthers *separate from one another or only loosely attached* and usually bearded on the back. Africa, mainly the southwestern Cape: ±60 spp. The tubers are edible. The vernacular name *baroe* derives from the original Khoi name.

▶ **STEM ERECT, NOT TWINING**

④ *Cyphia bulbosa*   J F M A M J J A S O N D

Erect perennial to 30 cm, with deeply divided leaves grading into the floral bracts, paler beneath, with the margins lightly rolled under, and a raceme of showy, 2-lipped, white to mauve flowers, 8–13 mm long, with the tube split down the sides; only 2 anthers bearded. Sandy and stony flats and slopes in the southwestern Cape, especially after fire.

⑤ *Cyphia phyteuma*   J F M A M J J A S O N D

Erect perennial to 40 cm, with slightly toothed leaves in a basal rosette, and a spiralled, spike-like raceme of ± sessile, 2-lipped, whitish to brown or mauve flowers, 16–20 mm long, with the tube split down the sides; all the anthers bearded. Sandy and stony flats and slopes in the southwestern Cape.

► STEM TWINING

① *Cyphia digitata*

Twining perennial with leaves usually deeply 3–7-lobed and ± toothed, and white to mauve, 2-lipped, flowers, 7–14 mm long, split down the sides, with stamens 5–9 mm long. Stony slopes in southwestern South Africa.

② *Cyphia volubilis*

Twining perennial with lance-shaped or deeply lobed, toothed leaves, and showy, 2-lipped, white to purple flowers, 10–26 mm long, split down the sides, with short stamens, 3–5 mm long, less than half as long as the floral tube. Sandy flats and slopes in southwestern South Africa.

► SUBFAMILY LOBELIOIDEAE FLOWERS ± 2-LIPPED, THE ANTHERS PRESENT AT FLOWERING AND JOINED IN A TUBE

Monopsis MONOPSIS

(Greek mon, one; opsis, appearing, alluding to the almost regular flowers in many species) Small annual or perennial herbs. Leaves opposite or alternate, toothed. Flowers in racemes or solitary in the axils, often yellow or purple, ± 2-lipped, with the pedicels twisted so that the upper lip is 3-lobed and the lower lip 2-lobed, split down the middle to the base; stamens sometimes attached to the base of the petals, with the anthers joined to one another in a ring, with a brush-like tuft of straight white hairs at the tips; stigma with 2 slender lobes. Africa: ±20 spp.; South Africa: 18 spp.

③ *Monopsis lutea*

Yellow Monopsis, Yellow Lobelia Sprawling or trailing perennial herb to 60 cm, with narrowly elliptical, toothed leaves, often oriented along the upper side of the stem, and spikes of sessile, 2-lipped, bright yellow flowers, 10 mm in diameter. Damp flats and lower slopes, often along seeps or streams, in the southwestern and southern Cape. *Monopsis flava*, from Namaqualand to Ceres, has stalked flowers; *M. variifolia*, in the Breede River valley, has fewer flowers, which nestle among the leaves.

④ *Monopsis debilis*

Pansy Monopsis, Pansy Lobelia Loosely sprawling or tufted annual herb to 25 cm, with narrowly elliptical, toothed leaves, and solitary, almost regular, purple flowers with a darker centre and broad, rounded petals, on slender pedicels in the leaf axils. Damp sandy slopes and flats, often along seeps, in western South Africa.

⑤ *Monopsis unidentata* Wild Violet

Erect or sprawling perennial herb to 60 cm, with narrow to elliptical, often coarsely toothed leaves, and 2-lipped, purple or brown flowers with a darker centre, 10 mm in diameter, on long, slender pedicels at the branch tips. Damp sandy flats and rocky slopes from the southern Cape to KwaZulu-Natal.

⑥ *Monopsis stellarioides*

Sticky-leaved Monopsis Sprawling perennial or annual herb with minutely barbed stems, narrow, toothed leaves, and solitary, 2-lipped, dull yellow, pink, brown or purple flowers with 2 yellow crests, 10 mm in diameter, on slender pedicels in the leaf axils along the stem. Grassland and swampy places through eastern South Africa.

333

① *Monopsis decipiens* `J F M A M J J A S O N D`

Butterfly Monopsis, Butterfly Lobelia Erect, perennial herb, with narrow, awl-like leaves, hairy on the margins, and solitary, 2-lipped, blue and purple flowers with 2 yellow crests, 15–18 mm in diameter, on slender pedicels. Seasonally damp grassland through eastern South and tropical Africa.

Lobelia LOBELIA *(Named for Flemish botanist, Matthias de l'Obel, 1538–1616)*

Perennials or subshrubs, rarely annual herbs. Leaves variable, often toothed. Flowers in racemes or 1–few in the upper leaf axils, often blue or purple, *2-lipped,* the upper lip *2-lobed and split down the middle to the base* and the lower lip 3-lobed; stamens attached to the base of the petals, with the anthers *joined to one another in a ring* and a *brush-like tuft of straight white hairs at the tips.* Worldwide: ±300 spp.; South Africa: ±70 spp. Some species were used medicinally.

▶ **LEAVES NARROW OR NEEDLE-LIKE; ALL ANTHERS WITH A TUFT OF WHITE HAIRS AT THE TIPS**

② *Lobelia setacea* `J F M A M J J A S O N D`

Tufted, erect or sprawling, wiry-stemmed perennial to 60 cm, with scattered, thread-like leaves less than 1 mm wide, and branched racemes of hairless, blue or violet and white flowers, 10 mm long. Sandstone slopes and sandy flats in the southwestern and southern Cape.

③ *Lobelia pinifolia* `J F M A M J J A S O N D`

Pine-leaved Lobelia Erect, densely leafy shrublet to 50 cm, with overlapping, narrow or needle-like leaves, 1–2 mm wide, and 1–few hairy, blue flowers, 10–15 mm long, on short or long, hairless pedicels. Rocky sandstone slopes and flats in the southwestern Cape.

④ *Lobelia tomentosa* `J F M A M J J A S O N D`

Tufted shrublet to 40 cm, with ± sprawling, shortly hairy stems branching from the base, the leaves narrow to thread-like and toothed, 2–5 mm wide, the margins rolled under, and wiry, leafless stems of 1–4 finely hairy, blue, violet or pink flowers, 10–15 mm long. Stony lower slopes from the southwestern to Eastern Cape.

⑤ *Lobelia coronopifolia* `J F M A M J J A S O N D`

Tufted shrublet to 30 cm, with ± sprawling, shortly hairy stems branching from the base, the leaves narrow to lance-shaped and deeply toothed or lobed, 5–10 mm wide, the margins lightly rolled under, and wiry, leafless stems of 1–few large, hairless, dark blue, pink or white flowers, 15–30 mm long. Sandy and stony flats and lower slopes in the southwestern Cape.

335

LEAVES TRIANGULAR TO HEART-SHAPED; ALL ANTHERS WITH A TUFT OF WHITE HAIRS AT THE TIP

1 *Lobelia vanreenensis*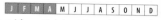
Delicate, clump-forming perennial to 45 cm, with petiolate, triangular, bluntly toothed leaves, 12–25 mm wide, and wiry, leafless stems of white flowers, 8–10 mm long. Damp, partially shaded cliffs and rock outcrops in the Drakensberg.

2 *Lobelia preslii*
Tufted perennial to 35 cm, with basal rosettes of petiolate, heart-shaped, bluntly toothed leaves, 12–35 mm in diameter, and wiry, leafless stems of deep blue flowers with a white centre, 15–25 mm long. Damp, partially shaded basalt cliffs and gullies in the Drakensberg.

LEAVES LANCE-SHAPED TO OVAL; ONLY THE LOWER 2 ANTHERS WITH A TUFT OF WHITE HAIRS AT THE TIP

3 *Lobelia comosa*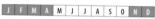
Soft shrublet with rod-like stems to 50 cm, branching from the base, with lance-shaped, hairless or thinly hairy, toothed leaves, 5–10 mm wide, and long-stemmed, loose or dense racemes of hairless, bright blue flowers, 10 mm long. Sandy coastal slopes in the southwestern Cape. *Lobelia valida* is a more robust plant with broad, paddle-shaped leaves, mostly 10–15 mm wide.

4 *Lobelia erinus* **Edging Lobelia**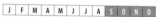
Erect or spreading, hairless annual or weak perennial to 10 cm, with narrowly lance- to paddle-shaped, toothed or lobed leaves, 5–15 mm wide, and leafy racemes of blue, violet, pink or white flowers, 10 mm long, usually with a white centre, and slender, awl-like sepals. Lower mountain slopes and coastal flats from the southwestern Cape to tropical Africa.

5 *Lobelia flaccida*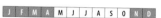
Similar to *Lobelia erinus* but with narrowly lance-shaped, toothed sepals. Moist mountain slopes and rock faces through eastern South Africa.

6 *Lobelia pubescens*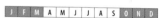
Spreading, hairy-stemmed annual or perennial to 50 cm, with finely hairy, petiolate, lance-shaped to broadly oval, toothed leaves, 8–20 mm wide, and leafy racemes of thinly hairy, white to pale blue flowers, 10–15 mm long. Sheltered rocky slopes and damp rocks near the coast from the southwestern to the Eastern Cape.

GOODENIACEAE Fan Flower family

Scaevola FAN FLOWER
(Named for Gaius Mucius Scaevola, the left-handed Roman hero of the 6th century BC, alluding to the shape of the flower)

Shrublets. *Flowers 5-lobed, with the tube slit to the base and thus fan-shaped; stigma concealed within a fringed cup.* Fruit fleshy. Mostly Australia: ±80 spp.; South Africa: 2 spp.

❶ *Scaevola plumieri* See-plakkie

Succulent shrublet to 50 cm, spreading underground to form large colonies, with fleshy, paddle-shaped leaves, and clusters of fan-shaped, white flowers, 25 mm in diameter, in the leaf axils. Coastal dunes above the high-tide mark from the southern Cape to tropical Africa. *Scaevola sericea* is a spreading shrub to 1.5 m, with apically toothed leaves and smaller flowers.

APIACEAE Carrot family

Alepidea TINSEL FLOWER
(Greek a, without; lepis, scale, possibly alluding to the joined involucral bracts) Tufted perennials. Leaves simple and toothed, *with coarse bristles on the margins,* basal leaves petiolate, upper leaves sessile. *Flowers sessile in heads, surrounded by a collar of white, petal-like bracts joined at the base.* Africa: 28 spp., mainly South Africa. Used in traditional medicine and magic.

❷ *Alepidea cordifolia*

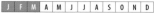

Giant Tinsel Flower Robust perennial to 2 m, with grooved, leafy stems and large, petiolate leaves with a lobed base and sharply toothed margins, and widely branched stems of greenish, star-like flowerheads, 10–15 mm in diameter; fruit smooth. Coarse grass near streams and in damp gullies through eastern South and subtropical Africa. *Alepidea amatymbica* from further south has leaves with a tapering base.

❸ *Alepidea woodii*

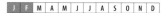

Wood's Tinsel Flower Tufted perennial to 60 cm, with a rosette of elliptical leaves with finely and evenly bristled margins, and shortly branched stems of white, star-like flowerheads surrounded by narrow, petal-like bracts, 10 mm in diameter; fruit warty. Damp grassy slopes and stream banks in the Drakensberg.

❹ *Alepidea thodei*

Thode's Tinsel Flower Tufted perennial to 30 cm, with a rosette of elliptical leaves with finely toothed and bristled margins, and unbranched stems of 1–3 large, white, daisy-like flowerheads with a dark blue centre, ±30 mm in diameter. Damp tuff at high altitudes in the Drakensberg.

339

Hermas TINDERLEAF, TONTELBLAAR *(Origin obscure)*

Tufted perennials or shrublets. Leaves *simple, leathery and felted or woolly, at least on the underside.* Flowers in dense, compound umbels resembling a simple umbel, *each umbel usually with a single female or bisexual flower surrounded by several male flowers* (thus only the central flower setting seed), white to cream-coloured. Fruit oblong or flattened, with the *two halves face to face.* Southwestern Cape: 7 spp. The woolly hairs were scraped from the leaves and dried for use in dressing wounds and in tinderboxes; hence the vernacular name.

1 *Hermas villosa*

J F M A M J J A S O N D

Robust 1–few-stemmed shrub to 1 m, with oblong to elliptical, finely toothed leaves, white-felted beneath, and crowded umbels of cream-coloured flowers. Rocky sandstone slopes in the extreme southwestern Cape.

Arctopus ARCTOPUS, PLATDORING

(Greek arktos, a bear; pous, foot, a fanciful allusion to the form of the leaves) *Stemless perennials* with a thick taproot and *sexes on separate plants.* Leaves prostrate, *oval and lobed with bristly or spiny margins.* Male flowers in stalked umbels, white or pinkish; *female flowers in sessile umbels* surrounded by 4 usually spiny bracts. Fruit oblong and tapering, ridged. Southwestern Cape: 3 spp. The thick taproot was used medicinally.

2 *Arctopus echinatus* Sieketroos

J F M A M J J A S O N D

Stemless perennial, with prostrate, glossy, lobed to fringed leaves with bristly margins, and white to pink male flowers; female involucral bracts joined at the base and spine-tipped, becoming hard and very spiny in fruit. Damp flats in southwestern South Africa. *Arctopus monacanthus* develops large, papery involucral bracts in fruit.

BRUNIACEAE   Brunia family

Berzelia BERZELIA, KOLKOL *(Named for Swedish chemist, Jacob J. Berzelius, 1779–1845)*

Ericoid shrubs. Flowers *many (>30) in ± spherical heads,* whitish, with the *stamens longer than the petals;* the ovary 1-chambered, with *1 style.* South Africa: 12 spp. Used in the cut-flower trade as 'Cape greens'. The vernacular name alludes to the appearance of the plants, which are visible from a distance as distinct patches *(kolle)* of bright green and white against the hillsides.

3 *Berzelia lanuginosa*

J F M A M J J A S O N D

Kolkol, Vleiknoppiesbos Willowy shrub to 2 m, with fine, needle-like leaves, and small, cream-coloured flowers in spherical heads, ±5 mm in diameter, on red, swollen peduncles. Damp slopes, seeps and stream banks in the southwestern Cape.

4 *Berzelia abrotanoides*

J F M A M J J A S O N D

Redlegs, Rooibeentjies Shrub to 1.5 m, coppicing from a woody base, with needle-like leaves, and clusters of small, white flowers in spherical heads, ±10 mm in diameter, on red, swollen peduncles. Drier sandy flats and slopes in the southwestern Cape.

Brunia BRUNIA, VOLSTRUISIES
(Named for the 18th-century apothecary and plant collector, Cornelius Brun) Ericoid shrubs. Flowers, *many (>30)* *in ± spherical heads*, whitish, with *stamens longer than the petals and unequal in length*; the ovary 2-chambered with *2 styles*. South Africa: 6 spp. The vernacular name *volstruisies*, originally applied to *Brunia noduliflora* in particular, alludes to the resemblance of the flowerheads to a brood of ostrich chicks.

1 *Brunia laevis* **Vaalstompie, Vaaltol**
Rounded shrub to 1.5 m, coppicing from a woody base, with oblong leaves incurved at the tips and minutely hairy on the upper surface, and small, cream-coloured flowers in spherical heads, 15–20 mm in diameter. Rocky slopes in the southwestern Cape.

2 *Brunia noduliflora* **Fonteinbos**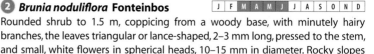
Rounded shrub to 1.5 m, coppicing from a woody base, with minutely hairy branches, the leaves triangular or lance-shaped, 2–3 mm long, pressed to the stem, and small, white flowers in spherical heads, 10–15 mm in diameter. Rocky slopes from the southwestern to Eastern Cape.

Staavia STAAVIA *(Named for Martin Staaf, a correspondent of Linnaeus)*

Ericoid shrublets. Leaves needle-like or oblong, *± spreading, the upper ones forming a conspicuous, whitish whorl or collar around the flowerhead*. Flowers small, in small heads, sometimes sticky; the *stamens shorter than the petals*. South Africa: 10 spp.

3 *Staavia radiata* **Altydbos**
Twiggy shrublet to 60 cm, coppicing from a woody base, with narrowly lance-shaped leaves, 4–10 mm long, and heads of small pink flowers surrounded by a whorl of small, white bracts. Sandy coastal flats in the southwestern Cape.

Identifying members of the Daisy family

The genera of daisies are grouped into several tribes distinguished primarily by microscopic characters of the stigmas and anthers that are of little practical use in a field guide. Most of the genera, however, may be identified by a combination of more obvious characters, notably:

▶ **Bracts:** Each daisy flowerhead is surrounded by overlapping involucral bracts. The number of rows, or series, of these bracts is important, as well as the shape and texture of the individual bracts, which may be entirely green or have conspicuous translucent membranous margins or tips, or be entirely dry and papery. Representative flowerheads with bracts from each of the Daisy genera included in this guide are illustrated on pages 345–347.

▶ **Florets:** Each flowerhead contains a number of individual, small flowers, or florets, which may differ in form and sex within the head. Button-like or discoid flowerheads contain only funnel-shaped florets, each with 5 (rarely only 4) triangular petals, and a fertile ovary and anthers. The more familiar radiate flowerheads, in contrast, comprise 2 different types of florets: funnel-shaped, male or bisexual disc florets in the centre, plus a peripheral ring of strap-shaped ray florets that usually lack stamens and are thus female. Most genera have narrow rays, but some have distinctive broad, wedge-shaped rays, and others have rays that are reduced to small, inconspicuous lobes. In a few genera with radiate flowerheads, 2 of the petals of the ray florets remain separate as thread-like appendages opposite the main ray, and are thus 2-lipped. An intermediate type of flowerhead, known as disciform, has several peripheral rows of tubular female florets surrounding the fertile disc florets. **HINT: Check the fruiting heads to determine which of the florets set seeds and are thus female/fertile. Those heads in which the disc florets are functionally male will set only a peripheral ring of seeds, developed from the outer florets.** The different types of floret are illustrated below.

▶ **Fruits:** One of the keys to the success of daisies lies in their highly specialised fruits, commonly misidentified as seeds. In many daisies each fruit is crowned with a ring of flat scales or thread-like bristles, known as the pappus, which aids in the dispersal of the fruits by wind. **HINT: The pappus is most evident at the fruiting stage, when it enlarges.** Fruits with a pappus of scales resemble miniature shuttlecocks or even dried florets, while those with bristles recall dandelions or dainty brushes. Relatively few daisies lack any form of pappus, having flattened or winged fruits instead.

FLORETS

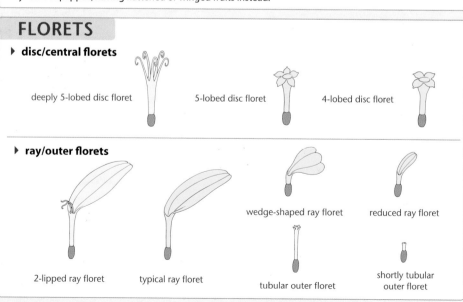

▶ **disc/central florets**

deeply 5-lobed disc floret   5-lobed disc floret   4-lobed disc floret

▶ **ray/outer florets**

2-lipped ray floret   typical ray floret   wedge-shaped ray floret   reduced ray floret

tubular outer floret   shortly tubular outer floret

▶ Plants ± felted; flowerheads discoid or disciform, **the involucral bracts papery, shining and colourful, more conspicuous than the florets**; pappus comprising bristles (everlastings and strawflowers) – p. 348

Helichrysum aureum

Syncarpha canescens

Edmondia sesamoides

Phaenocoma prolifera

▶ Thornless herbs or shrubs with mauve or purple, **discoid heads with several, overlapping rows of bracts**, and conspicuous long, thread-like style branches – p. 356

Vernonia capensis

▶ Plants often thistle-like, with large, usually radiate flowerheads; **involucral bracts spine-tipped, in 2 or more rows, often joined at the base into a cup**; ray florets sterile or absent; pappus comprising scales, sometimes narrow and bristle-like, rarely absent – p. 358

Dicoma capensis

Macledium zeyheri

Cullumia bisulca

Didelta carnosa

Berkheya armata

Gorteria diffusa

Hirpicium alienatum

Gazania lichtensteinii

▶ Flowerheads radiate; **all or at least the inner involucral bracts with large, rounded, membranous or papery tips**; pappus comprising scales – p. 370

Arctotis acaulis

Haplocarpha scaposa

Arctotheca calendula

Ursinia chrysanthemoides

FLOWERHEADS, ILLUSTRATING BRACTS

▶ **Involucral bracts entirely green and fleshy, in 1 row, cohering along the margins and sometimes joined below (sometimes with additional small bracteoles at the base);** ray florets curling back at night; pappus comprising barbed bristles (sometimes soon deciduous) – p. 380

Senecio arenarius

Cineraria geifolia

Othonna dentata

Euryops lateriflorus

Gymnodiscus capillaris

▶ Flowerheads radiate, with **involucral bracts in 1–4 rows, narrow and mostly green throughout;** fruit without an evident pappus, mostly large, >5 mm long – p. 392

Osteospermum polygaloides

Dimorphotheca nudicaulis

Osmitopsis asteriscoides

Eumorphia prostrata

Adenanthellum osmitoides

▶ Annuals, often with finely divided leaves; flowerheads discoid or with small white or yellow rays; **involucral bracts small, blunt, in several rows;** disc florets 4-lobed; receptacle often conical; pappus comprising scales or absent – p. 400

Oncosiphon grandiflorum

Foveolina tenella

Cotula barbata

▶ Flowerheads radiate with yellow rays but otherwise not as any of the above; **involucral bracts often partially dry and papery, in several rows** – p. 402

Heterolepis aliena

Leysera tenella

Rhynchopsidium pumilum

▶ Flowerheads either discoid, or radiate with white, pink, blue, purple, orange or red (rarely yellow) rays but otherwise not as any of the above; **involucral bracts narrow, in 2–several rows** – p. 404

Gerbera cordata

Callilepis laureola

Printzia polifolia

Athrixia rosmarinifolia

Microglossa mespilifolia

Chrysocoma coma-aurea

Felicia filifolia

Aster bakerianus

Amellus strigosus

Mairia coriacea

▶ PLANTS ± FELTED; FLOWERHEADS DISCOID OR DISCIFORM, THE INVOLUCRAL BRACTS PAPERY, SHINING AND COLOURFUL, MORE CONSPICUOUS THAN THE FLORETS; PAPPUS COMPRISING BRISTLES (EVERLASTINGS AND STRAWFLOWERS)

Helichrysum STRAWFLOWER, STROOIBLOM

(Greek helios, sun; chrysos, gold, for the glossy yellow bracts of some species) Annual or perennial herbs or shrubs, usually woolly or cobwebby. Leaves alternate, variously shaped and without teeth, flat or with the margins rolled under, mostly variously felted or woolly. Flowerheads solitary or often in flat-topped clusters at the branch tips, disciform, *with several rows of dry, chaffy or papery bracts* coloured white, yellow, straw-coloured, brown, pink, purple or red, at least *the inner with a translucent strip near the base*; receptacle without scales but sometimes fringed. Ray florets female, often narrowly tubular, yellow; disc florets fertile, 5-lobed, yellow. Fruit smooth or hairy, *pappus of barbed or somewhat feathery bristles*. Old World, mainly Africa: ±500 spp.; South Africa: ±250 spp. The leaves and twigs are an important traditional medicine, especially for chest complaints. *Helichrysum petiolare* is a popular horticultural plant.

▶ SPRAWLING, GREY-LEAVED SHRUBS WITH BELL-SHAPED TO ± SPHERICAL FLOWERHEADS, 5–10 MM ACROSS

1 *Helichrysum pandurifolium*

| J | F | M | A | M | J | J | A | S | O | N | D |

Straggling shrublet or shrub with grey-woolly, oval, crinkly leaves, narrowed and eared at the base and clasping the stem, and clusters of bell-shaped, discoid flowerheads, 5–8×6–10 mm, with hairless, pointed, cream-coloured bracts. Sandy flats and slopes in the southwestern and southern Cape.

2 *Helichrysum patulum*

| J | F | M | A | M | J | J | A | S | O | N | D |

Like *Helichrysum pandurifolium* but with blunt, cupped involucral bracts. Sandy flats and slopes along the coast in the southwestern Cape.

3 *Helichrysum petiolare*

| J | F | M | A | M | J | J | A | S | O | N | D |

Like *Helichrysum patulum* but the leaves have a conspicuous petiole and are not crinkly. Sheltered slopes and forest margins in the southern and Eastern Cape.

▶ ROBUST, ERECT, SOFT-LEAVED BIENNIALS OR PERENNIALS WITH FLATTENED-SPHERICAL FLOWERHEADS, 15–25 MM ACROSS

4 *Helichrysum tenax* **Sticky Everlasting**

| J | F | M | A | M | J | J | A | S | O | N | D |

Bushy subshrub to 2 m, sticky and foetid, with short stems terminating in rosettes of elliptical leaves, glandular-haired on both surfaces but sometimes also woolly, and 1–few, disciform, flattened-spherical flowerheads, 25–35 mm in diameter, with cream-coloured or pale to golden-yellow bracts. Rocky slopes or boulder beds, often along roads, in the Drakensberg.

5 *Helichrysum aureum*

| J | F | M | A | M | J | J | A | S | O | N | D |

Perennial with stems to 40(–80) cm, arising alongside rosettes of elliptical to paddle-shaped leaves, glandular-haired and sometimes woolly on both surfaces, and 1–few disciform, flattened-spherical flowerheads, 20–45 mm in diameter, with golden-yellow (rarely white) bracts. Grassland and cliffs through eastern South and tropical Africa.

1 *Helichrysum ruderale*

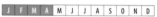

Robust, aromatic biennial to 1 m, with elliptical leaves, eared at the base and clasping the stem, glandular-haired on both surfaces, and white-woolly branches of disciform, flattened-spherical flowerheads, 25–30 mm in diameter, with bright yellow bracts. A pioneer, forming dense stands along roadsides and in old fields in KwaZulu-Natal. *Helichrysum cooperi* has little or no wool on the branches and flowers in late summer.

2 *Helichrysum foetidum*

Robust, foetid biennial to 1 m, with oblong to lance-shaped leaves, eared at the base and clasping the stem, glandular-haired above and grey-woolly beneath, and leafy clusters of flattened-spherical, disciform flowerheads, 15–25 mm in diameter, with cream-coloured to yellowish bracts. Damp rocky slopes in southern South Africa.

3 *Helichrysum elegantissimum*

Robust biennial to 1 m, with oblong to lance-shaped leaves, eared at the base and clasping the stem, glandular-haired above and woolly or cobwebby beneath, and leafy clusters of flattened-spherical, disciform flowerheads, 20–25 mm in diameter, with pink-flushed or crimson bracts. Damp slopes in scrub or on river banks in the southern Drakensberg.

▶ SMALL OR DWARF PERENNIALS WITH SPHERICAL OR TOP-SHAPED FLOWERHEADS, 15–40 MM ACROSS

4 *Helichrysum herbaceum*

Monkey-tail Everlasting Erect perennial with closely leafy stems to 40 cm, with a basal rosette of elliptical leaves and overlapping, narrow stem leaves, the margins often rolled under, cobwebby above and loosely felted beneath, and disciform, top-shaped flowerheads, 25–39 mm in diameter, with yellow and golden-brown bracts. Stony grasslands through eastern South and tropical Africa.

5 *Helichrysum ecklonis*

Large Pink Strawflower Perennial to 50 cm, with basal rosettes of oblong to elliptical leaves, usually loosely cobwebby-woolly on both surfaces but sometimes ± hairless above and then clearly 3–5-veined, the closely leafy flowering stems arising from the centre of a rosette, the upper stem leaves often papery, with a solitary, disciform, top-shaped flowerhead, 40–50 mm in diameter, the bracts glossy white to deep pink. Grassy, mostly montane slopes in eastern South Africa. *Helichrysum vernum* has ± hairless leaves with a single main vein.

6 *Helichrysum monticola*

Perennial to 50 cm, with basal rosettes of oblong to elliptical leaves, glandular-haired and cobwebby on both surfaces, the flowering stems arising from the centre of a rosette, with mostly several disciform, top-shaped flowerheads, 15–20 mm in diameter, the bracts glossy white or pink-tinged. Rocky montane grasslands through eastern South Africa.

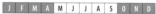

351

1 *Helichrysum adenocarpum*

J F M A M J J A S O N D

Pink Strawflower Perennial to 50 cm, with basal rosettes of elliptical to orbicular leaves, mostly grey-woolly or cobwebby on both surfaces, the flowering stems arising from beside a rosette, with 1–several disciform, top-shaped flowerheads, 25–35 mm in diameter, the bracts glossy white to carmine. Moist grassy slopes through eastern South Africa.

2 *Helichrysum marginatum*

J F M A M J J A S O N D

Silver-margined Strawflower Mat-forming perennial with crowded rosettes of elliptical, leathery, ± hairless leaves with white-woolly margins, and solitary spherical, disciform flowerheads, 30–40 mm in diameter, with dull white bracts. Alpine rock sheets in the Drakensberg and Maluti Mountains.

3 *Helichrysum confertum*

J F M A M J J A S O N D

Confetti Strawflower Mat-forming perennial with crowded rosettes of oval to elliptical leaves, grey-felted on both surfaces, and ± stalkless, disciform, bell-shaped flowerheads, ±16 mm in diameter, with opaque white bracts. Cliff faces and rock sheets in the high Drakensberg. *Helichrysum sutherlandii* has ± stalked flowerheads and flowers February to July.

4 *Helichrysum milfordiae*

J F M A M J J A S O N D

Spotted Strawflower Mat-forming dwarf perennial with crowded rosettes of paddle-shaped leaves, silvery-felted on both surfaces, and very shortly stalked, disciform, spherical flowerheads, ±20 mm in diameter, with glossy white bracts tipped pink or brown. Alpine rock sheets in the high Drakensberg.

5 *Helichrysum retortum*

J F M A M J J A S O N D

Sea Strawflower Straggling, closely leafy shrublet to 50 cm, with overlapping, oblong, channelled leaves, spreading or curved backwards with hooked tips, with silvery-silky, tissue paper-like hairs on both surfaces, and solitary, disciform, top-shaped flowerheads, ±40 mm in diameter, nestled in the leaves, with glossy white bracts, often flushed pink and brown. Coastal sands and cliffs in the southwestern Cape.

Syncarpha EVERLASTING, SEWEJAARTJIE

(Greek *syn, together*; *carpha, scale*, referring to the joined pappus bristles) Felted perennial herbs. Leaves alternate, narrow to lance-shaped, never toothed, *flat or slightly concave, densely grey- or silvery-felted on both surfaces*. Flowerheads solitary or in clusters, usually *large and conspicuous, discoid*, with several rows of glossy, dry, papery bracts coloured white, yellow, pink or brown; receptacle without scales but fringed. Florets all fertile, yellow, 5-lobed. Fruit oblong, warty, *pappus of feathery bristles joined at the base*. Southern Africa: 28 spp.

▸ FLOWERHEADS UP TO 20 MM ACROSS

6 *Syncarpha paniculata*

J F M A M J J A S O N D

Densely leafy, silvery-felted shrublet to 60 cm, with narrow, sharply pointed leaves, and clusters of hemispherical, discoid flowerheads, ±10 mm in diameter, with pointed, papery bracts, yellow or pink in bud but ageing to white or cream-coloured. Coastal and lower slopes in southwestern South Africa.

1 *Syncarpha argentea*

J F M A M J J A S O N D

Silver Everlasting Sprawling, silvery-felted shrublet to 60 cm, with paddle-shaped, 3-veined leaves curved back at the tips, and hemispherical, discoid flowerheads, 15–20 mm in diameter, on long, sparsely leafy stems, with pointed, papery, white bracts tipped pink. Coastal grassland and scrub in the Eastern Cape.

▶ **FLOWERHEADS >20 MM ACROSS**

2 *Syncarpha canescens*

J F M A M J J A S O N D

Pienksewejaartjie, Pink Everlasting Sparsely branched, grey-felted shrublet to 50 cm, with small, elliptical leaves, and mostly solitary, conical, discoid flowerheads, 25–35 mm in diameter, with pointed, papery, pink to red bracts. Drier rocky sandstone slopes and flats in southwestern South Africa.

3 *Syncarpha eximia*

J F M A M J J A S O N D

Strawberry Everlasting Robust, mostly single-stemmed, silvery-felted shrub to 40 cm, with oval leaves, and tight clusters of hemispherical, discoid flowerheads, 20–25 mm in diameter, nestled in the upper leaves, with rounded, papery, bright red bracts. Cool, moist, south-facing mountain slopes in the southern Cape.

4 *Syncarpha vestita* **Cape Snow**

J F M A M J J A S O N D

Softly woody, grey-woolly shrublet to 1 m, with paddle-shaped leaves, and loose clusters of conical, discoid flowerheads, 35–40 mm in diameter, often nestled in the upper leaves, with pointed, papery white bracts. Rocky slopes and flats in the southwestern and southern Cape.

5 *Syncarpha speciosissima*

J F M A M J J A S O N D

Cape Everlasting Sprawling, white-woolly shrublet with erect annual stems, 20–60 cm, with oblong to linear leaves clasping the stem at the base, and solitary, hemispherical, discoid flowerheads, 30–40 mm in diameter, on elongated peduncles, with pointed, papery, white to cream-coloured bracts. Sandstone slopes in the southwestern Cape.

Edmondia **EDMONDIA, SEWEJAARTJIE** (*Named for Scottish botanist, James Edmond, d. 1815*)

Slender shrublets. Leaves alternate, erect, overlapping, *hairless beneath and densely white-woolly above, ± differentiated into longer, needle-like leaves with upward-rolled margins on the vegetative branches and scale-like concave leaves on the flowering stems. Flowerheads solitary on slender stems, large and showy*, discoid or disciform, with several rows of large, glossy, dry, papery bracts coloured white, yellow or pink; receptacle without scales but fringed. Ray florets sometimes female and then narrower; disc florets fertile, 5-lobed, with glandular-haired petals. Fruit either ellipsoid and warty or flattened and smooth, pappus comprising ± feathery bristles joined at the base. Southwestern Cape: 3 spp.

6 *Edmondia sesamoides*

J F M A M J J A S O N D

Thinly woolly shrublet to 30 cm, with the lower foliage leaves needle-like, with upward-rolled margins, and the upper leaves scale-like, pressed against the peduncles, and solitary discoid flowerheads, 25–30 mm in diameter, with glossy white to pink or creamy yellow, papery bracts. Rocky flats and slopes in the southwestern Cape. *Edmondia fasciculata* (bright yellow bracts) and *E. pinifolia* (flattened, winged fruits) have the uppermost peduncular leaves grading into the involucral bracts through a series of brown scales.

Phaenocoma FALSE EVERLASTING, ROOISEWEJAARTJIE

(Greek phaino, shining; koma, head of hair, alluding to the glossy bracts) Stiffly branched shrublet with white-woolly stems bearing *numerous short shoots at right angles to the branches*, each in the axil of a brown bract. *Leaves small and granular or knob-like*, closely spaced, white-woolly on the upper surface, pressed against the branches. *Flowerheads solitary at the branch tips*, large, disciform, with several rows of large, dry, papery *bracts divided into a lower, woolly shaft, a central dark brown hinge, and an upper blade coloured glossy pink to red*. Ray florets female, slender; ray fruit flask-shaped and densely silky, with a pappus of ± feathery bristles. Disc florets male, 5-lobed, *with hairy petals*; sterile fruit smooth and glossy, with a pappus of several ± feathery bristles. Southwestern Cape: 1 sp.

① *Phaenocoma prolifera* J F **M** A **M** J J A **S** O N **D**

Stiffly branched, woolly-stemmed shrublet to 60 cm, with closely overlapping, granular leaves clustered on short shoots, and solitary, large, disciform flowerheads, 30–40 mm in diameter, with conspicuous glossy pink to red papery bracts. Rocky slopes in the southwestern Cape.

▸ THORNLESS HERBS OR SHRUBS WITH MAUVE OR PURPLE, DISCOID HEADS WITH SEVERAL OVERLAPPING ROWS OF BRACTS, AND CONSPICUOUS LONG, THREAD-LIKE STYLE BRANCHES

Vernonia VERNONIA, BLOUKWASBOSSIE

(Named for botanist William Vernon, d. 1811, active in the USA) Perennials or shrubs. Leaves alternate, narrow or broad, sometimes lobed, often felted beneath. Flowerheads usually in clusters, *discoid*, with several rows of bracts; receptacle without scales. Florets all fertile, *mauve to purple or magenta*, 5-lobed; *style branches long and thread-like*. Fruit narrow and ribbed, mostly ± hairy, the pappus comprising an inner series of barbed or feathery bristles and an outer series of scales or short bristles. Widespread: 1 000+ spp.; South Africa: 40 spp. Used medicinally.

▸ BRANCHED SHRUBS

② *Vernonia myriantha* J F M A **M** **J** **J** A S O N D

(=*Vernonia stipulacea*) **Tree Vernonia** Shrub to 4 m, with large, petiolate, elliptical, toothed leaves, to 300×120 mm, lobed towards base, thinly woolly beneath, and large panicles of discoid, pale mauve flowerheads, ±3 mm in diameter. Forest margins in northeastern South and tropical Africa. *Vernonia amygdalina* has more than 10 florets in each head; *V. colorata* has hairless fruits.

③ *Vernonia tigna* J **F** **M** **A** **M** J J A S O N D

(=*Vernonia neocorymbosa*) **Swartteebossie** Shrub to 1.8 m, with wedge-shaped, coarsely toothed leaves, to 60×40 mm, ± hairless above but grey-woolly beneath, and rounded panicles of discoid, pale to dark violet flowerheads, ±4 mm in diameter. Scrub and forest margins through eastern South Africa. *Vernonia crataegifolia* has the leaves loosely cobwebby beneath; *V. mespilifolia* has petiolate, ± hairless leaves.

▸ PERENNIALS WITH ± UNBRANCHED STEMS

④ *Vernonia hirsuta* J F M A M J J **A** **S** **O** **N** **D**

Quilted-leaved Vernonia Perennial with unbranched annual stems to 1 m, leafy throughout, with lance-shaped to oblong leaves, to 80×50 mm, coarsely hairy above but grey-woolly beneath, and rounded panicles of discoid, pinkish to purple flowerheads, 5–8 mm in diameter. Colonies in grassland and scrub through eastern South and tropical Africa.

357

① *Vernonia capensis*

Narrow-leaved Vernonia Perennial with mostly unbranched annual stems to 1 m, with narrow leaves, 40–70×1–3 mm, ± hairless above but silvery-silky beneath, and clusters of discoid, purple flowerheads to 10 mm in diameter. Colonies in grassland through southern and eastern South and tropical Africa. *Vernonia oligocephala* has elliptical to oval leaves.

② *Vernonia natalensis* Silver Vernonia

J F M A M J J A S O N D

Perennial with mostly unbranched annual stems to 1 m, with narrowly lance-shaped leaves, 30–60×3–20 mm, silvery-silky on both surfaces, and clusters of discoid, purple flowerheads to 10 mm in diameter. Grassland through eastern South and tropical Africa.

▶ PLANTS OFTEN THISTLE-LIKE, WITH LARGE, USUALLY RADIATE FLOWERHEADS; INVOLUCRAL BRACTS SPINE-TIPPED, IN 2 OR MORE ROWS, OFTEN JOINED AT THE BASE INTO A CUP; RAY FLORETS STERILE OR ABSENT; PAPPUS COMPRISING SCALES, SOMETIMES NARROW AND BRISTLE-LIKE, RARELY ABSENT

Dicoma DICOMA, DORINGBOSSIE (Greek di, two; coma, tuft, referring to the double pappus)

Perennials or shrublets. Leaves alternate or basal, *mostly not toothed, often soft-textured and white-felted*. Flowerheads discoid, thistle-like, with several rows of *narrow, dark-striped, ± hairy, spine-tipped bracts, often curved out at the tips*; receptacle without scales. *Florets white or purple*, deeply 5-lobed, *the petals curved back*. Fruit flask-shaped, *ribbed*, with a pappus of bristles and scales in several rows. Africa: ±40 spp.; South Africa: 12 spp. Used medicinally and as a tonic.

③ *Dicoma anomala*

J F M A M J J A S O N D

Erect or prostrate perennial, with narrow, sessile leaves, hairless above and white-felted beneath, and discoid, white to pink flowerheads, 15–30 mm in diameter, with narrow, spine-tipped bracts. Stony grassland and savanna through eastern and central South and tropical Africa. *Dicoma macrocephala* has elliptical to oval leaves.

Macledium MACLEDIUM, MAAGWORTEL (Origin uncertain)

Perennials with annual stems from a woody rootstock. Leaves alternate or basal, *mostly not toothed*, hairless or white-felted beneath. *Flowerheads discoid, protea-like*, with several rows of *hairless, spine-tipped, often silvery bracts*; receptacle without scales. *Florets white or purple*, deeply 5-lobed, *the petals ± erect*. Fruit flask-shaped, *smooth*, with a pappus of bristles and scales in several rows. Africa: ±30 spp.; South Africa: 6 spp. Used medicinally and as a tonic.

④ *Macledium zeyheri*

J F M A M J J A S O N D

(=*Dicoma zeyheri*) **Doll's Protea** Tufted perennial to 40 cm, with a basal tuft of narrowly paddle-shaped, ± petiolate leaves, hairless above and white-felted beneath, and discoid, purplish flowerheads, 40–60 mm in diameter, with long, spine-tipped, silvery bracts tinged purple. Rocky grassland and savanna in northeastern South Africa. *Macledium speciosa* has narrow, sessile leaves, ± hairless at maturity; *M. argyrophylla* has dense, needle-like leaves up the stem.

Cullumia   SNAKE THISTLE, STEEKHAARBOS

(Named for the Rev. Sir John Cullen, 1733–1862, and his brother Sir Thomas Cullen) Spiny shrublets, often sprawling, sometimes cobwebby. *Leaves alternate, overlapping, small, with spiny or bristly margins and often spine-tipped.* Flowerheads solitary and sessile, radiate, with *4 rows of stiff, hairless, often curved-back, involucral bracts with spiny margins, joined at the base*; receptacle honeycombed, without scales. Ray florets sterile, 4-toothed, yellow; disc florets fertile, deeply 5-lobed. Fruit oblong or ellipsoid, smooth, *without a pappus.* Winter-rainfall South Africa: 15 spp.

❶ *Cullumia squarrosa*

| J | F | M | A | M | J | J | A | S | O | N | D |

Sprawling, densely leafy shrublet to 50 cm, with spreading or arched, needle-like leaves (10–)15–25 mm long, with bristly margins rolled under, and radiate, yellow flowerheads, 30 mm in diameter; the inner involucral bracts unlike the outer and without prickles. Coastal bush in the southwestern Cape.

❷ *Cullumia setosa*

| J | F | M | A | M | J | J | A | S | O | N | D |

Sprawling, densely leafy shrublet to 60 cm, with arched, oval leaves, flexed down at the tips and with thickened margins bearing mostly 1 row of bristles, and radiate, yellow flowerheads, 20 mm in diameter. Lower mountain slopes in the extreme southwestern Cape.

Didelta   SALAD THISTLE, SLAAIBOS

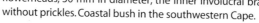

(Greek di, double; delta, △, referring to the triangular outer bracts) Perennial, ± succulent herbs or shrubs. Leaves alternate or opposite, with or without a few spiny teeth, hairless or felted. Flowerheads solitary and sessile or stalked, *with 2 rows of bracts, the outer comprising 3–5 large, leaf-like bracts and the inner comprising lance-shaped bracts,* sometimes with spiny margins; *receptacle deeply honeycombed, with the outer pits thick-walled, breaking into 3–5 woody outer segments, one attached to each of the outer bracts, with the fruits embedded in spine-fringed pits.* Ray florets sterile, yellow; disc florets fertile or inner ones male, deeply 5-lobed. Fruit flask-shaped, ribbed, smooth or hairy, with a pappus of narrow, fringed scales joined at the base. Winter-rainfall South Africa: 2 spp. The large, wing-like bracts aid in seed dispersal. The spiny pit margins deter seed predators, and the seeds germinate directly within the woody pits, 1 to a segment.

❸ *Didelta spinosa*

| J | F | M | A | M | J | J | A | S | O | N | D |

Greater Salad Thistle, Perdebos Shrub to 2 m, with opposite, oval to elliptical leaves, lobed at the base, with the margins slightly rolled under and sometimes prickly, and radiate, yellow flowerheads, 40–50 mm in diameter. Dry rocky slopes from southern Namibia to the West Coast.

❹ *Didelta carnosa*

| J | F | M | A | M | J | J | A | S | O | N | D |

Lesser Salad Thistle Rounded shrublet to 1 m, with narrowly elliptical, smooth or densely grey-felted leaves, tapering to the base, and radiate, yellow flowerheads, 40–50 mm in diameter. Coastal dunes and sandy flats from southern Namibia to the southwestern Cape.

Berkheya WILD THISTLE, WILDEDISSEL

(Named for Dutch botanist, M.J. Lefrancq van Berkhey, 1729–1812) *Thistle-like perennial herbs or shrubs*, often cobwebby or woolly. Leaves alternate or basal, rarely opposite, ± lobed and spine-toothed. Flowerheads usually several at the branch tips, radiate or discoid, with several rows of lance-shaped involucral *bracts joined only at the base*, usually with prickly or bristly margins and tips; *receptacle honeycombed with fringed pit margins*. Ray florets sterile, usually yellow, rarely white or lilac; disc florets fertile or inner ones male, deeply 5-lobed. Fruit flask-shaped, ribbed, smooth or hairy, with a pappus of short or long scales or barbed bristles. Southern and tropical Africa: ±75 spp.; South Africa: 71 spp. Used medicinally.

▶ PERENNIALS OR SHRUBLETS WITH LEAFY, UNWINGED STEMS

❶ *Berkheya cuneata* | J | F | M | A | M | J | J | A | S | O | N | D |

Vaaldissel, Vaalbietou Shrublet to 30 cm, with wedge-shaped, spine-toothed leaves, grey-felted on both surfaces, and mostly solitary, radiate, yellow flowerheads, 40–50 mm in diameter. Rocky slopes in the Little Karoo.

❷ *Berkheya fruticosa* Vaaldissel | J | F | M | A | M | J | J | A | S | O | N | D |

Shrub to 1.5 m, with grey-woolly branches, elliptical, prickly-toothed leaves, hairless and glossy dark green above but felted beneath, and clusters of radiate, yellow flowerheads, 40–50 mm in diameter. Dry, rocky slopes and plateaus in Namaqualand.

❸ *Berkheya spinosissima* | J | F | M | A | M | J | J | A | S | O | N | D |

Shrublet to 1 m, with reddish, thinly glandular-haired branches, opposite, elliptical, deeply spine-toothed leaves, ± hairless on both surfaces, and clusters of radiate, yellow flowerheads, 40–50 mm in diameter. Dry, rocky slopes in northwestern South Africa.

❹ *Berkheya barbata* | J | F | M | A | M | J | J | A | S | O | N | D |

Shrublet to 60 cm, with erect, white-felted stems sprouting from a woody rootstock, pairs of opposite, elliptical leaves, prickly-toothed, hairless and glossy dark green above but white-felted beneath, the margins rolled under, and solitary, radiate, yellow flowerheads, 50–60 mm in diameter. Rocky slopes in the southwestern Cape, flowering after fire.

❺ *Berkheya rosulata* | J | F | M | A | M | J | J | A | S | O | N | D |

Rosette Berkheya Bushy shrub to 1 m, with white-felted stems, clusters of elliptical, slightly prickly-toothed leaves at the branch tips, hairless and glossy dark green above but white-felted beneath, and solitary radiate, yellow flowerheads, 50–70 mm in diameter. Basalt cliffs at high altitude in the Drakensberg and Maluti Mountains.

❻ *Berkheya zeyheri* | J | F | M | A | M | J | J | A | S | O | N | D |

Grass-leaved Berkheya Perennial with clumps of erect stems to 60 cm from a woody rootstock, narrow leaves with slender bristles along the margins towards the base, ± hairless above but white-felted beneath, and radiate, yellow flowerheads, 50–70 mm in diameter. Grassland through northeastern South Africa, flowering after fire. *Berkheya insignis* has bristles all along the leaf margins.

▶ TUFTED PERENNIALS WITH A BASAL ROSETTE OF LEAVES AND UNWINGED STEMS

① *Berkheya speciosa*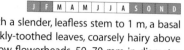
Skraaldisseldoring Perennial herb with a slender, leafless stem to 1 m, a basal rosette of petiolate, elliptical to oval, prickly-toothed leaves, coarsely hairy above but cobwebby beneath, and radiate, yellow flowerheads, 50–70 mm in diameter. Stony grassland through eastern South Africa.

② *Berkheya setifera*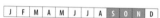
Similar to *Berkheya speciosa* but the leaves thickly covered in tawny bristles above and coarsely hairy beneath, and the pappus scales much longer than the fruits. Stony grassland through eastern South and subtropical Africa.

③ *Berkheya armata* **Grootdissel**
Tufted perennial to 40 cm, with a basal rosette of lance-shaped, prickly-toothed leaves, the margin slightly rolled under, hairless above but white-felted beneath, and 1–few radiate, yellow flowerheads, 40–50 mm in diameter; involucral bracts finely prickly along the margins. Stony and clay slopes and flats in the southwestern Cape. *Berkheya carlinoides* has stems covered in glandular hairs.

④ *Berkheya herbacea*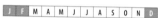
Kaaldissel Tufted perennial to 40 cm, with a basal rosette of lance-shaped leaves, often ± prickly-toothed, hairless above but white-felted beneath, and several radiate, yellow flowerheads, 40–50 mm in diameter; inner involucral bracts with broad, smooth, horny margins. Rocky sandstone slopes in the southwestern Cape.

⑤ *Berkheya multijuga*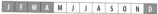
Spiny Berg-thistle Tufted perennial to 60 cm, with a lateral rosette of large, closely divided, spine-toothed leaves, thinly hairy above but cobwebby beneath, and clusters of radiate, yellow flowerheads, 60–100 mm in diameter. Damp rocky slopes below cliffs in the Drakensberg. *Berkheya macrocephala* has glandular hairs on the undersides of the leaves, and solitary flowerheads in spring.

▶ PERENNIALS WITH SPINE-TOOTHED WINGS ON THE STEMS

⑥ *Berkheya rhapontica*
Pagoda-flowered Berkheya Tufted perennial with a winged stem to 1 m, with a basal rosette of petiolate, elliptical to oval, prickly-toothed leaves pressed to the ground, coarsely hairy or smooth above but hairy or felted beneath, and a raceme-like spike of radiate, yellow flowerheads, 20–40 mm in diameter. Grassland and rock outcrops through eastern South Africa.

⑦ *Berkheya umbellata*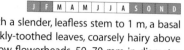
Mop-headed Berkheya, Klossiedissel Tufted perennial with a winged stem to 80 cm, with a basal tuft of paddle-shaped, lobed and spine-toothed leaves, densely bristled above and glandular-haired beneath, and discoid, yellow flowerheads, 20–30 mm in diameter. Colonies in moist grassland in the Eastern Cape and KwaZulu-Natal.

❶ *Berkheya echinacea*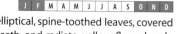

Perennial with winged stems to 1 m, with elliptical, spine-toothed leaves, covered in tawny spines above and ± hairless beneath, and radiate, yellow flowerheads, 50–60 mm in diameter. Colonies in stony grassland in northeastern South Africa.

❷ *Berkheya onopordifolia*

Branched perennial to 1.5 m, with oblong, deeply lobed and spine-toothed leaves, coarsely glandular-haired above but white-felted beneath, and radiate, pale yellow flowerheads, 60–70 mm in diameter; involucral bracts leaf-like, tipped with a short spine 3–4 mm long, less than one-fifth as long as the bract. Grassland and savanna, especially overgrazed land, through eastern South Africa.

❸ *Berkheya cirsiifolia*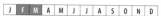

White Thistle-leaved Berkheya Branched perennial with a winged stem to 1.5 m, with oblong, deeply lobed and spine-toothed leaves, coarsely glandular-haired above but white-felted beneath, the basal leaves largest, and flowerheads 60–80 mm in diameter, with white rays and a yellow disc; involucral bracts leaf-like, tipped with a spine 5–10 mm long, ± half as long as the bract. Grassy mountain slopes in the Drakensberg.

❹ *Berkheya leucaugeta*

White Berkheya Tufted perennial with a winged stem to 80 cm, oblong, soft-textured, shallowly lobed and shortly spine-toothed leaves, glandular-haired above but white-woolly beneath, the basal leaves largest, and flowerheads 50–70 mm in diameter, with white rays and a yellow disc, in panicles; involucral bracts leaf-like. Marshy depressions and along streams in the Drakensberg.

❺ *Berkheya purpurea*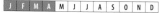

Purple Berkheya, Bloudisseldoring Tufted perennial with a winged stem to 80 cm, oblong, sharply lobed and spine-toothed leaves, coarsely and glandular-haired above but white-woolly beneath, the basal leaves largest, and radiate, pale to deep mauve flowerheads, 60–80 mm in diameter, in a raceme or spike; involucral bracts leaf-like. Grassy mountain slopes in the Drakensberg.

Gorteria **BEETLE DAISY** (Named for 18th-century Dutch botanist David de Gorter)

Annual herbs. Leaves alternate or basal, narrow or lobed, woolly beneath. *Flowerheads ± sessile,* radiate, with several rows of stiff bracts *joined below into a cup that becomes woody and encloses the seeds;* receptacle without scales. Ray florets sterile, yellow, orange or red, *mostly with dark marks at the base;* disc florets fertile or inner ones sterile, deeply 5-lobed. *Fruit remaining within the woody involucre,* ellipsoid, silky, with a pappus of small or bristle-like scales. Southern Africa: 3 spp. The vernacular name is a misnomer as the floral markings mimic and attract pollinating bee-flies.

❻ *Gorteria diffusa*

Sprawling annual to 10 cm, with narrow, sometimes lobed leaves, roughly hairy above and white-felted beneath, the margins rolled under, and radiate flowerheads, 20–35 mm in diameter, the rays orange with dark, beetle-like markings. Dry clay flats or rocky lower slopes in Namaqualand and the southwestern Cape.

367

Hirpicium HIRPICIUM *(Origin unknown)*

Shrubs, perennial or annual herbs. Leaves *narrow or needle-like*, usually *with the margins rolled under and white-felted beneath*. Flowerheads radiate, with several rows of stiff bracts *joined below into a smooth or hairy cup*; receptacle without scales. Ray florets sterile, yellow or white; disc florets fertile, deeply 5-lobed. Fruit flask-shaped, with rows of swollen cells, silky, the *pappus with an outer row of broad, overlapping scales and an inner row of small or absent scales.* Africa: 12 spp.; South Africa: 8 spp.

❶ *Hirpicium alienatum* Haarbossie   J F M A M J J A S O N D

Twiggy shrublet to 50 cm, with small leaves, white-felted beneath, and radiate yellow flowerheads, ±20 mm in diameter, with bristle-tipped involucral bracts. Dry, stony slopes from southern Namibia to the Eastern Cape. *Hirpicium integrifolium* has involucral bracts with feathery, thread-like tips.

❷ *Hirpicium armerioides*   J F M A M J J A S O N D

Mat-forming perennial to 25 cm, with rosettes of narrow, bristly leaves, white-felted beneath, and radiate flowerheads 25–50 mm in diameter, with white rays and yellow disc. Poor, stony patches or rock sheets in eastern South Africa.

Gazania GAZANIA, GOUSBLOM   *(Greek gaza, riches, alluding to the brilliant colours)*

Perennial or sometimes annual herbs, usually tufted, *with milky latex*. Leaves mostly basal or in a rosette, *narrow or deeply lobed into narrow segments*, usually *with the margins rolled under and white-felted beneath. Flowerheads solitary on hollow peduncles*, radiate, often brightly marked, with several rows of stiff bracts *joined below into a smooth or hairy cup*; receptacle without scales. Ray florets sterile, yellow, orange or red, *mostly with dark marks at the base*; disc florets fertile or inner ones sterile, deeply 5-lobed. Fruit flask-shaped with rows of swollen cells, silky, with a pappus of bristle-like scales. Southern Africa: 17 spp. The vernacular name derives from the Afrikaans *goud* (gold), alluding to the richly coloured flowerheads.

▸ **SPRAWLING OR CREEPING PERENNIALS ROOTING ALONG THE STEMS**

❸ *Gazania maritima*   J F M A M J J A S O N D

West Coast Gazania Creeping perennial to 10 cm, rooting along the stem, with leathery leaves, mostly divided into 3–7 elliptical lobes, the margins rolled under, white-felted beneath, often with bristly petioles, and radiate flowerheads 30–40 mm in diameter, the rays yellow to orange with dark marks at the base; the involucre ± hairless. Coastal rocks and sands in the southwestern Cape.

❹ *Gazania rigens* Strand Gazania   J F M A M J J A S O N D

Sprawling, mat-forming perennial to 20 cm, with most of the leaves lance-shaped, rarely lobed, on smooth petioles, the margins rolled under, white-felted beneath, and radiate flowerheads 30–40 mm in diameter, the rays yellow, with or without dark marks at the base; the involucre partially white-woolly. Coastal dunes and rocky outcrops along beaches from the southern Cape to southern Mozambique.

369

▶ TUFTED, STEMLESS PERENNIALS OR ANNUALS

① *Gazania krebsiana*

J F M A M J J A S O N D

Common Gazania Tufted perennial to 20 cm, with the leaves either simple or divided into narrow segments, the margins rolled under, white-felted beneath, and radiate flowerheads 30–40 mm in diameter, the rays yellow, orange or reddish, with dark marks at the base; the involucre hairless or thinly hairy. Roadsides, flats and lower slopes through southern and tropical Africa.

② *Gazania rigida* **Cape Gazania**

J F M A M J J A S O N D

Tufted perennial to 25 cm, with the leaves usually divided into elliptical lobes, sometimes undivided, the margins rolled under, white-woolly beneath, and radiate flowerheads 30–40 mm in diameter, the rays yellow or orange, usually with dark marks at the base; the involucre coarsely hairy. Flats and lower slopes in western South Africa.

③ *Gazania leiopoda*

J F M A M J J A S O N D

Namaqua Gazania Tufted perennial to 20 cm, with deeply and evenly lobed leaves, the margins rolled under, white-felted beneath, and radiate flowerheads 40–50 mm in diameter, the rays orange, often flushed reddish and darkly marked at the base; the involucre coarsely hairy and rounded at the base. Gravelly and stony flats in Namaqualand.

④ *Gazania lichtensteinii*

J F M A M J J A S O N D

Yellow Gazania Annual herb to 20 cm, with elliptical, toothed leaves, the margins lightly rolled under, ± hairless above but woolly beneath, and radiate flowerheads on hairless peduncles, 25–35 mm in diameter, the rays yellow to orange, marked with small green blotches at the base; the involucre smooth and pushed in at the bottom like a wine-bottle. Arid, gravelly and sandy flats, often in washes, in western South Africa.

▶ FLOWERHEADS RADIATE; ALL OR AT LEAST THE INNER INVOLUCRAL BRACTS WITH LARGE, ROUNDED, MEMBRANOUS OR PAPERY TIPS; PAPPUS OF SCALES

Arctotis ARCTOTIS, GOUSBLOM
(Greek arktos, bear; otis, ear, a fanciful reference to the tips of the bracts) Annual or perennial herbs or shrubs, *often felted and glandular*. Leaves alternate or basal, ± lobed and felted or woolly. Flowerheads solitary on short or long, hollow peduncles, radiate, often large, with 5 or 6 rows of bracts, the outer bracts often tailed and the *inner bracts broad with large, membranous or papery tips*; receptacle honeycombed, without scales. *Ray florets female,* white, yellow, orange, pink or purple, often with darker marks at the base; disc florets fertile, 5-lobed. *Fruit egg-shaped, with 3–5 ribs on 1 side enclosing 2 furrows,* hairless or silky and often with a *tuft of long hairs at the base, the pappus with 1 or 2 rows of scales.* Southern Africa: ±60 spp.

▶ ANNUAL HERBS

⑤ *Arctotis breviscapa*

J F M A M J J A S O N D

Sandveldgousblom Tufted annual to 20 cm, with a rosette of divided leaves, ± hairless above but woolly beneath, and radiate flowerheads 40–60 mm in diameter, the rays orange or yellow, red on the reverse, the disc dark; fruit with 2 elongated cavities, no pappus and a very small or absent basal tuft of hairs. Rocky slopes in the southwestern Cape.

① *Arctotis hirsuta* Gousblom

J | F | M | A | M | J | J | A | S | O | N | D

Slightly fleshy, often robust annual to 45 cm, with sparsely hairy, lyre-shaped, divided leaves, often with ear-like lobes at the base, and radiate flowerheads 40–60 mm in diameter, the rays orange, yellow or cream-coloured, the disc dark; fruit with 2 rounded cavities, a short pappus and a rudimentary basal tuft of hairs. Sandy slopes and flats, usually coastal, in the southwestern Cape.

② *Arctotis fastuosa*

J | F | M | A | M | J | J | A | S | O | N | D

Namaqualand Arctotis, Bittergousblom Slightly fleshy, thinly white-woolly annual to 45 cm, with deeply divided leaves, and radiate flowerheads, 50–70 mm in diameter, the rays orange, usually with a dark ring, the disc dark; fruit with a single elongated cavity, no pappus and no basal tuft of hairs. Sandy and gravelly flats and washes in Namaqualand.

③ *Arctotis leiocarpa* Karoo Arctotis

J | F | M | A | M | J | J | A | S | O | N | D

Stemless, sometimes branched, cobwebby annual to 20 cm, with narrowly paddle-shaped, roughly lobed or divided leaves, and radiate flowerheads 40–60 mm in diameter, the rays white or pale salmon-pink, the disc yellow; fruit with 2 elongated cavities, a well-developed pappus and a basal tuft of hairs. Gravel plains in western South Africa. *Arctotis venusta* has a dark disc.

▶ TUFTED PERENNIALS

④ *Arctotis acaulis*

J | F | M | A | M | J | J | A | S | O | N | D

Renostergousblom Tufted perennial to 20 cm, with a basal rosette of lance- to lyre-shaped, toothed leaves, coarsely hairy above but grey-felted beneath, and radiate flowerheads 40–60 mm in diameter, the rays orange, yellow or cream-coloured, the disc black; fruit with 2 rounded cavities, a well-developed pappus and a basal tuft of hairs. Clay, granitic and limestone flats in the southwestern Cape.

⑤ *Arctotis diffusa*

J | F | M | A | M | J | J | A | S | O | N | D

Roggeveld Arctotis Stemless perennial to 10 cm, with a basal rosette of paddle-shaped, deeply incised leaves, silvery-felted on both surfaces, and short-stalked, radiate flowerheads 50–70 mm in diameter, the rays white, the disc dark; fruit with 2 elongated cavities, a well-developed pappus and a basal tuft of hairs. Moist clay flats along the western escarpment.

⑥ *Arctotis campanulata*

J | F | M | A | M | J | J | A | S | O | N | D

Kamiesberg Arctotis Stemless perennial to 40 cm, with a basal rosette of lance-shaped leaves divided into elliptical lobes, with crinkly margins, silvery-felted on both surfaces, and radiate flowerheads 50–70 mm in diameter, the rays orange with a dark ring, the disc black; fruit with 2 elongated cavities, a well-developed pappus and a basal tuft of hairs. Seasonally damp gravelly flats in the mountains of Namaqualand.

▶ COARSELY HAIRY, SPRAWLING PERENNIALS OR SHRUBS

① *Arctotis decurrens*

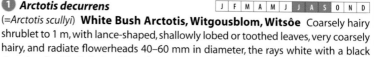

(=*Arctotis scullyi*) **White Bush Arctotis, Witgousblom, Witsôe** Coarsely hairy shrublet to 1 m, with lance-shaped, shallowly lobed or toothed leaves, very coarsely hairy, and radiate flowerheads 40–60 mm in diameter, the rays white with a black ring, the disc black; fruit with 2 elongated cavities, a well-developed pappus and a basal tuft of hairs. Coastal scrub in Namaqualand.

② *Arctotis aspera* Taaigousblom

J F M A M J J A S O N D

Sprawling, glandular-haired perennial to 2 m, with roughly glandular-haired leaves, divided 1 or 2 times into narrow lobes, the margins rolled under, sometimes grey-felted beneath, and radiate flowerheads 40–60 mm in diameter, the rays white to purplish, dark on the reverse, the disc black; fruit with 2 elongated cavities, a well-developed pappus and a basal tuft of hairs. Rocky slopes along the West Coast.

③ *Arctotis revoluta* Bush Arctotis

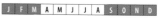

Softly woody, aromatic shrub to 2 m, with leaves usually divided 2 times into narrow segments, ± hairless or felted above but grey-felted beneath, the margins rolled under, and radiate flowerheads 40–60 mm in diameter, the rays yellow to orange, the disc dark; fruit with 2 wedge-shaped cavities, a well-developed pappus and a basal tuft of hairs. Rocky slopes, often coastal, in Namaqualand and the Western Cape.

④ *Arctotis arctotoides*

Creeping, mat-forming perennial, with lyre-shaped, lobed and toothed leaves, ± hairless above but thinly white-felted beneath, and radiate flowerheads 25–40 mm in diameter, the rays yellow, purplish on the reverse, the disc yellow; fruit with 2 elongated cavities, no pappus and no basal tuft of hairs. Marshy stream banks and drainage ditches through southeastern and central South Africa.

▶ GREY- OR SILVERY-WOOLLY, CREEPING PERENNIALS

⑤ *Arctotis stoechadifolia*

J F M A M J J A S O N D

Kusgousblom Creeping, silvery-woolly perennial with erect shoots to 35 cm, white-felted and lance-shaped to lobed leaves, and radiate flowerheads, the rays cream-coloured with a dark ring, reddish on the reverse, the disc dark; fruit with 2 elongated cavities, a well-developed pappus and a basal tuft of hairs. Dunes and sandy flats, mostly coastal, around the Cape Peninsula.

Haplocarpha HAPLOCARPHA, GOUSBLOM
(Greek apalos, soft; karphos, scale, referring to the pappus) Tufted or mat-forming perennial herb. Leaves toothed or lobed, *strongly bicoloured with the upper surface green and the lower densely white-felted.* Flowerheads solitary on hollow peduncles, with several rows of *bracts with broad membranous margins and tips.* Ray florets fertile, yellow, often with reddish reverse; disc florets fertile, deeply 5-lobed. *Fruit egg-shaped, weakly ribbed on 1 side, hairless or hairy, pappus of 2 or more rows of scales, or absent.* Tropical and southern Africa: 8 spp.; South Africa: 6 spp. Used medicinally; the felt from the leaves was used as tinder.

1 *Haplocarpha nervosa*

J F M A M J J A S O N D

Dwarf tufted perennial to 15 cm, frequently forming dense mats, with elliptical, irregularly toothed leaves on short petioles, white-felted beneath, and radiate yellow flowerheads 30–40 mm in diameter, on short, cobwebby scapes; fruit warty, with a rudimentary pappus. Marshy grassland in eastern South Africa.

2 *Haplocarpha scaposa*

J F M A M J J A S O N D

False Gerbera Tufted perennial to 30 cm, with paddle-shaped, toothed leaves, white-felted beneath, and radiate yellow flowerheads 40–60 mm in diameter, on long, cobwebby scapes; fruit warty, with a basal tuft of long hairs and long pappus scales. Grassland through eastern South and tropical Africa.

Arctotheca ARCTOTHECA
(Greek arktos, bear; theca, case, referring to the woolly fruits) Felted annual or perennial herbs, tufted or creeping. Leaves alternate, ± lobed and felted or woolly. Flowerheads solitary on hollow peduncles, radiate, with several rows of *bracts with broad membranous margins and tips;* receptacle honeycombed, without scales. *Ray florets sterile,* yellow, sometimes with a dark base; disc florets fertile, 5-lobed. *Fruit egg-shaped,* thinly ribbed, *usually woolly or silky, with a pappus of small scales or a crown of scales, or absent.* Southern Africa: 5 spp.

3 *Arctotheca calendula*

J F M A M J J A S O N D

Cape Weed, Cape Marigold, Tonteldoek Tufted or sprawling annual herb to 20 cm, with mostly basal leaves, scalloped to deeply lobed, roughly hairy above but white-woolly beneath, and radiate flowerheads 40–50 mm in diameter, on roughly hairy scapes, the rays pale to deep yellow, often paler or darker at the base, the disc black; fruit very woolly, with a small, chaffy pappus. Coastal areas or disturbed soil in southwestern South Africa.

4 *Arctotheca prostrata*

J F M A M J J A S O N D

Mat-forming perennial rooting along the creeping stems, with scalloped or lobed leaves, eared at the base, and radiate yellow flowerheads 40 mm in diameter; fruit silky. Coastal slopes and flats, often near streams, from the southwestern to the Eastern Cape.

5 *Arctotheca populifolia* Sea Pumpkin

J F M A M J J A S O N D

Creeping, mat-forming perennial with petiolate, white-felted, heart-shaped, sparsely toothed leaves, and radiate, yellow flowerheads on woolly, shortly leafy scapes; fruit woolly, with a small, crown-like pappus. Coastal dunes from Namaqualand to Mozambique.

Ursinia PARACHUTE DAISY, BERGMAGRIET

(Named for botanical author, Johann Ursinus, 1608–1666) Annual or perennial herbs or shrubs. Leaves alternate, usually toothed or lobed, often with thread-like segments. Flowerheads solitary or in loose clusters on *long, slender peduncles,* radiate, with several rows of bracts, the *outer bracts usually with dark margins* and the *inner bracts broad with large, rounded, membranous or papery tips; receptacle with scales enfolding the florets.* Ray florets usually sterile, yellow (rarely orange or red); disc florets fertile, 5-lobed. Fruit flask-shaped, straight or curved, sometimes with a basal tuft of web-like hairs, *the pappus comprising large, white, papery scales,* sometimes with an inner row of smaller scales. Mainly southern Africa, with 1 species extending to North Africa: ±40 spp.

▶ PAPPUS OF 5 SCALES ONLY

1 *Ursinia paleacea* **Geelmagriet**   J F M A M J J A S O N D
Shrub to 90 cm, with finely divided leaves, 20–60 mm long, and radiate flowerheads 20–50 mm in diameter, the rays yellow or brownish, sometimes greenish at the base and dark on the reverse, the disc yellow; pappus comprising 5 scales only. Sandstone slopes in the southwestern and southern Cape.

2 *Ursinia pilifera* **Grootbergmagriet**   J F M A M J J A S O N D
Thinly woolly shrublet to 35 cm, with leaves divided 2 times, 15–25 mm long, and radiate flowerheads ±30–60 mm in diameter, the rays white or yellow, dark on reverse; all involucral bracts with silvery papery tips; pappus comprising 5 scales only. Gravelly slopes in Namaqualand and the southwestern Cape interior.

3 *Ursinia anthemoides* **Magriet**   J F M A M J J A S O N D
Annual herb to 50 cm, with leaves divided 1 or 2 times, 20–50 mm long, and radiate flowerheads 15–60 mm in diameter, the rays yellow or orange, sometimes darker at the base and on the reverse, the disc dark; pappus comprising 5 scales only. Sandy and gravelly slopes and flats from southern Namibia to the Eastern Cape.

4 *Ursinia calenduliflora*   J F M A M J J A S O N D
Namaqua Parachute Daisy   Annual herb to 30 cm, with leaves finely divided 1 or 2 times, 20–60 mm long, and radiate flowerheads 30–40 mm in diameter, the rays orange, darker at the base, the disc dark; all involucral bracts with papery tips; pappus comprising 5 scales only. Rocky and gravelly slopes in Namaqualand.

▶ PAPPUS OF 5 SCALES AND 5 BRISTLES

5 *Ursinia cakilefolia*   J F M A M J J A S O N D
Sprawling annual herb to 45 cm, with leaves finely divided 2 times, 20–50 mm long, and radiate flowerheads 25–50 mm in diameter, the rays yellow or orange, the disc dark and glossy in bud; pappus comprising 5 scales and 5 bristles. Sandy flats and slopes in Namaqualand. *Ursinia speciosa* has involucral bracts with rounded and papery tips.

6 *Ursinia chrysanthemoides*   J F M A M J J A S O N D
Sprawling or creeping annual or weak perennial, rooting along the stem, with leaves finely divided 2 times, 20–50 mm long, and radiate flowerheads 25–50 mm in diameter, the rays yellow, orange, white or red, darker on the reverse, the disc yellow; pappus comprising 5 scales and 5 bristles. Sandy and gravelly slopes and flats from Namaqualand to the Eastern Cape.

▸ INVOLUCRAL BRACTS ENTIRELY GREEN AND FLESHY, IN 1 ROW, COHERING ALONG THE MARGINS AND SOMETIMES JOINED BELOW (SOMETIMES WITH ADDITIONAL SMALL BRACTEOLES AT THE BASE); RAY FLORETS CURLING BACK AT NIGHT; PAPPUS COMPRISING BARBED BRISTLES (SOMETIMES SOON DECIDUOUS)

Senecio GROUNDSEL, HONGERBLOM

(Latin senex, old man, alluding to the grey pappus bristles) Annual or perennial herbs, shrubs or climbers, sometimes succulent, hairless or hairy, sometimes glandular. Leaves alternate or basal, often toothed or lobed. Flowerheads radiate or discoid, *with 1 row of narrow green involucral bracts cohering along the margins, and additional minute bracteoles at the base*; receptacle without scales. Ray florets when present female, usually yellow, sometimes purple or pink to white; disc florets fertile, 5-lobed. *Fruit cylindrical* and ribbed, smooth or hairy, with a *pappus of barbed bristles*. Worldwide: ±1 250 spp.; South Africa: ±250 spp. Many species contain toxic alkaloids that are responsible for stock losses but have been used externally to promote healing. The vernacular name *hongerblom* derives from the purported use of certain species as a tea to enhance appetite.

▸ ANNUAL HERBS

1 *Senecio maritimus*   J F M A M J J A S O N D

Strandhongerblom Hairless, sprawling to creeping annual herb to 30 cm, with fleshy, slightly toothed, oblong, rather blunt leaves, and radiate, yellow flowerheads 10–15 mm in diameter. Coastal dunes and slopes from southern Namaqualand to the southwestern Cape.

2 *Senecio littoreus*   J F M A M J J A S O N D

Geelhongerblom Almost hairless to shortly hairy annual herb to 40 cm, with sessile, toothed to shallowly lobed, oblong to lance-shaped leaves, and radiate, yellow flowerheads 10–15 mm in diameter. Mainly coastal sands in southern Namaqualand and the southwestern Cape.

3 *Senecio abruptus*   J F M A M J J A S O N D

Bastergeelhongerblom Like *Senecio littoreus* but with deeply divided leaves. Stony slopes along the West Coast.

4 *Senecio cardaminifolius*   J F M A M J J A S O N D

Namaqua Groundsel, Geelhongerblom Similar to *Senecio littoreus* but the leaves deeply divided and distinctly petiolate. Gravelly and sandy slopes, often in disturbed places, in Namaqualand.

5 *Senecio arenarius* **Hongerblom**   J F M A M J J A S O N D

Glandular-haired (rarely almost hairless) annual herb, 15–40 cm, with sessile, toothed or lobed leaves, the margins sometimes rolled under, and radiate flowerheads 10–15 mm in diameter, the rays mauve or white, the disc yellow; involucre cylindrical and finely glandular-haired, with inconspicuous bracteoles at the base. Sandy flats from southern Namibia to the southwestern Cape.

6 *Senecio elegans* **Veld Cineraria**   J F M A M J J A S O N D

Densely glandular-haired annual herb to 1 m, with fleshy, deeply lobed or divided leaves, the margins rolled under, and radiate flowerheads 15–20 mm in diameter, the rays purple, the disc yellow; involucre cup-shaped, with conspicuous, black-tipped bracteoles at the base. Coastal sands from the West Coast to the Eastern Cape.

▶ ERECT PERENNIALS OR WOODY ANNUALS WITH LEAVES SCATTERED ALONG THE STEMS

① *Senecio umbellatus*

Hairless perennial to 80 cm, sometimes sparsely hairy below, with leaves either narrow and thread-like or divided into thread-like lobes, the margins rolled under and minutely toothed, and loosely branched clusters of radiate flowerheads, the rays magenta to pink or sometimes white, the disc yellow. Moist sandstone flats and slopes in southwestern South Africa.

② *Senecio polyanthemoides*

Single-stemmed, bushy annual with woody, leafy stems to 1.8 m, the narrow leaves smooth or toothed, hairless or minutely hairy above and thinly white-felted beneath, the margins rolled under, and radiate, yellow flowerheads, ±10 mm in diameter, each with ±8 rays. Forest margins, but often weedy along roadsides and in old fields, through eastern South Africa.

③ *Senecio pterophorus*

Like *Senecio polyanthemoides* but the flowerheads slightly larger, with ±13 rays. Forest margins and along roadsides in southern and eastern South Africa.

④ *Senecio cinerascens* Handjiesbos

Erect-stemmed shrub to 2 m, with white-woolly leaves, deeply divided into narrow segments, the margins rolled under, and radiate, yellow flowerheads, 15–20 mm in diameter. Rocky slopes in Namaqualand.

⑤ *Senecio isatidioides* Vlei Cabbage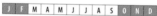

Robust, leafy-stemmed, hairless perennial to 2 m, with elliptical to oblong, finely toothed leaves with a greyish bloom, and large clusters of discoid, yellow flowerheads, ±5 mm in diameter. In colonies in marshy ground or along forest margins in northeastern South Africa. *Senecio isatideus* has leaves in a basal tuft.

▶ TUFTED PERENNIALS WITH LEAVES MOSTLY IN A BASAL ROSETTE

⑥ *Senecio macrocephalus* J F M A M J J A S O N D

Tufted, glandular-haired perennial to 60 cm, with a basal rosette of paddle-shaped, sometimes toothed leaves, and radiate, purple flowerheads, ±20 mm in diameter; involucre glandular-haired. Open grassland in eastern South Africa, often flowering after fire. *Senecio speciosus* has deeply toothed or lobed leaves on a distinct petiole.

⑦ *Senecio macrospermus* J F M A M J J A S O N D

Robust, tufted perennial to 1 m, grey-woolly, with a basal rosette of lance-shaped, minutely toothed leaves, and radiate, yellow flowerheads, ±30 mm in diameter; involucre grey-woolly. Damp montane grassland in the Drakensberg.

1 *Senecio erosus*

J F M A M J J **A S** O N D

Sticky-leaved Groundsel Tufted, glandular-haired perennial to 60 cm, with a woolly crown, leaves petiolate, lance-shaped, irregularly toothed to roughly lobed, mostly in a basal rosette, and radiate, yellow flowerheads, ±20 mm in diameter; involucre glandular-haired. Rocky slopes in southwestern South Africa.

2 *Senecio spiraeifolius*

J F M A M J **J A S** O N D

Fern-leaved Groundsel Tufted, glandular-haired perennial to 60 cm, with petiolate leaves, deeply and regularly divided into oblong, toothed and often twisted lobes, usually cobwebby beneath, in a basal rosette, and radiate, yellow flowerheads, ±20 mm in diameter; involucre hairless or thinly cobwebby. Stony flats in western South Africa.

▶ **CLIMBERS**

3 *Senecio pleistocephalus*

J F M **A M J** J A S O N D

Vigorous, hairless scrambler or climber to 2 m, with leathery, elliptical, toothed leaves, and dense clusters of discoid, yellow, honey-scented flowerheads, 5 mm in diameter; involucre 3–4 mm long. Hot scrub and savanna in eastern South Africa. *Senecio brachypodus* has radiate flowerheads.

4 *Senecio deltoideus*

J F M A **M J** J A S O N D

Hairless or thinly hairy climber with zigzag branching, soft, triangular, toothed leaves, eared at the base of the petiole, and clusters of radiate or discoid, yellow flowerheads, 5–10 mm in diameter; involucre 3–5 mm long. Forest margins and cliffs through southern and eastern South Africa.

5 *Senecio tamoides* **Canary Creeper**

J F M **A M** J J A S O N D

Vigorous, ± hairless climber, often covering trees, with fleshy, triangular, unevenly toothed, petiolate leaves, sometimes cobwebby beneath, and clusters of radiate, bright yellow flowers, 10–15 mm in diameter; involucre 8–9 mm long. Forest margins through eastern South and subtropical Africa.

6 *Senecio macroglossus*

J F **M A M J** J A S O N D

Natal Ivy, Flowering Ivy Slender, hairless climber, with fleshy, arrow-shaped, petiolate leaves, and large, mostly solitary, radiate, cream-coloured to pale yellow flowerheads, 40–50 mm in diameter; involucre 9–10 mm long. Forest margins, mostly coastal, in eastern South and subtropical Africa. *Senecio macroglossoides* from inland has heart-shaped, toothed leaves and long, spreading bracteoles at the base of the involucre.

▶ SUCCULENTS WITH CYLINDRICAL OR SPINDLE-SHAPED LEAVES

① *Senecio corymbiferus*

J F **M A M J J** A S O N D

Gnarled or erect succulent shrub with cane-like stems to 2 m, leafy at the tips, grey, spindle-shaped leaves, and small clusters of sparsely radiate, yellow flowerheads, 10–15 mm in diameter, nestled among the leaves. Dry, rocky hills in Namaqualand.

② *Senecio sarcoides*

J F M A M J **J A S O** N D

Thick-stemmed, hairless shrub to 75 cm, with fleshy, cylindrical, striped leaves in clusters at the branch tips, and stalked clusters of radiate, yellow flowerheads, 10 mm in diameter. Rocky areas from southern Namibia to the southwestern Cape.

③ *Senecio aloides*

J F M A M J **J A S O** N D

Thick-stemmed, hairless shrub to 75 cm, with fleshy, cylindrical, striped leaves in clusters at the branch tips, and mostly solitary, radiate, yellow flowerheads on long peduncles, 20 mm in diameter. Coastal rocks and dunes from southern Namibia to the southwestern Cape.

④ *Senecio radicans*

J F M **A M J J** A S O N D

Bobbejaantoontjies Trailing, succulent perennial, with spindle-shaped or almost spherical, upward-facing leaves, and peduncles of discoid, white or mauve, fragrant flowerheads, 10 mm in diameter. Rock outcrops on flats and hills through the drier southwestern, southern and central parts of South Africa.

Cineraria CINERARIA *(Latin cinerareus, of ashes, alluding to the greyish leaves of some species)*

Perennial herbs or subshrubs, sometimes grey-felted. Leaves alternate or sometimes basal, often *lyre-shaped and lobed and incised*, mostly distinctly petiolate, often eared at the base. Flowerheads in loose clusters, radiate (rarely discoid), *with 1 row of narrow green involucral bracts cohering along the margins, and additional minute bracteoles at the base*; receptacle without scales. Ray florets female, yellow; disc florets all or mostly fertile, 5-lobed. *Fruit elliptical and flattened, with a thickened rim*, smooth or hairy, with a *pappus of barbed bristles*. Africa and Madagascar: 35 spp.; South Africa: 32 spp.

⑤ *Cineraria deltoidea* Forest Cineraria

J F M **A M J J** A S O N D

Erect or scrambling perennial to 1.5 m, with hairless or cobwebby, triangular, irregularly toothed leaves and clusters of radiate, yellow flowerheads, 10–15 mm in diameter. Forest margins and among bushes in eastern South and tropical Africa.

⑥ *Cineraria canescens* Grey Cineraria

J F M A M J J A **S O** N D

Shrublet with grey-cobwebby stems to 50 cm, with rounded, irregularly lobed and toothed leaves, cobwebby above and grey-felted beneath, and clusters of radiate, yellow flowerheads, 10–15 mm in diameter. Drier rocky slopes in Namaqualand.

387

Othonna   OTHONNA, BOBBEJAANKOOL

(Greek othonne, linen, alluding to the soft leaves of some species) Perennial herbs, shrubs or climbers, ± *succulent and usually hairless*, although often woolly in the axils. Leaves alternate or basal, sometimes toothed or lobed, or cylindrical. Flowerheads solitary or several, radiate or discoid, with *1 row of smooth bracts joined at the base, without additional small bracteoles*; receptacle without scales. Ray florets when present usually yellow, rarely pink or white, fertile; ray *fruit ellipsoid, ribbed*, smooth or hairy, with a *pappus of long, fine, barbed bristles, often elongating markedly and banded with brown. Disc florets male*, 5-lobed. Southern Africa: ±120 spp.

▶ **PERENNIAL HERBS**

1 *Othonna filicaulis*

| J | F | M | A | M | J | J | A | S | O | N | D |

Bobbejaanklimop   Straggling perennial with annual stems to 70 cm from a woolly crown, with lance-shaped to rounded leaves, lobed at the base and clasping the stem, and discoid, white or yellow flowerheads, 10 mm in diameter. Sandy flats and slopes, often coastal, from southern Namibia to the Eastern Cape. *Othonna perfoliata* has radiate flowerheads.

2 *Othonna auriculifolia*

| J | F | M | A | M | J | J | A | S | O | N | D |

Stemless tuberous perennial to 15 cm from a woolly crown, with a rosette of petiolate, paddle-shaped, toothed to deeply lobed leaves, and radiate, yellow flowerheads, 15–20 mm in diameter, the rays often red on the reverse. Stony clay slopes and flats in the southwestern Cape interior.

▶ **SHRUBS**

3 *Othonna sedifolia*

| J | F | M | A | M | J | J | A | S | O | N | D |

Brittle-stemmed shrublet to 60 cm, with succulent, egg-shaped or spherical leaves at the branch tips, and radiate, yellow flowerheads, 15 mm in diameter. Stony slopes and banks in Namaqualand.

4 *Othonna cylindrica*

| J | F | M | A | M | J | J | A | S | O | N | D |

Brittle-stemmed shrub to 1 m, with fleshy, spindle-shaped to cylindrical leaves at the branch tips, and loose clusters of radiate, yellow flowerheads, 15–20 mm in diameter. Sandy and stony flats and rocks from southern Namibia to the West Coast.

5 *Othonna parviflora*

| J | F | M | A | M | J | J | A | S | O | N | D |

Bobbejaankool   Robust shrub to 2 m, with leathery, lance-shaped, smooth or finely toothed leaves, and large clusters of radiate, yellow flowerheads, 10 mm in diameter. Sandstone slopes in the mountains of southwestern South Africa.

6 *Othonna coronopifolia*

| J | F | M | A | M | J | J | A | S | O | N | D |

Semi-succulent shrub to 1.5 m, with lance-shaped, often irregularly toothed leaves, usually in tufts on short branchlets, and solitary, radiate, yellow flowerheads on long peduncles. Rocky sandstone and granite slopes along the West Coast. *Othonna ramulosa* has flowerheads on short peduncles; *O. leptodactyla* has narrower leaves.

Euryops **EURYOPS, HARPUISBOS** *(Greek eurys, large; ops, eye, referring to the showy flowerheads)*

Shrubs or shrublets. Leaves alternate, sometimes in tufts, *usually lobed or forked, sometimes needle-like.* Flowerheads *apparently axillary, on wiry peduncles,* radiate or discoid, with *1 row of smooth, oval bracts joined at the base, without additional small bracteoles*; receptacle without scales. Ray florets female, yellow; disc florets fertile, 5-lobed. *Fruit ellipsoid,* smooth to hairy, sometimes ribbed, with a *pappus of few, short, sinuous, barbed bristles that are soon deciduous.* Africa, mainly South Africa: 97 spp. The resin was used by early farmers as a substitute for mastic or gum.

▶ LEAVES UNDIVIDED OR LOBED ABOVE

❶ *Euryops tysonii*   J F M A M J J A **S** O N D
Densely leafy shrub to 1.5 m, with elliptical leaves, 10–30×2–8 mm, closely overlapping, and radiate, yellow flowerheads, ±25 mm in diameter; fruit hairless and ribbed. Rocky slopes and boulder beds in the Drakensberg. *Euryops evansii* has larger, 3-toothed leaves, 10–100×3–20 mm.

❷ *Euryops virgineus*   J F M A M J **J A S O N** D
Rivierharpuisbos Densely leafy shrub with stiffly erect stems to 3 m, with wedge-shaped, narrowly lobed or toothed leaves, 5–12×2–7 mm, and radiate, yellow flowerheads, 10 mm in diameter. Damp slopes in the southern and Eastern Cape.

❸ *Euryops tenuissimus*   J F M A M J J **A S O N** D
Resin Bush, Grootharpuisbos Shrub to 2.5 m, often mealy on the young parts, with needle-like, or sometimes 3-lobed leaves, 15–150 mm long, and radiate, yellow or orange flowerheads, 15–20 mm in diameter, clustered among the leaves; fruit hairy, becoming mucilaginous when wet. Stony karroid slopes from southern Namibia to the southern Cape. *Euryops thunbergii* has a thin woolly line beneath each leaf; *E. linifolius* from the West Coast has hairless fruits.

▶ LEAVES DIVIDED INTO NARROW SEGMENTS

❹ *Euryops euryopoides*   J F **M A M J J A S O N** D
Leafy shrub to 1 m, with leaves mostly 3-forked into thread-like segments, 10–30 mm long, and radiate, yellow flowerheads, ±20 mm in diameter, the florets without pappus bristles; fruit hairless and ribbed. Rocky slopes in scrub in the Eastern Cape.

❺ *Euryops abrotanifolius*   J F M A M J **J A S O N** D
Bergharpuisbos Densely leafy shrub to 1 m, with leaves divided into thread- or needle-like lobes, 60–90 mm long, and radiate, yellow flowerheads, 30–40 mm in diameter; fruit hairless and ribbed, with a fleshy appendage. Sandstone slopes in the southwestern and southern Cape.

❻ *Euryops speciosissimus*   J F M A M J J **A S O N** D
Pronkharpuisbos Slender shrub to over 2 m, with leaves divided into flexible, thread-like lobes, (40–)60–200 mm long, and radiate, yellow flowerheads, ±70 mm in diameter; fruit hairless and ribbed. Rocky sandstone slopes in western South Africa.

❼ *Euryops annuus* Annual Euryops   J F M A **M J J A S** O N D
Stemless annual to 30 cm, with a basal tuft of succulent leaves, divided 1 or 2 times into cylindrical segments, 20–100 mm long, and radiate, yellow flowerheads, 20–30 mm in diameter, on long, wiry peduncles; fruit hairy, becoming mucilaginous when wet. Dry gravelly flats in drainage lines in western South Africa.

Gymnodiscus YELLOWWEED, GEELKRUID
(Greek gymnos, naked; diskos, disc, alluding to the lack of pappus in the disc florets) Hairless annual herbs. Leaves in a basal rosette, leathery or succulent, elliptical and usually lobed, or spindle-shaped. Flowerheads small, in loose clusters on long, slender, almost leafless stems, radiate, with 1 row of smooth, oval bracts joined at the base, without additional small bracteoles; receptacle without scales. Ray florets female, yellow; ray fruit egg-shaped, warty or ± smooth, with a pappus of short, sinuous, barbed bristles soon deciduous (rarely absent). Disc florets male, 5-lobed, pappus absent. Winter-rainfall South Africa: 2 spp.

① *Gymnodiscus capillaris*

Tufted, succulent annual herb to 20 cm, with a rosette of lance- to lyre-shaped leaves, usually lobed below, and clusters of small, yellow flowerheads, with short rays, 8–10 mm in diameter. Sandy flats and lower slopes from Namaqualand to the southern Cape.

② *Gymnodiscus linearifolia*

Tufted, succulent annual herb to 30 cm, with a rosette of cylindrical or spindle-shaped leaves, and clusters of small, shortly radiate, yellow flowerheads, 8–10 mm in diameter. Gravelly slopes and flats in Namaqualand.

▶ FLOWERHEADS RADIATE, WITH INVOLUCRAL BRACTS IN 1–4 ROWS, NARROW AND MOSTLY GREEN THROUGHOUT; FRUIT WITHOUT AN EVIDENT PAPPUS, MOSTLY LARGE, >5 MM LONG

Osteospermum BONESEED, BIETOU
(Greek osteon, bone; spermum, seed, alluding to the hard fruits) Annual or perennial herbs or shrubs, sometimes thorny or glandular. Leaves usually alternate, mostly toothed or lobed. Flowerheads usually solitary on short peduncles, radiate, the rays curling back at night, with 2–4 rows of narrow or lance-shaped bracts; receptacle without scales. Ray florets female, bright yellow; ray fruit variously ± club-shaped to 3-angled or -winged, smooth, ribbed or warty, rarely fleshy, without a pappus. Disc florets male, 5-lobed. Mainly Africa but extending to the Middle East: ±85 spp; South Africa: ±80 spp. Some species produce prussic or hydrocyanic acid and are implicated in stock poisonings; selections of 1 or 2 species are widely cultivated. The vernacular name, *bietou*, is one of the very few Khoisan names still in use.

▶ FRUITS FLESHY AND EGG-SHAPED, GLOSSY BLACK WHEN RIPE

③ *Osteospermum incanum*

(=*Chrysanthemoides incana*) **Grey-leaved Tickberry, Grysbietou** Sprawling, white-woolly, sparsely thorny shrublet to 80 cm, with oval to elliptical, coarsely toothed leaves, and small clusters of radiate, yellow flowerheads, 15 mm in diameter, with woolly involucral bracts; fruit fleshy and glossy black when ripe. Coastal dunes or sandy inland slopes from Namibia to the southwestern Cape.

④ *Osteospermum moniliferum*

(=*Chrysanthemoides monilifera*) **Tickberry, Bosluisbessie** Rounded shrub to over 1.5 m, thinly woolly on the young parts, with oval to elliptical, toothed leaves, and small clusters of radiate, yellow flowerheads, 15–20 mm in diameter, with hairless or thinly woolly involucral bracts; fruit fleshy and glossy black when ripe. Sandy and stony slopes and flats from Namaqualand to tropical Africa.

► FRUITS HARD, WARTY OR SHORTLY WINGED, WITHOUT AN APICAL AIR CHAMBER

① *Osteospermum ilicifolium* | J | F | M | A | M | J | J | A | S | O | N | D |

(=*Gibbaria ilicifolia*) Coarsely hairy, sprawling, densely leafy, aromatic shrub to 1 m, sometimes thinly woolly on the young parts, with oval to lance-shaped leaves, the margins rolled under and usually sharply toothed, and radiate flowerheads, the rays and disc yellow; fruit kidney-shaped, warty and pitted, with a small cavity on 1 side, 4–5 mm long. Rocky and stony slopes in the southwestern Cape.

② *Osteospermum grandiflorum* | J | F | M | A | M | J | J | A | S | O | N | D |

Stinkbietou Coarsely hairy, foetid shrublet to 80 cm, with oval to lance-shaped, usually slightly toothed leaves, and loose clusters of radiate flowerheads, the rays and disc yellow or orange; fruit broadly 3-winged, ±12 mm long. Rocky slopes in Namaqualand.

► FRUITS DRY, CONSPICUOUSLY 3-WINGED, WITH AN APICAL AIR CHAMBER

③ *Osteospermum scariosum* | J | F | M | A | M | J | J | A | S | O | N | D |

(=*Tripteris aghillana*) **Skaapbos** Roughly hairy or bristly perennial to 30 cm, from a woody base, with mostly basal, lance-shaped, often sharply toothed leaves, and radiate flowerheads on elongated peduncles, the rays yellow or cream-coloured, sometimes with a dark base, the disc dark; fruit 3-winged, 9–12 mm long. Rocky slopes and hills through central South Africa.

④ *Osteospermum oppositifolium* | J | F | M | A | M | J | J | A | S | O | N | D |

(=*Tripteris oppositifolia*) **Dark-eyed Windowseed** Rounded, foetid, brittle-stemmed shrub to 1 m, with opposite, narrow, ± toothed leaves with a grey bloom, and radiate flowerheads, 30–40 mm in diameter, the rays pale to golden-yellow, the disc black; fruit 3-winged, 10–15 mm long. Dry rocky outcrops in Namaqualand. *Osteospermum sinuatum* is a smaller shrublet, with conspicuously toothed leaves.

⑤ *Osteospermum amplectens* | J | F | M | A | M | J | J | A | S | O | N | D |

(=*Tripteris amplectens*) **Springbok Windowseed, Dassiegousblom** Glandular-haired, aromatic annual herb to 50 cm, with elliptical, irregularly toothed leaves, and radiate flowerheads, 30–40 mm in diameter, the rays yellow, the disc dark purplish; involucral bracts with the membranous margins narrower than the central green portion; fruit 3-winged, 4–5 mm long. Rocky outcrops and gravelly flats, often along roadsides, in Namaqualand.

⑥ *Osteospermum hyoseroides* | J | F | M | A | M | J | J | A | S | O | N | D |

(=*Tripteris hyoseroides*) **Namaqua Windowseed, Dassiegousblom** Glandular-haired, aromatic annual herb to 50 cm, with elliptical, irregularly toothed leaves, and radiate flowerheads, 30–50 mm in diameter, the rays orange, the disc dark purplish; involucral bracts with the membranous margins broader than the central green portion; fruit 3-winged, 7–8 mm long. Stony flats in Namaqualand.

Dimorphotheca MARGUERITE, MAGRIET

(Greek dimorphe, of 2 forms; theca, case, alluding to the 2 forms of fruits in some species) Annual or perennial herbs or shrubs. Leaves alternate, usually coarsely toothed. *Flowerheads large,* radiate, the rays coming together at night, *with 1 or 2 rows of narrow bracts;* receptacle without scales. Ray florets female or sterile, *2 or 3 times as long as the involucral bracts, lilac, white, cream-coloured, or orange with darker reverse,* sometimes with a dark base; *ray fruit 3-angled, often with protuberances, without a pappus.* Disc florets sterile or fertile, 5-lobed; *disc fruit (when present) flattened and disc-like with a thickened rim, without a pappus.* Southern Africa: 13 spp. Some species contain prussic acid but have been used in traditional medicine; many are attractive garden plants.

▶ SHRUBS OR PERENNIAL HERBS

① *Dimorphotheca cuneata*   J F M A M J J A **S O N** D

Bosmagriet Rounded, glandular-haired, sticky shrublet to 50 cm, with wedge-shaped, toothed to lobed leaves, and radiate flowerheads, 30–40 mm in diameter, the rays white or orange, darker on the reverse, the disc yellow; ray fruit 3-angled and glandular, central fruit disc-like. Dry, stony ridges and flats in western and central South Africa.

② *Dimorphotheca nudicaulis*   J F M A M J J **A S O** N D

Witmagriet Glandular-haired perennial with annual stems to 30 cm from a woody base, with basal tufts of narrowly lance-shaped, usually toothed leaves with fringed margins, and radiate flowerheads, 40–50 mm in diameter, the rays white, purple to copper on the reverse, the disc purple; ray fruit very small or absent, central fruit disc-like. Sandstone slopes in southwestern South Africa. *Dimorphotheca tragus,* from Namaqualand and the northern West Coast, has orange or yellow rays.

③ *Dimorphotheca fruticosa*   J F M A M **J J A S** O N D

(=*Osteospermum fruticosum*) **Rankbietou** Sprawling to prostrate perennial, covered in short hairs, with petiolate, oval, minutely toothed leaves, and radiate flowerheads, 40–50 mm in diameter, the rays white or mauve, the disc purple; fruit smooth and 3-angled, ±6 mm long. Coastal dunes and rocks from the southwestern Cape to KwaZulu-Natal.

④ *Dimorphotheca caulescens*   J **F M** A M J J A **S O N D**

(=*Osteospermum caulescens*) Glandular-haired perennial on erect, tufted stems to 30 cm, with basal tufts of narrowly lance-shaped, usually toothed leaves, and radiate flowerheads, 30–40 mm in diameter, the rays white, bluish on the reverse, the disc yellow; fruit ellipsoid and 3-angled, 6 mm long. Rocky grassland through eastern and central South Africa.

⑤ *Dimorphotheca jucunda*   J F M A **M** J J A **S O N D**

(=*Osteospermum jucundum*) Glandular-haired perennial with trailing or erect stems to 30 cm, with basal tufts of narrowly lance-shaped, usually toothed leaves, and radiate flowerheads, 30–40 mm in diameter, the rays pink to mauve, purple to copper on the reverse, the disc yellow and black; fruit ellipsoid and 3-angled, 5 mm long. Moist rocky grassland and broken cliffs in eastern South Africa.

▶ ANNUAL HERBS

1 *Dimorphotheca pinnata*

J F M A M J J A S O N D

(=*Osteospermum pinnatum*) **Jakkalsbietou** Sprawling, glandular-haired annual herb to 20 cm, with leaves deeply divided into narrow or thread-like segments, and radiate flowerheads, 40–50 mm in diameter, the rays cream-coloured to orange, dark at the base, the disc yellow; fruit toothed or warty. Dry stony slopes and flats in western South Africa.

2 *Dimorphotheca pluvialis*

J F M A M J J A S O N D

Reënblommetjie Glandular-haired annual herb to 30 cm, with lance-shaped, lobed to toothed leaves, and radiate flowerheads, 40–50 mm in diameter, the rays white, purple at the base and darker on the reverse, the disc purple; the involucre shallowly cup-shaped; ray fruit slender and warty, central fruit disc-like. Sandy and clay flats and slopes from southern Namibia to the southern Cape.

3 *Dimorphotheca sinuata*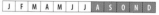

J F M A M J J A S O N D

Namaqualand Daisy Similar to *Dimorphotheca pluvialis* but with beige to orange rays and a deeply cup-shaped involucre. Sandy and gravelly flats and slopes in western South Africa.

Osmitopsis **MOUNTAIN DAISY, BELSKRUIE** *(Resembling the genus* Osmites*)*

Shrubs or shrublets, sometimes felted, *camphor-scented*. Leaves usually alternate, narrow and sometimes toothed, sometimes felted. *Flowerheads 1–few on short peduncles, radiate*, with 2–4 rows of green bracts; *receptacle with long, narrow scales.* Ray florets female or sterile, *white*; disc florets fertile, 5-lobed, yellow. Fruit egg-shaped and ± 3- or 4-angled, smooth, *pappus absent or comprising short scales*, often with the *stubby base of the style in the centre*. Southwestern Cape: 9 spp. Brandy tincture *(belsbrandewyn)* made from the leaves was a traditional tonic and antiseptic.

4 *Osmitopsis asteriscoides*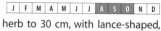

J F M A M J J A S O N D

Belskruie Sparsely branched, aromatic shrub with erect stems to 2 m, densely leafy above with erect, smooth or felted, lance-shaped leaves, 10–60(–80) mm long, and loose clusters of radiate flowerheads, 20–30 mm in diameter, the rays white, the disc yellow. Marshes and seeps in the southwestern Cape.

Eumorphia **EUMORPHIA** *(Greek* eu, *well;* morphe, *form, alluding to the neat foliage)*

Shrublets. *Leaves opposite, small and needle-like or cylindrical, often felted.* Flowerheads 1–few on short peduncles, radiate, with 3–5 rows of bracts; *receptacle usually with long, narrow scales.* Ray florets female, *white*; disc florets fertile, 5-lobed, yellow. *Fruit many-ribbed, hairless, with an apical rim but no pappus.* South Africa: 6 spp.

5 *Eumorphia sericea*

J F M A M J J A S O N D

Rounded, dwarf shrublet to 50 cm, with grey-woolly, narrow or 3-forked leaves crowded on short shoots, and radiate flowerheads, 15–20 mm in diameter, the rays white, sometimes flushed pink, the disc yellow, with scales; the involucral bracts with large orange oil glands on the inner face. Alpine grasslands, often along streams, at high altitude in the Drakensberg. *Eumorphia prostrata* is usually sprawling, with silky leaves, very small or no oil glands on the involucral bracts, and few or no scales on the disc.

Adenanthellum WILD CHRYSANTHEMUM

(Greek aden, gland; anthellum, small flower, alluding to the glandular underside of the rays) Perennial. Leaves
alternate, lance-shaped and toothed. Flowerheads on elongated stems, radiate, with overlapping,
narrow bracts with membranous margins; receptacle without scales. Ray florets female, *white,
glandular beneath, without a distinct tube;* disc florets fertile, yellow, *the tube merging into the fruit.*
Fruit oblong, with 10 ribs, *pappus absent.* South Africa: 1 sp.

1 *Adenanthellum osmitoides*   J F **M A M** J J **A** S **O N** D
Perennial with erect, rod-like stems to 50 cm, with hairless or sparsely hairy, lance-
shaped, sharply toothed leaves, and radiate flowerheads, ±30 mm in diameter, the
rays white, the disc yellow. Moist and marshy montane grassland in northeastern
South Africa.

▸ ANNUALS, OFTEN WITH FINELY DIVIDED LEAVES; FLOWERHEADS DISCOID OR WITH SMALL
WHITE OR YELLOW RAYS; INVOLUCRAL BRACTS SMALL, BLUNT, IN SEVERAL ROWS; DISC
FLORETS 4-LOBED; RECEPTACLE OFTEN CONICAL; PAPPUS OF SCALES OR ABSENT

Oncosiphon STINKWEED, STINKKRUID

(Greek onkos, tumour; siphon, tube, alluding to the swollen floral tube) Annual herbs, smooth or with glandular
hairs, usually foetid or aromatic. Leaves alternate, finely divided 1 or 2 times. Flowerheads solitary or
in clusters on peduncles, radiate or discoid, with several rows of bracts with narrow membranous
margins; receptacle without scales. Ray florets absent or female and then white; disc florets fertile,
4-lobed, with a swollen and brittle tube, yellow. Fruit flask-shaped and 4-ribbed with *glands between
the ribs,* with a pappus of small, irregular teeth. Southern Africa, mainly winter-rainfall region: 6 spp.
Traditionally used as an antispasmodic for stomach ailments.

2 *Oncosiphon suffruticosum*   J F M A M J J **A** S **O N** D
Stinkkruid, Wurmbossie Well-branched, aromatic annual herb to 50 cm, with
leaves finely divided 2 or 3 times, and flat-topped clusters of discoid, yellow
flowerheads, 5–8 mm in diameter. Sandy flats and slopes, often coastal in waste
ground, from southern Namibia to the West Coast.

3 *Oncosiphon grandiflorum*   J F M A M J J **A** S **O N** D
Grootstinkkruid Aromatic annual herb to 45 cm, with leaves finely divided
2 times, and 1–few discoid, yellow flowerheads, 8–10 mm in diameter, with thinly
woolly bracts. Sandy and stony flats and lower slopes from southern Namibia to the
West Coast.

Foveolina WILD CHAMOMILE, WILDEKAMILLE

(Latin fovea, small pit, referring to the minutely pitted fruits) Silky annual herbs. Leaves alternate, divided
2 times. Flowerheads *solitary on long peduncles,* discoid, disciform or radiate, with 3–5 rows of
blunt bracts with membranous margins; receptacle flat to conical, without scales. Outer florets
female, tubular or rayed and then white; disc florets fertile, 4- or 5-lobed, yellow. *Fruit small,
3-ribbed on 1 side and glandular,* with a crown- or ear-like pappus. Western South Africa: 5 spp.

4 *Foveolina tenella* **Lazy Daisy**   J F M A M **J J A** S **O N** D
Aromatic, thinly hairy annual herb to 25 cm, with leaves finely divided 2 times, and
radiate flowerheads, 15–20 mm in diameter, on slender peduncles, white with a
yellow disc. Sandy slopes and flats, mostly coastal, in Namaqualand.

① *Foveolina dichotoma* False Cotula J F M A M J J A S O N D

Aromatic, thinly silky, branched annual herb to 15 cm, with leaves finely divided 1 or 2 times, and discoid, yellow flowerheads, 10–15 mm in diameter, on long peduncles. Dry gravelly slopes and flats in northwestern South Africa.

Cotula BUTTONS, KNOPPIES *(Greek kotule, cup, alluding to the receptacle)*

Annual or perennial herbs. Leaves usually alternate, sometimes basal, *slender to finely divided 2 times*. Flowerheads *solitary on slender or wiry peduncles sometimes swollen beneath the head*, usually disciform, rarely with small or large rays, *with 2 rows of elliptical to round bracts with narrow membranous margins*; receptacle flat to conical, without scales. Outer or ray florets female, *mostly on short stalks*, white or yellow; disc florets fertile, *4-lobed, sometimes flattened or winged*, yellow. *Fruit usually stalked, flattened and elliptical*, usually warty, pappus absent. Southern hemisphere, mainly southern Africa: ±50 spp.; South Africa: ±45 spp.

② *Cotula turbinata* Ganskos J F M A M J J A S O N D

Softly hairy annual herb, 5–30 cm, with leaves finely divided 2 or 3 times, and radiate flowerheads, 8–12 mm in diameter, the rays short, white or yellow, the disc yellow, on wiry scapes that become swollen at the top in fruit; involucral bracts broad and 3-veined. Sandy or disturbed places in the southwestern Cape, often on waste ground. *Cotula duckittiae* is more robust, with larger yellow or orange flowerheads, 15–20 mm in diameter.

③ *Cotula barbata* Kleinganskos J F M A M J J A S O N D

Softly hairy annual herb to 15 cm, with leaves finely divided 2 or 3 times, in a basal tuft, and discoid, white or yellow flowerheads, 8–10 mm in diameter, on wiry scapes; involucral bracts with membranous margins. Gravelly slopes in Namaqualand.

▶ FLOWERHEADS RADIATE WITH YELLOW RAYS, BUT OTHERWISE NOT AS ANY OF THE ABOVE; INVOLUCRAL BRACTS OFTEN PARTIALLY DRY AND PAPERY, IN SEVERAL ROWS

Heterolepis ROCK DAISY

(Greek hetero, dissimilar; lepis, scale, alluding to the unequal pappus) Shrublets with cobwebby branchlets. *Leaves alternate, stiff and narrow or needle-like, the margins rolled under* and sometimes sparsely toothed, *sharply pointed and densely woolly beneath*. Flowerheads solitary on long or short, glandular peduncles, *large, radiate*, with 1–3 rows of green bracts with membranous margins, the inner bracts almost entirely membranous; receptacle honeycombed, without scales. Ray florets female, *with a thread-like lobe opposite the ray, yellow*; disc florets fertile, deeply 5-lobed. *Fruit flask-shaped, densely silky, with a pappus of 2 dissimilar rows of stout, tawny, barbed, bristle-like scales*. South Africa: 4 spp.

④ *Heterolepis aliena* J F M A M J J A S O N D

Sprawling shrublet to 30 cm, with cobwebby branches, needle-like, sparsely toothed leaves (10–)15–30 mm long, with the margins rolled under, densely woolly beneath, and radiate, yellow flowerheads, 40–50 mm in diameter, on short peduncles to 50 mm long. Rocky slopes and outcrops in the southwestern Cape.

Leysera LEYSERA, GEELTEE *(Named for German botanist, Friedrich Wilhelm von Leysser, 1731–1815)*

Slender shrublets or woody annuals, usually greyish-woolly. Leaves alternate, *needle-like, glandular.* *Flowerheads solitary on slender, wiry peduncles,* radiate, with 4–7 rows of oblong, firm-textured, glandular involucral bracts; receptacle without scales. Ray florets female, yellow; ray fruit slender, with a pappus of narrow scales. Disc florets fertile, 5-lobed; disc fruit slender, with a *pappus of feathery bristles surrounded by short scales.* Southern Africa and Mediterranean to Asia: 3 spp. South Africa: 2 spp. An infusion of the dried leaves was used as an emollient to treat coughs.

① *Leysera gnaphalodes*

J F M A M J J A S O N D

Skilpadteebossie Hairless or cobwebby shrublet to 40 cm, with glandular-haired, needle-like leaves, and radiate yellow flowerheads, 20 mm in diameter, on slender, wiry peduncles mostly at an angle and bent up at the tip; the pappus bristles feathery from the base. Sandy flats and slopes from southern Namibia to the Eastern Cape. *Leysera tenella* is a slender, more delicate annual with the pappus bristles feathery in the upper half only.

Rhynchopsidium RHYNCHOPSIDIUM, GEELSNEEU
(Greek rhyncho, beaked; opsis, appearance; idion, diminutive, alluding to the fruits) Annuals, usually greyish-woolly. Leaves alternate, needle-like, with glandular-hairs. Flowerheads solitary, sessile or on short peduncles, radiate, with 4–7 rows of oblong, papery-tipped involucral bracts; receptacle without scales. Ray florets female, yellow; disc florets fertile, 5-lobed. Fruit slender, densely hairy, with a pappus of small scales only. Southwestern South Africa: 2 spp.

② *Rhynchopsidium pumilum*

J F M A M J J A S O N D

Thinly cobwebby annual to 20 cm, with glandular-haired, needle-like leaves, and radiate yellow flowerheads 15–20 mm in diameter, on short peduncles. Mainly clay flats in the drier parts of western South Africa. *Rhynchopsidium sessiliflorum* has small, sessile flowerheads ±5 mm in diameter.

▸ FLOWERHEADS EITHER DISCOID, OR RADIATE WITH WHITE, PINK, BLUE, PURPLE, ORANGE OR RED (RARELY YELLOW) RAYS, BUT OTHERWISE NOT AS ANY OF THE ABOVE; INVOLUCRAL BRACTS NARROW, IN 2–SEVERAL ROWS

Gerbera GERBERA *(Named for German naturalist, Traugott Gerber, d. 1743)*

Tufted perennial herbs, often with a woolly crown. Leaves basal, elliptical and toothed or lobed, often *tough and leathery and densely felted beneath.* Flowerheads solitary on long scapes or peduncles, radiate, with several rows of bracts; receptacle without scales. Ray florets usually female, *2-lipped, the outer lip large and strap-shaped and the inner lip of 2 small, thread-like lobes,* white, pink or red, rarely yellow; disc florets fertile, 5-lobed and *irregularly 2-lipped with curled petals,* usually blackish. Fruit narrowly flask-shaped and ribbed, sparsely and shortly hairy, with a pappus of many barbed bristles. Africa and Asia: ±30 spp.; South Africa: 13 spp.

▸ PEDUNCLE WITH SMALL SCALE-LIKE BRACTS

③ *Gerbera crocea* **Dialstee**

J F M A M J J A S O N D

Tufted perennial to 40 cm, with a rosette of petiolate, lance-shaped to elliptical, lightly toothed leaves, the margins rolled under, ± hairless above and thinly cobwebby beneath, and radiate, white or pink flowerheads, maroon on the reverse, 20–35 mm in diameter, on scaly peduncles. Rocky slopes in the southwestern Cape, flowering after fire. *Gerbera wrightii* from the Cape Peninsula has heart-shaped leaves.

① *Gerbera serrata* J F M A M J J A S O N D

Tufted perennial to 30 cm, with a rosette of petiolate, elliptical, saw-toothed leaves, the margins rolled under, ± hairless above and yellow-felted beneath, and radiate, white flowerheads, maroon on the reverse, 20–35 mm in diameter, on scaly peduncles; involucral bracts in 2 rows. Rocky slopes in the southern Cape, flowering after fire. *Gerbera tomentosa* has several series of involucral bracts.

② *Gerbera linnaei* **Varingblom** J F M A M J J A S O N D

Tufted perennial to 40 cm, with a rosette of narrow leaves cut into round, twisted lobes, the margins rolled under, ± hairless above and yellow-felted beneath, and radiate, cream-coloured or sometimes yellow flowerheads, maroon on the reverse, 20–35 mm in diameter, on scaly peduncles. Rocky sandstone slopes in the southwestern Cape, flowering after fire.

▶ **PEDUNCLE WITHOUT BRACTS**

③ *Gerbera ambigua* J F M A M J J A S O N D

Tufted perennial to 35 cm, with a rosette of petiolate, elliptical leaves, thinly hairy or ± hairless above but white- or yellow-felted beneath, and white to yellow flowerheads, mostly reddish on the reverse, 20–35 mm in diameter, on naked scapes. Grassland and savanna through eastern South and tropical Africa.

④ *Gerbera viridifolia* **Pink Gerbera** J F M A M J J A S O N D

Tufted perennial to 35 cm, with a rosette of petiolate, elliptical leaves, thinly hairy or ± hairless on both surfaces, and white or pink to purple (rarely yellow) flowerheads, 25–40 mm in diameter, on naked scapes. Grassland and savanna through eastern South and tropical Africa. *Gerbera galpinii* has narrow leaves and yellow rays.

⑤ *Gerbera aurantiaca* **Hilton Daisy** J F M A M J J A S O N D

Tufted perennial to 30 cm, with a rosette of petiolate, elliptical leaves, velvety above but thinly woolly or hairless beneath, orange to red flowerheads, coppery on the reverse, 25–35 mm in diameter, on naked scapes. Rocky grassland in KwaZulu-Natal. Hybridises with *Gerbera ambigua*.

⑥ *Gerbera jamesonii* J F M A M J J A S O N D

Barberton Daisy Tufted perennial to 70 cm, with a rosette of petiolate, deeply undulating or lobed leaves, almost hairless except on the margins, and reddish flowerheads, 40–60 mm in diameter, on naked scapes. Rocky slopes in woodland in northeastern South Africa.

Callilepis CALLILEPIS, WILDEMAGRIET
(Greek kallos, *beauty;* lepis, *scale, perhaps referring to the involucral scales)* Perennials or shrublets. Leaves alternate, ± *hairless or with glandular hairs. Flowerheads solitary and pedunculate,* radiate, with 3 rows of bracts; *receptacle with boat-shaped scales.* Ray florets female, *white;* disc florets fertile, 5-lobed, *purple.* Fruit 3-angled or flattened, with a pappus of scale-like bristles. South Africa: 5 spp. Plants are highly poisonous but are used in traditional medicine.

⑦ *Callilepis laureola* J F M A M J J A S O N D

Perennial with erect annual stems from a tuberous rootstock, with narrow to lance-shaped, ± hairless leaves, 3-veined from the base, and radiate flowerheads, 40–60 mm in diameter, with white rays and a purplish-black disc. Grassland through eastern South Africa, flowering after fire.

Printzia   DAISY BUSH   *(Named for the 19th-century Danish botanist, H.C. Printz)*

Shrubs or perennial herbs. Leaves alternate, usually broad and toothed, *woolly or felted beneath*. Flowerheads in small clusters, ± sessile or shortly stalked, radiate or disciform, with 3–6 rows of ± *woolly bracts*; receptacle without scales. Ray florets female, white, mauve or purple; disc florets fertile, 5-lobed, yellow, *the anthers protruding in bud*. Fruit cylindrical, ribbed, hairy, with a *pappus of 2 or 3 rows of barbed or feathery bristles*. South Africa: 6 spp.

1 *Printzia polifolia*

J F M A M J **J A S O** N **D**

Stiffly branched shrub with ribbed, felted branches, 1–2 m, with paddle-shaped, weakly toothed and crinkly leaves, ± hairless above but felted beneath, and radiate flowerheads, 15–20 mm in diameter, with mauve rays and a yellow disc. Stony flats and lower slopes in southwestern South Africa.

Athrixia   ATHRIXIA, BOESMANSTEE   *(Greek thrix, hair, alluding to the hairy leaves)*

Shrubs or perennial herbs. Leaves alternate or basal, *narrow or needle-like and without teeth, woolly or felted beneath*. Flowerheads radiate, with *6–8 rows of spreading or downflexed, bristle-tipped, ± woolly bracts*; receptacle without scales. Ray florets female, white, mauve or purple; disc florets fertile, 5-lobed, yellow or white. Fruit cylindrical, ribbed, and hairy, with a *pappus of 2 rows of barbed bristles or scales*. Africa: 14 spp.; South Africa: 9 spp. *Athrixia phylicoides* was used medicinally.

2 *Athrixia phylicoides*

J F M A M J J A S O N D

Bushman's Tea   Sprawling shrublet to 1 m, with narrowly lance-shaped leaves, smooth and shiny above but felted beneath, 15–30×5–10 mm, and ± sessile radiate flowerheads, ±15 mm in diameter, with mauve rays and a yellow disc. Grassland and forest margins through eastern South and tropical Africa.

3 *Athrixia angustissima*

J F M A M J J A S O N **D**

Straggling perennial with slender, wiry stems to 30 cm, with scattered, spreading, needle-like stem leaves, smooth above and felted beneath, 30–50×1–3 mm, and radiate flowerheads, 15–25 mm in diameter, with white rays and a yellow disc. Moist grassland and cliffs in the Drakensberg. *Athrixia pinifolia* is a bush with clusters of leaves at the branch tips.

4 *Athrixia fontana*

J F M **A** M J **J** A S O N **D**

Tufted perennial to 30 cm, with rosettes of narrow to elliptical leaves, softly hairy and glandular above and felted beneath, up to 80×20 mm, and solitary, radiate flowerheads, 20–25 mm in diameter, on long stems, with white or pink-flushed rays and a yellow disc. Stream banks and wet slopes in the Drakensberg.

Microglossa   TRAILING DAISY
(Greek mikros, small; glossa, tongue, alluding to the short ray florets)   *Scrambling shrubs*. Leaves alternate, usually toothed. *Flowerheads in flat-topped clusters, radiate, the rays short*, with several rows of bracts, the inner shorter than the outer; receptacle without scales. Ray florets female, white; disc florets fertile, 5-lobed, yellowish. Fruit elliptical, faintly ribbed, smooth or hairy, with a *pappus of barbed bristles*. Africa: ±10 spp.; South Africa: 2 spp.

5 *Microglossa mespilifolia*

J F M A M J J A S O N D

Trailing Daisy   Vigorous scrambling shrub, with triangular, coarsely toothed leaves, and flat-topped clusters of radiate flowerheads, ±5 mm in diameter, with short, white rays and a yellowish disc. Forest margins and open scrub and woodland along the southeastern seaboard of South Africa.

Chrysocoma BITTERBUSH, BITTERBOS

(Greek chryso, golden; coma, head of hair, alluding to the golden flowerheads) Shrublets. Leaves alternate, usually *needle-like*. Flowerheads *solitary on slender peduncles*, usually *discoid*, with 4 rows of green bracts with narrow membranous margins; receptacle without scales. Florets 5-lobed, yellow. Fruit *flattened and elliptical with a thickened rim, and 2 small resin sacs at the top*, shortly hairy, with a *pappus of many barbed bristles* surrounded by an outer ring of minute scales. Southern Africa: ±20 spp. Although palatable to stock, the plants can cause illness if consumed in large quantities; they have, nevertheless, been used medicinally.

❶ *Chrysocoma ciliata*

Slender-stemmed shrublet to 60 cm, with ascending, hairless, needle-like leaves, 2–14 mm long, and discoid, yellow flowerheads, ±10 mm in diameter. Rocky slopes and flats through southern Africa.

❷ *Chrysocoma coma-aurea*

Shrublet to 50 cm, with spreading to curved-back, hairless, needle-like leaves, 3–20 mm long, often with upward-curving tips, and discoid, yellow flowerheads, ±10 mm long. Coastal flats and lower slopes in the southwestern Cape.

Felicia FELICIA, ASTERJIE *(Either from the Latin felix, happy, or for a German official of the same name)*

Annual or perennial herbs or shrublets. Leaves alternate, opposite or basal, narrow or broader, rarely toothed, usually hairy. Flowerheads solitary on peduncles, usually *radiate*, with 2–4 rows of green bracts with narrow membranous margins; receptacle without scales. Ray florets usually *fertile, blue, pink or white*; disc florets fertile, 5-lobed, yellow or rarely blue. *Fruit flattened and elliptical with a thickened rim*, usually hairy, and a *pappus of barbed bristles*. Africa to Arabia: 85 spp.; South Africa: 80 spp.

▸ **PERENNIALS OR SHRUBLETS**

❸ *Felicia fruticosa*

Wildeaster, Bosastertjie Shrublet to 1 m, with tufts of small, fleshy, lance-shaped leaves, and radiate flowerheads, 15–20 mm in diameter, with blue to mauve rays and a yellow disc; involucral bracts in 3 or 4 series. Rocky lower slopes in the extreme southwestern Cape and in the Soutpansberg in Limpopo.

❹ *Felicia filifolia* Draaibos

Shrublet to 1 m, with tufts of fleshy, needle-like leaves, and radiate flowerheads, 15–20 mm in diameter, with blue to mauve rays and a yellow disc; involucral bracts in 3 or 4 series. Stony flats and slopes, widespread through southern Africa.

❺ *Felicia aethiopica* Bloublommetjie

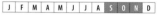

Thinly hairy, soft shrublet to 1 m, with elliptical to oval leaves, often flexed downward, and radiate flowerheads, 20 mm in diameter, with blue rays and a yellow disc; involucral bracts in 2 series, with 3 veins each. Rocky flats and slopes in southern South Africa. *Felicia amelloides* has 1-veined involucral bracts.

❻ *Felicia elongata*

Saldanha Bay Felicia Coarsely hairy, shrubby perennial to 30 cm, with lance-shaped leaves mostly clustered at the base, the margins rolled under, and radiate flowerheads, 30–40 mm in diameter, the rays white to pale mauve, with bold maroon markings at the base, the disc yellow; involucral bracts in 2 series. Coastal limestone sands around Saldanha Bay in the Western Cape.

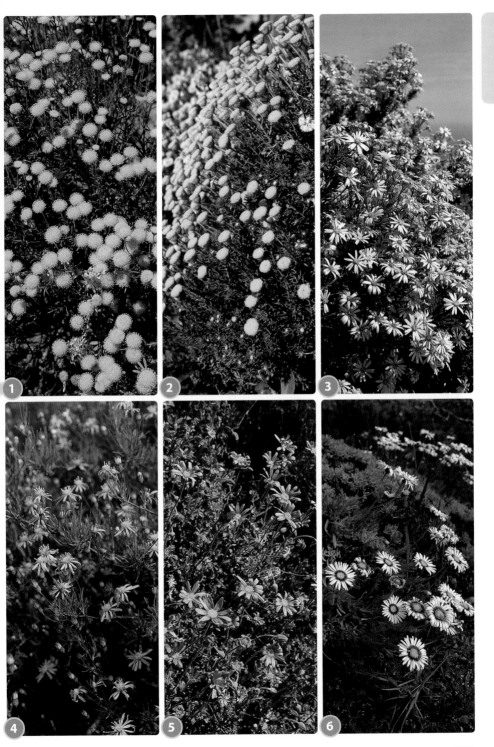

▶ ANNUAL HERBS

1 *Felicia australis* **Sambreeltjies**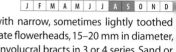
Thinly hairy, sprawling annual, 5–25 cm, with narrow, sometimes lightly toothed leaves, thinly hairy on the margins, and radiate flowerheads, 15–20 mm in diameter, with blue to mauve rays and a yellow disc; involucral bracts in 3 or 4 series. Sand or clay flats in western South Africa.

2 *Felicia tenella* **Sambreeltjies**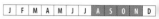
Thinly hairy annual, 5–25 cm, with narrow leaves, coarsely bristly on the margins, and radiate flowerheads, 15–20 mm in diameter, with blue, violet or white rays and a yellow disc; involucral bracts in 3 or 4 series. Damp places and coastal dunes in the southwestern Cape.

3 *Felicia merxmuelleri*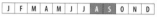
Namaqualand Felicia Shortly hairy annual herb to 25 cm, with spatula-shaped, shortly hairy leaves, and radiate flowerheads, 20–30 mm in diameter, with blue rays and a yellow disc; involucral bracts in 2 series; ray fruits without pappus bristles. Gravelly slopes and flats in Namaqualand.

4 *Felicia heterophylla*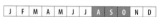
Blue-eyed Felicia, True-blue Daisy Roughly hairy annual with erect branches to 35 cm, with lance-shaped leaves, and radiate flowerheads, 20 mm in diameter, with blue rays and a blue (rarely yellow) disc; involucral bracts in 2 series; ray fruits without pappus bristles. Sandy flats and slopes in the southwestern Cape.

Aster **ASTER** *(Greek* astron, star, *alluding to the radiate flowerheads)*

Annual or perennial, often hairless herbs, distinguished from *Felicia* by the fruits with a combination of *pointed hairs and glandular hairs, and a pappus of barbed bristles plus an outer row of small scales.* Mainly northern hemisphere: ±250 spp.; South Africa: 16 spp. Used medicinally.

5 *Aster erucifolius*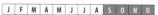
Drakensberg Aster Prostrate perennial, mostly 10–30 cm in diameter, with maroon stems and bracts, deeply lobed leaves, and radiate flowerheads, 20–30 mm in diameter, with mauve (rarely white) rays and a yellow disc. Damp gravelly patches and rock sheets in the high Drakensberg.

6 *Aster bakerianus* **Baker's Aster** J F M A M J J A S O N D
Perennial herb with roughly hairy, annual stems to 70 cm from a woody rootstock, with lance-shaped, ± coarsely hairy, slightly toothed leaves, 3–5-veined from the base, and radiate flowerheads, 15–20 mm in diameter, with blue or white rays and a yellow disc; involucral bracts ± hairy. Rocky grassland through eastern South and tropical Africa, flowering especially after fire.

7 *Aster harveyanus* J F M A M J J A S O N D
Harvey's Aster Like *Aster bakerianus* but stems, leaves and bracts hairless. Rocky grassland through eastern South and tropical Africa, flowering especially after fire.

413

Amellus   AMELLUS, GRYSASTERTJIE

(Name given by the Roman poet Virgil to a daisy with blue flowerheads)   Annual or perennial herbs or shrubs, *densely covered in grey hairs*. Leaves alternate, narrowly lance-shaped, sometimes toothed, *both surfaces equally grey-silky*. Flowerheads usually radiate, rarely discoid or disciform, with 2–7 rows of hairy bracts with narrow membranous margins; *receptacle with narrow scales*. Ray florets female, blue or purple; disc florets fertile, 5-lobed, yellow or white. *Fruit elliptical and flattened, hairy on the margins or throughout, with a pappus of fringed scales plus a few, deciduous, barbed bristles.* Winter-rainfall southern Africa: 12 spp.

1 *Amellus asteroides*

J F M A M J J A S **O** N D

Grey-silky shrublet to 40 cm, with spoon- or paddle-shaped leaves, and solitary, radiate or discoid flowerheads, 15–20 mm in diameter, with mauve or white rays and a yellow disc. Coastal dunes in southwestern South Africa.

2 *Amellus tenuifolius*

J F M A M J J A **S O N D**

Grey-silky perennial or shrublet with slender, erect stems to 50 cm, with narrow leaves, and loose clusters of radiate flowerheads, 15–20 mm in diameter, with mauve rays and a yellow disc. Sandy flats near the coast from southern Namibia to the West Coast.

3 *Amellus nanus*

J F M A M J **J A** S O N D

Annual herb to 20 cm, with short hairs, narrowly elliptical leaves, and solitary, radiate flowerheads, 15–20 mm in diameter, mauve with a yellow disc. Sandy washes in southern Namibia and the Richtersveld.

Mairia   FIRE DAISY, VUURASTER   *(Named for the 19th-century German plant collector, Louis Maire)*

Tufted, perennial herbs covered with thin, woolly hairs. Leaves in a basal tuft or rosette, leathery, coarsely toothed or scalloped. Flowerheads *solitary on softly hairy peduncles*, large, radiate, with 3–5 rows of green bracts; receptacle without scales. Ray florets female, white, pink or purple; disc florets fertile, 5-lobed, yellow. Fruit ellipsoid and hairy, with a *pappus of persistent, feathery bristles*, sometimes surrounded by small, fringed scales. Southwestern Cape: 5 spp.

4 *Mairia coriacea*

J **F M A** M J J A S O **N D**

Tufted perennial to 12 cm, with a basal rosette of erect, leathery, paddle-shaped leaves, often broadly toothed at the tips and softly hairy when young but hairless on both surfaces when mature, with a conspicuous tuft of silky hairs at the base of the petiole, and radiate flowerheads, 20–30 mm in diameter, with pink to purple rays and a yellow disc. Rocky slopes in the extreme southwestern Cape, flowering after fire.

5 *Mairia crenata*

J **F M** A M J J A **S O N D**

Tufted perennial to 15 cm, with a basal rosette of spreading, elliptical to oval, leathery, finely scalloped leaves, the margins rolled under, softly hairy when young but hairless above when mature, and radiate flowerheads, 15–20 mm in diameter, with pink to mauve or white rays and a yellow disc. Rocky sandstone slopes in southwestern South Africa, flowering mainly after fire.

6 *Mairia hirsuta*

J F M A M J **J A** S O N D

Short-stemmed perennial to 30 cm, with thinly felted, lance-shaped, slightly toothed leaves, more densely hairy beneath, the margins rolled under, and radiate flowerheads, 20–30 mm in diameter, with mauve to pink rays and a yellow disc. Cool mountain slopes in the southwestern Cape, flowering after fire.

DIPSACACEAE Scabious family

Cephalaria CEPHALARIA *(Greek kephale, a head, referring to the flowerheads)*

Herbs. Leaves opposite, often in a basal tuft, usually variously lobed or cut. Flowers in tight heads surrounded by *several rows of overlapping bracts*, white, *each flower in the axil of a bract or fringed sheath*; calyx of small scales; corolla obliquely funnel-shaped. Europe and Africa: ±60 spp.; South Africa: ±15 spp.

1 *Cephalaria galpiniana*

J F M A M J J A S O N D

Fern-leaved Cephalaria Tufted, mat-forming perennial to 30 cm, with a basal tuft of finely divided leaves, and small white flowers in solitary heads, 30 mm in diameter. Scree and rocky slopes at high altitude in the Drakensberg. Other species are larger, with lobed or simple leaves.

Scabiosa SCABIOUS, JONGMANSKNOOP
(Latin scabies, because the plants were used medicinally or they were rough and felted) Herbs or shrubs. Leaves opposite, often in a basal tuft, usually lobed or cut. Flowers in tight heads surrounded by *1 or 2 rows of overlapping bracts*, white or lilac, *each flower surrounded at the base by a shuttlecock-shaped epicalyx expanded at the top into a membranous, saucer-like collar; calyx of 5 long bristles; corolla funnel-shaped and ± 2-lipped, especially the outermost flowers*. Europe and Africa to Asia: ±100 spp.; South Africa: 9 spp. The leaves and roots have been used medicinally.

2 *Scabiosa africana* **Cape Scabious**

J F M A M J J A S O N D

Sprawling shrublet to 1 m, with large, soft-textured, velvety leaves that are toothed or cut, and heads of lilac flowers. Sheltered sandstone slopes on the Cape Peninsula.

3 *Scabiosa columbaria*

J F M A M J J A S O N D

Wild Scabious, Bitterbos Tufted perennial to 80 cm, with shortly hairy leaves of 2 markedly different types, the lower ones paddle-shaped and toothed or lobed, the upper ones deeply cut to the midrib into slender lobes, and heads of white to mauve flowers. Widespread on rocky slopes through South Africa.

VERBENACEAE Verbena family

Chascanum CHASCANUM *(Greek chascanon, a wide-mouthed mask, alluding to the flower shape)*

Perennial herbs or shrublets, variously hairy. Leaves often toothed. *Flowers in spikes*, white or cream-coloured; the calyx 5-toothed; the *corolla salver-shaped with a long tube*; stamens 4, of 2 types, *hidden within the tube*. Africa and Arabia: 30 spp.; South Africa: 14 spp.

4 *Chascanum latifolium*

J F M A M J J A S O N D

Broad-leaved Chascanum Robust perennial with annual stems to 50 cm, with paddle-shaped, hairless or velvety leaves without teeth, and white to pale mauve, salver-shaped flowers with a slender tube, ±15 mm long. Grassland in northeastern South Africa, flowering after fire.

LAMIACEAE

Mint family

▶ FERTILE STAMENS 2

Salvia   **SAGE, SALIE**   *(The classical name for the genus, from Latin salvare, to heal)*

Annual or perennial herbs or shrubs, variously hairy. Leaves entire, toothed or lobed. Flowers 2–many in whorls, with the bracts usually reduced, usually blue; the *calyx 2-lipped* with the upper lip mostly 3-toothed and the lower lip larger and 2-toothed; the corolla 2-lipped with the upper lip usually longer; *stamens 2, hinged at the elongated connective,* with the upper section longest and arching beneath the upper hood and the lower sterile. Worldwide: ±900 spp.; South Africa: 22 spp. Many species are grown ornamentally. The species hybridise readily and grade into one another, making identification difficult.

▶ **SOFT SHRUBS OR PERENNIALS, WITH FLASK-SHAPED CALYX NOT ENLARGING IN FRUIT**

① *Salvia repens*

J F M A M J J A S O N D

Creeping Sage, Kruipsalie   Perennial to 80 cm from a creeping rhizome, with ± hairless or hairy, paddle- to lyre-shaped, toothed leaves usually crowded below, and whorls of pale blue to purple flowers with darker spots, 12–25 mm long, the upper lip ± straight, the calyx shortly hairy. Grassland or woodland through southern and eastern South Africa.

② *Salvia disermas*

J F M A M J J A S O N D

Large Blue Sage, Grootblousalie   Soft shrub to 1.2 m, with roughly hairy, oval, toothed leaves, often crowded below, and whorls of whitish to mauve flowers with darker spots, 15–30 mm long, the upper lip deeply arched, the calyx hairy. Along temporary watercourses and roadsides across the drier interior of South Africa.

▶ **TWIGGY SHRUBS, WITH FLARED CALYX ENLARGING IN FRUIT**

③ *Salvia africana-caerulea*

J F M A M J J A S O N D

Blue Sage, Bloublomsalie   Shrub to 2 m, with softly hairy, paddle-shaped, sometimes toothed leaves, and whorls of mauve to blue or pink flowers with darker spots, 16–28 mm long, the calyx softly silky and enlarging in fruit. Sandy flats and slopes in Namaqualand and the southwestern Cape. *Salvia albicaulis* has slender, erect, white-velvety stems.

④ *Salvia chamelaeagnea*

J F M A M J J A S O N D

African Sage, Afrikaanse Salie   Shrub to 2 m, with almost hairless but gland-dotted, paddle-shaped, sometimes toothed leaves, and whorls of mauve to blue or pink flowers with darker spots, 16–28 mm long; the calyx coarsely hairy and enlarging in fruit. Sandy and granite slopes in the southwestern Cape.

⑤ *Salvia dentata*

J F M A M J J A S O N D

Namaqualand Sage   Shrub to 2 m, with paddle-shaped, toothed leaves, coarsely hairy beneath, and whorls of mauve to blue or whitish flowers with darker spots, 16–25 mm long; the calyx roughly hairy and enlarging in fruit. Stony slopes and rock outcrops in Namaqualand.

⑥ *Salvia dolomitica*

J F M A M J J A S O N D

Pilgrim's Rest Pink Sage   Shrub to 2 m, with elliptical, grey-haired leaves, and whorls of pink to lilac flowers with yellowish spots, 20–28 mm long; the calyx coarsely hairy and enlarging in fruit. Dolomite outcrops in northeastern South Africa.

① *Salvia lanceolata* J F M A M J J A S O N D

Red Sage, Rooisalie Shrub to 2 m, with grey-haired, paddle-shaped, sometimes toothed leaves, and mostly pairs of dull rose to reddish flowers, 25–35 mm long, the upper lip ±17 mm long; the bracts deciduous, the calyx shortly hairy and enlarging in fruit. Mainly coastal in fynbos on deep, acidic sands and rocky outcrops in Namaqualand and the southwestern Cape.

② *Salvia africana-lutea* J F M A M J J A S O N D

Brown Sage, Bruinsalie, Strandsalie Shrub to 2 m, with grey-haired, paddle-shaped, sometimes toothed leaves, and mostly pairs of golden-brown flowers, 30–50 mm long, the upper lip ±25 mm long; the calyx shortly hairy and enlarging in fruit. Coastal scrub on neutral or alkaline sands from Namaqualand to the Eastern Cape.

▶ **FERTILE STAMENS 4, SPREADING OUTWARDS**

Mentha MINT *(Classical Latin name for the genus)*

Perennial herbs, *smelling of mint when crushed*. Leaves usually toothed. Flowers *many, in whorls in a spike-like raceme*, small, white to lilac; *calyx 5-toothed with teeth all ± similar; corolla 4-lobed; stamens 4, ± equally spreading*. Worldwide temperate: 20–30 spp.; South Africa: 2 spp. Used medicinally and in food.

③ *Mentha longifolia* J F M A M J J A S O N D

Wild Spearmint, Horse Mint Rhizomatous perennial to 1.5 m, with sessile, narrow to lance-shaped, toothed or untoothed leaves, and whorls of white to lilac flowers, 3–5 mm long, in long, narrow spikes, 10–14 mm in diameter. River banks and damp places through South Africa.

④ *Mentha aquatica* Water Mint J F M A M J J A S O N D

Rhizomatous perennial to 1 m, with petiolate, lance-shaped to oval, toothed leaves, and whorls of pink to purple flowers, 3–5 mm long, in head-like spikes, 14–20 mm in diameter. Marshes and moist places in the southwestern Cape and southern and eastern South and tropical Africa.

Tetradenia IBOZA, MISTY PLUME
(Greek tetra, four; aden, gland, possibly referring to the stamens) Soft shrubs, *usually leafless at flowering, with the sexes on separate plants*. Leaves small or large, somewhat succulent. Flowers small, many in tight whorls *in branched spikes or panicles*, whitish to mauve; calyx 3-lobed; corolla 4-lobed; stamens 4 (absent in female flowers), *spreading*. Africa and Madagascar: 7 spp.; South Africa: 4 spp. Used medicinally.

⑤ *Tetradenia riparia* J F M A M J J A S O N D

Brittle-stemmed shrub to 5 m, leafless at flowering, with leaves oval, glandular-haired, 30–80 mm long, and flowers in large panicles, unisexual, whitish to mauve, 2–4 mm long. Wooded hillsides and stream banks in savanna in northeastern South and tropical Africa. *Tetradenia brevispicata* has smaller leaves, 10–30 mm long, with velvety undersides, and shorter male flower spikes, 10–20 mm long; *T. barberae* from Grahamstown has quilted leaves 8–15 mm long.

420 MINT FAMILY

▶ **FERTILE STAMENS 4, ARCHING UP BENEATH THE UPPER COROLLA LIP**

Rotheca **BUSH VIOLET** *(From the native Indian name for the genus)*

Shrubs or herbs. Leaves opposite or whorled, *often entire*. Flowers axillary; calyx 5-lobed; corolla 5-lobed and 1-lipped, blue; stamens 4, arching and of 2 lengths. *Fruit ± fleshy or leathery.* Africa and Asia: ±20 spp.; South Africa: 9 spp. Used medicinally.

❶ *Rotheca hirsuta*

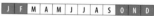

(=*Clerodendrum hirsutum, C. triphyllum*) **Wild Violet** Woody perennial with annual stems to 60 cm, with whorls of 2–4 ± hairy, elliptical to lance-shaped leaves, and bright blue, 1-lipped flowers, ±15 mm in diameter. Grassland and woodland through eastern and northern South Africa, flowering after fire.

Ajuga **BUGLE PLANT** *(Possibly from the classical Latin Abiga for a similar plant)*

Perennial herbs. Leaves in a basal rosette, usually toothed or lobed. Flowers in whorls, blue to purple; calyx 5-toothed; *corolla ± 1-lipped* (the upper lip reduced); stamens 4, *arching*. Worldwide temperate: ±100 spp.; South Africa: 1 sp.

❷ *Ajuga ophrydis*

Tufted perennial herb to 25 cm, with a basal rosette of leathery, paddle-shaped leaves, and a whorled spike of blue to mauve, 1-lipped flowers, 15–20 mm long. Grasslands through eastern South Africa.

Stachys **WOUNDWORT, TEEBOS** *(Greek stachus, spike, alluding to the inflorescence)*

Annual or perennial herbs or shrubs. Leaves narrow to broad, usually toothed. Flowers 2–several in whorls with the bracts mostly smaller than the leaves, usually white to purple; *calyx 5-toothed with teeth all ± similar*; corolla 2-lipped, usually with a ring of hairs near the base within; stamens 4, *arching* and of 2 lengths. Mainly southern hemisphere subtropical and temperate: ±400 spp.; South Africa: 40 spp. The leaves were used medicinally, as indicated by the vernacular names.

❸ *Stachys grandifolia*

Large-leaved Stachys Straggling perennial to 1 m, with heart-shaped, finely toothed leaves, 35–80 mm long, densely velvety beneath, and whorls of 4–6 white flowers with mauve spots, 10–15 mm long; calyx softly haired. Forest margins and stream sides in southern and eastern South Africa.

❹ *Stachys aethiopica*

African Stachys, Katbossie Sprawling perennial to 50 cm, with oval, toothed leaves, mostly 8–40 mm long, and whorls of 2–6 white or pink to mauve flowers with darker spots, 10–15 mm long; calyx with gland-tipped hairs. Scrub or grassland from southwestern South Africa to Swaziland.

❺ *Stachys natalensis* White Stachys

Sprawling perennial to 50 cm, with oval, toothed leaves, 10–40 mm long, and whorls of 2 white flowers with lilac spots, 10–15 mm long; calyx without gland-tipped hairs. Scrub or forest margins through eastern South Africa.

❻ *Stachys rugosa*

Grey Stachys, Vaaltee Shrub to 1.2 m, with sessile, grey-felted, lance-shaped, slightly toothed leaves, 15–80 mm long, and whorls of mostly 6 yellow or pink to purple, often mottled flowers, 8–15 mm long; calyx grey-felted. Rocky slopes along the western and southern escarpment.

Ballota   HOREHOUND, KATTEKRUIE   *(From the classical Greek name for the genus)*

Hairy perennials or shrublets. Leaves often quilted, toothed. Flowers in dense whorls with the bracts similar to the leaves; the *calyx with hairs on the inside* as well as on the outside and with 10–20 spreading, often awned, *teeth*; the corolla 2-lipped, with a ring of hairs in the throat; stamens 4, *arching* and of 2 lengths. Mostly Mediterranean and Eurasian: ±33 spp.; South Africa: 1 sp. Used medicinally as a sedative. The vernacular name *kattekruie* was transferred from Catnip, *Nepeta cataria*, a European species.

❶ *Ballota africana*

J F M A M J J A S O N D

Aromatic, soft-textured, greyish shrublet to 1.2 m, with softly hairy, heart-shaped, toothed leaves, and dense whorls of pink to purple flowers, 10–14 mm long; calyx sharply 10–20-toothed. Rocky or disturbed places through western and southern South Africa.

Leonotis   MINARET FLOWER, WILDEDAGGA

(Greek leon, lion; otis, ear, a fanciful allusion to the form of the flower)   Robust annuals or perennials. Leaves scalloped or toothed. Flowers in dense whorls with the bracts similar to the leaves; *calyx stiffly 8–10-toothed*, sometimes the upper lobe largest; *corolla usually orange*, 2-lipped, the upper lip *10–30 mm long and conspicuously fringed*; stamens 4, *arching* and of 2 lengths. Sub-Saharan Africa: ±10 spp.; South Africa: 3 spp. The dried leaves were used medicinally but, despite the vernacular name, are not known to be narcotic, or even tolerable as a tobacco substitute.

❷ *Leonotis leonurus*

J F M A M J J A S O N D

Narrow-leaved Minaret Flower Erect shrub to 2 m, with narrowly lance-shaped, toothed leaves, and whorls of velvety orange flowers, 40–50 mm long, with the lower lobes curled back; the calyx toothed, with teeth all ± similar. Forest margins, rough grassland and roadsides through southern and eastern South Africa.

❸ *Leonotis ocymifolia*

J F M A M J J A S O N D

Broad-leaved Minaret Flower Erect shrub to 2 m, with distinctly petiolate, oval, toothed leaves, and whorls of velvety orange flowers, 25–45 mm long, with the lower lobes joined at the base and spreading; the calyx 2-lipped, with the upper lip larger. Rocky slopes, grassland and forest margins through southern and eastern South and tropical Africa.

▸ FERTILE STAMENS 4, DIRECTED DOWNWARDS ALONG THE LOWER COROLLA LIP

Aeollanthus   SPUR BUSH   *(Greek Aiolos, god of the winds; anthos, flower; the allusion is unclear)*

Herbs or soft shrublets. Leaves fleshy and toothed. Flowers in *1- or 2-flowered whorls* with small bracts; calyx 5-toothed, *falling away cleanly from the fruit, like a collar*; corolla 2-lipped with the lower lip boat-like, white to blue; stamens 4, of 2 lengths, attached by the anthers, *directed downwards*. Africa: ±40 spp.; South Africa: 6 spp.

❹ *Aeollanthus rehmannii*

J F M A M J J A S O N D

Bushveld Spur Bush Brittle shrublet to 50 cm, with petiolate, oval leaves, shortly hairy beneath and with red, scalloped margins, and white to mauve flowers, 7–11 mm long. Rock outcrops in savanna and woodland through northeastern South and tropical Africa.

Pycnostachys HEDGEHOG SAGE, PYCNOSTACHYS

(Greek pyknos, dense; stachys, spike, referring to the inflorescence) Perennial herbs or soft shrublets. Leaves opposite or whorled. *Flowers in dense, conical spikes* with small bracts; *calyx 5-toothed with spine-like teeth*; corolla 2-lipped with the lower lip boat-like, mauve to blue; stamens 4, of 2 lengths, *shortly joined at the base, directed downwards.* Africa and Madagascar: 4 spp.; South Africa: 2 spp. Used as a mouthwash and grown as ornamentals.

❶ *Pycnostachys reticulata*

J F M A M J J A S O N D

Pale Blue Pycnostachys Erect perennial to 2 m, with sessile, oblong to lance-shaped, hairless to hairy, toothed leaves, and dense spikes of pale mauve or sky-blue flowers, 10–18 mm long. Moist, grassy places throughout eastern South Africa.

❷ *Pycnostachys urticifolia*

J F M A M J J A S O N D

Dark Blue Pycnostachys, Blue Boys Erect perennial to 2 m, with distinctly petiolate, oval, hairless to hairy, scalloped leaves, and dense spikes of gentian blue flowers, 12–20 mm long. Moist, grassy places and forest margins in northeastern South and tropical Africa.

Plectranthus PLECTRANTHUS, SPUR-FLOWER

(Greek plektron, spur; anthos, flower, referring to the floral spur) Annual or pennial herbs, or shrublets. Leaves opposite. Flowers in panicles, racemes or spikes, *with small bracts well-differentiated from the leaves;* calyx 5-toothed, and often 2-lipped; corolla 2-lipped, *usually bent and sac-like at the base,* with lower lip boat-like, usually blue; stamens 4, sometimes joined at the base, *directed downwards.* Africa to Asia and Australasia: ±350 spp.; South Africa: ±45 spp. Used medicinally and widely cultivated.

❸ *Plectranthus ecklonii*

J F M A M J J A S O N D

Large Spur-flower Shrub to 2.5 m, with oval, toothed leaves, 60–170 mm long, dotted with reddish glands beneath, and pale blue to mauve flowers with a slender, straight tube, 16–20 mm long, expanding gradually and evenly from the base. Forest margins through eastern South Africa.

❹ *Plectranthus ciliatus*

J F M A M J J A S O N D

Speckled Spur-flower Soft, often sprawling shrublet to 60 cm, with oval, toothed leaves, 40–80 mm long, with conspicuous hairs on the margins, dotted with golden glands and often purple beneath, and whitish flowers densely speckled with purple, with a sharply flexed tube, ±10 mm long, sac-like at the base. Forest glades and wooded stream sides through southern and eastern South Africa.

❺ *Plectranthus fruticosus*

J F M A M J J A S O N D

Forest Spur-flower Soft shrublet to 2 m, with oval, toothed leaves, 40–140 mm long, dotted with golden glands and often purple beneath, and bluish-mauve flowers with a sharply flexed tube, ±10 mm long, sac-like at the base. Forest and scrub through southern and eastern South Africa.

❻ *Plectranthus grallatus*

J F M A M J J A S O N D

Mountain Spur-flower Soft perennial with erect, annual stems to 1.5 m, with oval, toothed leaves, 50–160 mm long, dotted with red glands beneath, and white, sparsely spotted flowers with a sharply flexed tube, ±10 mm long, sac-like at the base. Montane forest and scrub through eastern South Africa.

Rabdosiella FLY BUSH *(Diminutive of Greek rhabdos, rod, alluding to the wand-like branches)*

Erect shrublet. Leaves opposite or whorled. *Flowers in a dense, closely branched panicle, with leaf-like bracts; calyx 5-toothed;* corolla 2-lipped and sac-like, with the lower lip boat-like, cream-coloured flushed pink; stamens 4, of 2 lengths, *directed downwards.* Africa and India: 2 spp.; South Africa: 1 sp. The common name is derived from the unpleasant smell of the crushed leaves; an attractive garden plant.

1 *Rabdosiella calycina*

J F M A M J J A S O N D

Soft shrub with annual stems to 1.5 m, with ± sessile or shortly petiolate, oval to lance-shaped leaves, toothed or scalloped, and a densely branched panicle of cream-coloured flowers flushed pink or mauve, 8–11 mm long. Moist grassland and rocky outcrops through eastern South Africa.

Syncolostemon PINK PLUME, SAGE BUSH
(Greek syn, united; kolos, stunted; stemon, stamen, referring to the joined lower stamens) Perennials or soft shrubs.
Leaves often toothed. Flowers in racemes or panicles; calyx 5-toothed or 2-lobed; corolla 2-lipped with the lower lip boat-like, short or long-tubed, white to pink; stamens 4, of 2 types, *upper pair arising within the lower half of the corolla tube, lower pair* arising at the mouth of the tube and joined for most of their length. Mainly Africa: ±45 spp.; South Africa: 40 spp. Recently enlarged to include the genus *Hemizygia.* Used medicinally.

2 *Syncolostemon densiflorus*

J F M A M J J A S O N D

Common Pink Plume Shrub to 2 m, with petiolate, elliptical to oval, leaves, and dark (rarely pale) pink flowers, 18–23 mm long, in whorls of 4–6; calyx teeth all similar, corolla tube 15–20 mm long. Rough grassland and forest margins near the coast in eastern South Africa. *Syncolostemon parvifolius* from the Eastern Cape has flowers in pairs, with the corolla tube 20–23 mm long.

3 *Syncolostemon macranthus*

J F M A M J J A S O N D

Large-flowered Pink Plume Shrub to 2.5 m, with petiolate, oval to lance-shaped leaves, and pale pink to mauve flowers, 25–30 mm long, in whorls of 4–6; the upper calyx tooth larger, the corolla tube 20–25 mm long. Stream banks and forest margins in the northern Drakensberg foothills.

4 *Syncolostemon albiflorus*

J F M A M J J A S O N D

(=Hemizygia albiflora) **Erica-leaved Sage Bush** Gnarled, twiggy shrublet to 1 m, with sessile, small, narrow leaves, rolled under along the margins, white-felted beneath, and white flowers, 12–15 mm long, in whorls of 4–6; the upper calyx tooth larger, the corolla tube 10–15 mm long. Crevices in quartzite rock along the northeastern escarpment.

Ocimum SWEET BASIL *(The classical Greek name for the genus)*

Herbs or shrublets. Leaves opposite or in whorls. Flowers in whorls; calyx 5-toothed and 2-lipped; corolla 2-lipped with the lower lip cupped, whitish to mauve; stamens 4, of 2 types, *the upper pair arising near the bottom of the corolla tube and with a hairy knee-bend near the base.* Africa and Mediterranean: ±16 spp.; South Africa: 10 spp. Used medicinally.

5 *Ocimum obovatum*

J F M A M J J A S O N D

(=Becium obovatum) **Cat's Whiskers** Perennial with annual stems to 30 cm, with narrow to broad, weakly toothed leaves, and white to pale mauve flowers streaked with purple, 10–17 mm long, in whorls crowded near the tip of the stem. Grasslands through eastern South and tropical Africa, flowering after fire.

UTRICULARIACEAE   Bladderwort family

Utricularia BLADDERWORT (Latin utriculus, a small sac, referring to the leaf traps)

Small, aquatic or terrestrial *insectivorous herbs*. Leaves in the terrestrial species often withered at flowering; some *developing into minute, bladder-like traps*. Flowers mostly in racemes, *resembling miniature snapdragons*; the *calyx 2-lipped*. Worldwide, mainly tropical and subtropical: ±180 spp.; South Africa: 18 spp.

❶ *Utricularia bisquamata*

Delicate annual herb to 12 cm, with small, narrow leaves at the base, and thin, wiry racemes of 2-lipped, white to lilac or yellowish flowers, with a scale-like upper lip and smooth, yellow palate at the base of the lower lip, 5–10 mm long. Boggy, acidic sandstone soils through southern Africa. *Utricularia livida* has a wrinkled palate.

ACANTHACEAE   Acanthus family
▸ FLOWERS 1-LIPPED

Acanthopsis ACANTHOPSIS, STEKELKRUID (Resembling the genus Acanthus)

Shrublets or stemless perennials. *Leaves usually spine-toothed*. Flowers in dense spikes; bracts spine-toothed; *corolla 1-lipped, with a short tube, blue or white; stamens 4, stiff and hard, protruding*. Southern Africa: 8 spp.

❷ *Acanthopsis disperma* Skietpit

Dwarf perennial to 10 cm, with a basal rosette of narrowly elliptical, spine-toothed leaves, and a dense, cylindrical spike of 1-lipped, blue (rarely white) flowers, 20 mm long, among spiny bracts that bend down in fruit. Dry stony flats in western South Africa and Namibia.

Blepharis BLEPHARIS (Greek blepharis, eyelash, referring to the fringed anthers)

Shrublets, perennials or annuals. Leaves often in dissimilar pairs, *usually spine-toothed*. Flowers in dense spikes; bracts usually spine-toothed; *corolla 1-lipped with a short tube, blue or white; stamens 4, stiff and hard, protruding, the upper pair flattened above and horned*. Africa to India: 126 spp.; South Africa: ±50 spp.

❸ *Blepharis subvolubilis*

Rounded shrublet to 30 cm, with elliptical to lance-shaped, sharply spine-toothed leaves, and short, dense spikes of pale to deep mauve, 1-lipped flowers with dark veining, 20 mm long, usually 2 or 4 open at a time; bracts finely hairy, ±20 mm long, oval and sharply spined, becoming papery. Dry grassland and open savanna in northeastern South Africa.

Crossandra CROSSANDRA, ROOIBLOM
(Greek krossos, fringe; andra, male, alluding to the hairy anthers in some species) Shrublets or stemless perennials. Leaves often large and elliptical. Flowers in dense, pedunculate racemes; bracts usually large and ± spiny; *corolla 1-lipped with a long, slender tube, yellow to red; stamens 4, concealed within the tube*. Africa to India: ±50 spp.; South Africa: 4 spp.

① *Crossandra greenstockii*   J F M A M J **J A** S **O N D**

Bushveld Crossandra Stemless perennial to 30 cm, with a basal tuft of elliptical leaves, and dense racemes of orange to reddish, 1-lipped flowers with a lightly notched upper edge, 20 mm in diameter; bracts softly glandular-haired and slightly spiny on the margins. Open savanna and woodland in northeastern South and tropical Africa.

② *Crossandra zuluensis*   J F **M A M** J J **A** S **O N D**

Zululand Crossandra Stemless perennial to 30 cm, with a basal tuft of elliptical leaves, and dense racemes of orange to reddish, 1-lipped flowers with a flat upper edge, 20 mm in diameter; bracts ± hairless and strongly spined on the margins. Open savanna and woodland in northeastern South Africa. *Crossandra fruticulosa* is a shrublet with petiolate leaves. .

▶ **FLOWERS 2-LIPPED**

Ruttya   **RUTTYA**   *(Named for Irish naturalist, Dr John Rutty, 1697–1775)*

Shrublet. Leaves petiolate, untoothed. Flowers in dense panicles; bracts small and narrow; calyx 5-lobed *with thread-like lobes; corolla 2-lipped*, white; *stamens 2, with 1-chambered anthers*; style not enclosed in a channel in the upper lip, stigma 2-lobed. Fruit club-shaped. Africa: 3 spp.; South Africa: 1 sp.

③ *Ruttya ovata*   J **F** M A M J J A S O N D

Hairless shrublet to 3 m, with petiolate, lance-shaped leaves, and dense panicles of white, 2-lipped flowers speckled with purple on the lower lip, 20 mm in diameter. Forest margins and woodland through eastern South Africa.

Adhatoda   **ADHATODA**   *(A Malabar name for the genus)*

Perennials resprouting from a woody rootstock. Leaves sessile. Flowers in dense panicles; bracts narrow; calyx deeply 5-lobed; *corolla 2-lipped with lips ± similar, white, upper lip deeply hooded with a central channel containing the style; stamens 2, bending back when old.* Fruit club-shaped. Africa and Asia: ±150 spp.; South Africa: 2 spp. Used in traditional medicine.

④ *Adhatoda densiflora*   J F M A M J J A S **O N** D

Perennial with annual stems to 40 cm from a woody rootstock, with ± sessile, softly hairy, elliptical to ovate leaves, and a panicle of 2-lipped, white flowers with pinkish streaks on the wrinkled lower lip, 15 mm long. Stony grassland in KwaZulu-Natal. *Adhatoda andromeda*, from higher altitudes, has narrower, almost hairless leaves.

Justicia   **JUSTICIA**   *(Named for Scottish horticulturist, James Justice, 1698–1763)*

Herbs or shrubs. Leaves sessile or petiolate. Flowers in clusters or panicles; bracts narrow; calyx deeply 5-lobed; *corolla 2-lipped, the lips dissimilar, white, blue or yellow, upper lip smaller and shallow, with a central channel containing the style; stamens 2, bending back when old.* Fruit club-shaped. Worldwide in the tropics: ±420 spp.; South Africa: 23 spp. Used in traditional medicine.

⑤ *Justicia petiolaris* Blue Justicia   J **F** M **A M** J J A S **O N** D

Perennial to 1 m, with petiolate, lance-shaped leaves, and dense panicles of blue and white flowers, 15 mm long. Woodland and forest margins through eastern South and tropical Africa.

433

Peristrophe FALSE BUCKWHEAT

(Greek peri, around; strophos, a twisted band, alluding to the bracts surrounding and enclosing the calyx) Herbs or
shrublets. Leaves often small, not toothed. Flowers in axillary clusters; bracts broad or narrow;
corolla white to purple, funnel-shaped, *2-lipped, twisted through 180°; stamens 2, anthers with 2 lobes.*
Africa and East Indies: ±15 spp.; South Africa: 11 spp. Used medicinally.

1 *Peristrophe cernua*   J F **M A M J J A** S O N D
Hairless, slender-stemmed, sprawling shrublet to 1 m, with scattered, lance-
shaped leaves, and small axillary clusters of 2-lipped, finely hairy, mauve or pink
flowers with purple speckles, ±25 mm long. Dry woodland and valley bushveld
through southeastern South Africa.

Hypoestes RIBBON BUSH

(Greek hypo, beneath; estia, house, referring to the calyx being covered by the bracts) Herbs or shrublets. Leaves
not toothed. Flowers crowded in interrupted, spike-like inflorescences; bracts small and narrow;
corolla white to purple, funnel-shaped, *2-lipped, twisted through 180°; stamens 2, anthers with
1 lobe.* Africa to Australasia: ±40 spp.; South Africa: 3 spp.

2 *Hypoestes aristata*   J F **M A M J J A** S O N D
Purple Ribbon Bush Leafy shrublet to 1.5 m, with petiolate leaves, and dense
whorls of 2-lipped, finely hairy, pink flowers with purple speckles, ±30 mm long. Dry
thicket and forest through southern and eastern South and tropical Africa.

3 *Hypoestes forskaolii*   J **F M A M J J A S O N D**
White Ribbon Bush Straggling perennial to 1 m, with petiolate leaves, and
scattered, 2-lipped, white to pale pink flowers with purple spots, ±20 mm long, finely
hairy. Thicket, woodland and rocky grassland through southern and eastern South
and tropical Africa.

▶ FLOWERS WITH 5 ± SIMILAR LOBES

Thunbergia THUNBERGIA *(Named for Carl Thunberg, 1743–1828, the father of South African botany)*

Climbers or shrublets. Leaves oval or arrow-shaped. Flowers large, axillary or in clusters, *with
2 large bracts concealing the calyx; calyx 5-lobed or with 10–18 narrow teeth; corolla trumpet-shaped,
with 5 ± similar lobes; stamens 4, with bearded, spurred anthers. Fruit spherical, with a blade-like
beak, sessile.* Tropical Africa and Asia: ±100 spp.; South Africa: 11 spp. Plants are eaten and used
medicinally, and some species are cultivated.

4 *Thunbergia natalensis*   J **F** M **A** M J J A S **O N** D
Blue Thunbergia, Natal Blue Bell Erect, almost hairless perennial to 1 m, with
± sessile, oval, toothed leaves, and pale blue, funnel-shaped flowers with a yellow
throat, 50–60 mm in diameter. Forest and bush margins in rank grassland through
eastern South and tropical Africa.

5 *Thunbergia atriplicifolia*   J **F** M **A** M J J A S **O N** D
Natal Primrose Hairy perennial to 40 cm, resprouting from a woody base, with
± sessile, narrow to broad, oval leaves, and pale creamy, trumpet-shaped flowers with
a yellow throat, 40–50 mm in diameter. Grassland through eastern South Africa.

1 *Thunbergia pondoensis* J F M A M J J A S O N D

White Thunbergia Hairy creeper to 2 m, with petiolate, arrow-shaped leaves with pointed lower angles, and white, trumpet-shaped flowers with a yellow throat, 30 mm in diameter. Woodland in eastern South Africa. Other species with white or pale yellow flowers have heart-shaped leaves with rounded lower angles.

2 *Thunbergia alata* J F M A M J J A S O N D

Black-eyed Susan, Swartoognooi Hairy creeper to 4 m, with oval or arrow-shaped, often toothed leaves on winged petioles, and orange, trumpet-shaped flowers with a purplish-black throat, 30–40 mm in diameter. Forest margins through southeastern and eastern South and tropical Africa.

Ruellia VELD VIOLET *(Named for 16th-century French naturalist, Jean de la Ruelle)*

Shrublets. Leaves mostly untoothed. Flowers axillary, *lilac to purple*; bracts narrow; calyx ± 2-lipped; *corolla funnel-shaped, with 5 ± similar lobes*; stamens 4. Worldwide in the tropics: ±150 spp.; South Africa: 8 spp. Used magically.

3 *Ruellia cordata* J F M A M J J A S O N D

Hairy perennial to 20 cm, resprouting from a woody base, with ± sessile, oval leaves, and funnel-shaped, lilac flowers with purple streaks, 15–20 mm in diameter. Grassland and open woodland through eastern and northern South Africa.

Asystasia ASYSTASIA *(Greek asystasio, disordered, referring to the unequal corolla lobes)*

Herbs or shrubs. Flowers in *raceme-like inflorescences, white*; bracts small and narrow; corolla *funnel-shaped, with 5 ± similar lobes*; stamens 4. *Fruit club-shaped*, with a stalk. Africa to Australasia: ±70 spp.; South Africa: 7 spp. Eaten as a vegetable.

4 *Asystasia gangetica* J F M A M J J A S O N D

Spreading perennial to 60 cm, with opposite, petiolate leaves, and scattered, white, funnel-shaped flowers with a puckered, purple-streaked lower lip, ±15 mm in diameter. Coastal dunes in forest or woodland, through eastern South and tropical Africa to India.

Barleria BARLERIA *(Named for French amateur botanist, Rev. James Barrelier, 1606–1673)*

Shrublets, sometimes spiny. Leaves ± sessile. Flowers funnel-shaped, often blue or purple; *calyx 4-lobed with the outer pair of lobes large and leaf-like*; corolla funnel-shaped, *with 5 ± similar lobes*; stamens 2 or 4. Fruit ellipsoid or flask-shaped, sessile. Worldwide, mainly tropics: ±250 spp.; South Africa: ±60 spp.

▸ STAMENS 4

5 *Barleria ovata* J F M A M J J A S O N D

Grassland Barleria Hairy perennial to 50 cm, resprouting from a woody base, with elliptical leaves, and magenta, funnel-shaped flowers, 30 mm in diameter, with 4 stamens and a club-shaped stigma; fruit ellipsoid. Stony grassland through eastern South Africa.

437

▶ STAMENS 2

① *Barleria obtusa* Bush Violet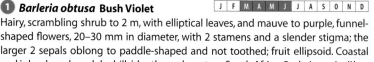
Hairy, scrambling shrub to 2 m, with elliptical leaves, and mauve to purple, funnel-shaped flowers, 20–30 mm in diameter, with 2 stamens and a slender stigma; the larger 2 sepals oblong to paddle-shaped and not toothed; fruit ellipsoid. Coastal and inland scrub and dry hillsides through eastern South Africa. *Barleria gueinzii* has oval, sharply toothed outer sepals.

② *Barleria meyeriana*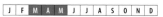
Straggling, shortly hairy shrublet to 1 m, with greyish leaves, and flaring, pale mauve flowers, 30–40 mm in diameter, with 2 stamens and a slender stigma; fruit flask-shaped with a blade-like beak. Savanna and woodland through eastern South Africa.

③ *Barleria elegans*
White Bushveld Barleria Sprawling shrublet with shortly hairy branches to 1 m, oval leaves, and crowded, axillary spikes of narrowly funnel-shaped, white flowers, 20–30 mm in diameter, clustered among oval, spine-toothed bracts, with 2 stamens and a slender stigma; fruit ellipsoid, 15 mm long. Thicket and woodland through northeastern South and tropical Africa.

PEDALIACEAE — Sesame family

***Ceratotheca* WILD FOXGLOVE** *(Greek kerato, horned; theke, case, referring to the fruits)*
Annual or perennial herbs. Leaves opposite, variable. Flowers solitary in the axils, funnel-shaped, sac-like at the base. Fruit with 2 similar pairs of spreading horns at the tip. Africa: 5 spp.; South Africa: 4 spp. Some species are cultivated for their seeds and are used medicinally; *Ceratotheca triloba* is grown as an ornamental.

④ *Ceratotheca triloba*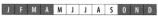
Annual or short-lived perennial to 2 m, glandular-haired and foetid, with petiolate, mostly heart-shaped or 3-lobed and toothed leaves, and racemes of hanging, foxglove-like, lilac flowers with dark streaks in the throat, 40–70 mm long; fruit cylindrical with 4 spreading horns at the tip. Often in disturbed places through eastern South and tropical Africa.

***Sesamum* SESAME, OLIEBOSSIE** *(The classical Greek name for sesame)*
Annual or perennial herbs. Leaves opposite, variable. Flowers solitary in the axils, funnel-shaped. Fruit tapering to a sharp point or beak. Tropics: ±15 spp.; South Africa: 10 spp. *Sesamum orientale* is the source of sesame seeds.

⑤ *Sesamum alatum*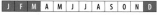
Annual to 1.5 m, glandular-haired and foetid, with lower leaves petiolate, narrowly 3–5-lobed, upper leaves thread-like, and racemes of hanging, funnel-shaped, pink to purple flowers, 20–30 mm long; fruit narrowed into a short beak at the tip; seeds 2-winged. Often in disturbed places, through northeastern South and tropical Africa. *Sesamum capense* has 3-winged seeds; *S. triphyllum* has ± wingless seeds.

Rogeria **ROGERIA** *(Probably named for 18th-century French horticulturist, Thomas Roger)*

Robust annual or perennial herbs. Leaves opposite, variable, mealy beneath. Flowers 1–few in the axils, *tubular and salver-shaped with a basal sac or spur. Fruit obliquely beaked, often with warts or horns near the middle on 1 side.* Africa and Brazil: 7 spp.; South Africa: 4 spp.

❶ *Rogeria longiflora*

J F M **A M J J A S** O N D

White-flowered Rogeria Robust annual to 2 m, glandular-haired and foetid, with petiolate, rounded leaves, paler beneath, and clusters of hanging, trumpet-shaped, fragrant, white flowers, 60–80 mm long; fruit beaked, with a pair of horns near the base on the upper side. Dry sandy and stony flats, dry streambeds and roadsides in Namibia and western South Africa.

BIGNONIACEAE   Bignonia family

Rhigozum **RHIGOZUM, GRANAAT** *(Greek rhigios, stiff; ozos, branch)*

Stiffly branched shrubs, sometimes thorny. Leaves simple or 3-lobed, usually *in tufts on short shoots.* Flowers in clusters on short shoots, bell- or funnel-shaped, white or pink to yellow; *stamens 5.* Fruit oblong *with a stiff beak.* Africa: 7 spp.; South Africa: 5 spp.

❷ *Rhigozum obovatum*

J F M A M J **J A S O N D**

Karoo Rhigozum, Wildegranaat Stiffly branched, spiny shrub to 4.5 m, with elliptical, shortly petiolate leaves in tufts, and clusters of 1–3 funnel-shaped, yellow flowers, 20–30 mm in diameter; fruit flattened. Dry stony slopes and flats in karroid scrub through central South Africa. *Rhigozum brevispinosum* has sessile leaves; *R. zambesiacum* has pinnate leaves with a winged axis.

Tecoma **CAPE HONEYSUCKLE** *(Contraction of the Mexican name Tecomaxachitl for 1 species)*

Shrubs, sometimes sprawling. Leaves compound with a terminal leaflet. Flowers in short terminal racemes, *trumpet-shaped, yellow or orange; stamens 4. Fruit narrow and flattened.* Africa and the Americas: ±13 spp.; South Africa: 1 sp.

❸ *Tecoma capensis*

J F M A M J **J A** S O N D

Cape Honeysuckle, Trompetters Scrambling shrub or small tree to 6 m, with compound leaves divided into several toothed leaflets, and dense terminal racemes of curved, trumpet-shaped, orange flowers, 50–60 mm long; fruit slender and flattened. Thicket and forest margins through southeastern and eastern South and tropical Africa.

Podranea **PODRANEA** *(Anagram of the related genus Pandorea)*

Scrambling shrubs. Leaves compound with a terminal leaflet. Flowers in terminal panicles, large, *trumpet-shaped, pink; calyx inflated; stamens 4. Fruit very long, narrow and flattened.* Africa: 2 spp.; South Africa: 1 sp.

❹ *Podranea ricasoliana*

J F M A M J J A S O N D

Port St John's Creeper Scrambling shrub to 10 m or more, with dark green, compound leaves divided into oval, serrated leaflets, and terminal panicles of trumpet-shaped, pink flowers, 50–70 mm long, with darker streaks in the throat. Thicket and forest margins around Port St Johns in the Eastern Cape. The widely cultivated Zimbabwe Creeper, *Podranea brycei*, has narrower, paler leaflets, and a bell-shaped, strongly flattened floral tube with thick white hairs in the throat.

GESNERIACEAE African Violet family

Streptocarpus STREPTOCARPUS
(Greek streptos, twisted; karpos, fruit, referring to the spirally coiled fruits) Mainly stemless perennials. Leaves *1–few in a basal rosette, velvety, quilted.* Flowers 1 or more, white or pink to blue, 2-lipped; calyx 5-lobed; corolla funnel- or trumpet-shaped, 5-lobed; stamens 2, the anthers usually cohering face to face. *Fruit splitting open spirally like a corkscrew.* Africa: ±125 spp.; South Africa: ±45 spp. Popular indoor and garden plants; used magically.

① Streptocarpus cyaneus

J F **M A M** J J **A** S **O** N D

Stemless perennial to 20 cm, with a rosette of several velvety leaves, and slender stalks of 1–12 funnel-shaped, rosy pink to blue (rarely white) flowers with a yellow band in the throat and darker streaks on the lower lip, 30–60 mm long, the tube straight and ± cylindrical. Coastal forest floor and mossy banks along the northeastern escarpment.

② Streptocarpus rexii

J F **M A** M J J **A** S **O** N D

Cape Primrose Stemless perennial to 20 cm, with a rosette of several velvety leaves, and slender stalks of 1 or 2(–6) funnel-shaped, pale blue flowers with darker streaks on the lower lip, 40–75 mm long, the tube straight and ± cylindrical. Shaded banks on forest margins and forest floor in the Eastern Cape. *Streptocarpus primulifolius* has larger, darker flowers, 65–110 mm long.

③ Streptocarpus gardenii

J **F M A** M J J **A** S O **N** D

Stemless perennial to 15 cm, with a rosette of several, velvety leaves, and slender stalks of 1 or 2(–6) funnel-shaped, pale blue flowers with darker streaks on all petals around the pale green mouth, 50 mm long, the tube straight and slightly flattened from above at the mouth. Damp rocks and stream banks in forest, mainly in KwaZulu-Natal.

④ Streptocarpus dunnii

J **F** M A M J J A S O **N** D

Crimson Streptocarpus Stemless perennial to 20 cm, with 1–several velvety leaves, and an elongated raceme of trumpet-shaped, dull reddish flowers with darker streaks in the throat, 40 mm long, the tube curved and ± cylindrical. Sheltered situations at the foot of rocks in grassland and moist bush in northeastern South Africa.

OROBANCHACEAE Broomrape family

Buttonia CLIMBING FOXGLOVE
(Named for Edward Button, 1836–1900, geologist and plant collector) *Scrambler or climber. Leaves opposite, petiolate, oval and lobed or dissected. Flowers solitary in the axils, large, mauve;* calyx 5-lobed, inflated in fruit; corolla funnel-shaped, 5-lobed; stamens 4, joined in pairs by the anthers. Africa: 3 spp.; South Africa: 2 spp.

⑤ Buttonia superba

J F **M A M** J **J** A S **O** **N** D

Large-flowered Climbing Foxglove Scrambling climber to 2 m, with petiolate, deeply 3–5-lobed leaves, and large, funnel-shaped, mauve flowers streaked with purple in the throat, 50–60 mm long. Thicket and woodland through northeastern South Africa. *Buttonia natalensis* has deeply 5–7-lobed leaves and smaller flowers, ±35 mm long.

443

Graderia WILD PENSTEMON *(An anagram of Gerardia)*

Shrublets from a woody rootstock. Leaves sessile, opposite, alternate or whorled, toothed or not. *Flowers solitary in the upper axils, pink;* calyx 5-lobed; *corolla funnel-shaped, 5-lobed; stamens 4,* 1 anther lobe of each pair usually narrower. Africa and Socotra: 5 spp.; South Africa: 3 spp. Used medicinally.

❶ *Graderia scabra*

| J | F | M | A | M | J | J | A | S | O | N | D |

Pink Ground-bells Shrublet to 60 cm from a woody rootstock, with overlapping, sessile, sparsely toothed leaves, and pink to mauve, funnel-shaped flowers in the upper axils, ±30 mm long. Grassland through southern and eastern South Africa.

Alectra YELLOW WITCHWEED, VERFBLOMMETJIE
(Greek alektor, a cock, for the cockscomb-shaped leaves)

Herbs. Leaves opposite or alternate, lance-shaped to oval, usually toothed, sometimes scale-like. Flowers in spikes, *yellow to orange with darker veins;* calyx 5-lobed to ± halfway; *corolla bell-shaped,* slightly oblique, 5-lobed to ± halfway; *stamens 4,* with the anthers 2-celled and cohering in pairs. Asia and Africa: ±40 spp.; South Africa: ±17 spp. The vernacular name *verfblommetjie* refers to the early use of the rootstock as a source of an orange-yellow dye used for colouring fabric.

❷ *Alectra sessiliflora*

| J | F | M | A | M | J | J | A | S | O | N | D |

Hemiparasitic perennial to 25 cm, with spreading, lance-shaped leaves, coarsely toothed below and longer than the flower buds, and spikes of yellow to orange flowers, the stamens in 2 very dissimilar pairs, with hairless filaments. Damp flats and lower slopes from southwestern South to tropical Africa.

Melasma MELASMA *(Greek melas, black, as the plants turn black when dry)*

Herbs. Leaves opposite, lance-shaped or lobed, usually toothed. Flowers in loose racemes, *yellow with a purple eye; calyx large, inflated, 5-lobed,* becoming balloon-like in fruit; *corolla widely funnel-shaped, 5-lobed; stamens 4,* with the anthers 2-celled. Tropical America and Africa: 5 spp.; South Africa: 1 sp.

❸ *Melasma scabrum*

| J | F | M | A | M | J | J | A | S | O | N | D |

Hemiparasitic perennial to 60 cm, with narrow, roughly hairy, lance-shaped leaves, sometimes lobed below, and a loose raceme of pale yellow flowers with a purple eye, ±30 mm in diameter. Marshes and wet grassland through southern and eastern South Africa.

Sopubia SOPUBIA *(The Indian vernacular name)*

Hemiparasitic annual or perennial herbs with stiffly erect, felted or woolly stems. Leaves opposite or whorled, or alternate above, *narrow. Flowers in racemes or spikes, pink;* calyx 5-lobed; *corolla widely bell-shaped* with 5 spreading lobes; stamens 4, 1 lobe of each anther reduced and sterile. Asia and Africa: 25–30 spp.; South Africa: 4 spp.

❹ *Sopubia cana* Silvery Sopubia

| J | F | M | A | M | J | J | A | S | O | N | D |

Parasitic herb with erect, wand-like stems to 45 cm, densely covered with silvery-grey hairs throughout, with narrow leaves bearing short, leafy shoots in the axils, and racemes of pink flowers, 20 mm in diameter, with delicate petals spreading horizontally from a very short tube. Grassland through eastern South and tropical Africa.

445

Cycnium MUSHROOM FLOWER, INK PLANT

(Greek kyknos, swan, alluding to the elegantly bent floral tube) *Hemiparasitic herbs, turning black when dry.* Leaves mostly opposite, narrow to oval, usually toothed. Flowers solitary in the axils or in racemes, *white to pink*; calyx 5-lobed and 10-ribbed; *corolla salver-shaped, 5-lobed; stamens 4, with the anthers 1-celled.* Plants are root parasites on grasses and sedges; used medicinally. The vernacular name alludes to the superficial resemblance of the clusters of white, parasol-like flowers of *Cycnium adonense* to mushrooms.

1 *Cycnium racemosum*

| J | F | M | A | M | J | J | A | S | O | N | D |

Large Pink Mushroom Flower Roughly or shortly hairy, hemiparasitic herb with erect stems to 75 cm, with narrow, toothed leaves, and open racemes of salver-shaped, white to deep pink flowers, turning black when faded, 50–60 mm in diameter, the calyx tubular and ribbed, with very short, hooked teeth; fruit elongated and enclosed within the calyx at maturity. Moist grassland through eastern South and tropical Africa.

2 *Cycnium tubulosum*

| J | F | M | A | M | J | J | A | S | O | N | D |

Small Pink Mushroom Flower Hairless, hemiparasitic herb with slender, erect stems to 50 cm, with narrow, untoothed leaves, and an open raceme of salver-shaped, white to pale pink flowers, turning black when faded, 30–40 mm in diameter, the calyx cup-shaped with slender teeth; fruit short and transversely oriented, exposed above calyx at maturity. Moist or marshy grassland through eastern South and tropical Africa.

3 *Cycnium adonense*

| J | F | M | A | M | J | J | A | S | O | N | D |

White Mushroom Flower, Handkerchief Flower Low-growing, roughly hairy, hemiparasitic herb to 20 cm, with elliptical, sharply toothed leaves, and large, white, salver-shaped flowers in the leaf axils, turning black when faded, 60–70 mm in diameter, the calyx tubular, with blunt teeth. Grassland, often in rocky places, through eastern South and tropical Africa, flowering especially after fire.

Harveya INKFLOWER, INKBLOM

(Named for Dr William Harvey, 1811–1866, chief author of Flora Capensis) *Fleshy parasitic herbs, turning black when drying.* Leaves scale-like and lacking chlorophyll, usually yellowish. Flowers usually large, in spikes or racemes, pink, red, white or yellow; calyx deeply 5-lobed, sometimes ± 2-lipped; corolla bell-shaped to salver-shaped, *5-lobed and slightly oblique to 2-lipped; stamens 4, each with 1 anther lobe sterile, the other fertile and often hooked.* Africa and the Mascarenes: ±35 spp.; South Africa: 12 spp. The plants are root parasites on grasses and shrubby daisies; they turn black when dry and were used by early colonists as a source of writing ink, hence the vernacular name; also used medicinally.

▶ **FLOWERS WHITE, PINK OR PURPLE**

4 *Harveya speciosa*

| J | F | M | A | M | J | J | A | S | O | N | D |

Large White Inkflower Showy parasitic herb to 1 m, with a dense raceme of large, trumpet-shaped, creamy-white flowers with a yellow throat, fragrant at night, 50–70 mm long, the calyx tubular and shortly lobed. Mainly montane grassland and damp thicket through eastern South Africa.

447

① *Harveya huttonii*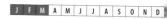

Parasitic herb to 50 cm, with a short or loose raceme of broadly funnel-shaped, pink to lilac flowers with a white or pale yellow throat, 30–50 mm long, the calyx cup-shaped and 2-lipped, with short lobes. Grassland and damp scrub at higher elevations in eastern South Africa. *Harveya pauciflora* from lower elevations has smaller flowers, 20–30 mm long.

② *Harveya purpurea* Pers Inkblom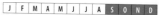

Parasitic herb to 15 cm, with a short or loose raceme of broadly funnel-shaped, fragrant, pale yellow or white to pink flowers with yellow blotches in the throat, 25–35 mm long, the calyx cup-shaped and lobed more than halfway. Sandstone slopes in southwestern South Africa.

▶ FLOWERS ORANGE OR RED

③ *Harveya bolusii* Rooi-inkblom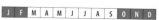

Parasitic herb to 25 cm, with a dense raceme of narrowly funnel-shaped, red to orange flowers with a yellow throat and short petals, 25–35 mm long, the calyx cup-shaped and lobed ± halfway. Sandstone slopes in southwestern South Africa. *Harveya bodkinii*, from the mountains along the interior West Coast, has larger, cylindrical flowers.

④ *Harveya scarlatina*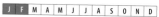

Parasitic herb to 28 cm, with a dense spike of ± sessile, trumpet-shaped, orange to red flowers with a yellow throat, 50–70 mm long, the calyx tubular and 2-lipped, with short lobes. Montane grassland and low scrub along the Drakensberg.

⑤ *Harveya squamosa*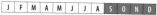

Parasitic perennial herb to 15 cm, with a long spike of sessile, tubular, orange flowers with a yellow throat and short petals, 35–45 mm long, the calyx tubular and 2-lipped, with short lobes. Deep sandy soils in Namaqualand and on the West Coast.

Hyobanche SCARLET BROOMRAPE, KATNAELS, WOLWEKOS

(Greek *anche*, *strangler*, refers to the parasitic nature, but complete derivation uncertain) *Fleshy parasitic herbs.* *Leaves scale-like and lacking chlorophyll.* Flowers large, in dense, often head-like spikes, pink, red or dark maroon, cylindrical; calyx 5-lobed and usually 2-lipped; corolla tubular, 3-*lobed and hooded*; stamens 4, with *1 anther lobe each*. Southern Africa: 7 spp. The plants are root parasites on shrubby daisies; the origin of the vernacular name *wolwekos* is unknown but may allude to the resemblance of the plants to scraps of fresh carrion.

⑥ *Hyobanche glabrata*

Root parasite with scale-like leaves, and sparsely hairy, scarlet or red flowers, 40–60 mm long, with conspicuously protruding stamens. Clay slopes and flats in western South Africa.

⑦ *Hyobanche sanguinea*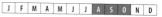

Root parasite with scale-like leaves, and densely hairy, crimson-red or pink flowers, 40–60 mm long, with the stamens concealed within but the style protruding. Sandy slopes and flats from southern Namibia to the Eastern Cape. *Hyobanche rubra* from the southern Cape coast has dark red flowers.

SCROPHULARIACEAE
Sutera family

▶ FLOWERS SESSILE IN DENSE SPIKES, WITH THE CALYX JOINED TO THE BRACT BELOW

Dischisma FALSE SLUGWORT *(Greek di, two; schizein, to split, referring to the divided corolla)*

Annual or perennial herbs or shrublets. Leaves alternate or the lower opposite, mostly narrow and toothed. Flowers *sessile in dense spikes*, white; *calyx 2-lobed* and *joined to the bract below*; *corolla 1-lipped with a funnel-shaped tube, slit down the front* and expanded above into a 4-lobed upper lip; stamens 4 in dissimilar pairs inserted at different levels; *ovule/seed 1 per chamber.* South Africa: 11 spp.

❶ *Dischisma ciliatum*

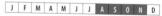

Sprawling perennial to 40 cm, with narrow to elliptical, spreading, toothed leaves, and long spikes of unscented or fragrant white flowers, 10 mm long, with densely hairy bracts. Rocky slopes and flats in western and southern South Africa.

Hebenstretia SLUGWORT, SLAKBLOM

(Named for Johan Hebenstreit, 1720–1791, professor at Leipzig and St Petersburg) Annual or perennial herbs or shrublets. Leaves alternate or the lower opposite, sometimes with axillary tufts, mostly narrow and toothed. Flowers *sessile in dense spikes*, white, usually with an orange patch in the throat; *calyx boat-shaped, sometimes notched, joined to the bract below; corolla 1-lipped with a funnel-shaped tube, slit down the front* and expanded above into a 4-lobed upper lip; stamens 4 in dissimilar pairs inserted at different levels; *ovule/seed 1 per chamber.* Southern and tropical Africa: ±25 spp.; South Africa: 25 spp. Mixed with fat to make a perfumed ointment.

❷ *Hebenstretia robusta*

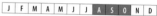

Large Slugwort Shrublet with erect branches, spreading, narrow, slightly toothed leaves, and long spikes of white, honey-scented flowers with orange to red marks, 10 mm long, anthers ± sessile. Rocky soils in southwestern South Africa.

❸ *Hebenstretia oatesii*

Willowy Slugwort Slender perennial with wand-like stems to 2 m, branching above, with narrow, toothed leaves, and spikes of fragrant white flowers with a red mark, 10 mm long. Marshy grassland through eastern South and tropical Africa.

Pseudoselago POWDERPUFF *('False' Selago, referring to its resemblance to that genus)*

Annual or perennial herbs, usually with *winged stems*. Leaves opposite below, usually becoming alternate above, mostly toothed. Flowers small, sessile, in spikes that are usually grouped into rounded or flat-topped clusters, white or mauve, sometimes with an orange patch; calyx 5-lobed, *joined to the bract below*; corolla tubular, 5-lobed and 2-lipped; stamens 4, in dissimilar pairs; *ovule/ seed 1 per chamber.* Southwestern Cape: 28 spp.

❹ *Pseudoselago serrata*

Stout, leafy perennial to 40 cm, with closely overlapping, oval, sparsely toothed leaves with the tips curved over, continuing down the stem in narrow wings, and dense, flat-topped clusters of mauve, funnel-shaped flowers. Mountain slopes in the southwestern Cape.

❺ *Pseudoselago spuria*

Sparsely hairy perennial with rod-like stems to 75 cm, with narrow leaves toothed above, often with axillary tufts of smaller leaves, continuing down the stem in narrow wings, and loose clusters of mauve, funnel-shaped flowers. Mountain slopes in the southwestern Cape.

Zaluzianskya DRUMSTICK FLOWER, VERFBLOMMETJIE
(Named for Czech botanist, Adam Zaluziansky von Zaluzian, 1558–1613)

Annual or perennial herbs with hairy stems. Leaves opposite below but often alternate above, usually toothed. Flowers ± sessile in elongated or head-like spikes, either colourful and open during the day or white with dull red reverse and nocturnal; calyx 2-lipped, *strongly 5-ribbed and pleated*; corolla with 5 ± similar lobes, the lobes often notched or forked, tubular, often with a ring of hairs in the mouth; stamens 4 in dissimilar pairs or 2; *stigma tongue-like with 2 marginal strips of hairs.* Southern Africa, mainly Western Cape: 55 spp. The vernacular name *verfblommetjie* refers to the use of the flowers of certain species as a source of dye.

① *Zaluzianskya villosa*

Southern Purple Drumsticks Annual herb to 30 cm, the stems densely covered in spreading hairs, with densely hairy, rather blunt, lance-shaped leaves, and spikes of white to mauve flowers with a yellow or red star in the centre, with deeply notched petals and a tube 10–25 mm long, honey-scented at night; stamens 2. Sandy flats along the coast in the extreme southwestern Cape.

② *Zaluzianskya affinis*

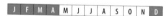

Northern Purple Drumsticks Annual herb to 30 cm, the stems covered in spreading hairs, with sparsely hairy, rather sharp, lance-shaped leaves, and spikes of white to mauve flowers with a yellow or red star in the centre, with deeply notched petals and a tube 10–25 mm long, honey-scented at night; stamens 2. Sandy flats along the coast in Namaqualand.

③ *Zaluzianskya violacea*

Hantam Purple Drumsticks Annual herb to 15 cm, the stems covered in down-facing hairs, with shortly hairy, oval to elliptical, ± toothed leaves, and spikes of mauve flowers with a yellow or red star in the centre, with deeply notched petals and a tube 10–23 mm long, honey-scented at night; stamens 4. Stony flats in the southwestern Cape, mainly near Calvinia.

④ *Zaluzianskya crocea*

Drakensberg Purple Drumsticks Dwarf annual herb to 12 cm, the stems covered in short, spreading hairs, with sparsely hairy, paddle-shaped leaves, and short spikes of mauve flowers with a minute yellow or red eye and a tube 18–30 mm long; stamens 4. Gravel patches on rock sheets in the high Drakensberg.

⑤ *Zaluzianskya microsiphon*

Two-lipped Drumsticks Perennial herb to 40 cm, the stems covered in shaggy hairs, with elliptical, sometimes toothed leaves in a basal rosette, and spikes of side-facing, 2-lipped, white flowers flushed dull red on the reverse, with deeply notched petals and a tube 20–50 mm long. Montane grassland in the Drakensberg.

Glumicalyx GOOSENECK FLOWER (Alluding to the glume-like, or chaffy, calyx)

Perennial herbs or shrublets *with downward-facing hairs on the stems. Leaves opposite below but often alternate above, leathery, usually toothed. Flowers ± sessile, in nodding, elongated or head-like spikes; calyx 5-lobed; corolla with 5 ± similar lobes, tubular or funnel-shaped; stamens 4 in dissimilar pairs; stigma tongue-like with 2 marginal strips of hairs.* South Africa: 6 spp.

❶ *Glumicalyx goseloides*

J F M A M J J A S O N D

Greater Gooseneck Flower Perennial herb to 45 cm, with sparsely hairy, oblong-elliptical, ± scalloped leaves, and nodding heads of orange flowers, white on the reverse, petals round, tube 20–30 mm long, with only 2 stamens protruding. Boulder beds and gravelly places in the high Drakensberg. Hybridises with *Glumicalyx nutans*.

❷ *Glumicalyx nutans*

J F M A M J J A S O N D

Lesser Gooseneck Flower Similar to *Glumicalyx goseloides* but the flowers have oblong petals and a tube 12–16 mm long. Boulder beds and gravelly places in the high Drakensberg.

❸ *Glumicalyx flanaganii*

J F M A M J J A S O N D

Flanagan's Gooseneck Flower Perennial herb to 60 cm, with sparsely hairy, oblong-elliptical, toothed leaves, and nodding heads of orange flowers, white on the reverse, with oblong to round petals, a tube 13–18 mm long, and all 4 stamens protruding. Stream gulllies and damp cliffs in the high Drakensberg.

▶ **FLOWERS USUALLY STALKED AND WITH 5 SIMILAR LOBES; SHRUBLETS WITH ± WOODY STEMS**

Aptosimum KAROO VIOLET (Greek a, not; ptosimos, deciduous, alluding to the persistent fruits)

Dwarf shrublets, often cushion-forming. Leaves alternate, not toothed, often crowded. Flowers solitary in the axils, ± sessile, dark blue to purple; calyx 5-lobed; corolla trumpet-shaped, with 5 ± similar lobes, with a broadly cylindrical tube; stamens 4 in dissimilar pairs, anthers of 1 pair smaller. Southern and tropical Africa: ±40 spp.; South Africa: ±20 spp.

❹ *Aptosimum procumbens*

J F M A M J J A S O N D

Creeping, mat-forming dwarf shrublet, with petiolate, paddle-shaped leaves, 10–30 mm long, and violet flowers with purple marks, 10–20 mm long. Dry, rocky flats through the drier parts of South Africa.

❺ *Aptosimum indivisum*

J F M A M J J A S O N D

Cushion-forming dwarf shrublet to 7 cm, with spatula-shaped leaves, 10–25 mm long, on long petioles, and violet flowers with purple marks around a white throat, 25 mm long. Dry, rocky flats in open scrub through the drier parts of southern Africa.

Phygelius RIVER BELLS, RIVIERKLOKKIE
(Greek phugo, to shun; helios, sun, referring to the partly shaded habitat) *Shrubs, ± hairless. Leaves opposite, petiolate, toothed. Flowers nodding in panicles, orange with a yellow throat; calyx 5-lobed; corolla trumpet-shaped, with 5 ± similar lobes, with a broadly cylindrical tube; stamens 4, dissimilar pairs, all protruding.* Southern Africa: 2 spp. Used medicinally and magically; attractive garden plants.

455

❶ *Phygelius aequalis* J F M A M J J A S O N D

Eastern River Bells Shrub to 2 m, with opposite, elliptical, toothed leaves, and dense panicles of nodding, tubular, reddish flowers with a yellow throat and level mouth, 40 mm long. Montane stream banks and gullies in the Drakensberg.

❷ *Phygelius capensis* J F M A M J J A S O N D

Western River Bells Shrub to 1 m high, with opposite, elliptical, toothed leaves, and open panicles of backward-flexed, tubular, orange flowers with a yellow throat and oblique mouth, 30–40 mm long. Montane stream banks and moist gullies in the Drakensberg and Maluti mountains.

Oftia OFTIA *(Derivation unknown)*

Shrubs or shrublets with sprawling, leafy stems. Leaves mostly opposite, *sessile, closely toothed, with the margins ± rolled under.* Flowers solitary in the upper axils, white; calyx 5-lobed; *corolla with 5 ± similar lobes with the tube longer than the petals;* stamens 4, *all similar,* with *parallel anther lobes. Fruit a small fleshy drupe.* South Africa: 3 spp.

❸ *Oftia africana* J F M A M J J A S O N D

Sprawling, roughly hairy shrublet with trailing branches to 1 m, with toothed, lance-shaped leaves, 10–40 mm long, and fragrant white flowers in the upper axils, 10 mm in diameter. Rocky slopes in southwestern South Africa. *Oftia glabra* from the Little Karoo is a more erect shrub with smaller leaves, 7–12 mm long; *O. revoluta* from Namaqualand has narrower leaves, with the margins rolled under.

Chaenostoma SKUNK BUSH, STINKBOSSIE

(Greek chaeno, *gaping;* stoma, *mouth, alluding to the funnel-shaped floral tube)* *Shrublets or woody perennials* (rarely annuals), often aromatic or foetid. Leaves usually opposite, usually toothed. Flowers mostly solitary in the leaf axils, usually white, pink or mauve to blue, with a yellow throat; calyx 5-lobed and ± 2-lipped; *corolla with 5 ± similar lobes;* stamens 4, in dissimilar pairs, *all or only 2 protruding from the tube.* Africa, mainly South Africa: 46 spp. The genus *Chaenostoma* has recently been resurrected to accommodate all but 3 of the erstwhile species of *Sutera.*

❹ *Chaenostoma caeruleum* J F M A M J J A S O N D

(=*Sutera caerulea*) Erect, glandular-haired perennial to 1 m, with lance-shaped, usually sparsely toothed leaves, and long racemes of mauve or violet flowers with a yellow, shortly funnel-shaped tube, 3–5 mm long; all 4 stamens protrude. Stony soils in scrub in southwestern South Africa.

❺ *Chaenostoma uncinatum* J F M A M J J A S O N D

(=*Sutera uncinata*) Glandular-haired shrublet with narrowly winged stems to 60 cm, narrow, mostly untoothed leaves, with the margins sometimes rolled under, and racemes or narrow panicles of pink to purple flowers with a yellow throat and narrowly funnel-shaped tube, 10–19 mm long; only 2 stamens protrude. Sandy or rocky places in scrub in southwestern South Africa.

Jamesbrittenia JAMESBRITTENIA *(Named for British botanist, James Britten, 1846–1924)*

Shrublets, woody perennials or annual herbs, *usually glandular-haired and foetid*. Leaves usually opposite, variously shaped, usually toothed. Flowers solitary in the leaf axils to form racemes, often mauve to blue, with a yellow throat; calyx 5-lobed; *corolla salver-shaped, with 5 ± similar lobes, with a slender, cylindrical tube widening abruptly and kinked near the top*; stamens 4, in dissimilar pairs, *the upper 2 extending down the inside of the tube as hairy wings or ridges*. Mainly central and southern Africa: 83 spp.; South Africa: 56 spp. The yellow to purple flowers of *Jamesbrittenia atropurpurea* were used as a substitute for saffron in medicine and dyeing.

❶ *Jamesbrittenia grandiflora*

J F **M A M J J** A S O N D

Slender shrublet to 1.5 m, with tufts of glandular-haired, paddle-shaped, toothed leaves, and mauve flowers, 20–30 mm in diameter, with a tube ±20 mm long. Rocky slopes in rough grassland and scrub in northeastern South Africa. *Jamesbrittenia macrantha* from northwest of Lydenburg has almost hairless, folded leaves.

❷ *Jamesbrittenia calciphila*

J F **M A M J J A S O N** D

Gnarled, very twiggy, glandular-haired shrublet to 45 cm, with minute, rounded, almost granular leaves, mostly 1–2 mm long, crowded on short shoots, and pink to blue, rarely white, flowers with a wedge-shaped yellow to red patch at the base of each petal, with a tube 9–11 mm long. Coastal limestone rocks and cliffs in the southwestern Cape.

❸ *Jamesbrittenia albomarginata*

J F **M A M J J A S O N D**

Dwarf, glandular-haired shrublet to 40 cm, with small leaves, ±3 mm long, often toothed above, and brownish-yellow or orange to maroon flowers edged in white, with a tube 12–18 mm long. Scrub on coastal limestone flats and dunes in the southwestern Cape.

❹ *Jamesbrittenia fruticosa*

J F M A M J J **A S** O N D

Aromatic, twiggy shrublet to 1 m, with elliptical, sparsely glandular-haired leaves, and clustered racemes of mauve to purple flowers with a dark purple eye, 15–20 mm in diameter, with a tube 20–26 mm long. Sandy and stony flats in open scrub in southern Namibia and Namaqualand.

❺ *Jamesbrittenia racemosa*

J F M A M **J J A** S O N D

Aromatic annual herb to 50 cm, covered in glistening, glandular hairs, with oval, coarsely toothed leaves, and white to pale lilac flowers with a star-like purplish eye and notched petals, 12–24 mm in diameter, with a tube 15–18 mm long. Granite outcrops in the shelter of boulders or crevices and gravelly watercourses in Namaqualand.

❻ *Jamesbrittenia pristisepala*

J **F M A M** J J A S O **N D**

Dwarf shrublet to 30 cm, covered in glistening glandular hairs, with greyish, elliptical, deeply lobed leaves, and long racemes of creamy-white to mauve flowers in long racemes, ±10 mm in diameter, with a tube 8–12 mm long. Cliffs and boulder beds in the Drakensberg. Hybridises with *Jamesbrittenia breviflora* and other species.

❼ *Jamesbrittenia breviflora*

J **F M** A M J J A **S O N D**

Aromatic, sprawling perennial, covered in glistening glandular hairs, with oval, scalloped leaves, and long, leafy racemes of red to pink flowers with a yellow throat, 10–20 mm in diameter, with a tube 4–6 mm long. Open grassy and rocky slopes in the Drakensberg.

459

① *Jamesbrittenia jurassica* `J F M A M J J A S O N D`

Sprawling, mat-forming perennial, covered in glistening glandular hairs, with oblong, lobed leaves, and axillary, pink to violet flowers with a yellow throat, ±15 mm in diameter, with a tube 7–9 mm long. Gravelly rock sheets at high altitude in the Drakensberg.

▶ **SOFT-STEMMED ANNUAL OR PERENNIAL HERBS; FLOWERS STALKED, WITH 5 ± SIMILAR LOBES, WITHOUT POCKETS OR SPURS**

Lyperia **LYPERIA** *(Greek lyperos, mournful, alluding to the dull-coloured flowers)*

Perennial or annual herbs, usually glandular, *with narrowly winged stems*. Leaves usually opposite, variously shaped, usually toothed. Flowers solitary in the leaf axils to form racemes, greenish, or white to mauve with a yellow throat; calyx 5-lobed; *corolla with 5 ± similar lobes, with a slender, cylindrical tube that widens abruptly near the top*; stamens 2 or 4, and then in dissimilar pairs, *the upper pair extending down the inside of the tube as hairy wings or ridges*. Southwestern Cape: 6 spp.

② *Lyperia lychnidea* `J F M A M J J A S O N D`

Glandular-haired perennial to 1 m, with leaves mostly in axillary tufts, shortly toothed above, and racemes of greenish to yellow flowers, clove-scented at night, with a slender tube, 23–28 mm long; fruit 13–23 mm long. Coastal scrub along the southwestern Cape coast.

③ *Lyperia tristis* `J F M A M J J A S O N D`

Glandular-haired annual herb to 60 cm, with leaves sometimes toothed, and racemes of whitish to yellow or brown flowers, clove-scented at night, with a slender tube, 20–29 mm long; fruit 4–15 mm long. Sandy, gravelly or stony ground from Namibia to the Eastern Cape.

Manulea **MANULEA, VINGERTJIES**
(Latin manus, hand, referring to the finger-like petals of some species)

Annual or perennial herbs, usually hairy. Leaves usually opposite and toothed. Flowers in racemes or panicles, white or greenish-yellow to red or brown; calyx 3-lobed and 2-lipped; corolla with 5 ± similar lobes or 2-lipped, usually tubular; stamens usually 4 in dissimilar pairs, the upper pair arising well within the tube, *all enclosed within the tube*; stigma tongue-like, with 2 marginal strips of hairs. Africa and India: 74 spp.; South Africa: 73 spp.

④ *Manulea tomentosa* `J F M A M J J A S O N D`

Grey-haired perennial to 60 cm, with toothed leaves, and crowded clusters of orange to brown flowers with narrow, longitudinally rolled petals, the tube 7–10 mm long, the stamens attached in the outer third. Coastal sands in the southwestern Cape.

⑤ *Manulea altissima* `J F M A M J J A S O N D`

Glandular-haired, foetid, short-lived perennial to 1 m, with ± toothed leaves crowded at the base, and head-like racemes of scented white flowers with a yellowish centre and rounded petals, the tube 8–10 mm long, the stamens attached near the middle. Deep sandy soils in Namaqualand.

⑥ *Manulea corymbosa* `J F M A M J J A S O N D`

Glandular-haired annual herb to 45 cm, with toothed leaves crowded at the base, and head-like racemes of creamy-white flowers with an orange centre and rounded petals, the tube 8–12 mm long, the stamens attached in the outer third. Sandy flats along the West Coast.

1 *Manulea silenoides* **Mauve Manulea**
Annual herb to 15 cm, with a basal tuft of elliptical, sparsely hairy leaves, and crowded racemes of mauve flowers with a yellow eye and Y-shaped petals, 6–12 mm in diameter, the tube 3.5–5.5 mm long. Sandy and gravelly soils in Namaqualand.

▶ **SOFT-STEMMED ANNUAL OR PERENNIAL HERBS; FLOWERS STALKED, SOLITARY OR IN RACEMES AND STRONGLY 2-LIPPED, USUALLY WITH 1 OR MORE POCKETS OR SPURS**

Craterostigma MOLE'S SPECTACLES *(Greek krater, crater, alluding to the cup-like stigma)*

Perennial, rhizomatous herbs, sometimes with orange roots. *Leaves in a basal tuft, mostly not toothed,* ± hairless above, *several-veined from the base.* Flowers solitary or in racemes, on slender stalks, white or pink; calyx 5-lobed; corolla 4- or 5-lobed and 2-lipped, with *the upper lip hooded;* stamens 4 in 2 dissimilar pairs, *the upper pair hidden beneath the hood and the lower pair curved inwards.* Africa: ±9 spp.; South Africa: ±4 spp.

2 *Craterostigma wilmsii*
Tufted perennial to 15 cm, with a basal rosette of paddle-shaped, slightly cupped leaves, finely hairy beneath, and a raceme of pale to deep pink, 2-lipped flowers, 10–15 mm in diameter. Seasonally wet rock sheets in northeastern South Africa.

Colpias ROCK FLOWER, KLIPBLOM
(Greek kolpos, breast, alluding to the paired pouches on the flowers) Soft-stemmed shrublet. Leaves alternate, toothed, usually softly hairy. Flowers solitary in the axils on slender stalks, white, yellow or orange; calyx 5-lobed; corolla bell-shaped, 5-lobed and 2-lipped, with *a cylindrical tube excavated into 2 sacs;* stamens 4 in 2 dissimilar pairs. South Africa: 1 sp.

3 *Colpias mollis*
Soft-stemmed, dwarf shrublet to 20 cm, usually softly hairy but sometimes hairless, with oval, toothed leaves, and pale yellow to white flowers on slender stalks in the leaf axils, funnel-shaped, with a pair of small pouches beneath, spice-scented, 20–30 mm in diameter. Shaded, south-facing rock crevices in Namaqualand. The fruits curve away from light so that the seeds are thrust into rock cracks.

Nemesia NEMESIA, LEEUBEKKIE *(Ancient Greek name for a similar plant)*

Annual or perennial herbs. Leaves opposite, variously toothed. Flowers solitary in the axils or in loose, leafy racemes, combinations of white, yellow, orange, pink or blue; calyx 5-lobed; corolla 5-lobed and strongly *2-lipped, snapdragon-like* with the lower lip bulging upwards at the base, with *a very short tube bearing a single pouch or spur;* stamens 4 in 2 dissimilar pairs twisted around one another. Southern Africa, mainly southwestern Cape: ±60 spp. Some of the annual species are popular garden plants.

▶ **SHORT-LIVED PERENNIALS OR SOFT SHRUBLETS; LEAVES MOSTLY 3–5-VEINED FROM THE BASE**

4 *Nemesia sylvatica* **Forest Nemesia**
Bushy perennial herb to 1 m, with stalked, oval, toothed leaves, and leafy racemes of white flowers, with a cushion-like hump on the lower lip, and a slender, pointed spur 6–9 mm long; racemes become long and slender in fruit. Forest margins in eastern South Africa.

1 *Nemesia rupicola*   J F M A **M** J J A S O **N D**
Mountain Nemesia Well-branched perennial herb to 70 cm, with stalked, oval, toothed leaves, and short racemes of white, pink or pale mauve flowers, with a white or yellowish cushion-like hump on the lower lip, and a short, pointed spur to 3.5 mm long. Boulder beds, scree or mountain slopes on the eastern escarpment.

2 *Nemesia denticulata* **Blue Nemesia**   J F **M A M J J A S** O N D
Tufted perennial herb with annual stems to 40 cm high from a woody rootstock, with sessile, oval, toothed leaves, and pink or mauve flowers with 2 yellow or orange crests on the lower lip, a pair of raised yellow bumps inside the throat, and a pointed spur, 2–3 mm long. Stony grassland and open woodland in eastern South Africa.

3 *Nemesia caerulea*   J F M A M J J A **S O** N **D**
Drakensberg Nemesia Very similar to *Nemesia denticulata* but without the raised bumps inside the throat of the flowers. Rocky grassland in the Drakensberg and Maluti mountains.

4 *Nemesia fruticans*   J F M A M J J A **S O** N D
Common Wild Nemesia Shrublet to 40 cm, with narrowly lance-shaped, toothed leaves, the margins slightly rolled under, and pink or lilac flowers, with an oblong cushion-like hump on the lower lip, and a pointed spur, ±4 mm long; fruit as long as or longer than wide. Stony slopes and roadsides from southern to northeastern South Africa.

▶ **ANNUAL HERBS; FLOWERS WITH A SLENDER SPUR >3 MM LONG, OFTEN BICOLOURED YELLOW AND WHITE**

5 *Nemesia karroensis* **Karoo Nemesia**   J F M A M J **J A** S O N D
Annual herb to 30 cm, with oval, toothed leaves and heart-shaped bracts, and white or purple and yellow flowers, with narrow, often folded upper petals, a cushion-like hump on the lower lip, and a strongly curved spur, 10–13 mm long, clove-scented; fruit as long as wide. Dry gravelly flats in western South Africa.

6 *Nemesia anisocarpa*   J F M A M J J **A S** O N D
Namaqua Nemesia Annual herb to 40 cm, with elliptical to lance-shaped, toothed leaves, and white or pink or orange and yellow flowers, with narrowly oblong upper petals, a cushion-like hump on the lower lip, and a tapering spur, ±3 mm long; fruit longer than wide, with an oblique base. Stony flats and slopes in Namaqualand.

7 *Nemesia ligulata*   J F M A M J J **A S O** N D
Club-spurred Nemesia Annual herb to 40 cm, with elliptical to lance-shaped, toothed leaves, and white and yellow to orange or blue, or entirely yellow flowers, with narrowly oblong upper petals, 2 velvety crests on the lower lip, and a curved spur, often blunt or slightly swollen at the tip, 6–12 mm long. Sandy slopes and flats in Namaqualand.

8 *Nemesia cheiranthus*   J F M A M J **J A** S O N D
Long-eared Nemesia Annual herb to 40 cm, with lance-shaped, toothed leaves, and white and yellow flowers, sometimes marked purple, with long, slender upper petals, 2 velvety crests on the lower lip, and a pointed spur, 3–5 mm long; fruit as long as wide. Mainly sandy slopes and flats in Namaqualand.

1 *Nemesia bicornis*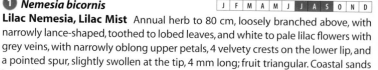

Lilac Nemesia, Lilac Mist Annual herb to 80 cm, loosely branched above, with narrowly lance-shaped, toothed to lobed leaves, and white to pale lilac flowers with grey veins, with narrowly oblong upper petals, 4 velvety crests on the lower lip, and a pointed spur, slightly swollen at the tip, 4 mm long; fruit triangular. Coastal sands in southwestern South Africa.

2 *Nemesia affinis*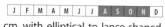

Varicoloured Nemesia Annual herb to 30 cm, with elliptical to lance-shaped, toothed leaves, and white, blue, yellow, or sometimes red flowers, with oblong upper petals, a raised, cream-coloured to yellow palate with 2 velvety crests, and a pointed spur, 3–5 mm long; fruit as long as or slightly longer than wide. Sandy and granite slopes and flats from southern Namibia to the Eastern Cape.

▶ **ANNUAL HERBS; FLOWERS WITH A SAC-LIKE OR CONICAL SPUR LESS THAN 3 MM LONG**

3 *Nemesia leipoldtii*

Leipoldt's Nemesia Annual herb to 30 cm, with oval, toothed leaves, and white to mauve flowers with a cushion-like yellow hump on the lower lip, oblong upper petals, and a pointed, sac-like spur; fruit as long as wide. Clay flats in the Northern Cape.

4 *Nemesia barbata*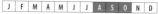

Bearded Nemesia Annual herb to 30 cm, with oval, toothed leaves, and crowded racemes of white and blue to blackish flowers, with small, rounded upper petals, a hairy hump on the lower lip, and a short, blunt spur, up to 2 mm long; fruit longer than wide. Sandy flats and slopes in southwestern South Africa, often flowering after fire.

5 *Nemesia strumosa*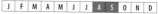

Cape Snapdragon Annual herb to 40 cm, with narrowly lance-shaped, toothed leaves, and rounded racemes of white, cream-coloured, pink, mauve, or sometimes red flowers, mottled brown and coarsely hairy in the throat, with rounded upper petals, and a broad, sac-like spur; fruit longer than wide. Sandy flats along the West Coast; widely cultivated.

Diascia **TWINSPUR, PENSIES**
(Greek di, *two;* askion, *bladder, alluding to the paired pouches or spurs*) Annual or perennial herbs. Leaves basal or opposite, the upper ones sometimes alternate, usually toothed or lobed and hairless. Flowers solitary in the axils on long pedicels or in racemes, mostly *pink to purple* with a darker centre and *bright yellow windows;* calyx 5-lobed; corolla cup-shaped, 5-lobed and 2-lipped, with 4 small upper petals and 1 large lower one, with a *very short tube bearing 2 pouches or spurs;* stamens 4 in 2 dissimilar pairs twisted around one another. Southern Africa: ±70 spp. The Afrikaans vernacular name is a 17th-century corruption of the English 'pansy'; a few species are popular garden plants.

▶ **PERENNIAL HERBS; FLOWERS IN RACEMES**

6 *Diascia cordata*

Heart-leaved Twinspur Sprawling perennial to 60 cm, with oval, sharply toothed leaves, and sparse racemes of pale pink flowers, ±18 mm in diameter, with a pair of yellow and black windows at the base of the upper petals, and widely spreading spurs, 8–9 mm long, the stamens clustered in the centre. Stream sides and damp slopes in the Drakensberg.

1 *Diascia integerrima* J F M **A** M J J **A** S O N **D**

Narrow-leaved Twinspur Tufted perennial with slender, erect, wand-like stems, very narrow, toothed leaves, and racemes of pale pink flowers, ±18 mm in diameter, with a central keel covered in black glands and down-facing spurs, 4–6 mm long, the stamens clustered under the upper petals. Basal cliffs, scree, roadsides and boulder beds in the Drakensberg and Maluti mountains.

2 *Diascia anastrepta* **Greater Twinspur** J F **M** A M J J A S O N **D**

Loosely tangled perennial herb to 40 cm, with oval, sharply toothed leaves, and racemes of pink flowers, ±20 mm in diameter, with a single, elongated yellow and black window in the upper lip, 2 patches of scattered black glands on the lower lip, and spreading spurs, 6–7 mm long, the stamens in 2 diverging pairs, with the lower anthers green. Damp basalt cliffs and stream sides in the Drakensberg.

▶ **ANNUAL HERBS; FLOWERS SOLITARY IN THE LEAF AXILS**

3 *Diascia namaquensis* J F M A M J J **A** S O N D

Namaqua Twinspur Annual herb, 10–50 cm, with elliptical, toothed or deeply lobed leaves, and reddish-purple flowers, ±10 mm in diameter, with a single, large, elongated spot at the base of the upper 2 petals, and spreading spurs, ±20 mm long. Gravelly loam soils, often in fallow lands, in northern Namaqualand.

4 *Diascia tanyceras* J F M A M J J **A** S O N D

Long-horned Twinspur, Bokhorinkies Annual herb, 10–50 cm, with elliptical, toothed or deeply lobed leaves, and reddish-purple flowers, ±15 mm in diameter, with a pair of elliptic spots at the base of each of the upper 2 petals, and spreading spurs, ±20 mm long. Gravelly loam soils, often in fallow lands, in central Namaqualand.

5 *Diascia capensis* **Cape Twinspur** J F M A M J J **A S** O N D

Erect or sprawling annual herb to 35 cm, with deeply lobed leaves, and greyish-purple flowers, 12–23 mm in diameter, with a dark magenta centre and 2 shallow yellow sacs, the stamens on a yellow boss and arching sharply downwards. Mainly coastal sandveld in the southwestern Cape.

Hemimeris **HEMIMERIS, GEELGESIGGIES**

(Greek hemi, half; meros, a part, alluding to the 2-lipped flowers) Annual herbs. Leaves opposite, the upper ones sometimes alternate, usually toothed or lobed. Flowers solitary in the axils on long pedicels or in dense, flat-topped racemes, *bright yellow with dark spots in the centre;* calyx 5-lobed; corolla cup-shaped, *4-lobed and 2-lipped,* the lower lip larger, with *a very short tube with 2 pouches or spurs;* stamens 2, sharply bent. Southwestern South Africa: 5 spp.

6 *Hemimeris racemosa* J F M A M J **J A S O** N D

Annual herb, 3–50 cm, with oval, toothed or lobed leaves, and yellow flowers, 7–13 mm long, with 2 spurs, 1.5–3 mm long. Coastal and inland sand and clay soils from Namaqualand to the Eastern Cape.

7 *Hemimeris sabulosa* J F M A M J **J A S O** N D

Annual herb, 3–50 cm, with lobed or toothed leaves, and yellow flowers, 9–12 mm long, with 2 sacs, 1–2 mm deep and with lateral pockets folded over the stamens. Sandy coastal flats in Namaqualand and the southwestern Cape.

GLOSSARY OF TERMS

See illustrated glossary on the front or back endpaper for additional terms.

annual plant that germinates from seed, then flowers and produces new seeds, and dies within a single season. It typically has fine, fibrous roots.

apical of the tip or apex.

awn stiff bristle, often present on the fruits of grasses.

axil the upper angle between a stem and an attached leaf or branch; **axillary** of structures in this position.

basal of the base.

boss protuberance or swelling.

bract leaf-like organ subtending a flower or inflorescence.

bracteole small, second-order bract.

carpel single element or segment of an ovary containing ovules.

compound comprised of several individual units.

coppice to resprout from near the base.

corm underground storage structure formed from a short, swollen stem; **cormous** of plants with a corm.

cupule small cup-like structure or organ.

cyathium modified inflorescence of *Euphorbia* species resembling a single flower.

dehiscent opening spontaneously to shed seeds or pollen.

dichotomy division into two equal parts; **dichotomously** divided in this manner.

digitate completely divided to a central point, like fingers.

disciform of daisy flowerheads with several peripheral rows of tubular, female florets surrounding the funnel-shaped, bisexual disc-florets (see also p.344).

discoid button-like; of daisy flowerheads with only funnel-shaped, bisexual florets (see also p.344).

ellipsoid rugby ball-shaped.

epicalyx series of small, sepal-like bracts forming a calyx-like whorl beneath the true calyx.

epiphyte plant that grows on another plant but is not parasitic on it.

ericoid small, stiff, needle-like leaves with the margins rolled under, as in many *Erica* species; shrubs with such leaves.

flowerhead head-like inflorescence containing a number of individual small flowers or florets.

foliolate comprising separate leaflets.

funicle thread-like stalk attaching an ovule or seed to the wall of the ovary.

geophyte perennial plant with underground storage organs that propagates by means of buds below the soil surface.

glaucous covered with a grey, waxy or powdery bloom.

glume dry, chaffy bract of the flower spike in grasses, restios and sedges.

heterostylous having styles of different lengths in different flowers.

hilum the scar on a seed at the place where it was attached to the funicle or stalk during development.

keeled bearing a median longitudinal ridge, like the keel of a boat.

mucilage glutinous carbohydrate secreted by certain plants; **mucilaginous** of or producing mucilage.

nectary glandular structure secreting nectar.

New World Americas; western hemisphere.

Old World Europe, Asia, Africa; eastern hemisphere.

palmate lobed or incompletely divided to a central point, like a hand.

papilla small, pimple-like projection; **papillate** bearing papillae.

pappus ring of scales or fine bristles on the fruit of many members of the Daisy family (see also p.344).

peduncle stalk of a plant bearing an inflorescence or solitary flower; **pedunculate** with a peduncle.

perennial herbaceous plant that persists for several years. It typically has fleshy or carrot-like roots, and leaves clustered at the base of the stem.

perianth outer, sterile parts of a flower, comprising the calyx and corolla.

pollinium mass of cohering pollen grains in the Orchid and Milkweed families; **pollinia** (plural).

porose with an apical pore or short slit.

radiate of daisy flowerheads with peripheral, strap-shaped, ray florets surrounding funnel-shaped disc-florets (see also p.344).

rhizome horizontal plant stem creeping along the surface or underground, usually with buds and scale-like leaves; **rhizomatous** with or like a rhizome.

rostellum small, beak-like outgrowth from the stigma in orchid flowers.

salver-shaped of flowers with a narrow, cylindrical tube and flat, spreading petals.

scape naked flower stalk lacking leaves or bracts and arising directly from the root of the plant.

sessile without a stalk.

sheath tubular protective structure, as in the lower portion of a grass leaf that clasps the stem.

short shoot small, highly contracted branch bearing tufts of leaves or flowers.

shrub woody plant smaller than a tree and with several main stems from the base instead of a single trunk; **shrublet** small shrub.

simple undivided or unbranched.

spathe large leaf- or petal-like bract enclosing an entire or partial flower cluster.

staminode sterile stamen, often flattened and colourful or petal-like.

tuber swollen subterranean storage stem or root; **tuberous** bearing or resembling a tuber; **tuberculate** covered with small, rounded nodules or tubercles.

zygomorphic bilaterally symmetrical; capable of division into two equal parts only along the vertical axis.

REGIONAL WILD-FLOWER GUIDES

South Africa has many local and regional wild-flower guides and these should be consulted for more complete coverage of specific areas of the country.

Northwest

Van Rooyen, N. 2001. *Flowering Plants of the Kalahari Dunes*. Ekotrust, Pretoria.

West and southwest

Bean, A. & Johns, A. 2005. *Stellenbosch to Hermanus: South African Wild Flower Guide 5*. Botanical Society of South Africa, Cape Town.

Le Roux, A. 2004. *Namaqualand: South African Wild Flower Guide 1*. Botanical Society of South Africa, Cape Town.

Manning, J. 2007. *Field Guide to Fynbos*. Struik Publishers, Cape Town.

Manning, J.C. & Goldblatt, P. 2007. *Nieuwoudtville, Bokkeveld Plateau and Hantam: South African Wild Flower Guide 9*. Botanical Society of South Africa, Cape Town.

Manning, J.C. & Goldblatt, P. 2007. *West Coast: South African Wild Flower Guide 7*. Botanical Society of South Africa, Cape Town.

Moriarty, A. 1997. *Outeniqua, Tsitsikamma and Eastern Little Karoo: South African Wild Flower Guide 2*. Botanical Society of South Africa, Cape Town.

Mustart, P., Cowling, R. & Albertyn, J. 1997. *Southern Overberg: South African Wild Flower Guide 8*. Botanical Society of South Africa, Cape Town.

Shearing, D. 2008. *Karoo: South African Wild Flower Guide 6*. Botanical Society of South Africa, Cape Town.

Trinder-Smith, T. 2006. *Wild Flowers of the Table Mountain National Park: Stellenbosch to Hermanus: South African Wild Flower Guide 12*. Botanical Society of South Africa, Cape Town.

Van Rooyen, G. & Steyn, H. 2004. *Cederberg, Clanwilliam and Biedouw Valley: South African Wild Flower Guide 10*. Botanical Society of South Africa, Cape Town.

East and southeast

Manning, J.C. 2001. *Eastern Cape: South African Wild Flower Guide 11*. Botanical Society of South Africa, Cape Town.

Pooley, E. 1998. *A Field Guide to Wild Flowers: KwaZulu-Natal and the Eastern Region*. Natal Flora Publications Trust, Durban.

Pooley, E. 2003. *Mountain Flowers: a Field Guide to the Flora of the Drakensberg and Lesotho*. Natal Flora Publications Trust, Durban.

Vanderplank, H.J. 1998. *Wildflowers of the Port Elizabeth Area: Swartkops to Sundays Rivers*. Bluecliff Publishing, Port Elizabeth.

Vanderplank, H.J. 1999. *Wildflowers of the Port Elizabeth Area: Gamtoos to Swartkops Rivers*. Bluecliff Publishing, Port Elizabeth.

North and northeast

Germishuizen, G. & Clarke, B. 2003. *Illustrated Guide to the Wildflowers of Northern South Africa*. Briza, Pretoria.

Germishuizen, G. & Fabian, A. 1997. *Wild Flowers of Northern South Africa*. Fernwood Press, Cape Town.

Onderstall, J. 1984. *Transvaal Lowveld and Escarpment: South African Wild Flower Guide 4*. Botanical Society of South Africa, Cape Town.

INDEX TO SCIENTIFIC NAMES

CAPITAL LETTERS denote families
Bold denotes genera

Bold italics denotes alternative generic names
Italics denotes alternative species names

A
ACANTHACEAE 430
Acanthopsis 430
A. disperma 430
Adenandra 210
A. uniflora 210
A. villosa 210
Adenanthellum 400
A. osmitoides 346, 400
Adenium 258
A. multiflorum 258
Adhatoda 432
A. andromeda 432
A. densiflora 432
Aeollanthus 424
A. rehmannii 424
AGAPANTHACEAE 52
Agapanthus 52
A. africanus 52
A. campanulatus 52
A. inapertus 54
A. praecox 52
Agathosma 212
A. bisulca 212
A. capensis 212
A. thymifolia 212
AIZOACEAE 304
Ajuga 422
A. ophrydis 422
Albuca 84
A. abyssinica 84
A. canadensis 84
A. flaccida 84
A. maxima 84
A. nelsonii 84
A. setosa 84
Alectra 444
A. sessiliflora 444
Alepidea 338
A. amatymbica 338
A. cordifolia 338
A. thodei 338
A. woodii 338
ALLIACEAE 52
Aloe 74
A. affinis 82
A. alooides 76
A. arborescens 78
A. boylei 78
A. castanea 76
A. ciliaris 78
A. cooperi 78
A. dichotoma 76

A. ecklonis 78
A. ferox 76
A. fosteri 82
A. framesii 80
A. greatheadii 82
A. immaculata 82
A. khamiesensis 80
A. kniphofioides 78
A. krapohliana 80
A. lineata 76
A. longibracteata 82
A. maculata 80
A. marlothii 76
A. melanacantha 80
A. microstigma 80
A. mitriformis 78
A. mudenensis 82
A. nubigena 78
A. parvibracteata 82
A. perfoliata 78
A. petricola 80
A. pillansii 76
A. plicatilis 76
A. striata 80
A. tenuior 78
A. variegata 80
A. verdoorniae 82
AMARYLLIDACEAE 54
Amaryllis 62
A. belladonna 62
Amellus 414
A. asteroides 414
A. nanus 414
A. strigosus 347
A. tenuifolius 414
Ammocharis 60
A. coranica 60
A. longifolia 60
Anchusa 232
A. capensis 232
Androcymbium 100
A. latifolium 100
A. melanthioides 100
Aneilema 50
A. aequinoctiale 50
Anemone 186
A. fanniniae 188
A. tenuifolia 188
A. transvaalensis 188
Anisodontea 216
A. elegans 218
A. julii 218
A. scabrosa 216

ANTHERICACEAE 66
Antherotoma 324
A. debilis 324
A. phaeotricha 324
Apatesia 306
A. helianthoides 306
A. pillansii 306
APIACEAE 338
APOCYNACEAE 258
Aponogeton 46
A. angustifolius 46
A. distachyos 46
APONOGETONACEAE 46
Aptosimum 454
A. indivisum 454
A. procumbens 454
ARACEAE 46
Arctopus 340
A. echinatus 340
A. monacanthus 340
Arctotheca 376
A. calendula 345, 376
A. populifolia 376
A. prostrata 376
Arctotis 370
A. acaulis 345, 372
A. arctotoides 374
A. aspera 374
A. breviscapa 370
A. campanulata 372
A. decurrens 374
A. diffusa 372
A. fastuosa 372
A. hirsuta 372
A. leiocarpa 372
A. revoluta 374
A. scullyi 374
A. stoechadifolia 374
A. venusta 372
Argyroderma 320
A. delaetii 320
A. fissum 320
Argyrolobium 290
A. baptisioides 290
A. robustum 290
A. sandersonii 290
Aristea 106
A. abyssinica 108
A. africana 108
A. angolensis 108
A. bakeri 106
A. capitata 106
A. compressa 108

A. dichotoma 108
A. major 106
A. torulosa 108
A. woodii 108
Asclepias 262
A. cucullata 262
Aspalathus 296
A. astroites 296
A. callosa 298
A. capensis 296
A. capitata 298
A. cephalotes 298
A. chenopoda 296
A. cordata 296
A. crenata 296
A. ericifolia 296
A. nigra 298
A. quinquefolia 298
ASPHODELACEAE 66
Aster 412
A. bakerianus 347, 412
A. erucifolius 412
A. harveyanus 412
ASTERACEAE 344
Asystasia 436
A. gangetica 436
Athrixia 408
A. angustissima 408
A. fontana 408
A. phylicoides 408
A. pinifolia 408
A. rosmarinifolia 347

B
Babiana 132
B. ambigua 134
B. angustifolia 134
B. attenuata 134
B. bainesii 134
B. curviscapa 134
B. dregei 134
B. hirsuta 134
B. mucronata 134
B. nana 134
B. ringens 136
B. scabrifolia 134
B. stricta 132
B. thunbergii 134
Baeometra 100
B. uniflora 100
Ballota 424
B. africana 424
BALSAMINACEAE 272

Barleria 436
B. elegans 438
B. gueinzii 438
B. meyeriana 438
B. obtusa 438
B. ovata 436
Bartholina 152
B. burmanniana 152
Bauhinia 276
B. galpinii 276
Becium obovatum 428
Begonia 320
B. sonderiana 320
B. sutherlandii 320
BEGONIACEAE 320
Berkheya 362
B. armata 345, 364
B. barbata 362
B. carlinoides 364
B. cirsiifolia 366
B. cuneata 362
B. echinacea 366
B. fruticosa 362
B. herbacea 364
B. insignis 362
B. leucaugeta 366
B. macrocephala 364
B. multijuga 364
B. onopordifolia 366
B. purpurea 366
B. rhapontica 364
B. rosulata 362
B. setifera 364
B. speciosa 364
B. spinosissima 362
B. umbellata 364
B. zeyheri 362
Berzelia 340
B. abrotanoides 340
B. lanuginosa 340
BIGNONIACEAE 440
Blepharis 430
B. subvolubilis 430
Bobartia 108
B. indica 108
B. orientalis 110
Bonatea 150
B. speciosa 150
BORAGINACEAE 228
Brachycarpaea 192
B. juncea 192
BRASSICACEAE 190
Brownleea 158
B. macroceras 158
Brunia 342
B. laevis 342
B. noduliflora 342

BRUNIACEAE 340
Brunsvigia 62
B. bosmaniae 62
B. grandiflora 62
B. josephinae 62
B. marginata 64
B. orientalis 62
B. radulosa 62
BUDDLEJACEAE 268
Bulbine 66
B. abyssinica 68
B. annua 68
B. capitata 68
B. narcissifolia 68
B. praemorsa 68
Bulbinella 70
B. caudafelis 70
B. latifolia 70
B. nutans 70
Buttonia 442
B. natalensis 442
B. superba 442

C
Cadaba 190
C. aphylla 190
Callilepis 406
C. laureola 347, 406
CAMPANULACEAE 326
Canavalia 282
C. rosea 282
Carpanthea 306
C. pomeridiana 306
Carpobrotus 308
C. acinaciformis 308
C. deliciosus 308
C. dimidiatus 308
C. edulis 308
C. mellei 308
C. quadrifidus 308
CARYOPHYLLACEAE 252
Cephalaria 416
C. galpiniana 416
Cephalophyllum 310
C. caespitosum 310
C. pillansii 310
C. spissum 310
C. spongiosum 310
Ceratotheca 438
C. triloba 438
Ceropegia 264
C. ampliata 264
Chaenostoma 456
C. caeruleum 456
C. uncinatum 456
Chamaecrista 276
C. comosa 276

C. mimosoides 276
C. plumosa 276
Chascanum 416
C. latifolium 416
Chasmanthe 136
C. aethiopica 136
C. floribunda 136
Cheiridopsis 316
C. denticulata 316
C. namaquensis 316
C. rostrata 316
Chironia 256
C. baccifera 256
C. jasminoides 256
C. linoides 256
C. palustris 256
C. purpurascens 256
C. tetragona 256
Chlorophytum 66
C. bowkeri 66
C. comosum 66
C. cooperi 66
C. krookianum 66
C. triflorum 66
C. undulatum 66
Chrysanthemoides incana 392
C. monilifera 392
Chrysocoma 410
C. ciliata 410
C. coma-aurea 347, 410
Cineraria 386
C. canescens 386
C. deltoidea 386
C. geifolia 346
Clematis 188
C. brachiata 188
Cleome 190
C. angustifolia 190
C. hirta 190
Cleretum 306
C. papulosum 306
Clerodendrum hirsutum 422
C. triphyllum 422
Clivia 56
C. caulescens 56
C. gardenia 56
C. miniata 56
C. nobilis 56
Coccinea 322
C. adoensis 322
C. palmata 322
Codon 228
C. royenii 228
COLCHICACEAE 98
Colchicum 100
C. coloratum 100

C. melanthioides 100
C. orienticapense 100
Colpias 462
C. mollis 462
Commelina 50
C. africana 50
C. benghalensis 50
C. eckloniana 50
C. erecta 50
COMMELINACEAE 50
Conicosia 306
C. elongata 308
C. pugioniformis 306
Conophytum 318
C. minusculum 318
C. minutum 318
C. subfenestratum 318
Conostomium 324
C. natalense 324
CONVOLVULACEAE 222
Convolvulus 222
C. capensis 222
Corycium 156
C. carnosum 156
C. crispum 156
C. dracomontanum 156
C. nigrescens 156
C. orobanchoides 156
Cotula 402
C. barbata 346, 402
C. duckittiae 402
C. turbinata 402
Cotyledon 238
C. barbeyi 238
C. orbiculata 238
C. velutina 238
C. woodii 238
Crassula 234
C. coccinea 236
C. columnaris 234
C. fascicularis 236
C. obtusa 236
C. perfoliata 234
C. rupestris 234
C. setulosa 234
C. vaginata 234
CRASSULACEAE 234
Craterocapsa 328
C. tarsodes 328
Craterostigma 462
C. wilmsii 462
Crinum 60
C. bulbispermum 60
C. campanulatum 62
C. macowanii 60
C. moorei 60
C. variabile 60

Crocosmia 136
C. aurea 136
C. mathewsii 136
C. paniculata 136
C. pearsei 136
Crossandra 430
C. fruticulosa 432
C. greenstockii 432
C. zuluensis 432
Crotalaria 292
C. capensis 292
C. excisa 292
C. globifera 292
C. laburnifolia 292
CUCURBITACEAE 322
Cullumia 360
C. bisulca 345
C. setosa 360
C. squarrosa 360
Cyanella 102
C. alba 102
C. hyacinthoides 102
C. lutea 102
C. orchidiformis 102
Cyanotis 50
C. lapidosa 50
C. speciosa 50
Cybistetes longifolia 60
Cyclopia 300
C. genistoides 300
Cycnium 446
C. adonense 446
C. racemosum 446
C. tubulosum 446
Cyphia 330
C. bulbosa 330
C. digitata 332
C. phyteuma 330
C. volubilis 332
Cyrtanthus 54
C. angustifolius 54
C. breviflorus 56
C. elatus 54
C. flanaganii 56
C. sanguineus 54
C. tuckii 54
C. ventricosus 54
Cysticapnos 270
C. cracca 270
C. pruinosa 270
C. vesicaria 270

D
Delosperma 312
D. cooperi 312
D. wethamae 312
Desmodium 280

D. repandum 280
Dianthus 252
D. basuticus 252
D. mooiensis 252
D. zeyheri 252
Diascia 466
D. anastrepta 468
D. capensis 468
D. cordata 466
D. integerrima 468
D. namaquensis 468
D. tanyceras 468
Diastella 180
D. divaricata 180
D. proteoides 180
Dicoma 358
D. anomala 358
D. capensis 345
D. macrocephala 358
D. zeyheri 358
Didelta 360
D. carnosa 360
D. spinosa 360
Dierama 122
D. argyreum 122
D. floriferum 122
D. latifolium 122
D. pallidum 122
Dietes 110
D. grandiflora 110
D. iridoides 110
Dilatris 104
D. corymbosa 104
D. ixioides 104
D. pillansii 104
D. viscosa 104
Dimorphotheca 396
D. caulescens 396
D. cuneata 396
D. fruticosa 396
D. jucunda 396
D. nudicaulis 346, 396
D. pinnata 398
D. pluvialis 398
D. sinuata 398
D. tragus 396
Dipogon 282
D. lignosus 282
DIPSACACEAE 416
Disa 160
D. atricapilla 160
D. bivalvata 160
D. chrysostachya 160
D. cooperi 164
D. cornuta 162
D. crassicornis 164
D. draconis 164

D. ferruginea 162
D. flexuosa 162
D. graminifolia 162
D. harveiana 164
D. longicornu 164
D. nervosa 162
D. polygonoides 160
D. purpurascens 162
D. racemosa 160
D. scullyi 164
D. tenuifolia 160
D. thodei 164
D. uniflora 162
D. versicolor 160
D. woodii 160
Dischisma 450
D. ciliatum 450
Disperis 158
D. capensis 158
D. fanniniae 158
D. stenoplectron 158
D. wealei 158
Dissotis 326
D. canescens 326
D. phaeotricha 324
D. princeps 326
Dorotheanthus 304
D. bellidiformis 304
D. maughanii 304
D. rourkei 304
Drimia 82
D. altissima 82
D. capensis 82
D. macrocentra 84
Drosanthemum 312
D. bicolor 312
D. hispidum 312
D. speciosum 312
Drosera 190
D. cistiflora 190
D. pauciflora 190
DROSERACEAE 190

E
Edmondia 354
E. fasciculata 354
E. pinifolia 354
E. sesamoides 345, 354
Empodium 96
E. plicatum 96
Erica 240
E. abietina 244
E. cerinthoides 240
E. coccinea 240
E. curviflora 242
E. densifolia 244
E. discolor 244

E. grandiflora 244
E. longifolia 244
E. mammosa 240
E. mariae 242
E. massonii 242
E. patersonia 242
E. patersonii 242
E. perspicua 242
E. phylicifolia 244
E. pinea 242
E. plukenetii 240
E. purpurea 244
E. regia 242
E. sessiliflora 242
E. speciosa 244
E. versicolor 244
E. vestita 242
E. viscaria 244
ERICACEAE 240
Eriosema 288
E. cordatum 288
E. distinctum 288
E. kraussianum 288
E. psoraleoides 288
E. salignum 288
Eucomis 90
E. autumnalis 90
E. bicolor 90
E. comosa 90
E. humilis 90
E. pallidiflora 90
Eulophia 148
E. angolensis 148
E. clavicornis 150
E. ensata 148
E. ovalis 150
E. parvilabris 148
E. speciosa 148
E. streptopetala 148
E. welwitschii 148
E. zeyheriana 150
Eumorphia 398
E. prostrata 346, 398
E. sericea 398
Euphorbia 232
E. caput-medusae 232
E. mauritanica 232
EUPHORBIACEAE 232
Euryops 390
E. abrotanifolius 390
E. annuus 390
E. euryopoides 390
E. evansii 390
E. lateriflorus 346
E. linifolius 390
E. speciosissimus 390
E. tenuissimus 390

475

E. thunbergii 390
E. tysonii 390
E. virgineus 390
Eurystigma clavatum 304

F
FABACEAE 276
Felicia 410
F. aethiopica 410
F. amelloides 410
F. australis 412
F. elongata 410
F. filifolia 347, 410
F. fruticosa 410
F. heterophylla 412
F. merxmuelleri 412
F. tenella 412
Ferraria 110
F. crispa 110
Foveolina 400
F. dichotoma 402
F. tenella 346, 400
Freesia 120
F. alba 120
F. caryophyllacea 120
F. grandiflora 120
F. laxa 120
FUMARIACEAE 270

G
Galaxia fugacissima 112
Galtonia candicans 86
G. regalis 86
Gazania 368
G. krebsiana 370
G. leiopoda 370
G. lichtensteinii 345, 370
G. maritima 368
G. rigens 368
G. rigida 370
Geissorhiza 130
G. aspera 130
G. exscapa 130
G. monanthos 130
G. ovata 130
G. radians 130
G. splendidissima 130
GENTIANACEAE 254
GERANIACEAE 200
Geranium 200
G. brycei 202
G. flanaganii 202
G. incanum 200
G. pulchrum 202
G. robustum 200
G. schlechteri 202
G. wakkerstroomianum 202

Gerbera 404
G. ambigua 406
G. aurantiaca 406
G. cordata 347
G. crocea 404
G. galpinii 406
G. jamesonii 406
G. linnaei 406
G. serrata 406
G. tomentosa 406
G. viridifolia 406
G. wrightii 404
GESNERIACEAE 442
Gibbaria ilicifolia 394
Gladiolus 138
G. alatus 140
G. angustus 144
G. aurantiacus 144
G. brevifolius 138
G. caeruleus 140
G. cardinalis 144
G. carinatus 142
G. carmineus 138
G. carneus 142
G. caryophyllaceus 142
G. crassifolius 144
G. cunonius 142
G. dalenii 144
G. debilis 142
G. densiflorus 144
G. ecklonii 144
G. equitans 140
G. floribundus 144
G. gracilis 140
G. inflatus 138
G. liliaceus 140
G. monticola 138
G. mortonius 146
G. oppositiflorus 146
G. papilio 146
G. patersoniae 138
G. saccatus 142
G. saundersii 144
G. scullyi 142
G. teretifolius 140
G. tristis 140
G. undulatus 144
G. venustus 142
G. virescens 140
G. watermeyeri 140
G. watsonius 140
Gloriosa 98
G. modesta 98
G. superba 98
Glumicalyx 454
G. flanaganii 454
G. goseloides 454

G. nutans 454
Gnidia 246
G. anthylloides 246
G. caffra 246
G. capitata 246
G. compacta 246
G. deserticola 246
G. geminiflora 248
G. juniperifolia 248
G. kraussiana 246
G. oppositifolia 248
G. penicillata 248
G. pinifolia 248
G. simplex 248
G. squarrosa 248
G. tomentosa 248
Gomphocarpus 262
G. cancellatus 262
G. fruticosus 262
G. physocarpus 262
Gomphostigma 268
G. virgatum 268
GOODENIACEAE 338
Gorteria 366
G. diffusa 345, 366
Graderia 444
G. scabra 444
Grielum 322
G. grandiflorum 322
G. humifusum 322
Gymnodiscus 392
G. capillaris 346, 392
G. linearifolia 392

H
Habenaria 150
H. clavata 152
H. cornuta 152
H. dregeana 152
H. epipactidea 150
H. falcicornis 152
H. lithophila 152
Haemanthus 58
H. albiflos 58
H. coccineus 58
H. humilis 58
H. sanguineus 58
HAEMODORACEAE 104
Haplocarpha 376
H. nervosa 376
H. scaposa 345, 376
Harveya 446
H. bodkinii 448
H. bolusii 448
H. huttonii 448
H. pauciflora 448
H. purpurea 448

H. scarlatina 448
H. speciosa 446
H. squamosa 448
Hebenstretia 450
H. oatesii 450
H. robusta 450
Helichrysum 348
H. adenocarpum 352
H. aureum 345, 348
H. confertum 352
H. cooperi 350
H. ecklonis 350
H. elegantissimum 350
H. foetidum 350
H. herbaceum 350
H. marginatum 352
H. milfordiae 352
H. monticola 350
H. pandurifolium 348
H. patulum 348
H. petiolare 348
H. retortum 352
H. ruderale 350
H. sutherlandii 352
H. tenax 348
H. vernum 350
Heliophila 192
H. africana 194
H. arenaria 194
H. carnosa 192
H. cornuta 192
H. coronopifolia 194
H. elata 192
H. formosa 192
H. juncea 192
H. rigidiuscula 192
H. variabilis 194
Hemimeris 468
H. racemosa 468
H. sabulosa 468
Hemizygia 428
H. albiflora 428
Hermannia 214
H. alnifolia 216
H. althaeifolia 216
H. cristata 214
H. geniculata 214
H. grandiflora 214
H. hyssopifolia 216
H. saccifera 214
H. scabra 214
H. stricta 214
H. trifurca 216
Hermas 340
H. villosa 340
Herschelia graminifolia 162
Hesperantha 130

H. bachmannii 132
H. baurii 132
H. coccinea 132
H. cucullata 132
H. falcata 132
H. scopulosa 132
Heterolepis 402
H. aliena 347, 402
Hexaglottis lewisiae 112
Hibiscus 218
H. aethiopicus 220
H. barbosae 218
H. calyphyllus 220
H. cannabinus 222
H. coddii 218
H. dongolensis 220
H. engleri 220
H. pedunculatus 218
H. pusillus 218
H. saxatilis 220
H. trionum 220
H. vitifolius 220
Hirpicium 368
H. alienatum 345, 368
H. armerioides 368
H. integrifolium 368
Homeria 110
H. miniata 112
H. ochroleuca 112
Hoodia 268
H. gordonii 268
HYACINTHACEAE 82
Hybanthus 270
H. capensis 270
H. enneaspermus 270
Hyobanche 448
H. glabrata 448
H. rubra 448
H. sanguinea 448
HYPERICACEAE 252
Hypericum 252
H. aethiopicum 252
H. revolutum 252
H. roeperanum 252
Hypoestes 434
H. aristata 434
H. forskaolii 434
HYPOXIDACEAE 94
Hypoxis 94
H. colchicifolia 96
H. hemerocallidea 96
H. rigidula 94

I
Impatiens 272
I. hochstetteri 272
I. sylvicola 272

Indigofera 278
I. brachystachya 278
I. hedyantha 278
I. heterophylla 278
I. hilaris 278
I. oxytropis 280
I. procumbens 278
Ipomoea 224
I. crassipes 224
I. holubii 224
I. oblongata 224
I. obscura 224
I. pellita 224
I. pes-caprae 224
IRIDACEAE 106
Ixia 122
I. dubia 124
I. maculata 124
I. paniculata 122
I. polystachya 124
I. rapunculoides 122

J
Jamesbrittenia 458
J. albomarginata 458
J. breviflora 458
J. calciphila 458
J. fruticosa 458
J. grandiflora 458
J. jurassica 460
J. macrantha 458
J. pristisepala 458
J. racemosa 458
Jordaaniella 310
J. cuprea 310
J. dubia 310
J. spongiosa 310
Justicia 432
J. petiolaris 432

K
Kalanchoe 238
K. luciae 238
K. rotundifolia 240
K. thyrsiflora 238
Kniphofia 72
K. buchananii 74
K. caulescens 72
K. ensifolia 72
K. fluviatilis 74
K. hirsuta 72
K. laxiflora 74
K. linearifolia 72
K. porphyrantha 74
K. ritualis 72
K. sarmentosa 74
K. thodei 74

K. triangularis 74
K. tysonii 72
K. uvaria 72
Knowltonia transvaalensis 188

L
Lachenalia 90
L. aloides 92
L. bulbifera 92
L. mutabilis 92
L. pustulata 92
L. rubida 92
LAMIACEAE 418
Lampranthus 314
L. amoenus 314
L. aureus 314
L. bicolor 314
L. watermeyeri 314
Lanaria 94
L. lanata 94
LANARIACEAE 94
Lebeckia 290
L. cytisoides 292
L. plukenetiana 290
L. sepiaria 290
L. sericea 292
L. simsiana 290
Ledebouria 88
L. cooperi 88
L. revoluta 88
L. socialis 88
L. zebrina 90
Leonotis 424
L. leonurus 424
L. ocymifolia 424
Lessertia 276
L. canescens 278
L. frutescens 278
L. perennans 276
Leucadendron 174
L. argenteum 174
L. daphnoides 176
L. laureolum 178
L. meridianum 176
L. salicifolium 174
L. salignum 176
L. sessile 176
L. spissifolium 176
L. xanthoconus 176
Leucospermum 182
L. bolusii 182
L. calligerum 182
L. catherinae 186
L. conocarpodendron 184
L. cordifolium 184
L. cuneiforme 184

L. hypophyllocarpodendron 184
L. lineare 184
L. muirii 182
L. oleifolium 182
L. patersonii 184
L. prostratum 184
L. reflexum 186
L. rodolentum 182
L. tomentosum 182
L. tottum 184
L. vestitum 186
Leysera 404
L. gnaphalodes 404
L. tenella 347, 404
Limonium 226
L. capense 226
L. perigrinum 226
Liparia 302
L. splendens 302
Littonia modesta 98
Lobelia 334
L. comosa 336
L. coronopifolia 334
L. erinus 336
L. flaccida 336
L. pinifolia 334
L. preslii 336
L. pubescens 336
L. setacea 334
L. tomentosa 334
L. valida 336
L. vanreenensis 336
Lobostemon 228
L. argenteus 230
L. dorotheae 228
L. echioides 230
L. fruticosus 230
L. glaucophyllus 228
L. montanus 230
L. trichotomus 228
Lotononis 294
L. corymbosa 294
L. galpinii 294
L. lotononoides 294
L. prostrata 294
L. pulchella 294
L. sericophylla 294
L. umbellata 294
Lyperia 460
L. lychnidea 460
L. tristis 460

M
Macledium 358
M. argyrophylla 358
M. speciosa 358

M. zeyheri 345, 358
Mairia 414
M. coriacea 347, 414
M. crenata 414
M. hirsuta 414
MALVACEAE 214
Manulea 460
M. altissima 460
M. corymbosa 460
M. silenoides 462
M. tomentosa 460
Melasma 444
M. scabrum 444
MELASTOMATACEAE 324
MELIANTHACEAE 272
Melianthus 272
M. comosus 272
M. elongatus 272
M. major 272
M. pectinatus 272
Mentha 420
M. aquatica 420
M. longifolia 420
Merremia 222
M. kentrocaulos 222
M. tridentata 222
Merwilla 88
M. dracomontana 88
M. plumbea 88
Mesembryanthemum 304
M. eurystigmatum 304
M. guerichianum 304
Microglossa 408
M. mespilifolia 347, 408
Microloma 264
M. calycinum 264
M. namaquense 264
M. sagittatum 264
M. tenuifolium 264
Mimetes 178
M. argenteus 178
M. cucullatus 178
M. fimbriifolius 178
M. hirtus 178
Momordica 322
M. foetida 322
Monilaria 316
M. moniliformis 316
Monopsis 332
M. debilis 332
M. decipiens 334
M. flava 332
M. lutea 332
M. stellarioides 332
M. unidentata 332
M. variifolia 332

Monsonia 202
M. attenuata 202
M. camdeboense 204
M. ciliata 204
M. crassicaule 204
M. glauca 204
M. multifida 204
M. patersonii 204
M. speciosa 202
Montinia 320
M. caryophyllacea 320
MONTINIACEAE 320
Moraea 110
M. alticola 114
M. angusta 112
M. anomala 112
M. brevistyla 116
M. ciliata 112
M. elliotii 114
M. fugacissima 112
M. fugax 114
M. galaxia 112
M. huttonii 114
M. inclinata 114
M. lewisiae 112
M. miniata 112
M. moggii 114
M. neglecta 112
M. ochroleuca 112
M. polystachya 114
M. ramosissima 114
M. serpentina 112
M. spathulata 114
M. trifida 116
M. tripetala 116
M. unguiculata 116
M. villosa 116
Muraltia 274
M. heisteria 274
M. scoparia 274
M. spinosa 274
Myosotis 230
M. afropalustris 230
Mystacidium 146
M. capense 146
M. venosum 146

N
Nemesia 462
N. affinis 466
N. anisocarpa 464
N. barbata 466
N. bicornis 466
N. caerulea 464
N. cheiranthus 464
N. denticulata 464
N. fruticans 464

N. karroensis 464
N. leipoldtii 466
N. ligulata 464
N. rupicola 464
N. strumosa 466
N. sylvatica 462
Nerine 64
N. angustifolia 64
N. appendiculata 64
N. bowdenii 64
N. humilis 64
N. krigei 64
N. sarniensis 64
NEURADACEAE 322
Nivenia 106
N. stokoei 106
Nylandtia spinosa 274
Nymphaea 46
N. nouchali 46
NYMPHAEACEAE 46

O
Ocimum 428
O. obovatum 428
Oftia 456
O. africana 456
O. glabra 456
O. revoluta 456
Oncosiphon 400
O. grandiflorum 346, 400
O. suffruticosum 400
Onixotis 100
O. stricta 100
Oophytum 318
O. nanum 318
Orbea 266
O. namaquensis 268
O. variegata 266
O. verrucosa 266
ORCHIDACEAE 146
Ornithogalum 86
O. candicans 86
O. dubium 86
O. pruinosum 86
O. regale 86
O. saundersiae 86
O. thyrsoides 86
O. xanthochlorum 86
OROBANCHACEAE 442
Orphium 256
O. frutescens 256
Oscularia 316
O. deltoides 316
Osmitopsis 398
O. asteriscoides 346, 398
Osteospermum 392
O. amplectens 394

O. caulescens 396
O. fruticosum 396
O. grandiflorum 394
O. hyoseroides 394
O. ilicifolium 394
O. incanum 392
O. jucundum 396
O. moniliferum 392
O. oppositifolium 394
O. pinnatum 398
O. polygaloides 346
O. scariosum 394
O. sinuatum 394
Otholobium 284
O. bracteolatum 284
Othonna 388
O. auriculifolia 388
O. coronopifolia 388
O. cylindrica 388
O. dentata 346
O. filicaulis 388
O. leptodactyla 388
O. parviflora 388
O. perfoliata 388
O. ramulosa 388
O. sedifolia 388
OXALIDACEAE 198
Oxalis 198
O. flava 200
O. hirta 200
O. luteola 198
O. melanosticta 198
O. obliquifolia 198
O. obtusa 198
O. pardalis 200
O. pes-caprae 198
O. polyphylla 200
O. purpurea 198
O. semiloba 198

P
Pachycarpus 260
P. campanulatus 260
P. concolor 260
P. grandiflorus 260
P. scaber 260
P. schinzianus 260
Pachypodium 258
P. namaquanum 258
P. saundersii 258
Papaver 188
P. aculeatum 188
PAPAVERACEAE 188
Pavonia 216
P. burchellii 216
PEDALIACEAE 438
Pelargonium 204

P. alchemilloides 206
P. betulinum 210
P. capitatum 210
P. crispum 210
P. cucullatum 210
P. elegans 206
P. fulgidum 208
P. incrassatum 206
P. inquinans 208
P. lobatum 204
P. luridum 206
P. myrrhifolium 206
P. ovale 206
P. peltatum 208
P. scabrum 210
P. schlechteri 206
P. suburbanum 208
P. tongaense 208
P. triste 204
P. zonale 208
PENAEACEAE 244
Pentanisia 324
P. prunelloides 324
Peristrophe 434
P. cernua 434
Phaenocoma 356
P. prolifera 345, 356
Phygelius 454
P. aequalis 456
P. capensis 456
Plectranthus 426
P. ciliatus 426
P. ecklonii 426
P. fruticosus 426
P. grallatus 426
PLUMBAGINACEAE 226
Plumbago 226
P. auriculata 226
P. zeylanica 226
Podalyria 302
P. calyptrata 302
P. myrtillifolia 302
P. sericea 302
Podranea 440
P. brycei 440
P. ricasoliana 440
Polygala 274
P. fruticosa 274
P. myrtifolia 274
P. virgata 274
POLYGALACEAE 274
Polystachya 146
P. pubescens 146
Printzia 408
P. polifolia 347, 408
Prismatocarpus 330
P. diffusus 330

P. fruticosus 330
Protea 166
P. acaulos 166
P. amplexicaulis 166
P. aurea 166
P. burchellii 172
P. caffra 168
P. compacta 170
P. coronata 174
P. cynaroides 170
P. dracomontana 170
P. eximia 170
P. gaguedi 168
P. glabra 168
P. laurifolia 172
P. lepidocarpodendron 174
P. longifolia 172
P. lorifolia 174
P. nana 166
P. neriifolia 172, 174
P. nitida 168
P. obtusifolia 172
P. punctata 168
P. repens 170
P. roupelliae 170
P. scolymocephala 166
P. simplex 168
P. subvestita 170
P. susannae 172
P. welwitschii 168
PROTEACEAE 166
Pseudarthria 280
P. hookeriana 280
Pseudoselago 450
P. serrata 450
P. spuria 450
Psoralea 284
P. aculeata 284
P. affinis 284
P. aphylla 284
P. pinnata 284
Pterygodium 156
P. alatum 156
P. catholicum 156
P. magnum 156
Pycnostachys 426
P. reticulata 426
P. urticifolia 426

R
Rabdosiella 428
R. calycina 428
Rafnia 300
R. angulata 300
R. perfoliata 300
RANUNCULACEAE 186

Ranunculus 186
R. baurii 186
R. multifidus 186
Raphionacme 258
R. hirsuta 258, 260
R. palustris 260
Rhigozum 440
R. brevispinosum 440
R. obovatum 440
R. zambesiacum 440
Rhodohypoxis 96
R. baurii 96
R. milloides 96
Rhynchopsidium 404
R. pumilum 347, 404
R. sessiliflorum 404
Rhynchosia 286
R. cooperi 286
R. monophylla 286
R. villosa 286
Roella 328
R. ciliata 328
R. incurva 328
R. maculata 330
R. triflora 330
Roepera 196
R. cordifolia 196
R. flexuosa 196
R. foetida 196
R. morgsana 196
Rogeria 440
R. longiflora 440
Romulea 128
R. cruciata 128
R. hirsuta 128
R. monadelpha 128
R. rosea 128
R. sabulosa 128
R. tabularis 128
Rotheca 422
R. hirsuta 422
RUBIACEAE 324
Ruellia 436
R. cordata 436
Ruschia 314
R. tecta 314
R. tumidula 314
RUTACEAE 210
Ruttya 432
R. ovata 432

S
Saltera 244
S. sarcocolla 244
Salvia 418
S. africana-caerulea 418
S. africana-lutea 420

S. albicaulis 418
S. chamelaeagnea 418
S. dentata 418
S. disermas 418
S. dolomitica 418
S. lanceolata 420
S. repens 418
Sandersonia 98
S. aurantiaca 98
Sarcocaulon
    camdeboense 204
S. crassicaule 204
S. multifidum 204
S. patersonii 204
Satyrium 152
S. carneum 154
S. coriifolium 154
S. cristatum 154
S. erectum 154
S. hallackii 154
S. longicauda 154
S. neglectum 154
S. odorum 154
S. parviflorum 152
Scabiosa 416
S. africana 416
S. columbaria 416
Scadoxus 56
S. membranaceus 56
S. multiflorus 58
S. puniceus 58
Scaevola 338
S. plumieri 338
S. sericea 338
Schizocarphus 88
S. nervosus 88
Schizodium flexuosum
    162
Schizostylis coccinea 132
Scilla natalensis 88
SCROPHULARIACEAE
    450
Sebaea 254
S. albens 254
S. aurea 254
S. exacoides 254
S. grandis 254
S. marlothii 254
S. natalensis 254
S. sedoides 254
S. spathulata 254
Senecio 380
S. abruptus 380
S. aloides 386
S. arenarius 346, 380
S. brachypodus 384
S. cardaminifolius 380

S. cinerascens 382
S. corymbiferus 386
S. deltoideus 384
S. elegans 380
S. erosus 384
S. isatideus 382
S. isatidioides 382
S. littoreus 380
S. macrocephalus 382
S. macroglossoides 384
S. macroglossus 384
S. macrospermus 382
S. maritimus 380
S. pleistocephalus 384
S. polyanthemoides 382
S. pterophorus 382
S. radicans 386
S. sarcoides 386
S. speciosus 382
S. spiraeifolius 384
S. tamoides 384
S. umbellatus 382
Serruria 178
S. acrocarpa 180
S. decipiens 180
S. fasciflora 180
S. fucifolia 180
S. villosa 180
Sesamum 438
S. alatum 438
S. capense 438
S. triphyllum 438
Sisyndite 194
S. spartea 194
SOLANACEAE 226
Solanum 226
S. africanum 226
S. guineense 228
Sopubia 444
S. cana 444
Sparaxis 124
S. bulbifera 124
S. elegans 124
S. grandiflora 124
S. pillansii 124
S. tricolor 124
S. variegata 124
S. villosa 124
Spiloxene 96
S. aquatica 98
S. canaliculata 98
S. capensis 98
S. serrata 98
Staavia 342
S. radiata 342
Stachys 422
S. aethiopica 422

S. grandifolia 422
S. natalensis 422
S. rugosa 422
Stapelia 266
S. gigantea 266
S. grandiflora 266
S. hirsuta 266
Strelitzia 48
S. alba 48
S. caudata 48
S. juncea 48
S. nicolai 48
S. reginae 48
STRELITZIACEAE 48
Streptocarpus 442
S. cyaneus 442
S. dunnii 442
S. gardenii 442
S. primulifolius 442
S. rexii 442
Struthiola 250
S. argentea 250
S. ciliata 250
S. dodecandra 250
S. leptantha 250
S. myrsinites 250
S. striata 250
S. tomentosa 250
Stylochaeton 46
S. natalensis 46
Sutera 456
S. caerulea 456
S. uncinata 456
Sutherlandia 276
S. frutescens 278
Syncarpha 352
S. argentea 354
S. canescens 345, 354
S. eximia 354
S. paniculata 352
S. speciosissima 354
S. vestita 354
Syncolostemon 428
S. albiflorus 428
S. densiflorus 428
S. macranthus 428
S. parvifolius 428

T
Tecoma 440
T. capensis 440
TECOPHILAEACEAE 102
Tephrosia 280
T. grandiflora 280
T. macropoda 280
Tetradenia 420
T. barberae 420

T. brevispicata 420
T. riparia 420
Thunbergia 434
T. alata 436
T. atriplicifolia 434
T. natalensis 434
T. pondoensis 436
THYMELAEACEAE 246
Trachyandra 68
T. asperata 68
T. divaricata 70
T. falcata 68
T. muricata 70
T. revoluta 70
T. saltii 68
Tribulus 194
T. cristatus 196
T. terrestris 194
Tricliceras 212
T. lacerata 212
T. longipedunculata 212
Trifolium 286
T. africanum 286
T. burchellianum 286
Tripteris aghillana 394
T. amplectens 394
T. hyoseroides 394
T. oppositifolia 394
Tritonia 126
T. crocata 126
T. deusta 126
T. disticha 126
T. drakensbergensis 126
T. flabellifolia 126
T. gladioloides 126
T. laxifolia 126
T. lineata 126
T. nelsonii 126
T. pallida 126
T. securigera 126
T. squalida 126
Tritoniopsis 138
T. antholyza 138
T. burchellii 138
T. triticea 138
Tulbaghia 52
T. acutiloba 52
T. alliacea 52
T. capensis 52
T. cernua 52
Turbina holubii 224
T. oblongata 224
TURNERACEAE 212
Tylecodon 236
T. grandiflorus 236
T. paniculatus 236
T. wallichii 236

U
Ursinia 378
U. anthemoides 378
U. cakilefolia 378
U. calenduliflora 378
U. chrysanthemoides 345, 378
U. paleacea 378
U. pilifera 378
U. speciosa 378
Utricularia 430
U. bisquamata 430
U. livida 430
UTRICULARIACEAE 430

V
VELLOZIACEAE 94
Veltheimia 92
V. bracteata 92
V. capensis 92
VERBENACEAE 416
Vernonia 356
V. amygdalina 356
V. capensis 345, 358
V. colorata 356
V. crataegifolia 356
V. hirsuta 356
V. mespilifolia 356
V. myriantha 356
V. natalensis 358
V. neocorymbosa 356
V. oligocephala 358
V. stipulacea 356
V. tigna 356
Vigna 282
V. unguiculata 282
V. vexillata 282
Viola 270
V. decumbens 270
VIOLACEAE 270

W
Wachendorfia 104
W. multiflora 104
W. paniculata 104
W. thyrsiflora 104
Wahlenbergia 326
W. androsacea 326
W. annularis 326
W. capensis 326
W. cuspidate 328
W. polytrichifolia 328
W. undulata 328
Watsonia 116
W. aletroides 116
W. borbonica 118
W. densiflora 118

W. fourcadei 118
W. knysnana 118, 120
W. laccata 116
W. lepida 118
W. meriana 120
W. pillansii 118, 120
W. schlechteri 120
W. strubeniae 118
W. tabularis 120
W. watsonioides 118
Wiborgia 298
W. fusca 298

W. mucronata 298
W. obcordata 300
Witsenia 106
W. maura 106
Wurmbea 100
W. elatior 100
W. stricta 100

X
Xenostegia 222
X. tridentata 222
Xerophyta 94

X. retinervis 94
X. viscosa 94
Xysmalobium 262
X. undulatum 262

Z
Zaluzianskya 452
Z. affinis 452
Z. crocea 452
Z. microsiphon 452
Z. villosa 452
Z. violacea 452

Zantedeschia 48
Z. aethiopica 48
Z. albomaculata 48
Z. jucunda 48
Z. pentlandii 48
Z. rehmannii 48
ZYGOPHYLLACEAE 194
Zygophyllum 196
Z. cordifolium 196
Z. flexuosum 196
Z. foetidum 196
Z. morgsana 196

INDEX TO COMMON NAMES

A
Aalwyn 74
Aambeibossie 256
Aandblom 130
Aardboontjie 330
Aasblom 266
Aas-uintjie 112
Acanthosis 430
ACANTHUS FAMILY 430
Adenium 258
Adhatoda 432
African Blue-bell 326
African Clover 286
African Fumitory 270
African Mallow 216
African Potato 96
African Sage 418
African Stachys 422
African Sugarbush 168
AFRICAN VIOLET FAMILY 442
Afrikaanse Salie 418
Agapanthus 52
AGAPANTHUS FAMILY 52
Agretjie 126
Agtdaegeneesbos 228
Albany Vlei Lily 62
Albertinia Pincushion 182
Aloe 74
ALOE FAMILY 66
Alpine Saffron Bush 246
Altydbos 342
AMARYLLIS FAMILY 54
Amellus 414
Aneilema 50
Anemone 186
Anemoon 186
Angelier 252
Annual Bulbine 68
Annual Euryops 390
ANTHERICUM FAMILY 66

Antherotoma 324
Apatesia 306
APONOGETON FAMILY 46
Apple-blossom Orchid 160
April Fool 58
Arctopus 340
Arctotheca 376
Arctotis 370
Arid Pincushion 182
Aristea 106
ARUM FAMILY 46
Arum Lily 48
Aster 412
Asterjie 410
Astral Pachycarpus 260
Asystasia 436
Athrixia 408
Aunt Eliza 136
Autumn Star 96

B
Bababoudjies 320
Babiana 132
Baker's Aster 412
Ballerina 132
Balloon Pea 276
Balsam Apple 322
BALSAM FAMILY 272
Banded Aloe 80
Bandjiesbos 236
Barberton Daisy 406
Barleria 436
Baroe 330
Basbos 248
Bastergeelhongerblom 380
Bauhinia 276
Baur's Hesperantha 132
Beach-bean 282
Beaded Ice Plant 316
Bearded Nemesia 466
Beesmelkbos 232

Beetle Daisy 366
Beetle Lily 100
Begonia 320
BEGONIA FAMILY 320
Bell Agapanthus 52
Belladonna 62
BELLFLOWER FAMILY 326
Belskruie 398
Bergharpuisbos 390
Bergmagriet 378
Bergroos 216
Berzelia 340
Bicoloured Pineapple Lily 90
Bietou 392
BIGNONIA FAMILY 440
Bindweed 222
Birdflower 292
Bird-of-Paradise Flower 48
Bitteraalwyn 76
Bitterbos 410, 416
Bitterbush 410
Bittergousblom 372
Bitterwortel 256
Blaasertjie 276
Black-bearded Protea 174
Black-bud Indigo 278
Black-eyed Berg Lily 86
Black-eyed Bindweed 222
Black-eyed Susan 436
Black-faced Orchid 156
Black-stick Lily 94
BLACK-STICK LILY FAMILY 94
Black-thorned Aloe 80
Bladder Hibiscus 220
Bladderwort 430
BLADDERWORT FAMILY 430
Blepharis 430
Bloedwortel 104

Blombiesie 108
Blood Flower 58
Blood Lily 56, 58
Bloodroot 104
BLOODROOT FAMILY 104
Blou Afrikaner 142
Blouaalwyn 80
Bloublommetjie 410
Bloublomsalie 418
Bloudisseldoring 366
Bloukalossie 122
Bloukelkie 130
Bloukeurtjie 284
Blouklokkie 138, 326
Bloukwasbossie 356
Bloulelie 52
Bloupypie 140
Blouriet 192
Blousuurkanol 106
Blousyselbos 226
Blou-uintjie 116
Blue Boys 426
Blue Commelina 50
Blue Disa 162
Blue Justicia 432
Blue Nemesia 464
Blue Pea 284
Blue Sage 418
Blue Sceptre 106
Blue Sequins 130
Blue Squill 88
Blue Thunbergia 434
Blue Tulp 114
Blue Waterlily 46
Blue-eyed Felicia 412
Blue-eyed Grass 108
Blushing Bride Orchid 154
Bobbejaanarm 190
Bobbejaanklimop 388
Bobbejaankool 388
Bobbejaanstert 94

Bobbejaantjie 132
Bobbejaantoontjies 386
Bobbejaanuintjie 200
Boegoe 212
Boertee 300
Boesmanpyp 264
Boesmanskers 202
Boesmanstee 408
Bokbaaivygie 304
Bokhorinkies 264, 468
Bokmakieriestert 106
Boneseed 392
Bonnet Orchid
Bontaalwyn 80
Bontrokkie 132
Bontviooltjie 92
Bosastertjie 410
Bosklimop 282
Bosluisbessie 392
Bosmagriet 396
Bosveld Slymlelie 84
Bot River Protea 170
Botterboom 236
Brakslaai 304
Brandbossie 246
Brandui 82
Broad-leaved Chascanum
    416
Broad-leaved Grass Aloe 78
Broad-leaved Minaret
    Flower 424
Broad-leaved Pentanisia
    324
Broad-leaved Stargrass 96
Broad-leaved Sugarbush
    170
BROOMRAPE FAMILY 442
Brown Bonnets 288
Brown Sage 420
Bruinsalie 420
Brunia 342
BRUNIA FAMILY 340
Bryce's Geranium 202
Buchu 212
BUDDLEJA FAMILY 268
Bug-catcher Bush 280
Bugle Plant 422
Bulbine 66
Bulbinella 70
Burchell's Clover 286
Burchell's Sugarbush
    172
Bursting Beauty 322
Bush Arctotis 374
Bush Iris 106
Bush Lily 56
Bush Tea 300

Bush Turbina 224
Bush Violet 422, 438
Bushman's Candle 204
Bushman's Tea 408
Bushveld Arum 46
Bushveld Crossandra 432
Bushveld Monsonia 204
Bushveld Slime Lily 84
Bushveld Spur Bush 424
Buttercup 186
Butterfly Bush 274
Butterfly Gladiolus 146
Butterfly Lily 104
Butterfly Lobelia 334
Butterfly Monopsis 334
Buttons 402

C
Cadaba 190
Calla 48
Callilepis 406
Canary Creeper 384
Canavalia 282
Candelabra Lily 62
Cape Agapanthus 52
Cape Anemone 188
Cape Bindweed 222
Cape Cowslip 92
Cape Everlasting 354
Cape Forget-me-not
    232
Cape Garlic 52
Cape Gazania 370
Cape Gorse 296
Cape Honeysuckle 440
Cape Kokerboom 76
Cape Marigold 376
Cape Poker 72
Cape Primrose 442
Cape Scabious 416
Cape Snapdragon 466
Cape Snow 354
Cape Speckled Aloe 80
Cape Star 96
Cape Sweetpea 282, 302
Cape Twinspur 468
Cape Weed 376
CARNATION FAMILY 252
Carpanthea 306
Carpet Bellflower 328
Carrion-flower 266
CARROT FAMILY 338
Cat's Whiskers 428
Cat's-tail Aloe 76
Catherine-wheel
    Pincushion 186
Centaury 256

Cephalaria 416
Cephalophyllum 310
Ceropegia 264
Chascanum 416
Cheiridopsis 316
Chestnut Sugarbush 168
China Flower 210
Chincherinchee 86
Chinese Lantern Lily 98
Christmas Bells 98
Christmas Berry 256
Cigarettes 316
Cineraria 386
Cistus-flowered Bushman's
    Candle 204
CITRUS FAMILY 210
Clematis 188
Cleome 190
Cleretum 306
Cliff Gladiolus 138
Climbing Aneilema 50
Climbing Foxglove 442
Clivia 56
Clockflower 112
Clover 286
Club-spurred Nemesia
    464
Cluster Disa 162
Cobra Lily 136
Codon 228
COFFEE FAMILY 324
COLCHICUM FAMILY 98
Commelina 50
COMMELINA FAMILY 50
Common Agapanthus 52
Common Blue Moraea 114
Common Buttercup 186
Common Candelabra
    Lily 62
Common Cape Nerine 64
Common Cone Plant 318
Common Devil's-thorn 194
Common Gazania 370
Common Grass Aristea 108
Common Grassland
    Monsonia 202
Common Grassland
    Sugarbush 168
Common Ledebouria 88
Common Liquorice Bean
    290
Common Marsh Poker 72
Common Pagoda 178
Common Pin Spiderhead
    180
Common Pineapple Lily 90
Common Pink Plume 428

Common Pink Sorrel 198
Common Rootstock
    Spiderhead 180
Common Silkypuff 180
Common Speckled
    Gladiolus 144
Common Spotted Aloe 82
Common Stargrass 96
Common Turkey Bush 272
Common Wild Nemesia
    464
Concertina Plant 234
Cone Bush 174
Cone Plant 318
Confetti Strawflower 352
Conicosia 306
CONVOLVULUS FAMILY 222
Cooper's Grass Aloe 78
Cooper's Ledebouria 88
Cooper's Rhynchosia 286
Coral Aloe 80
Cotyledon 238
Cowled Friar 156
Cowpea 282
Crane Flower 48
CRANE FLOWER FAMILY 48
Crane's-bill 200
Crassula 234
CRASSULA FAMILY 234
Creeping Sage 418
Crested Hermannia 214
Crimson Streptocarpus 442
Crocosmia 136
Crossandra 430
CUCUMBER FAMILY 322
Curry Bush 252
CYANELLA FAMILY 102
Cyphia 330

D
Dainty Pavonia 216
Daisy Bush 408
DAISY FAMILY 344
DAPHNE FAMILY 246
Dark Blue Pycnostachys
    426
Dark-eyed Bellflower 326
Dark-eyed Dwarf Hibiscus
    218
Dark-eyed Windowseed
    394
Dassiegousblom 394
Delosperma 312
Desert Broom 194
Desert Primrose 322
DESERT PRIMROSE FAMILY
    322

Desert Rose 214
Desmodium 280
Devil Orchid 152
Devil's-thorn 194
Dialstee 404
Dicoma 358
Dierama 122
Dietes 110
Disa 160
Dissotis 326
Doll's Powderpuff 50
Doll's Protea 358
Doll's Rose 214
Dongola Hibiscus 220
Doringbossie 358
Doringpapawer 188
Dorotheanthus 304
Doublom 190
Douvygie 312
Douwurmbos 230
Draaibos 410
Drakensberg Aster 412
Drakensberg Carnation 252
Drakensberg Cliff Hesperantha 132
Drakensberg Nemesia 464
Drakensberg Purple Drumsticks 452
Drakensberg Sugarbush 170
Drakensberg Tritonia 126
Drakensberg Watsonia 118
Drip Disa 164
Dronkbessie 226
Drooping Agapanthus 54
Drosanthemum 312
Drumstick Flower 452
Duikerwortel 322
Dune Morning Glory 224
Dwarf Arum Lily 48
Dwarf Blood Lily 56
Dwarf Cassia 276
Dwarf Dissotis 324
Dwarf Grassland Sugarbush 168
Dwarf Hibiscus 220
Dwarf Pineapple Lily 90

E
Eastern River Bells 456
Ecklon's Commelina 50
Edging Lobelia 336
Edmondia 354
Elephant Trunk 258
Elephantine Ceropegia 264
Elim Heath 242

ERICA FAMILY 240
Erica-leaved Sage Bush 428
Eriosema 288
Ertjiebos 274
Eumorphia 398
Euphorbia 232
EUPHORBIA FAMILY 232
Euryops 390
Everlasting 352

F
Fairy-bell Pachycarpus 260
Falling Stars 136
False Buckwheat 434
False Cotula 402
False Everlasting 356
False Gentian 258
False Gerbera 376
False Nerine 64
False Slugwort 450
Fan Flower 338
FAN FLOWER FAMILY 338
Featherhead 250
Felicia 410
Fenestrate Cone Plant 318
Fern-leaved Cephalaria 416
Fern-leaved Groundsel 384
Fibrous Slime Lily 84
Fire Daisy 414
Fire Heath 240
Fire Lily 54
Fireball Lily 58
Fish Bean 280
Flame Lily 98
Flanagan's Geranium 202
Flanagan's Gooseneck Flower 454
Fleshy-leaved Pink Sorrel 198
Flissie 120
Flowering Ivy 384
Fluweeltjie 124
Fly Bush 428
Fonteinbos 284, 342
Forest Cineraria 386
Forest Iris 110
Forest Nemesia 462
Forest Primrose 252
Forest Rattle Pod 292
Forest Spur-flower 426
Forget-me-not 230
FORGET-ME-NOT FAMILY 228
Foster's Spotted Aloe 82
Fragrant Candelabra Lily 62
Freesia 120

Fried Egg Orchid 162
Froetang 128
FUMITORY FAMILY 270

G
Gansiebos 262
Gansies 306
Ganskos 402
Gazania 368
Geel Piesang 48
Geelgesiggies 468
Geelhongerblom 380
Geelklokkie 98
Geelkruid 392
Geelmagriet 378
Geelmelkbos 232
Geeloogsuring 198
Geelsneeu 404
Geelsuring 198
Geeltee 404
Geeltjienk 86
Geelvarkoor 48
Geldjiesbos 196
GENTIAN FAMILY 254
George Lily 54
Geranium 200
GERANIUM FAMILY 200
Gerbera 404
Ghaap 268
Ghost Orchid 150
Giant Anemone 188
Giant Candelabra Lily 62
Giant Chincherinchee 86
Giant Ledebouria 90
Giant Nerine 64
Giant Pineapple Lily 90
Giant Rhynchosia 286
Giant Stapelia 266
Giant Tinsel Flower 338
Giant Vygie 310
Giant White Ornithogalum 86
Gifbossie 246
Gladiolus 138
Golden Orchid 162
Golden Spiderhead 180
Golden Vlei Moraea 114
Golden-haired Morning Glory 224
Gooseneck Flower 454
Gordon's Bay Pincushion 182
Gousblom 368, 370, 372, 376
Granaat 440
Grand Duchess Sorrel 198
Grand Pachycarpus 260

Granny Bonnet 158
Graskop Aloe 76
Graskop Cloud Aloe 78
Graslelie 66
Grass Lily 66
Grassland Barleria 436
Grassland Cross-flower 192
Grass-leaved Berkheya 362
Grass-leaved Nerine 64
Greater Bellflower 326
Greater Gooseneck Flower 454
Greater Salad Thistle 360
Greater Twinspur 468
Green Heath 242
Green Sugarbush 174
Green Wood Orchid 150
Green-tipped Fire Lily 54
Grey Cineraria 386
Grey Stachys 422
Grey-leaved Chincherinchee 86
Grey-leaved Poker 72
Grey-leaved Sugarbush 172
Grey-leaved Tickberry 392
Grootbergmagriet 378
Grootblousalie 418
Grootdissel 364
Grootharpuisbos 390
Grootstinkkruid 400
Ground Lily 60
Ground Protea 166
Groundsel 380
Grysastertjie 414
Grysbietou 392
Guernsey Lily 64

H
Haarbossie 368
Haasoor 266
Hairbell 122
Halfmens 258
Handjiesbos 382
Handkerchief Flower 446
Hangertjie 240
Hantam Purple Drumsticks 452
Haplocarpha 376
Harlequin Orchid 148
Harlequin-flower 124
Harpuisbos 390
Harvey's Aster 412
Heart-leaved Eriosema 288
Heart-leaved Twinspur 466
Heath 240
Hedgehog Sage 426
Heide 240

483

Hellthorn 204
Hemimeris 468
Hemp-leaved Hibiscus 222
Hen-and-chickens 66
Herfspypie 138
Hesperantha 130
Heuningblom 272
Heuningtee 300
Hibiscus 218
HIBISCUS FAMILY 214
Highveld Marsh Poker 72
Hilton Daisy 406
Hirpicium 368
Hoenderbos 210
Honeybush Tea 300
Honeyflower 272
Hongerblom 380
Hooded Meadow-star 262
Hoodia 268
Horehound 424
Horse Mint 420
Hottentotsuintjie 114
HYACINTH FAMILY 82

I
Iboza 420
Ice Plant 304
ICE PLANT FAMILY 304
Impala Lily 258
Impatiens 272
Inanda Lily 54
Indigo 278
Ink Pea 300
Ink Plant 446
Inkblom 446
Inkflower 446
Inkpotjie 110
IRIS FAMILY 106
Ivy-leaved Geranium 208
Ixia 122

J
Jaagsiektebossie 292
Jakkalsbietou 398
Jamesbrittenia 458
Jeukbol 82
Jongmansknoop 416
Jordaaniella 310
Juffertjie-roer-by-die-nag
   250
Justicia 432

K
Kaaldissel 364
Kalanchoe 238, 240
Kalkoentjie 126, 140
Kalossie 122

Kamiesberg Arctotis 372
Kandelaar 62
Kandelaarbos 236
Kaneeltjie 204
Kanferblaar 210
Kankerbos 278
Kannetjies 264
Kanniedood 80
Kapok Lily 94
Karkaarblom 138
Karoo Arctotis 372
Karoo Iris 114
Karoo Nemesia 464
Karoo Rhigozum 440
Karoo Rose 214
Karoo Snow 304
Karoo Violet 454
Katbossie 422
Katjietee 126
Katnaels 448
Katoenbos 262
Katstert 70
Kattekruie 424
Keeled Indigo 280
Kei Lily 54
Keiserkroon 236
Kerriebossie 246
Kersbos 204
Keurtjie 302
Kewerlelie 100
Khakibutton 234
King Protea 170
Klappertjies 270
Kleinganskos 402
Klimop 222
Klipblom 236, 462
Klokkiebos 214
Klossiedissel 364
Knikkertjie 128
Knoppies 402
Knysna Lily 54
Kokerboom 76
Kolkol 340
Koningskandelaar 62
Kopieva 66, 68
Koringblommetjie 124
Kouteriebos 238
Kransaalwyn 78
Kreupelhout 184
Kroesbossie 274
Kruidjie-roer-my-nie 272
Kruipsalie 418
Krulletjie 110
Kudu Lily 258
Kusgousblom 374
Kusmalva 210
Kwaslelie 58

L
Lachenalia 90
Lady's Hand 102
Lady's Slipper 270
Lampranthus 314
LANARIA FAMILY 94
Large Blue Sage 418
Large Blue Squill 88
Large Brown Afrikaner 140
Large Liquorice Bean 290
Large Pink Mushroom
   Flower 446
Large Pink Strawflower 350
Large Pink Watsonia 118
Large Salmon Gladiolus
   146
Large Slugwort 450
Large Snake-head 84
Large Spur-flower 426
Large Stapelia 266
Large White Forest Iris 110
Large White Inkflower 446
Large White Pachycarpus
   260
Large Yellow Moraea 114
Large Yellow Wild Hibiscus
   220
Large-flowered Climbing
   Foxglove 442
Large-flowered Pink Plume
   428
Large-flowered Tephrosia
   280
Large-leaved Stachys 422
Lazy Daisy 400
Leadwort 226
Leafy-flowered Morning
   Glory 224
Lebeckia 290
Ledebouria 88
Leeubekkie 462
Leipoldt's Nemesia 466
Lemoenbloeisels 188
Lepelblom 142
Lesotho Cornflag 144
Lesotho Poker 72
Lesser Bellflower 326
Lesser Gooseneck Flower
   454
Lesser Salad Thistle 360
Lesser Yellow-head 246
Lewertjie 278
Leysera 404
Lilac Disa 164
Lilac Mist 466
Lilac Nemesia 466
Lilac Pachycarpus 260

Lion's Eye 212
Liquorice Bean 290
Little Painted Lady 142
Littonia 98
Livingstone Daisy 304
Lobelia 334
Lobostemon 228
Long-eared Nemesia 464
Long-horned False
   Gentian 260
Long-horned Twinspur 468
Lotononis 294
Luisbos 230
Lyperia 460

M
Maagbossie 108
Maagwortel 358
Maartblom 62
Macledium 358
Maerbos 196
Maerman 82
Magriet 378, 396
Malgas Lily 60
Malgaslelie 60
Malva 204
Mandarin Poker 74
Manulea 460
March Pagoda 178
Marguerite 396
Maritzwater 322
Marsh Afrikaner 140
Marsh Dissotis 326
Mauve Manulea 462
Meadow Flower 100
Mealie Heath 242
Medusa's Head 232
Melasma 444
MELIANTHUS FAMILY 272
Melkbos 232
Melktou 264
Men-in-a-boat 100
Mielieheide 242
Milkweed 262
MILKWEED FAMILY 258
Milkwort 262
Minaret Flower 424
Mint 420
MINT FAMILY 418
Misryblom 58
Misty Plume 420
Mitre Aloe 78
Moederkappie154, 158
Mole's Spectacles 462
Monilaria 316
Monkey-tail Everlasting
   350

Monkshood Orchid 156
Monopsis 332
Monsonia 202
Montbretia 136
Montinia 320
MONTINIA FAMILY 320
Moore's River Lily 60
Mop-headed Berkheya 364
Moraea 110
Morning Glory 224
Moss-leaved Bellflower 328
Mountain Aloe 76
Mountain Dahlia 302
Mountain Daisy 398
Mountain Spur-flower 426
Mountain Fumitory 270
Mountain Mallow 218
Mountain Nemesia 464
Mountain Pea 302
Mountain Rose 166
Muden Spotted Aloe 82
Muishondghaap 268
Mushroom Flower 446
MUSTARD FAMILY 190

N
Namakwakannetjies 264
Namaqua Creeping Vygie 310
Namaqua Gazania 370
Namaqua Groundsel 380
Namaqua Kalkoentjie 140
Namaqua Nemesia 464
Namaqua Parachute Daisy 378
Namaqua River Lily 60
Namaqua Stork's-bill 206
Namaqua Turkey Bush 272
Namaqua Twinspur 468
Namaqua Windowseed 394
Namaqualand Arctotis 372
Namaqualand Beauty 206
Namaqualand Daisy 398
Namaqualand Felicia 412
Namaqualand Sage 418
Narrow-leaved Bulbine 68
Narrow-leaved Minaret Flower 424
Narrow-leaved Sugarbush 172
Narrow-leaved Twinspur 468
Narrow-leaved Vernonia 358
Nasturtium-leaved Buttercup 186
Natal Blue Bell 434

Natal Ivy 384
Natal Lily 144
Natal Primrose 434
Natal River Lily 60
Needle-leaved Pincushion 184
Nelson's Slime Lily 84
Nelspruit Rock Aloe 80
Nemesia 462
Nerina 64
Nerine 64
New Year Lily 144
Ninepin Heath 240
Northern Purple Drumsticks 452
Northern Spiderhead 180
Northern White Lady 238
Nylandtia 274

O
Oftia 456
Oktoberlelie 150
Oliebossie 438
ONION FAMILY 52
Orange Desmodium 280
Orange Poppy 188
Orange River Lily 60
Orange Tritonia 126
ORCHID FAMILY 146
Oscularia 316
Ossetong 232
Otholobium 284
Othonna 388
Otterbossie 268
Overberg Pincushion 182
OXALIS FAMILY 198

P
Pachycarpus 260
Pachypodium 258
Pagoda Bush 178
Pagoda-flowered Berkheya 364
Paintbrush Lily 58
Painted Lady 142
Pale Blue Pycnostachys 426
Pale Harlequin-flower 124
Pale Yellow Eriosema 288
Pansy Lobelia 332
Pansy Monopsis 332
Papierblom 226
Parachute Daisy 378
Parrot Gladiolus 144
Partridge Aloe 80
Partridge Moraea 116
Patrysblom 100

Pavonia 216
PEA FAMILY 276
Peacock Flower 98
Peacock Moraea 116
Pebble Plant 318
Pelargonium 204
PENAEA FAMILY 244
Pencilled Tritonia 126
Penny-leaved Twinleaf 196
Pennypod 298
Pensies 466
Pentanisia 324
Peperbos 320
Pepper-and-salt Flower 100
Perdebos 360
Perdekapok 94
Pers Inkblom 448
Perskalkoentjie 142
Peultjiesbos 190
Piempiempie 136
Pienksewejaartjie 354
Pienk-trewwa 154
Pienkvarkoor 48
Pietsnot 322
Pilgrim's Rest Pink Sage 418
Pincushion 182, 184
Pincushion Lotononis 294
Pineapple Lily 90
Pine-leaved Lobelia 334
Pink 252
Pink Candle Orchid 154
Pink Everlasting 354
Pink Forest Hibiscus 218
Pink Gerbera 406
Pink Ground-bells 444
Pink Lady's Slipper 270
Pink Plume 428
Pink Strawflower 352
Pink Trailing Pelargonium 206
Platdoring 340
Plectranthus 426
Ploegtydblommetjie 96
Plumbago 226
PLUMBAGO FAMILY 226
Podranea 440
Poison Squill 82
Poker Grass Aloe 78
Pokkiesblom 216
POLYGALA FAMILY 274
Pondblossom 46
Poppy 188
POPPY FAMILY 188
Poppy-flowered Sundew 190
Poprosie 214

Porseleinblom 210
Port St John's Creeper 440
POTATO FAMILY 226
Powderpuff 450
Pride-of-De Kaap 276
Primrose Gentian 254
Prince-of-Wales Heath 242
Prismatocarpus 330
Pronkharpuisbos 390
Protea 166
PROTEA FAMILY 166
Purple Berkheya 366
Purple Chironia 256
Purple Gorse 274
Purple Hermannia 216
Purple Ribbon Bush 434
Pycnostachys 426
Pyjama Flower 100
Pypie 138
Pypkalossie 122

Q
Quilted-leaved Vernonia 356

R
Raaptol 102
Rabbit's Ears 58
Rankbietou 396
RANUNCULUS FAMILY 186
Raphionacme 258
Rattle Pod 292
Red Bush Indigo 278
Red Crassula 236
Red Disa 162
Red Heath 244
Red Hibiscus 218
Red Nerine 64
Red Sage 420
Red Star 96
Red Treasure 234
Red Tritonia 126
Red-hot Poker 72
Redlegs 340
Reënblommetjie 398
Renostergousblom 372
Resin Bush 390
Rhigozum 440
Rhynchopsidium 404
Rhynchosia 286
Ribbokblom 140
Ribbon Bush 434
Ribbon Pincushion 184
Ribbon-leaved Nerine 64
Rietpypie 138
River Bells 454
River Lily 60

485

River Poker 74
River Stars 268
Rivierharpuisbos 390
Rivierklokkie 454
Rock Daisy 402
Rock Flower 462
Rocket Pincushion 186
Roella 328
Roemanaggie 250
Rogeria 440
Roggeveld Arctotis 372
Roggeveld Poker 74
Romulea 128
Rooi Afrikaner 140
Rooibeentjies 340
Rooibergpypie 138
Rooiblom 430
Rooibobbejaantjie 134
Rooihaartjie 240
Rooiheide 244
Rooi-inkblom 448
Rooikanol 104
Rooikappie 154
Rooiklossieheide 240
Rooimalva 208
Rooinaeltjie 92
Rooisalie 420
Rooisewejaartjie 356
Rooisterretjie 96
Rooistompie 178
Rooisuikerblom 236
Rooitrewwa 154
Rosette Berkheya 362
Rotstert 136
Round-pod Rattle Bush 292
Royal Berg Lily 86
Ruiksissie 236
Ruik-trewwa 154
Ruschia 314
Rush Iris 108
Ruttya 432
Rysblommetjie 100

S
Sabie Star 258
Sabie Watsonia 118
Saffraan 246
Saffron Bush 246
Sage 418
Sage Bush 428
Salad Thistle 360
Saldanha Bay Felicia 410
Saldanha Pincushion 182
Salie 418
Saltera 244
Sambreeltjie 202
Sambreeltjies 412

Sandlelie 92
Sandpypie 142
Sandroos 216
Sandsteenvygie 316
Sandsuring 198
Sandveld Pincushion 182
Sandveld Spiderhead 180
Sandveldgousblom 370
Sandviooltjie 92
Satinflower 130
Satyr Orchid 152
Scabious 416
SCABIOUS FAMILY 416
Scarlet Broomrape 448
Scarlet Eriosema 288
Scarlet Pelargonium 208
Scarlet River Lily 132
Schlechter's Geranium 202
Scrambling Twinleaf 196
Sea Pumpkin 376
Sea Rose 256
Sea Strawflower 352
Sea-pink 226
Sebaea 254
See-plakkie 338
Sentkannetjie 234
Septemberbos 274
Serpentine Moraea 112
Sesame 438
SESAME FAMILY 438
Sewejaartjie 352, 354
Showy Geranium 202
Shrubby Eriosema 288
Sieketroos 340
Silky-haired Pincushion 186
Silkypuff 180
Silver Everlasting 354
Silver Pagoda 178
Silver Sugarbush 170
Silver Tree 174
Silver Vernonia 358
Silver-leaved Stargrass 94
Silver-margined
  Strawflower 352
Silvery Sopubia 444
Sjielingbos 196
Skaamblom 302
Skaapbos 394
Skaapbostee 284
Skaapvygie 312
Skietpit 430
Skilpadbessie 274
Skilpadbos 196
Skilpadteebossie 404
Skollie 166
Skraaldisseldoring 364
Skunk Bush 456

Slaaibos 360
Slakblom 450
Slangkop 84, 86
Slender Poker 74
Slime Lily 84
Slugwort 450
Slymbos 196
Slymlelie 84
Small Black-stick Lily 94
Small Forest Iris 110
Small Pink Mushroom
  Flower 446
Small Salmon Gladiolus 146
Small St John's Wort 252
Small White Poker 74
Small Wild Gladiolus 144
Snake Thistle 360
Snake-stemmed
  Pincushion 184
Snotrosie 190
Snout Orchid 146
Soap Aloe 80
Social Ledebouria 88
Soetgonna 250
Soetkalkoentjie 140
Soetuintjie 114
Sonder's Begonia 320
Sopubia 444
Sorrel 198
Sosaties 234
Sour Fig 308
Southern Purple
  Drumsticks 452
Sparaxis 124
Speckled Spur-flower 426
Spekbos 196
Speldekussing 182
Spider Lily 110
Spider Orchid 152
Spiderhead 178
Spike Lily 100
Spinnekopblom 110
Spinnekopbos 178
Spiny Berg-thistle 364
Sporrie 192
Spotted Sorrel 200
Spotted Squill 88
Spotted Strawflower 352
Spotted-leaved Arum
  Lily 48
Springbok Windowseed
  394
Spur Bush 424
Spur-flower 426
St John's Wort 252
ST JOHN'S WORT FAMILY
  252

Staavia 342
Starburst Pelargonium 206
Stargrass 94
STARGRASS FAMILY 94
Steekhaarbos 360
Steelvrug 330
Steenbokboegoe 212
Stekelkruid 430
Stekeltee 296
Sterretjie 96
Sticky Everlasting 348
Sticky Heath 244
Sticky-leaved Groundsel 384
Sticky-leaved Monopsis 332
Stiff-leaved Stargrass 94
Stinging Hibiscus 220
Stinkbietou 394
Stinkblaarsuikerbos 172
Stinkbossie 456
Stinkkruid 400
Stinkweed 400
Stompie 178
Stone Plant 320
Stonecrop 234
Strand Gazania 368
Strandhongerblom 380
Strandlelie 134
Strandroos 226
Strandsalie 420
Strandvygie 310
Strap-leaved Bulbine 68
Strap-leaved Sugarbush 174
Strawberry Everlasting 354
Strawflower 348
Streptanthera 124
Streptocarpus 442
Striped Aloe 76
Strooiblom 348
Stroopbossie 250
Sugarbush 166, 170
Suikerbos 170
Suikerkannetjie 142
Suikerkelk 228
Sundew 190
SUNDEW FAMILY 190
Sunflax 192
Suring 198
SUTERA FAMILY 450
Sutherlandia 278
Suurkanol 116
Suurvy 308
Swartoognooi 436
Swartstormbos 190
Swartteebossie 356
Sweet Basil 428
Syblom 130
Sysie 130

T

Taaigousblom 374
Table Mountain Watsonia 120
Tall White Squill 82
Tamarak 84
Tawny-haired Dwarf Hibiscus 220
Teebos 422
Tephrosia 280
Terblansbossie 220
Thode's Poker 74
Thode's Tinsel Flower 338
Thread-leaved Bindweed 222
Thread-leaved Sorrel 200
Thunbergia 434
TIBOUCHINA FAMILY 324
Tickberry 392
Tinderleaf 340
Tinsel Flower 338
Tjienk 86
Toad Plant 266
Tolbos 174
Tontelblaar 340
Tonteldoek 376
Toontjies 318
Trachyandra 68
Trailing Daisy 408
Trailing Dwarf Cassia 276
Transvaal Anemone 188
Transvaal Balsam 272
Transvaal Blister-leaf 188
Transvaal Clivia 56
Traveller's Joy 188
Tree Orchid 146
Tree Pagoda 178
Tree Vernonia 356
Trembling Heath 242
Trewwa 152
Trilheide 242
Tritonia 126
Tritoniopsis 138
Trompetters 140, 440
True-blue Daisy 412
Tufted Stone Plant 320
Tulbagh Bell 138
Tulp 110, 112
Turbina 224
Turkey Bush 272
TURNERA FAMILY 212
Twinleaf 196
TWINLEAF FAMILY 194
Twinspur 466
Two-lipped Drumsticks 452
Two-tiered Pelargonium 206

Tylecodon 236
Tyson's Poker 72

U

Uzura 262

V

Vaalbietou 362
Vaaldissel 362
Vaalstompie 342
Vaaltee 422
Vaaltol 342
Varicoloured Nemesia 466
Varingblom 406
Varklelie 48
Varkoor 238
Varkslaai 306
Veerheide 242
Veertjie 250
Veld Cineraria 380
Veld Violet 436
Veldkool 68
Veldskoenblaar 58
Veltheimia 92
Velvet Bean 280
VERBENA FAMILY 416
Verfblommetjie 444, 452
Vernonia 356
Vetkousie 306
Vierkleurtjie 92
Vine-leaved Hibiscus 220
Vingerpol 232
Vingertjies 460
Violet 270
VIOLET FAMILY 270
Viooltjie 90
Visboontjie 280
Vlam-van-die-vlakte 276
Vlei Cabbage 382
Vlei Disa 160
Vlei Orchid 148
Vleiklapper 262
Vleiknoppiesbos 340
Vleipypie 144
Vlei-uintjie 114
Vlieëbossie 244
Volstruisies 342
Volstruisuintjie 112
Volstruisvygie 310
Vuuraster 414
Vuurlelie 54
Vuurpyl 72
Vygie 314

W

Waaiertjie 106
Waboom 168

Warty-stemmed Pincushion 184
Waspypie 120
Water Hawthorn 46
Water Heath 242
Water Mint 420
Waterblommetjie 46
Waterbos 242
Waterlily 46
WATERLILY FAMILY 46
Waterlily Sugarbush 170
Watersterretjie 98
Watsonia 116, 118
Wax Creeper 264
West Coast Gazania 368
Western River Bells 456
White Afrikaner 142
White Arum Lily 48
White Berg Lily 86
White Berkheya 366
White Bush Arctotis 374
White Bushveld Barleria 438
White Geranium 202
White Hermannia 214
White Lady 238
White Mushroom Flower 446
White Paintbrush Lily 58
White Ribbon Bush 434
White Squill 88
White Stachys 422
White Stonecrop 234
White Thistle-leaved Berkheya 366
White Thunbergia 436
White-flowered Rogeria 440
Wild Balsam 272
Wild Banana 48
Wild Carnation 252
Wild Chamomile 400
Wild Chrysanthemum 400
Wild Cotton 262
Wild Cowpea 282
Wild Cucumber 322
Wild Foxglove 438
Wild Fumaria 270
Wild Garlic 52
Wild Geranium 200
Wild Orange Begonia 320
Wild Penstemon 444
Wild Pentas 324
Wild Scabious 416
Wild Spearmint 420
Wild Stock 192
Wild Sweetpea 282
Wild Thistle 362
Wild Tibouchina 326

Wild Violet 270, 332, 422
Wilde Kapok 262
Wilde Stokroos 222
Wildeaster 410
Wildedagga 424
Wildedissel 362
Wildegranaat 440
Wildekamille 400
Wildemagriet 406
Wildepynappel 90
Wildestokroos 218
Wildeviolette 290
Willow-leaved Eriosema 288
Willowy Slugwort 450
Winged Devil's-thorn 196
Wit Sporrie 194
Witch Orchid 158
Witgousblom 374
Witkoppie 100
Witmagriet 396
Witsenia 106
Witsôe 374
Wittamarak 84
Witteboom 174
Wolweghaap 268
Wolwekos 448
Wood Orchid 150
Wood's Aristea 108
Wood's Tinsel Flower 338
Woodland Painted Petals 120
Woundwort 422
Wurmbossie 400
Wynkelkie 130

Y

Yellow Arum Lily 48
Yellow Commelina 50
Yellow Crassula 234
Yellow Dobo Lily 56
Yellow Fire Lily 56
Yellow Gazania 370
Yellow Lobelia 332
Yellow Monopsis 332
Yellow Morning Glory 224
Yellow Mouse-whiskers 190
Yellow Trailing Pincushion 184
Yellow Watsonia 118
Yellow Witchweed 444
Yellowweed 392

Z

Zig-zag Crocosmia 136
Zonal Pelargonium 208
Zululand Crossandra 432

487

ILLUSTRATED GLOSSARY

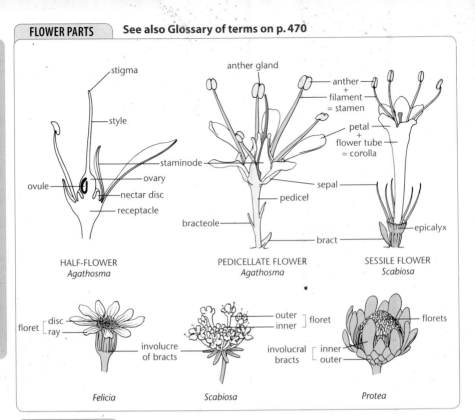

HALF-FLOWER
Agathosma

PEDICELLATE FLOWER
Agathosma

SESSILE FLOWER
Scabiosa

Felicia

Scabiosa

Protea

FLOWER SHAPES

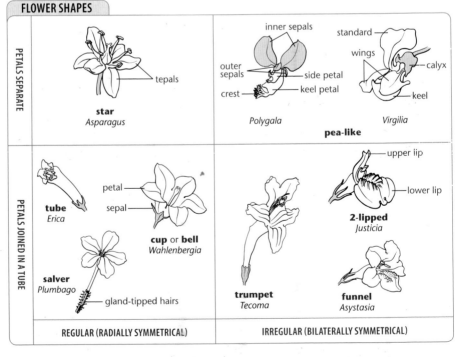

PETALS SEPARATE

star
Asparagus

Polygala

Virgilia

pea-like

PETALS JOINED IN A TUBE

tube
Erica

cup or **bell**
Wahlenbergia

salver
Plumbago

2-lipped
Justicia

trumpet
Tecoma

funnel
Asystasia

REGULAR (RADIALLY SYMMETRICAL)   IRREGULAR (BILATERALLY SYMMETRICAL)

ASTRONOMY ™

The Characteristics and the Life Cycle of Stars

An Anthology of Current Thought

Edited by Larry Krumenaker

The Rosen Publishing Group, Inc., New York

To D, L, J, and K, the constellation into which planet Z has always been welcome to wander.

Published in 2006 by The Rosen Publishing Group, Inc.
29 East 21st Street, New York, NY 10010

First Edition

Library of Congress Cataloging-in-Publication Data

The characteristics and the life cycle of stars: an anthology of current thought/edited by Larry Krumenaker.—1st ed.
    p. cm.—(Contemporary discourse in the field of astronomy)
ISBN 1-4042-0395-8 (library binding)
1. Stars.
I. Krumenaker, Larry. II. Series.
QB801.C45 2005
523.8—dc22

                         2004025550

Manufactured in the United States of America

On the cover: Bottom right: Hubble photograph of Unusual Planetary Nebula. Bottom left: Galileo Galilei. Center left: the Dumbell Nebula. Top right: solar flares.

CONTENTS

Introduction   **5**

1. Star Formation   **10**

"Style & Substance" by Ray Jayawardhana   11

"Rethinking an Astronomical Icon" by Ron Cowen   17

"Space Invaders" by Alexandra Goho   25

"Gorgeous Gas" by Ron Cowen   35

"A Stellar Relic from the Early Milky Way"
    by N. Christlieb, M. S. Bessell, T. C. Beers, B. Gustafsson,
    A. Korn, P. S. Barklem, T. Karlsson, M. Mizuno-
    Wiedner, and S. Rossi   41

**2. The Lives and Characteristics of Stars and
Their Planetary Systems**   **51**

"Solar System Like Ours Is Called 'Missing Link'"
    by Lee McFarling   52

"Solving the Solar Neutrino Problem" by Arthur B.
    McDonald, Joshua R. Klein, and David L. Wark   57

"Keep an Eye on Hypergiant Rho Cassiopeiae"
    by Alex Lobel   73

"Peering into Stardust" by A. G. Tielens   87

3. The End of Life for a Solar Mass Star   **95**

"When Stars Collide" by Michael Shara   96

"Butterflies and Crabs of the Southern Sky"
    by Sun Kwok   108

"Fluorine" by Ken Croswell   112

"Gems from the Stars" by Sun Kwok   123
"When a White Dwarf Explodes" by David Branch 133

4. The End of Life for a High Mass Star   **138**
"A Millennium of Shattered Stars"
   by F. Richard Stephenson and David A. Green   139
"Black Holes Reveal Their Innermost Secrets"
   by A. C. Fabian and J. M. Miller   153
"Black Hole's Velocity Links It to Supernova"
   by William Harwood   158
"Astronomers Link Gamma-Ray Bursts to Supernovas"
   by Dennis Overbye   162
"In the Line of Fire" by Steve Nadis   167

Web Sites   177
For Further Reading   178
Bibliography   179
Index   181

Introduction

The stars on a clear evening can thrill us with their beauty. Most of us enjoy a starry sky for aesthetic reasons alone, but a person with an inquiring mind might look at stars and wonder what they are and how they came to be. The answers to these questions are amazing, but the ways we get the answers are also amazing, especially considering that these answers come from three things we can observe about any star. These three things are its brightness in our sky, its position, and its colors. Astronomy is science at a distance; we cannot handle and experiment upon the objects of our interest. All we can do is gather the light of the stars and passively measure each star's color, brightness, and position.

The brightness of a star's light depends on two things: the star's true luminosity and its distance, which makes it appear brighter or fainter in our sky than it might actually be. A brilliant star can be close and dim or it can be a cosmic lighthouse at some faraway location. Measuring the brightness of stars over time often reveals variations that give us clues that something is happening to the star.

Perhaps, for example, it throbs in response to changes in size or a companion object's influence. If it is a young object, it may be pulsing erratically as its stellar furnaces stabilize or as it blows away an obscuring cocoon of dust. If it is old, it may be in its death throes, which may be mildly disruptive or totally explosive.

Stars may not change position in their constellations in a way that is noticeable during a human lifetime, but the stars do move, if minutely. These changes in position can indicate the orbit of a star around the galaxy or the presence of objects otherwise invisible to us. All objects have gravity, so when a single point of light fails to move along a straight line, we know something must be causing it to stray from the path. Could it be a planetary system? Perhaps it is the corpse of a dead companion, a neutron star or black hole with which the star travels in a macabre dance through space? This information can be revealed simply by tracking the position of the star in the sky.

The most precise tool in the astronomer's tool kit is the star's color. The overall color of the star is a clue to the star's temperature, but we can be more precise than that. By separating the light into a spectrum—a continuum of color resembling a rainbow—we can examine components of the star's light, including individual lines or wavelengths of color. The red lines of hydrogen light, the green glow of oxygen atoms, the yellow of sodium—these colors can reveal a lot about a star. Studying the color reveals the star's makeup and allows us to measure its temperature, quantity, and movement.

In fact, modern astronomical knowledge comes mostly by looking at stars in various parts of the spectrum. Not only do we study the visible colors, but we also study the components invisible to our eyes: radio waves, X-rays, gamma rays, and infrared and ultraviolet light. When we do, we see a far more interesting, less placid universe, a universe filled with violent star deaths and magnificent star creations. We solve mysteries about the origin of the atoms that make up our world and even our bodies. Humans are sometimes said to be star-stuff, and this star-stuff is looking out at itself to see where it came from.

All stars are created in stellar nurseries called nebulae. Enough material collects itself in space that its own gravity causes knots of gas to condense together into spheres that become hot enough to ignite in nuclear fusion and glow as stars. Disks of materials surrounding the spheres often form planetary systems.

Once a star stabilizes, most of the gas and dust of formation is ejected into space. The star itself burns hydrogen, its predominant constituent, into helium deep inside its core. This produces light and heat, and in a delicate balance between radiation pressure outward and gravity pulling inward, the star shines for millions or billions of years, depending on how much mass the star has. Heavier elements are built up inside the star.

Like everything else, all good things must come to an end. At some point the hydrogen fuel in the core is used up. If the star is solar-sized in mass (anything up to 1.4 solar masses), the star will expand into a red giant star, as large as Earth's orbit. The outside of the star is cool because it is so swollen and far from its hot core, now shrunken and burning helium, the ash of its hydrogen-burning days. The red giant phase is a temporary time of late-life glory. Shortly (in an astronomical time sense) the outer gases will be gently blown off into a planetary nebula, a beautiful fluorescing shell of debris more closely resembling a soap bubble and having nothing to do with planets at all. The star's insides shrink into a cooling white dwarf that harbors its last feeble amounts of energy into a miserly ghost of its former self, dimly glowing for billions of years before it becomes a dark ember.

Stars of more than 1.4 solar masses—high mass stars—experience a more spectacular demise. Following the red giant phase, the star's core collapses and tears the star apart as a supernova. For a few days or weeks, the one star can outshine the entire galaxy it is in, spewing gas; dust; heavy elements; and X-ray, gamma, and radio radiation into space. A small fragment of the star's core gets compressed into the nearly crystalline form of a neutron star or the gravitational trap of a black hole, from which not even light escapes. But surrounding these stellar corpses may be surviving companion stars and disks of material falling back into the well of gravity surrounding the former stars. These give us clues as to what is happening now around these once stable balls of light. Some of the material blown away in the explosions seeds the nebulae in the galaxy with new elements, some of which form stars and planets.

In this book we examine the lives of the stars in four segments. The first part looks at new research into how stars are formed and what they are like when they are young. The second chapter examines an area little mentioned in most astronomy texts—what goes on during the stable lives of the stars, which is the longest period of a star's life. It may not be as spectacular as a newly glowing nebula or the fireworks display of a star's death, but like the human life that occurs between birth and death, it is the most important period of a star's life cycle. The last two chapters present articles about the way stars die and what happens to their atoms when they do. One chapter foretells what will happen to our Sun by examining stars of one solar mass that have run their course ahead of us, while the final chapter looks into what happens to the behemoths of the sky, the heavy mass stars. That is not an altogether tragic story, for from these come the readers of the book, or at least their atoms. —*LK*

1

Star Formation

Though each season has its highlights, the skies of winter are perhaps the most brilliant and beautiful. The winter sky also tells a story, one that took years for humankind to understand. Look closely among the constellations of winter and you'll see that some objects are clearly different. Sometimes the difference is obvious, sometimes subtle: a red star here, a blue one there, a group of stars over there. Here in one natural tableau is the life history of stars, from birth to death.

The first chapter of that history lies in the centerpiece constellation of winter, Orion. Below his distinctive belt of three bright stars lies one point of light that appears fuzzy. It's not a star. It's a nebula, the nearest and brightest of all the stellar nurseries in the galaxy.

Ray Jayawardhana opens this chapter about the origin of stars with an analysis of the great Orion Nebula, birthplace of stars. In the Orion Nebula are thousands of stars, most of which cannot be seen with mere telescopes *because of the tremendous amounts of gas and dust in which they are still cocooned. The Hubble Space Telescope has seen young stars cocooned in disks that appear to be forming planetary systems. Debris resembling comets has been detected orbiting far beyond the realm of our own planets. In this one patch of sky lie stars that observers a few thousand years from now will visualize as a brilliant cluster of stars, perhaps with planetary systems with primitive life-forms similar to that of our own Earth more than 4 billion years ago. — LK*

"Style & Substance"
by Ray Jayawardhana
Astronomy, October 2003

A resplendent gem in the eyepiece, the Orion Nebula is not just another pretty face. It may hold the key to how stars and planets form.

Orion the Hunter is a familiar constellation in winter's evening sky. A little below the three stars that make up the Hunter's belt, near the middle of his sword, shines a giant cloud of gas and dust known as the Orion Nebula, illuminated by several hot stars that make up the famous Trapezium Cluster at its core. The nebula's beauty—not to mention its scientific mysteries—has long mesmerized both amateur astronomers and professionals. In the past two decades, researchers have published nearly a thousand papers on the nebula,

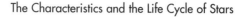

which, at a distance of about 1,500 light-years, is the closest stellar nursery harboring massive stars.

The Orion Nebula, also called M42, is a thin, concave blister of hot, ionized gas in front of a vast molecular cloud complex that drapes across much of the constellation Orion. Most of the cloud is extremely cold and dark, made up of hydrogen molecules (hence the name "molecular cloud") and a smidgen of dust. Newborn stars ionize and illuminate M42 and other well-known landmarks such as the Horsehead Nebula and Barnard's Loop.

Oriented nearly face-on to us, the nebula lies behind a cavity carved out by the hot young stars of the Trapezium and their brethren. In the foreground, a thin veil of interstellar gas and dust appears as the "dark bay" to the east of the Trapezium stars.

In the 1990s, C. Robert O'Dell and Zheng Wen, both then at Rice University, produced a detailed model of the nebula based on a variety of observations. A few years ago, computer graphics experts at the San Diego Supercomputer Center used the model to create a stunning 3-D visualization of M42 for New York's Hayden Planetarium at the American Museum of Natural History.

In the nebula's blazing heart, about 3,000 very young stars, most less than a million years old, crowd into a volume just a few light-years across. Only a few of the brightest penetrate dust in the natal cloud to shine through as the Trapezium Cluster. But detectors sensitive to infrared or x-ray wavelengths pierce the dust to reveal the majesty of thousands of young suns.

When the Hubble Space Telescope imaged the Orion Nebula in 1992, the silhouettes of dusty disks around many baby stars stood out against the nebula's bright background. Because dust absorbs a star's light and re-emits it as infrared radiation (heat), stars with disks glow more brightly in the infrared than do diskless stars. Surveys of nearby star-forming regions such as the Trapezium Cluster previously had revealed that 50 to 80 percent of newborn stars harbor an "infrared excess" consistent with the presence of disks. But it was reassuring to see the disks directly with Hubble.

These disks are typically a few hundred astronomical units across, or several times the size of Pluto's orbit around the Sun, and their masses range from about 1 to 10 percent of the Sun's mass. That's more than enough stuff to make a planetary system like ours. But many of the disks won't survive long enough to grow planets; intense ultraviolet radiation from hot stars in the Trapezium boils off material from the surfaces of many of these protoplanetary disks, or "proplyds."

Hubble images show a comet-like coma of evaporating material cocooning each proplyd, the coma's tail pointing away from nearby hot stars. The disks are losing material at the furious rate of about a half-Earth mass per year. They will evaporate completely within a few hundred thousand years, probably before planets will have had a chance to form. Living so close to the Trapezium's bigwigs presents "an environmental hazard to planet formation," as astronomer John Bally of the University of Colorado in Boulder puts it.

Space- and ground-based telescopes also show pairs of long, thin jets emanating from some very young stars. Twisting magnetic field lines send a fraction of the material that spirals toward the star from the disk hurtling into space along jets perpendicular to the plane of the disk. Many of the jets contain clumps, suggesting that material is being shot out in machine-gun-like fashion every few decades. Since the origin of the jets is intimately linked to infalling material from the disk, the presence of clumps implies the material falls onto the star in spurts.

Moving at hundreds of thousands of miles per hour, the jets slam into the surrounding interstellar gas, creating a bow shock similar to that made by a speedboat skimming across a lake. The violent collision heats up the stationary gas, and the result is glowing shock regions known as Herbig-Haro objects, after George Herbig and Guillermo Haro who discovered them in the 1950s.

In addition to the jets, which are narrow, hot, and fast-moving, some young stars harbor broader and slower outflows of cold gas. The jets are usually nested inside these vast outflows. While the ionized gas in jets can be seen in optical and near-infrared images, the colder outflows are best detected through the emission of specific molecules at radio wavelengths.

When the Chandra X-ray Observatory took a long exposure of the Orion Nebula recently, it came up with a rich bounty—thousands of young stars glowing more brightly in x rays than our middle-aged Sun. These x-ray powers, as well as observations of flares much stronger than those on the Sun, are probably the result of elevated magnetic activity due to the stars' youth. "We found a much higher rate of flares than expected," says Eric Feigelson of Pennsylvania State University. In fact, the flares are energetic and frequent enough that if the Sun had experienced such flares in its past, they could account for the creation of unusual isotopes found in ancient meteorites. "If the young stars in Orion can do it, then our Sun should have been able to do it too," argues Feigelson.

Although a few massive, hot stars dominate the Trapezium, the vast majority of objects in the Orion Nebula are less massive than the Sun. Some of these bodies are too puny to fuse hydrogen at all. These failed stars, with masses below 75 Jupiters, are known as brown dwarfs and glow only by converting gravitational energy into heat as they slowly contract in size. A recent, deep-infrared image of the region from Hubble, obtained by Kevin Luhman of the Harvard-Smithsonian Center for Astrophysics and his colleagues, reveals swarms of brown dwarfs, many of which had never been seen before. Some may be stranger objects yet—planetary-mass objects with masses as low as a few Jupiters that don't orbit host stars. How such free-floating "planemos" form is a topic of much current research. A finding, by myself and others, that they harbor dusty disks, like those seen around stars, suggests brown dwarfs and planemos form the same way stars do: by a gradual accumulation of gas. One theory proposes these objects are stellar embryos ejected from newborn multiple-star systems before they gather enough mass to fuse hydrogen.

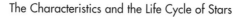

To the northwest and southwest of the Trapezium are two clusters of heavily enshrouded protostars best seen in the infrared. The brighter of the two, to the northwest, contains a remarkable protostar called the Becklin-Neugebauer object, which shines with a luminosity of 10,000 Suns. Named after its discoverers, Eric Becklin of the University of California in Los Angeles and Gerald Neugebauer of the California Institute of Technology, the BN object illuminates an extended infrared nebula.

Named Kleinmann-Low after Susan Kleinmann of the University of Massachusetts at Amherst and Frank Low of the University of Arizona who first imaged it, this nebula hosts powerful outflows and strong shocks that may be caused by the BN object or its luminous neighbors. Even after decades of intense multi-wavelength observations, the BN-KL region remains somewhat enigmatic.

The southwestern source, called Orion-S, is probably denser than the BN-KL region, so radiation from the neighboring Trapezium stars has penetrated it even less. Two bipolar outflows emanate from Orion-S, probably launched by deeply embedded protostars that remain invisible even in the near-infrared. Charles Lada at the Harvard-Smithsonian Center for Astrophysics and his colleagues have recently identified a candidate protostar for these outflows in Orion-S by observing in the mid-infrared.

It is hard to overstate how much our present understanding of star formation owes to studies of the Orion Nebula and its neighboring clouds. The nebula is often where a new phenomenon is uncovered or a new theory is put to the observational test. But this ethereal beauty has not revealed all its mysteries yet. Astronomers will be intrigued by the Orion Nebula for centuries to come.

"The Three Pillars of Creation," a magnificent photograph of dust columns in the Eagle Nebula made by the Hubble telescope, has become an iconic image for astronomy enthusiasts. On the edges of the pillars are lozenge-shaped disks, where new stars are enshrouded. Trailing out behind some of those disks are tails that resemble tails of comets and may be evidence of stellar winds. Or are they? This story shows how scientific explanations are often temporary and how the first explanation can often be supplanted by a better one as studies move on from their initial conclusions. —LK

"Rethinking an Astronomical Icon"
by Ron Cowen
Science News, March 16, 2002

The Eagle's EGG's: Not so fertile

In 1995, less than 2 years after astronauts installed a device to correct the Hubble Space Telescope's blurry

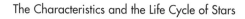
vision, NASA released a picture that captivated millions. In it, eerie blue-green pillars of gas and dust rise up like stalagmites in a cave. In a glimpse of the universe that's both science and art, a team of Arizona astronomers captured what they thought were nests brimming with stellar embryos. "I distinctly recall the first time I saw the image, in my office on a quiet holiday, a few days before the press release came out," says astronomer Mark J. McCaughrean of the Astrophysical Institute in Potsdam, Germany. "I was blown away . . . and immediately went in search of someone to show it to."

The picture landed on the covers of magazines around the world. Jay Leno displayed it on the *Tonight Show*. The heavenly portrait not only restored Hubble's tarnished reputation but became an astronomical icon.

Now, images taken with infrared detectors show that icon in a new light.

Composed of cold hydrogen gas and dust, the pillars reside in the Milky Way's Eagle nebula, a star-forming region 7,000 light-years from Earth. The columns are the dense remnants of what had been a giant gas cloud. Harsh ultraviolet light and fierce winds from a nearby cluster of hot, massive stars blasted away most of that cloud, leaving the pillars behind. As the ultraviolet light continues to bombard the pillars, it both hinders and fosters star birth. It hinders it by continuing to erode material and fosters it by compressing gas, hastening its collapse into stars.

When their original visible-light image was released, Hubble astronomers Paul Scowen and J. Jeff

Hester of Arizona State University in Tempe drew special attention to a group of dense, comet-shaped protrusions at or near the tips of the pillars. They suggested that the protrusions, which they called "evaporating gas globules," or EGGs, are havens where stars are forming.

Taking the findings one step further, Hester and his colleagues proposed that the EGGs represent a novel aspect of star formation. The unrelenting ultraviolet radiation from the neighborhood bullies wasn't only laying bare the EGGs, it was stripping material from these would-be stellar nurseries, stopping newborn stars from packing on additional girth. According to Hester's team, the erosion of material by bombardment of ultraviolet radiation, a process dubbed photoevaporation, may be the primary factor in limiting the heft of newborn stars across the galaxy.

Hester had estimated that hundreds to thousands of stars are currently forming in the 73 EGGs recorded by the Hubble camera. That interpretation prompted NASA to issue a press release that called the dusty columns "pillars of creation."

But there remained one problem with this interpretation, notes McCaughrean. The images were taken in visible light, and visible light doesn't penetrate dust. More recently, several researchers, including Hester and McCaughrean, have independently examined the EGGs with infrared detectors, which can probe the interior of the dusty columns.

The resulting images paint a different portrait of the pillars of creation. Only 15 percent of the EGGs contain newborn stars; the rest are sterile, too sparse in dust and gas to support star formation. Nonetheless, researchers disagree about whether ultraviolet light limits the growth of these infants.

Eyes of the Beholder

"The [visible-light] image was and is one of the most stunning things to come out of the Hubble Space Telescope," says McCaughrean. "On the other hand, much of the EGG-star formation theory was rather speculative, and after it got sound-bitten a few times, the public ended up thinking this revolutionized everything we ever knew about how stars are made."

To examine the pillars, McCaughrean and Morten Andersen, a colleague at Potsdam, recently used one of the quartet of 8-meter telescopes collectively known as the Very Large Telescope (VLT) in Paranal, Chile. Their findings will be published in an upcoming *Astronomy and Astrophysics*. A group of Japanese researchers also studied the pillars in the infrared, using the University of Hawaii's 2.2-m telescope. They report their findings in the Jan. 20 *Astrophysical Journal Letters*.

Hester maintains, however, that the new findings only confirm his original view, that ultraviolet light has been limiting the final mass of stars forming in the Eagle nebula's EGGs. He and his collaborators had studied the pillars with Hubble's near-infrared camera and multi-object spectrometer (NICMOS) in 1998, about a year before the device ran out of its solid nitrogen coolant and stopped operating. They found that few of the EGGs contain stars.

NASA unveiled this infrared image at a press briefing last month, where officials described plans for an ambitious mission to tune up Hubble. In that mission, astronauts attached a refrigerator to NICMOS to revive it. A report by Hester and his colleagues Rodger I. Thompson of the University of Arizona in Tucson and Bradford A. Smith of the University of Hawaii in Honolulu is scheduled for publication in the *Astrophysical Journal.*

"I'll admit that my original guess was that a larger fraction of the EGGs would contain young stellar objects," Hester says. The infrared images taken by the three teams imply that within the pillars an amount of gas equivalent to one-thousandth the sun's mass is converted into stars each year. Although that rate is one-tenth the amount he had calculated in 1995, Hester says it's "still a remarkably high star-formation rate."

The pillars, estimated to contain only a few hundred solar masses of material, could only sustain that rate of star formation for 100,000 years, he notes.

"We are seeing a brief, fairly intense period of star formation, with an ongoing competition between material being tied up in stars and material being dispersed by photoevaporation," says Hester. "The bottom line is that the [new] star-formation rate for the columns is both significant and the right magnitude to support the idea that photoevaporation plays a key role in shaping what is going on."

Same Images, New Ideas

McCaughrean says the new infrared images, which show that only about 11 EGGs contain stars, make it even more of a stretch to suggest that nearby massive stars and the ultraviolet radiation they emit limit the maximum mass of stars in the Eagle's pillars, let alone the rest of the Milky Way galaxy.

Moreover, he notes, many models of star formation indicate that massive stars take longer to assemble than do lower-mass stars, such as the typical stars within the EGGs. If that's the case, then EGG stars would reach maturity before neighboring stars could have grown massive enough to emit the disruptive ultraviolet radiation. The ultraviolet light would therefore have little affect on the overall mass of the newborn, he contends.

In this scenario, the radiation might still disperse the disks of gas and dust that surround newborn stars, interfering with their ability to form planets from this material, McCaughrean notes.

Hester interprets the same data differently. "The process that is revealed by the infrared and other observations is frankly remarkably close to the process that we originally suggested," he says.

Mario Livio of the Space Telescope Science Institute in Baltimore agrees that the early interpretations of the image were plausible. "I don't think the [original] image was hyped too much," he says. And although he notes that the picture's influence "was always because of its breathtaking beauty, not necessarily because of its scientific impact," the image did inspire astronomers to search for similar structures in other star-forming regions of the Milky Way.

"We now know that in many star-forming regions, such as 30 Doradus, you find such pillars," Livio adds.

The best observations to date indicate that there's little if any variation in the typical mass of newborn stars, whether they form in low-density regions of the Milky Way, which contain no massive stars, or regions bombarded by ultraviolet radiation from heavyweights, notes Stephen E. Strom of the National Optical Astronomy Observatory in Tucson. "The issue of triggering star formation, in which ultraviolet radiation could play a role, should be isolated from the ability of the radiation to determine the mass of stars—there's no evidence of that," he says.

"This whole theory of truncated star formation was always just hype," says astronomer Lynne Hillenbrand of the California Institute of Technology in Pasadena. Ultraviolet radiation from massive stars "surely is impacting the pillars, but once a star has started to form, I doubt the radiation dominates over gravity anywhere but in the outermost [layers] of the star-forming core," she notes.

When the original pillar images came out in 1995, Hubble's flawed optics had only recently been corrected. To both the scientific community and the public, the orbiting telescope was no longer a symbol of high-tech failure, says Hester. He adds, "The image became attached to the larger story—the recovery of Hubble and the dreams that had originally accompanied its launch."

Scientists don't find it surprising that interpretations of an astronomical image—even an icon like the pillars—may need revising, says McCaughrean. Hester "was doing science when he made a hypothesis based on his observations, and we're also doing science in checking his hypothesis and finding it to be less substantial than he hoped," McCaughrean notes. "The problem with press releases is that they tend to obscure this to-and-fro process, making science sound like it's all unimpeachable Eureka moments."

The new findings also highlight how much astronomers still have to learn about star formation. The arguments may not be settled until researchers can take ultrasharp, longer-wavelength images of the region. Infrared images and spectra obtained at these longer wavelengths can penetrate more of the dust in the pillars and provide a better estimate of the number and masses of stars that reside there, says McCaughrean.

He emphasizes that Hubble has an unavoidable case of tunnel vision—a small field of view. Just around the corner from the pillars, a much larger drama is unfolding. "There's a huge cluster of young stars, several thousand of them, which are home to the [handful of] massive stars whose ultraviolet light is destroying the pillars," McCaughrean notes. There's no clear evidence that the ultraviolet radiation from these massive stars determine the size of the thousands of low-mass stars in the cluster, he asserts.

In their *Astronomy and Astrophysics* report, McCaughrean and his colleagues summarize the findings this way: "The ongoing destruction of the columns and the relatively limited star formation taking place within them may ultimately prove to be a sideshow in the grander scheme of things—albeit a beautiful one."

They're out there, quietly traveling from star to star. Patient, they can wait millions of years for a world to conquer. Then they'll drop out of the skies like stealth bombers, dissolving into the oceans. Rendezvousing deep within the sea, they come together as simple life-forms that colonize a new sterile world. Sort of like Earth a long time ago.

That's the scene that some scientists see when they examine the material between the stars. There's neither pure vacuum nor more than a few random hydrogen atoms and dust floating in space. There are organic molecules, the same kinds found in life on Earth. So maybe, somewhere out there are some siblings made of star-stuff just like us. —LK

"Space Invaders: The Stuff of Life Has Far-flung Origins"
by Alexandra Goho
Science News, May 1, 2004

When most people look up at the night sky, they see emptiness. Stars, to be sure, but mostly a black void.

When Louis Allamandola, an astrochemist based at NASA's Ames Research Center in Moffett Field, Calif., looks up, he sees life. Everywhere. Perhaps not life in the literal sense, but its building blocks—materials just like those delivered to Earth via comets or meteorites some 4.5 billion years ago. Understanding how these molecules formed within the interstellar medium, he says, could offer scientists a rare glimpse of our chemical heritage and the complex processes that gave rise to life on Earth.

Until recently, "space was perceived as a sterile environment, and there was nothing of any significant molecular complexity out there," says Allamandola. Only in the past several years has a new picture emerged of interstellar space—one that portrays it as chemically diverse and complex. That view is now beginning to take hold in the scientific community.

Buried in the Milky Way are interstellar clouds that block out distant stars, thereby creating the effect of dark patches on the night sky as viewed by the naked eye. These clouds arise when stars, nearing the ends of their lives, eject their outer shells into the surrounding space. This fog of gas and dust particles then coalesces into cold, dense clouds that eventually give rise to a new generation of stars. From observations by ground-based telescopes and satellites, scientists have identified in interstellar clouds and cooling stars hundreds of molecules, most of which contain carbon and so are classified as organic.

"We know there are a lot of these molecules present in space, but we don't know what kind of molecules were delivered to the Earth or to Mars," says Alexander Tielens of the University of Groningen in the Netherlands. "If we are to understand the origin of life, we have to know what it is we started with."

Laboratory experiments under simulated-space conditions have shown that the environment within these clouds can foster an array of chemical reactions that result in organic molecules even more complex than those so far observed in space. Such experiments not only serve to confirm what astronomers have found in our galaxy but also provide clues as to what other molecules might be present in the interstellar medium.

Complex organic molecules readily forming in space could have contributed to life's beginnings on Earth some 3.5 billion years ago. Scientists have long assumed that combinations of simple molecules on Earth eventually formed individual cells that replicated on their own. Some scientists have argued that the time between when Earth became habitable and when life emerged was too short to have generated the complexity required of self-replicating cells. However, if precursor molecules for making proteins, RNA, and DNA came from space, life-creating chemical reactions within Earth's primordial soup could have greatly accelerated.

What's more, if complex organic materials are forming in space and being delivered to the planet even now, it's conceivable that these same materials are also being delivered to other planets. Says

Allamandola: "The fact that life could be widespread now seems to me is inescapable."

They're Everywhere

A star emits an enormous amount of radiation in all directions. When that radiation passes through the dust in a molecular cloud or surrounding a dying star in the Milky Way, organic molecules absorb some of the emissions and release that radiation at different wavelengths. As a result, the molecules display a unique optical spectrum that researchers can detect and compare with the spectra of similar molecules measured in the lab. By detecting the emissions of specific wavelengths of light from space, astronomers can identify types of organic molecules in the interstellar medium.

Some 30 years ago, astronomers discovered a series of spectra dubbed the unidentified infrared bands. They suspected that these spectra came from simple molecules on interstellar dust particles, but it wasn't until the late 1990s that scientists confirmed the source of these bands: polycyclic aromatic hydrocarbons (PAHs). These extremely stable organic molecules contain rings of carbon atoms and are widespread on Earth. For instance, they're a standard by-product of gasoline combustion in automobiles.

Originally, scientists thought that PAHs in outer space existed only around the edges of dense clouds or dying stars. Recent observations suggest that these molecules also reside in the diffuse interstellar medium and in galaxies beyond the Milky Way. For example,

NASA's Spitzer Space Telescope has revealed PAHs in the Milky Way and more-distant regions.

Now, astronomers' big challenge is to determine the size and structure of these molecules. They have recently begun the arduous task of creating a detailed inventory. For instance, Adolf Witt at the University of Toledo and his colleagues this year determined the nature of some PAHs by looking at the Red Rectangle nebula, a star located 1,000 light-years away and surrounded by a cloud of dust and gas.

The star is in the very late stages of its life and is firing off large amounts of material from its outer shell. Although emissions in the infrared range can identify a class of molecules, they can't describe its chemical structure. So, Witt looked instead at the ultraviolet part of the spectrum. The type of ultraviolet radiation that an organic molecule emits corresponds to its size.

Using observations made with telescopes in Chile and in Arizona, the researchers identified ultraviolet spectra characteristic of PAHs such as anthracene and pyrene, which have three-and four-carbon rings, respectively. Anthracene contains 24 atoms of which 14 are carbon, and pyrene has 26 atoms, including 16 carbons, says Witt. He presented his findings in January at the American Astronomical Society meeting in Atlanta.

"These nebulae are like chemical factories," says Witt. They start off producing simple molecules such as acetylene, which has just two carbons and two hydrogens. These molecules, in turn, combine and grow into more-complicated structures, such as single-ring benzene and multiring pyrene. "Eventually, you have very large organic molecules," says Witt.

This delicate process takes place only because the nebula, which is cooling, provides a protective environment for small molecules. Only after the organic molecules reach a certain size—perhaps 40 atoms or so, says Witt—can they survive ejection from the nebula into the harsh ultraviolet light of the diffuse medium and stay there for millions of years.

Increasing Complexity

If organic molecules such as PAHs can form in space, Allamandola wondered, what other kinds of complex molecules might arise? To answer that question, he and his colleagues have been re-creating molecular clouds in the laboratory to simulate the different chemical reactions that might occur within that extremely frigid environment. One of his group's first findings was that, inside a cold vacuum chamber, photochemistry takes place within the tiny ice mantles that form on microscopic grains of dust. When the researchers create ice particles containing simple molecules and irradiate them with ultraviolet light, the molecules begin to interact.

Using this irradiation technique, the NASA team and scientists at the University of California, Santa Cruz converted simple molecules—water, methanol, ammonia, and carbon monoxide—into compounds that form vesicles with cell-like membranes. When the scientists exposed the vesicles to ultraviolet light, the membranes glowed. The researchers speculate that the glowing molecules guard the membrane against ultraviolet radiation, a protection that would be required for a cell to survive.

In simulated molecular clouds, the NASA team has also created amino acids, the main components of proteins. The researchers trapped three simple compounds—methanol, ammonia, and hydrogen cyanide—inside an ice particle and exposed it to ultraviolet light. After warming the particles to room temperature, the researchers detected three different amino acids: alanine, serine, and glycine. The process might underlie the origins of amino acids that have been found in meteorites that have landed on Earth.

"There's a driving force, even under harsh conditions, to make molecules like these," says Allamandola.

Most recently, Allamandola has found that replacing one of the carbons in a PAH compound with a nitrogen atom yields molecules with absorption spectra similar to some recently observed unexplained spectra from space. Intriguingly, these nitrogen-containing molecules resemble components of DNA and its cousin RNA. "It's almost as if in this simple simulation of interstellar particles, which are widespread throughout our galaxy, you have all the basic building blocks of life" says Allamandola.

Not only do these experiments explain some space observations, they're also influencing astronomical observations. "The lab studies are getting better at predicting what we should be looking for," says Steven Charnley of NASA's Ames Research Center.

In the Aug. 20, 2003 *Astrophysical Journal*, Charnley and researchers from Taiwan and Poland reported evidence of the amino acid glycine in space. Between 1997 and 2001, the international team carried out a series of observations with the University of Arizona's Arizona Radio Observatory telescope near Tucson. The researchers found signs of the amino acid in the radio-wave region of the spectra from three giant molecular clouds.

Charnley adds that his group is now in hot pursuit of a pyrimidine, a particular component of DNA and RNA.

Unsettling Dust

Many scientists have suspected that life on Earth stems from complex organic molecules delivered via meteorites, comets, and the dust particles that populate space. Cosmic dust containing carbon continues to enter Earth's atmosphere and settle on the planet's surface. However, chemical evidence pinpointing the extraterrestrial origins of this organic material has remained elusive.

But recently, when scientists at Washington University in St. Louis and Lawrence Livermore (Calif.) National Laboratory analyzed an interplanetary dust particle collected by a NASA aircraft from Earth's stratosphere, they discovered organic material older than the solar system. The researchers say in the Feb.

27 *Science* that the particle must have formed in an interstellar molecular cloud.

Other researchers had reported finding isotopic signatures of hydrogen and nitrogen indicative of an interstellar origin, but never of carbon. However, Christine Floss of Washington University and her colleagues succeeded in finding an isotopic signature both in the nitrogen and the carbon elements.

When the researchers analyzed the ratio of carbon isotopes in the sample, they found an isotopic signature that arises only in the extremely cold environment of interstellar molecular clouds. This signature differs from that of anything found on Earth or in the solar system, says Floss.

The researchers' analysis so far hasn't determined whether the organic material is a PAH or some other type of hydrocarbon. They plan tests to further elucidate the sample's molecular structure.

Floss says that there's growing evidence to suggest that dust particles spill onto Earth from comets. These icy bodies predate the solar system and bear the chemical signatures of their interstellar environment.

The NASA Stardust mission to Comet Wild 2 has already collected dust particles near a comet and is scheduled to return to Earth in January 2006. Researchers hope to find a wealth of organic molecules in these particles.

"That's something we're all very excited about," Floss says. "I think it's going to be a big step forward for this field."

Allamandola, for one, says he won't be surprised if the comet-dust samples contain wildly complex molecules. Perhaps not an entire bacterium, virus, or even strand of DNA. "That's pushing it," he admits. Still, he notes, "just in the last 5 years, we've opened up this whole new magical world. I think in the next 10 years, it's going to get more and more incredible."

Among the youngest of stars no longer bedded down in their gaseous nursery are stars that send out a lot of their own gas, making their own nebulae that look like abstract works of art. Wolf-Rayet stars are so hot that they can't contain themselves but spin off great whirls of glowing gas. It's possible that they are responsible for the starburst galaxies, great pinwheels of stars where massive amounts of supernovae and stellar nebulae coexist. They may have been responsible for the killing off of life at some of the earliest times of Earth's existence. And they may give clues to how the earliest stars first came into existence. There are very few such stars, a result of the fact that they don't last long. Scientists are studying those few they can find now, before one of these babies has a temper tantrum to end all tantrums and showers Earth with deadly debris. —LK

"Gorgeous Gas: New Observations of Space Clouds Reveal Stellar Histories"
by Ron Cowen
Science News, May 24, 2003

Fierce winds of particles and radiation from massive stars can sculpt the universe. What would otherwise be dim regions of amorphous gas become transformed into luminous works of art. Resembling bright bubbles, these diaphanous expanses of gas and dust belong to the category of astronomical phenomena known as nebulas. Unlike most of the nebulas that populate the universe, these clouds are limned by arcs or rings and bathed in the blue light emitted by helium ions. That makes these cosmic beauties really hot stuff.

Last year, astronomers observed four of the nearest such nebulas with one of the quartet of 8-meter telescopes that make up the Very Large Telescope (VLT) in Paranal, Chile. Images of the nebulas, located just a few hundred thousand light-years away, provide the first detailed look at these comely clouds and the hot, massive stars that power them.

Beyond their undeniable beauty, the images may reveal properties of the very first stars to light up the cosmos. Models of stellar formation suggest that pioneer stars, which lived and died nearly 14 billion years ago, were unusually hot and massive compared with typical stars today. The new observations, which home in on nebulas from two satellite galaxies of the Milky Way, may also provide insight into the strong

visible-light emissions that have been observed coming from some distant galaxies. Astronomers suspect that the distant emissions may emanate from the same type of nebulas.

Yaël Nazé of the Institute of Astrophysics and Geophysics in Liege, Belgium, and her colleagues, including You-Hua Chu of the University of Illinois at Urbana-Champaign, describe the findings in an upcoming *Astronomy and Astrophysics*.

Windy Stars

Any hot, young star can set a surrounding nebula aglow by stripping hydrogen atoms of their single electron. The light emitted by the ionized hydrogen atoms gives these regions a ruddy hue. One well-known example is the Orion nebula. But it takes an even hotter, more massive star, with a surface temperature greater than 75,000 kelvins and a mass heavier than 20 times that of the sun, to strip helium atoms of their two electrons. These completely ionized helium atoms then grab a single electron, becoming singly ionized helium, which astronomers refer to as HeII. These ions emit a particular wavelength of blue light, 488.6 nanometers.

It's these special nebulas, known as HeII nebulas, that astronomers observed last year with the VLT.

To fully ionize helium, a massive star must be extremely hot. That requirement disqualifies most massive stars, which typically haw temperatures lower than 50,000 kelvins and can't radiate enough energy to strip helium atoms of both of their electrons, notes Donald R. Garnett of the University of Arizona in Tucson. Hotter stars "are not predicted by normal stellar evolution, so the presence of the HeII nebulas is a bit of a mystery," comments Garnett, who has observed such nebulas with the Hubble Space Telescope.

The ultraviolet light radiated by massive stars can't be seen by ground-based telescopes. But if a high density of hydrogen and helium atoms surrounds the star, much of the ultraviolet radiation is reemitted as visible light, which reveals these gases in the form of glowing nebulas. Because so much of the ultraviolet light is absorbed, studying the nebulas is the only way to learn about the ultraviolet emissions and general nature of these unusually powerful stars, says Garnett.

Several of the new observations provide evidence for one of the many models astronomers have formulated to account for the stars, says Chu. According to this model, a type of star called Wolf-Rayet, known for its strong winds and intense radiation, ionizes the helium. Wolf-Rayet stars, which last for only 100,000 years, appear to be the descendants of massive O stars, which also produce winds. Akin to the winds of ionized particles blowing out from the sun, these winds of O and Wolf-Rayet stars are much more powerful, with speeds of 2,000 to 4,000 kilometers per second.

Most Wolf-Rayet stars either aren't hot enough or don't have enough gas surrounding them to produce bright, easy to see HeII nebulas, notes Claus Leitherer of the Space Telescope Science in Baltimore. "The only good candidates are outside the Milky Way, making it hard to obtain high-quality data," he says. "The new VLT data finally allow us to derive precise temperatures

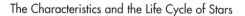

and measure the radiation field" produced by these stars, he says.

One of the new images depicts the nebula surrounding the star BAT99-2, which is in the nearby Large Magellanic Cloud galaxy. The star is the hottest Wolf-Rayet star known, with a surface temperature of 120,000 kelvins, nearly 20 times that of the sun. Before the star became hot enough to be classified as a Wolf-Rayet, it emitted a strong wind that swept up interstellar debris like a snowplow, suggest Nazé, Chu, and their colleagues.

This wind apparently created a bubble of hydrogen and helium gas, which can be seen as a large semicircle to the south of the star. After evolving into its Wolf-Rayet phase, the star blew an even stronger wind, some 20,000 to 40,000 km/s which slammed into gaseous material previously ejected by the star. This created a new bubble, visible as a small arc to the northwest of the star. "We are apparently witnessing an ongoing merger of these two bubbles," Chu says.

Wolf-Rayet stars are the probable power sources for two other HeII nebulas examined in detail by Nazé's group. But a fourth image poses a puzzle.

The nebula known as N44C contains two massive stars, but even the hottest, most massive one lacks the oomph to ionize helium. The astronomers propose that this nebula harbors a third, unseen star that's extremely dense and circled by the nebula's most massive visible star. When these two stars are closest together, the dense, unseen star siphons a large amount of material from its partner. As the material falls onto the dense star, it reaches searing temperatures of up to millions of kelvins, emitting both X rays and ultraviolet light— enough to fully ionize helium atoms. At other times, when the two stars are farther apart, the compact star can cannibalize very little mass and the energetic radiation dwindles on a time scale of decades to centuries.

So far, however, observations of N44C reveal little or no fading of the radiation.

Says Nazé, "We were able to understand three nebulas, but we must now look more closely at N44C."

Nebulous Riddles

There are other puzzles to solve, notes Garnett. Even for the HeII nebulas that are clearly powered by Wolf-Rayet stars, it's uncertain how these stars arise. They may be the descendants of massive stars, or they might be produced through the interaction of binary stars. What's more, astronomers don't fully understand how hot, massive stars can produce so much high-energy ultraviolet radiation.

Part of the uncertainty stems from the difficulty of modeling the ultraviolet output of hot, massive stars. Not only is the light readily absorbed by atoms, preventing direct measurements, but modelers must also take into account the effects of the stellar wind and the shape of the nebulas. The new observations will help, Garnett says, because once astronomers calculate the ultraviolet output of the stars imaged, they can use that information to model other Wolf-Rayet stars.

On a grander scale, the new nebula observations could hold clues to star formation in distant galaxies, including so-called starburst galaxies, in which stars are forming like gangbusters. The energetic stars that power HeII nebulas "may be common in starburst galaxies, especially in those with low abundances of heavy elements, notes Garnett.

It's also possible that the first stars in the universe were at least as hot and massive as the stars that power HeII nebulas today, he adds.

Theory predicts that O stars were far more abundant in the early universe than there are today. "If there were many O stars, then there should also be many Wolf-Rayet stars as well," notes Leitherer.

Astronomers propose that a group of ancient, massive stars ended the so-called cosmic Dark Ages by ionizing hydrogen and helium atoms, lighting up the universe for the first time since the Big Bang. But to say this for certain, says Garnett, "we need to understand the ultraviolet emissions from present-day massive stars and the breathtaking nebulas that surround them."

The astronomical mind must seek out the tiniest clues, as this somewhat technical article illustrates. Our own Sun is made from the debris of stars that have long since died. It isn't a pure, pristine star, but is filled with other atoms, called metals, unlike the stars that were first made

shortly after the big bang. That's a long time ago, when the universe was essentially one big collection of hydrogen atoms. Is it possible that a star from that early era still shines some-where? The writers of this article tell of a star that appears to be almost totally devoid of iron, a slow-burning, low-mass, billion-octogenarian star of that first era that survived the passing of its brethren. —LK

"A Stellar Relic from the Early Milky Way"
by N. Christlieb, M. S. Bessell, T. C. Beers,
B. Gustafsson, A. Korn, P. S. Barklem,
T. Karlsson, M. Mizuno-Wiedner, and S. Rossi
Nature, October 31, 2002

The chemical composition of the most metal deficient stars reflects the composition of the gas from which they formed. These old stars provide crucial clues to the star formation history and the synthesis of chemical elements in the early Universe. They are the local relics of epochs otherwise observable only at very high red-shifts;[1, 2] if totally metal-free ("population III") stars could be found, this would allow the direct study of the pristine gas from the Big Bang. Earlier searches for such stars found none with an iron abundance less than 1/10,000 that of the Sun,[3, 4] leading to the suggestion[5, 6] that low-mass stars could only form from clouds above a critical iron abundance. Here we report the discovery of a low-mass star with an iron abundance as low as 1/200,000 of the solar value. This discovery suggests

that population III stars could still exist, that is, that the first generation of stars also contained long-lived low-mass objects. The previous failure to find them may be an observational selection effect.

The star HE 0107–5240, at coordinates right ascension R.A.(2000.0) = 01h 09m 29.1s and declination δ = -52° 24' 34'' , is a giant star of the Galactic halo population with apparent magnitude B = 15.86. It was found during medium-resolution spectroscopic follow-up observations of candidate metal-poor stars selected from the Hamburg/ESO objective prism survey (HES).[7,8] This survey, which covers the entire southern high-galactic-latitude sky to an apparent magnitude limit of $B \approx$ 17.5, extends the total survey volume for metal-poor stars in the Galaxy by almost one order of magnitude compared to the total volume explored by previous spectroscopic surveys.

A medium-resolution ($\delta\lambda \approx$ 0.2 nm) spectrum of HE 0107-5240 was obtained by M.S.B. with the Siding Spring Observatory 2.3-m telescope on 12 November 2001. The Ca II K (λ = 393.4 nm) line was barely visible in that spectrum, indicating that the star was likely to be extremely metal deficient. Shortly thereafter, a high-resolution, high signal-to-noise ratio spectrum was obtained with the 8-m Unit Telescope 2 (UT2) of the Very Large Telescope at the European Southern Observatory (ESO), Paranal, Chile.

We derive an effective temperature T_{eff} = 5100 ± 150K for HE 0107–5240 by means of broad-band visual and infrared photometry. The absence of Fe II lines, through the Fe I/Fe II ionization equilibrium, constrains the star to have a logarithmic surface gravity of $\log(g) > 2.0$ dex, while main-sequence gravities are excluded by the relative strengths of Balmer lines, and the strength of the Balmer jump seen in the medium-resolution spectrum. Hence we conclude that the star is located on the red giant branch. By interpolation in a 12-Gyr pre-helium-flash stellar evolutionary track,[9] we estimate the surface gravity of HE 0107–5240 to be $\log(g) = 2.2 \pm 0.3$, and its mass M $\approx 0.8 M_{\odot}$. We derive [Fe/H] $\approx -5.3 \pm 0.2$ for HE 0107-5240, where [A/X] = $\log_{10}(N_A/N_X) - \log_{10}(N_A/N_X)_{\odot}$ and the subscript "$\odot$" refers to the Sun. In the determination of the iron abundance, as well as the Fe I/Fe II ionisation equilibrium, we took into account deviations from local thermodynamical equilibrium (LTE) in the formation of iron lines in the atmosphere of the star, which led to a correction of $+0.1$ dex for the Fe I abundance. The quoted error in the iron abundance includes uncertainties in the derived model atmosphere parameters T_{eff} (resulting in δ [Fe/H] = ± 0.20 dex) and $\log (g)$ (δ [Fe/H] = ± 0.02 dex), the adopted oscillator strengths (δ [Fe/H] = ± 0.1 dex), and in the line-strength measurement uncertainties (δ [Fe/H] = ± 0.07 dex). An LTE analysis, conducted differentially with respect to CD $-38°$ 245 (with [Fe/H] = -3.98, previously the most iron-deficient giant star known),[1] shows that HE 0107–5240 is 1.4 dex more iron-poor. This is in very good agreement with our non-differential LTE value of [Fe/H] = -5.4 for HE 0107–5240.

Extreme iron deficiencies have also been observed in some post-asymptotic giant branch (post-AGB) stars.[10, 11] However, extensive studies have revealed that their observed elemental abundances were altered substantially from their primordial compositions by selective dust depletion and subsequent radiation-driven gasdust separation.[10, 12] The most extreme cases are HR 4049 and HD 52961, which have [Fe/H] = −4.8. Other elements, such as Ca and Mg, are depleted by a similar amount, while the abundances of elements such as C, N, O, and Zn are close to the solar values.[11] For HE 0107-5240, on the other hand, we derive an upper limit for the Zn abundance that is significantly below solar ([Zn/H] < −2.7). We also note that these post- AGB stars occupy a stellar physical parameter space[11] that is not shared by HE 0107–5240, that is, T_{eff} = 6,000–7,600 K, $\log(g)$ = 0.5–1.2. Furthermore, typically many lines in the spectra of post-AGB stars exhibit prominent emission features owing to a strong stellar wind, while other lines have a complex absorption structure resulting from the presence of circumstellar gas.[11, 13] Such features are not seen in the spectrum of HE 0107-5240. Finally, we note that infrared photometry of our star does not reveal any indications of an excess of infrared flux due to hot dust.

We conclude that HE 0107-5240 likely formed from a gas cloud with a metal abundance corresponding to [Fe/H] ≈ −5.3. The abundance pattern of elements heavier than Mg can be well fit by the predicted elemental yields[14] of a $20 - 25 M_{\odot}$ star that underwent a type II supernova explosion, indicating that the gas cloud from which HE 0107–5240 formed could have been enriched by such a supernova [see Fig. 1 in the original article]. Alternatively, HE 0107–5240 could have formed from a zero metallicity gas cloud, with its present metallicity being due to accretion of material during repeated passages through the Galactic disc.[15]

The large overabundances of C and N, and possibly Na, in HE 0107-5240 can be explained by either mass transfer from a previously more massive companion during its AGB phase, or else by self-enrichment. The mass-transfer scenario has been proposed as the likely explanation for the so-called metal-poor CH stars.[16] Recent model computations of the structure, evolution and nucleosynthesis of low-mass and intermediatemass stars of zero or near-zero metallicity have shown[17–19] that such stars undergo extensive mixing episodes at or shortly after the helium-core flash, resulting in a dredge-up of helium burning and CNO-cycle processed material to their surfaces, especially carbon and nitrogen. The surface abundance ratios of CNO, Na, and Mg, predicted by Siess et al.[19] for stars in the mass range 1–$2M_\odot$, agree reasonably well with the abundances observed in HE 0107–5240, within the large uncertainties arising from the input physics adopted in the model calculations.

Our derived upper limits for Ba and Sr indicate that HE 0107-5240 is not strongly overabundant in neutron-capture elements. In this respect, our star is similar to the extremely metal-poor giant[20] CS 22957–27, a star with [Fe/H] = -3.4 and [C/Fe] = $+2.2$, as well as to the recently discovered class of mildly carbon-enhanced

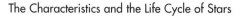
metal-poor stars that are underabundant in neutron-capture elements.[21] This abundance pattern implies that helium burning and some CNO burning may have occurred. However, if this scenario is correct, the observations suggest that the reactions involved have produced little ^{13}C, or that the ^{13}C produced has been consumed by proton captures. We note that if α captures on ^{13}C were dominant, neutrons would have been produced through the reaction ^{13}C(α, n)^{16}O, giving rise to s-process nucleosynthesis.

It was once believed that the lowest-metallicity objects to have formed in the Galaxy (at least those that survived until the present) were the halo globular clusters, such as M92, with [Fe/H] = −2.5, a factor of 300 times below the solar value. This belief was based on several assumptions, most importantly that star formation in the early Galaxy would have been strongly inhibited at low masses, owing to the difficulty of forming stars from nearly primordial gas without cooling channels arising from heavy elements such as iron. A number of early studies[22, 23] suggested that cooling from molecular species including hydrogen might allow low-mass star formation before the production of heavy metals significantly polluted the interstellar medium, but no examples of stars approaching such low metallicities as HE 0107–5240 were then known. This view received support from early objective-prism surveys[3] that failed to detect significant numbers of low-mass stars with [Fe/H] < −2.5. For the past two decades, more extensive surveys have pushed the low-metallicity limit to [Fe/H] = −4.0, that is, the iron abundance of

CD $-38°$ 245, but no lower.[4] On the basis of the numbers of metal-poor stars thus far identified in these surveys, which include some 1,000 stars with [Fe/H] < -2.0, a simple extrapolation of the distribution of metal abundances suggested that if stars with [Fe/H] < -4.0 existed in the Galaxy, at least a handful should have been found. The dwarf carbon star G 77–61 has been suggested to have[24] [Fe/H] = -5.5, if a logarithmic solar Fe abundance of 7.51 (on a scale where the logarithmic abundance of hydrogen is 12) is adopted, as we did for our analysis of HE 0107–5240. However, the analysis of the cool (T_{eff} = 4,200 K)[24] dwarf G 77–61 is much less certain than the analysis of HE 0107–5240, because the spectrum of the former is dominated by molecular bands of carbon that are much stronger than in HE 0107–5240. Clearly, the existence of at least one example of a star with an iron abundance as low as [Fe/H] = -5.3 provides evidence that the limiting metallicity of halo stars may not yet have been reached.

This has implications for the nature of the first mass function (FMF) of early star formation. Although some studies[5, 6] have suggested that metal-poor gas clouds fragment into low-mass objects only above a certain critical metallicity, $Z_{crit} \approx 10^{-4} Z_{\odot}$ ([Fe/H] = -4), our discovery provides evidence in favor of other studies suggesting that the FMF included not only very massive stars but also lower-mass stars.[25] The FMF may also have been bimodal[26] and may have included stars with masses around $1 M_{\odot}$ as well as around $100 M_{\odot}$. Other authors[27] have speculated on the possible presence of ancient (presumably extremely low

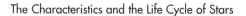

metallicity) objects that could have formed before re-ionization of the early Universe. In this view, the "gap" between the iron abundance of HE 0107–5240 and other extremely metal-poor stars may represent the period of reheating and reionization, when star forma-tion was strongly suppressed owing to destruction of the molecular hydrogen that was needed for cooling. As an alternative, it remains possible that the [Fe/H] = −4.0 "limit" is an artefact caused by the brighter magnitude limits of surveys that have been carried out up to now. Indeed, it may be no coincidence that the fainter magnitude limit of the HES allowed for the detection of HE 0107–5240 at a distance of about 11 kpc from the Sun, whereas most previous surveys have been limited to searches for extremely metal-poor stars within the inner halo of the Galaxy. Further tests of this hypothesis are currently targeting the faintest giants from the HES, which extend to 20 or more kpc from the Sun. If additional stars with iron abundances substantially lower than [Fe/H] = −4.0 are identified, these will provide important new tools with which, for example, we could directly compare observed elemen-tal abundance patterns with the predicted yields of the first generation of supernova type II explosions, make a definitive measurement of the primordial lithium abundance (which strongly constrains "big bang" nucleosynthesis),[28] and obtain tighter constraints on the nature of the FMF. If any examples of the so-called r-process-enhanced stars are found with [Fe/H] < −4.0, we may be able to use nucleochronometry[29] to obtain a direct estimate of the epoch of first star formation in the Universe, possibly resulting in an improved lower limit for the age of the Universe.

Received 1 July; accepted 24 September 2002

1. Norris, J. E., Ryan, S. G. & Beers, T. C. Extremely metal-poor stars. VIII. High-resolution, high signal-to noise ratio analysis of five stars with [Fe/H] < -3.5. *Astrophys. J.* **561**, 1034–1059 (2001)

2. Cohen, J. G., Christlieb, N., Beers, T. C., Gratton, R. & Carretta, E. Stellar Archaeology: A Keck pilot program on extremely metal-poor stars from the Hamburg/ESO survey. I. Stellar parameters. *Astron. J.* **124**, 470–480 (2002)

3. Bond, H. E. Where is population III? *Astrophys. J.* **248**, 606–611 (1981)

4. Beers, T. C. In: *The Third Stromlo Symposium: The Galactic Halo* (eds. Gibson, B. K., Axelrod, T. S.& Putman, M. E.) *Astron. Soc. Pacif. Conf. Ser.* **165**, 202–212 (1999)

5. Bromm, V., Ferrara, A., Coppi, P. S. & Larson, R. B. The fragmentation of pre-enriched primordial objects. *Mon. Not. R. Astron. Soc.* **328**, 969–976 (2001)

6. Schneider, R., Ferrara, A., Natarajan, P. & Omukai, K. First stars, very massive black holes, and metals. *Astrophys. J.* **571**, 30–39 (2002)

7. Wisotzki, L. et al. The Hamburg/ESO survey for bright QSOs. III. A large flux-limited sample of QSOs. *Astron. Astrophys.* **358**, 77–87 (2000)

8. Christlieb, N. et al. The stellar content of the Hamburg/ESO survey. I. Automated selection of DA white dwarfs. *Astron. Astrophys.* **366**, 898–912 (2001)

9. Yi, S. et al. Towards better age estimates for stellar populations: The Y2 isochrones for solar mixture. *Astrophys. J. Suppl.* **136**, 417–437 (2001)

10. Mathis, J. S. & Lamers, H. J. G. L. M. The origin of the extremely metal-poor post-AGB stars. *Astron. Astrophys.* **259**, L39–L42 (1992)

11. Van Winckel, H., Waelkens, C. & Waters, L. B. F. M. The extremely iron-deficient "post-AGB" stars and binaries. *Astron. Astrophys.* **293**, L25–L28 (1995)

12. Waters, L. B. F. M., Trams, N. R. & Waelkens, C. A scenario for the selective depletion of stellar atmospheres. *Astron. Astrophys.* **262**, L37–L40 (1992)

13. Bakker, E. J. et al. The optical spectrum of HR 4049. *Astron. Astrophys.* **306**, 924–934 (1996)

14. Woosley, S. E. & Weaver, T. A. The evolution and explosion of massive stars. II. Explosive hydrodynamics and nucleosynthesis. *Astrophys. J.* **101**, 181–235 (1995)

15. Yoshii, Y. Metal enrichment in the atmospheres of extremely metal-deficient dwarf stars by accretion of insterstellar matter. *Astron. Astrophys.* **97**, 280–290 (1981)

16. McClure, R. D. &Woodsworth, A.W. The binary nature of the Barium and CH stars. III. Orbital parameters. *Astrophys. J.* **352**, 709–723 (1990)

17. Fujimoto, M. Y., Ikeda, Y. & Iben Jr., I. The origin of extremely metal-poor carbon stars and the search for population III. *Astrophys. J.* **529**, L25–L28 (2000)

18. Schlattl, H., Salaris, M., Cassisi, S. & Weiss, A. The surface carbon and nitrogen abundances in models of ultra metal-poor stars. *Astron. Astrophys.* (2002) (in the press); also preprint astro-ph/0205326 at http://xxx.lanl.gov

19. Siess, L., Livio, M. & Lattanzio, J. Structure, evolution, and nucleosynthesis of primordial stars. *Astrophys. J.* **570**, 329–343 (2002)

20. Norris, J., Ryan, S. G. & Beers, T. C. Extremely metal poor stars. The carbon-rich, neutron capture element-poor object CS 22957–027. *Astrophys. J.* **489**, L169–L172 (1997)

21. Aoki, W., Norris, J. E., Ryan, S. G., Beers, T. C. & Ando, H. The chemical composition of carbon-rich, very metal poor stars: a new class of mildly carbon rich objects without excess of neutron-capture elements. *Astrophys. J.* **567**, 1166–1182 (2002)

22. Yoshii, Y. & Sabano, Y. Stability of a collapsing pregalactic gas cloud. *Publ. Astron. Soc. Jpn.* **31**, 505–521 (1979)

23. Palla, F., Salpeter, E. E. & Stahler, S. W. Primordial star formation: the role of molecular hydrogen. *Astrophys. J.* **271**, 632–641 (1983)

24. Gass, H. Liebert, J. & Wehrse, R. Spectrum analysis of the extremely metal-poor carbon dwarf star G77-61. *Astron. Astrophys.* **189**, 194–198 (1988

25. Yoshii, Y. & Saio, H. Initial mass function for zerometal stars. *Astrophys. J.* **301**, 587–600 (1986)

26. Nakamura, F. & Umemura, M. On the initial mass function of population III stars. *Astrophys. J.* **548**, 19–32 (2001)

27. Ostriker, J. P. & Gnedin, N. Y. Reheating of the universe and population III. *Astrophys. J.* **472**, L63–L67 (1996)

28. Ryan, S. G., Norris, J. E. & Beers, T. C. The Spite lithium plateu: ultrathin but postprimordial. *Astrophys. J.* **523**, 654–677 (1999)

29. Cayrel, R. et al. Measurement of stellar age from uranium decay. *Nature* **409**, 691–692 (2001)

The Lives and Characteristics of Stars and Their Planetary Systems

2

Once a star is stable, out of the nebula from which it formed, it settles down and converts hydrogen to helium and energy. The disk of material from which it formed is ejected by stellar winds. And it seems ever more likely that planets form around the star.

Until recently we only had evidence for a few planetary systems—ours and a few nearby stars that wobbled as they moved slowly across our sky. (The wobbling was evidence that large Jupiter-like planets were orbiting the stars.)

We've gotten better at detecting planetary systems in the past few years. In fact we know of more than a hundred planets, a few in systems of two or more. But virtually all such systems are filled with big gas giants like Jupiter. What about Earth-type worlds? So far those are too small to detect. And there's another problem: most of the big bloated gas worlds we've discovered orbit close to the star, where Mercury or Venus would orbit. Therefore, Mercury and Venus would not be able to form, let alone orbit!

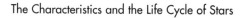

How do we get a planetary system like ours when those gas giants are in the way? The scientists mentioned in this article think they have a solution to the problem. The gas giants form first, move outward, and rocky worlds like ours form afterward, when it's safe. —LK

"Solar System Like Ours Is Called 'Missing Link'"
by Lee McFarling
Los Angeles Times, June 14, 2002

Astronomers searching for worlds around distant stars announced the discovery Thursday of the first solar system like Earth's, boosting hopes that there are other habitable spots in the universe.

"One of the big questions in science is, 'Are we alone?'" said Anne Kinney, who directs the astronomy and physics division at NASA headquarters. This "brings us one step closer to answering that."

While scientists did not find an Earth, they found a close cousin: a Jupiter. It is the first planet scientists have found with a roughly circular orbit that is a healthy distance from its star, like many of Earth's neighbors.

"It's got the smell of our own solar system," said Geoff Marcy, the UC Berkeley astronomer who leads the planet-hunting team. "In a sense this solar system is a missing link."

Since the first extrasolar planet was discovered seven years ago, 91 have been discovered. But many have been so odd—many times the size of Jupiter, so close to their suns they'd be permanently scorched or on wild, elliptical orbits—scientists began to wonder whether our home solar system was unique. Looks like it's not.

The planet, a gas giant known as "55 Cnc d," circles around the star 55 Cancri, about 41 light-years from Earth. The middle-aged star is about the same size as our sun and is visible to the naked eye.

The new planet is about four times the size of Jupiter and is about the same distance from its sun as Jupiter is from ours. While that planet looks comfortingly familiar, the solar system also contains some strange elements: two other large planets hundreds of times larger than Earth that circle very close to the sun.

Those oddities carry the "wacky stink of some of the strange solar systems we've been finding over the past few years," Marcy said. They underscore that while Earth's orderly solar system is not unique, neither is it the norm.

Finding planets is difficult work. They are not visible, even to the powerful Hubble Space Telescope, because they give off only a faint glow of reflected light, light that is imperceptible in the glare coming from the stars they circle. Instead, Marcy's team detects planets using a sensitive technique that measures the slight wobble of stars caused by the gravitational yank of planets circling them.

The technique has a bias that explains why most findings so far have been of big, close-in planets—"oddballs" that are easiest to find because they perturb their stars the most. The smallest planet discovered so far, one of 14 others also announced Thursday, is about half the size of Saturn, or 40 times the size of Earth.

Planets the size of Earth would not be visible. For example, if the team looked at our own solar system from afar with its technique, it could detect only the two largest planets, Jupiter and Saturn.

The reason many of the early discoveries have been of planets close to stars is because their full orbits take only days. The wobbles caused by the planets cannot be analyzed until at least one full orbit has been made. A planet farther away, that takes years to orbit its star, takes years of monitoring to detect.

The newly discovered Jupiter-like planet took 13 years to orbit its sun, and therefore took 13 years to detect.

"There's a tremendous amount of persistence required for this work," said Alycia Weinberger, an astronomer at the Carnegie Institution of Washington who was not involved in the research. "It's an experiment that doesn't necessarily give its most exciting results right away."

Astronomers are debating whether a smaller planet could exist in a temperate zone among 55 Cancri's three Jupiter-like planets.

The outer Jupiter might serve, as ours does, to absorb the blows of comets and asteroids that could otherwise explode into our planet and wipe out life.

Theories suggest that gas giant planets form in the outer part of the solar system and exist near stars only if they migrate there. Behemoths spiraling toward the core of a solar system could pummel smaller planets out of existence. But Weinberger said enough dusty material might survive this transit to allow an Earth-sized planet to form after the monsters passed by. UC Santa Cruz theoretical astronomer Greg Laughlin has shown that a small planet could survive in a stable orbit between two giants.

Marcy and Paul Butler, an astronomer at the Carnegie Institution, have spent 17 years perfecting the process of planet hunting and waited nearly a decade before finding their first planet. Now, their system works so smoothly, "we're actually drowning in planets," Marcy said. Last week, the team had planned to announce 13 new planets at its news conference. It found two more over the weekend.

Given the length of time the astronomers have been monitoring some stars, they expect to find more and more "normal" planets in these distant regions from their suns that have never been probed. "We're entering virgin territory," Butler said.

The team plans to conduct a census of the 2,000 stars within 150 light-years of Earth in an attempt to see how common our solar system is. "Are we one in a hundred? One in a thousand? We have no idea right now," Butler said.

The scientists do not expect that they—or anyone else—will find another Earth for at least a decade. That will have to wait for new technology now being developed at the Jet Propulsion Laboratory.

The NASA center working on several space telescopes to be launched this decade and next will continue the search for new planets with far more powerful tools and attempt to take the first images of these distant worlds.

The Jupiter-like planet announced Thursday is a good candidate for the first portrait, scientists said, because it is relatively close to Earth and far from the blinding light coming from its home star.

Some astronomers study the Sun from—surprise!—below Earth's surface; they are observing the particles called neutrinos. Back in the 1960s and 1970s, we thought we knew how the Sun was powered. Hydrogen fused into helium, and we got energy and some massless particles called neutrinos. Neutrinos go through everything like a hot knife through warm butter. Still, every once in a while, one can be stopped when it hits a molecule just right, such as those in huge underground vats of heavy water, water in which there is an extra neutron in each hydrogen atom. When we count the hits, we see only one-third as much as we ought to see. But scientists in the underground Sudbury Neutrino Observatory in Canada may have solved the thirty-year mystery of the missing neutrinos, making us secure once again in our knowledge of solar power. —LK

"Solving the Solar Neutrino Problem"
by Arthur B. McDonald, Joshua R. Klein, and David L. Wark
Scientific American, April 2003

The Sudbury Neutrino Observatory has solved a 30-year-old mystery by showing that neutrinos from the sun change species en route to the earth.

Building a detector the size of a 10-story building two kilometers underground is a strange way to study solar phenomena. Yet that has turned out to be the key to unlocking a decades-old puzzle about the physical processes occurring inside the sun. English physicist Arthur Eddington suggested as early as 1920 that nuclear fusion powered the sun, but efforts to confirm critical details of this idea in the 1960s ran into a stumbling block: experiments designed to detect a distinctive by-product of solar nuclear fusion reactions ghostly particles called neutrinos observed only a fraction of the expected number of them. It was not until last year, with the results from the underground Sudbury Neutrino Observatory (SNO) in Ontario, that physicists resolved this conundrum and thereby fully confirmed Eddington's proposal.

Like all underground experiments designed to study the sun, SNO's primary goal is to detect neutrinos, which are produced in great numbers in the solar core. But unlike most of the other experiments built over the previous three decades, SNO detects solar neutrinos using heavy water, in which a neutron has been added to each of the water molecules' hydrogen atoms (making

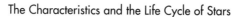

deuterium). The additional neutrons allow SNO to observe solar neutrinos in a way never done before, by counting all three types, or "flavors," of neutrino equally. Using this ability, SNO has demonstrated that the deficit of solar neutrinos seen by earlier experiments resulted not from poor measurements or a misunderstanding of the sun but from a newly discovered property of the neutrinos themselves.

Ironically, the confirmation of our best theory of the sun exposes the first flaw in the Standard Model of particle physics—our best theory of how the most fundamental constituents of matter behave. We now understand the workings of the sun better than we do the workings of the microscopic universe.

The Problem

The first solar neutrino experiment, conducted in the mid-1960s by Raymond Davis, Jr., of the University of Pennsylvania and his co-workers, was intended to be a triumphant confirmation of the fusion theory of solar power generation and the start of a new field in which neutrinos could be used to learn more about the sun. Davis's experiment, located in the Homestake gold mine near Lead, S.D., detected neutrinos by a radio-chemical technique. The detector contained 615 metric tons of liquid tetrachloroethylene, or dry-cleaning fluid, and neutrinos transformed atoms of chlorine in this fluid into atoms of argon. But rather than seeing one atom of argon created each day, as theory predicted, Davis observed just one every 2.5 days. (In 2002 Davis shared the Nobel Prize with Masatoshi Koshiba of the

University of Tokyo for pioneering work in neutrino physics.) Thirty years of experiments following Davis's all found similar results despite using a variety of different techniques. The number of neutrinos arriving from the sun was always significantly less than the predicted total, in some cases as low as one third, in others as high as three fifths, depending on the energies of the neutrinos studied. With no understanding of why the predictions and the measurements were so different, physicists had to put on hold the original goal of studying the solar core by observing neutrinos.

While experimenters continued to run their neutrino experiments, theorists improved the models used to predict the rate of solar neutrino production. Those theoretical models are complex, but they make only a few assumptions—that the sun is powered by nuclear reactions that change the element abundances, that this power creates an outward pressure that is balanced by the inward pull of gravity, and that energy is transported by photons and convection. The solar models continued to predict neutrino fluxes that exceeded the measurements, but other projections they made, such as the spectrum of helioseismologic vibrations seen on the solar surface, agreed very well with observations.

The mysterious difference between the predictions and the measurements became known as the solar neutrino problem. Although many physicists still believed that inherent difficulties in detecting neutrinos and calculating their production rate in the sun were somehow the cause of the discrepancy, a third alternative became widely favored despite its somewhat revolutionary

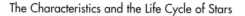

implications. The Standard Model of particle physics holds that there are three completely distinct, massless flavors of neutrinos: the electron-neutrino, muon-neutrino and tau-neutrino. The fusion reactions in the center of the sun can produce only electron-neutrinos, and experiments like Davis's were designed to look exclusively for this one flavor—at solar neutrino energies, only electron-neutrinos can convert chlorine atoms to argon. But if the Standard Model were incomplete, and the neutrino flavors were not distinct but instead mixed in some way, then an electron-neutrino from the sun might transform into one of the other flavors and thus escape detection.

The most favored mechanism for a change in neutrino flavor is neutrino oscillation, which requires that the neutrino flavors (electron-, muon- and tau-neutrinos) are made up of mixtures of neutrino states (denoted as 1, 2 and 3) that have different masses. An electron neutrino could then be a mixture of states 1 and 2, and a muon-neutrino could be a different mixture of the same two states. Theory predicts that as they travel from the sun to the earth, such mixed neutrinos will oscillate between one flavor and another.

Particularly strong evidence of neutrino oscillation was provided by the Super-Kamiokande collaboration in 1998, which found that muon-neutrinos produced in the upper atmosphere by cosmic rays were disappearing with a probability that depended on the distance they traveled. This disappearance is explained extremely well by neutrino oscillations, in this case muon-neutrinos that are probably turning into tau-neutrinos.

The former are easily detected by Super-Kamiokande at cosmic-ray energies, but the latter mostly evade detection [see "Detecting Massive Neutrinos," by Edward Kearns, Takaaki Kajita and Yoji Totsuka; *Scientific American*, August 1999].

A similar process could explain the solar neutrino deficit. In one scenario, the neutrinos would oscillate during their eight-minute journey through the vacuum of space from the sun to the earth. In another model, the oscillation is enhanced during the first two seconds of travel through the sun itself, an effect caused by the different ways in which each neutrino flavor interacts with matter. Each scenario requires its own specific range of neutrino parameters—mass differences and the amount of intrinsic mixing of the flavors. Despite the evidence from Super-Kamiokande and other experiments, however, it remained possible that neutrinos were disappearing by some process other than oscillation. Until 2001 scientists had no direct evidence of solar neutrino oscillation, in which the transformed solar neutrinos themselves were detected.

The Observatory

The Sudbury Neutrino Observatory was designed to search for this direct evidence, by detecting neutrinos using several different interactions with its 1,000 tons of heavy water. One of these reactions exclusively counts electron-neutrinos; the others count all flavors without distinguishing among them. If the solar neutrinos arriving at the earth consisted only of electron-neutrinos—and therefore no flavor transformation was occurring—then

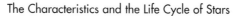

the count of neutrinos of all flavors would be the same as the count of electron-neutrinos alone. On the other hand, if the count of all flavors was far in excess of the count of the electron-neutrinos, that would prove that neutrinos from the sun were changing flavor.

The key to SNO's ability to count both electron-neutrinos alone and all flavors is the heavy water's deuterium nuclei, also called deuterons. The neutron in a deuteron produces two separate neutrino reactions: neutrino absorption, in which an electron-neutrino is absorbed by a neutron and an electron is created, and deuteron breakup, in which a deuterium nucleus is broken apart and the neutron liberated. Only electron-neutrinos can undergo neutrino absorption, but neutrinos of any flavor can break up deuterons. A third reaction detected by SNO, the scattering of electrons by neutrinos, can also be used to count neutrinos other than electron-neutrinos but is much less sensitive to muon- and tau-neutrinos than the deuteron breakup reaction.

SNO was not the first experiment to use heavy water. In the 1960s T. J. Jenkins and F. W. Dix of Case Western Reserve University used heavy water in a very early attempt to observe neutrinos from the sun. They used about 2,000 liters (two tons) of heavy water aboveground, but the signs of solar neutrinos were swamped by the effects of cosmic rays. In 1984 Herb Chen of the University of California at Irvine proposed bringing 1,000 tons of heavy water from Canada's CANDU nuclear reactor to the bottom of INCO Ltd.'s Creighton nickel mine in Sudbury—a location that was deep enough to enable a clear measurement of both neutrino absorption and deuteron breakup for solar neutrinos.

Chen's proposal led to the establishment of the SNO scientific collaboration and ultimately to the creation of the SNO detector. The 1,000 tons of heavy water are held in a 12-meter-diameter transparent acrylic vessel. The heavy water is viewed by more than 9,500 photomultiplier tubes held on an 18-meter-diameter geodesic sphere. Each tube is capable of detecting a single photon of light. The entire structure is submerged in ultrapure ordinary water filling a cavity carved out of the rock two kilometers below the surface of the earth.

SNO's Measurement

Solar neutrinos can be observed deep underground because of the extreme weakness of their interaction with matter. During the day, neutrinos easily travel down to SNO through two kilometers of rock, and at night they are almost equally unaffected by the thousands of kilometers that they travel up through the earth. Such feeble coupling makes them interesting from the perspective of solar astrophysics. Most of the energy created in the center of the sun takes millions of years to reach the solar surface and leave as sunlight. Neutrinos, in contrast, emerge after two seconds, coming to us directly from the point where solar power is created.

With neither the whole sun nor the entire earth able to impede the passage of neutrinos, capturing them

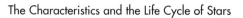
with a detector weighing just 1,000 tons poses something of a challenge. But although the vast majority of neutrinos that enter SNO pass through it, on very rare occasions, one will—by chance alone—collide with an electron or an atomic nucleus and deposit enough energy to be observed. With enough neutrinos, even the rarity of these interactions can be overcome. Luckily, the sun's neutrino output is enormous—five million high-energy solar neutrinos pass through every square centimeter of the earth every second—which leads to about 10 neutrino events, or interactions, in SNO's 1,000 tons of heavy water every day. The three types of neutrino reaction that occur in SNO all generate energetic electrons, which are detectable through their production of Cerenkov light—a cone of light emitted like a shock wave by the fast-moving particle.

This small number of neutrino events, however, has to be distinguished from flashes of Cerenkov light caused by other particles. In particular, cosmic-ray muons are created continually in the upper atmosphere, and when they enter the detector they can produce enough Cerenkov light to illuminate every photomultiplier tube. The intervening kilometers of rock between the earth's surface and SNO reduce the deluge of cosmic-ray muons to a mere trickle of just three an hour. And although three muons an hour is a far greater rate than the 10 neutrino interactions a day, these muons are easy to distinguish from neutrino events by the Cerenkov light they produce in the ordinary water outside the detector.

A far more sinister source of false neutrino counts is the intrinsic radioactivity in the detector materials themselves. Everything inside the detector—from the heavy water itself to the acrylic vessel that holds it to the glass and steel of the photo-multiplier tubes and support structure—has trace amounts of naturally occurring radioactive elements. Similarly, the air in the mine contains radioactive radon gas. Every time a nucleus in these radioactive elements decays inside the SNO detector, it can release an energetic electron or gamma ray and ultimately produce Cerenkov light that mimics the signal of a neutrino. The water and the other materials used in SNO are purified to remove the bulk of the radioactive contaminants (or were chosen to be naturally pure), but even parts per billion are enough to overwhelm the true neutrino signal with false counts.

The task before SNO is therefore very complex—it must count neutrino events, determine how many are caused by each of the three reactions, and estimate how many of the apparent neutrinos are caused by something else, such as radioactive contamination. Errors as small as a few percent in any of the steps of analysis would render meaningless SNO's comparison of the electron-neutrino flux to the total neutrino flux. Over the 306 days of running, from November 1999 to May 2001, SNO recorded nearly half a billion events. By the time the data reduction was complete, only 2,928 of these remained as candidate neutrino events.

SNO cannot uniquely determine whether a given candidate neutrino event was the result of a particular

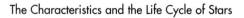

reaction. Typically [such] an event could equally well be the result of deuteron breakup as neutrino absorption. Fortunately, differences between the reactions show up when we examine many events. For example, deuteron breakup, the splitting of a deuterium nucleus in the heavy water, always leads to a gamma ray of the same energy, whereas the electrons produced by neutrino absorption and electron scattering have a broad spectrum of energies. Similarly, electron scattering produces electrons that travel away from the sun, whereas the Cerenkov light from deuteron breakup can point in any direction. Finally, the locations where the reactions occur differ as well—electron scattering, for instance, occurs as easily in the outer layer of light water as in the heavy water; the other reactions do not. With an understanding of those details, SNO researchers can statistically determine how many of the observed events to assign to each reaction.

Such an understanding is the result of measurements that were complete nuclear physics experiments in their own right: to determine how to measure energy using Cerenkov light, sources of radioactivity with known energies were inserted inside the detector. To measure how the Cerenkov light travels through and reflects off the various media in the detector (the water, the acrylic, the photo-multiplier tubes), a variable wavelength laser light source was used. The effects of radioactive contamination were assessed by similar experiments, including radioassays of the water using new techniques designed specifically for SNO.

For the final SNO data set, after statistical analysis, 576 events were assigned to deuteron breakup, 1,967 events to neutrino absorption and 263 to electron scattering. Radioactivity and other backgrounds caused the remaining 122. From these numbers of events, we must calculate how many actual neutrinos must be passing through SNO, based on the tiny probabilities that any particular neutrino will break up a deuteron, be absorbed or scatter an electron. The upshot of all the calculations is that the observed 1,967 neutrino absorption events represent 1.75 million electron-neutrinos passing through each square centimeter of the SNO detector every second. That is only 35 percent of the neutrino flux predicted by solar models. SNO thus first confirms what other solar neutrino experiments have seen—that the number of electron-neutrinos arriving from the sun is far smaller than solar models predict.

The critical question, however, is whether the number of electron-neutrinos arriving from the sun is significantly smaller than the number of neutrinos of all flavors. Indeed, the 576 events assigned to deuteron breakup represent a total neutrino flux of 5.09 million per square centimeter per second—far larger than the 1.75 million electron-neutrinos measured by neutrino absorption. These numbers are determined with high accuracy. The difference between them is more than five times the experimental uncertainty.

The excess of neutrinos measured by deuteron breakup means that nearly two thirds of the total 5.09 million neutrinos arriving from the sun are either muon- or tau-neutrinos. The sun's fusion reactions can produce only electron-neutrinos, so some of them must be transformed on their way to the earth. SNO has therefore demonstrated directly that neutrinos do not behave according to the simple scheme of three distinct massless flavors described by the Standard Model. In 20 years of trying, only experiments such as Super Kamiokande and SNO have shown that the fundamental particles have properties not contained in the Standard Model. The observations of neutrino flavor transformation provide direct experimental evidence that there is yet more to be discovered about the microscopic universe.

But what of the solar neutrino problem itself—does the discovery that electron-neutrinos transform into another flavor completely explain the deficit observed for the past 30 years? It does: the deduced 5.09 million neutrinos agrees remarkably well with the predictions of solar models. We can now claim that we really do understand the way the sun generates its power. Having taken a detour lasting three decades, in which we found that the sun could tell us something new about neutrinos, we can finally return to Davis's original goal and begin to use neutrinos to understand the sun. For example, neutrino studies could determine how much of the sun's energy is produced by direct nuclear fusion of hydrogen atoms and how much is catalyzed by carbon atoms.

The Future

The implications of SNO's discovery go even further. If neutrinos change flavor through oscillation, then they cannot be massless. After photons, neutrinos are the second most numerous known particles in the universe, so even a tiny mass could have a significant cosmological significance. Neutrino oscillation experiments such as SNO and Super-Kamiokande measure only mass differences, not masses themselves. Showing that mass differences are not zero, however, proves that at least some of the masses are not zero. Combining the oscillation results for mass differences with upper limits for the electron-neutrino mass from other experiments shows that neutrinos make up something between 0.3 and 21 percent of the critical density for a flat universe. (Other cosmological data strongly indicate that the universe is flat.) This amount is not negligible (it is roughly comparable to the 4 percent density that arises from gas, dust and stars), but it is not quite enough to explain all the matter that seems to be present in the universe. Because neutrinos were the last known particles that could have made up the missing dark matter, some particle or particles not currently known to physics must exist—and with a density far in excess of everything we do know.

SNO has also been searching for direct evidence of the effects of matter on neutrino oscillations. As mentioned earlier, travel through the sun can enhance the probability of oscillations. If this occurs, the passage of neutrinos through thousands of kilometers of the earth could lead to a small reversal in the process—the sun might shine more brightly in electron-neutrinos at night than during the day. SNO's data show a small excess of electron-neutrinos arriving

at night compared with during the day, but as of now the measurement is not significant enough to decide whether the effect is real.

The results reported by SNO so far are just the beginning. For the observations cited here, we detected the neutrons from the critical deuteron breakup events by observing their capture by other deuterium atoms—an inefficient process that produces little light. In May 2001 two tons of highly purified sodium chloride (table salt) were added to the heavy water. Chlorine nuclei capture neutrons with much higher efficiency than deuterium nuclei do, producing events that have more light and are easier to distinguish from background. Thus, SNO will make a separate and more sensitive measurement of the deuteron breakup rate to check the first results. The SNO collaboration has also built an array of ultraclean detectors called proportional counters, which will be deployed throughout the heavy water in mid-2003 to look for the neutrons directly. Making these detectors was a technical challenge of the first order because they must have a spectacularly low level of intrinsic radioactive background—corresponding to about one count per meter of detector per year. Those devices will essentially check SNO's earlier results by an independent experiment.

SNO has unique capabilities, but it is not the only game in town. In December 2002 the first results from a new Japanese-American experiment called KamLAND were reported. The KamLAND detector is at the Super-Kamiokande site and studies electron-antineutrinos produced by all the nuclear reactors nearby in Japan and Korea. If matter-enhanced neutrino oscillations explain the flavor change seen by SNO, theory predicts that these antineutrinos should also change flavor over distances of tens or hundreds of kilometers. Indeed, KamLAND has seen too few electron-antineutrinos, implying that they are oscillating en route from the nuclear reactors to the detector. The KamLAND results imply neutrino mass differences and mixing parameters similar to those seen by SNO.

Future neutrino experiments might probe one of the biggest mysteries in the cosmos: Why is the universe made of matter rather than antimatter? Russian physicist Andrei Sakharov first pointed out that to get from a big bang of pure energy to the current matter-dominated universe requires the laws of physics to be different for particles and antiparticles. This is called CP (charge-parity) violation, and sensitive measurements of particle decays have verified that the laws of physics violate CP. The problem is that the CP violation seen so far is not enough to explain the amount of matter around us, so phenomena we have not yet observed must be hiding more CP violation. One possible hiding place is neutrino oscillations.

To observe CP-violating neutrino oscillations will be a multistage process. First physicists must see electron-neutrinos appear in intense beams of muon-neutrinos. Second, higher-intensity accelerators must be built to produce beams of neutrinos so intense and pure that their oscillations can be observed in detectors located across continents or on the other side of the earth. Studies of a rare radioactive process called neutrinoless double beta decay will provide further information about neutrino masses and CP violation.

It will probably be more than a decade before these experiments become a reality. A decade may seem a long way off, but the past 30 years, and the sagas of experiments such as SNO, have shown that neutrino physicists are patient and very persistent—one has to be to pry out the secrets of these elusive particles. These secrets are intimately tied up with our next level of understanding of particle physics, astrophysics and cosmology, and thus persist we must.

Back when people thought that a bad thing happened because of cosmic interference, they called it a "disaster," which comes from the Greek words for "bad star." There's a star up there preparing to be a disaster. Rho Cassiopeiae is more than a red giant and even more than a supergiant—it's a hypergiant, a star using up its fuel like there's no tomorrow. In fact, for Rho, there may not be many more tomorrows left. And when that fuel goes, there will be an explosion the likes of which we haven't seen in at least a few hundred years, perhaps even longer. Every once in a while, Rho gives an indication

that the day is coming and then settles down again. One day, the error of its spendthrift days will bring a reckoning. —LK

"Keep an Eye on Hypergiant Rho Cassiopeiae"
by Alex Lobel
Mercury, January–February 2004

An eruption in 1946 of mighty Rho Cassiopeiae put the astronomy community on guard, and recent, exciting changes in the star may portend something big and explosive for it in the near future.

She goes without a proper name, but recently the 17th brightest star of the northern constellation Cassiopeiae is drawing the attention of amateur and professional astronomers worldwide. In the spring of 2000 Rho Cassiopeiae, or ρ Cas, brightened up to magnitude 4.0, then dimmed to an astonishing 5.3 over the next half year, while changing its usual yellowish-white color to the red-orange glare of Betelgeuse (α Orionis). Such a rapid, extraordinary change was also observed for the star in 1946, bringing it to the attention of astronomers everywhere.

Various types of variable stars are known to change their visual brightness in a rather predictable way—stars such as Mira (o Ceti) and Algol (β Persei). And the R Coronae Borealis stars can suddenly dim by several magnitudes; they are much fainter and less intrinsically luminous than ρ Cas, however.

Indeed, shining at about half a million times the Sun's luminosity, Queen ρ Cas is known to be one of the most luminous cool stars of our Galaxy. Tucked away in the Orion spiral arm of the Galaxy, at an approximate distance of ten thousand light-years, it is possibly the most distant star with a surface temperature comparable to that of our Sun that can easily be observed with the unaided eye.

The study of luminous cool (yellow to red) and hot (blue to white) stars addresses a number of key astrophysical questions that pertain to the very existence of stellar objects in general.

- Why do we observe many more luminous hot stars than luminous cool stars in the Galaxy?

- Why do we not see cool stars more luminous than about a million Suns?

- What physical mechanisms determine the relationship between a star's luminosity and its mass, the most fundamental parameter?

- Are these mechanisms universal in the sense that they always operate regardless of other intrinsic stellar parameters such as radius, surface temperature, composition, age, and rotation, or external properties like binarity, group or association membership, or even the star's location in the Galaxy?

To phrase the last question differently: why do we observe stars with, for instance, comparable surface temperatures and total intrinsic magnitudes, but possessing very different spectral signatures?

ρ Cas is a distant star for which modern, space-borne imaging does not reveal clearly discernible structures in its surrounding environment—for example, there appears to be no reflection nebula—and this is real hindrance to our efforts at inferring its stellar properties. But ρ Cas does have one formidable advantage over all other luminous stars: its extraordinary optical brightness.

Spilling the Light Fantastic

More than a century ago astronomers noticed that when the light of stars is split into colors, the stars can be classified according to the presence (or absence) of dark features called "spectral absorption lines," first cataloged for sunlight by Joseph von Fraunhofer in 1814. These spectral signatures contain a wealth of information about the physical circumstances of the stellar atmospheres in which they form but that cannot be deduced from observing the brightness of a star of its variability over time. The spectrum (Latin for "ghost") of a star contains the unique fingerprints of the chemical elements present and is determined by the physical mechanisms that distribute the energy of photons into various visible colors and those invisible to the human eye—from energetic gamma rays and x rays to lower-energy infrared, microwave, and radio waves.

X rays and radio waves have yet to be detected from ρ Cas, but the spectrum of its visible light has been recorded with high precision for more than a century.

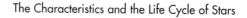
In particular, we have discovered that ρ Cas is one of very few cool stars for which recurrent spectral changes can be linked with the star's semi-regular brightness changes: the positions of the spectral absorption lines change periodically with time, shifting right to left and back again, while the lines' shapes and darknesses change as well. They are occasionally even brighter than the surrounding, continuous spectrum and become bright "emission lines."

As a doctoral student at Utrecht, the Space Research Organization of The Netherlands, I organized in 1993 a small group of researchers with the goal of combining spectral observations of ρ Cas from two telescopes. Since then, however, the group's efforts have grown to include continuous monitoring programs from six different telescopes in the United States and Europe. One would normally require a large telescope for the ground-based, high-resolution observations we collect from ρ Cas, but the star is so bright in the optical portion of the electromagnetic spectrum that a high-quality and high-resolution spectrum can be collected within an hour using one- to two-meter telescopes. Fortunately, we have access in the northern hemisphere to such telescopes with high-resolution spectrographs, which permits us year-round, spectroscopic access to ρ Cas. Indeed, our observational campaign on this star is one of the largest ground-based, high-resolution, spectral-monitoring programs ever conducted.

But ρ Cas is more than just a cool, luminous star. Unlike many other bright stars in the sky, there is no observational evidence that ρ Cas is part of a binary or multiple-star system. This was suspected before 1993 and has in the meantime been confirmed by our spectral monitoring program. This fact may appear to be only a detail in a much bigger picture, yet for a stellar spectroscopist the difference between binarity or other multiplicity and not is as great as that between day and night. The observed shifts of the spectral lines could be influenced, if not solely produced, by gravitational tugs on large ρ Cas by smaller but sufficiently massive companions. If this were the situation, it would be practically impossible for one to directly correlate the remarkable line shifts with the brightness changes of the star itself, compromising the ultimate goal of our monitoring program to document and unravel the physical cause for this dependence.

In the summer of 2000, after more than six years of continuous spectral monitoring, ρ Cas finally revealed more than we had ever hoped for. The star brightened and then abruptly dimmed by more than a full magnitude—almost three times dimmer—all the while displaying tremendous spectral changes. After more than half a century since its similar, dramatic event in 1946, enigmatic ρ Cas revealed its deepest secrets through a new eruption—likely a once-in-a-career event for an astronomer. Our continuous, high-resolution spectral monitoring program yielded an amazing result: the highest rate of mass-loss by a star during a single outburst. At the same time, ρ Cas disclosed in an unequivocal way its true nature: it is a "yellow hypergiant." Our observations of the star have continued in the aftermath of the outburst, and the most recent spectral evolution reveals new, dramatic, dynamical changes in its outer atmosphere.

How Hyper Is Your Giant?

ρ Cas is among the most massive, cool stars presently known. Theoretical models employed to predict the evolution of very luminous stars indicate that the stars' lives are relatively short: the heavier a star is at birth, the sooner it dies with a blinding flash of light in a supernova explosion.

Indeed, different masses at birth spell different lives for stars. Stars with ten to about sixty times the Sun's mass burn hydrogen in their cores and eventually evolve from the hottest, bluest, type-O spectral class to become first blue supergiants and then to redder, cooler, type-M supergiants. Stars with forty to sixty solar masses loop back from their red-supergiant phase into hotter and smaller blue supergiants. Above sixty solar masses, stellar-evolution theory suggests that stars never reach cool spectral-class M and remain hot, extreme supergiants. These curious evolutionary loops are predicted only for luminous stars born with masses within a limited range.

Evolutionary tracks for ρ Cas—with its total lifespan of ten million years, one or two million of which will be spent as a red supergiant—show that it is either becoming a red supergiant or is on its way back from being one. In general and after the hydrogen in their cores is depleted, stars begin fusing hydrogen to helium in a shell just outside their hot, helium-rich cores. Models predict that near the end of its red-supergiant stage, a massive star reacts to the constant drain of energy from this shell source of energy by raising its central temperature to more than 100 million kelvins and initiating the fusion of the core helium into carbon. Following an extended period of different nuclear fusion regimes (e.g., carbon fusion, oxygen fusion, etc.) and concomitant structural changes, the outer layers of the red supergiant contract, which increases the surface temperature. The red supergiant is now evolving "blueward."

This scenario is rather sketchy because we know that red supergiants are convective, large quantities of energy carried by hot parcels of gas from a star's depths to its surface, and release enormous amounts of atmospheric gas into space. Consider, for illustration, that M-class supergiant Betelgeuse, which if placed at the Sun's position would have a surface somewhere between Mars's and Jupiter's orbits, sheds each year about a millionth of a solar mass; the mass loss comes from steady wind leaving the star's huge surface. Red supergiants are, therefore, one of the most important cosmic factories for replenishing the interstellar medium with material processed through nuclear fusion reactions. More specifically in this case, the copious loss of mass from a cool luminous star is believed to have a decisive influence on the star's blueward evolution, which may last only as long as 50,000 years, less than one percent of the star's entire lifetime.

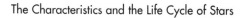

Only a handful of cool luminous stars known in the Milky Way Galaxy are thought to be post-red supergiants, and they are notorious for their changing spectral properties. HR 8752, for example, is a cool hypergiant that increased its surface temperature by 3000 kelvins over the past thirty years, while the temperature of star IRC + 10420 increased at least 2000 kelvins over the last two decades. It is presently unclear if such large temperature changes can be directly attributed to active reconstruction of the stellar interior on human time scales, but the stars' spectra do indicate a very advanced evolutionary stage.

Mysterious ρ Cas is even more extreme. It usually has an optical spectrum corresponding to a surface temperature of about 6000 to 7000 kelvins and with unusually broad absorption lines not commonly observed in the spectra of other, "normal" yellow supergiants such as δ Canis Majoris and φ Cassiopeiae, which have luminosities comparable to ρ Cas. As with ρ Cas, the visual brightness of these supergiants fluctuates somewhat due to oscillations of the stellar atmosphere, yet ρ Cas differs in that it frequently shows very strong emission components in an important line in the red part of the spectrum.

This spectral line, called Balmer H α and corresponding to a wavelength of 6563 Å, is produced by atomic hydrogen gas, the most abundant chemical element in the star's pulsating atmosphere. The line's shape provides us a precise indicator for gas movements in the extended hypergiant atmosphere, where it forms. The emission-portion of the H α line is caused by Doppler-shifted photons from a strong stellar wind, indicative of a very high rate of mass loss. Indeed, before ρ Cas's dramatic dimming of 2000 my group occasionally measured mass-loss rates a hundred million times higher than that observed for the Sun's solar wind.

The broad absorption lines of ρ Cas are formed by supersonic, turbulent gas movements. Spectral changes indicate the star's atmosphere is very unstable, with surging upward and downward currents of material, a strong stellar wind blowing material outward, and other atmospheric activities that together give rise to pulsations of the surface temperature, brightness and size, in quasi-regular periods of about 320 days. During ρ Cas's pulsations in surface temperature of about 750 kelvins, the average radius of its visible surface changes by forty percent and averages a mean size of 400 to 500 times the radius of the Sun.

ρ Cas is, thus, smaller than red supergiant Betelgeuse with a mean radius around 700 times the Sun's radius. But Betelgeuse is not a hypergiant. The term "hypergiant" does not refer to the large size or luminosity of a massive star, but instead to its exceptional spectral properties indicative of a distended and dynamically active atmosphere. One out of a million stars in our Galaxy is a normal supergiant star, yet fewer are hypergiants. And the cool hypergiants are extremely scarce, their erratic atmospheric behavior thought to result from their advanced evolutionary stage on a blueward loop. They are so luminous that one cool hypergiant has even been identified in the spiral galaxy M33.

Mysterious Changes

In the summer of 1946, ρ Cas dimmed by 1.5 magnitudes to become fainter than 6.0 magnitudes. During this unexpected event, the star temporarily changed its spectral class from F to much cooler M and showed prominent spectral absorption bands attributed to titanium-oxide molecules, whose presence signals low atmospheric temperature. Such broad absorption bands are common for the optical spectra of M-class stars, such as Betelgeuse and μ Cepheus, but are absent in spectra of F-class stars. During ρ Cas's 1946 event, more than spectral changes were observed: the atmosphere's average temperature decreased by more than 3000 kelvins, causing the star to dim in the visible but to brighten in the infrared. The visible dimming lasted for about 400 days, and the star returned to normal brightness levels in late 1947. Spectra from this period clearly show absorption lines that are Doppler-displaced toward shorter wavelengths during the brightness decline, signaling atmospheric gases rushing outward. However, these old spectroscopic data are rather coarse and too sparse, and we can not infer much about the dynamics or thermal conditions in ρ Cas's atmosphere during this historical eruption.

Since that time the quality of spectroscopic measurements has improved considerably. Over the past ten years we collected from ρ Cas a total of about 100, high-resolution, optical spectra on different nights. The combined data sets yield the surprising result that the visual brightness changes of ρ Cas are, in fact, matched by Doppler shifts observed in the photospheric spectral lines about one hundred days earlier. In other words, the upward and downward movements of atmospheric gases are mimicked by intensity variations of continuous light emission from the star due to temperature changes in the lower atmosphere. In general, when ρ Cas's atmosphere collapses, it heats up over the following three months. After re-inflating, it cools down again.

In early 2000 large shifts of the absorption lines showed that the atmosphere was strongly collapsing. Roughly one hundred days later the brightness reached an unprecedented 4.0 magnitudes. Over the following hundred days, ρ Cas's atmosphere expanded, reaching a maximum velocity of about 35 km/sec in a massive eruption, and subsequently chilled by at least 3000 kelvins later that year. We were able to measure the wavelength shifts of the newly formed titanium-oxide bands: the combined measurements reveal that 10,000 Earth masses of gas were blasted off into space over a period of 200 days.

Many other strange features are observed in the outburst spectra from 2000, such as peculiar and normally absent (save for the 1946 eruption) emission lines of sodium. The most striking feature, however, is the broad, red-shifted H α absorption line that shows emission at its short-wavelength side. The emission component is very strong in the months during the collapse and before the visible outburst but disappears completely during the deep dimming of ρ Cas. From this profound and time-dependent spectral line shape, we infer that the star's entire upper atmosphere falls down onto the star's photosphere, which subsequently warms under the strong compression. Further, our spectral monitoring of the Balmer H α line reveals that high layers of the atmosphere oscillate with a longer period than those lower. As the gas shoots upward from deep atmospheric layers, it temporarily exceeds the gravitational pull of the star; some of the gas escapes into the environment around ρ Cas.

The energetics of the massive gas layers expelled from the star are subtle but very important. Freed atoms can bind into molecules such as titanium oxide, and, as the ejected layers expand and cool, free protons and electrons recombine into neutral hydrogen atoms. Both these combinations release energy to the ejected layers, which results in an increase in the layers' expansion velocity. Detailed calculations show that the hydrogen recombination mechanism is very effective in accelerating the explosion of the atmosphere of a yellow hypergiant, leading, in fact, to what we call a "superwind" from the star. The outburst results from the synchonization of outward acceleration with the thermal cooling rate, causing an avalanche of hydrogen recombination. A similar recombination mechanism for helium atoms is a possible cause for the faster eruptions of the smaller R Coronae Borealis stars. And in the spectra of RV Tauri variables, titanium-oxide bands reminiscent of those in ρ Cas appear during brightness minimum, whereas strong H α emission occurs during brightness maximum. Stars of this type are also semiregular pulsators and possess spectra that can vary between spectral classes F-G and K-M. Yet even though their spectral changes suggest kinship with the yellow hypergiants, these stars far less massive and smaller than ρ Cas.

The advanced evolutionary stage of all these cool-star types indicates a prominent atomic process that strongly enhances the elasticity of the stars' dynamic atmospheres. Pulsations in deep levels of the atmosphere can become amplified and grow into circumstellar shock waves that strongly inflate and cool the upper atmosphere. Outburst spectra of ρ Cas reveal that its atmosphere more than doubles in size, and then retreats during about three months after the shell ejection.

Keeping Our Eyes Peeled

Over the past three years, the bright emission at the short-wavelength side of ρ Cas's Hα line has reappeared with an unusually broad absorption trough, signaling the collapse of the star's extended upper atmosphere. This peculiar Hα profile was also observed in ρ Cas before a moderate brightness decrease in 1986, but it has never been observed over a period this long. The recent spectral velocity measurements reveal that since early 2003, layers of the deeper atmosphere were rapidly expanding but did not reach the very fast expansion velocities observed during the millenium outburst. The lower photosphere started to contract quickly again in the fall of 2003, so we have not observed a new eruption as we imagined we might.

Our continuous monitoring reveals, however, a new, strange, spectral phenomenon. The shape of the Hα line has rapidly and dramatically transformed during the past ten months, signaling that the upper atmosphere reversed from contraction into a fast global expansion with enhanced mass loss. This remarkably fast phenomenon has not before been observed in ρ Cas or in any other star. We are left wondering what is in store for ρ Cas in the coming months—could the millennium eruption have been only the precursor of a stronger eruption still preparing to blow?

The critical thing for my group to do is to continue our monitoring of ρ Cas. When a new outburst occurs, we must collect high-quality spectra during the star's fast brightness decrease because they will provide important clues to and information about the acceleration mechanism of the atmosphere, and, more generally, such observations will help us uncover the physical mechanisms that instigate and drive these gargantuan stellar explosions. In addition, our and others' continued studies of cool hypergiants like ρ Cas will address the basic question of why these stars are rare compared to the blue luminous stars. Finally, our work will hopefully permit us to say how hypergiants end their stellar days—through a series of mass-losing eruptions separated by half centuries and occurring over a few tens of millennia or perhaps as super- or even hypernovae. All we can do is wait. And keep an eye on ρ Cassiopeiae.

If you think the dust bunnies under your bed must have come from some other world, you're not as far off as you might think. The dust may not have come from the solar system, but that doesn't mean the solar system is exactly clean. Much of the dust that formed the solar system has been ejected away from us. However, scientists have meticulously cleaned some space dust captured in meteorites and found a few compounds that don't have the same amount of elemental isotopes that our own solar system has. It appears that these grains of material managed to make their way into our own area, leading us to believe that red giant stars have created their own cosmic dust bunnies. —LK

"Peering into Stardust"
by A. G. Tielens
Science, April 4, 2003

The smallest components of the Milky Way, the (sub)micrometer-sized grains of stardust, may provide crucial insights into star and planet formation. Most interstellar dust is thought to form in the ejecta of red giants or supernovae.[1] Stardust locks in the characteristics of its stellar birthplace, particularly its anomalous isotopic composition, which is often used to identify presolar grains in solar system materials. But as may be concluded from the study by Messenger et al.,[2] isotopically anomalous stardust particles may not be the only presolar grains in the solar system.

Some 15 years ago, Anders and co-workers[3] isolated the first genuine stardust grains from meteorites. Searching for the carrier of noble gas isotopic anomalies in meteorites, they burned the haystack to find the needle. Removing all material except for a few very resistant compounds, they localized the isotopic anomalies in nanometer-sized diamond stardust grains. Analogous procedures following the trail of different noble gas anomalies led to the isolation of other stardust components, including SiC and graphite grains. In each case, the presolar nature of the grains was established by their anomalous isotopic composition, not only in the trapped noble gases but essentially in all elements.

Messenger et al.[2] now report the results of another technique to find stardust. Instead of searching for a needle, they study the haystack itself. They thus overcome one of the key drawbacks of the technique of Anders and co-workers: the removal of silicates. Astronomical studies show that a major fraction of interstellar dust is in the form of small silicates rather than carbonaceous grains.

In their study, Messenger et al. mapped the oxygen isotope composition of micrometer-sized interplanetary dust particles (IDPs) with a NanoSIMS (SIMS, Scanning Ion Microprobe Spectrometer). In that way, they were able to identify isotopically anomalous silicate stardust grains. Once identified, various techniques can be brought to bear on these isolated mineral stardust grains to determine their composition, mineralogy, and textural relationship with their environments.

The big surprise was not the discovery of genuine silicate stardust, but rather how little was found: Only 6 out of some 1000 grains, or 0.5 % by mass, are isotopically anomalous. Messenger *et al.* focused on the analysis of GEMS, glass with embedded metal and sulfides, a major phase in chondritic, porous IDPs.[4] GEMS consist of 10-nm-diameter FeNi metal and sulfide grains embedded in a silicate glass. The elemental composition, mineralogy, morphology, and texture of GEMS suggests that they were produced through high-energy particle irradiation of silicate precursor grains.[4]

Comets, the likely source of these IDPs, are thought to represent rather pristine reservoirs of presolar material and should be replete with stardust grains. Among IDPs, GEMS are the most obvious stardust candidates. Many of their characteristics are similar to those expected for presolar silicate grains. Consequently, GEMS have often been identified with surviving presolar interstellar silicates.[4] The fact that GEMS are isotopically normal[2] forces us to reassess their evolution and perhaps that of comets and of the solar nebula as well.

The key assumption made by Messenger *et al.* is that presolar grains are characterized by a nonsolar isotope distribution. The evidence for this rests on astronomical observations of the nonsolar oxygen isotope ratio in the photospheres of red giants, the birthplaces of silicate stardust.[5] Theoretical studies of nucleosynthesis in red giants and supernovae also predict large oxygen isotope anomalies.[6, 7] The measured oxygen isotope distribution of graphite stardust is highly anomalous as well.[8]

Hence, we would expect presolar oxygen isotope ratios to differ from solar ones by more than a factor of 2 and up to a factor of 10. In contrast, the overwhelming majority of GEMS investigated by Messenger *et al.* show solar abundance ratios within 10%. Thus, most of these GEMS appear to have equilibrated with the gas phase and acquired the average composition of the interstellar medium.

Although most silicon injected into the interstellar medium is expected to be in the form of silicate stardust, various processes will influence its evolution. Strong interstellar shock waves will sputter some atoms into the gas phase, some of which may reaccrete during the evolution of the grain to form a (protective) mantle. However, abundance considerations and the low temperature of the interstellar medium suggest that this mantle should be dominated by volatile species such as carbon, oxygen, and hydrogen.

Hence, although such a putative mantle would have a normal isotopic composition, it would be carbon- rather than silicate-based. Formation of silicates with an isotopically normal composition is only likely in the inner solar system, or the inner protoplanetary disk around any protostar, where most of the incoming presolar dust will sublime and recondense.

There is additional evidence for major processing of silicate dust in comets. Astronomical observations have shown that interstellar silicate dust is largely amorphous, with a crystalline fraction of at most 2%.[1] In contrast, infrared spectroscopy studies with the Short Wavelength Spectrometer aboard the Infrared Space Observatory have revealed that comet Hale-Bopp has a very high crystalline-silicate fraction.[9] That seems to be a general characteristic of solar system comets.[10] Silicates in circumstellar disks around isolated intermediate-mass protostars also show high crystalline-silicate fractions.[11]

The amorphous-crystalline transition of silicates occurs at 1000 K, well above the temperatures experienced by comets or the observed temperature of silicate dust around protostars. These observations provide further support for large-scale, radial mixing of materials in planetary disks around newly formed stars such as the early solar nebula, with transport of freshly crystallized (and likely freshly condensed) materials from the inner solar nebula out to the region where the comets were formed.[12] The evidence and line of reasoning are different from those of Messenger *et al.*,[2] but the conclusion is the same.

By pinning the GEMS to a local protosolar or protostellar origin, Messenger *et al.* have identified a further puzzle. The GEMS have experienced extensive energetic-particle irradiation,[4] which in view of the observed textural and mineralogical structures must have occurred before the IDPs agglomerated. The obvious protosolar/protostellar environment for such process-ing is high-velocity jets, which often accompany low-mass star formation.[13]

Perhaps presolar material is processed rapidly through inner protoplanetary disks, subliming and recondensing silicates with complete loss of any preso-lar signature. They are then ejected through the fast winds of protostars, converting a large fraction or even all into GEMS. This processed material may be mixed into the infalling core forming the Sun or, more likely, stirred throughout the whole molecular cloud (which contains many protostars). The total amount of mate-rial involved in protostellar outflows is a fair fraction of the protostellar mass (and much more than the solar system's planetary mass). This may lead to a prepon-derance of GEMS in the outer protosolar nebula with an isotopically normal composition either from the inner solar nebula by way of the jet and the envelope or even from neighboring protostars.

Such dust formation in protostellar environments could be a source of dust for the interstellar medium com-parable to that from the classical stardust sources, red giants and supernovae. Hence, isotopically normal silicates in the form of GEMS could be abundant in the general interstellar medium. However, crystalline silicate grains in comets have not experienced a radiation environment, and silicates in molecular clouds are amorphous. A more gentle radial transport mechanism therefore has to exist to transport newly condensed, crystalline silicates from the inner solar nebula outwards where the comets formed.[12]

Silicate stardust formed in red giant ejecta may be processed by the jets and hot gases associated with the planetary nebulae phase, which immediately follows the red giant phase in the evolution of low-mass stars. Silicate stardust formed in supernova ejecta will be processed in the hot gas of the supernova blast wave. Hence, although their origins may be different, presolar and solar/protostellar dust may have experienced similar environments, leading to very similar GEMS-like textures, structures, and morphologies. Of course, solar system GEMS will be characterized by a solar isotopic composition, whereas presolar stardust still has its anomalous isotopic composition.

Perhaps it is too early to conclude from the study of Messenger *et al.* that GEMS are not presolar and that comets are not pristine. The Stardust mission may help to answer the many open questions. It is designed to return samples of genuine, interstellar, and cometary dust to Earth in 2006. The number of grains will be limited (100 interstellar and 1000 cometary grains), but determination of cosmic ray exposure ages of interstellar dust, cometary GEMS/IDPs, and crystalline silicates will be very revealing.

Techniques are also being developed to identify, in samples collected in Earth orbit, those grains that are true interstellar dust grains among IDPs that may have been processed in the solar system.[14] Collectors in Earth orbit using such techniques would provide a relatively cheap way to collect large samples of fresh interstellar dust. Moreover, this would yield IDPs that have not been exposed and altered by the heating events associated with their entry into Earth's atmosphere.

Studies of captured IDPs and interstellar dust will help to address the issue of the presolar nature of GEMS and the origin of comets and will be an important step toward putting the planetary formation jigsaw puzzle together on a grain-by-grain basis.

References

1. J. S. Mathis, *Annu. Rev. Astron. Astrophys.* **28**, 37 (1990).
2. S. Messenger, L. P. Keller, F. J. Stadermann, R. M. Walker, E. Zinner, *Science* **300**, 105 (2003); published online 27 February 2003 (10.1126/science.1080576).
3. R. S. Lewis, M. Tang, J. F. Wacker, E. Anders, E. Steel, *Nature* **326**, 160 (1987).
4. J. P. Bradley, *Science* **265**, 925 (1994).
5. V. Smith, D. Lambert, *Astrophys. J. Suppl. Ser.* **72**, 387 (1990).
6. A. I. Boothroyd, I.-J. Sackmann, *Astrophys. J.* **510**, 232 (1999).
7. B. S. Meyer, T. A. Weaver, S. E. Woosley, *Meteoritics* **30**, 325 (1995).
8. S. Amari, E. Zinner, R. S. Lewis, *Astrophys. J.* **447**, L147 (1995).
9. J. Crovisier et al., *Science* **275**, 1904 (1997).
10. M. Hanner, *Space Sci. Rev.* **90**, 99 (1999).
11. K. Malfait et al., *Astron. Astrophys.* **332**, L25 (1998).
12. D. Bockelee-Morvan et al., *Astron. Astrophys.* **384**, 1107 (2002).
13. B. Reipurth, J. Bally, *Annu. Rev. Astron. Astrophys.* **39**, 403 (2001).
14. G. Dominguez, A. J. Westphal, M. L. F. Phillips, S. M. Jones, in preparation.

The End of Life for a Solar Mass Star

There is plenty of space between the stars—in the Sun's part of the galaxy. Elsewhere, it is like cosmic bumper cars. Collisions are especially common in dense star clusters called globulars. For evidence of collisions, we need only look at the cast-aside hulks and smoking wrecks that are left behind.

There are many sources for X-rays in the sky, but a preponderance of them are found in globular clusters, huge balls of stars that orbit around galaxies like our Milky Way. The X-rays come from binaries, pairs of objects orbiting around a common center of mass, of which one component is a black hole or neutron star. In the normal course of evolution, some stars explode as supernovae. Some become black holes or neutron stars that are sent flying through the pinball machine of gravitational fields that is a globular cluster. In our neck of the cosmic woods, two stars colliding would just curve around each other and go merrily on their separate ways, in new directions. Not so in the

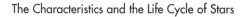
high-density world of globulars. Two or even three stars might come together, rob each other of energy, and form a partnership, a dangerous one in which all are bathed in X-rays. —LK

"When Stars Collide"
by Michael Shara
Scientific American, September 2004

When two stars smash into each other, it can be a very pretty sight (as long as you're not close by). These occurrences were once considered impossible, but they have turned out to be common in certain galactic neighborhoods.

Overview/Stellar Collisions

- This article represents one of those cases in which the textbooks need to be revised. The conventional wisdom that stars can never hit each other is wrong. Collisions can occur in star clusters, especially globular clusters, where the density of stars is high and where gravitational interactions heighten the odds of impact.

- The leading observational evidence for collisions is twofold. Globular clusters contain stars called blue stragglers that are best explained as the outcome of collisions. And globulars contain an anomalously high number of x-ray sources—again the likely product of collisions.

Of all the ways for life on Earth to end, the collision of the sun and another star might well be the most dramatic. If the incoming projectile were a white dwarf—a superdense star that packs the mass of the sun into a body a hundredth the size—the residents of Earth would be treated to quite a fireworks show. The white dwarf would penetrate the sun at hypersonic speed, over 600 kilometers a second, setting up a massive shock wave that would compress and heat the entire sun above thermonuclear ignition temperatures.

It would take only an hour for the white dwarf to smash through, but the damage would be irreversible. The superheated sun would release as much fusion energy in that hour as it normally does in 100 million years. The buildup of pressure would force gas outward at speeds far above escape velocity. Within a few hours the sun would have blown itself apart. Meanwhile the agent of this catastrophe, the white dwarf, would continue blithely on its way—not that we would be around to care about the injustice of it all.

For much of the 20th century, the notion that stellar collisions might be worth studying seemed ludicrous to astronomers. The distances between stars in the neighborhood of the sun are just too vast for them to bump into one another. Other calamities will befall the sun (and Earth) in the distant future, but a collision with a nearby star is not likely to be one of them. In fact, simple calculations carried out early in the 20th century by British astrophysicist James Jeans suggested that not a single one of the 100

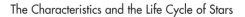
billion stars in the disk of our galaxy has ever run into another star.

But that does not mean collisions are uncommon. Jeans's assumptions and conclusion apply to the environs of the sun but not to other, more exotic parts of the Milky Way. Dense star clusters are a veritable demolition derby. Within these tight knots of stars, observers in recent years have discovered bodies that are forbidden by the principles of ordinary stellar evolution—but that are naturally explained as smashed-up stars. Collisions can modify the long-term evolution of entire clusters, and the most violent ones can be seen halfway across the universe.

A Star-Eat-Star World

The 1963 discovery of quasars was what inspired skeptical astronomers to take stellar collisions seriously. Many quasars radiate as much power as 100 trillion suns. Because some brighten or dim significantly in less than a day, their energy-producing regions must be no larger than the distance light can travel in a day—about the size of our solar system. If you could somehow pack millions of stars into such a small volume, astronomers asked, would stars crash? And could this jostling liberate those huge energies?

By 1970 it became clear that the answer to the second question was no. Nor could stellar slam dancing explain the narrow jets that emanate from the central powerhouses of many quasars. The blame fell instead on supermassive black holes. (Ironically, some astronomers have recently proposed that stellar collisions could help feed material into these holes.)

Just as extragalactic astronomers were giving up on stellar collisions, their galactic colleagues adopted them with a vengeance. The Uhuru satellite, launched in 1970 to survey the sky for x-ray-emitting objects, discovered about 100 bright sources in the Milky Way. Fully 10 percent were in the densest type of star cluster, globular clusters. Yet such clusters make up only 0.01 percent of the Milky Way's stars. For some reason, they contain a wildly disproportionate number of x-ray sources.

To express the mystery in a different way, consider what produces such x-ray sources. Each is thought to be a pair of stars, one of which has died and collapsed into a neutron star or a black hole. The ex-star cannibalizes its partner and in doing so heats the gas to such high temperatures that it releases x-rays. Such morbid couplings are rare. The simultaneous evolution of two newborn stars in a binary system succeeds in producing a luminous x-ray binary just once in a billion tries.

What is it about globular clusters of stars that overcomes these odds? It dawned on astronomers that the crowded conditions in globulars could be the deciding factor. A million stars are crammed into a volume a few dozen light-years across; an equivalent volume near the sun would accommodate only a hundred stars. Like bees in a swarm, these stars move in ever changing orbits. Lower-mass stars tend to be ejected from the cluster as they pick up energy during close encounters with more massive single and double stars, a process

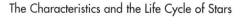

referred to as evaporation because it resembles the escape of molecules from the surface of a liquid. The remaining stars, having lost energy, concentrate closer to the cluster center. Given enough time, the tightly packed stars will begin to collide.

Even in a globular cluster, the average distance between stars is much larger than the stars themselves. But Jack G. Hills and Carol A. Day, both then at the University of Michigan at Ann Arbor, showed in 1975 that the probability of impact is not a simple matter of a star's physical cross section. Because the stars in a globular cluster move at a lackadaisical (by cosmic standards) 10 to 20 kilometers a second, gravity has plenty of time to act during close encounters. Without gravity, two stars can hit only if they are aimed directly at each other; with gravity, each star pulls on the other, deflecting its path. The stars are transformed from ballistic missiles with a preset flightpath into guided missiles that home in on their target. A collision becomes up to 10,000 times more likely. In fact, half the stars in the central regions of some globular clusters have probably undergone one or more collisions over the past 13 billion years.

Around the same time, Andrew C. Fabian, James E. Pringle and Martin J. Rees of the University of Cambridge suggested that a grazing collision or a very near miss could cause two isolated stars to pair up. Normally a close encounter of two celestial bodies is symmetrical: they approach, gather speed, swing past each other and, unless they make contact, fly apart. But if one is a neutron star or a black hole, its intense gravity can contort the other, sapping some of its kinetic energy and preventing it from escaping, a process known as tidal capture. The neutron star or black hole proceeds to feast on its ensnared prey, spewing x-rays.

If the close encounter involves not two but three stars, it is even more likely to produce an x-ray binary. The dynamics of three bodies is notoriously complex and sometimes chaotic; the stars usually redistribute their energy in such a way that the two most massive ones pair up and the third gets flung away. The typical situation involves a loner neutron star that comes a little too close to an ordinary binary pair. One of the ordinary stars in the binary is cast off, and the neutron star takes its place, producing an x-ray source. The bottom line is that three-body dynamics and tidal capture lead to a thousandfold increase in the rate at which x-ray sources form in globular clusters, neatly solving the puzzle raised by Uhuru.

Crash Scene

What happens when two stars smack into each other? As in a collision involving two vehicles, the outcome depends on several factors: the speed of the colliding objects, their internal structures and the impact parameter (which specifies whether the collision is head-on or a sideswipe). Some incidents are fender benders, some are total wrecks and some fall in between. Higher-velocity and head-on collisions are the best at converting kinetic energy into heat and pressure, making for a total wreck.

Although astronomers rely on supercomputers to study collisions in detail, a few simple principles govern the overall effect. Most important is the density contrast. A higher-density star will suffer much less damage than

a tenuous one, just as a cannonball is barely marked as it blows a watermelon to shreds. A head-on collision between a sunlike star and a vastly denser star, such as a white dwarf, was first studied in the 1970s and 1980s by me and my colleagues Giora Shaviv and Oded Regev, both then at Tel Aviv University and now at the Technion Israel Institute of Technology in Haifa. Whereas the sunlike star is annihilated, the white dwarf, being 10 million times as dense, gets away with only a mild warming of its outermost layers. Except for an anomalously high surface abundance of nitrogen, the white dwarf should appear unchanged.

The dwarf is less able to cover its tracks during a grazing collision, as first modeled by me, Regev and Mario Livio of the Space Telescope Science Institute. The disrupted sunlike star could form a massive disk in orbit around the dwarf. No such disks have yet been shown to exist, but it is possible that astronomers might be mistaking them for mass-transferring binary stars in star clusters.

When the colliding stars are of the same type, density and size, a very different sequence of events occurs. The case of two sunlike stars was first simulated in the early 1970s by Alastair G. W. Cameron, then at Yeshiva University, and Frederick G. P. Seidl, then at the NASA Goddard Institute for Space Studies. As the initially spherical stars increasingly overlap, they compress and distort each other into half-moon shapes. Temperatures and densities never climb high enough to ignite disruptive thermonuclear burning. As a small percent of the total mass squirts out perpendicular to the direction of stellar motion, the rest mixes together. Within an hour, the two stars have fused into one.

It is much more likely that two stars will collide somewhat off-axis than exactly head-on; it is also more likely that they will have slightly different rather than identical masses. This general case has been studied in detail by Willy Benz of the University of Bern in Switzerland, Frederic A. Rasio of Northwestern University, James C. Lombardi of Vassar College, Joshua E. Barnes of the University of Hawaii at Manoa and their collaborators. It is a beautiful mating dance that ends in the perpetual union of the two stars.

The object that results is fundamentally different from an isolated star such as our sun. An isolated star has no way of replenishing its initial allotment of fuel; its life span is preordained. The more massive the star is, the hotter it is and the faster it burns itself out. Given a star's color, which indicates its temperature, computer models of energy production can predict its life span with high precision. But a coalesced star does not follow the same rules. Mixing of the layers of gas during the collision can add fresh hydrogen fuel to the core, with a rejuvenating effect rather like tossing twigs on a dying campfire. Moreover, the object, being more massive than its progenitors, will be hotter, bluer and brighter. Observers who look at the star and use its color and luminosity to deduce its age will be wrong.

For instance, the sun has a total life span of 10 billion years, whereas a star twice its mass is 10 times brighter and lasts only 800 million years. Therefore, if two sun-like stars merge halfway through their lives, they will

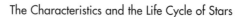

form a single hot star that is five billion years old at the moment of its creation but looks as though it must be younger than 800 million years. The lifetime remaining to this massive fused star depends on how much hydrogen fuel was thrown to its center by the collision. Usually this lifetime will be much shorter than that of each of its parents. Even in death the star distinguishes itself. When it dies (by swelling to become a red giant, a planetary nebula and finally a white dwarf), it will be much hotter than other, older white dwarfs of similar mass.

Got the Blues

In a globular cluster, massive merged stars will stand out conspicuously. All the members of a globular are born at roughly the same time; their temperature and brightness evolve in lockstep. But a coalesced star is out of sync. It looks preternaturally young, surviving when others of equal brightness and color have passed on. The presence of such stars in the cores of dense star clusters is one of the most compelling predictions of stellar-collision theory.

As it happens, Allan R. Sandage of the Carnegie Institution of Washington discovered in the early 1950s that globular clusters contain anomalously hot and bright stars called blue stragglers. Researchers have since advanced a dozen theories of their origin. But it is only in the past decade that the Hubble Space Telescope has provided a strong link with collisions.

In 1991 Francesco Paresce, George Meylan and I, all then at the Space Telescope Science Institute, found that the very center of the globular cluster 47 Tucanae is crammed with blue stragglers, exactly where collision theory predicted they should exist in greatest number. Six years later David Zurek of the Space Telescope Science Institute, Rex A. Saffer of Villanova University and I carried out the first direct measurement of the mass of a blue straggler in a globular cluster. It has approximately twice the mass of the most massive ordinary stars in the same cluster—as expected if stellar coalescence is responsible. Saffer and his colleagues have found another blue straggler to be three times as massive as any ordinary star in its cluster. Astronomers know of no way other than a collisional merger to manufacture such a heavy object in this environment.

We are now measuring the masses and spins of dozens of blue stragglers. Orsola De Marco of the American Museum of Natural History in New York City and her colleagues have recently detected disks of gas orbiting several blue stragglers-perhaps remnants of their violent births. Meanwhile observers are also looking for the other predicted effects of collisions. For instance, S. George Djorgovski of the California Institute of Technology and his co-workers have noted a decided lack of red giant stars near the cores of globular clusters. Red giants have cross sections thousands of times as large as the sun's, so they are unusually big targets. Their dearth is naturally explained by collisions, which would strip away their outer layers and transform the stars into a different breed.

To be sure, all this evidence is circumstantial. Definitive proof is harder to come by. The average time between collisions in the 150 globular clusters of the

Milky Way is about 10,000 years; in the rest of our galaxy it is billions of years. Only if we are extraordinarily lucky will a direct collision occur close enough—say, within a few million light-years—to permit today's astronomers to witness it with present technology. The first realtime detection of a stellar collision may come from the gravitational-wave observatories that are capturing data. Close encounters between stellar-mass objects should lead to distortions in the spacetime continuum. The signal is especially strong for colliding black holes or neutron stars. Such events have been implicated in the enormous energy releases associated with gamma-ray bursts.

Collisions are already proving crucial to understanding globulars and other celestial bodies. Computer simulations suggest that the evolution of clusters is controlled largely by tightly bound binary systems, which exchange energy and angular momentum with the cluster as a whole. Clusters can dissolve altogether as near-collisions fling stars out one by one. Piet Hut of the Institute for Advanced Study in Princeton, N.J., and Mison Sills of McMaster University in Ontario have argued that stellar dynamics and stellar evolution regulate each other by means of subtle feedback loops.

The fates of planets whose parent stars undergo close encounters is another addition to the topic of stellar collisions. Numerical simulations by Jarrod R. Hurley of the American Museum of Natural History show that the planets often fare badly: cannibalized by their parent star or one of their planetary siblings, set adrift within the star cluster, or even ejected from the cluster and doomed to tramp through interstellar space. Recent Hubble observations by Ron Gilliland of the Space Telescope Science Institute suggest that stars in a nearby globular cluster do indeed lack Jupiter-size planets, although the cause of this deficiency is not yet known for sure.

Despite the outstanding questions, the progress in this field has been astonishing. The very idea of stellar collisions was once absurd; today it is central to many areas of astrophysics. The apparent tranquility of the night sky masks a universe of almost unimaginable power and destruction, in which a thousand pairs of stars collide somewhere every hour. And the best is surely yet to come. New technologies may soon allow direct and routine detection of these events. We will watch as some stars die violently, while others are reborn, phoenix-like, during collisions.

When the hydrogen in the core of our star, the Sun, is depleted, it will undergo some real changes. The core, which burns hydrogen into helium for energy, will collapse, raising its temperature until it can start to burn that helium as fuel. This sends out a lot of energy that lifts the yellow photosphere outward until the Sun is many times its original size. The outer edge is now so far away that it is comparatively cool

and glows red. For a time, this midlife crisis will cause the aged star to shine even more brilliantly than it did in its youth, but the energy won't last. Eventually the star will shed its red cape of glory, creating a brief but showy bubble of glowing gas, a planetary nebula. Inside the nebula will be a white dwarf, the feeble end of a star's life.

They don't last long and they no longer have the simple soap-bubble shape that the planetary nebulae that were first discovered all seemed to have. (They are called planetary nebulae, or planetaries, because those first observed through nineteenth-century telescopes resembled the solar system's gas giant planets, Jupiter and Saturn. The name stuck even though it has nothing to do with planets or planetary formation.) Now we see that planetaries are a bit more complicated and have other fanciful shapes that tell us more about the red giant atmosphere shedding than we ever knew before. —LK

"Butterflies and Crabs of the Southern Sky"
by Sun Kwok
Sky & Telescope, January 2002

Of all the spectacles in our galaxy, few are as colorful or captivating as the ethereal bubbles of glowing gas known as planetary nebulae. Bright and easy to see, many rank among the most popular targets for telescopic observers at all levels. Yet planetary nebulae have nothing at all to do with planets—William Herschel coined the term because through his telescopes they had much the same size, shape, and color as Uranus, the planet he discovered in 1781. And even though Herschel soon convinced himself that they were actually globs of incandescent gas, the misnomer stuck.

Although the nature of planetary nebulae was not understood for almost 200 years, we now realize that these glowing clouds have been ejected by red-giant stars nearing the ends of their lives. The process begins as the red giant sheds its atmosphere into space, creating a broad, diffuse cloud of matter. Eventually the star's outer layers completely dissipate, exposing its core. The stellar winds, now energized by light pressure from the hot core, race away at much greater speed and plow into the slower, outer envelope. The light we see marks the pileup zone.

Unlike stars, which radiate in all colors from violet to red interspersed by dark lines due to absorption by atoms in the stellar atmosphere, planetary nebulae emit predominantly in specific colors like neon signs. In addition to the red (H-alpha) light of hydrogen atoms, the spectra of planetary nebulae show the characteristic green line of doubly ionized oxygen atoms. It is through the detection of these lines that new planetary nebulae are discovered.

Although we usually think of them as extended objects with symmetrical shapes, most of the 1,500 known planetary nebulae in our galaxy look unassumingly starlike. In fact, planetary nebulae are usually

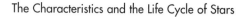

identified as such by their emission-line spectrum, rather than by appearance. This is particularly true for those in the southern hemisphere. Many of them lie in the direction of the galactic center and are too distant and too small to have their nebulosities resolved by ground-based telescopes.

This all changed with the launch of the Hubble Space Telescope (HST). From its orbit high above Earth, HST does not suffer from the image-degrading effects of atmospheric turbulence and thus can routinely achieve much higher resolution than ground-based telescopes. In recent years, astronomers have exploited this advantage to observe an increasing number of "stellar" planetary nebulae, especially those at southern declinations.

Some of the newly resolved objects, such as the one known as He2-131, show round shells reminiscent of the most famous planetary, the Ring Nebula (M57) in Lyra. Others, like He2-86, have two-lobed (bipolar) shapes similar to NGC 6302, the well-known Butterfly Nebula. Although bipolar planetary nebulae have been observed for almost a century, they were dismissed as rare and exotic—just a deviation from the normal ring-like structures seen among their siblings. Recent studies, however, have revealed that these winged forms are more common than previously thought. In fact, the Ring Nebula itself may be a butterfly viewed down its long axis.

Just when astronomers thought they were making progress in understanding these perplexing objects, new HST observations posed further challenges. Consider the bizarre aspect of He2-320. Instead of the round-ended lobes commonly seen in NGC 6302 and elsewhere, He2-320 terminates in lobes that are pointed and sharp—as if guided and shaped by an unseen hand. Between the two lobes is a very tight waist. Astronomers conjecture that an unseen doughnut of dust wraps around the waist and channels the gas flow to create the bipolar lobes.

Other examples of HST's strange revelations are He2-447 and He2-299, which sport two and three pairs of lobes, respectively. Such structures are not expected in any of our current theoretical models. Nor are the crab-like claws of objects like He2-104. Some astronomers have argued that He2-104 is not really a planetary nebula but rather a peculiar object with a hot-and-cool pair of central stars.

Further amazement awaited us as observers used HST to track down more southern planetary nebulae. He3-1475 defies all conventional wisdom in having an S-shaped structure. The two thin lobes seem to have been swung out from a slingshot. In contrast, He3-1357 has a disklike structure with a bubble bursting out on each side.

All these discoveries have raised new questions about the origin of the morphologies of planetary nebulae. As this issue of *Sky & Telescope* reaches subscribers, more than 200 researchers will be gathering in Canberra, Australia, for a symposium on planetary nebulae sponsored by the International Astronomical Union. Perhaps such a high-power brainstorming session will shed some new light on how these objects fashion their diverse and beautiful shapes.

Sun Kwok, "Butterflies and Crabs of the Southern Sky," *Sky and Telescope,* January 2002.

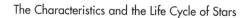

Red giants in your toothpaste? Fluorine, the element that fights bacteria and fluoridates water, seems to have its origins in the hearts of red giant stars. Some of these stars burn fuel in two places: an outer shell of hydrogen burning into helium, and an inner, somewhat sputtering shell where helium flashes in a runaway reaction. The fluorine forms in the outer burning shell, which normally would turn around and destroy the fluorine. However, the occasional helium flash sends fluorine outward to where cool temperatures and stellar winds carry it off safely into space. —LK

"Fluorine: An Elementary Mystery"
by Ken Croswell
Sky & Telescope, September 2003

Every chemical element on Earth tells a story written in the heavens. The nitrogen in our atmosphere and in your body's proteins blossomed in stars somewhat heavier than the Sun, like Capella, which cast their outer layers away as planetary nebulae when they died. The oxygen you breathe and the neon gas in storefront lights were cooked up in massive stars like Antares, which later spewed these elements into the galaxy by exploding as supernovae. And supernova explosions themselves forged much of the iron in your blood and the gold in your jewelry.

One element, however, abounds in mystery: fluorine. Although fluorine seems familiar—it's in toothpaste and fluoridated water, as well as in the beautiful mineral fluorite—no one knows how it arose. According to one intriguing idea, fluorine owes its existence to neutrinos, the ghostly particles that shoot through us every second from the core of the Sun. A competing idea holds that the element originates when red giants fuse nitrogen, while another theory maintains that massive blue stars that have blown off their outer layers—Wolf-Rayet stars—do the trick.

An Element Apart

Astronomically and chemically, fluorine (atomic number 9, for 9 protons in its nucleus) stands apart. For one thing, it's rare. Rank the elements by their cosmic abundances: its neighbors—carbon (atomic number 6), nitrogen (7), oxygen (8), and neon (10)—all make the top six, right after hydrogen and helium. But fluorine doesn't even appear in the top 20. It's like a shack stuck between mansions.

Fluorine's scarcity offers astronomers a vital clue—and a possible opportunity. The clue is simple: whatever makes fluorine doesn't make much. Indeed, the nuclear reactions by which stars churn out so much carbon, nitrogen, oxygen, and neon must largely bypass the element.

And that, in turn, means fluorine's very existence may probe hitherto unknown nucleosynthetic processes.

"The rarest isotopes can actually be diagnostics of some very interesting physics," says Stan E. Woosley (University of California, Santa Cruz), "because they take special circumstances to make. It's very easy to make iron, for example; but it turns out to be very hard to make fluorine." As a result, the little fluorine born in exotic processes doesn't get swamped by huge quantities created elsewhere.

Fluorine is the element most spectroscopists have never seen. Because of its rarity, the few spectral lines it produces are weak. Although the Milky Way galaxy abounds with 100 billion stars or more, astronomers have seen the element in fewer than 100 of them.

Even to chemists, fluorine stands apart as the most reactive of all the elements. It's so hyperactive that it coaxes such unsociable atoms as krypton and xenon— both noble gases—into making molecules. When paired with hydrogen, it becomes hydrofluoric acid (HF), a substance so corrosive that it will dissolve the test tube that holds it. Fluorine is a so-called halogen, occupying the periodic table's next-to-last column, along with chlorine, bromine, iodine, and astatine.

To a nuclear scientist, fluorine is fragile. Unlike most elements it has only one stable isotope, fluorine-19. Although stars normally manufacture elements, they typically destroy the little fluorine they inherit. That's because their most common elements, hydrogen and helium, annihilate it. In a star's hot interior, hydrogen nuclei—protons—split fluorine into oxygen and helium, while helium-4 nuclei convert it into neon.

Thus, any fluorine that manages to arise faces a universe stacked against it.

An Explosive Idea

In 1988 Woosley and University of Washington physicist Wick C. Haxton suggested a way around this problem. They proposed that fluorine can be both created and saved by supernovae. The stellar explosions fling the fluorine into space fast enough to protect it from the elements that would destroy it. In a 2002 paper, Woosley and others declared that neutrinos in supernovae probably make most of the universe's fluorine. If so, the fluorine in your toothpaste wouldn't exist without phantom particles that pass through almost anything.

When a massive star like Antares goes supernova, 10^{58} neutrinos storm through the exploding star. Although neutrinos are normally harmless—trillions of solar neutrinos pass through us each second—supernova-born neutrinos carry so much energy and blow through such a dense medium that 1 in 200 of these normally ghostly particles interact with matter outside the newborn neutron star. If such a supernova happened at the Sun's position, the neutrino burst alone would kill us.

Such an interaction, wrote Woosley and Haxton, produces fluorine. Before it explodes, a massive star creates an enormous store of neon-20, which has 10 protons and 10 neutrons. During the explosion the neutrinos race through the star's neon layer, and some knock off a proton to make fluorine-19 or remove a neutron to make radioactive neon-19, which then decays into fluorine-19. Either way, fluorine is born. Unfortunately, no one has ever observed fluorine in a supernova or supernova remnant, so the neutrino process remains speculative.

A Giant Discovery

In 1992 three astronomers did report the discovery of fluorine—not in supernovae, but in dozens of red-giant stars. Says Alain Jorissen (Free University of Brussels), "That was one of these few moments in a career when you think, 'Wow—that's really great,' because theory meets observations, and without any trigger from one or the other." While completing his thesis in Belgium, Jorissen developed a theory for fluorine's production, without even knowing that two Texas astronomers had already confirmed it. At a conference in Indiana, Jorissen bumped into David L. Lambert (University of Texas, Austin). Lambert told Jorissen that he and Verne V. Smith (University of Texas, El Paso), while studying other elements in giant stars, had accidentally detected the infrared signature of gaseous hydrogen fluoride (HF). Up to that time fluorine had been seen only in the Sun, Venus, Betelgeuse, the interstellar medium, cosmic rays, the envelope of a carbon star, and a planetary nebula or two. Before long the astronomers had measured the fluorine abundance in 65 giant stars.

Some of the stars were ordinary giants, such as K-type Arcturus in Bootes and M-type Mirach in Andromeda. And most of the K and M stars had fluorine abundances that roughly matched the Sun's. The story changed dramatically, though, when the astronomers scrutinized the carbon stars. They all had more fluorine than the Sun—up to 65 times more, indicating that the stars created the fluorine themselves, just as Jorissen's thesis predicted. The discovery caused Grant J. Mathews (University of Notre Dame) to wax alliterative in the pages of Nature: "[F]luorine is probably formed in the frequent furious fusion flashes of an inflated florid star."

The responsible party is a so-called asymptotic giant branch star, which powers itself by two fusion reactions. The first, which occurs in an outer shell, converts hydrogen into helium via the CNO cycle, whereby carbon, nitrogen, and oxygen catalyze the hydrogen-to-helium reaction. The CNO cycle also converts carbon and oxygen into nitrogen-14.

The second fusion reaction occurs sporadically in a shell deeper inside the star, where the ash of hydrogen burning—helium—gets transformed into carbon. Helium-shell burning is unstable. When the helium shell ignites, it produces so much heat that the reaction causes a nuclear runaway, known as a helium-shell flash. When the reaction is over, convection in the star's outer envelope dredges the carbon up to the star's surface, changing a normal giant into a carbon star.

The same dredge-up also lifts fluorine to the surface. Because the hydrogen-burning CNO cycle produces nitrogen-14, this element is mixed with the helium ash. Once it's there, reactions during the helium-shell flash can transform it into fluorine-19.

Normally that fluorine wouldn't stand a chance—it's surrounded by fluorine-fleecing helium nuclei apt to destroy it—but in this case the fluorine is forged faster than the helium can eliminate it and gets raised into the star's cooler upper levels. So when the star dies, it launches its fluorine-enriched atmosphere into space by way of a beautiful planetary nebula.

The progenitors of the Milky Way's red giants were born with between about 1 and 8 solar masses. (More massive stars become supergiants, rather than giants, and explode as supernovae.) The lesser giants—those less than 4 Suns—actually produce the most fluorine, because the helium-shell flashes in more massive giants get too hot and may destroy more fluorine than they create.

The few observations of fluorine in planetary nebulae support this mass-dependent trend. In 1997 Xiao-wei Liu (Peking University) found a fairly high abundance of fluorine in the planetary nebula NGC 4361 in Corvus. Its progenitor probably had between 1 and 2 solar masses. Earlier, astronomers had detected high fluorine levels in the envelope around the mass-losing carbon star CW Leonis, whose mass is between 1.5 and 4 Suns. But in 2001 Jaime L. Highberger (University of Arizona) and her colleagues reported a much lower fluorine abundance in the Egg Nebula, a planetary-nebula-to-be that arose from a star about seven times as massive as the Sun. The astronomers suggest that the Egg Nebula's lower fluorine abundance may be due to its progenitor's greater mass.

Blowing in the Wind

Meanwhile, Georges Meynet (Geneva Observatory) and Marcel Arnould (Free University of Brussels) have advised fluorine seekers to look not to red stars but to blue ones known as Wolf-Rayet stars. These originate from the most massive O-type main sequence stars. As a typical O star evolves, it expands, which causes its surface to cool until the star swells into a red supergiant like Antares. However, the brightest O stars—those born with masses of more than 40 Suns—shine so immensely that their light blows their hydrogen envelopes into space. As a result the star stays hot and blue, becoming a Wolf-Rayet star that unveils the elements it has manufactured beneath its blown off surface.

One of those elements is nitrogen-14, which the star produces while burning hydrogen into helium via the CNO cycle. When the star ignites its helium core, some of the nitrogen-14 gets converted into fluorine-19 through the same nuclear reactions that occur in red giants.

Normally this fluorine wouldn't do any good because as helium burning progresses, the temperature rises, causing helium to bombard the fluorine and convert it into neon. In a Wolf-Rayet star, however, the fluorine may meet a happier end. "The wind is important," says Meynet, "because it can save the element from destruction." The star's wind spirits the newly minted fluorine into space, rescuing it from the helium that would otherwise destroy it. According to Meynet and Arnould's calculations, Wolf-Rayet winds should possess up to 70 times the Sun's fluorine abundance, making them a major source of the element. Unfortunately, no one has yet found fluorine in a Wolf-Rayet star.

Testing Time

New observations now under way may finally pinpoint fluorine's origin among the three competing possibilities of supernovae, red giants, and Wolf-Rayet stars.

The trick is to track how fast fluorine formed in the young Milky Way by comparing it with oxygen and iron. Oxygen formed quickly, because it came from massive stars that burned fast and furiously and exploded soon after birth. As a result, the young galaxy had oxygen, and so do the old, metal-poor stars (those with few elements heavier than hydrogen and helium) that inhabit the galactic halo. In contrast, iron diffused throughout the galaxy more slowly, because much of it came from type 1a supernovae, which erupt when white dwarfs explode. Such stars typically require billions of years to develop and then blow up.

The three theories for fluorine's production predict different histories of the element and thus different abundance patterns in metal-poor stars. If supernovae from short-lived massive stars produce fluorine via the neutrino process, fluorine formed in the Milky Way fast, and halo stars should have some quantity of the element. On the other hand, if red giants produce most of the universe's fluorine, halo stars should have less, because red giants originate from longer-lived stars like the Sun.

The Wolf-Rayet theory predicts a third pattern—that the galaxy produced fluorine only after it attained a critical metallicity. That's because metallicity determines whether a Wolf-Rayet star can form in the first place. An O star becomes a Wolf-Rayet star by blowing off its atmosphere; but to do that, its light has to push against metals in the atmosphere. So no metals, no Wolf-Rayet star—and no fluorine.

Trouble is, observing fluorine in metal-poor stars is even harder than observing it in "normal" stars, because all three theories predict lower fluorine abundances at low metallicities. Nevertheless, in the September 2003 Astronomical Journal, Katia Cunha (National Observatory, Rio de Janeiro), Verne Smith, David Lambert, and Kenneth H. Hinkle (National Optical Astronomy Observatory) report tantalizing observations of hydrogen fluoride in metal-poor stars. Using the 8.1-meter Gemini South telescope in Chile, Cunha and her colleagues obtained fluorine abundances for nine such stars in the Large Magellanic Cloud. The astronomers even detected fluorine in two stars in the globular cluster Omega Centauri that have iron abundances of just 5 and 10 percent solar, indicating great age.

By comparing the fluorine abundances with those of oxygen and iron, the astronomers conclude that fluorine originates chiefly in high-mass stars—either when these stars explode and shoot neutrinos through their neon, or via nuclear reactions in Wolf-Rayet stars, or both. Red giants, in contrast, seem to make little contribution.

Thus, if neutrinos never interacted with matter and the brightest stars hadn't blown off their outer layers, most fluorine wouldn't exist—and we'd probably have a lot more cavities. Who would have guessed that such exotic processes could save your teeth?

Still, Cunha cautions that more observations are needed, especially at the low metallicities that yield such crucial insights. Within a year, she hopes to report the full story behind the fluorine in your toothpaste.

The universe is an ancient alchemist's dream. It's filled with more rare gems than Earth can contain. Granted, the gems are microscopic and you'd have to vacuum up the dust of the entire solar system to get a handful. But the universe is a pretty big place, and there's enough room for everybody to get their hands on a load of diamonds. The only problem is how to get at them.

Astronomers are more interested in how these precious gems are formed. Some, like calcite, need water on Earth. So how can they form in the waterless planetary nebulae? Diamonds are a form of carbon. How can you tap into the atmospheres of red giants and get enough carbonaceous material to make a diamond?

In this story, author Sun Kwok describes astronomy as a branch of geology. Now that's a cosmic twist! —LK

"Gems from the Stars"
by Sun Kwok
Sky & Telescope, October 2002

Diamonds, rubies, and sapphires have always been treasured for their beauty and rarity, so it may come as a surprise that stars are producing these "rare" gem minerals in vast quantities. Astronomers once thought the dust of interstellar space was relatively simple. But recent observations from ground- and space-based telescopes have found signatures of many different solids that are blowing like smoke from stars and floating in the spaces between them—from substances making up common sand to the most treasured minerals on Earth. Interstellar dust is not very plentiful. It amounts to only about 1 percent of interstellar matter; the rest is gas. But dust plays a disproportionate role in many cosmic processes. Among these are the heating and cooling of nebulae—processes that regulate where stars will be born and what their masses will be—and the interstellar chemistry that creates the raw materials for planets. Dust also determines how much of our Milky Way galaxy we see, or don't. On a dark night, vast black clouds are visible silhouetted along the midline of the Milky Way, blocking most of the galaxy from our view. The gas that dominates these dark nebulae is generally transparent and invisible; what we see is the dust.

Although the presence of dust in interstellar space has been known for almost a century, its origins and chemical compositions have remained a mystery. Interstellar dust is too cold to radiate in the visible part

of the spectrum, so its nature was first studied through its selective absorption of starlight. Based on an ultraviolet absorption feature in stellar spectra at a wavelength of 220 nanometers (2200 angstroms), astronomers long thought that interstellar dust is made of graphite. This may still be an ingredient, but recent infrared observations have found an amazing variety of minerals in space, especially around dying stars. Among them are some of the gemstones that have been treasured throughout human history.

Long regarded as signs of wealth, luxury, and power, gems in many cultures are thought to possess medicinal or magical powers. Modern science has shown that precious stones are nothing more than minerals made up of the same elements found in common rocks, such as carbon, oxygen, silicon, aluminum, magnesium, and iron. Their luster and colors are well understood from the physical principles of refraction, reflection, and dispersion. Their internal structures can be accurately determined through the technique of X-ray crystallography. We now know that, with a few exceptions such as amber and opal, precious stones are atoms arranged in periodic, crystalline structures. These various geometric patterns give them their unique optical properties.

According to some myths and legends, gems come from the sky. Could there be any truth to this idea? Sadly, the diamond in your ring did not originate around some other star. Geologists know very well how precious stones are formed in Earth's crust, and in any case interstellar particles are generally much too small. They typically range in size from about a micron (a thousandth of a millimeter) down to clumps of just a few hundred atoms a thousand times smaller still. However, scientists are now pondering the possibility that some microscopic gemstones now on Earth may indeed have come from space and may be older than our planet.

The first evidence for such a possibility came from the study of meteorites. In 1987 researchers found that some meteorites contain diamonds a nanometer (thousandth of a micron) in size. Following this discovery, meteorite investigators turned up tiny grains of silicon carbide (SiC) and graphite. The isotopes in all these grains suggest that they did not arise within our solar system but originated elsewhere and were later incorporated into meteoric material intact.

In 1997 scientists analyzing meteorites at Washington University in St. Louis found many corundum particles (Al_2O_3), the class of aluminum oxides to which rubies and sapphires belong. Again, the grains seemed to be interstellar in origin.

Where were they made and how did they get here? From studying stellar spectra in the infrared, we have established definite links between grains found in meteorites and the minerals being thrown out in the winds of certain old red-giant stars. We have learned that dying stars manufacture vast quantities of solid matter and distribute it throughout the galaxy. The discovery of this link between heaven and Earth is one of the most remarkable stories of modern astronomy.

Mineralogy in Space

The beginning of stellar mineralogy dates from the late 1960s and the first infrared telescopes. A number of old red giants showed an emission feature at the mid-infrared wavelength of 10 microns. These stars have masses similar to the Sun's but have evolved to such an advanced stage that they are shedding massive stellar winds and are only about a few million years from becoming planetary nebulae. The 10-micron feature was quickly identified as the signature of micron-size silicate grains. Silicates comprise a wide variety of minerals based on silicon-oxygen bonds, often including magnesium and iron—many of the same substances making up common rocks.

While rock dust in space may not seem to be a big deal to geologists, it is to astronomers. Since the 1950s we have known that all atoms heavier than helium are made within stars. In the atmospheres of cool stars, some of these assemble into gaseous molecules; dozens of such chemicals have been found in stellar surroundings, first by optical spectroscopy and later by microwave and infrared spectroscopy. Astronomers can conceive many ways to make gas molecules in stellar and space environments, but not solids—certainly not under the very low-density conditions in a red giant's atmosphere, which is less than a billionth as dense as the Earth's.

Worse yet, solids melt at high temperatures. Red giants may be cool by stellar standards, but their surfaces are still around 3,000°K, far hotter than the melting or vaporizing points of most metals and minerals. Apparently solid dust grains condense above the stellar atmosphere, where the temperature is less hot. However, the fact that the gas density here must be even lower makes the process even harder to understand.

The Infrared Astronomical Satellite (IRAS) opened a new era in space mineralogy in 1982. During 10 months it surveyed 97 percent of the sky in the mid- and far-infrared spectral bands. Onboard was a Dutch-built infrared spectrometer, the first to be flown in space. It obtained spectra of more than 50,000 sources, including more than 4,000 red giants in which our research group has found silicate emission at 10 and 18 microns. (The former comes from Si-O bonds vibrating by stretching and compressing; the latter is due to the bending vibration of Si-O-Si lineups.) So there is no doubt that the manufacture of silicates is very common among old stars.

While the stellar silicates show some similarity to those in Earth's crust, they are not the same. In fact, no terrestrial mineral exactly matches the spectroscopic properties of this celestial dust. Most terrestrial silicates are in crystalline form, showing narrow, sharply defined spectral signatures not seen in their stellar counterparts. Apparently the silicon-oxygen bonds near stars are not in crystal structures but in a disorganized, "amorphous" form more like glass.

Another solid material commonly seen in old stars, especially red giants that are rich in carbon, is silicon carbide (SiC). On Earth its artificial crystal form is known as carborundum. The IRAS spectrometer found more than 700 stars displaying it. Generally speaking, old red giants show either silicates or silicon carbide, depending on whether they are oxygen- or carbon-rich.

If solid bits of silicate and silicon carbide can condense in stellar atmospheres, could other minerals be present too? The first solid materials to condense out of a hot gas ought to be those that form solids at the highest temperatures. Aluminum and titanium oxides are good candidates, not only because of their high melting points but also because of the relatively high abundance of these two elements. In the IRAS spectroscopic data, Irene Little-Marenin (Wellesley College) detected a feature at 13 microns in a number of red giants. Astronomers from the University of Amsterdam suggested that it could signal an amorphous, glasslike form of aluminum oxide, Al_2O_3. Its crystal form, corundum, is a colorless mineral that is the hardest known natural substance after diamond. Following up on this idea, and using infrared observations by NASA's Kuiper Airborne Observatory, William Glaccum (University of Chicago) suggested that the source of the mysterious feature at 13 microns is actually sapphire. This is a form of corundum in which some aluminum atoms have been replaced by titanium, giving the clear crystal a bluish color.

These suggestions were difficult to test due to a lack of good infrared laboratory spectra of corundum and sapphire. Not many facilities can do these measurements, but one that can is at the Max Planck Institute in Jena, Germany. Scientists at Jena considered rutile (titanium dioxide, TiO_2) and spinel (magnesium aluminum oxide, $MgAl_2O_4$) in addition to corundum as the possible source of the 13-micron feature. Rutile is a reasonable possibility because gaseous TiO is widely present in the optical spectra of red giants that are rich in oxygen. On Earth, very fine needles of rutile sometimes appear in rubies and sapphires, creating a star-shaped pattern of reflected light.

In 1995 the European Space Agency launched the Infrared Space Observatory (ISO), which carried infrared spectrometers much more sensitive than the one on IRAS. Working with colleagues from Vienna, the Jena group compared their laboratory results with the superior data from ISO and concluded that the most likely candidate for the 13-micron feature is spinel. On Earth this mineral exists in a variety of colors from red to blue, the result of some of the magnesium atoms being replaced by iron, zinc, or manganese, and aluminum atoms being replaced by iron or chromium. Red spinels are sometimes confused with rubies; the 17-carat "Black Prince's Ruby" in the British Imperial State Crown is in fact a spinel.

Whether sapphire, ruby, or spinel, old stars have clearly demonstrated their ability to synthesize gemstone dust without difficulty, even under unforgiving high-temperature, low-density conditions.

Rocks and Limestones

Despite our natural human interest in gems, we should mention some more down-to-earth minerals. One of the ISO mission's legacies is the detection of crystalline silicates and carbonates, the constituents of common rocks and limestones, respectively. Clear detections of forsterite (Mg_2SiO_4) and enstatite ($MgSiO_3$) have been made in a number of planetary nebulae, including NGC 6302 and NGC 6537.

Both these nebulae have butterfly or hourglass shapes. The ISO measurements were made toward the waist of the objects, where we believe most of the solid minerals lie. The gases in these nebulae are as hot as 10,000°K, and the central star of NGC 6302 is one of the hottest stars known, at about 250,000°K. How these nebulae manage to produce large quantities of crystalline silicates and carbonates is completely unknown.

Planetary nebulae are gaseous ejecta from former red giants (both the oxygen- and carbon-rich varieties) that have reached the ends of their lives (S&T: July 1996, page 38). The fact that *crystalline* silicates are found in planetary nebulae suggests that something may have changed the red giants' amorphous, glassy silicate articles into crystals. Alternatively, the crystalline grains may have formed in the nebulae on their own. Since these nebulae are only a few thousand years old, condensation within them would have been rapid and efficient.

Another common class of minerals is the limestones, which on Earth are products of weathering. Calcite ($CaCO_3$) and dolomite ($CaMg(CO_3)_2$), the main components of limestone, are believed to form in the sea. How a hot planetary nebula like NGC 6302 manages to produce large quantities of calcite and dolomite without water is a complete mystery. This issue was hotly debated at an International Astronomical Union symposium on planetary nebulae in Canberra, Australia, in November 2001. No theory has yet come close to explaining the observed abundance of these minerals.

Diamonds Are Forever

Diamond is a form of pure carbon. The abundance of carbon in the universe has long led astronomers to speculate about interstellar diamonds, so the 1987 discovery of submicroscopic diamond grains in a meteorite was seen as a nice confirmation of our suspicions that extraterrestrial diamonds do exist. On Earth diamonds are created deep underground at high pressures, temperatures, and densities. Interstellar diamonds are conjectured to form in strongly shocked gas, perhaps in supernovae, though new studies suggest that nanodiamonds may be made in protostellar disks, and possibly in the solar nebula itself.

Diamonds are nearly transparent in visible light and also lack distinct spectral features in the infrared, so interstellar diamonds are extremely difficult to detect directly. By the end of the 20th century the outlook for finding them in space was bleak. However, in the early 1980s astronomers found a pair of unidentified infrared features at 3.43 and 3.54 microns in young stellar objects called Herbig *Ae/Be* stars. The best examples of stars displaying them are HD 97048 in the Chamaeleon dark cloud and Elias 1 in the Taurus dark cloud. Using ISO, a group of Belgian astronomers observed these two stars and confirmed the ground-based results but were unable to offer any new insights into their origin.

Oliver Guillois (French Atomic Energy Commission), who has been studying the infrared properties of carbonaceous compounds, took a strong interest in these astronomical results. He searched the literature and found that a group of scientists at the Institute of

Atomic and Molecular Science of the Academia Sinica in Taiwan had successfully taken infrared spectra of diamonds. The Taiwanese group, led by Huan C. Chang, irradiated synthetic diamond with hydrogen—and found that hydrogen atoms attached themselves to the corners of diamond crystals. While pure diamonds have very few infrared signatures, the hydrogenated crystals produced exactly the two emission features seen at the stars. Since interstellar gas is mostly hydrogen, it's not surprising that interstellar diamonds would be covered with it. This identification represents the first definite detection of diamond in space.

Guillois and his colleagues estimate that the region around HD 97048 contains about 100,000 to 1,000,000 trillion (10^{17} to 10^{18}) tons of diamond dust—enough to make a pile some 200 to 400 kilometers wide and tall. When we consider that on Earth we measure diamonds in units of carats (0.2 gram), such a vast quantity of diamond at a star is truly mind-boggling.

At the beginning of the 21st century we have entered a new era of stellar mineralogy. It is clear that old red giants make a variety of minerals, including some real gems. They do so under the most unfavorable conditions, at extremely low densities and high temperatures. Furthermore, the synthesis takes place on a large enough scale to strew the entire galaxy with these substances. Most amazingly, we now can hold in our hands (in the form of grains in meteorites) materials that were made beyond the solar system.

It may be centuries before humans travel to stars, but it is comforting to know that every year, stars deliver to us presents in the form of tiny gems to study and treasure.

Normally, a white dwarf just fades away over billions of years. The Sun will have a similar quiet retirement. But the Sun is a rarity, a star with no stellar companion. As the stars leave the stellar nebular nurseries, they often take a companion along for the ride. That companion is a killer. If the solar mass star becomes a white dwarf first, it may be so close that it draws off matter from the surviving companion. As it does, the white dwarf gains mass. If it gains enough to reach 1.4 solar masses or more, it crosses over into the territory of the high solar mass stars. Then the star explodes as a supernova. There are two kinds of these exploding behemoths that destroy themselves. These binary-formed supernovae become the kind that astronomers can use as a scale to measure the distance to other galaxies. —LK

"When a White Dwarf Explodes"
by David Branch
Science, January 3, 2003

The 10^{28}-megaton stellar explosions called type Ia supernovae are brighter than a billion suns.

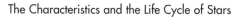
Observations show that there is little variation between different type Ia explosions. Thanks to their brilliance and homogeneity, they are used as "standard candles" for determining the relation between distance and redshift in our expanding universe: The dimmer a type Ia supernova looks, the more distant it must be. On page 77 of this issue, Gamezo *et al.*[1] report an important step toward understanding how type Ia supernovae explode.

Observations of remote (high-redshift) type Ia supernovae—some so remote that they erupted before Sun and Earth formed—have provided strong evidence that the cosmic expansion is accelerating.[2, 3] It does so under the influence of some "dark energy" that may correspond to Einstein's cosmological constant, also called the vacuum energy.

As astronomers prepare to probe the nature of the dark energy by observing type Ia supernovae at even higher redshifts,[4] a better understanding of the physics of these explosions is urgently required. For example, very distant (high-redshift) type Ia supernovae might have reached different peak brightnesses than their closer (low-redshift) counterparts. If this is the case, then the derived distances to the high-redshift events, and hence the inferred history of the cosmic expansion, will be in error.[5]

Type Ia supernovae are the most homogeneous and luminous supernovae, but not the most frequent. Other supernovae are powered by the gravitational potential energy that is released when the iron cores of massive stars collapse to form neutron stars or black holes. In contrast, a type Ia supernova is the complete thermonuclear disruption of a carbon-oxygen white dwarf, without leaving behind a black hole or neutron star.[6]

Eight billion years from now, the Sun will have burned the hydrogen in its core to helium and then to a mixture of carbon and oxygen. It will lose its gravitational grip on its outer layers and expose its dense core, which will become a white dwarf supported against gravity by the pressure of degenerate electrons. The white dwarf will cool at constant radius to become, after further billions of ears, a black dwarf. No supernova explosion will ensue.

A very different fate awaits a white dwarf that accretes mass from a close binary companion star. Such a white dwarf contracts, increasing its temperature and density. As the mass approaches 1.4 solar masses (the Chandrasekhar mass), carbon fusion ignites deep in the interior. The resulting thermonuclear instability is followed by a nuclear burning front that rages outward and explodes the whole star in seconds. The nuclear reactions change the white dwarf's composition, unbind it, and provide the kinetic energy of the ejected matter. At first, the expanding matter cools, but then radioactive decay of freshly synthesized ^{56}Ni and ^{56}Co reheats it and makes the supernova shine.

Explosion at the Chandrasekhar mass provides an explanation for the observed homogeneity of type Ia supernova explosions. Slight variations [see the first figure in the original article] could be caused, for example, by the white dwarf's initial carbon/oxygen ration or the time history of accretion.

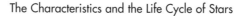
Numerical explosion models have shed some light on the physics behind type Ia supernova explosions. Models that create about 0.6 solar masses of ^{56}Ni yield light curves (brightness versus time) consistent with observations. Radial stratification, with the heaviest elements on the inside and the lightest on the outside, appears necessary for reproducing observed spectra [see the first figure in the original article].[7-9]

So far, however, these comparisons have been carried out only for spherically symmetric (one-dimensional, 1D) explosion models of two kinds. In a deflagration model, the burning front is a subsonic nuclear flame. In a delayed detonation model, the deflagration makes a transition to a supersonic detonation. In both models, the velocity of the deflagration is crucial to the outcome, but it has to be treated as an adjustable parameter because the flame is inherently three-dimensional (3D). The density at which the deflagration-detonation transition (DDT) takes place also cannot be calculated in a 1D model.

Gamezo et al.[1] have now calculated a self-consistent 3D deflagration explosion. The total amount of fuel burned, and therefore the kinetic energy and the amount of ^{56}Ni, are about right to be consistent with observed light curves. The compositional structure, however, is quite unlike those of 1D models that are consistent with observation. Instead of being radially stratified, the elements coexist at all radii. The model spectra are unlikely to be consistent with observations.

The radially mixed compositional structure appears to be an inevitable characteristic of deflagration models, because buoyant burned matter such as ^{56}Ni and its decay products has time to rise relative to the denser unburned carbon and oxygen. Gamezo et al.[1] conclude that type Ia supernovae must undergo a DDT. Thus, by solving one problem they present another: Calculating DDT will be computationally challenging, especially considering the likelihood that DDT initiates almost simultaneously at various places in the ejected matter.[10]

Now that 3D explosion models are beginning to appear, astronomers are gearing up to do 3D radiative transfer calculations so that the spectra of the models can be calculated and compared with observations.[11-12] Supernova research is entering a new realm of computational complexity.

References and Notes

1. V.N. Gamezo, A.M. Khokhlov, E.S. Oran, A.Y. Chtchelkanova, R.O. Rosenberg, *Science* **299**, 77 (2003); published online 21 November 2002 (10.1126science.1078129).
2. S. Perlmutter et al., *Astrophys. J.* **517**, 565 (1999).
3. A.G. Riess et al., *Astron. J.* **116**, 1009 (1998).
4. See http://snap.lbl.gov.
5. B. Leibundgut, *Annu. Rev. Astrophys.* **39**, 67 (2001).
6. K. Nomoto, K. Iwamoto, N. Kishimoto, *Science* **276**, 1378 (1997).
7. P.A. Mazzali et al., *Astron. Astrophys.* **269**, 423 (1993).
8. P. Ruiz-Lapuente et al., *Astrophys. J.* **439**, 60 (1995).
9. E.J. Lentz, E. Baron, D. Branch, P.H. Hauschildt, *Astrophys. J.* **557**, 266, (2001).
10. E. Livne, *Astrophys. J.* **527**, L97 (1999).
11. D.A. Howell, P. Hoflich, L. Wang, J.C. Wheeler, *Astrophys. J.* **556**, 302 (2001).
12. R.C. Thomas et al., *Astrophys. J.*, in press.
13. I thank M. Hamuy, R. Lopez, and A. Pastorello for providing the data for the first figure.

4 The End of Life for a High Mass Star

Unlike our Sun, big stars don't go out with a whimper. They go out with a king-sized bang.

Any star with more than 1.4 solar masses (40 percent more atoms than what our Sun possesses) can't just shed its atmosphere, become a planetary nebula, and fade out as a white dwarf star. In that red giant phase, when the fuel runs out, the star may temporarily burn another source of fuel or two, but eventually it gets a core filled with iron. Nothing converts iron into usable energy in a star, so the star collapses under its own weight. The collapsing outer shells compress the core, igniting it one last time in a tremendous outpouring of energy, and a supernova results, temporarily outshining the entire galaxy. A cloud of glowing gaseous debris, filled with the products of billions of years of cosmic cooking, spreads out into the universe as a supernova remnant. The core itself compresses into a neutron star, essentially a big superatomic nucleus, or a black hole.

It's been a while since we've had a supernova in the Milky Way. This article examines those known in history over the past 1,000 years or so and what astronomers have since learned about them as they examine the sky with photographs, X-ray and radio telescopes, and more. —LK

"A Millennium of Shattered Stars: Our Galaxy's Historical Supernovae"
by F. Richard Stephenson and David A. Green
Sky & Telescope, May 2003

Of the various stellar explosions that astronomers observe from time to time in our own galaxy and others, supernovae are among the most violent. In the course of such an outburst, a star is either disrupted completely or split apart, its outer layers hurled outward at supersonic speeds while its core is crushed to extraordinary density.

When a star becomes a supernova, its luminosity typically increases by a factor of at least 100 million, after which it fades slowly. For several weeks a supernova's light output may rival that of all the other stars in its home galaxy combined. Within months or at the very most a few years, however, the star is destined to fade to invisibility at visual wavelengths. However, physical evidence of its cataclysmic death may survive for millennia.

The material ejected during a supernova outburst gradually expands into interstellar space, producing a supernova remnant (SNR)—a powerful source of radio emission and X-rays that may remain detectable for many thousands of years. In some cases the star's rapidly rotating core survives as a neutron star and continues to pump energy into the center of the remnant. The neutron star maybe seen as a pulsar, its radio or X-ray emission periodically sweeping Earth like a lighthouse beam (and pulsars can remain observable for billions of years).

More than 200 supernova remnants have been identified in our galaxy, and the frequency of supernovae in a galaxy like our own is estimated to be one or two per century. Yet only five such events are known with a fair degree of certainty to have been seen in the Milky Way over the past millennium. (The solar system's location close to the Milky Way's mid-plane, where obscuring interstellar dust is densest, is responsible for the apparent shortfall.) All of these supernovae were witnessed before the birth of telescopic astronomy. Hence, unaided-eye observations made centuries ago have proved to be of outstanding importance.

Sifting for Supernovae

Historical records from a variety of civilizations contain references to strange stars appearing for some time and then disappearing. These stars are probably mainly novae (lesser but still substantial outbursts that do not destroy the stars involved) or comets, along with the occasional supernova. How, then, do we identify likely supernovae in historical records?

The new star's duration is key. If a "guest star" remained visible for several months—and there is no indication of motion—then it is fairly likely that the object was stellar in nature. (A comet, by contrast, would move across a considerable portion of the sky in such a time.) A supernova's brightness usually declines more slowly than a nova's, so a lengthy period of visibility is an encouraging indicator.

Another useful criterion is a smoothly varying brightness, which is evident in the cases of Tycho's supernova and Kepler's, as the 1572 and 1604 supernovae, respectively, are known (by contrast, a nova's brightness varies both rapidly and erratically). Another good hint is a low galactic latitude. Type II supernovae—those that result from the abrupt collapse of short-lived, massive stars—are likeliest to occur in the galaxy's gas-rich mid-plane, where starbirth continues apace. Novae, by contrast, can be seen in essentially any direction.

As stated above, just five Milky Way supernovae satisfying these criteria have been documented in the past millennium: in 1006, 1054, 1181, 1572, and 1604. Each of these new stars temporarily ranked among the brightest in the night sky. In some instances they were visible even in daylight (*S&T*: August 1999, page 30).

Old Records, New Insights

Our galaxy's historical supernovae have been studied for decades by astronomers and historians alike. However, previously unknown observations continue to come to light in China, Korea, and the Arab world. These discoveries have been particularly significant for the 1006 supernova.

Furthermore, new techniques enable us to better interpret descriptions that already are familiar to

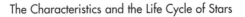

historians. These have improved our understanding of the terminology used in Chinese texts and have enabled us to more accurately identify the star groups near which the supernovae appeared. Progress of this sort has been especially noteworthy in the case of the 1054 supernova, the one that spawned the Crab Nebula.

Cutting-edge observations of their remnants, particularly those carried out by the Chandra X-ray Observatory, also have greatly aided our understanding of the historical supernovae. Not only is Chandra significantly more sensitive than its predecesors; its X-ray images have unprecedented angular resolution. These factors have enabled astronomers to make new discoveries such as the long-suspected pulsar within 3C 58, the remnant of the 1181 supernova.

Several of the historical supernovae were observed in Europe. The supernovae of 1604 and 1572 were studied extensively by European astronomers, most notably Johannes Kepler and Tycho Brahe. However, the only viable European sources of pre-Renaissance supernova observations have been somewhat unexpected monastic records and town chronicles. Annalists frequently noted impressive celestial occurrences, particularly eclipses and comets, and certain chronicles mention the especially bright supernova that appeared in 1006.

For their part, medieval Arab astronomers had little interest in "temporary stars." Following the traditional views of the ancient Greeks, Arab astronomers regarded comets and other impermanent celestial sights merely as atmospheric phenomena; the celestial vault beyond was believed to be unchanging. Fortunately Arab chroniclers were not influenced by such restrictive views. As a result, many reports of the brilliant 1006 supernova are found in Arab annals, though these accounts tend to be only qualitative. There is also an isolated Arab reference to the supernova of 1054.

In general, East Asia has been the most important source of historical supernova observations. The Chinese, Japanese, and Koreans chronicled all five of the certifiable Milky Way supernovae that appeared during the past millennium, along with several earlier events. Official court astronomers in China, Japan, and Korea regularly noted all kinds of unusual celestial phenomena, mainly for their astrological importance. The early invention of printing in China (around A.D. 700) greatly contributed to the preservation and accessibility of East Asian texts.

But enough introduction. Now let's meet each of the supernovae that skywatchers discerned in the Milky Way during the past millennium.

A Superlative Supernova
SN 1006

The new star that appeared in the constellation Lupus in 1006 was extensively observed in China and Japan. It also was recorded in Europe and in the Arab dominions. The Chinese reports are by far the most detailed, not only giving a fairly accurate position for the star but also demonstrating that it remained visible for at least three years.

Discovery in both China and Japan took place on May 1, 1006, and the supernova was apparently still visible well into 1009. Chinese records emphasize the

star's extreme brilliance: it was "huge . . . like a golden disk"; "its appearance was like the half Moon and it had pointed rays"; "it was so brilliant that one could really see things clearly [by its light]." Nearly 3½ years after the supernova first was sighted, the Chinese Emperor Zhen-zong instituted a regular sacrifice to the star, implying that the supernova was still attracting considerable attention even at this late date.

Brief Arab reports of the new star are preserved in chronicles from several regions: Egypt, Iraq, Yemen, and either northwestern Africa or Spain. The most likely date for the new star's discovery by an Arab observer is April 30th—one day earlier than in China and Japan. By far the most detailed Arab account is by the Cairo physician and astrologer Ali ibn Ridwan, who witnessed the star as a boy. His report not only emphasizes the supernova's brilliance; it also states the star's position to the nearest degree.

Two European accounts—in the respective chronicles of the St. Gallen (Switzerland) and Benevento (Italy) monasteries—clearly refer to the new star. The former source indicates that the star was visible for three months. It also mentions that this visibility was frequently interrupted, implying that the star no more than skimmed the mountainous southern horizon. This has provided a valuable upper limit on the supernova's declination.

Working from Australia in 1965, astronomers Frank Gardner and Douglas Milne identified this supernova's likely remnant with the radio source PKS 1459-41, also known as G327.6 + 14.6 from its galactic coordinates. Subsequent (and more precise) observations confirmed this connection when the remnant was revealed as a hollow shell about a half degree in diameter. P. Frank Winkler (Middlebury College) and his colleagues have used new visible-light images of the remnant's faint, filamentary shell to accurately determine its distance. The result—7,200 light years—is consistent with the 1006 supernova being of Type Ia. It also implies an extremely bright peak apparent magnitude of –7.5, in agreement with historical records.

A Crab Is Born
SN 1054

The Crab Nebula (Messier 1) in Taurus is an unusually bright nebula at both radio and X-ray wavelengths. Spanning approximately 7' x 5', the Crab has been known since the early 18th century. It has generally been recognized as the remnant of the 1054 guest star since 1942, when Dutch historian Jan J. L. Duyvendak assembled a substantial number of Chinese and Japanese records of the supernova.

Chinese Observers sighted the guest star in the eastern sky at daybreak on July 4, 1054; the star remained visible until April 6, 1056. Both Chinese and Japanese sources agree that the star appeared close to 3rd-magnitude Zeta (ζ) Tauri (the Bull's southernmost horn), and that it remained stationary for the whole of its very long period of visibility. Noting that the star was visible in daylight (for 23 days, as it turned out), Chinese astronomers compared it to Venus.

This supernova appeared during the reign of the Chinese Emperor Renzong. Observing from

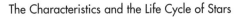
Bian—present-day Kaifeng—his official astronomers kept the star in view for 21 months. At the time, Yang Weide was the court's chief astrologer, a position he had held for almost a half century. Yang was able to dispel any alarm the star's appearance might have caused by giving a favorable interpretation—namely, that it indicated a virtuous ruler.

It also is likely that this supernova was recorded in Constantinople (now known as Istanbul, Turkey), then the seat of the Byzantine Empire. Al-Makhtar ibn Butlan, a Christian physician, provides a brief record of a new star seen at this time.

Some have suggested that there are European records of the Crab supernova, but no such report is definitive. It has also been suggested that this supernova—which was close to the ecliptic—is recorded in cave paintings in the American Southwest, which depict a (presumably lunar) crescent close to a circle or star symbol. However, only a very approximate date range can be deduced for these paintings.

The Crab Nebula is one of the Milky Way's few supernova remnants known to contain a pulsar, a spinning neutron star with the mass of our Sun (or more) packed into a sphere only 10 kilometers or so across. The violently compressed core of the exploded star, this pulsar is extremely important for explaining the energetics and structure of the whole remnant, which is the prototype for a special SNR class, the *filled-center* supernova remnants. There are a small but growing number of these remnants, which are brightest toward their centers. Presumably each of these remnants contains a central source of energy like the Crab pulsar, but these energy sources have not always been directly identified.

Radio waves from the Crab Nebula were first identified in 1963 (resulting in the designations 3C 144 and G184.6-5.8); X-rays were identified in 1964. The 1968 discovery of its pulsar—one of the first known—attracted huge interest internationally. No other supernova remnant has achieved such notoriety or been the subject of so many research papers.

A Poet and a Pulsar
SN 1181

As with the 1006 supernova, both the Chinese and Japanese extensively observed the new star of 1181. We are indebted to the 13th-century Japanese poet and courtier Fujiwara Sadaie for preserving valuable reports of this supernova and the two that preceded it.

How did this poet become a critical archivist of matters astronomical? After witnessing a guest star—actually a comet—in 1230, Fujiwara searched Japanese history for reports of similar events. He included the accounts of the three supernovae, as well as other temporary stars, in his diary: the *Meigetsuki* (Diary of the full Moon).

There are three Chinese records of the star, from the North and South Chinese empires, both in existence at the time. There also are five Japanese accounts, Fujiwara's included. None of these sources report any motion. The star was first seen in South China on August 6, 1181; independent discovery in Japan followed only one day later. The star remained visible for 185 days.

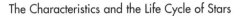
The Chinese and Japanese records place the guest star in Cassiopeia, close to the radio source 3C 58, or G130.7 + 3.1, which one of us (Stephenson) first proposed as the remnant of this guest star in 1971. Like the Crab Nebula, 3C 58 is a filled-center supernova remnant. It spans roughly 9' x 5'. A pulsar spinning approximately 15 times per second has recently been detected in X-rays with the Chandra satellite. However, while this remnant shares these properties with (and is similar in age to) the Crab Nebula, it is much less luminous than the Crab, and in 1992 one of us (Green, along with University of Cambridge colleague Peter Scheuer) found that the two objects' spectra differ when examined closely. This implies that filled-center SNRs have a wide range of intrinsic properties.

A New Star Circles the Pole SN 1572

The supernova that appeared in the far-northern constellation Cassiopeia during the late autumn of 1572 was recorded in both Europe and East Asia. Since the most detailed European observations of the supernova were made by Tycho Brahe (1546-1601), this temporary star is often referred to as Tycho's supernova.

This supernova was discovered in Korea on November 6th and sighted two days later in China. The star finally disappeared from sight sometime between April 21st and May 19th in 1574, so it was visible for about 18 months. Chinese records assert that the star was visible in daylight, while in Korea, its brightness was compared to that of Venus. It seems that the supernova's apparent magnitude peaked at around −4.0.

Virtually all the important European observations of the supernova are contained in Tycho's *Astronomiae instauratae progymnasmata* (Introduction to the new astronomy), published in 1602. The first European detection was probably that of Maurolycus, abbot of Messina (Italy), on November 6, 1572, if not a day or two earlier. Tycho first observed it on November 11th, though he remained skeptical of the star's existence until he questioned both passersby and his servants. Once he realized that this was a new star, however, Tycho "began to measure its situation and distance from the neighboring stars of Cassiopeia and to note extremely diligently those things which were visible to the eye concerning its apparent size, form, color, and other aspects."

These accurate observations enabled Tycho to determine the supernova's position with a few arcminutes' precision—a boon to modern studies. Moreover, Tycho concluded that the new star lay far beyond the Moon, among the fixed stars, contravening the widely accepted Aristotelian doctrine that change could occur only in the sublunar realm.

Working at the United Kingdom's Jodrell Bank radio observatory in 1952, pioneering radio astronomers Robert Hanbury Brown and Cyril Hazard tentatively identified the remnant of Tycho's supernova when they found a celestial source of radio waves near the position then available for the supernova. This subsequently was confirmed by later radio observations, which in turn led optical astronomers in 1957 to the faint nebulosity associated with the radio source. At radio and X-ray wavelengths this remnant—often called either 3C 10 or G120.1 + 1.4—shows a hollow shell approximately 8' in diameter. As the remnant's age is definitely known from historical records, astronomers have been able to study its dynamics and energetics quantitatively.

At the Foot of the Serpent Holder SN 1604

Although it was observed in both China and Korea, the bright star that appeared in 1604 is usually designated Kepler's supernova, and deservedly so. Over the 12 months it was visible, Johannes Kepler (1571-1630) observed the new star extensively. He measured its position with arcminute precision and repeatedly compared its brightness to those of planets and other stars. His observations are contained in his 1606 treatise, *De stella nova in pede Serpentarii* (On the new star on the foot of the serpent holder, as Ophiuchus then was known). In Korea, King Sonjo's official astronomers extensively observed the new star from the royal observatory in Hanyang (present-day Seoul).

Discovery in Europe (in Italy) took place on October 9th. Only a day later the star was sighted in China; Korean astronomers first saw it on the 13th. Bad weather delayed discovery in much of northern Europe, and Kepler—then in Prague—did not himself see the star until the 16th of the month.

Both Kepler and David Fabricius (in Friesland, on the North Sea) systematically measured the supernova's angular distance from other stars with impressive accuracy. Their main objective in making these measurements was to determine whether the star showed any parallax. As was the case with the new star of 1572, Kepler's supernova showed no parallax and hence was taken to lie far beyond the planets, among the "fixed" stars, where change was traditionally thought impossible.

Astronomers in both China and Korea also estimated the new star's position, but their observations were relatively crude. However, frequent Korean estimates of the star's changing brightness have proved a valuable supplement to the European observations.

Guided by Kepler's and Fabricius's observations, the German-born astronomer and cosmology pioneer Walter Baade (1893-1960) discovered the supernova's remnant optically in 1943. Subsequently (in 1957) this remnant was identified with a source of radio waves. Known as 3C 358 or G4.5 + 6.8, this radio source was revealed (in 1975, by University of Cambridge astronomer Steve Gull) as a hollow shell approximately 3' across. The remnant also manifests itself as a shell of X-ray emission. As with the other shell-type supernova remnants described here, 3C 358's radio emission is synchrotron radiation produced by relativistic electrons that spiral around magnetic-field lines, while the X-ray emission is the thermal glow of gas at temperatures measured in millions of degrees.

Our Galaxy's Next Supernova?

One more supernova remnant—and a particularly spectacular one at that—merits discussion. Cassiopeia A (or "Cas A") is one of the night sky's brightest sources of radio waves, and it has been regarded as a young supernova remnant since the late 1950's, when a nearly circular collection of expanding optical filaments a few arcminutes across was associated with the radio emission. Optical, radio, and X-ray observations all show that the remnant is expanding and is only about 300 years old. Recently the remnant has been revealed in great detail at X-ray wavelengths by the Chandra satellite, which identified a compact X-ray source, thought to be a neutron star, near its center.

A quarter century ago, University of Missouri historian William B. Ashworth Jr. suggested that 3 Cassiopeiae—a star that was cataloged by John Flamsteed in 1680 but does not exist—was in fact a sighting of the supernova that produced Cas A (*S&T*: April 1980, page 295). However, the positional difference between Cas A and 3 Cas is very much larger than Flamsteed's measurement errors. Instead, as R. Peter Broughton and the late Karl W. Kamper asserted in 1979, it seems that Flamsteed had mixed up his measurements for two separate stars in Cassiopeia.

We conclude that history records no more than five definite sightings of supernovae that exploded in our Milky Way. This brings us to the subject of the next supernova. All five of the supernovae described appeared at random moments decades or centuries apart. From our vantage on Earth, the next supernova could appear very soon or hundreds of years in the future; we have no way of knowing. Let us hope we do not have to wait too long.

It sounds like a contradiction: although nothing can escape the inside of a black hole, that doesn't mean we don't see anything from the black hole. In fact, some black holes are among the most luminous objects in the universe. How can that be? It isn't the hole itself that we see, but rather evidence of a disk of material that surrounds the hole. The disk itself is not directly visible to us on Earth. This material is often pulled out of a visible companion star. As it falls into the black hole, it gets hotter. The atoms in the material give off radiation as they heat up, spiraling faster into the trap. This radiation creates an X-ray–like image of the disk. From this intimate portrait, we can find out how much mass there is in the disk and the black hole and perhaps even get some idea about how the black hole is spinning. —LK

"Black Holes Reveal Their Innermost Secrets"
by A. C. Fabian and J. M. Miller
Science, August 9, 2002

Black holes can be luminous sources of radiation. During accretion of matter from their surroundings, they release enormous amounts of gravitational energy as gas spirals through an accretion disk into the hole. Recent studies indicate that one component of this emission can provide unprecedented insights into the innermost regions of stellar mass black holes.

The emission spectrum of a black hole is dominated by a broad peak caused by thermal emission within the disk. Emissions extending to hard x-rays, which follow a power law, are produced by interactions between disk photons and hot electrons in a corona above the disk. This type of spectrum is observed for black holes of stellar mass (typically 5 to 15 times the mass of our Sun) in orbit around a normal star. It is also found for super-massive black holes (with typical masses of 10^7 solar masses) in the nuclei of galaxies. However, the temperatures in a disk around a supermassive black hole are cooler than around one of stellar mass.

A further feature, first clearly seen in the spectra of one class of accreting supermassive black holes, the Seyfert galaxies, is an iron emission line, produced by the irradiation of the disk by the coronal radiation. In its simplest form, it is a fluorescent iron line at 6.4 keV. This line is distorted into a characteristically skewed frequency profile by the combined effects of Doppler shifts, relativistic beaming, and gravitational redshifts. The latter result from the emitting matter that orbits at high velocities deep in the gravitational potential well surrounding the black hole.[1, 2] Such a line shape was originally used to describe the spectrum of a stellar mass black hole, Cygnus X-1,[1, 3] but was first clearly resolved in the Seyfert galaxy MCG-6-30-15.[4, 5]

Until recently, evidence for such skewed emission lines from stellar mass black holes was very limited. Stellar mass black holes are much brighter because they are much closer than the supermassive black holes in Seyfert galaxies. But if the disk were highly ionized, little evidence for iron emission would be found. Now, however, the Chandra and XMM-Newton satellites have provided evidence for such lines in data from Cygnus X-1[6] and other stellar mass black holes.

Reanalysis of archival data from recent x-ray satellites such as BeppoSAX[6,9] is revealing further evidence for iron lines. Most previous workers misinterpreted these features as breaks in the continuum emission, or had serious problems with the detectors because the sources were too bright. It is of course possible that we are the ones who are misled. But the similarities between the stellar mass black hole lines now found and those from the Seyfert galaxies appear compelling.

Particularly exciting is the extent of the red (lower energy) wing on some of the lines, for example, in Cygnus X-1 and XTE J1650-500. These lines indicate extreme gravitational redshifts, which can only arise when the emitting matter is extremely close [at about one gravitational radius[10]] to the black hole's event horizon, from beyond which no information can escape.

The iron lines are the most direct signature from the innermost region around a black hole. The frequency of quasi-periodic oscillations (QPOs) in the x-ray flux from some of these objects[11] may be tied to orbital motion and may also point to the inner regions. However, there is no clear consensus on what modulates the QPOs or why high-frequency QPOs are not observed continuously. They therefore do not yet represent as effective a diagnostic probe.

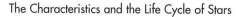
The shape of the broad iron line allows us to determine the inner radius of the emission and the emission profile on the disk. Sometimes it is steeply peaked inward,[6, 12, 13] suggesting an additional power source; for example, rotational energy may be extracted from a spinning black hole via magnetic connections to the inner accretion disk.[14]

Spinning (Kerr) black holes have been postulated, but evidence for the spin itself is only now emerging. For several black holes, the inner radius of the disk deduced from the iron line indicates that matter is orbiting much closer than is possible for a nonspinning black hole. The orbit is closer to the stable orbit of a spinning black hole. The hypothesis that the fastest spinning black holes are those with the strongest radio emission remains untested.

A further quantity determined by the profile of the broad iron line is the disk inclination. The Doppler shifts are larger when the disk is seen more edge on, affecting mostly the blue (high energy) wing of the line. It is reasonable to suppose that the disk inclination is the same as that of the orbit of the binary companion, in the case of a stellar mass black hole. This has been demonstrated for some systems with optical measurements.

The iron line is a powerful diagnostic of the immediate environment of stellar mass black holes. It will enable us to test strong gravity, catalog black hole spin, and test models for the accretion inflow and jetted outflows from these objects. Further observations with Chandra and XMM-Newton, combined with the Rossi X-ray Timing Explorer (RXTE),[15] promise more revelations about stellar mass black holes.

References and Notes

1. A. C. Fabian, M. J. Rees, L. Stella, N. E. White, *Mon. Not. R. Astron. Soc.* **238**, 729 (1989).

2. A. Laor, *Astrophys. J.* **376**, 90L (1991).

3. P. Barr, N. E. White, C. Page, *Mon. Not. R. Astron. Soc.* **216**, 65 (1985).

4. Y. Tanaka *et al.*, *Nature* **375**, 659 (1995).

5. K. Iwasawa *et al.*, *Mon. Not. R. Astron. Soc.* **306**, 19L (1999).

6. J. M. Miller *et al.*, *Astrophys. J.*, in press.

7. J. M. Miller *et al.*, *Astrophys. J.* **570**, 69L (2002).

8. J. M. Miller *et al.*, in preparation.

9. A. Martocchia *et al.*, *Astron. Astrophys.* **387**, 215 (2002).

10. A gravitational radius is $G*mBH/c2$, where G is Newton's gravitational constant, mBH is the mass of the black hole, and c is the speed of light.

11. T. E. Strohmayer, *Astrophys. J.* **552**, 49L (2001).

12. J. Wilms *et al.*, *Mon. Not. R. Astron. Soc.* **328**, 27L (2001).

13. A. C. Fabian *et al.*, *Mon. Not. R. Astron. Soc.*, in press.

14. R. D. Blandford, R. L. Znajek, *Mon. Not. R. Astron. Soc.* **179**, 433 (1977).

15. RXTE can measure fast timings and covers a broad spectrum, thereby complementing the high resolution over a narrow spectrum of Chandra and XMM-Newton.

BLACK HOLE HEADING TOWARD EARTH! Sounds like a hokey Hollywood movie plot, but it's real. However, there's no reason to take shelter yet (not that it would really help anyway). Such a black hole won't arrive for some millions of years into the future.

Black holes have been theorized for years, accepted for a few years less. Do they really come from exploding stars? Here's some evidence that may solve that mystery. That black

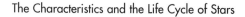
hole heading our way is moving at such a high speed that the only way it could go that fast is if it was ejected by a supernova explosion. —LK

"Black Hole's Velocity Links It to Supernova"
by **William Harwood**
Washington Post, **November 19, 2002**

Astronomers have spotted a black hole speeding through the Milky Way as it gobbles up the outer layers of a doomed companion star locked in a fatal gravitational embrace.

The discovery provides direct observational evidence that black holes with masses comparable to single stars can, as long theorized, form in supernova explosions, the catastrophic end result for the most massive stars in the universe.

"This is the first black hole found to be moving fast through the plane of our galaxy," Felix Mirabel, of the French Atomic Energy Commission and the Institute for Astronomy and Space Physics of Argentina, said in a statement. "This discovery is exciting because it shows the link of a black hole to a supernova."

The black hole, known as GRO J1655-40, is heading in the general direction of Earth, racing through space at about 250,000 mph in the constellation Scorpius. Lest anyone worry about some future collision, the black hole is 6,000 to 9,000 light years away, putting it more than 16 million years from Earth's vicinity in the Milky Way.

"It is much more likely that a normal star could produce discernible effects than a black hole, simply because they are much more numerous," Mirabel said in an e-mail from Madrid.

While GRO J1655-40 itself cannot be directly observed, the companion star is visible, as are the effects of the black hole's titanic gravity.

The hole is slowly consuming the companion sun, which whirls around GRO J1655-40 once every 2.6 days. Huge jets of debris stream away from the poles of the black hole at sizable fractions of the speed of light.

Mirabel says the black hole probably formed in the inner disk of the Milky Way galaxy, where star formation is at its highest. The supernova explosion that created the hole provided the energy to send it careening away through space at such high velocity.

It is that velocity that provides the best evidence yet that black holes with masses comparable to individual suns are formed in supernova explosions.

"What this does say is yes, it did form in a supernova because there's nothing else that can impart that kind of velocity," said Paul Hertz, a senior scientist at NASA headquarters in Washington.

Stars like our sun remain stable by balancing the inward pull of gravity with the outward pressure generated by nuclear fusion in their cores. When the fuel for nuclear fusion eventually runs out, gravity triumphs and the core collapses.

What happens at that point depends on the mass of the star and its core. For stars with up to about eight times the mass of Earth's sun, the core collapses

to a point where gravity is held at bay by quantum mechanical effects that limit how tightly electrons can be crammed together.

The result is a white dwarf, a star about the size of Earth that slowly cools and fades away over billions of years. Such stars frequently blow off their outer layers as they run out of fuel, producing spectacular expanding clouds of glowing gas.

For stars with more than eight times the mass of the sun, the effects that produce white dwarf stars are not sufficient to hold off the inward pull of gravity.

If the planet-size core of the doomed star is between about 1.4 and three times the mass of the sun, the end result is a neutron star, an object about the size of a large city, the mass of a normal star and the density of an atomic nucleus. Gravity is held at bay by quantum nuclear forces that represent a star's last line of defense.

When the core reaches this enormous density, the collapse stops and material still falling inward hits what amounts to a brick wall and rebounds. The resulting shock wave blows the rest of the star apart in a supernova explosion.

For rare stars with more than 25 to 30 times the mass of the sun—and with cores containing more than three solar masses—no known force can stop gravity once the star's nuclear fuel runs out. Again, a supernova results, but in those cases the core collapses into a black hole, an object with such extreme gravity not even light can escape.

That's the theory, but observational evidence is slim, in large part because black holes are difficult, by definition, to detect. Finding a solar mass black hole like GRO J1655-40, one with a velocity of 250,000 mph, is strong evidence black holes do, in fact, form in supernova explosions.

Mirabel said a neutron star or black hole can be accelerated to high velocities in a supernova detonation by either an asymmetrical collapse of the core or because of the offset center of gravity in a binary star system.

GRO J1655-40 was observed by the Hubble Space Telescope in 1995 and 2001. Those observations were combined with ground-based measurements of its radial velocity to determine the binary star system's actual speed through space. Mirabel's results are discussed in the Nov. 19 issue of *Astronomy and Astrophysics*.

Reprinted with permission from William Harwood.

Gamma-ray bursts are some of the most exasperating, powerful events in the universe. One moment they are here. In seconds or minutes they are gone. Often, they vanish before telescopes and satellite observatories can be used to observe them in detail. But in the incident described in this story, the culprit was caught in the act. Over days, the location of the burst was filled with a spot of light, an afterglow that, as it cooled off, gave all the right indicators for a supernova explosion. For the first time, astronomers could link one of these

energy sources to a real object, a black hole being formed in the death throes of a star. —LK

"Astronomers Link Gamma-Ray Bursts to Supernovas"
by Dennis Overbye
New York Times, June 20, 2003

Alien space wars and antimatter comets are but two of the more exotic explanations that have been proffered in the last three decades for the flashes of high-energy radiation known as gamma-ray bursts that have appeared sporadically in the cosmic night, tantalizing and frustrating astronomers.

An only slightly more prosaic theory has taken hold among astronomers in recent years: that these violent flashes are the yowls of giant stars imploding, perhaps into black holes, the inky gravitational sinks that swallow light and all else.

Now there is evidence that those astronomers are right, at least about some of the bursts. On March 29 a gamma-ray burst was detected that went off unusually near Earth—a mere two billion light-years away—prompting a deluge of observations that discerned the unmistakeable hint of a supernova explosion, the cataclysm in which a massive star ends its life, in the debris of the burst.

"There should no longer be doubt in anybody's mind" that gamma-ray bursts and supernovas are connected, said Dr. Thomas Matheson, of the Harvard-Smithsonian Center for Astrophysics in Cambridge, Mass.

Dr. Stan E. Woosley, an astrophysicist at the University of California at Santa Cruz, said, "It looks like a black hole was born that day." Dr. Woosley is an author of a series of three papers on the burst by an international array of astronomers that appeared yesterday in *Nature*.

In interviews, astronomers described the results as the "smoking gun" they had long suspected must be there connecting the two most violent phenomena in nature.

"It's just ironclad now," said Dr. Donald Lamb, an astrophysicist at the University of Chicago.

In a commentary accompanying the *Nature* papers, Dr. Peter Meszaros, an astronomer at Pennsylvania State University, called the recent work "a watershed event." Dr. George Ricker, a gamma-ray astronomer at the Massachusetts Institute of Technology, said the detailed observations of this burst would serve as a template for theorists for years to come. "It's a very lucky event for us," Dr. Ricker said.

Gamma-ray bursts have led astronomers on a merry chase since the 1960's, when they were accidentally discovered by satellites intended to look for nuclear tests on Earth.

Efforts to understand these bursts were hampered at first because they last only a few seconds or minutes and do not repeat. The satellites that detected them could not fix their locations in the sky precisely enough for astronomers to link them to particular stars or galaxies.

It was not until 1997, using coordinates relayed from the Dutch-Italian satellite Beppo-Sax, that astronomers found a visible afterglow to one burst in a galaxy seven

billion light-years away, establishing these flashes as some of the most violent events in the universe.

Then on March 29, the High Energy Transit Explorer, operated by NASA and a multinational collaboration led by the Center for Space Research at M.I.T., recorded a blast in the constellation Leo and sent its coordinates to a network of astronomers.

Whereas most gamma-ray bursts had been traced to galaxies typically 10 billion light-years away, the afterglow from this one was so bright that the astronomers joked about its casting shadows, said Paul Price, a graduate student at Mount Stromlo Observatory in Australia, who was among the first to identify the glow and who is the lead author of one of the *Nature* papers.

"Up close and personal with a cosmic explosion," as Dr. Price put it in an e-mail message. The result was that the burst afterglow could be studied in unprecedented detail.

A crucial breakthrough came when Dr. Krzysztof Stanek and Dr. Matheson, of the Center for Astrophysics, and Dr. Peter Garnavich of the University of Notre Dame, aided by astronomers around the world recording observations 12 nights in a row, discovered the spectral signature of a supernova peeking out from the fading afterglow about a week after the burst. It was the first direct evidence that at least some gamma-ray bursts come from supernovas. Their results were published earlier this month in the online edition of *Astrophysical Journal Letters*.

Significantly, both this supernova and one in 1998 were of a type known as Ic, which seem to involve certain very massive stars, giving support to what is termed the "collapsar" model of bursts.

Under this theory, Dr. Woosley said, the story begins with a rapidly aging rotating star, perhaps 30 times the mass of the Sun. When the core of such a star, made of iron, finally collapses of its own weight, it creates a black hole or a dense neutron star in its middle.

Material trying to fall onto this object forms a hot swirling disk and a narrow jet, which shoots out of the star in six or seven seconds. The gamma rays are formed when this jet, moving at nearly the speed of light, plows into material in interstellar space, forming a "fireball" of magnetic fields and high-energy particles.

Meanwhile, the rest of the star blows up as a supernova, but for a few days that violence is masked by the greater fury of the gamma-ray fireball that surrounds it.

"We can't see inside until it fades," Dr. Woosley said.

The new papers both validate and complicate this picture, the astronomers say. In one, Dr. Makoto Uemura, an astronomer at Kyoto University, and his colleagues report that the afterglow from the March 29 burst did not fade steadily in its first few hours. Rather it rose and fell in brightness sporadically. These "bumps" in the light curve could provide important clues to the nature of gamma-ray bursts, Dr. Uemura said in an e-mail message.

One possibility, he explained, is that the black hole, the central engine of the burster, sputters, emitting jets in more than one puff, which then catch up to each other in the outer world and collide, "refreshing" the fireball.

The connection between the supernova and the March 29 gamma-ray burst has been strengthened by the observations reported in another paper by several astronomers led by Dr. Jens Hjorth of the University of Copenhagen. They concluded that the gamma-ray burst and the supernova explosion occurred within two days of each other, eliminating models in which the star's collapse happens in two stages.

The spectral data also suggest that the supernova associated with this gamma-ray burst was unusually violent, with gas flying outward at 36,000 kilometers a second, "faster than a supernova has ever been seen to expand," Dr. Woosley said.

How some stars attain such savage explosive energies and the rapid spins needed to power the jets are mysteries that await elucidation. The Hubble Space Telescope will be able to study the afterglow from the March 29 event for another year, astronomers say, and radio telescopes might be able to track it longer. A new satellite known as Swift, designed to hunt and study the bursts, is scheduled to be launched this winter.

"My head is spinning," Dr. Lamb said.

That old philosophical question, "If a tree falls in the forest, and there is no one around to hear it, does it make a sound?" has an astronomical counterpart. It now appears that those puzzling gamma-ray bursts (GRBs), which show up without warning, have various luminosities, and die off

quickly, are visible to us only when the energy is channeled in our direction. If the channel doesn't face us, we don't ever "hear" the sound of the burst. This last story combines new research in GRBs with research in black holes—especially those that emit jets of radiation—into an explanation of these high-powered mysteries. —LK

"In the Line of Fire"
by Steve Nadis
Astronomy, January 2004

Astronomers are closing in on the universe's most powerful explosions: gamma-ray bursts. They are beams of matter and energy, and many are aimed straight at Earth.

Since their discovery some thirty years ago by military satellites monitoring nuclear explosions, gamma-ray bursts (GRBs) have endured as one of astronomy's greatest mysteries. They appear at seemingly random spots in the sky several times a day, unleashing —between a fraction of a second and about a minute—prodigious blasts of energy that, by some accounts, rival the Big Bang itself. The origins of these bursts have stumped researchers for decades, but the picture is now coming into sharper focus. Scientists have found that the burst energy is not sprayed in all directions but instead is channeled into narrow, cone-shaped beams or jets. Most of these jets pass by unseen, but occasionally one is pointed right at us, as if we were sitting at the end of a gun barrel. Far from feeling uneasy, gamma-ray astronomers live for the chance to be shot through with high-energy photons.

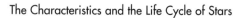

Awareness of the beamed nature of GRBs has enabled investigators to estimate, in one fell swoop, both the energy of individual bursts and their frequency. "If you didn't know the geometry, and assumed spherical emission when it's really conical, you could infer an energy release a thousand times bigger than it really is," notes Shri Kulkarni of the California Institute of Technology. "And if the beams are as narrow as we think they are, for every GRB I see there are a thousand I don't see."

One of the most telling clues about the origin of GRBs was uncovered on March 29, 2003, when NASA's High Energy and Transient Explorer (HETE-2) satellite detected a burst from the constellation Leo. The burst's subsequent "afterglow" revealed the GRB arose just 2.6 billion light-years away and was associated with a bright supernova that occurred around the same time. Now theorists believe they're converging on a plausible explanation for GRBs, linking the most common class of bursts (those typically lasting about twenty seconds) to the creation of black holes when massive stars (originally about 30 or more times the mass of the Sun) collapse and die in a blaze of supernova glory.

The suggestion that gamma rays are shot through space from a two-way cosmic cannon has been around for at least a decade, and nature holds other examples of jetted flows from stars and active galactic nuclei. But it is difficult to determine if the gamma-ray pulses periodically detected by our orbiting instruments are beamed in jets or radiated in all directions.

This problem is compounded by special relativity. In the standard "fireball" model, gamma rays are thought to be produced from the extreme heat generated by internal collisions within a torrent of material ejected from a dying star at close to the speed of light. If photons are emitted from a hot, high-velocity source, they don't wander all over the place but instead are concentrated in discrete, laser-like beams, traveling perpendicular to the surface. The faster the surface expands, the narrower the beam. One consequence of relativity, Kulkarni explains, is that "very fast-moving surfaces do not reveal themselves fully. You see only a small portion. And if you see only a little bit, you can't tell if it's an entire sphere or a small section of a sphere like a cone."

The First Afterglow

The model sharpened dramatically in 1997 with the discovery of GRB afterglows—X-ray, optical, and radio emissions that persist for weeks and months after bursts. Afterglows, according to the fireball model, are produced when jets bump into the interstellar media and other matter spewed out by the star. Due to these collisions, jets slow down steadily during the afterglow phase. When the speed dips below a critical value, it becomes possible to see the jet's "edge"—proof that the emission is not spherical because spheres, by definition, have no edges.

In 1997, James Rhoads, an astronomer at the Space Telescope Science Institute, encapsulated these ideas in a simple diagnostic test called the "jet break." After running into surrounding material, Rhoads said, a jet will lose speed and start to expand sideways. When this happens, the luminosity of the afterglow falls off sharply as light focused into a narrow cone becomes more diluted. This should appear as a change in the slope of the "light curve"—a graph of luminosity versus time—at the precise point where brightness begins to decline more abruptly.

In a 1999 study, Re'em Sari of the California Institute of Technology and his colleagues found indications of "jet-like behavior" in three previously observed GRBs. Luminosity was dropping so quickly in those cases that they concluded the afterglow observations must have begun after the jet break.

But a broader analysis of a larger observational sample was needed to draw more meaningful comparisons between bursts. This came recently when Dale Frail of the National Radio Observatory, Kulkarni, Sari, and eleven other astronomers examined the light curves of seventeen GRB afterglows in a variety of wavelengths. After confirming the gamma-ray energy was focused in jets, the team went on to calculate the angular size of those jets based on the time of the jet break: The later the break occurred after the burst, the bigger the "opening angle" of the cone. Most jets, they concluded, were just a few degrees wide. An independent analysis by Alin-Daniel Panaitescu of Princeton and Pawan Kumar of the University of Texas reached similar conclusions.

Clocking GRB Energies

Knowledge of beaming angles is important because scientists now think different angles account for different luminosities observed in gamma-ray bursts, with tightly focused jets appearing brighter than those that are more widely dispersed. "Early on, people didn't realize how small the beams are," says Stan Woosley, a theorist at the University of California, Santa Cruz. "They assumed angles of about twenty degrees, but now it looks closer to four degrees."

Narrow beams mean that for every GRB we observe, there are 500 to 1,000 bursts invisible to us because they're pointing in another direction. Statistically, the data suggest that at least 1,500 GRBs occur in the visible universe each day, which is equivalent to a birthrate of one stellar-mass-size black hole each minute. This figure seems reasonable enough to Woosley as it means just "one percent of the stars massive enough to die as supernovae end up as GRBs."

Angular calculations also permit estimates of the total gamma-ray energy release, which appears to be fairly constant from one burst to the next: roughly 10^{51} ergs. GRBs are like "standard bombs," just slightly more energetic than supernovae, according to Woosley. They retain the title of "nature's grandest explosions" by a slim margin, but they are easily "the brightest explosions since the Big Bang."

Before beaming was taken into account, theorists had little luck concocting workable scenarios that yielded an energy output of 10^{54} ergs—what the biggest GRBs were clocked at. The lower, revised estimate fits well with models that equate GRBs with run-of-the-mill supernovae.

Death Throes

Jet flows are an integral feature of the so-called "collapsar" model developed by Woosley and collaborators. In this model, arguably the leading one at present, the GRB and supernova happen at the same time and are powered by the same energy source: the terminal collapse of a massive, rotating star that creates a black hole in the center surrounded by a spinning disk of matter. The rotating black hole and disk wind up magnetic fields, which may funnel particles from the disk out into jets along the star's rotation axis. A powerful wind blowing from the disk, along with the jets, rips the star apart. The relativistic jets that shoot out in opposite directions give rise to gamma-ray emissions. The rest of the star's outer shell expands at a more modest pace because the same amount of energy is imparted to a greater bulk of matter; as a result, it moves more slowly. Although GRBs and supernovae traditionally are considered separate phenomena, in this model, they're different manifestations of the same explosion (at least some of the time—perhaps one percent of supernovae are involved with GRBs, while 99 percent are thought to be powered by neutron star formation or neutrinos).

Additional support for the link between GRBs and supernovae comes from observations that show bursts tend to originate in star-forming regions. "In places where lots of stars are born, a lot of massive stars will also be dying," notes theorist Tsvi Piran of Hebrew University in Israel. Andrew Fruchter, an astronomer at the Space Telescope Science Institute, agrees. "The hosts show signs of being unusually star-forming: They are blue and have strong emission lines," he says. "They also show disturbed morphologies." Other suggestive evidence comes from a study of the X-ray afterglow of a recent GRB using the XMM-Newton space telescope. James Reeves of the University of Leicester in England and his colleagues conducted a detailed spectral analysis of the afterglow that revealed the presence of light chemical elements—magnesium, silicon, sulfur, argon, and calcium—typically flung into space by a supernova explosion.

With the various pieces of evidence combined, Woosley believes the case tying GRBs to star death is pretty compelling. "We have a working model, and there's even some consensus in the community, but that doesn't make it right," he says. As an example, he points out that a dozen years ago, many people believed in the "thermonuclear" model, which assumed gamma rays were produced by rapid accretion of matter onto a neutron star, with magnetic confinement generating the requisite heat. Although the idea makes perfect sense, it is absolutely wrong, Woosley says. "I should know because it was my model."

Uncertainties afflict almost every aspect of the currently favored "collapsar" model. "Even if we know the GRB is caused by the explosion of a massive star, that still doesn't tell us how it blew up," Woosley says. On the most basic level, researchers can't describe how jets are made, nor what they are made of, although it is often assumed they consist of the universe's standard material, hydrogen, in the form of protons and electrons.

There are fundamental questions, as well, about the enigmatic source that accelerates jets to relativistic velocities and focuses the beams to such an exquisite degree. "What is the mysterious engine that produces so much energy yet can operate with such fine precision?"

asks Kulkarni. "It's a rare combination of the delicate and the powerful." He is particularly intrigued by the collimation mechanism. "Making a cone of just one degree is like cutting a pizza into three hundred sixty slices. How does nature make these incredible pizzas?"

Kumar is mystified by the apparent "constancy of energy" among bursts, which he believes must be an important clue to what is behind the explosion. "Why isn't there a bigger variation in energy, and why are you only tapping about one percent of the total?" he asks. "It's as if you had $100,000 in a group bank account and everybody can only take out $1,000. There has to be a reason. Otherwise, people might take out $10, $100, or $10,000."

The GRB Future Is Bright

Kumar also is trying to understand the properties of jets in a more precise way. "In our models, we think in terms of a cone carved out of a sphere, but things may not be as neat as a uniform cone," he says. "Different parts of the jets could be propagating at different speeds." He's now doing theoretical work to figure out what to look for when new data are available from SWIFT, NASA's orbiting GRB observatory, which is set to be launched in May.

With all the unanswered questions still swirling about bursts and jets, high hopes are being pinned on SWIFT. The mission is expected to spot about 300 GRB afterglows a year and monitor at least 1,000 afterglows in all, greatly expanding the number of bursts with known locations, which presently stands at about fifty. "We have a small sample right now and want to make sure it's representative of the entire class of GRBs," Kumar says.

"It's not only a matter of quantity, but quality," says Sari of SWIFT's potential contributions. "Burst positions will be given to people on Earth within seconds rather than hours, so we can look at the afterglows very quickly. That means we can catch jets with the smallest angles and earliest breaks."

Meanwhile, an independent strategy is being pursued, a strategy based on another test proposed by Rhoads in 1997. If GRBs truly are broadcast in discrete beams, then we should be able to see afterglows in some cases where it is impossible to see the bursts themselves. These "orphan afterglows," as Rhoads calls them, will be hard to find because they're much fainter and rarer than supernovae. "But they have to exist if this picture is right," he says.

Even without an orphan afterglow sighting, it appears that after thirty years of detective work, researchers finally are getting to the bottom of the gamma-ray burst mystery—at least as far as long-duration bursts are concerned.

Unfortunately, short-duration bursts, which last less than two seconds, remain "as mysterious as ever," according to Piran. A different mechanism may be responsible for short bursts, namely the merger of two neutron stars. The impetus for this explanation is timing—in the stellar collapse model, the jet has to force its way through the shell of the dead star, a process that takes at least a few seconds. In theory, merging neutron stars release high-energy radiation quickly enough to explain momentary GRBs. While a strong case ties long-duration bursts to the deaths of massive stars, Piran notes, "we don't even have indirect evidence for this other (merging neutron star) scenario."

For his part, Kulkarni speculates the standard energy output that he and his colleagues find perplexing may be "due to the fact that we're only seeing the brightest events. In time, I think we'll see fainter ones and that constancy will go away."

Woosley also is prepared for the prospect that the variety of bursts observed to date is just the tip of the iceberg. A broad range of "optical transients"—emanating from supernovae, novae, flare stars, and active galactic nuclei—has been cataloged in the past, he says, "and there are likely to be forms of gamma-ray transients we don't know anything about."

So it looks like gamma-ray sleuths won't be putting themselves out of business anytime soon. Just as one GRB mystery is solved, other quandaries draw our attention back to these errant jets from the far reaches of the cosmos.

Web Sites

Due to the changing nature of Internet links, the Rosen Publishing Group, Inc., has developed an online list of Web sites related to the subject of this book. This site is updated regularly. Please use this link to access the list:

http://www.rosenlinks.com/cdfa/clcs

For Further Reading

Cassé, Michel. *Stellar Alchemy: The Celestial Origin of Atoms*. New York, NY: Cambridge University Press, 2003.

Cole, K. C. *Mind Over Matter: Conversations with the Cosmos*. Orlando, FL: Harcourt, Inc., 2003.

Inglis, Mike. *Observer's Guide to Stellar Evolution*. New York, NY: Springer-Verlag, 2003.

Kaler, James B. *Extreme Stars: At the Edge of Creation*. New York, NY: Cambridge University Press, 2001.

Kaler, James B. *The Hundred Greatest Stars*. New York, NY: Copernicus Books, 2002.

O'Dell, C. Robert. *The Orion Nebula: Where Stars Are Born*. Cambridge, MA: Harvard University Press, 2003.

Schilling, Govert. *Flash! The Hunt for the Biggest Explosions in the Universe*. New York, NY: Cambridge University Press, 2002.

Wilford, John Noble, ed. *Cosmic Dispatches*. New York, NY: WW Norton & Co, 2001.

Bibliography

Branch, David. "When a White Dwarf Explodes." *Science*, January 3, 2003, pp. 53–54.

Christlieb, N., M. S. Bessell, T. C. Beers, B. Gustafsson, A. Korn, P. S. Barklem, T. Karlsson, M. Mizuno-Wiedner, and S. Rossi. "A Stellar Relic from the Early Milky Way." *Nature*, October 31, 2002, pp. 904–906.

Cowen, Ron. "Gorgeous Gas: New Observations of Space Clouds Reveal Stellar Histories." *Science News*, May 24, 2003, pp. 328–329.

Cowen, Ron. "Rethinking an Astronomical Icon." *Science News*, March 16, 2002, pp. 171–172.

Croswell, Ken. "Fluorine: An Elementary Mystery." *Sky & Telescope*, September 2003, pp. 30–35.

Fabian, A. C., and J. M. Miller. "Black Holes Reveal Their Innermost Secrets." *Science*, August 9, 2002, pp. 947–948.

Goho, Alexandra. "Space Invaders: The Stuff of Life Has Far-flung Origins." *Science News*, May 1, 2004, pp. 280–281.

Harwood, William. "Black Hole's Velocity Links It to Supernova." *Washington Post*, November 19, 2002, p. A.2.

Jayawardhana, Ray. "Style & Substance." *Astronomy*, October 2003, pp. 42–47.

Kwok, Sun. "Butterflies and Crabs of the Southern Sky." *Sky & Telescope*, January 2002, pp. 48–53.

Kwok, Sun. "Gems from the Stars." *Sky & Telescope*, October 2002, pp. 38–43.

Lobel, Alex. "Keep an Eye on Hypergiant Rho Cassiopeiae." *Mercury*, January–February 2004, pp. 13–19.

McDonald, Arthur B., Joshua R. Klein, and David L. Wark. "Solving the Solar Neutrino Problem." *Scientific American*, April 2003, pp. 40–49.

McFarling, Lee. "Solar System Like Ours Is Called 'Missing Link.'" *Los Angeles Times*, June 14, 2002, p. A.1.

Nadis, Steve. "In the Line of Fire." *Astronomy*, January 2004, pp. 42–47.

Overbye, Dennis. "Astronomers Link Gamma-Ray Bursts to Supernovas." *New York Times*, June 20, 2003, p. A21.

Shara, Michael. "When Stars Collide." *Scientific American*, September 2004, pp. 50–56.

Stephenson, F. Richard, and David A. Green. "A Millennium of Shattered Stars: Our Galaxy's Historical Supernovae." *Sky & Telescope*, May 2003, pp. 40–48.

Tielens, A. G. "Peering into Stardust." *Science*, April 4, 2003, p. 68.

Index

A

Algol (star), 73
Allamandola, Louis, 26, 27, 30, 33, 34
Antares (star), 112, 115

B

Becklin-Neugebauer object, 16
Beppo-Sax satellite, 163
Betelgeuse (star), 73, 79, 81, 116
big bang, 41, 167, 171
  star from, 41–49
black holes, 6, 8, 95, 98, 101, 106, 134, 138, 153–156, 157–161, 162, 165, 167
blue straggler stars, 104, 105
Brahe, Tycho, 142, 148–149
Butterfly Nebula, 110

C

Cassiopeiae (constellation), 73, 86, 148, 149, 151, 152
Cerenkov light, 64–65, 66
charge-parity (CP) violation, 71, 72
Chen, Herb, 62–63
Chu, You-Hua, 36, 37, 38
comets, 11, 17, 89, 91, 92, 94, 141, 162
constellations, 6, 10, 11, 12, 73
cosmic rays, 62, 64
Crab Nebula, 142, 145–147, 148
Cunha, Katia, 121, 122

D

Davis, Raymond, Jr., 58–59, 60
diamonds, 131–133
DNA, 27, 31, 32, 34

E

Eagle Nebula, 17–25
  "pillars of creation," 17, 19, 21, 22
Earth, 11, 18, 25, 27, 28, 31, 33, 34, 51, 52, 53, 54, 55, 93, 97, 112, 122, 124, 125, 126, 128, 130, 131, 134, 140, 153, 159, 162, 163
  atmosphere of, 94
  black hole heading toward, 157–161, 167
  crust of, 127
  orbit of, 8
Eddington, Arthur, 57
Einstein, Albert, 134
European Space Agency (ESA), 129
evaporating gas globules (EGGs), 17, 19–20, 22, 118

F

Fabricius, David, 150, 151
55 Cancri (star), 53, 54
Floss, Christine, 33
fluorine, 112–122
Fujiwara Sadaie, 147

G

gamma rays, 7, 8, 75
  bursts (GRBs), 161–176
Garnett, Donald R., 36–37, 39, 40
gemstones, 122–133
giant branch star, 117
globular clusters, 95–96, 99, 100,
  104–106, 121

H

Hale-Bopp (comet), 91
halo stars, 120
HeII (nebula), 36, 37, 38, 39, 40
Herbig-Haro objects, 14
Herschel, William, 109
Hester, J. Jeff, 18–19, 20, 21, 22, 24
High Energy Transit Explorer, 164
Horsehead Nebula, 12
Hubble Space Telescope (HST),
  11, 13, 17, 18, 19, 20, 21, 23,
  24, 37, 104, 107, 110, 111, 166
hypergiant stars, 72, 77, 80, 81,
  85, 86

I

Infrared Astronomical Satellite
  (IRAS), 127, 128, 129
interplanetary dust particles
  (IDPs), 88, 89, 91, 93–94
interstellar dust, 87, 93, 94,
  123–124

J

Jeans, James, 97–98
Jet Propulsion Laboratory, 55
Jorissen, Alain, 116, 117
Jupiter, 15, 51, 52, 53, 54, 108

K

KamLAND, 70–71
Kepler, Johannes, 142, 150, 151
Kleinmann-Low Nebula, 16
Koshiba, Masatoshi, 58–59
Kulkarni, Shri, 168, 169, 170, 176

Kumar, Pawan, 170, 174–175
Kwok, Sun, 122

L

Lamb, Dr. Donald, 163, 166
Lambert, David L., 116, 121
Large Magellanic Cloud galaxy,
  38, 121
Leitherer, Claus, 37–38, 40
Leo (constellation), 164
Livio, Mario, 22–23, 102

M

Marcy, Geoff, 52, 53
Matheson, Dr. Thomas,
  162, 164
McCaughrean, Mark J., 18, 19,
  20, 21, 24
M-class stars, 78, 79, 82
Mercury, 51
Milky Way, 18, 22, 23, 26, 28,
  29, 35, 37, 74, 80, 87, 95,
  98, 99, 106, 114, 118, 120,
  123, 139, 140, 141, 143,
  146, 152, 158, 159
Milne, Douglas, 144
Mira (star), 73
Mirabel, Felix, 158, 159, 161
M33 (spiral galaxy), 81

N

NASA, 18, 26, 29, 30, 31, 32, 52,
  102, 128, 159, 164, 168
Nazé, Yäel, 36, 38, 39
nebulae, 7, 8, 9, 10, 11–12, 30, 34,
  35, 51, 75, 91, 92, 123
neutron star, 6, 8, 95, 101, 106,
  134, 138, 140, 161
N44C (nebula), 38, 39

O

Omega Centauri, 121
Orion (constellation), 11, 12, 74
Orion Nebula (M42), 10–17, 36
O star, 119, 120

P

particle physics, standard model of, 58, 60, 68
Piran, Tsvi, 172, 175, 176
planetary nebulae, 93, 104, 108–111, 118, 122, 126, 130, 138
planetary systems, 6, 7, 11, 51, 52
    formation of, 52–56
planets
    extrasolar, 52–53
    55 Cnc d, 53
    formation of, 51, 54–55, 87, 94, 123
    gas giants, 51, 52, 53, 54–55, 108
Pluto, 13
polycyclic aromatic hydrocarbons (PAHs), 28–29, 30, 31, 33
protostar, 16, 92

Q

quasars, 98

R

R Coronae stars, 73, 84
red giant stars, 7–8, 72, 87, 89–90, 92, 93, 104, 105, 108, 109, 112, 116, 120, 121, 125, 126, 127
Red Rectangle Nebula, 29
Rhoads, James, 169, 175
Rho Cassiopeiae, 72–86
Ring Nebula, 110
RNA, 27, 31, 32

S

Sakharov, Andrei, 71
Sari, Re'em, 170, 175
Saturn, 54, 108
Scorpius (constellation), 158
solar neutrinos, 56–72
solar power, 56, 58, 63
solar system, 52, 53, 55, 93, 108, 122, 125
    dust in, 87–94

space-time continuum, 106
spectral absorption lines, 75, 80, 82, 83–86
star(s)
    age of, 53
    brightness/luminosity of, 5–6, 36, 73, 74, 75, 78, 81, 85, 86, 104, 122
    collisions, 95–107
    color of, 6, 103, 104, 109
    death of, 7, 9, 161–162, 173
    distance of, 5, 74, 95, 100
    formation of, 19, 21, 25–41, 87, 91
    high-density stars, 101–102
    high mass stars, 138–176
    low-mass stars, 41, 92, 93, 99
    massive, 38, 39, 40, 103, 112, 115, 158, 159–160, 165
    movement of, 6
    newborn, 22, 23, 99
    radiation from, 28, 38, 39, 40
    temperature of, 6, 36, 38–39, 40, 74, 81, 83, 102, 103
    variable, 73
starburst galaxies, 40
Stardust mission, 33, 93
stellar mineralogy, 126–128
stellar winds, 51, 109, 112, 125
Sudbury Neutrino Observatory, 55
    solar neutrino studies by, 56–72
Sun, the, 9, 14, 15, 40, 41, 48, 55, 74, 78, 81, 95, 97, 103, 105, 112, 113, 115, 117, 118, 134, 135, 138, 159, 160, 165
    hydrogen depletion in, 107–108
    neutrinos in, 56–72, 115
supergiant stars, 72, 78, 79, 80, 81, 118
supernovae, 8, 34, 48, 78, 87, 90, 93, 95, 112, 115–116, 118, 120, 158, 159, 160, 161, 162–166, 171, 172, 173, 175
    brightness of, 141

history of, 139–152
type Ia, 133–135, 145
type Ic, 164
type II, 141
supernova remnant (SNR),
    139–140, 146, 148

T
Trapezium Cluster, 11, 12, 13,
    15, 16

U
Uhuru satellite, 99, 101
ultraviolet light/radiation, 7, 13,
    19, 20, 22, 23, 29, 30, 37, 38,
    39, 40, 124

V
Venus, 51, 116

Very Large Telescope (VLT), 20,
    35, 37, 42

W
Weinberger, Alycia, 54, 55
white dwarf stars, 8, 97, 102,
    104, 160
  explosions of, 133–137
Witt, Adolf, 29–30
Wolf-Rayet stars, 34, 37, 38, 39,
    40, 113, 119–121
Woosley, Stan E., 114, 115, 163,
    165, 166, 171, 173, 176

X
X-rays, 7, 8, 12, 14, 39, 75,
    95, 96, 99, 101, 139, 140,
    150, 151–152, 153–154,
    169, 172

About the Editor

The author of numerous articles published in science journals in the United States and abroad, Larry Krumenaker is a member of the National Association of Science Writers and the International Science Writers Association. He has degrees in astronomy and science education and currently teaches high school physics in Atlanta.

Photo Credits

Front cover (top inset) © Royalty-Free/Corbis; (center left inset) © Digital Vision/Getty Images; (bottom right inset) © Reuters/Corbis; (bottom left inset) © Library of Congress Prints and Photographs Division; (background) Brand X Pictures/Getty Images. Back cover (top) © Photodisc Green/ Getty Images; (bottom) © Digital Vision/Getty Images.

Designer: Geri Fletcher; Editor: Christine Poolos